Letters from a Life : The Selected Letters
and Diaries of Benjamin Britten 1913–1976

EDITOR-IN-CHIEF: DONALD MITCHELL

Letters from a Life:
The Selected Letters and
Diaries of Benjamin Britten
1913–1976

VOLUME ONE
1923–1939

EDITED BY
DONALD MITCHELL
ASSISTANT EDITOR:
PHILIP REED
ASSOCIATE EDITORS: ROSAMUND STRODE,
KATHLEEN MITCHELL, JUDY YOUNG

faber and faber

First published in 1991
by Faber and Faber Limited
3 Queen Square London WC1N 3AU

Phototypeset by Input Typesetting Ltd, London
Printed in Great Britain by Clays Ltd, St Ives Plc

A CIP record for these books is available from the British Library

ISBN 0–571–164056
ISBN 0–571–15221–x Vol. One
ISBN 0–571–16058–1 Vol. Two

Endpaper: Lowestoft in the twenties

To the memory of Hans Keller
1919–1985

CONTENTS

INDEX OF CORRESPONDENTS
to Volumes One and Two

LIST OF PLATES

Note: Pictures from a Life (PFL, 1978) remains the most extensive picture documentation of Britten's life. We have tried to avoid duplication, but some overlap has proved necessary.

1 Britten's parents, an engagement photograph, 1900

2 Edith Rhoda Hockey, before her marriage to Robert Victor Britten

3 The wedding: St John's Smith Square, London SW1, 5 September 1901

4 R.V. Britten, 1909

5 Edith Britten, 1909

6a The family home, 21 Kirkley Cliff Road, Lowestoft, where Britten was born on 22 November 1913; Mr Britten's dental practice was on the ground floor

6b The first floor sitting room, known to the family – because of its upper location – as 'Heaven'

7 Beth; Edith Britten and her infant son, Benjamin; Barbara; Robert, 1914

8a Nursery theatricals; back row from left: Barbara; unidentified; Robert; Benjamin cross-legged in front row; Beth kneels on his right

8b Mrs Scarce, Nanny, with Benjamin, 1914

8c Benjamin, c.1915

9a Invitation to the theatricals, probably in Nanny's hand

9b Benjamin and battleship, c.1916

9c Beth and Benjamin, c.1916

ACKNOWLEDGEMENTS AND
EDITORIAL METHOD

First and foremost we must thank all those who have so generously placed at our disposal their correspondence with Britten and often supplied us with much illuminating information. Without their collaboration these volumes, self-evidently, would not exist. The names of all correspondents appear on pp. ix–xiii. We are no less grateful to those owners of Britten letters, whether individuals or institutions, for their indispensable co-operation.

The texts of the letters and diaries: we have preserved throughout Britten's idiosyncratic spelling and punctuation in his letters and diary entries. We have not, however, extended this principle to cover letters or documents by other hands, where obvious mistakes have been silently corrected.

Format: in the lay-out of the letters we give addresses and dates in their original form. Editorial information about location (in the case of some diary entries) or the type of communication, i.e. when it is a postcard or telegram that is reproduced, is contained within square brackets, ranged left at the head of each item. We also indicate where letters are typed (as distinct from handwritten) and where handwritten additions have been made. It was often Britten's custom, on finishing a letter, to add a postscript at the top of the first page, above the address and date. We have preserved this feature where it occurs. Where addresses have been supplied or dates conjectured, this information appears in square brackets, ranged right.

All Britten's letters and diary entries, and Pears's letters and diaries, are set *unjustified*, as are quotations from these sources in the annotations. All other written and published sources appear justified.

Omissions: in Britten's wartime letters to his sisters we have occasionally omitted duplications of news and information. In a very small

number of instances we have omitted a remark which might cause
hurt or pain directly to a living person. In the case of one correspondent, we have acceded to the request that the letters should not be
given in their entirety. All editorial omissions are indicated thus:
[. . .].

We owe a special debt to the Trustees of the Britten–Pears Foundation, the owners of the copyright in Britten's letters and diaries,
his other writings and his unpublished music; and to the Trustees
of the late Sir Peter Pears, owners of the copyright in his letters and
other writings. We acknowledge with special gratitude the unique
contributions Peter Pears made to our knowledge of Britten and his
times.

We express our warmest thanks to our editorial colleagues,
Kathleen Mitchell, Rosamund Strode (Keeper of Manuscripts and
Archivist of the Britten–Pears Library) and Judy Young, for their
many skills, encouragement, patience and enthusiasm, and not least
their ability to keep the editors at their editing.

We acknowledge gratefully the contribution of Dr John Evans, who
participated at an early stage in the selection and documentation of
the letters.

We have been helped in the preparation of these volumes for
publication by the following friends and colleagues at (or associated
with) Faber and Faber: Helen Sprott, James Butler (the designer), Jill
Burrows, Dave Fairey, Daphne Tagg and Ingrid Grimes.

We wish to thank the following individuals and institutions for
the help given us throughout the preparation of this project. Without
their particular assistance our task would not just have been difficult
– it would have been impossible: the late Hedli Anderson; Lady
Berkeley (the widow of Sir Lennox Berkeley) and Michael Berkeley;
John Bishop and the Frank Bridge Trust; Lady Bliss (widow of Sir
Arthur Bliss); Paul Bowles (Tangier); Joy Bowesman; Henry Boys;
Alan Britten; the late Barbara Britten; Mrs H. Marjorie Britten; the
late Robert Britten; the late Mrs Antonio Brosa; Jill Burrows; Hugh
Cobbe; Mr and Mrs Eric Crozier; the late Sir Clifford Curzon; the
Estate of the late Ronald Duncan; Albert Goldberg (Pasadena); Paul
Hagland (Chicago); the late Trevor Harvey; the late Imogen Holst;
the Revd Michael Mayer; Professor Edward Mendelson (New York)
and his co-Executors of the Estate of W.H. Auden; George Neigh-
bour; Sir Sidney Nolan, OM; Daphne Oliver; John Pounder; Hans
Erik Pringsheim (Tokyo); Dr Basil Reeve (Colorado); Bobby Rothman
(Southold, Long Island); the late David Rothman (Southold, Long

Island); Beata Sauerlander (New York); Wulff Scherchen; Marion Thorpe; the late Elizabeth Welford (Beth Britten); Paul Wilson (former Librarian) and the Staff of the Britten–Pears Library (Gary Coward, Jennifer McGough, Sylvia Rush, Anne Surfling and Pamela Wheeler).

We also wish to acknowledge the following individuals for their valuable assistance: John Alston; John Amis; Mrs Harold Bailey (Chicago); Dr Paul Banks; Mr and Mrs George Barker; Professor Cyrilla Barr (Catholic University of America, Washington, DC); Mr and Mrs Paul Bechgaard; George Behrend; Eileen Bell; the late Max Bennett, and Mrs Bennett; Bailey Bird (Toronto); Susan Briggs; Anthony Burton (BBC); Humphrey Carpenter; Colin Chambers (Royal Shakespeare Company); Marion Coate; the late Sir William Coldstream; the Revd Charles Coleman; Dr Mervyn Cooke; Joan Cross; Jeremy Cullum; Caroline Cuthbert; Mr and Mrs Norman Del Mar; Peter Dickinson; David Dorward; Basil Douglas; Neville Dove; Barbara Dunkerley; Dr Graham Elliott; Ethel Farrell; Tony Fell (Boosey & Hawkes Ltd); Howard Ferguson; Christopher Finzi; Lewis Foreman; Ellis J. Freedman (New York); the late Anthony Friese-Green; Dr Malcolm Gillies; Sir William Glock; Humphrey Gyde; Mrs Daphne Hayter (Canberra); Christopher Headington; Frances Heinsheimer Wainright (CBC, Montreal); Hans W. Heinsheimer (New York); Charles Hobday; Alan Hollinghurst; Dr Laton E. Holmgren (Palm Desert); John Hurst; Professor Samuel Hynes; the late Christopher Isherwood; the late Lotte Jacobi; Arthur Jacobs; Marjorie King; Bridget Kitley; Eardley Knollys; Professor Mary Lago (University of Missouri); Julia Lang; Anita Lasker Wallfisch; Remo Lauricella; David Layton; Marion Leigh (Paris); John Lindsay; John Lucas; Nigel Luckhurst; William MacDougall; Neil Mackie; Anne Macnaghten; Corinna MacNeice; Dame Elizabeth Maconchy; the late Anna Mahler; Colin Matthews; Robert Medley; Sir Yehudi Menuhin, OM; Professor Atsushi Miura (Yokohama); Nell Moody; Miss M.E. Morling; Michael Nicholas; Patricia Nicholson; Arthur Oldham (Paris); Mrs Frances Palmer; Tony Palmer; J. Allan Pearce; Carlos Pemberton (Buenos Aires); Vivian Perlis (Yale); Christopher Pollard (Gramophone); Tony Pool (Boosey & Hawkes Ltd); Julian Potter; Sir Richard Powell; Christopher Raeburn; Lady Jean Redcliffe-Maud; Jonathan Rennert (St Michael's, Cornhill); Bernard Richards; John von Rhein (Chicago); Winifred Roberts; James Rusbridger; Mr and Mrs Peter du Sautoy; the late Ian Scott-Kilvert; Caroline Seebohm (Mrs Walter Lippincott) (New York); Dr Michael Sells; Donald Sewell; Desmond Shawe-Taylor; the late Enid Slater; the late Dr Milton Smith (New York); Brigid (Brigitte) Steiner (New York); Professor Kamtorn Snidvongse

(Bangkok); Leonard Thompson; Rita Thomson; Richard Toeman (Josef Weinberger Ltd); the late Julian Trevelyan; Mr and Mrs Theodor Uppman (New York); Malcolm Walker; the late R.N. White; Robin Whitworth; Ninka Willcock; Dr Wynne Willson; Mrs Hilde Wittgenstein (New York); A.W.P. Woodard; Sir Paul Wright.

The following institutions, libraries and other organizations have been consistently helpful in answering our enquiries: Aldeburgh Foundation; Arts Council of Great Britain; Austrian National Library (Information Section, Christine Bader); Bibliothèque historique de la ville de Paris (Jean Derens); Bibliothèque Nationale (Bibliothèque et Musée de l'Opéra, M.J. Kerhoas); Ballet Rambert (Jane Pritchard); Boosey & Hawkes Ltd (Archive Department, Andrew Kemp and Malcolm Smith); Boosey & Hawkes (Canada) Ltd (George Ullman); Boosey & Hawkes Inc., New York; Boston Symphony Orchestra (Eleanor McGourty, Archives Coordinator); BBC Music Library; BBC Written Archives Centre (John Jordan); British Film Institute (F. Margaret Binnie); British Library (Rutland Boughton Collection); Byron Society (Elma Dangerfield); University of California at Los Angeles (Stephen Fry and Alva Moore Stevenson); Cambridge City Library; Central Music Library, Westminster; Centre Belge de Documentation Musicale (Anna Van Steenbergen); Chester Music (Christine Smith); Cleveland Orchestra (Program Editor); Music Division, Library of Congress, Washington, DC (Elmer Booze and Wayne D. Shirley); Constable Publishers (Christine Senior); Courtauld Institute of Art (Witt Library, Kate Liley); Dartington College of Arts; Decca International Ltd (Maureen Fortey and John Parry); Library Staff of the University of East Anglia; Finsbury Local History Library; French Embassy (Cultural Counsellor); Glyndebourne Festival Opera Archive (Rosy Runciman); Goldsmith's Library (Leicester Public Libraries); Benny Goodman Estate (William F. Hyland); Grand Rapids Symphony Orchestra (Peter W. Smith); Gresham's School, Holt (Michael Barrett); Guildhall School of Music; The Hulton Picture Company (Harriet Orr); Ibbs and Tillett Ltd (Beryl Ball and Tim Bullamore); Ipswich Public Library (County Information Service); Islington Council Libraries Department (Hazel Vanderhoeven); John Ireland Trust; Kurt Weill Foundation for Music (Dr Kim H. Kowalke); Lancing College; Law Society Reference Library; London Philharmonic Orchestra (John Willan); Los Angeles Philharmonic Association; Lowestoft Local History Library; Raymond Mander and Joe Mitchenson Theatre Collection; Marylebone Local History Library; Mendelssohn Scholarship Foundation (Hon. Sec., Pamela Harwood); Library of the University of Michigan (Tom Burnett); Moulsford Preparatory School (D.R. Jarman); NBC Orchestra (New York); National Sound Archive (Judith Barnes); Newberry Library, Chicago (Diana Haskell); University of New Mexico, Albuquerque (Barbara Johnson, Special Collections Department); University of New Jersey (Institute of Jazz Studies, Dan Morgenstern); News International Newspapers Ltd (R. Cain); New York Philharmonic Orchestra (Mark C. Young); New York Public Library (Henry W. and Albert A. Berg Collection, Astor, Lenox and Tilden Foundations, Curator, the late Dr Lola L. Szladits, and Wayne Furman, Music Division); Norfolk Record Office; Norwich Public Library; *Observer* Reference Library; Oriel College, Oxford; Oxford University Press, Music Department (Sally Broadhurst and Liz Burrell); Peace Pledge Union (William Hetherington); Paul Sacher Foundation, Basel (Niklaus Röthlin); Performing Right Society (John Billingham and Peter L.T. Stroud); Science Museum Library; the Library (Barbirolli papers) of the Royal Academy of Music (Joan Slater (Librarian) and Kathy Adamson, Nazlin Bhimani and Rosalind Woodall); Royal College of Music (Christopher Bornet, Celia Clarke, Paul Collen and Oliver Davies); Royal College of Physicians (Geoffrey Davenport); Royal Harwich Yacht Club (Commodore David Hall); Royal Liverpool Philharmonic Orchestra (Paul Meacham); St Helen's Local History Library, Merseyside; Arnold Schoenberg Institute (R. Wayne Shoaf); Sion College Library; South African Library, Johannesburg (Vallein Haddad); Suffolk Record Office; H.M. Tennent Ltd; Theatre Museum (Andrew Kirk); *The Times* Reference Library; Music Library, Yale University (Harold E. Samuel).

We are specially pleased to be able to acknowledge the following copyright holders of letters to Britten, Pears and others which appear in our annotations; for their co-operation we are extremely grateful: the Executors of the Estate of W.H. Auden; Don Bachardy (Executor of the Estate of the late Christopher Isherwood); Boosey & Hawkes Music Publishers Ltd; Rutland Boughton Music Trust; Frank Bridge Trust (John Bishop); BBC Written Archives Centre; the late Aaron Copland; Peter Cox; Eric Crozier; Fritz Curzon; Winton Dean; Mrs Rose Marie Duncan; Marina Fistoulari-Mahler; Professor Alexander Goehr; Humphrey Gyde; Bridget Kitley; Eardley Knollys; Performing Right Society (Michael Freegard); Sir Stephen Spender; Leonard Thompson; Marion Thorpe; Sir Michael Tippett, OM; Lady Walton; John Woolford; C.C. Wright and Charles Saunders (the Executors of the Estate of the Revd Walter Hussey).

Copyright material from the following newspapers, journals and magazines has been reproduced with permission: *Christian Science Monitor*; *Cincinnati Enquirer*; *Daily Mail*; *Daily Telegraph*; *East Anglian*

Daily Times; Eastern Daily Press; Evening Standard (*Express Newspapers* plc); *The Gresham; Journal of Commerce; Journal of the English Folk Dance and Song Society; The Listener; Liverpool Daily Post; London Magazine; Los Angeles Times; Lowestoft Journal; Music Survey; Musical Opinion; Musical Times; New Statesman* (reproduced with permission of *New Statesman & Society*); *New York Times; Observer; Opera News; Sight and Sound; Sunday Telegraph; Sunday Times* (Times Newspapers Ltd); *Tempo; Time* Magazine; *The Times* (Times Newspapers Ltd).

Copyright material from the following publishers' books has been reproduced with permission: Aitken and Stone Ltd; Anchor Books (Doubleday and Co. Ltd); Chatto & Windus Ltd; The City University; Ernst Eulenburg Ltd; Faber and Faber Ltd; Faber Music Ltd; Grafton Books; Harper & Row, Publishers, Inc.; Jonathan Cape Ltd; The Macdonald Group; Macmillan Publishers Ltd; Michael Joseph Ltd; Oxford University Press; Secker & Warburg; Sigmund Freud Copyrights; Tate Gallery; Thomas Nelson and Sons Ltd; Unwin Hyman Ltd. All titles from which copyright material has been quoted are included, with full bibliographical details, in the Bibliography, pp. 1293–1331.

We are pleased to be able to include the pair of music examples used on p. 931: the extract from Ravel's *Histoires naturelles* is reproduced by permission of Editions Durand S.A., Paris/UMP Ltd; the extract from Britten's *Michelangelo Sonnets* is reproduced by permission of Boosey & Hawkes Ltd.

We have made every effort to trace copyright owners and shall be glad to hear from those that we have been unable to locate or have inadvertently omitted, to whom we extend our apologies.

DM, PR

KEY TO BIBLIOGRAPHICAL ABBREVIATIONS

BBAA   Benjamin Britten, *On Receiving the First Aspen Award*, London, Faber and Faber, 1964

BBST   Benjamin Britten, 'Britten Looking Back', *Sunday Telegraph*, 17 November 1963, p. 9

BC   Christopher Palmer (editor), *The Britten Companion*, London, Faber and Faber, 1984

DMBA   Donald Mitchell, *Britten and Auden in the Thirties: The Year 1936*, London, Faber and Faber, 1981

DMHK   Donald Mitchell and Hans Keller (editors), *Benjamin Britten: A Commentary on His Works from a Group of Specialists*, London, Rockliff, 1952

DMPB   W.H. Auden, *Paul Bunyan: The Libretto of the Opera by Benjamin Britten*, with an essay by Donald Mitchell, London, Faber and Faber, 1988

DNB   *The Dictionary of National Biography*

DVDM   Donald Mitchell (compiler and editor), *Benjamin Britten: Death in Venice*, Cambridge, Cambridge University Press, 1987

EMWHA   W.H. Auden, *The Complete Works of W.H. Auden: Plays (with Christopher Isherwood) and other Dramatic Writings, 1928–1938*, edited by Edward Mendelson, London, Faber and Faber, 1989

EWB   Beth Britten, *My Brother Benjamin*, Bourne End, The Kensal Press, 1986

EWW   Eric Walter White, *Benjamin Britten: His Life and Operas*, 2nd edition, edited by John Evans, London, Faber and Faber, 1983

GE   Graham Elliott, *Benjamin Britten: The Things Spiritual*, Ph.D. dissertation, University of Wales, 1985

HCWHA   Humphrey Carpenter, *W.H. Auden: A Biography*, London, Allen & Unwin, 1981

IHB   Imogen Holst, *Britten* (The Great Composers), 3rd edition, London, Faber and Faber, 1980

LFBML   Lewis Foreman, *From Parry to Britten: British Music in Letters*, London, Batsford, 1987

MKWW   Michael Kennedy, *Portrait of Walton*, Oxford, Oxford University Press, 1989

PFL   Donald Mitchell and John Evans, *Pictures from a Life: Benjamin Britten 1913–1976*, London, Faber and Faber, 1978

PGPB   Philip Brett (compiler), *Benjamin Britten: Peter Grimes*, Cambridge, Cambridge University Press, 1983

PHFB   Paul Hindmarsh, *Frank Bridge: A Thematic Catalogue*, London, Faber Music, 1983

PPT   Marion Thorpe (editor), *Peter Pears: A Tribute on His 75th Birthday*, London, Faber Music/The Britten Estate, 1985

PPTMS   *A Tenor Man's Story*, Central Television/Barrie Gavin, 1985

PR   Philip Reed, *The Incidental Music of Benjamin Britten: A Study and Catalogue of His Music for Film, Theatre and Radio*, Ph.D. dissertation, University of East Anglia, 1988

RDBB   Ronald Duncan, *Working with Britten: A Personal Memoir*, Welcombe, The Rebel Press, 1981

TBB   Anthony Gishford (editor), *Tribute to Benjamin Britten on His Fiftieth Birthday*, London, Faber and Faber, 1963

TP   *A time there was . . . : A Profile of Benjamin Britten*, London Weekend Television/Tony Palmer, 1980

INTRODUCTION

Donald Mitchell

I LIFE

The Pattern of Life: Britten's Diaries

A diary is a kind of private bulwark against
the endless inroads made upon the memory by time.
Erich Heller

Andrew Motion, the poet and biographer, must surely be our ideal reader. In the *Sunday Times* (Books section, 26 March 1989), commenting on a new biography of Wordsworth, he wrote: 'I regret the absence of personal detail which even the most vigorous biography needs to bring it to life. I want to know when people had their hair cut as well as when they wrote their great works.'

He might be joined by Roy Jenkins, politician and biographer, who, on reviewing the Leo Amery Diaries in the *Observer* (7 August 1988), propounded 'two propositions: First, that although rashes of footnotes can be both ugly and irritating, it is better to put up with a moderate quantity than to be left constantly floundering. And second, that it is too austere to believe that the content of conversations is always more interesting than the framework in which they took place. Half the fun of diaries is provided by "pattern of life" details.' (We learn, almost as we go to press, that each volume of the monumental edition of *The Gladstone Diaries* (Vols. 9–11, Oxford, Clarendon Press, 1986–9) concludes with a section 'Where Was He?', showing where he spent the night. We wish the idea had occurred to us.)

Others, we recognize, may protest at an epidemic of footnotes. But to establish the pattern of Britten's life – the music and the haircuts – has been our aim, and in the achievement of that objective footnotes have been indispensable. In any case – as the late and sorely missed Hans Keller might have said – doesn't it all depend on the footnotes and how interesting or necessary they are? We must confess to finding very little in Britten's life that has not proved of interest and of some significance for his evolution as a composer.

When it comes to articulating the 'pattern of life', Britten's pocket diaries, naturally, have offered vital information about almost every sphere of his activities from 1928 to 1939 – music, people, politics, schooldays, family life, personal history, successes, disappointments, his training, employment, and yes – as it happens – when and where he had his hair cut. It was not our first intention to make such ample use of the diaries: how they first surfaced is explained below (see pp. 56–7). These extraordinary documents are of such interest and importance in their own right that we had thought their (complete) publication should follow publication of the letters. But the longer we worked on the letters, the more we found ourselves relying on the diaries to clarify or amplify references in the letters and, above all, to fill out extensive chronological gaps in the correspondence. For example, few letters are extant for the years 1931 and 1932, and here we have called on the diaries extensively to maintain the narrative thread. We have also tried to include many of the diary entries relating to principal national and political events that happened during the decades covered by this first volume of letters, and, naturally, all major entries relating to the composition and performance of Britten's works, of all kinds. But much remains still be to published, and the complete publication of the diaries, comprehensively annotated, must be one of the next steps to be taken in Britten studies. It will certainly involve a lot more footnotes.

Even the sampling of the diaries that appears in these volumes shows, we suggest, their richness as a source. They inform us about the closeness of family life at Lowestoft and also how the texture of that life was replicated in London during Britten's student days and early manhood, when he shared a flat with sister Beth and was a regular madrigalist with sister Barbara, who was secretary of the Arnold Foster choir. If London was, in some respects, a continuation of life at Lowestoft, with tennis and church-going sustained, and his mother a frequent visitor, in other major respects it was revelatory. For a start there was a wealth of new musical experience – all faithfully recorded in the diaries – to absorb the attention and imagination of the boy from the provinces: new music and new friends. There was life at the Royal College of Music, and lessons with John Ireland. The diaries for the first time, we think, allow us to assess that teacher/pupil relationship and to realize that it was by no means a wholly negative experience: there were some very good lessons (Britten seems to have forgotten these in later life and remembered only the bad ones). As for the College, the conjunction of diaries and letters permits us to document in detail the history of his student years and reflect a little on the prevailing attitudes to his exceptional gifts. As we shall see, the charge of unacceptable 'cleverness' was one that would stick. But of course it was not from the College that Britten received his 'training'. It was Frank Bridge who was his teacher. The diaries are crowded with references to Bridge, to his music, to his prowess as a conductor and viola player, entries that go a little way towards compensating us for what seems to be the irretrievable loss of the Britten side of the correspondence with his mentor. (It was probably the rough ride given to Bridge by the

English press in the thirties that contributed to his pupil's dislike of critics.) The diaries record the concerts and operas he attended, his intense musical enthusiasms, some of which endured – Mahler – some of which fell away – Beethoven, Wagner – and his keen, evaluating observation of performance and performers. They remind us too of his concentration on his own talents as a performer: incessant piano practice (when it was envisaged that he might have to become a pianist to survive economically: it was about the only time in his life he *did* practise) and viola studies (while it was not unknown for him on occasions to take up his brother Robert's violin). Penetrating this mass of activity, involvement and comment like a piercing searchlight is the ambition to compose, to be a composer; and it is the diaries that provide us with the evidence of the unremitting drive, energy and application the child, the boy and the young man brought to this central goal. As we shall observe more than once, the work ethic was always strong in him. The diaries show just how early it emerged, and brought him rewards at an unusually early stage in his professional career: he was talking to the publisher, Hubert Foss, in 1932, while still at the College.

As for the narrative of Britten's personal life – his inner life – we have not hesitated to use the diaries whenever they had a significant statement to make or indicated an important decision or change of position or attitude. It is probably only a reading of the diaries in their entirety that will convey to the full the constancy of his preoccupations, and their importance for his creativity. His need for children, his observation of them, and his enjoyment of their company: these are characteristics that are confirmed by the diaries and make sense of the creative energy that Britten put into writing music for them. A frieze of boys runs through the diaries, rather like the procession of girls along the front at Balbec in Proust's *A la Recherche du temps perdu*, an integral part of *his* seascape.

In this area the diaries show Britten located somewhere between a commitment to innocence and an appetite for experience, not always comfortably so. Uncomfortable for him, maybe. We can look to the music, in which the conflicts, if there were such, were resolved.[1] These passing diary entries, or the Dunkerley story (see note 3 to Diary for January 1936, pp. 40–8) and others like it, make especially telling a remark of Britten's in a letter to Pears, 17 November 1964, when Pears was away and Britten had had one of his protégés in the house: 'Little John has cheered me up a bit. He is a sweet affectionate child – makes one feel rather what one has missed in not having a child.' He adds ruefully, 'But one must remember the

Butler (notebook) bit – about choosing the mother & "Besides, he would probably be a girl".[2] But John is a little bit of a substitute & I'm really lucky.' The pattern of life, once set, rolled inexorably on.

The diaries often predict a future that can hardly have been guessed at. For example, this historic entry for 1 June 1932, which initiated what must be the longest period of gestation in Britten's work, even for a composer who often meditated on a project for a long time before embarking on it: '[. . .] listen to wireless – Saint-Saëns Carnival des Animaux – and a wonderful, impressive but terribly eerie & scarey play "The Turn of the Screw" by Henry James.'

There are many like instances: a search in 1935 for a Latin text appropriate for an intended *Hymn to St Cecilia* (Auden was eventually to oblige in the 1940s); or in the same year a setting of Blake's 'Poison Tree' (the text, though not the music, was to be incorporated into the Blake cycle of 1965).

Britten's dissatisfaction with his College days is amply documented. He gave expression to it in his diary on 13 October 1932: 'More copying before going to R.C.M. in morning for the most atrocious of all rehearsals of my Sinfonietta. Only 8 inst. out of the 10 (& of these 3 new!) What an institution. [. . .] Dinner with Bridges with moaning about R.C.M.'

He was to find his reputation for 'cleverness', which was established at the College and caused difficulties for him there, was by no means a passing phenomenon. On the contrary, it was a view that was formidably to mould English critical opinion up to and beyond the war (hence the fascination of the diaries and auxiliary documentation which show that opinion in the making). One might have expected something better of Edmund Rubbra (who had written well of *A Boy was Born*) than his comment on *Our Hunting Fathers*: 'dry, cocktail cleverness, unrelieved by any real beauty of line'. Of course composers are unreliable witnesses, but the choice of words is revealing and suggests how current and widely received this particular opinion was. It was promoted to the status of doctrine in the fifth edition of *Grove*, edited by Eric Blom and published in 1954, in which Frank Howes, in his main entry on the composer, enshrines a judgement which he attributes to others without acknowledging that it was a judgement he himself shared:

Critical opinion, towards which his attitude is somewhat gunpowdery, is divided not so much on the question of his extraordinary talent, which can hardly be denied, as on the question how much is heart and how much is head. 'Clever' is often applied to him with its usual [sic] pejorative implication: there is universal agreement that Britten is extremely clever, but the imputation is left that feelings do not go deep enough in his music. The question is of interest only for its bearing on estimates of what he may yet achieve. In what he has already accomplished it may be enough to affirm that to his cleverness he certainly adds an imagination of extraordinary fertility.

'Clever' and 'cleverness' toll like a bell in the space of a very short paragraph. The ensuing letters and diaries not only document, among many other things, the reception and assessment of a composer's music. They also document and, one may think, throw a revelatory light on the characterizing features and institutional attitudes of English musical culture in the thirties. One wonders, sometimes, how he survived them.

I have used as a motto for the first section of my Introduction some words from Erich Heller's outstanding essay, 'Thomas Mann's diaries and the search for identity' (from *In the Age of Prose*, Cambridge, Cambridge University Press, 1984), in the course of which he develops the theme of an artist's private diaries functioning as a means of self-identification, of answering the question 'Whom am I?' He introduces Schopenhauer's observation that 'the "true artist" must "disown for some time his whole personality and survive alone as . . . a medium of lucid visions" '; Keats's confession 'that he is a poet and, *therefore*, has no identical nature'; T.S. Eliot's ' "continual extinction of personality" as the condition for "the progress of an artist" '; and – perhaps most shrewd of all – Nietzsche's comment that 'the perfect artist is for ever and ever shut off from all "reality" '.

Professor Heller concludes:

It is . . . the desire . . . to define and ultimately even reveal himself as a 'real person' that accounts for Thomas Mann's pedantic zeal of keeping diaries . . .

diaries which

abound with every imaginable wavering and indecision, ambivalence and contradiction; yet toothaches and indigestion, insomnia and sleeping tablets, haircuts, having tea with so-and-so – all these trivia are at least irrefutably, unironically, unambiguously 'real'.

With hindsight, it is not at all surprising that long, long after he had ceased being a diarist himself, Britten was to undertake a diarist's opera, *Death in Venice*, in which indeed the very issues raised so eloquently in Heller's essay, and by others before him, are precisely addressed, and in particular the abyss that opens up between the 'perfect artist' and 'reality'.

Thus Britten's diaries, limited through the period of his keeping

them was (only from 1928 to 1939), open up perspectives on his life
as a whole and on his life's work. I have no doubt that one of the
reasons for his handing over the diaries to me in 1976 was to affirm
that he was – had been – a 'real person', toothache, haircuts and all.
(How appropriate that a haircut should have such significance attached to it in *Death in Venice*, both in Mann's story and Britten's opera!)

'Who am I? Who *was* I?': the diaries help us to answer both questions. They were part of Britten's search for, and establishing of, an
identity.

Mr and Mrs R.V. Britten

> . . . if a man has been his mother's undisputed darling he retains
> throughout life the triumphant feeling, the confidence in success,
> which not seldom brings actual success along with it.
>
> Sigmund Freud*

The only letters of Britten's that match his letters to Pears in intensity
of feeling are those to his mother, Edith, especially those from his
childhood and adolescence. They too were love letters, albeit of a
different kind. His relationship with his mother was beyond doubt
an extremely powerful one, one that very clearly – and it would seem
intendedly – shaped and guided the development of his character,
defined his life's goals and generated in him the ambition to achieve
them.

The sometimes painful intensity of the feelings – above all the
sense of separation – show up in his schoolboy diaries. I choose a
sequence of diary entries from January and February 1930, when
Britten was at Gresham's aged sixteen:

22 January
No letter from Mummy. She hasn't written since Friday, & then only a
note.

23 January
I really am getting alarmed at the lack of a letter from Mummy. Especially
as I dreamed about death 2ce last night, & both times tho' not she, it
was connected with her. I don't like to write in case our letters cross, but
I shall certainly write soon [. . .]

24 January
The long-waited for letter arrives by the last post; it has relieved me
enormously [. . .]

A Childhood Recollection from *Dichtung und Wahrheit*, quoted in *Sigmund Freud: His Life
in Pictures and Words*, edited by Ernst Freud, Lucie Freud and Ilse Grubrich-Smitis
(Harmondsworth, Penguin, 1985), p. 71.

The next month, on the 11th, Britten records another anxious, death-haunted family dream (small wonder that in his *Quatre Chansons Françaises*, written in 1928 and dedicated to his parents, the schoolboy composer set a poem of Victor Hugo's, 'L'Enfance', in which a young child sings while the sick mother lies dying):

I really think that last night was the most miserable night of my existance. 1. I couldn't get to sleep (not unusual). 2. I had litterally about 6 terrible dreams, seperated by a about ½ hr. of sleeplessness. in 1. Mummy was killed by a chimneystack falling through the roof. 2. Pop was killed when driving a bus (!) over Kessingland dam [south of Lowestoft]. 3. Beth (or Barbara) was burned in the house catching fire. I cannot remember the others.

But perhaps the most telling and revealing entry is also one of the shortest, made on 21 June, after Britten's return to school from days in London spent with his mother:

Quite a successful day considering it is the first away from my darling.

There was not, I think, to be another 'my darling' in Britten's life until Pears came into it.

In the light of 'existance', 'litterally' and 'seperated' in the diary entry for 11 June, it is the moment perhaps to reiterate an important editorial principle: we print the texts of the diaries and letters exactly as they appear in Britten's hand, and do not attempt to correct his punctuation or highly idiosyncratic spelling. To the end of his life he wrote letters always with a dictionary nearby.

Mrs Britten was the first musician, the first *performer* her son ever met, perhaps at a very early age. It must have been a memory of his own infancy that prompted him to make this reply to a 1968 interview[3] for the Canadian Broadcasting Corporation:

I think that the acme of perfection in the art – in music art – is the human voice singing beautifully [. . .]

and quote as an example:

[. . .] one's mother [singing] over one, trying to make one go to sleep when one's two years old and having a restless night [. . .]

The detail of that recollection suggests that Britten was drawing on his own experience. His sister Beth, in a 1973 interview for the BBC, confirmed that her brother was 'Always very nervy, yes; never a very good sleeper' (their father was to write to his wife on 27 April 1915, when Britten was seventeen months old, 'Benjy, I believe, is a bit of a bother in getting to sleep, Nurse says "he is so knowing he knows the <u>instance</u> I move from him" '), and paid tribute to her 'very musical' mother. She continued:

She used to play and sing. In fact, if she hadn't married she might have been a professional singer, and she was also a very good pianist, they [her mother and younger brother] always played duets on Sunday afternoons [. . .]

But to the life of what was undoubtedly a musical household, Britten's father, so Beth remembered (in an interview with Charles Ford in 1976), contributed 'absolutely nothing at all'. (She further recalled the odd fact that he enjoyed music only if it were 'in the minor key'.) In the same interview she remarked that her mother spoilt her youngest child 'terribly':

I think my father was extra hard on him because he felt he had to make up for it and I think he was always rather afraid for him [. . .] about what his life was going to be like and whether he was strong enough.

A somewhat similar impression, though more forcefully expressed, emerges from an interview given me in 1986 by Basil Reeve, a close boyhood friend of the composer's, himself an able pianist and friend, in his eyes, sanctioned by Mrs Britten: 'I could only see him with her permission.' But see him often he did (see note 2 to Diary for 1 January 1931), as Britten's diaries testify. Dr Reeve's vivid memories are of exceptional interest because they survive from a period when Britten's sisters were away from home[4] and he was invited into the household by Mrs Britten as an appropriate companion for her son. He recalls the father in these terms:

. . . I don't think [he] was at all musical. He was, I suppose, one of the best dentists in Lowestoft – perhaps the best dentist – very busy, down-to-earth. He never thought that Ben could do a thing, musically . . . [i.e.] he didn't see how anyone could make a living at it . . . He was rather a hard man, I'd say; but a good person.[5]

'Hard' is an adjective used by both the daughter and the school-friend. But I do not think one should underestimate the genuine anxiety on the part of Britten's parents, and his father in particular, about the future of their prodigiously endowed son, a 'gift' (in more senses than one) that could never have been predicted and left them uncertain about how best to act, as Beth recalled in 1976:

. . . it was difficult for my parents, because they didn't quite know whether he was going to be able to make the grade.

In her memoir [EWB] she wrote,

My father was not a mean man, but expenses weighed heavily on him. He had four children to educate and there were no grants in those days (p. 51).

What later she refers to as 'our father's anxiety about finance' (p. 52),

was doubtless one of the reasons for the impression he made of
being 'hard' with or on his son. However, the letters he exchanged
with him are affectionate enough in tone, and – when responding
to early musical successes – admiring and proud (see, for example,
Letter 37). The dedication of Britten's opus 3, *A Boy was Born*,[6] to
'my father' probably carried a more complex weight of feeling than
one might at first suspect.[7]

Mrs Britten's impact on her son was of an altogether different
order, and its influence, beyond question, more lasting. Britten's
letters to his mother, and his diaries, speak eloquently of the bond
between them. Oddly, and perhaps significantly, when Britten met
Dr Reeve in 1964, at Aspen, Colorado – Britten was there to receive
the first Aspen Award – he reacted to his old friend's reminder –
'You know, your mother used to do so-and-so' – by remarking, 'Did
she? You know, I can't remember anything about my mother'; and
it is the case that, the letters and diaries apart, there are no further
first-hand reminiscences of his mother from Britten, only a very
occasional reference prompted by the calendar – for example, birthday or other festivity (Christmas, New Year). After her death in
January 1937, and his immediate response to it, the rest was silence,
and we have to rely on the memories of her daughter, Beth, and the
testimony of family friends and acquaintances. It is precisely here
that Dr Reeve's memories of the home at Lowestoft in 1928–32 are
so valuable and revealing.

'I think Ben's mother decided I was a good person for Ben to
know,' Dr Reeve recalls. 'That's really how it happened. So she
arranged his life. His mother really made him a great musician.
That's absolutely clear to me.' The 'control' factor was something he
insists on more than once:

At times, we had very good times together, till we were eighteen or so,
when I guess we were too much for the mother – till we went up to London
[Britten at the Royal College of Music] . . . and I was at Oxford. Then she
couldn't take control. Everything was absolutely controlled before; the length
of time that we two could be together, what we could do together – absolutely
controlled . . . Entirely determined by the mother; absolutely structured,
you know – might have been a Communist state . . . It was astonishing; but
when we got away it wasn't like this at all, you see . . . She was a very
formidable woman with him. No, I could only see him with her permission.

Dr Reeve also touched on the sense of driving ambition generated
by the mother:

DONALD MITCHELL: . . . it's clear from the early letters and the diaries
   that she certainly was the dominant figure in Ben's early life.

BASIL REEVE: Absolutely.

DM: And you were aware of that, were you?

BR: Oh yes . . . these astonishing things happened, that, for
       instance, when we would walk out to Morlings [the music
       shop in Lowestoft] and back again, we would have a lot of
       conversation, and quite often we would talk about the three
       Bs, or the four Bs. The three Bs were Bach, Beethoven and
       Brahms, and the fourth B was Britten, and when I told this to
       Beth, she said, 'I don't believe it; because if my father had
       ever heard this he'd have pooh-poohed it, he'd have said,
       "This is ridiculous." '⁸ So she had this tremendous drive; but
       also I think she must have had a hell of a lot of sense to make
       him into an outstanding musician.

It was a crucial point in this interview to which we returned:

BR: And this terrible drive – 'You've got to do it, you've got to do
       it', you see –

DM: Become the fourth B?

BR: Yes.

DM: Do you think that was something the mother really – do you
       think she saw him as a fourth B?

BR: Oh yes; oh yes. We talked about this perfectly seriously . . .
       No, the mother was *determined* that he should be a great
       musician.

It was a combination, Dr Reeve suggests, of the mother's 'drive'
and the father's 'down-to-earth attitude' ('She must have done all
this management without the father's knowledge, or with very little
of the father's knowledge') that was influential in shaping the boy's
character. Certainly ambition remained with Britten as a conspicuous
feature of his personality, though perhaps of a rather different kind
from the ambition his mother had for him. It was not part of his
personality to see himself as a fourth B: the idea, in later life, would
have appalled him. Small wonder that he kept quiet about, or sup-
pressed, the memory from childhood. (In any event, he was eventually to ditch two of the Bs whom his mother admired.) But the drive
which motivated his own form of ambition, which maybe he owed
ultimately to his mother's determination, stayed with him. I quote
from a 1963 BBC interview, on the occasion of his fiftieth birthday
celebrations:

BBC: What would you like to achieve in the years ahead?

BB: Write better music.⁹

And he was writing despondently to Pears in Denmark just a year later on 17 November – his impending fifty-first birthday may have brought on another fit of self-doubt –

I've been madly low & depressed – you being away mostly I expect, but worried about my work [first Cello Suite, Op. 72] which seems so bad always. If I could only have a longer stretch at it – these "Screws" are a ruddy bore [performances of *The Turn of the Screw* at Oxford which Britten was to conduct] but I fear the fault lies really in me. I must get a better composer some how – but how − − − but how − − − ? [Cf. Albert's *scena* in *Albert Herring*, Act II scene 2, 7 bars before Fig. 97.]

Not a fourth B, not necessarily the best, but always to be *better*: that was surely part of Mrs Britten's legacy to her son. If Frank Bridge was his conscience with regard to his technique, his mother was the source of expectations of himself that were never satisfied. (Bridge was also a substitute parent figure – the musical father his own father wasn't – and one of the first of those dominating sources of authority and influence which were an indispensable part of Britten's life, from which, needless to add, he was obliged to free himself, from Bridge eventually, as from others.)

Music was central to family life at Lowestoft; on occasion, it might seem, music-making was raised to the status of a ritual. On those Sunday afternoons when Britten and his mother played piano duets, it was Wagner who was the chosen composer. Beth remembers the repertory as '*Mastersingers* and *Siegfried Idyll*'. Dr Reeve recalls more specifically that when Britten was young,

I think after lunch every day he had to play the . . . *Siegfried Idyll* to his mother, and he played it from a score. It was extremely good . . .

Even though the details of timing and frequency may differ, the two accounts significantly match up in the emphasis they give to the *Siegfried Idyll*; and in the Archive we find the very score that Dr Reeve mentions, a well-thumbed miniature score of the work, inscribed 'E.B. Britten' and numbered 'No. 16', which allows us accurately to attribute its acquisition to 1926. It was this score, undoubtedly, that serviced the curious domestic rite at 21 Kirkley Cliff Road, when Britten rendered at the piano Wagner's famous declaration of love to Cosima.

There were of course many other differently constituted musical occasions. Reeve recalls Mrs Britten's 'private concerts' in which he, Britten and (later) Charles Coleman (see note 1 to Diary for 1 January 1931) were conscripted to play:

We had to play in these goddamn concerts, and Miss Astle [see note 1 to

Letter 4] would come and she would always play her one piece . . . one piece that she always played, and played quite well . . . and it absolutely horrified me, the whole performance.

He adds that Mrs Britten always saw to it that her son, marked out by his 'great ability', felt himself to be

the centre of everything . . . and so it became, I'm sure, later, very easy for him to be at the centre of things, because this was how he'd been brought up.[10]

Thus music was at the centre of the household – by Mrs Britten's command, so to speak – and at the centre of that was the son 'fifty times more gifted than anyone else'. But central to his musical experience had been, and still was, the talented singer who was his mother;[11] and it is about her voice that Dr Reeve remembers something wholly remarkable:

. . . this is another strange thing. Peter Pears's voice – [Mrs Britten] used to sing a lot, and Ben used to accompany her. His mother's voice and Peter Pears's voice were fantastically similar . . . that's the first thing I noticed.

Dr Reeve was unable to remember what Mrs Britten sang, but he was in no doubt about the character of the voice:

Oh, that voice, it's the same voice. He [Britten] couldn't miss it. And I told this to Beth, and she said, 'My God, yes!'[12]

One has to be careful not to appear to trivialize the relationship of two great artists. Psycho-history cannot account for the composer's genius or Pears's incomparable interpretative gift. But it can tell us something about choice; and it seems clear that a significant history was influential in determining Britten's choice of a *singer* as lifelong companion. His mother's voice, all the evidence suggests, had been at the centre of his earliest musical and emotional life. Now Pears's voice was to be a central creative preoccupation, with momentous consequences for the history of Britten's music. A letter from November 1943 (No. 438) makes the point in his own words:

It was heaven to hear your voice, & to know you're feeling better. Practise hard & get the golden box back in its proper working order again. Something goes wrong with my life when that's not functioning properly.

That last sentence speaks – sings – for itself; and what was true in 1943 held true for the remaining thirty years of partnership and prodigious compositional fertility.

Mrs Britten Dies

Mrs Britten died, in tragically ironic circumstances, in January 1937. The event is fully documented in the letters and diary entries appearing in this first volume.[13]

Her son's grief was profound,[14] and in 1940, perhaps when all the passion of grieving was spent, he was to memorialize *both* parents in the *Sinfonia da Requiem*, the history of which was to become so oddly entangled with the *amour propre* of Imperial Japan. But it was clear to his friends that throughout 1937 the impact of his mother's death was the cause of conspicuous distress and disarray. At the end of the year he went to Sussex, to stay with Marjorie Fass, an immediate neighbour and leading member of the circle surrounding Bridge, and there was much concern over his health and a hectic life-style that was perhaps a means of keeping personal miseries at bay. His host wrote anxiously to Daphne (Bi) Oliver:

Benjy has gone up to town for the day & I'm having a bit of a rest, as he's so tired & over worked he simply can't be still for one second, & will go on having music on the grammy & getting excited whenever he isn't doing a bit of his own scoring. The Brits [Bridges] were so worried abt him being on the verge of a complete mental & physical breakdown – & as he'd been fainting about lately we thought his heart might be groggy (it's not) – so I got [Dr] Downing to vet him yesterday – & she was fine with him, & evidently gave him just the same kind of lecture that Mr Brit had given him in the morning – that it rested with him to refuse work that wasn't worth while – not to stay up till 2.a.m. every night & get up at 8 & instead of decent meals fortifying himself with brandy, when he felt rotten. Mr Brit had told him if he went on like this he'd find one day he was so tired his legs would simply refuse to support him & his brain cease to work – & Downing said he was half starved & simply must contrive to get a decent midday meal [. . .] & when he said he was too awfully busy she just looked at him & smiled for a moment & then said it was quite possible to feed properly even for busy people [. . .] & he looked back at her & felt a fool. He ought to go to bed for a week so that his mind doesn't for ever go on with the work he's trying to do. So instead of going up to town until next Wed: as he meant he's coming back here tonight, & I'll try & keep him in bed for a couple of days – just a case of over excitement & bad management.

And in another letter from these same days, Fass, with a remarkably sure touch, identifies the source of much of Britten's disorientation:

After dinner he sat looking the picture of misery & depression as I know he is in a mental muddle abt a great deal & dreads the future, so I had to go & put my arms round him & give him a good hug & he said 'thank you, Marj, that was nice of you'. He really hates growing up & away from a very happy childhood that ended only with his Mother's death last Christmas – so he dreads this one.

These fascinating reports from a critical year in Britten's life have all the immediacy and verisimilitude of snapshots. They also suggest that Marjorie Fass, a singularly gifted woman in her own right, was the first of the long line of motherly women who were to play such a prominent role in Britten's life: in 1939, Elizabeth Mayer was to assume the mantle.

Inevitably, however, the death of Mrs Britten, as wholly unwished for and arbitrary as it was, must have brought with it some sense of relief.

Dr Reeve was not alone in finding Mrs Britten a powerful and dominating woman, and perhaps especially so after the death of her husband in 1934. For example another close musical friend of Britten's during his young manhood, Henry Boys, 'found her a little intimidating. She was a newly made widow, as it were . . .' It seems clear that when the mitigating, albeit strict (and maybe sceptical) father was no longer a presence, the 'control' factor in Mrs Britten's personality was significantly heightened.[15]

It is absolutely not my intention to make out some sort of a case 'against' Mrs Britten. Others saw her differently, particularly in those years when the family was together and much younger: John Alston, for example, a boyhood friend of the composer's (his mother taught Britten the viola and introduced him to Bridge), 'liked her very much. She was a charming person, but I can't remember very much except that. I was only a kid at the time. Of course, the sisters were around, Beth and Barbara . . .' [16] John Pounder, comparing her with her husband, remembered her as 'very much softer and gentler' though 'more strait-laced'. In any event, if a 'case' were to be made, it could be made as much positively as negatively. She was not only a loving, talented mother but, as Dr Reeve reminded me more than once in his interview, determined both to nourish and to protect her son's exceptional gift. 'Determined' is a word that crops up in Beth's family recollections:

She was a very determined lady . . . If she thought her ewe lamb was being ill-treated or overworked down the hill she would run [to South Lodge Preparatory School] in order to protest. She insisted always that he must have time to practise and write his music.

(EWB, pp. 52–3)

Dr Reeve was to suggest in his interview that although the mother, in his estimation, 'made' Britten, 'she didn't really give him – she didn't release all that enormous warmth that was in him, I think' – which was another way of saying, perhaps, that in this intense relationship the son's capacity freely to feel, to make external relationships, was repressed.

If we were obliged to rely solely on Dr Reeve's witness, it would be no more than prudent to bear in mind that he is clearly a man of strong views, views moreover that include a distinct antipathy for Peter Pears and an implied regret for what he feels to be the impoverishment of Britten's homosexuality. These are views that, I think, undeniably colour his memories, but do not necessarily distort them. One can accept the accuracy of the observations, without accepting all the conclusions Dr Reeve draws. There is, indeed, striking evidence to confirm, not any inability on Britten's part to feel in and through his music (no lack there of passionate engagement), but a difficulty in feeling *outside* it, in the particular sense of making positive commitments to other human relationships, and perhaps especially physical commitments. This, surely, is the conclusion that has to be drawn from the crucial and influential friendship with W.H. Auden, which began in the summer of 1935, and which is fully documented here for the first time. It is neither here nor there whether or no Auden was a successful or unsuccessful 'suitor' (it is improbable, in fact, that this was a role he played). What is more to the point are certain of the revelatory poems he addressed to the young composer during the first years of their brilliant association, poems that testify to the refrigeration of feeling that seems to have been a consequence of the bonding with his mother. We explore all this in considerable detail (see note 3 to Letter 71), and a couple of anticipatory quotations here must suffice. In a poem addressed to Britten, that Britten was himself to set in 1936, 'Underneath the Abject Willow', Auden enjoins his friend, whose 'unique and moping station' has proved him 'cold', to

> Stand up and fold
> Your map of desolation

and ends,

> Coldest love will warm to action,
> Walk then, come,
> No longer numb,
> Into your satisfaction.[17]

'Cold', 'coldest', 'ice', 'numb' – these are all key words in the poem. The assessment, the message and the injunction are clearly spelled out. Further, there is the hope expressed by Auden in his 'Last Will and Testament' from *Letters from Iceland* (with Louis MacNeice, 1937, p. 238): '. . . I beg/That fortune send him soon a passionate affair.'

There is little doubt that the new friends that Britten made in London soon after leaving the College – and in particular Auden and *his* friends – recognized the young composer's seeming emotional 'block' and set about dismantling it; while at the same time encouraging him to come to terms with his own sexuality.[18] But until Mrs Britten died in 1937 – when Britten had known Auden for some eighteen months ('Underneath the Abject Willow' was written in 1936) – all the evidence points to her son existing in a strange kind of void, in which the most intense human relationships were extensions – or perhaps attempted replicas – of the friendships and above all the hierarchies of school. The extraordinary story of Piers Dunkerley (one of the dedicatees of *War Requiem*, see note 3 to Diary for January 1936), whom the twenty-year-old Britten met when Dunkerley was thirteen, powerfully illumines this whole area of the young Britten's emotional life. The relationship – so close to the public-school concept of the senior boy who is his junior's mentor – is fully documented in the diaries, where, one may note in passing, the language often reflects schoolboy slang: things are 'beastly nice', 'simply topping', or 'absolutely ripping'. Dunkerley is a 'first-rate kid'.

But post-January 1937, Britten, however gingerly, begins to allow himself to be led out of his time warp and away from low-temperature, non-physical relationships. On 5 March, he writes in his diary: 'I lunch with David Green – who is very decent – & emphasises the point (very truly) that now is the time for me to decide something about my sexual life.' A crucial entry, one might think.[19] He begins to explore, to experiment.[20] His letters and diaries from this period (and letters from friends) give sufficient indication of the 'liberation' that followed in the wake of his mother's death; and it is not surprising that it was a friend of Auden's – Christopher Isherwood – who had become a friend of Britten's, who was one of his guides:

3 July 1937
After dinner I go out with Christopher Isherwood, sit for ages in Regent's Park & talk very pleasantly & then on to Oddeninos & Café Royal – get slightly drunk, & then at mid-night go to Jermyn St. & have a turkish Bath. Very pleasant sensations – completely sensuous, but very healthy. It is extraordinary to find one's resistance to anything gradually weakening. The trouble was that we spent the night there – couldn't sleep a wink on the hard beds, in the perpetual restlessness of the surroundings.

(The Jermyn Street Turkish Baths (off Piccadilly Circus) were well-known pre- and post-war as a meeting place for homosexuals.)

These new friends – Auden, Isherwood, the GPO Film Unit crowd – broke the mould of old friendships and introduced tensions into existing circles. The observant Marjorie Fass, writing in December 1937 to Daphne Oliver in a series of remarkable letters, which throw much fresh light on how the young Britten was perceived by at least some of his old friends and mentors, singles out Isherwood for a candid commentary:

I'm having a bit of fun with him [Benjy] by not being bowled over with everything that Auden & Christopher Isherwood do – I'm definitely <u>bored</u> with Christopher's adolescent 'smartness' & his unwise interest in prostitutes male & female – & Benjy so hoped I'd like his last book called 'Sally Bowles' [1937] that he insisted on giving it me – & I find it even <u>more</u> boring & not so good as 'Mr Norris' [1935] –   I've just read it this afternoon & shall tell Benjy that the theme is <u>so</u> stale, the prostitute with the heart of gold, having been done in every possible way ever since 'La Dame aux Camélias' of Dumas, that I think it a sheer waste of 3/6. Yesterday to keep him quiet I read aloud to him, his eyes are very inflamed, & he said he loved being read aloud to, but the only other person who'd read to him was Christopher – so I said <u>I</u> didn't compete & had no 'method' of reading aloud & only read because I liked things. So I read first two Theocritus Idylls, neither of which he knew, & both of which he adored – & then began a short story of Somerset Maugham that I find a bit dull but he got interested in – & couldn't finish it by tea time.
In the evening he told me he wished I'd meet Auden as I'd 'got the same kind of brain'!!!! Oh oh said I, no no – but that I was sure I'd like him & we might meet some day. Dear Benjy he <u>is</u> so young & <u>so</u> dazzled – & we 3 sober unshockable Brits <u>are</u> so good for him!!

In August 1938 there was the first performance at the Proms of the Piano Concerto and, according to Fass, a 'happy party at Pagani's afterwards, Brosi, Brits, Audrey & John Alston & a friend or two of Benjy's', a happy occasion, maybe, but one on which the contrasted circles of friends clearly did *not* overlap:

[Benjy] came & sat with us rather than the noisy others who make so much of him, & with whom he shld make it his business to keep in – which shews that his heart is still entire even if his head rather goes up in smoke. [. . .] He knows we <u>know</u>, & that he can't fake to take us in – & we love him so much some day he'll have to hear and bear exactly what we feel abt him but at the moment it's difficult.

The Piano Concerto was not much admired by members of the Bridge circle (see note 1 to Letter 145); and the features of the work they deplored were seen, one may safely assume, to be a consequence of Britten's hijacking by a new set of acquaintances: 'The thing that is bad for him', Fass had written a few months earlier at the end of 1937, 'is that he's meeting brilliant people who are not brilliant in <u>his</u> sphere, but their own, & so make a mutual admiration society – & if one pricks his bubble he bleeds – .'

The year 1937, however, was also to see the beginning of a friendship with someone who did indeed belong to Britten's sphere, an
aspiring young tenor, Peter Pears.[21] They were to set up home
together in a flat in Nevern Square in March 1938. (See PPT, pp.
109–12.) Finding a flat was not easy, and while the search was on
Britten was himself without a settled address: the Old Mill at Snape
was under conversion and part of his time was spent at Peasenhall,
at the home of Beth's parents-in-law. It is this fact, I am confident,
that explains the entry in his diary for 9 February, 'Sleeping with
Peter P.' This does not mean what it means in contemporary par-
lance, but is a characteristic documentary note in the diary of where
Britten found a bed when he was in London in this period (a suitable
flat was signed up on the 25th).

It is a necessary and important point to make because in fact the
evolution of the relationship was altogether slower and more complex
than an incautious reading of the entry for 9 February might suggest.
As these volumes of letters reveal, there were other relationships
first to be discarded or dismantled, some of which were sustained
in parallel with the new and still to be tested relationship that was
in train with Pears (and one of which, at least, was an obsessive,
passionate attachment that had found some form of physical
expression). It is Pears's 1974 letter to Britten, which I quote in full
below on pp. 60–61, that enables us to establish when and where it
was that the final act of possession and commitment was made.
(Peter sometimes spoke of the moment as a mutual 'pledge'.)

We know that Britten and Pears were in Grand Rapids between
12 and 17 June 1939. It was then, precisely, as Pears's letter makes
clear, that their love was consummated, physically and completely
for the first time, though it seems to have been mutually recognized
a few days before, in a hotel on Toronto's University Avenue; Pears
was to recall the occasion in 1959 when writing to Britten from
Toronto, on 28 February: 'I wonder if you remember what happened
in Toronto $19\frac{1}{2}$ years ago? It is a place which cannot help having a
certain importance in my life.' Pears was always the fervent, unin-
hibitedly physical lover[22] and the dominant partner. In 1974 he was
to write, '[. . .] it is you who have given me everything, right from
the beginning, from yourself in Grand Rapids!' It was with the gift
of himself to Pears in June 1939 that the bond was sealed, and Britten
at last entered into the 'satisfaction' that his friends had wished for
him and which was to endure until his death. Already, in 1937, he
had composed an orchestral song specifically for Pears's voice (in *The
Company of Heaven*). The seventh song, 'Being Beauteous', of *Les*

Illuminations (completed in the USA in 1939) was dedicated to him. (No.3b, 'Antique', was dedicated to Wulff Scherchen.) In March 1940, at Amityville – less than a year on from Grand Rapids – he embarked on the *Michelangelo Sonnets*, a sequence of love poems, and the first song-cycle written expressly for, and dedicated to, Pears. When the two men returned from the States to wartime England in 1942, their relationship had fundamentally changed. Henceforth, as I was to suggest in 1978 (PFL, p. 234), the two lives were one.

And Mrs Britten? Laid to rest? Expelled? Dispersed? Extirpated? There can be no doubt at all that the relationship with Pears was the 'passionate affair' that his friends had wished for him, as an escape, one must suppose, from his mother's spell. It was an 'affair' with a man and a voice that was not only a release in that sense, but also the agent of a release of creativity embodied in the extraordinary series of vocal works and operatic roles that poured out of Britten from 1940 until the very end of his life, music destined for and generated by Pears. The huge cycle of compositions opened with a dedication, 'To Peter' – the *Michelangelo Sonnets* – and closed with one – *Death in Venice* – again, 'To Peter'. In between, there was a phenomenal mass of music, written for, round and about Pears: 'It may not seem like it to you,' Britten wrote to Pears in April 1966, 'but what you think or feel is really the most important thing in my life. It is an unbelievable thing to be spending my life with you; I can't think what the Gods were doing to allow it to happen!' The music flowed out of this overwhelming sense of gratitude and admiration.

There was also in the relationship, on Britten's side at least, a strong dependency (he was always anxious when Pears was away and eager for him to return); and this, coupled with the musical format of the partnership and the obsession with the 'golden box', suggests that combined with the release was also a continuation of the pattern of life, exterior and interior, from the earliest Lowestoft days, in which Britten's mother's role had been so dominant and influential and her absence a source of pain.[23]

Britten, post-Pears and post-*Grimes*, it is clear, was in some important respects a different sort of composing animal from what he had been pre-Pears. That had to be, given the pre-history of the relationship and, yet more importantly, the qualities of Pears as an interpreter: fortune, in 1937, had sent Britten not only a passionate lover but also an incomparable artist. (One cannot but wonder what the case might have been if Pears had been all passion but a lesser artist. Odder still, one reflects on the fortune that sent Pears not only a man of creative genius but a pianist who proved to be one of the greatest accompanists of the century.)

The extraordinary release and fulfilment, then, that was Pears also brought necessary and inevitable constraints. We can hardly regret the succession of masterpieces Pears inspired; and in any event, the impulse to compose for the voice and for specific voices – Sophie Wyss, Hedli Anderson[24] – was strong in Britten well before Pears appeared on the scene. But his joining the composer meant, from 1940 onwards, an intense concentration on and upgrading of the vocal dimension. Despite this, Britten continued to work extensively in other genres, as indeed he had done in his works up to and including the first years of the war. One might well conclude that his non-vocal works post-1940 never received the attention that was their due, and perhaps remain relatively unfamiliar and undervalued, simply because he came to be regarded as a composer whose vocal music was predominant. Dominant, maybe, but *predominant*? Our view of the post-1940 music has been distorted by crippling omissions and gaps. It is only comparatively recently, for example, that a monumental orchestral score like *The Prince of the Pagodas* (1957) has been first recorded in its entirety, and the score published, the longest orchestral work that Britten ever wrote.[25] Growing familiarity with it will alter our perception of him as a composer. Likewise, the picture we had of his pre-war works was a partial one. A handful of pieces were well known, but major scores, like *Our Hunting Fathers* (1936), and other essential works from the thirties and forties, especially from the American years – *Paul Bunyan* (1941), for example – have only recently come to public notice.[26] As a result, we find ourselves in possession of a prolific pre-war composer, with some features quite distinct from the composer we knew post-1942, after his return from the States and with Pears as his partner, though I think we can assume that Britten would have devoted himself to the musical theatre however his personal life might have shaped itself. The dramatic compulsion was there from early days onwards (nursery theatricals at Lowestoft, which surely provided the precedent for *The Little Sweep*!).

The contrast in character: it is this, I believe, that is the interesting distinction to be made between (roughly) pre- and post-war Britten. The mix of vocal and instrumental works was present from the start. What changed in the music were some things that went out of it. Whereas up to the mid-point of the war satire, parody, a certain scepticism and a passionate indignation were often uppermost in the music – indeed, it was precisely in these areas that the composer's

feelings declared themselves unreservedly – these were characteristics that were not sustained, or at least not with the same unsettling
intensity. Other characteristics took their place, perhaps more important or enduring ones. *War Requiem* (1961), to be sure, is not wanting
in passion or protest. None the less it is permissible to miss and
regret a little the caustic, sardonic, wild brilliance of some of the
early works, and to reflect on the reasons for its muting, a particular
brilliance of which we have become aware only through our recla-
mation of the music from the thirties and the American years. One
wonders if these singular manifestations of feeling – the attachment
to parody and satire, for example – were not in fact tied in with the
character of Britten's emotional life in young manhood. Did the
'tone', the 'voice', change along with the fulfilment of his feelings in
a passionate human relationship?

And Mrs Britten, I ask myself again: was she laid to rest? Dispelled?
We shall never be able to answer that question with total confidence.
Sometimes it seems to me that the extraordinary history of Britten's
life is close to that of Michael Ransom, the hero of Auden's and
Isherwood's *The Ascent of F6* who reaches the summit of the mountain
only to find there a mysterious figure, 'whose draperies fall away,
revealing Mrs Ransom as a young mother':

RANSOM: Mother!
MOTHER (MRS RANSOM):   My boy! At last!

One cannot doubt that Mrs Britten helped her son to scale his Everest. Was she always there, beckoning him on with the litany of her
four Bs? Did she, in some sense, create the need for a dominant or
dominating personality in his life?[27] And did she live on, her voice
encapsulated within Pears's? But the mountain, the magic mountain
of Britten's music: that was his creation. It is the mountain that
matters to us.

II LETTERS

Words

Britten was always fond of saying that he had no facility with words, that *notes* were his business. Words, he gave us to believe, did not come naturally to him; and beyond that, in later life at least, he was overtly suspicious of words in many of their manifestations. Criticism is a familiar example of that suspicion, not only adverse opinions, but verbal 'explanations' of music, even when they were positive. Britten cared for none of this. Words in the service of analytic method were largely anathema to him: the relentlessly, unstoppably 'clever' talker (see note 7) made him feel uncomfortable. One might well conclude that he was happy with words only when setting them, when consuming them musically, a process that required no verbal-ization – when his response to them was embodied in the notes.

The music is sufficient evidence of just how analytic and superbly penetrating was his response to language, indeed to literary experi-ence in general. That much we know or could guess from his close reading of the texts of his songs and the sources for his operas. To choose only one example, *Death in Venice*, the opera itself constitutes a brilliant interpretation of Mann's novella, in which not a single point is missed: everything is made articulate in music. Everything that Britten might have wanted to 'say' about Mann is said in the score.

It might appear then – and I think did appear to be so during his lifetime – that his relationship to words was a singular one in the sense that, music apart, the relationship was unproductive, intend-edly so. It was a picture that the composer himself did nothing to modify. On the contrary, he encouraged an impression of verbal disengagement.

Like so many conclusions about Britten's personality, this one demands reconsideration. The reality, we shall find, is something different from the appearance, which may have been an appearance that he wanted to make but was none the less misleading for that. In our rethinking of his relationship to words, his use of them, his facility with them, his letters and diaries, naturally, have a crucial role to play. I shall want to suggest that far from having a passive relationship, and despite the buttressing across the years of an impression of verbal diffidence, he was in fact quite exceptionally and verbally articulate – how indeed could it really have been otherwise? – and more than that, that the *written* word was for him a vital means of communication and self-expression. His letters, and to a lesser but still significant degree the pocket diaries, speak for a compulsive, necessary relationship with words, which allow us no longer to subscribe to a view of a word-less Britten. The truth was otherwise.

Perhaps the first thing to remark upon is the extent of the letters. Since Britten's death one of the main tasks of the Britten–Pears Library and Archive has been to locate the whereabouts, and wherever possible secure copies, of his correspondence. This has been a remarkably successful operation which has led to the recovery of a very large quantity of letters and postcards, the majority of them in his own hand. Undoubtedly some important correspondence has been lost or destroyed. There are instances where we know that significant correspondence must have been exchanged but where we must now assume that Britten's side of it no longer exists; for example, as I have mentioned above, his letters to Frank Bridge, and those to W.H. Auden, of which, to date, we can report only one survivor (Letter 182). In Bridge's case it seems virtually certain that Britten's letters were lost at the time of the dispersal of Bridge's papers. He was concerned about the fate of his old teacher's manuscripts; but it would not have occurred to him, I think, to make a point of conserving correspondence, and least of all his part in it. Quite rightly, it was the legacy of manuscripts he exerted himself to protect.

The loss of his side of the correspondence, however, was grievous. Were it available, it is hard not to believe that we should learn a great deal more about this crucial relationship. Its enduring significance is not in doubt. But as the important Fass letters have already revealed, the relationship with Bridge and his entourage began – inevitably – to show signs of stress and dissension. There was the invasion of new friends and, as the 'son' no less inevitably grew up and away from the 'father', assertions of musical independence. One such incident is vividly described by Marjorie Fass in a letter from December 1937:

As Franco [Frank Bridge] got out of his car he muttered to me that never again wld he try to help Benjy over his work, as some of the things he pointed out, the boy simply wldn't alter, so why waste his time & energy? And as I drove home with Benjy & asked if he'd had a good afternoon he said he'd had to 'stick up for himself' a thing he'd never done before with Mr Brit – so I said that was allright, but surely it was of value to him to have Mr Brit's criticism & he said, 'Yes, but they're _my_ songs' & I said 'certainly', but since Mr Brit knows so infinitely more about music than you do I shld have thought his wisdom & experience were worth your accepting' which left spoilt young Benjy in a silent temper – & I had to have a quite light hand over everything at dinner & afterwards & didn't touch again on his work.

The songs in question were Britten's settings of Auden's *On this Island*, Op. 11.

What Fass reports gives us an indication of complexities in the relationship with Bridge which have been very little documented. There were, it seems, and especially as the thirties came to an end, not only doubts about Britten's new friends, but doubts too about the direction his music was taking. The year 1937 saw Britten struggling to accommodate himself to the death of his mother. One emancipation had already, as it were, been thrust upon him. One wonders, in the light of this fresh evidence, if there were not something a shade claustrophobic about the atmosphere at Friston which provoked further demonstrations of emancipation: the affirmations of independence that disconcerted Fass and the Brits and the accumulation of new, and in Friston's terms, iconoclastic friends? The influence of the latter was no doubt responsible for generating the occasional political discussions that Fass did not like (she preferred to share 'beautiful things').

Ironically enough, Britten's letters to one of the suspect new friends, W.H. Auden, were to suffer a similar fate to those he wrote to Bridge, though in the case of Auden, it was not indifference or malign neglect that led to the loss of Britten's letters but the known custom of the recipient: the poet's policy was not to keep personal correspondence, but to get rid of it, a policy he wanted his friends to adopt after his death with regard to his own letters, an injunction Britten was to ignore.

He, by way of contrast, kept virtually everything, and in particular preserved – perhaps hoarded would not be too strong a word – a wealth of material of significance in and from his early years. There is no doubt that this was a period of fundamental importance to him, as a man and as a creator. It is scarcely appropriate to think in conventional terms of him growing *out* of his childhood. He certainly grew up. But he did not discard his childhood so much as preserve it intact within him, and protect and conserve it throughout his adult life. The outward signs of this inner preoccupation show up in the care with which he kept his musical juvenilia which, naturally enough, mattered specially to him, and of which, at the age of thirteen or fourteen, he compiled a characteristically meticulous list (see p. 102), perhaps in preparation for studying with Bridge. But there were also associated documents and memorabilia, for example his letters to his parents, which they carefully preserved and which he as carefully kept after their deaths. These indeed are the letters that open this first volume, letters that vividly record Britten's childhood experiences and his family relationships. I think one is not exaggerating if one senses in these letters a genuine impulse, perhaps even a compulsion, to record not only experience but the facts surrounding or giving rise to the experience. The childhood letters are indeed lively responses to events and experience – what one might expect from a lively child who clearly had, and wanted to sustain when separated from them, an intense and busy line of communication with his family, with his parents, with his mother above all.

But the diaries are something else, and surely unusual in their methodical concentration on fixing in words the 'pattern', the daily round, a means, above all, of documenting the facts, setting them down and getting them right. They are also a defence against memory's infinite capacity for suspect improvement: as Primo Levi reminds us, 'The further events fade into the past, the more the construction of convenient truth grows and is perfected.' This insistence on accuracy was an early manifestation of a feature of Britten's personality that remained constant throughout his life. It was certainly not a preoccupation with the importance of his autobiography. It was, however, a conviction that the record of a life, if made at all, should be precise.

There are many instances of this insistence on factual precision: whether it was an event in Britten's life or an aspect of his work, the facts had to be correct. He was pained, aggrieved, on occasion angered, by wrong information, as if the imprecise somehow damaged the sense he had of the integrity of his experience. It would be grotesque to suggest that there was anything self-conscious about this self-documentation. He was certainly not documenting himself for posterity. And yet one has to recognize that the conjunction of letters and diaries leaves one with an impression of an artist, a personality, who – whatever his denials of skills with the written word – used words to record, to order, to document, confirm and communicate, many of the most important experiences and events of his life, to keep an account of the 'real'.

We have adopted a chronological order for the letters throughout. Thereby one gains a sometimes day-by-day impression of his life, the continuity of it and the variety of its texture. One gets a real sense across the years of the bombardment of experience, musical and otherwise, the multiplicity of commitments, the diversity of friends, colleagues and acquaintances, the diversity of his involvements and the many faces he presents to the world: like the rest of us, the personality of the writer changes along with the addressee. The alternative was to group the letters by using the recipient as the organizing principle. This would undeniably have had the advantage of allowing a more immediate assessment of the important correspondents in Britten's life. It would have shown the progress of a friendship and in some cases the evolution of an idea, the development of a work. But then life itself does not flow tidily along and works of art are often created in circumstances that one would have thought scarcely conducive to their making: a case in point is surely the music that Britten wrote on his journey home by convoy across the Atlantic in 1942, which is vividly described in Letter 372. Chronology has the merit of unfolding things as they happened and sharpens up the contrasts and confusions that surround the creativity.

An Analytic Ear

We have naturally been on the look out for early signs of musical activity and impingement. There is, indeed, among the juvenilia evidence of the musical documentation of family events, e.g. a 'composition' by the six-year-old Britten entitled 'Do you no that my Daddy has gone to London today' (see p. 106). But in the letters and diaries too there are frequent observations that rivet the reader's attention. A letter to his parents from his later schooldays, from Gresham's, in January 1930 (Letter 18), is an example of the richness and diversity of resonance that a single letter may disclose. It opens with a paragraph that makes it amusingly clear that when the resident composer of the GPO Film Unit in the 1930s came to write his celebrated score for *Night Mail*, an awareness of the mechanics by which mail was delivered by rail round the country had long been part of his consciousness:

This is the first of eleven epistles to leave my hand, travel via M. & G. N. [Midland & Great Northern Railway], pass through the G.P.O. and be disposited on your doorstep at a quarter to eight approximately on the following Monday morning.

This same letter also contains a striking aural observation which shows that a composer's ear was already in evidence, taking note of the sounds of his immediate environment – in this case boys snoring in the dormitory, who summon up for him another aural memory, the warning to shipping emitted by buoys afloat on the surface of the sea:

I hope the buoys are as good as ever, Pop, and just as regular. I was reminded strongly of them the other night – there were two boys snoring in bed next to me; one of them snored taking breath both in and out while the other only when breathing in. For about five or even six times they agreed, & then gradually they got out of time, & they took quite a time to get in again. It fascinated me so much that I could not get to sleep.

And finally, again from this same letter, an exasperated comment from the schoolboy composer ('Gog' was Mr Greatorex, the music master at Gresham's):

Gog seems to have meant what he said last term about performing one of my bally works this term. He asked me for one yesterday; and so I thrust the nicer modern one into his hands – but he nearly choked & so I had to show him the silly small one, and he even calls that one <u>modern</u>!!!

This is an especially interesting passage, revealing as it does the particular friction between Britten and his teachers (more of that below) and the particular source of the friction, the supposed 'modernity' of the music he was writing. His letter tells us something about the attitudes prevailing in England in the 1930s (he was to meet them again during his College years) when 'modernity', i.e. the influence of the new music from Europe, was perceived as something specifically pernicious, to be resisted at all costs.

This issue of 'modernity' was never to pack up and go away during his lifetime. Ironically (and just as mindlessly) it became a discrimination that in later years was used against him, i.e. his music was *not* (or insufficiently) 'modern'. It was a post-war and perhaps peculiarly sixties evaluation of Britten, rooted in the assumption that the present was always in a state of perpetual crisis in relation to the past: it was for the future that composers should be writing. It was not a philosophy that he found persuasive; and its adherents were deaf to the unpublicized radical innovations that were a marked feature of the composer's development. The eighties have allowed us to see – to hear – things differently.

I doubt if Mr Greatorex was troubled by such considerations. He may well have been made uneasy, however, by the remarkable gifts his pupil possessed, and disconcerted by his opinions, and especially by his opinions of the musical standards and literacy of his teachers, to which the schoolboy Britten gave caustic expression in his letters and diaries. His comments leave us in no doubt of the exceptional sensitivity of his ear, for example this, from a letter (No. 17) to his parents in October 1929:

They [visitors from Germany] went to the Music Recital last night, and what an opinion they must have of the music of Gresham's School! It was the worst Music recital on record – even the least critical boys say that. It was silly, that is the only adjective which can qualify the playing. All three of them, Gog, Mr Taylor, Miss Chapman (who played on a small viola, which sounded like a cracked muted violin), sounded as if they were bad sight-readers, had never seen the music before, and had never had an hour of coaching.

And this was also an *analytic* ear, one attuned in particular to precise dynamics and rhythmic co-ordination at the keyboard, as an earlier letter (No. 10) to his mother at the end of his first week at Gresham's in September 1928 shows (he had, in fact, already passed Associated Board Grade VIII at the age of twelve):

After nearly eight years of study, I had a very flimsy technick(?); he [Greatorex] as good as said I had none at all. His words were, when I finished playing, "And who taught you that?" Afterwards he made out that it was hopeless for a boy of my age to play later Beethoven, and that my love of Beethoven will soon die, as it does with everyone! I afterwards played the Chopin polanaize. You might ask Bobby to look up and tell me by letter whether the bars, 5–8, you know

etc. are marked p or f, I played them f, he said that they ought to be marked pp practically, and then demonstrated how, playing with no two notes together, and a gripping touch, and terrible tone. I don't think much of his ~~technick~~ (oh I don't know) technich(?)!

If Britten was ever active as a music critic, it was during his schooldays at Gresham's, though in 1952 he was to contribute a review of *Figaro* (Covent Garden, 8 February) to *Opera* (May 1952, 3/5, pp. 308–9). 'Something [. . .] went wrong with the tempi relations of the last finale,' he observed, and went on to protest at 'the tradition of cutting Basilio's and Marcellina's arias in the last act' of an opera which, he reminded us, was 'exactly considered from every point of view'. 'Could we not once give Mozart the benefit of the doubt and include them?' he asked. The tone may have softened since the days of Mr Greatorex but this is still a critic who speaks up for the composer.

The American Dream

> Every day America's destroyed and re-created,
> America is what you do,
> America is I and you,
> America is what you choose to make it.
>
> W.H. Auden, *Paul Bunyan* (1941)

We find that a period of Britten's life which is among the most richly documented are the years he spent in the USA, from 1939 to 1942. By the time he left England with Pears, in May 1939, both his parents had died, which meant his shouldering the responsibility of keeping the lines of communication open with his family, with his two sisters especially (the relationship with his elder brother, Robert, was less close). Indeed, he clearly felt responsible not only for maintaining as best he could the traditional links with the family but also for the welfare of his sisters. We have a clear picture of an anxious, dutiful, caring brother giving his sisters the best advice he can and lending them financial support. There was certainly a ready assumption of obligations. I have sometimes wondered if this was not, so to speak, the younger son 'proving' himself retrospectively to the sceptical father; the fulfilment of that sense of obligation ensured a constant flow of letters to England to his sisters and other friends. This in itself would have ensured a regular exchange of correspondence between North America and England. But the outbreak of war introduced a further obligation to keep the letters flowing, and he wrote to his sisters alternately on a roughly fortnightly basis, providing us with what is virtually a diary of the North American years.

It would be a redundant exercise to dwell for too long on the perspectives opened up on these years by this particular sequence of letters, when Britten himself recounts his American experiences with such exceptional clarity and verve. But there are a few points worth singling out for special attention. First, and possibly for the first time, we are able for ourselves to gauge the importance for his development of his stay in America. We have known, of course, of the major works that were completed, or written and first performed, in America – the Violin Concerto, *Les Illuminations*, *Sinfonia da Requiem*, and – a more recent acquisition – *Paul Bunyan* – but the letters permit us to apprehend fully the context in which those works were created: in particular, the story of the commission and rejection of the *Sinfonia* by the Japanese government is unfolded in all its labyrinthine and bizarre detail. (Our research has extended to the Japanese press of the period.) And in the conjunction of untiring creativity and sequence of first and repeat performances we can follow the shaping of Britten's professional career – the letters to Elizabeth Sprague Coolidge, Albert Goldberg and Serge Koussevitzky are of special importance in this respect – and the public reception his music enjoyed, at least as expressed in the press at the time. We have spared no effort, throughout these volumes, to document what the press said about major events, not because we have much more confidence than Britten did himself in critical judgements, but because press reviews and notices fascinatingly reveal the changing profile of public attitudes and opinions. We note his responses to his American critics, to his successes and his failures. There are many indications of the kind of responses that he was to make in similar circumstances throughout his life, but also some differences, to which I shall return.

The second point: did Britten and Pears mean to stay? It seems that initially, at least, the family was left with the impression that the two friends 'had decided to go together to make a new life in the United States'. This was Beth's recollection (EWB, p. 109), and she also remembered her relief, as 1939 drew to its close, and war had been declared, that 'There had been no more talk of his taking out papers to become a citizen of the USA and we hoped that was the end of that idea.'

There must undoubtedly have been some influence from Auden's and Isherwood's disillusioned exit from England to the USA a few months earlier, and no less an impulse to explore a fresh continent and fresh possibilities: these were points that Beth made in an interview with the BBC producer Anthony Friese-Green, c.1977. Pears had already travelled to the States, while Britten would have heard about the country and especially the potentialities of patronage from Bridge. There was another motive too, which Beth does not touch on. Although he had not yet committed himself finally to Pears, there was strong reason for him detaching himself from other close relationships which had become burdensome, demanding and difficult to manage: to cross the Atlantic was one way of reducing the temperature and removing proximity at a single stroke. This may not have been the sole factor but was certainly a contributing one (see Letter 174).

In any event, whatever the declared intention may have been at the outset, what emerges from the letters, and the actuality of the American experience, is something far less clear cut: occasional thoughts about staying on were inextricably counterpointed with expressions of resolve to return home. Already in January 1940 (Letter 244) Britten is writing to his sister, Barbara:

You see I am fairly O.K. as regards money. R.H. [Ralph Hawkes] will continue as long as possible with the guarantee, & I can pick up odd things. I had such a good success in Chicago, that I'm sure I can get dates playing in future. Anyhow – as soon as poss. Peter & I are going to get on the British Quota – which allows us to work normally instead of being just 'visitors'. We shall go probably to Mexico or Cuba (a formality) & return as under this Quota. A curse & an expense but it must be done. I didn't want to do it as it seemed somehow to cut another English tie – but it isn't binding at all and I can return to England whenever I can (pray God – soon!), and Ralph & all are insistent.

The complications of the American quota system and the bureau-cratic complexities of visa extensions run like an anxious theme throughout the letters. But after war had been declared, the 'official' British advice – often referred to – was to stay put, and it was not only Britten and Pears who were so advised. This was forgotten or ignored by vocal groups at home which were not slow to denounce them for their lack of patriotism. We give some space to the docu-mentation of this unattractive episode (see note 2 to Letter 292 and note 7 to Letter 326). In fact, Britten's sense of English ties that could not, must not, be broken continually surfaces in his letters home. In April 1940, the American experience seems to have stimulated him to thinking about himself in terms that remarkably anticipate a key passage in his Aspen Award speech of 1964 (be it noted, an American award!). This is how Britten saw himself, in Amityville, Long Island, in a letter (No. 253) to his brother-in-law, Kit Welford:

You see – I'm gradually realising that I'm English – & as a composer I suppose I feel I want more definite roots than other people.

It was a sentiment that was to find virtually identical, though much more elaborate, expression in the speech, which acknowledged the importance of the American years (personal relationships, one notes, were still what mattered: Britten prefers to salute Americans rather than America), and gives us a glimpse of how, a quarter of a century on, he remembered himself (and his ambitions) at the start of his American period. It is a justly famous passage; and the letters permit us to experience, along with the composer, the clarifying of the realization, already adumbrated as early as this, that roots had to be put down, and in England:

I first came to the United States twenty-five years ago, at the time when I was a discouraged young composer – muddled, fed-up and looking for work, longing to be used. I was most generously treated here, by old and new friends, and to all of these I can never be sufficiently grateful. Their kindness was past description; I shall never forget it. But the thing I am most grateful to your country for is this: it was in California, in the unhappy summer of 1941, that, coming across a copy of the Poetical Works of George Crabbe, in a Los Angeles bookshop, I first read his poem Peter Grimes; and, at this same time, reading a most perceptive and revealing article about it by E.M. Forster, I suddenly realized where I belonged and what I lacked. I had become without roots, and when I got back to England six months later I was ready to put them down [. . .] I believe in roots, in associations, in backgrounds, in personal relationships. I want my music to be of use to people, to please them, to 'enhance their lives' (to use Berenson's phrase). I do not write for posterity – in any case, the outlook for that is somewhat uncertain. I write music, now, in Aldeburgh, for people living there, and further afield, indeed for anyone who cares to play it or listen to it. But my music now has its roots, in where I live and work. And I only came to realize that in California in 1941.

Only three days after he had written to his brother-in-law about his 'roots', he was writing to John Pounder, Letter 254:

Personally I'm crazily homesick, & if it were not that Peter looks after me like a lover, & the family Mayer were surely made in heaven, & that Wystan Auden's about the place & always coming down here, I should be home, war or no war, like a shot.

The same letter ends:

I suppose America will be in this war within a year and then I'll be back ——

A sentence that reminds us that, for Britten, what was absolutely central to the whole preceding decade, the thirties, was his pacifism. After the outbreak of war in Europe in 1939, and even though, as we have just seen, he was quick to apprehend that the USA would not long remain neutral, America was *not*, as he emphatically put it (Letter 253), 'engaged solely with killing people (altho' she may be thinking of it more every day)'. This was no minor consideration in his eyes. It was surely responsible for continually prompting him to suggest that his sisters and relations should find ways of leaving wartime England and join him in the States. There are constant references to this plan in his letters home. His brother-in-law, Kit Welford (Beth's husband), was a doctor (Letter 253):

What I want so much is for you to come out here for a visit before you decide anything. I'm going to try to find out for you the medical possibilities here. You know that every emigré has to pass an exam.? Luckily speaking English, you won't have to take the language exam, which is one of the worse bogies. I have an idea that there are some states which have no exam. – I'll find that out for you. We could easily find affidavits for you – & by that time I may have taken out my 1st Citizen papers – which, incidentally, arn't binding in the least.

Again, the same appeal to his sister, Beth (Letter 275):

Now for a serious word. I do want you all to realize – if by hook or by crook you can get visas to come across, I will guarantee everything this end – if the authorities won't take my guarantee I can easily get the necessary ones from friends. This goes for any other relatives or friends you know.

Not, one might think in retrospect, a very realistic proposal. But the letter reminds us that fear of invasion (of England by Germany) was a real fear at the beginning of the war; and that during the period of the so-called 'phoney war', that strange year when the war itself appeared to be stationary, it was still possible to plan and plot family affairs as if the war were not in fact an insuperable hindrance to one's ability to carry them out. That suspended situation was soon to come to an end and Britten makes no further references to his schemes to get the family over to the States. Evidence they were, however, of his deep roots in family ties and sense of family obligation.

As the war years progressed, and more and more nations and continents were involved in the conflict, the making of one decision came to dominate Britten's and Pears's lives: the timing of their return home. There were endless complications about visas, and constant checks on their status with British representatives in the USA. In September 1940 (Letter 291) Britten was writing to Beth, 'Officially one must stay put', in a letter that at the same time speaks for the paralysing difficulty of choosing the best course of action:

There are lots of problems to be settled at this moment, & it is very worrying. There are so many alternatives as to what to do, & what one wants to do too – that I, who never was good at decisions, don't know where I am. I wish to God I could be back with you, but that's no use, because obviously if I were back I couldn't be <u>with</u> you – so that's not much sense. One feels bad about not suffering as well – & of course many militant people here are very cross with us for being alive at all (esp. old ladies) – but one must try & be realistic, & that's what I'm trying to work out now – where one is most use & least bother. If you have any ideas let me know!

And in September to Mrs Coolidge (Letter 289):

I expect to spend the winter in New York as it seems that still the British Government does not wish anyone to return – one's absence and possible means of sending currency being more precious than one's presence. I feel very lucky in being in a country where one is able to work and to think about other things than destruction, but it is a terribly anxious time. My family is scattered over the East of England and in London & I have friends in every part of the country.

In October Britten was writing to his publisher (Letter 292):

I have been desparately worried, not really about what people are saying (I feel that one's real friends in England will be unselfishly pleased that one is being spared the horrors – that is in fact what every letter says so far), but about the fact that one is doing nothing to alleviate any of the suffering, that both of us again asked official advice on what we had better do. The answer is always the same – stay where you are until called back; you can't do anything if you do go back; get on with your work as artistic ambassadors etc. etc.

The ceaseless, nagging questioning and uncertainty went on, with yet another flurry of activity about visa extensions in July 1941. But by October an irrevocable decision was taken, and Britten was writing to Mrs Coolidge (Letter 344):

I want to tell you something on my part. I have made up my mind to return to England, at anyrate for the duration of the war. I am not telling people because it sounds a little heroic, which it is far from being – it is really that I cannot be separated any longer from all my friends and family – going through all they are, and I'm afraid will be, in the future. I think I shall be able to continue with my work over there, which is what I most want to do, of course. I don't actually know when I shall be sailing, since boats are so scarce & heavily booked up – and anyhow I have so much to get finished here, so I may not be leaving much before Christmas.

In fact, Britten and Pears did not leave the States until March 1942, so difficult did it prove to secure a passage.

It was during the visit to California that the famous encounter occurred with Forster's *Listener* article on Crabbe, and then with Crabbe's poem, which led not only to the birth of *Peter Grimes* but also, it has commonly been supposed, to the decision to return to England. It was clearly the case that these potent reminders of home and Suffolk were influential in reaching that decision. But the letters from America make cumulatively clear that from the very start – that is, after the declaration of war in September 1939 had converted a temporary stay into one without a perceived limit to its duration – Britten's preoccupation was with home and England. These were extraordinary times and extraordinary years, and his circumstances were peculiar. It is scarcely surprising that he should have shown the same confusion of motives, schemes and actions as almost everybody else during a particularly confused period. But behind the confusion – behind the uneasy acceptance of 'staying put', the plans to relocate the family, the recognition that America, for the time being at least, was at peace while Europe and England were at war – behind all these considerations, some of them contradictory or competing, there was a clear perception on his part that his fate, destiny, call it what one will, was inextricably bound up with his own country, and perhaps even his own county: one catches a whiff of Britten's intense sense of place – and his overwhelming nostalgia – when he writes somewhat intemperately about the USA to Enid Slater in April 1940 (Letter 255) and then adds:

I'm sorry – it's probably Spring that makes one so bad tempered – England is so heavenly at this time – & I've got to let Snape [the Old Mill] – o dear, o dear . . .

It was a period of anxiety and continuous uncertainty about the future. How he felt, when writing to Beth in the same month (No. 256), was how he was to continue to feel until the decision to return home had been taken:

I think it's probably just one's mental condition that gets one down these days. One just feels so hopeless & helpless – & impossible to settle-down. In the normal way it wouldn't be so difficult to decide whether to stay British or change to American – but at the moment I am just marking time until I can get back to England! I suppose there wouldn't be much sense in coming at the moment – because my work is the most important thing, & I suppose it is best to stay where [I] can work most easily, & that is it over here.

This same letter continues:

But the idea of spending one's life here appalls me at the moment. Probably in normal times it would be O.K. — but at the present time one is inclined to see all America's bad points & England's good ones.

It will not only be American admirers of Britten's who may be surprised by the strength of his adverse opinion of the States, above all of 'metropolitan' America – that is to say, New York. In a letter to Kit Welford (No. 253), he writes:

You see, Kit, in so many ways this country is such a terrible disappointment. Sometimes it seems to have, forinstance, all the infuriating qualities of youth without any of its redeeming qualities. Of course I judge mostly from this State – & the little of New England that I've seen – the Middle-West when I went there was quite different, and had nothing of the ultra-sophistication of, say, New York. I hate New York – Wystan compares it to a great Hotel & it's a damn good comparison. It is like the Strand Palace – all glitter, & little gold – nothing stable – everyone on the move – & terribly fashionable (in the worst sense of the word). Everything here is crazes – crazes – crazes.

In a letter (No. 254) written a few days later to John Pounder, after the comparison of New York to a 'great hotel' has surfaced once again, Britten was to continue:

The country scenery (or what I've seen of it) can be very striking, but it's not like England as it hasn't been lived in – it's dead & colourless. The best part I've seen so far is the Middle-West – I went there to play in January, & found it much more serious & honest than the East coast – but terribly narrow of course, & reactionary. But America in general is reactionary – particularly at the moment – to be a liberal is dangerous – to be a communist is fatal (vide Fascist Dies committee). The present Bertrand Russell case has shocked us all – because of his ideas of Marriage, he was removed from his Higher Maths. lecturing position at the N. York University. America is nationalist & chauvanistic – her interest in Europe is

patronising – full of advice but refusing to take the consequences. When I
saw the way things were going in Europe I used to think that the only
hope was America – now I'm sadly disillusioned.

The disillusionment had been rapid, though in fact he had already
shown a conspicuous *European* orientation both musically – for
instance, his ambition to study with Berg – and in terms of personal
experience. The trip to Vienna and elsewhere he made in 1934,
accompanied by his mother, and documented in detail in Letters
56–61, consolidated his feelings for Europe, besides providing him
with his first contacts with European musical personalities, some of
whom were later to play an important role in his life, for example
Erwin Stein (see Letter 59). Britten had brought with him to the
States his European inheritance. It was the measure by which he
judged, fairly or unfairly, what America had to offer. It also explains
part of the happiness he enjoyed as a member of the remarkable
Mayer household on Long Island, to the history of which we attempt
to do justice in note 1 to Letter 194. The Mayers themselves represented an island of European culture and values within America
(see Letter 212 and EWB, pp. 121–2). There were many such islands;
and when one takes into account the menacing world situation in
the 1930s, one should add, preserved not only within but *by* America.
Britten and Pears were lucky to attach themselves to a family at the
centre of a particularly gifted circle of European writers, painters and
musicians. The Old World was still theirs even while they were
exploring the New, though, as it happened, it was a new friend (a
patient of Dr Mayer's) from the New World – the Canadian-born
composer Colin McPhee (1901–1964) – whose influence, unacknow-
ledged at the time, was to cast a long shadow on Britten's own
development (see note 12 to Letter 312).

The relationship with the Mayers had yet another significant
dimension to it. It gave Britten a secure and sympathetic environment
in which to work. These new friends on Long Island guaranteed him
the family context that was so important to him and from which the
accidents of mortality (both his parents dead) and history (the outbreak of war and its consequences) had divorced him. The family
that had been lost to him was now miraculously reconstituted in
Amityville. The need for the family, or at least to feel himself to
be part of a family, was powerful in him; furthermore Mrs Mayer
undeniably played the role of surrogate mother. There was never to
be a repeat of this family relationship of quite the same order of
intensity, the precedent for which was created in his own past; but
it was to provide a model – pioneered, as we have seen, by Marjorie

Fass – for many of the relationships in his adult life: there were to be many other motherly women whose role had something in common with Mrs Mayer's.

Soon after the return of Britten and Pears from America they were, indeed, to relocate themselves in a family environment that in many aspects replicated the Amityville experience, but now it was the Steins, Erwin and Sophie, and their daughter, Marion, who played the roles hitherto assumed by the Mayers. (Mrs Stein kept house for the two men in London from 1944 to 1953; oddly enough, she had been born and brought up in the same part of northern Germany as Mrs Mayer, and her father too was a pastor.) There were, naturally, many differences; and in particular Stein (see note 9 to Letter 59), as a musician of the first rank, was able to counsel Britten on musical affairs in a way that had not been within the reach of the amiable and generous Dr Mayer. (It was his wife who was the musician.) But transcending the differences was a common characteristic of much interest. Like the Mayers, the Steins represented another island of Europeanism, though this time within England, not the USA. There is something to ponder on in these two powerful alliances with families originally from Europe who had found themselves uprooted.[28] There were many excellent, practical, even mundane reasons for the overlapping of the lives of Britten and Pears with the Mayers and the Steins, but at the centre of the relationships there was also surely an altogether deeper appeal – the call, as it were, of Europe, of cosmopolitanism, which had always been strong in Britten's life and sometimes sat rather oddly alongside his vigorous assertion of regional roots. And finally, in these family circles, we find an anticipation of the need for the orderly domesticity with which Britten surrounded himself when he settled with Pears in Aldeburgh.

Although Britten's judgements often seem harsh and narrow, one should not, I suggest, conclude that these letters of disillusionment represent the whole truth about his attitude to America. It is important, not in this context alone but elsewhere, to remind ourselves that letters tend to represent the vivid moment, the immediate response – hence, indeed, their value. But it can well be the case that no sooner is the envelope sealed and in the mailbox that the writer's mood entirely changes, from depression to high spirits or vice versa. This is a caution that we must exercise not just for the duration of the years in America, but throughout these volumes of letters and their successors. Moreover, it was not only place that could excite his alternating approbation and disapprobation. People too were sometimes subjected to the same volatile swings of opinion. Once again, it is of the first importance to remember that a letter that reveals a decisive dip in esteem probably arose from a local or momentary irritation and should not be read in any sense as an ultimate judgement. One of the interesting and enlightening things we learn from his correspondence – and I am looking ahead here to the volumes that will bring us to the end of his life – is what one might describe as the staying power of old friendships and associations, among them some of the stormiest and most vulnerable to the temperamental fluctuations I have referred to above.

Britten's long friendship with Lennox Berkeley is a case in point. If the sometimes choleric letters from America were all we had before us, then we might conclude that this was a relationship that had foundered. But we should be entirely wrong. There is no doubt that the extraordinary anxieties and tensions of the period and difficulties of transatlantic communication contributed to Britten's outbursts of impatience and bad temper which seem to have led him, on occasion, to forget the generosity and encouragement that Berkeley had consistently offered as a friend. There was, too, a divergence of views about the war between the two men which further exacerbated already ruffled feelings. But as later letters will show – and indeed the long history of the continuing relationship – the friendship survived the wartime crisis and was publicly embodied in the commissioning of the *Stabat Mater* (1947) and productions of new operas by Berkeley at successive Aldeburgh Festivals: *A Dinner Engagement* in 1954, *Ruth* in 1957 and *Castaway* in 1967. It was a distinction accorded no other of Britten's contemporaries.

The Berkeley–Britten association was of special significance. But there were other friendships too that came near to collapse, in fact *did* collapse but later were valuably and productively renewed – an example here is provided by Britten's long – but interrupted – friendship with Clifford Curzon.

There were undoubtedly exceptions, and some famous (and complex) ones among them – the relationship with Auden, for instance, which finally expired (though it persisted, as we reveal, for much longer than has hitherto been supposed). But in general old friendships and associations, even though the exceptional circumstances of Britten's life when he was working at the height of his powers may not have permitted an unbroken continuity of relationship, were remembered and valued with warmth and gratitude; and if contact was re-established, the old warmth and recollection of a valued past were there. Too many people, and perhaps not those especially close to Britten, were too quick to remember slights and affronts and other hurts, which were as much part of him (an unwelcome part) as they are of most human beings, and forget (or are unaware of) the profounder, enduring attachments.

But I must return to his relationship with America, about which there is much more to be said. Something a good deal more positive about the country was said and no doubt felt by Britten himself very shortly after his return to England in 1942. He now reacted to a reversed culture shock. For example he writes to Elizabeth Mayer on 4 May 1942 (Letter 374):

Do tell her [Beata] from me that returning to Europe isn't all that one imagines – it is pretty sordid, and although the country is <u>unbelievably</u> beautiful (& the cuckoo!!), the accent is horrible, and there is a provincialism & lack of vitality that makes one yearn for the other side.

And again to Mrs Mayer on 5 June (Letter 383):

I'm greedy about letters – it seems so easy to lose touch with things over the other side, and it is a thing I am so particularly keen not to do. Not that people are being nasty over here; remarkably (and suspiciously!) nice, and nothing is too much trouble for them to do – Louis MacNeice has been particularly helpful. It is merely that, however much I love this country, I feel that, come what may, half of my life is now tied up with America.

And to Beata on 6 June (Letter 384):

I was amused by your description of the Ulli visit. The woman seems a poor specimen. But I'm not so sure that I shouldn't agree with some of the things she said about my countrymen. They can be very annoying, especially when you've known Americans. Awfully snooty, & lacking in vitality. But there are lots of nice things about them – & I do think they live in the most beautiful country in the world.

This incomplete letter ends:

We have been very lucky so far; no unpleasantness about being away; in fact people think it's rather nice of us to have come back – certainly very silly! I still really don't know why I did it – except that I happened to feel that it was the right thing. But I am quite certain that when this mess is over (& Astrologers say hostilities will cease in Europe in the late fall!!) I'll come running [. . .]

It is not difficult to conjecture that the next and missing word was 'back'.

And finally, to David Rothman on 29 September (Letter 394):

I was delighted to get your letter – really thrilled & both Peter and I read & re-read it lots of times. It gave such a wonderful picture of your life, that I know so well and cannot hear too much about. I really felt very homesick for you all – which I am afraid I very frequently do feel! Life is so completely different over here, one's perspectives are so absolutely changed, that those three glorious years I spent in the States are becoming more & more dreamlike in quality – and a very beautiful dream it was too!

The wheel, one feels, has turned full circle. Here is Britten, in September 1942, homesick now for his friends in the USA! It is a chastening thought that if by some mischance the last batch of letters had been lost or destroyed, we should have been left with a significantly partial account of his attitudes to America.

To be sure he continued to be sceptical about the values and mode of life of what one might describe as metropolitan America, i.e. the big-city life of New York or Los Angeles (though he seems to have liked Chicago). Isherwood took a similarly jaundiced view of New York: 'The nervous breakdown expressed in terms of architecture.' But the truth was that Britten was never a metropolitan-inclined man, a happy urbanite. Had he had the occasion to write about London, for example, I have little doubt that he would have come up with a description quite as unflattering as his commentary on New York. This scepticism and suspicion of metropolitan values made him a reluctant visitor to the States in later years (in fact on only two occasions, 1949 and 1969), a reluctance reinforced by a sense that for a significant period after his return to England it was in America that his music seemed to be least successful in making headway and by his and Pears's falling foul of a post-war act of Congress (the Immigration and Nationality Act, Section 212(a)(28)) which debarred those belonging, subscribing to or supporting 'proscribed' organizations from easily acquiring a visa to enter the USA. (Pears was finally rid of this impediment,[29] Britten not: to be sure, he made no effort in his lifetime to have the ban lifted.) In July 1944 (Letter 470), he remarked to Elizabeth Mayer:

Things go well with me here – in Sweden, Portugal, Switzerland, & other pleasant places. But I don't worry that America is so hard to conquer, except that it means you hear so few performances.

And at the end of December 1945, the topic comes up again in a letter (No. 514) to Ralph Hawkes:

[. . .] don't be too depressed if things aren't too good about me in the U.S.A. Let matters take their course there. I'm afraid that I am conceited enough to feel that eventually they'll come round, as this country & the continent have – but at the moment my music is neither ordinary enough or shocking enough to hit them. I'm sorry, but only because of the good orchestras on your side – not because of the audiences, the critics, or the impressarios for whom I can't care much!

Britten, of course, had always had his American admirers; and his partnership with Pears enjoyed an even wider constituency. But in later years it seemed as if there were a fundamental change of attitude to his music in the States, which must have pleased him; and since his death the change has been even more marked.

A perception of the American years as a period of growth and evolution, both personal and professional, is reflected in a letter to his sister Beth, written in May 1941 (No. 312):

I am glad you'd the feeling that I have 'grown up' – well, may be I have at last! If I haven't with all this, I don't think there's much chance of me ever doing so!

And the letter concludes:

I am just about to leave for Brooklyn by train (about an hour away). I have a lot of business to do in the city & I shall stay a few nights in our house there – the house that Peter, Wystan & I share with a man called George Davis (one of the editors of Harper's Bazzaar). It is quite nice & convenient, tho' a trifle too bohemian for my liking – I like the ordinary dull routine more & more, the older I get! I can't live wildly and work! I don't think your brother would shock you, my dear, if you met him. He is still quite a sober, God-fearing person – & altho' you never believe it, he does work pretty hard! But he only lives for the day, when he can meet his sisters & bro.-in-law & nephew – whom he thinks of continually, altho' he fails to write as often as he should.

There is one phrase there that has a special resonance to it: 'I can't live wildly and work!' It was a guiding principle throughout Britten's life, though this particular letter was written out of his experience of the bohemian environment of the house in Brooklyn that he and Pears shared for a time with Auden and others in 1940–41 (see note 2 to Letter 291). The order/anarchy dichotomy was a preoccupation; and it surfaced yet again, in a rather more elaborate form, in a letter to Kit Welford (No. 367) written in March 1942:

I am so pleased that you have thought things out so carefully. From a very different angle I have come to an identical point-of-view (re discipline & obedience) – but in art, as you know, the bias is to the other direction, that of anarchy and romantic 'freedom'. A carefully chosen discipline is the only possible course.

The American years were not only an exploration of the fabled New World but also, and equally importantly, a period of *self*-exploration and discovery in which were laid down, at every level of personal and professional life, recurrent basic motivations and inspirations. Is it not the case that in *Death in Venice*, his last opera, some thirty-four years later, Britten returned to the juxtaposition of anarchy and self-discipline that is the theme of the letter from 1942?

'I have "grown up" – well, may be I have at last!': it is a point that Pears makes in a letter from England to Elizabeth Mayer on Long Island, written in August 1944 (No. 473):

My roots are stronger than they were, I fancy – so are Ben's too – He is a lovely mature person, no less vital but stronger and broader [. . .].

Some part of that maturing must be ascribed to the experience of the American years, which also saw a comparable stretching and extension of his creative powers.

This was something of which Britten himself was aware, however disillusioned he may have been about other aspects of his residence in America. When he writes to Enid Slater in April 1940 (No. 255) one gets the sense of an irrepressible creative exuberance and fertility – and, along with that, an early intimation of the composition of a key work, the *Michelangelo Sonnets*, the first and one of the most important fruits of the just beginning partnership with Pears. The pattern initiated here was to continue for the next three decades and more:

I have now got lots of things on the stocks. I've got a sudden craze for the Michael Angelo Sonnetts & have set about half a dozen of them (in Italian – pretty brave, but there are people here who speak good Italian, & after Rimbaud in French I feel I can attack anything! I've got my eye on Rilke, now & Hölderlin!) And a crazy commission from the Japanese government has come up again & I'm planning a work with plenty of 'peace-propaganda' in it – if they will accept it – And a string quartet – & arranging some Tschaikovsky, etc. etc.

On the very same day that he wrote that letter, he also wrote to another friend, John Pounder, a letter from which I have already quoted (No. 254). He ends, however, on a creative upbeat:

This country has all the faults of Europe & none of its attractions. Where that hope is to be found now I can't think – except of course in art, & in one's friends. I personally have never worked so well as at the moment – perhaps as an escape, but I don't think so – but that is a long story & must wait till we meet.

Whatever his doubts and reservations about his temporary exile may have been, his sense of getting into his stride as a composer was surely justified by the productivity of the American years and the exceptional quality of the works themselves. By April 1940 he had already completed *Young Apollo*, the Violin Concerto, *Canadian Carnival* and *Les Illuminations*. Shortly to come were *Sinfonia da*

Requiem, Diversions, Michelangelo Sonnets and *Introduction and Rondo alla Burlesca* for two pianos, all of them works that belong to the same year. In 1941, he completed *Paul Bunyan* and composed the *Matinées Musicales*, First String Quartet, *Mazurka Elegiaca* for two pianos, *Occasional Overture* (see note 2 to Letter 343) and *Scottish Ballad*; and to this roll-call could be added the radio features (in which Britten collaborated with Auden) and arrangements for the ballet, all of which were part of his professional activities as a composer. He committed himself to the American musical scene with impressive energy. It was typical of the composer, with his conviction that communication was a prime responsibility, that in these 'American' works he addressed his audiences with a distinctly North American accent. *Paul Bunyan* is the pre-eminent example of the quickness of his ear in absorbing a vernacular style; but both *Canadian Carnival* and *Occasional Overture* show a similar skill in their incorporation of typically American gestures.

The letters from these years tell us a lot about his relationships with fellow musicians in the States, with Copland in particular: in fact, a fascinating comparison might be made between his specifically 'American' works and Britten's. Britten was swift not only to recognize Copland's great gifts but also to be of practical assistance to him. It was he who prompted his own publisher, Ralph Hawkes, to offer his friend a contract, even before he himself had left for the States. Hawkes replied on 1 July 1938:

[Copland] is already an old friend of ours. I met him in New York in February and arranged to take care of the Score and Parts of 'EL SALON MEXICO' for him. If he is back in London before the 12th, I shall be pleased to see him again with you but I am getting in touch with him with a view to taking over this work and others for our catalogue. Many thanks for the kind recommendation you gave him. I agree he is likely to turn out a 'winner'.

As John Harbison, an American composer of a later generation, has remarked (*Musical Quarterly*, New York, 71/1, 1985, p. 98), 'Copland was fortunate in his musical friendships, especially with Chávez and Britten, who helped to make him our first truly international composer.'

Thus the American years, compositionally speaking, reveal *two* Brittens, one continuing to write what might be described as mainstream works (concerto, symphony, song-cycle, string quartet), the other, with an extraordinary combination of technical versatility and sharp instinct for the available market, involving himself in American musical life, and going about it with characteristic seriousness, skill and determination.

There were, naturally, setbacks and disappointments (*Paul Bunyan* was one of them). But Britten in America wore his tribulations rather more lightly than was the case in later years. He shrugged off adverse criticism with a cheerfulness that he seemed unable to muster, paradoxically, when his reputation was established. A letter (No. 310) he wrote to Albert Goldberg, the Chicago-based conductor, administrator and critic, and important early advocate of his music in the States, is typical in its exuberant disregard of criticism of the *Bridge Variations* and Goldberg's reactions to the *Sinfonia da Requiem* (the broadcast of the first performance):

I am sorry the press was so bitter about the Variations – I thought that old piece was accepted by them now; certainly in most places it is – but perhaps Chicago is behind (or in front of) the times! Anyhow the audience liked it, & that's what matters. Koussevitsky did it last week – by-the-way.

I'm sorry that you didn't like the Sinfonia, because I think it's the best so far – & people here (intelligent people – ha! ha!) think so too. Maybe something happens in the air between Carnegie Hall & Chicago. But you'll hear it again – don't worry!

His skin was to grow altogether thinner. But there was one attitude that was never to undergo modification: his belief that it was only composing that was his business and a consequent refusal to be sidetracked into any other activity. An invitation from Douglas Moore (in June 1941) to undertake a teaching appointment prompted the following response (Letter 321):

[. . .] at the present time, when one hasn't the foggiest idea of what the future will show, I feel that I want to spend my whole time writing down what musical ideas may be in my head, and unless threatened with starvation I don't want to spend my time doing what would be primarily an executive job, which incidentally I feel would be much more efficiently done by many other people. Also, at the moment, I do not want to spend much time away from the East Coast, where I have so many friends and where most of my occupation lies. Later on I may find it necessary to hold such a position, but for the time being I think I'll risk just being a freelance composer, doing hack-work maybe, but in the composing line, and what little teaching just confined to composition. I do hope you understand.

It was a statement of intent to which he remained faithful for the rest of his life, his 'teaching', i.e. compositional advice, he confined to close friends and contemporaries, like Lennox Berkeley or Grace Williams, and young colleagues, among them Jonathan Harvey, Oliver Knussen, Arthur Oldham and Robert Saxton, none of them, strictly speaking, a 'pupil', and yet all of whom, I believe, would acknowledge the insights and encouragement Britten had to offer.

(The same might be said of performers, who were advised in an identical spirit.)

A response to the public reception of his music rather more complex than his jolly rejoinder to Albert Goldberg, shows up in a letter to Beth (No. 312):

Well – I have produced my first Symphony (the Requiem one, in memory of Mum & Pop, paid for by the Japanese Government – nice touch that – don't you think?) & my first opera. Neither could be called an unqualified success, but the reaction was everywhere violent which I suppose is a good thing, but personally I hate it. I'd much rather it was praised mildly everywhere – I feel embarrassed at being the subject of animated debate. Roughly speaking – the reaction of the public has been excellent – in every case much applause (three or four calls for me at each performance of the Symphony) – the reaction of the intellectual composers has been bad (I am definitely disliked (a) because I am English (no music ever came out of England) (b) because I'm not American (everything is nationalistic) (c) because I get quite alot of performances (d) because I wasn't educated in Paris – etc. etc.) – the reactions of the press mixed – usually the respectable papers (like the Times) bad or puzzled – the rag papers or picture papers good – funny, isn't it?

The key phrase is, surely, 'I feel embarrassed at being the subject of animated debate', which seems to have disconcerted him even more than the hostile reactions of the press. It represents, I think, an early manifestation of what was to become a prominent feature of his character. He was distinctly not, by temperament, a controversial personality; on the contrary, he shrank from controversy, from overt conflict, friction and debate. It was something that distinguished him from many of his contemporaries, who were either controversial by nature or by intent; and it singled him out perhaps especially in an age when to be pugnaciously articulate about being 'modern' (or innovative, or radical or revolutionary) was part of the very concept of 'modernity'. There was nothing of the confrontational publicist about Britten. Manifestos did not come naturally to him. It is impossible to imagine him undertaking, and even less relishing, the role, say, of Stravinsky, of whose personality controversy and debate were an integral part, even a necessary creative part. (Boulez is a later example of an artist for whom controversy is a natural fuel.) Does one regret his reluctance to engage himself in aesthetic issues, in verbal combat? There were certainly enough of them about in his lifetime; and he held strong views about most of them. His shying away from the controversial, his distaste for debate, for confrontation, undeniably had its negative side. Had he participated in open debate, or if not in debate, then at least in discussion, his influence on the course of musical events – about which he often privately expressed dismay and scepticism – might have been greater; and, possibly more important still, he might have avoided the impression of self-imposed isolation that in some cases impeded his relationships with the younger generation of composers. The reluctance to debate sometimes made a dialogue across the generations difficult to achieve, as the production at the 1968 Aldeburgh Festival of Harrison Birtwistle's opera, *Punch and Judy*, which became a veritable *cause célèbre*, was to prove.

But however intriguing the speculation, the truth is that a debating or controversial Britten was neither the composer we know nor the composer that he wanted to be. If there is one thing the letters reveal it is the extraordinary consistency and integrity (i.e. wholeness) of the personality from the early years onwards. What – who – Britten was, one might say, was established early, and though subjected to infinite variation and development, the fundamental constituents remained constant, even stubbornly so. It is this fact that makes these first volumes of letters so important: we find in them most of the keys to the later life and work, and – remarkably – rather few contradictions.

The consistency emerges in a letter to Elizabeth Mayer (No. 430), after the return to England, where, in May 1943, he professes himself uncertain about an excess of 'success':

I am a bit worried by my excessive local success at the moment – the reviews that the Sonnetts, St. Cecilia, the Carols, & now the Quartet have had, & also the fact that Les Illuminations is now a public draw! It is all a little embarrassing, & I hope it doesn't mean there's too much superficial charm about my pieces. I think too much success is as bad as too little; but I expect it's only a phase which will soon pass. Luckily Peter & Michael [Tippett] are rigorous critics – but how I miss you & Wystan. There is one great critic here, Erwin Stein (late of Universal, Vienna), who is a great help. But I think I told you about him and his charming wife (from Mechlanburg, not Schwerin, but I think Strelitz) – who are so good to us both – they are almost second Mayers – but no, that's just not possible. The Mayers are unique.

This letter strikes a sceptical note with which we were to become familiar in later years. Success certainly came to him; but he rarely courted it and remained, I think, surprised by it, and suspicious of it to the end of his life. Recognition and above all recognition of what in his work as an artist he was trying to achieve, that was something else, and something, I think, he valued. Perhaps too, and particularly during the American years, he perceived 'success' as too closely allied to 'publicity', the success-manufacturing machine of which he had become uncomfortably aware when in New York: '[. . .] everything in this country', he writes to Enid Slater in April 1940 (Letter 255), 'is valued by publicity'. And again, perhaps contributing to his suspicion of success, there was his nervy suspicion of himself: 'success' prompted him to ask of himself if he was as good as he was made out to be (see also Letter 450). This indeed, for Britten, must have been one of the unwanted burdens of success. His insecurity, so hard to believe in, and yet ineradicably there, was paradoxically stimulated rather than soothed by the outward success that would have brought balm to most other composers. This is another instance of the cumulative compilation of character traits which can be made from the letters and which results ultimately in a portrait painted by himself.

The Writing of Grimes

Early on in the American years, in a letter (No. 254) from which I have already quoted, Britten was writing to John Pounder, 'I personally have never worked so well as at the moment.' That sense of creative well-being was not uninterrupted. A feature of these years was the occurrence and recurrence of composing 'blocks' and fits of creative depression. He was never entirely to rid himself of them (there was a 'bad patch' again in 1943 (EWB, p. 181)), but in the States they were of an unusual severity. They may have been the by-products of the momentous decisions he was required to take in his personal life. But principally, I suggest, these were part and parcel of the conflicts, insecurities and fears attendant on the reappraisal and reassessment of his compositional goals and ambitions which I believe he undertook during these critical and often self-critical years; and which, consciously or unconsciously, was another motivation – perhaps the most serious one – of his temporary abandonment of England. He returned knowing the composer he wanted to be.

In a letter (No. 367) to Kit Welford, written only a couple of weeks before leaving New York on the start of the journey home, he remarks, 'I have reached a definite turning point in my work.' Another key phrase: the history of Britten's American period seems to me to be contained between his sense, in April 1940, of working at the then height of his powers, while embarked on a voyage of self-reflection, of self-definition, and the conclusion which that voyage was to lead him two years later, his sense of having reached in his compositional development a decisive 'turning point'. Not only

a turning point, but also a re-turning point. It is clear that the decision
to return home and the bout of creativity that was finally to discharge
itself in the completion of *Peter Grimes* (already outlined as an idea
in California in the summer of 1941) were inextricably linked
together. The aftermath of the 'turning point' to which Britten refers
is mapped out for us in terms of the works he composed between
1942 and 1945. We shall want to pay particular attention to the
evolution of *Peter Grimes*.

References to the opera begin soon after Britten's arrival in England. In April 1942 (Letter 374) he writes to Mrs Mayer:

M. [Montagu Slater] has taken to Grimes like a duck to water & the opera
is leaping ahead. It is very exciting – I must write & tell Koussey about
it. He has splendid ideas. It is getting more and more an opera about the
community whose life is 'illuminated' for this moment by the tragedy of the
murders. Ellen is growing in importance, & there are fine minor characters,
such as the Parson, pub-keeper, 'quack'-apothecary, & doctor.

In June, again to Mrs Mayer (Letter 383) he is confident that his
ideas 'are crystalizing nicely, and I think that, given opportunity, we
can make a really nice thing of it'. On 10 March 1943, however, in a
letter to Slater's wife, Enid, he writes: 'the more I think of P. Grimes
the more I like it & get excited over it. The trouble is that I don't
think anyone'll be able to bear it on the stage.'

In this same month, perhaps somewhat unexpectedly, we find
Britten studying the score of Richard Strauss's *Rosenkavalier*, which
he had asked for from his publisher, Ralph Hawkes, to whom he
writes (Letter 417):

Thank you, more than I can say. I can scarcely contain myself to write this
note – you see, I've never seen a score of Rosenkavalier, & I am impatient
to see how the old magician makes his effects! There's a hell of a lot I can
learn from him!

He continues:

I am afraid my opera won't be as lush or glittering as this one – after all
there is a difference between Vienna & Suffolk!! – but I have great hopes
of it, once we get the libretto right. I am working on it again now, with
some new improvements in view.

And this same letter continues further with one of those extraordinary penetrations of the future which we realize in retrospect to have
been so characteristic of the artist and the man. 'By-the-way,' he
adds,

I have a feeling that I can collaborate with Sadlers Wells opera abit in the future – it would be grand to have a permanent place to produce one's operas (& I mean to write a few in my time!) It may mean cutting down means a bit (no 4 flutes or 8 horns!) – but that doesn't hurt anyone – look at the Magic Flute or Figaro, with just a tiny orchestra. It's the ideas that count. This is only a scheme at the back of my mind, but I have a hunch that it's at the back of theirs too, as Joan Cross & Tony Guthrie want to see me about something. Don't say anything about it yet tho'.

In this one paragraph, in a letter from 1943, we find outlined the history yet to come of the English Opera Group[30] and even more importantly the idea of chamber opera; and this even before *Peter Grimes*, which remains Britten's grandest operatic conception, was composed, and while he was studying the score of *Rosenkavalier*! It is an arresting example of the penetrating insights the letters offer us into the working of his mind, one that obliges us radically to rethink the chronology of the chamber opera concept, which we can no longer analyse as a reaction against or divergence from *Grimes* but was clearly already part of his thinking pre-*Grimes*. We should note too his declaration to Hawkes of his firm commitment to future operas: 'I mean to write a few in my time!' This, surely, was also part of the sense of having reached a 'turning point', i.e. the discovery in himself of the fully fledged opera composer he was about to become. *Paul Bunyan* was behind him; *Grimes* beckoned.

It was again in March 1943, while in a London hospital, that Britten writes a letter (No. 418) to Erwin Stein, in which he discloses his thoughts about the character of Grimes. It shows the composer to have been among the first to be aware of the problems to which the psychology of his anti-hero gave rise and which have remained a preoccupation of analysts of the opera ever since 1945:[31]

[. . .] one bit of good work I'm doing is on the opera libretto – I am finding lots of possibilities of improvement, especially the character of Grimes himself which I find doesn't come across nearly clearly enough. At the moment he is just a pathological case – no reasons & not many symptoms! He's got to be changed alot.

This, one notes, was work on the *libretto*. Britten would certainly have had some musical ideas by this stage but the actual committal of the music to paper did not begin until early in 1944.

In April 1943 (Letter 426) he has come to a crucial decision about who is to sing the title role in the opera. He writes to Dr Mayer:

He [Peter] is singing so well, & acting with such abandon, that he is well on the way to becoming an operatic star. I wish you could see him, &

we all could discuss his performances. When I write it, & if it is put on
here, I hope he'll do the principal part in Peter Grimes. The ideas are
going well, but I haven't had time to start it yet.

It was to Pears, on 10 January 1944 (Letter 446), that he announces
that he has started work on the composition of the opera – an historic
letter by any reckoning, and a particularly valuable example of how
the correspondence with Pears enables us precisely to time the
moment of the work's inception:

Well, at last I have broken the spell and got down to work on P.G.. I have
been at it for two days solidly and got the greater part of the Prologue
done. It is very difficult to keep that amount of recitative moving, without
going round & round in circles, I find—but I think I've managed it. It is
also difficult to keep it going fast & yet paint moods and characters abit. I
can't wait to show it to you. Actually in this scene there isn't much for
you to do (I haven't got to the love-duet yet); it is mostly for Swallow, who
is turning out quite an amusing, pompous old thing! I don't know whether
I shall ever be a good opera composer, but it's wonderful fun to try once
in a way!

The note of exhilaration while composing Grimes remains pretty
constant; but there were occasional dips into acute depression, as in
June 1944, when he writes to Pears (Letter 464):

My bloody opera stinks, & that's all there is to it. But I daresay I shall be
able to de-odourise it before too long – or I'm hoping so.

The hope was fulfilled; and a month later he informs Elizabeth Mayer
(Letter 470):

The opera is going well – I've just finished Act II, & it is the next production
after Così at the Wells. Isn't that thrilling! It is becoming a bigger and bigger
affair than I expected and so topical as to be unbearable in spots! I am
yearning to see it on the stage – with Peter, Joan Cross, & Kenneth's
sets, & perhaps me conducting!

The progress of the composition of the opera was monitored by
Pears who writes to Mrs Mayer in August 1944 (No. 473):

Peter Grimes is now two-thirds done. The 2nd Act is finished, & Ben is
starting the Third with confidence. We are planning to do it with the
Sadler's Wells Opera next April. The first Act is quite terrifyingly intense,
from first note to last. Quite shattering. The 2nd is warmer & more
relaxed, though it has the death of the boy at the end. It will be terribly
difficult to do, for me especially, as the part is so dramatic it needs a
Chaliapin – & my voice is still lyrical and not dramatic. However, it was a
year before I could tackle the Sonnets, do you remember, and now they say
I sing them best of anything. So perhaps I shall reach Grimes by April!

The pace of the composition was extraordinary: two acts completed in just over six months. And there is the use of just one word by Britten – 'topical' – that suggests how, in his own mind, the violence and pain of *Grimes* were bound up with the violence and pain of the war years.[32]

7 June 1945

Britten, I have suggested, was not a seeker after conventional success, and was sometimes surprised by it when it came. (*War Requiem* in 1962, was a case in point: Lord Harewood writes well about it in his chapter on Britten in his autobiography, *The Tongs and the Bones* (London, Weidenfeld and Nicolson, 1981), p. 148.) But after the triumphant first performance of *Grimes* at Sadler's Wells it is clear from a letter he wrote to Imogen Holst on the 26 June (Letter 503) that he was aware that what he had achieved had an altogether special resonance about it. Its implications were far reaching:

> Thank you for your kind letter about Peter Grimes. I am so glad that the opera came up to your expectations, & it is sweet & generous of you to write so warmly about it. I must confess that I am very pleased with the way that it seems to 'come over the foot-lights', & also with the way the audience takes it, & what is perhaps more, returns night after night to take it again! I think the occasion is actually a greater one than either Sadler's Wells or me, I feel. Perhaps it is an omen for English Opera in the future. Anyhow I hope that many composers will take the plunge, & I hope also that they'll find as I did the water not quite so icy as expected!

The première of *Peter Grimes*, as we know now, represented a particular point of culmination in Britten's work and an altogether particular moment in the history of English music. These first volumes of letters allow us to observe the development of the composer towards that climactic achievement. We follow him through childhood and youth, through his schooldays, student and apprentice years, to his first years as a professional composer, and stay with him during his temporary exile in America, which was to lead to the crucial 'turning point' and to the return home, to England, to Suffolk, and finally to the composition of *Grimes*.

Above all, the letters testify to the extraordinary *preparation* that preceded the composition of the works that placed him at the forefront of English composers of his generation. And by that I mean the ceaseless accumulation, elaboration and practice, from a very early age, of the techniques that would eventually nourish, and indeed permit, the creation of a work like *Grimes*, techniques that draw on his experience in an unusual number of fields – film, radio, theatre as well as the concert hall. From the earliest days, these letters show, this was a life dedicated wholly and unremittingly to music. There can be no doubt that he accepted the destiny that his superior endowment shaped out for him. Indeed, a significant sub-theme that surfaces throughout his letters is the sense of duty he felt towards the protection and development of his compositional talents, all the more striking in an artist who was scarcely given to excessive self-esteem. For Britten, creativity entailed obligations. He looked after his creativity soberly, as if it were a responsibility, not just a heaven-sent gift to be exercised or squandered at whim.

Grimes brings these volumes to an end on a high plateau of achieve-ment: the opera was a consummation of virtually everything that had been learned in preceding years. But the fame of *Grimes* should not blind us to the exceptional riches and achievements of the periods leading up to the opera. There has been some satisfaction in witness-ing since Britten's death in 1976 a growing appreciation of the totality and consistency of his work. One of the significant merits of the letters is that they document so faithfully the integral continuity of the creative life and are free of the discriminations and judgements – often false judgements – that have been introduced retrospectively by poorly informed criticism or superficial fashion. The letters get us as close as we can possibly hope to get to apprehending the context in which and for which so much of his music in the 1930s and 1940s was written.

His post-*Grimes* letter to Imogen Holst, with its key phrase – 'I think the occasion is actually a greater one than either Sadler's Wells or me' – shows his awareness of that extra dimension which was certainly part of the *Grimes* phenomenon. But that same awareness was already part of his consciousness, even before he had started work on the composition of the opera. It was engendered by the response to that group of works which had been initiated by the critical 'turning point' reached at the end of the American years, among them the *Hymn to St Cecilia*, *Ceremony of Carols*, *Rejoice in the Lamb* and *Serenade*. It was these works, along with the *Michelangelo Sonnets*, their public reception, and the public interest they stirred, that provide the backcloth to the letter (No. 436) that Britten wrote to Imogen Holst on 21 October 1943 (a few days after the first per-formance of the *Serenade* had taken place at the Wigmore Hall):

I am not so self-confident ever to be blasé about appreciation, but when it comes from a musician of your standing, & from a section of musical life

which I have hitherto imagined so unsympathetic to me, it is inexpressibly
moving & valuable to me. It is also encouraging that you too sense that
'something' in the air which heralds a renaissance. I feel terrifically
conscious of it, so do Peter, & Clifford [Curzon], & Michael Tippett & so
many that I love & admire – it is good to add you to that list! Whether we
are the voices crying in the wilderness or the thing itself, it isn't for us
to know, but anyhow it is so very exciting. It is of course in all the arts,
but in music, particularly, it's this acceptance of 'freedom' without any
arbitrary restrictions, this simplicity, this contact with the audiences of our
own time, & of people like ourselves, this seriousness & above all this
professionalism.

It is a letter that is virtually an artist's credo, entirely spontaneous,
and yet disclosing principles and beliefs that were to remain fundamental to Britten's thinking until the end of his life: freedom from
arbitrarily imposed constraints (did he have serial dogma in mind?);
simplicity (clarity?); the obligation to communicate; seriousness; and
– 'above all' – professionalism (shades of Bridge!). The last item in
the litany was something that still needed to be emphasized in England in the 1940s. As for his surprise at praise from an unexpected
quarter – 'a section of musical life which I have hitherto imagined so
unsympathetic to me' – it reminds us of his uneasy relationship with
the music of the pastoral, folksong school of English composers
where 'professionalism', at least to Britten's ears, was discounted.

One of the more important letters, one may think, of the composer,
who, more than any other, was responsible through his music for
the renaissance to which he refers and of which he was aware of
being part, and published here for the first time. The consequences
of the extraordinary release of creativity in the early 1940s and the
seismic shock of 1945, when *Grimes* was first launched, are still with
us today.

The Pears Letters

It was Peter Pears whose idea it was that I should divert my attention
from compiling materials for Britten's biography and concentrate
instead on bringing out an edition of Britten's letters, though he
could scarcely have foreseen the challenging scale and complexity of
the finished publication.

I had originally discussed with Britten the character of the book
that I would write about him, in response to his invitation, in the
summer preceding his death in December 1976. We talked at length
one afternoon sitting in the garden of the Red House, and that same

night I drew up an outline scheme which he approved next morning. It is a book that I still intend to write.

There were two further important consequences of this discussion. The first was that Britten handed over to me in a shoebox the twelve volumes of his pocket diaries, which he kept from 1928 to 1939. There had been a few occasions when he had consulted his diaries, notably when he wanted to correct the faulty memory of Ronald Duncan. But this was the first time, I believe, that he had ever offered the diaries to be read and absorbed in their entirety (indeed, I had not known of their existence before the summer of 1976). I took the shoebox and its contents to Bangkok in July, where I had rented a house to work in, and started to assimilate the mass of information the diaries contained and to prepare a rudimentary index. Progress was slow, but out of that working vacation emerged the 1979 T.S. Eliot Memorial Lectures, *Britten and Auden in the Thirties: The Year 1936* (published 1981). The theme of the lectures arose directly from my experience of the diaries and was an indication of my growing interest in a decade that has proved to be of fundamental importance to our understanding of the history and evolution of Britten's creative life. I was also struck by the prodigious amount of work he got through and how *hard* he worked to get things right. He was particularly pleased to hear this from me on my return to England, and I can still remember him turning to Pears with unaffected delight: 'Did you hear that, Peter? I told you so; and now Donald says those old diaries back me up.' Even in 1976, Britten was gratified to know that the work ethic, which was so strong in him, had been alive and well in the 1930s and earlier.

The second consequence did not take the shape of a shoebox but of an injunction: 'I want you', he said to me when we were talking about my outline scheme, 'to tell the truth about Peter and me.' He said no more than that and indeed it was the only direct wish he expressed with regard to the biographical dimension of the book I was planning to write. His words, not surprisingly, have a special bearing on his letters to Pears, which I discuss below.

Well before Pears made his suggestion about publishing the letters in advance of my own study of the composer, it had already begun forcefully to strike me that Britten's letters and diaries together formed a source that could provide a comprehensive documentation of his life and works *in his own words*. Had he lived, it was improbable that he would ever have contemplated an autobiography – perhaps not improbable, but impossible. And yet in some sense, as I have already remarked, the impulse to self-documentation, and above all accurate self-documentation, was a powerful one. It had the result, I believe, of our having access to an autobiography embodied in the letters and diaries; and it is the extrapolation and release of that autobiography that has been one of the editors' principal goals. When complete, this series of volumes might be said to contain the autobiography that Britten himself would never have written. But write it, in fact, he did.

It scarcely needs to be said that no book that concerns itself with Britten's life would be complete without including Pears's life; and a volume of his letters would have been unthinkable without including his letters to his lifelong partner and supreme interpreter. A significant number of these letters were in Pears's possession, and after reading them – and by now the project Pears himself had motivated was well under way – I approached him to seek his agreement on which letters could be included and how they should be presented. I was aware, of course, that highly sensitive issues were involved. It was an altogether special relationship and the letters themselves were intimate personal documents. I was not at all sure how much, while Pears was alive, he would want published, for which reason I made some editorial suggestions about omissions and exclusions. But everything of musical importance stayed in. There were certain aspects of the history of Britten's music in the 1940s, for example, that were only documented in his letters to Pears.

In the event, Pears – in retrospect, I believe with much more wisdom than I had shown – rejected any notion of editing and agreed in principle to the use of the final selection of letters appearing without cuts.

I should not, perhaps, have been surprised by this decision. On at least two occasions known to me he had referred in public, and positively, to the publication of these letters. In the interview I conducted with him for Tony Palmer's documentary film, *A time there was* (1980), he remarked: 'I have had some quite wonderful letters from Ben and I propose one day to publish them . . . he liked to take the line that he would never have done anything without me. There is a really wonderful letter to that effect which I'd love one day everybody to know'; and again in an interview published in the *Advocate* (San Francisco, 271, 12 July 1979, pp. 37–9), he replied to the question, 'How do you see yourself mentioned in the biographies of Britten? I've just seen Donald Mitchell's book . . . *Pictures from a Life*':

Well, he does stress, charmingly, I think, the fact that it isn't the story of one man. It's a life of the two of us. And that, it seems to me, is where I stand. That's where I belong. I hope one day that we shall publish some of Ben's letters. I hope the climate will be right then for publishing some of the most marvellous letters that one can imagine, which he wrote to me. And which will put it clearly.

There was no hurry on my part to reach a final decision about which letters, precisely, should appear, and I left a batch with Pears to reflect on and choose. There the matter rested, while work on the project continued. But not for long. Pears was to write to me – the letter is undated but must belong to late 1985 – and in effect withdrew his sanction:

Dearest Donald,

I have been mulling over Ben's letters to me which you kindly left for me to think about. I should really prefer not to include them as the only letters in the first volume, and would prefer to include them in my own book which is beginning to take shape at last and where they would be more at home, I think.

Much love to you both

PETER

I confess that I was somewhat disconcerted by this reversed decision. I found it hard to envisage a volume of Britten's correspondence *without* any letters to Pears; moreover, as I have said, there was musical documentation – especially about the composition of *Peter Grimes* – to be found nowhere else. I was also in difficulty with the biographical dimension. If the letters were to give a faithful account of the texture of Britten's life – let alone the complexity of it – I could not see how that was to be achieved without at least some of – or some parts of – the letters to Pears.

On the other hand his own proposal, to write a book of his own, was clearly of overriding importance; and had it happened – and his friends, colleagues and co-Trustees did everything in their power to create the conditions in which it might happen – it would have been a unique narrative; and indisputably Britten's letters to him would have belonged to it. (What Pears left amounts to thirty pages of a draft account of his childhood and youth, to the age of eighteen or thereabouts.) I recognized that, naturally, but still hoped that before it came to the point of submitting these volumes for publication I might succeed in persuading him to allow me at least to include those parts of the letters that had a direct bearing on the history and chronology of Britten's music. But Pears's death intervened, in 1986, and I never had the opportunity to discuss the matter with him again.

While I had certainly conceded the unquestioned appropriateness of Pears's letters from Britten appearing in the context of his own book, if it came to be written, I had not perceived that other, perhaps deeper, feelings on his part were involved. It was only after his death that I learned from others, close to him, that he took the view that including 'his' letters in a volume that necessarily included the fullest possible representation of Britten's friends, relatives, acquaintances, colleagues and collaborators, somehow detracted from the special character of the relationship: to put not too fine a point upon it, downgraded it.

Perhaps a rather closer reading of his public statements on the letters, from which I quote above, might have given me advance warning of the change of mind I was to encounter. But while one may understand Pears's anxiety, especially in his last years, when he seemed to feel the need to keep his own profile high – as if he feared that his unique role in Britten's life and creativity might somehow be overlooked or undervalued – I find it difficult to believe that his forebodings were realistic. After his death – and after the discovery of a further batch of letters from Britten, equal in number and importance to those that he and I had first discussed, I did wonder momentarily if a separate volume of letters might be the answer. But thinking along those lines only confirmed my earlier conviction, that far from taking anything away from the unique nature of the relationship, placing the letters in the context of Britten's life, and thereby in the context of the life he came to share with Britten, could only enhance and illumine our understanding of it. Britten, I think, wrote many fascinating letters, but his letters to Pears are like no others (perhaps with one exception). There is no conceivable sense in which they might be thought to be lost amid or overwhelmed by the letters that surround them.

I have already mentioned the importance of the Pears letters for the chronology of Britten's music. There is another aspect which I think of no less significance. Pears, as we have seen, liked the concept I had introduced into *Pictures from a Life*: '. . . it isn't the story of one man. It's the life of the two of us.' It seems to me that these volumes expand on that precedent: the letters from Britten to Pears, and no less Pears's letters to Britten – he was himself an extraordinarily observant, witty and colourful correspondent – reveal precisely how those two lives merged to become (for them, at least) one life. It was not immediate. There was an exceptionally rich personal and creative life, as it were, pre-Pears. The crucial pre-war period of achievement and evolution, the influence of Auden and his circle, the first meetings with Pears, the growth of the friendship, the gradual disengagement (on Britten's part) from other commitments, wished for or wished on him – all of this documented by the *totality* of the letters, down to the exact moment when, as we can know now and have read above, a final pledge was made, when we can safely assume the two lives fused.

'Tell the truth about Peter and me': I have tried to fulfil that injunction in the way that I believe was the only possible way; and if there remains even the palest shadow of doubt in anyone's mind about the relationship that was distinct in kind from all the other relationships in Britten's life, let me dispel it for ever by quoting an exchange of letters between Britten and Pears in November 1974, when Britten was convalescing from his open heart surgery, and writing from Germany, while Pears (at the age of sixty-four!) was making his début at the Metropolitan Opera, New York, as Aschenbach in *Death in Venice*.

Britten's letter was dated Sunday 17 November 1974:

My darling heart (perhaps an unfortunate phrase – but I can't use any other) I feel I must write a squiggle which I couldn't say on the telephone without bursting into those silly tears – I do love you so terribly, not only glorious you, but your singing. I've just listened to a re-broadcast of Winter Words (something like Sept. '72) and honestly you are the greatest artist that ever was – every nuance, subtle & never over-done – those great words, so sad & wise, painted for one, that heavenly sound you make, full but always coloured for words & music. What have I done to deserve such an artist and man to write for? I had to switch off before the folk songs because I couldn't [take] anything after "how long, how long" [the last song of the Hardy cycle]. How long? – only till Dec. 20th[33] – I think I can just bear it.

> But I love you,
> I love you
> I love you — —
> B.[34]

Pears's reply was undated but postmarked New York, 21 November:

My dearest darling

No one has ever ever had a lovelier letter than the one which came from you today – You say things which turn my heart over with love and pride, and I love you for every single word you write. But you know, Love is blind – and what your dear eyes do not see is that it is you who have given me everything, right from the beginning, from yourself in Grand Rapids! through Grimes & Serenade & Michelangelo and Canticles – one

thing after another, right up to this great Aschenbach – I am here as your
mouthpiece and I live in your music – And I can never be thankful
enough to you and to Fate for all the heavenly joy we have had together
for 35 years.

> My darling, I love you –
>
> P.

If these volumes show how the Britten–Pears relationship began,
these two letters from 1974 show how it ended, with their love for
each other magnificently intact. There are no words to be added to
their words. I would only entreat the reader – and this, I hope, will
allow Peter to rest easy – to read the correspondence between the
two men published here in the radiant perspective that the 1974
letters unfold. Just two years later Britten was dead, after thirty-
seven years of life with 'the greatest artist that ever was'.

*Bangkok – Hua Hin – Ban Surae – Horham – London – Hong Kong – Bangkok –
London – Horham*
March 1986 – August 1989

NOTES

1 Or generated, as Hans Keller put it, the 'conquest of new musical territory so far as the use of children's voices in and outside the opera house was concerned, a conquest which, in 1954, contributed to what may be his greatest operatic achievement altogether – *The Turn of the Screw*'. Keller adds, 'however little Britten may have been alive to the fact, his psychosexual organization placed him in the privileged position of discovering and defining new truths which, otherwise, might not have been accessible to him at all'. ('Introduction: Operatic Music and Britten', in *The Operas of Benjamin Britten*, ed. David Herbert (London, Hamish Hamilton, 1979), pp. xxv–vi.)

It was Pears's strongly held view that there were no 'conflicts'. For example, when Michael Kennedy was working on his 1981 study of Britten, he addressed a question to Pears about Britten's 'anguish through guilt', to which Pears forcefully replied in his undated, draft response:

Forget it! Ben never regarded his own passionate feelings for me or his earlier friends as anything but good, natural, and profoundly creative. In that direction there was never a moment of guilt. I do not believe that Ben's private life plays any role in the 'assessment of his artistry & personality'. He was a musical genius.

Is one really interested in the sex life of the great musicians – In Bach, Mozart, or the less great – Gounod, Stanford or Wm Walton? I don't think so. ~~Only if one is bored by their music, do we have to find something to blame~~. I'm sorry to be vague throughout.

One day before long I hope I shall write about Ben & perhaps help to clear up some ~~doubts~~ queries & ~~print some letters~~.

Britten's diaries, however, do not allow us to be quite so confident that feelings of 'guilt' were not attached to his perception of his sexuality.

2 Britten refers to the posthumously published *Notebooks* of Samuel Butler (1835–1902), the author of *Erewhon*.

3 On 11 April, when Henry Comer was the interviewer.

4 'I knew them all, but Barbara and Robert were, you know, away from home when I was there, and Beth I knew quite well, though she left, you see. In a way the only person that saw him at this time I guess was me!'

5 An almost exactly similar formulation was used by another childhood friend, John Pounder (Interview with Donald Mitchell, 24 June 1988, Aldeburgh) who described Mr Britten as 'severe . . . but not in a nasty sort of way – severe in a nice sort of way'.

6 Basil Reeve, incidentally, helped his friend correct the words in *A Boy was Born* and was rewarded with the inscription 'To the noble proof-reader'.

7 It was not, however, Britten's thriftiness, sober dress and taste for plain living alone that may be attributed to his following his father's example. We learn from Beth's family recollections that for many years he wore his father's tails 'and always looked extremely good in them' (EWB, p. 52); and it seems likely that it was Mr Britten who was the source of his son's fondness for cold baths (p. 46), a consequence of the 'character training' (along with 'cold bedrooms') that Beth remembered as part of her childhood. Rather more interestingly it is possible that her brother's suspicion of those who were conspicuously articulate may have had its roots in a like reaction by the father, who was never comfortable with Bridge, for example, because 'He had long hair, was very excitable and talked a lot. Our father was very conservative and could not stand anyone who talked as much *thinking it showed an empty mind*' (p. 54; my italics). More than a trace of that scepticism about excessive volubility was inherited by the son.

Beth makes a further, singular observation: '. . . my father', she writes (p. 29), 'never intended to have children at all: there was no birth control at that time.'

8 See also RDBB, p. 23, where the Bs turn up again in a different formulation.

9 Many of Britten's friends – I among them – will remember a street game (the subject of a poem by A.A. Milne) he played while out walking which reflected this same preoccupation. In Britten's version he would hop from square to square of the paving stones and if he could complete a stretch without his feet touching any of the lines he would claim that this showed that after all he was a good composer – or going to be. See also RDBB, p. 86.

10 Britten describes in his diary, on 26 February 1937, a party that took place after the first performance of *The Ascent of F6* and concludes: 'In fact have a good & merry time (& me not far from being the centre of attraction strange as it may seem!)'.

11 To whom was dedicated the song, 'The Birds', with words by Hilaire Belloc, composed at Holt in June 1929 (and revised in 1934), the first title in the chronological catalogue of Britten's published words. (He wrote in his diary on the 3rd, 'Write song for voice & strings, "The Birds" by H. Belloc'; and on the 4th: 'I touch up my song [. . .] and am more satisfied.') But the song is only the tip of the iceberg. Between 15 October 1925 and 30 January 1926 Britten dedicated to his mother no fewer than twelve works for solo piano, including four suites and five sonatas. There was also an earlier work for piano duet dedicated to her, 'The March of the Gods into Paridise' [*sic*]. Two sets of songs were also written for her, the 'Twelve Songs for the mezzo-soprano and contralto voice' (1923/4), which carried a special inscription – 'N.B. all these songs are dedicated to my mother – Mrs. E.B. [*sic*] Britten' – and imprint – 'published by "Home Songs" 21 Kirkley Cliff Road, Lowestoft' – and 'Six Songs for voice and piano' (1926). There were also works jointly dedicated to his parents: a 'Suite Fantastique' in A minor, for large orchestra and pianoforte obbligato (for their silver wedding anniversary in 1926); 'Chaos and Cosmos', a symphonic poem for large orchestra (for their twenty-sixth wedding anniversary in the following year); and the 'Quatre Chansons

Françaises', for soprano and small orchestra (for their twenty-seventh wedding anniversary in 1928, published posthumously in 1982). To 1927 also belonged another joint dedication: the Symphony in D minor for large orchestra. There are no individual dedications to Britten's father among his son's juvenilia, which makes the later dedication of *A Boy was Born* all the more exceptional.

12 In her memoir of her brother, EWB, p. 109, Beth writes:

> . . . his chief creative power was writing for the voice, and there was something about Peter's voice which gave Ben what he needed. A close friend of Ben's who had known my mother well and heard her voice, remarked to me recently that Peter's voice was very like my mother's, and she had just died.

In October 1973, when he was inevitably much preoccupied with the past and contemplating a programme of gramophone records (probably for local consumption), Britten included an item, 'Songs my mother used to sing, such as: Roger Quilter, "Now sleeps the crimson petal"; Cyril Scott, "Lullaby"; and Schubert, any of the better known songs: "Who is Sylvia?", "Hark! Hark! the lark!", "Heidenröslein".' The programme was never given, no doubt because of his health: he was convalescing after his heart operation in May.

One cannot but remark, in this context, on the Quilter setting of Tennyson's poem. Britten was himself to set the text when working on the *Serenade*, but then chose to exclude the song – unequivocally addressed to Pears – from the cycle. (See note 2 to Letter 419.)

The first item in the programme was to be Beethoven's *Coriolan* overture: 'Beethoven was my earliest love; until I was in my teens he completely dwarfed all other composers.'

13 In RDBB p. 47, Duncan writes: '[Britten] told me that soon after his return [from Paris, in January 1937] his mother had been taken ill and had become delirious before she died. "During the delirium," he said simply, "she spoke to me, not as though I were her son, but her lover . . ." '

14 There is extant only one example of the many letters Britten wrote to friends and relatives in response to his mother's death, a letter to John Pounder, 8 February 1937 [see Letter 97]: 'It is a terrible feeling, this loneliness, and the very happy & beautiful memories I have of Mum don't make it any easier [. . .]'

Later diary entries speak for themselves:

9 May
Feel terribly lonely for Mum to-night – it is so hard to realise that this all has happened. I have some gramophone records on – but can't have many, because it is through music that our contact was perhaps greatest.

15 May
Look at photos alot after supper – heart rending one's of Mum & Pop included – Mum being shown as an absolute beauty, such a girl as ever I could lose my heart to.

One of the very few public references by Britten to his mother's death was made in the course of a broadcast in 1942 about the *Sinfonia da Requiem*, on the occasion of its first performance in England at the Proms on 22 July:

For me to produce my best music it is always essential for the purely musical idea or germ to precede the external stimulus. In the case of the *Sinfonia da Requiem* this external stimulus was the death of my mother a few years ago. It had an especially powerful emotional effect on me and set me, in self-defence, analysing my feelings in regard to suffering and death. To this personal tragedy were soon added the more general world tragedies of the Spanish and the present wars.

('How a musical work originates', *Listener*, 30 July 1942, p. 138)

15 This must surely have made its contribution to the extraordinary depth-charge of feeling at the heart of *Albert Herring* (1947), which surfaces and erupts in Act II, scene 2. It seems to me now not far fetched to suppose that something essential is said in the opera about the composer's relationship to his own mother. Hitherto, one has read the opera, principally, as an allegory, as a parable of the transition from youth to adulthood and in particular the obligatory achievement of sexual liberation and emancipation. The opera is indeed all that, and many other things besides. But now it seems to me that, while the opera marvellously transcends and transforms the purely autobiographical, the musicalization of the relationship of Albert and his Mum must have been fuelled directly by Britten's experience. In this light, Albert's longings and yearnings for freedom take on fresh significance, as must his final dismissal of his mother at the end of Act III. Perhaps it was in *Albert Herring*, in truth, that Britten wrote the final act of a long-running, domestic drama: 'That'll do, Mum!' (Fig. 73–4).

In RDBB, p. 21, Duncan writes of his pre-war friendship with Britten:

Both of us were without a father, both of us were hopelessly tied to our mothers . . . Britten's mother remained a considerable influence on him. She was a small bird-like woman with great energy and appeared to be most possessive about her son.

16 Interview with Donald Mitchell, 21 May 1988, Aldeburgh; Britten–Pears Library.

17 Britten's setting of the text pointedly declines to accept the reproach. In his diary, on 17 November 1936, he describes his setting thus: 'very light & Victorian in mood!' Did Britten perhaps mean Victorian in its 'moral' stance? See also DMBA, pp. 163–5.

18 The influence of these same friends meant that Britten began to question some of the rules of conduct which his mother still wished him to observe. For example, on 11 April 1936 he writes at home in his diary: 'Before bed we have the periodical row about going to Communion (for to-morrow). It is difficult for Mum to realise that one's opinions change at all – tho it would be a bad outlook if they didn't!' Politics too – clearly an early consequence of his meeting Auden – were a source of conflict. On 2 August 1935, he writes: '[. . .] try to talk communism with Mum, but it is impossible to say anything to anyone brought up in the old order without severe ruptions. The trouble is that fundamentally she agrees with me & won't admit it.' But these manifestations of friction occur only infrequently and then only after 1935 and the influx of radical friends with their 'subversive' views. By January 1937, Britten was writing to John Pounder about (probably) a politicized Christmas card on the mantelpiece, 'Mum never objects, in fact silently acquiesces, & my sisters are well-trained now!' See also DMBA, p. 39 and pp. 77–8.

19 The need for a decision had already begun to surface in 1936. On 5 June
   Britten writes in his diary: 'Life is a pretty hefty struggle these days – sexually
   as well. Decisions are so hard to make, & its difficult to look unprejudiced
   on apparently abnormal things.'

20 Ironically enough, Mrs Britten's death followed almost immediately on her
   son's return from Paris, where, in the company of Henry Boys and Ronald
   Duncan, he was led off to a brothel (see note 1 to Letter 95): 'It is revolting
   – appalling that such a noble thing as sex should be so degraded.'

21 A fateful sequence of events unfolded in the early months of 1937. In January,
   Mrs Britten died. In April, Pears's close friend, Peter Burra, was killed in an
   air accident. It was these *two* deaths, one might say, that created the conditions that allowed the Britten–Pears relationship in the first instance to
   happen and then to flourish.

22 Britten was ardent in his letters to Pears but, characteristically, rarely
   amorous.

23 In a letter to Wulff Scherchen from Amityville, postmarked 29 September
   1939 (Letter 210), Britten writes: 'Peter sends his love, & says he's looking
   after me – as he certainly is – like a mother hen! He's a darling — — — '

24 After an evening of listening to gramophone recordings of Lehmann, Schumann, Flagstad *et al.*, Britten wrote in his diary on 28 March 1937, 'I have
   such a passion for sopranos that I may some time become "normal".' Wyss
   had given the first performance of *Our Hunting Fathers* six months earlier,
   the biggest work Britten had yet composed for high voice and orchestra; and
   he was soon to embark on *On this Island*, and *Les Illuminations*, again for
   Wyss.

25 It was this work that prompted Imogen Holst in an interview with me (22
   June 1977, Aldeburgh) to remark:

   I must tell you that I got the impression very strongly throughout *The Prince of the
   Pagodas*, which lasted a long time and was a terrible burden to Ben . . . that Peter had
   no interest in it, because it hadn't got singing things in it, and that therefore *all* that
   support that he gave Ben in *all* his compositions with a part for him in, which kept
   Ben going, was absolutely cut off at the main, not going there.

26 I remember Britten saying to me how surprised he was at the revival of
   interest in his Violin and Piano Concertos: 'I had been told so often that
   they were no good that I had come to believe it myself.' Of course, one of
   the reasons why these works were written off was because of the received
   opinion that Britten's real strength rested only in his vocal music. The rest
   could be safely disregarded.

27 For example, before Pears there was the powerful and intoxicating Auden
   ('Ben told me that Peter got him away from Auden', EWB, p. 177); and it
   may not seem altogether fanciful to perceive in the stimulus to create that
   Britten found in specific events and specific performers a reflection of the
   fundamental relationship in his life. The setting up of goals – exterior, in
   the first instance, however much they would then become interiorized – was
   an indispensable part of his creative process. Some of the key texts quoted
   so often from Britten's Aspen Award speech (1964) – e.g. 'I want my music
   to be of use to people, to please them'; 'There should be special music made

and played for all sorts of occasions' – might also be scrutinized afresh from this angle.

28 There was also an element of the 'outsiders' (in more than one respect) finding themselves most at home among those who were themselves, culturally speaking, from outside rather than inside.

29 Those interested in following up this singular political episode can consult the relevant file in the Archive.

30 Likewise, in a letter (No. 337) from September 1941, Britten, in commenting adversely on the ISCM Festival which had been held in New York in May – 'the Festival itself was a wash-out – no real community feeling – no friendliness – all the people there one knew already, they're living here anyhow – no trips, or local colouring' – reveals by implication the very characteristics that were to distinguish the Aldeburgh Festival when it came to be conceived.

31 In a message designed to accompany the first Swedish production of *Grimes* in 1946, Britten wrote:

I can't help feeling that there is a kinship between our Crabbe and your Strindberg. They both broke with the romantic tradition in literature. They both had a keen eye for the seamy side of life. They were without embellishments. They were perhaps, each in his own way, epoch-making in his harsh realism.

(BBC European Service, Swedish transmission, 19 March 1946)

32 From a letter to Beth (No. 256) we learn that the *Sinfonia da Requiem* of 1940 was not only a memorial to his parents but also reflected the explosive tension of the immediately preceding decade.

33 The date of the last performance of *Death in Venice* at the Met, after which Pears returned to Aldeburgh.

34 The letter ends with a postscript: 'The Folk Song Suite ("Up she goes"?) is just finished – good I hope.' Britten refers to *A time there was . . .* , Op. 90.

Volume One
1923–1939

Letters of thanks, letters from banks,
Letters of joy from the girl and boy,
Receipted bills and invitations
To inspect new stock or visit relations,
And applications for situations,
And timid lovers' declarations,
And gossip, gossip from all the nations;
News circumstantial, news financial,
Letters with holiday snaps to enlarge in,
Letters with faces scrawled in the margin,
Letters from uncles, cousins and aunts,
Letters to Scotland from the South of France,
Letters of condolence to Highlands and Lowlands,
Notes from overseas to the Hebrides;
Written on paper of every hue,
The pink, the violet, the white and the blue.
The chatty, the catty, the boring, adoring,
The cold and official and the heart's outpouring,
Clever, stupid, short and long,
The typed and the printed and the spelt all wrong.

. . . none will hear the postman's knock
Without a quickening of the heart,
For who can bear to feel himself forgotten?

W.H. Auden
'Night Mail' (1935)

Childhood and Schooldays:
South Lodge and Gresham's
1923–1930

Chronology: 1913–1930

Year	Events	Compositions
1913	*22 November*: Born at 21 Kirkley Cliff Road, Lowestoft, the youngest child of Mr and Mrs R.V. Britten. The other children were Barbara (1902–1982), Robert (1907–1987) and Elizabeth (Beth; 1909–1989)	
*c.*1919	First music lessons from his mother, an active amateur singer and later Secretary of the Lowestoft Musical Society	First compositions
*c.*1921	Piano and music theory lessons with Miss Ethel Astle, a local teacher at the pre-preparatory school he attended with the younger of his two sisters, Beth	
1922–3		Early piano compositions and songs, including 'Beware!'
1923	Enters South Lodge Preparatory School, Lowestoft, as a day boy	
*c.*1923	Viola lessons with Audrey Alston at Framingham Earl, near Norwich	
1924	*30 October*: Hears Frank Bridge's orchestral suite, *The Sea*, conducted by the composer at the Norwich Triennial Festival	
1925		More songs and piano music, including waltzes, scherzos, fantasias, bourrées, suites and four sonatas
1926	*January*: Passes finals (Grade VIII) Associated Board piano examinations with honours. *July*: Submits his orchestral 'Ouverture' to the BBC's	Composes much chamber music and his first orchestral pieces

Year	Events	Compositions
	Autumn Musical Festival Prize Competition *December*: Advice sought from Charles Macpherson, organist of St Paul's Cathedral	
1927	*September*: Head Boy of South Lodge 27 *October*: Hears Bridge's *Enter Spring* at Norwich and meets Bridge for the first time through Audrey Alston. Begins composition lessons with Bridge at his homes in London and Friston, near Eastbourne, during school holidays	More chamber and orchestral works, including a Symphony in D minor
1928	*Summer Term*: Captain of cricket and *Victor Ludorum* 20 *September*: Enters Gresham's School, Holt, Norfolk. Continues composition lessons with Bridge *November*: Begins piano lessons with Harold Samuel in London	*June–August*: *Quatre Chansons Françaises* (Hugo and Verlaine), for soprano and orchestra
1929		*January–March*: Rhapsody, for string quartet *June*: 'The Birds' (Belloc), for voice and piano (rev. 1934)
1930	*1 March*: Bagatelle, for violin, viola and piano, performed at Gresham's by Joyce Chapman, Britten and Walter Greatorex *July*: Leaves Gresham's (School Certificate with five credits) after winning an open scholarship to the Royal College of Music, London	*January–April*: *Quartettino* *May*: A Wealden Trio: *The Song of the Women* (rev. 1967) *July*: *A Hymn to the Virgin* (rev. 1934) *August*: Elegy, for viola solo *September*: 'I saw three ships' (rev. 1967 as *The Sycamore Tree*)

1   To Mr and Mrs R.V. Britten[1]

[88 Berners Street]
Ipswich
25 April, 1923

My Darling Mums & Daddy

I have had a most Lovely time, Auntie[2] & I have juse been to the station & saw about 20 L & N e r [London & North Eastern Railway] Engines please tell Bobby I saw A 4.6.0 L & N.E.R. Engine a Lovely one a new one! It had got on the side plates

it was green with a gold rim round its chimmeny.

Mummie I am practising every day and have the C.L.O. [Cod Liver Oil] in malt every day too. thank you so much for letting me stay till saterday. I have writter a "sonata Fantaste"[3] Please thank Daddy for the lovely letter.

With love
Your loveing son
BENJAMIN
XXXXX
OO
XXX

1 Britten's parents. His father, Robert Victor, was born in Birkenhead on 4 January 1877. He died at Lowestoft, where he practised as a dental surgeon, on 6 April 1934 (see also Letters 46–48 and note 2 to Letter 136). He married Edith Rhoda Hockey on 5 September 1901. She was born on 9 December 1872 and died in London on 31 January 1937 (see also Letter 96, and Diaries for 27–31 January and 1–3 February, 1937). There were four children by the marriage: Edith Barbara (b. 11 June 1902; d. 20 December 1982); Robert [Bobby] Harry Marsh (b. 28 January 1907; d. 12 June 1987); Charlotte Elizabeth [Beth] (b. 10 June 1909; d. 16 May 1989); and Edward Benjamin (b. 22 November 1913; d. 4 December 1976). For further details of the Britten and Hockey families see EWB, pp. 15–21, 29–33 and 201–5.

2 Jane Hockey (née Holbrook; 1869–1942). She was Britten's aunt, sister-in-law of his mother. Britten was visiting his Aunt Janie at Ipswich when he wrote this letter.

     She married Henry William Hockey ('Willie'), Mrs Britten's brother

(1870–1948) in 1900. Willie was organist at the Tower Church (St Mary-le-Tower), Ipswich, and conductor of the Ipswich Choral Society and taught singing both in Ipswich and London. There were two children by the marriage (Britten's cousins): Elsie Mary (1902–1984) and George William (b. 1906). The Hockey family home was at 88 Berners Street, Ipswich. (See also note 1 to Diary for 10 September 1932.) Elsie, who became a prominent dancing teacher in Ipswich, took part in the documentary television film, TP, made in 1979 and first shown on 6 April 1980.

3 This work, for piano solo, survives among Britten's juvenilia. It was subsequently, though no less oddly, entitled 'sonata fantasti'. The first page (of seven) is reproduced below.

Britten, in the 1950s, was to write a sleeve note for a recording of the *Simple Symphony* (see note 2 to Letter 40) which took the shape of a vividly remembered account of his prep school days. It is the only document of its kind and we reproduce it here in full:

Once upon a time there was a prep-school boy. He was called Britten mi., his initials were E.B., his age was nine, and his locker was number seventeen. He was quite an ordinary little boy; he took his snake-belt to bed with him; he loved cricket, only quite liked football (although he kicked a pretty 'corner'); he adored Mathematics, got on all right with History, was scared by Latin Unseen; he behaved fairly well, only ragged the recognised amount, so that his contacts with the cane or the slipper were happily rare (although one nocturnal expedition to stalk ghosts left its marks behind); he worked his way up the school slowly and steadily, until at the age of thirteen he reached that pinnacle of importance and grandeur never to be quite equalled in later days: the head of the Sixth, head-prefect, and Victor Ludorum. But . . . there was one curious thing about this boy: he wrote music. His friends bore with it, his enemies kicked a bit but not for long (he was quite tough), the staff couldn't object if his work and games didn't suffer. He

wrote lots of it, reams and reams of it. I don't really know when he had
time to do it. In those days, long ago, prep school boys didn't have much
. free time; the day started with early work at 7.30, and ended (if you were
lucky not to do extra prep.) with prayers at 8.0 – and the hours in between
were fully organised. Still there were odd moments in bed, there were half
holidays and Sundays too, and somehow these reams and reams got written.
And they are still lying in an old cupboard to this day – String Quartets (six
of them), twelve piano sonatas; dozens of songs; sonatas for violin, sonatas
for viola and cello too; suites, waltzes, rondos, fantasies, variations; a tone-
poem 'Chaos and Cosmos'; a tremendous symphony, for gigantic orchestra
including eight horns and oboe d'amore (started on January 17th and finished
February 28th); an oratorio called Samuel: all the opus numbers from 1 to
100 were filled (and catalogued) by the time Britten mi. was fourteen.

Of course they aren't very good, these works; inspiration didn't always
run very high, and the workmanship wasn't always academically sound,
and although our composer looked up oboe d'amore in the orchestra books,
he hadn't much of an idea what it sounded like; besides, for the sake of
neatness, every piece had to end precisely at the bottom of the right-hand
page, which doesn't always lead to a satisfactory conclusion. No, I'm afraid
they aren't very great; but when Benjamin Britten, a proud young composer
of twenty (who'd already had a work broadcast) came along and looked in
this cupboard, he found some of them not too uninteresting; and so, rescor-
ing them for strings, changing bits here and there, and making them more
fit for general consumption, he turned them into a SIMPLE SYMPHONY, and
here it is.

The recording of the work, in November 1953, was made by the New
Symphony Orchestra of London Strings under Eugene Goossens,
and issued in 1956 by Decca on LW 5163.

In an interview for the CBC (on 11 April 1968) Britten was asked
about a childhood oratorio and 'an aria for God in C minor', to which
he replied, 'Yes, yes. I hoped it was a key He'd like'. It is probable
that this aria belonged to Samuel, the oratorio he composed at the
age of ten (sixteen pages, on thirty-stave manuscript paper) and
which he makes a point of mentioning in his Simple Symphony note.

2   To Mr and Mrs R.V. Britten

[EWB, plate 17, between pp. 54–5
Picture postcard: Two fluffy kittens]

[Postmark 18 June 1923]

My darling Mums & Dad

I am just composing another peace of mine. it is not a very nice
but is good 'nough to put down. I have just come home from
Elizabeth Boyd's and Mrs. Boyd[1] has asked me to go next sunday
too is'nt it kind of her

[Written upside down]
Lazy[2] has been out with her dog

Love me – please Love me   give to Beth!!

Love me – BENNY!

Mrs & Mrs RV Britten
C⁰ of Lowe House
School of St Mary & Anne[3]
Abbots Bromley
Staffordshire
England

1 Mrs Doveton Boyd, a friend of Mrs Britten's and her daughter, Elizabeth. Mrs Boyd lent the Brittens a square piano, which was housed in the boys' bedroom at Kirkley Cliff Road. See EWB, p. 44. There was another family of Boyds in Lowestoft whom the Brittens knew: see note 4 to Diary for 18 April 1931.

2 Edith Ellen Hayes [sometimes spelled Haes], Mr Britten's secretary. Beth Britten recalls in EWB, p. 37:

Benny was about three when she came and he could not say his 's's', so he called her 'Milhale'. Then, she became known, quite undeservedly, as 'Lazy', which she remained for the eighteen years she stayed with us. Lazy was a good and loyal friend to all of us. After her aged mother died and she left the practice she went to live with her sister in Kettering [Northamptonshire] where we went to see her when we could.

Miss Hayes was still in touch with the composer in 1946.

3 Britten's parents were visiting the school at which both his sisters were educated.

3 To Mrs Britten

[PFL, *plate 30*]

21 Kirkley Cliff Road, Lowestoft.[1]
Telephone No. 112
June 19th 1923

My darling Mummy

I hope you are enjoying yourself   How's Beth   I hope She's quite well   It's Lowestoft and Oulton broad[2] carnavle week   Last night we saw a ripping proseshion   the Fire Engine Life boat, edvertisments etc: Edwards the taylor had a

ripping edvertisment   a man with a very big mask on and a
Huge straw hat[3]

1 The Britten family home from 1908 where Mr Britten had his surgery
  on the ground floor. The house stands today much as it did throughout Britten's childhood and youth.
2 The Broads (Broadlands): extensive inland stretches of water in
  Norfolk and North Suffolk used for sailing.
3 In an interview after her brother's death, Beth recalled that he 'used
  to draw most beautifully . . . everybody thought he was going to be
  an artist, not a [composer] . . . It's funny but it might have switched
  the other way . . .' (Interview with Charles Ford, c.1976/7, Aldeburgh; Archive at the Britten–Pears Library.)

21 Kirkley Cliff Road, a pen-and-ink drawing (by Aunt Queenie?) preserved among
Britten's papers

4   To Mrs Britten

21, Kirkley Cliff Road, Lowestoft
November 7th, 1923.

My Mummie darling,

Oh! Mummie what a life, (!) a piece of news was given to me this morning by Miss Ethel — —[1]   My Exam (Thery) is on the 12th wednesday Next and you wont be home, I suppose it would be noosty of me to ask you to be home, so I wont but oh! I wish you could be. The 'Xam' zam is at 2 till five' W've got to be there at a quarter to 2.   Dummy! I have given the notice to Beak[2] and he was supprised that It was so early and he wondered what he could do about it. "Lazy" said that she'd take me out on Sunday with Duffer.[3] Rose[4] is stoneing raisens (but I've eaten more than she's stoned). She's just put the raisan in the cup (for pips) and pips in the bigone. Pounder[5] has just lent me a story about nice bugalers and murderers called Raffles 6d edition.[6] Alice is sewing and so's Mary,[7] I'm writing as you see, so arn't we an industrious family of kittens immortles. I hope you arrived safely and did Bobby meet you on the Stamford road?[8] I hope the car ran well, and you did not run over any bodie, (or doggie). I hope "Didern Like" ("Littlen")[9] is allright and pa. There is a match to-morrow agin the Choir (St. John's),[10] I hope we win but I don't think there is much chance because they bring such hefty great chaps. I came home early and Pounder came in and we had some some [sic] together. My music lessen went quite well this morning I did all thery and no playing. Miss Ethel said that she'd send me down and other paper to work. I am going to have a lesson on Miss Ethel's piano, and I am only to take my exam list and scales so Heaven only knows when I'm to do my paper because I've got to show it up on Monday and to-day's Friday. I shall have to go to bed in a minute so I can't say Much more. By-the-way when are you going to Beth, please let me know when because I'll want to write to you.

With tons and cwts. and lbs. and ozs. of pakages of Love,
Your own tiny little (sick-for-Muvver)
BENI

1 Ethel M.K. Astle (1876–1952), ARCM, was Britten's first piano teacher. With her sister, she ran 'Southolme' (52 Kirkley Cliff Road), the pre-preparatory school which Britten attended from 1921 to 1923 (see EWB, pp. 36–7). She also taught music theory (Britten had rudi-

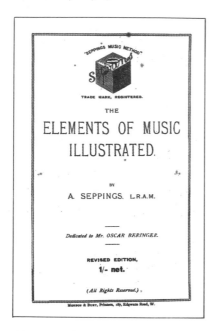
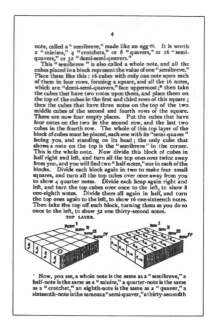

The 'Seppings Music Method', title page and p. 4

mentary harmony lessons from her at the age of eight) and the 'Seppings method' of sight-reading. Britten dedicated his 'Piano Sonata No. 9', composed in March 1926, to Miss Astle. A prominent local music teacher, she placed an advertisement in the *Lowestoft Journal* (21 April 1923):

Miss E.M.K. Astle, ARCM: pianoforte, singing, harmony & a Preparation for Examinations.
Qualified teacher of the Seppings method of sight reading and transposition.

Britten and 'Miss Ethel' kept in touch while the family remained in Lowestoft (like Mrs Britten, Miss Astle was a Christian Scientist) and indeed later after Mrs Britten's death. On 30 September 1937 he wrote: 'I spend morning writing letters – a testimonial for Miss Ethel Astle who's setting up in Frinton (how that name makes my heart ache!)'. Britten had written:

[. . .] I hear that it is the people of the Frinton district who are going to benefit now from your teaching. I know that they will appreciate your great skill, understanding and really infinite patience. You will be using, I suppose, the Seppings' Method. I have a great respect for it and remember that my early musical days, instead of being the usual wearying grind, were always interesting and entertaining – my progress was extremely rapid – and I cannot have been an easy child! In this method transposition is made so simple, because the pupil is taught to feel a great sense of key relationships – which is valuable even in these days of atonality.

Technically your teaching was of course impeccable; later, when I studied with Harold Samuel and Arthur Benjamin, both commented on the really first-rate ground-work that I had received. Frank Bridge and John Ireland said the same thing referring to theory and composition.

So I feel that the musical aspirants of Essex are going to be very fortunate to have you there.

See also note 3 to Letter 92 and Letter 388. On her death Britten was reported in the *Eastern Daily Press* (24 April 1952) as saying: 'I had a great personal affection for her and I owed her a tremendous debt.'

Miss Astle and her pupil were unlikely to have known that a month after the date of this letter a distinguished pianist who was also a composer was to give a piano recital at Belstead Hall, in nearby Aldeburgh: Béla Bartók, whose programme on 4 December included his own music and works by Scarlatti and Debussy. See Malcolm Gillies, *Bartók in Britain: A Guided Tour* (Oxford, Clarendon Press, 1989), pp. 56–8.

2 The headmaster, Thomas Jackson Elliott Sewell, MA, MC (1888–1972), of South Lodge, Kirkley Cliff Road, Lowestoft, the preparatory school (founded in 1862) that Britten attended from September 1923 until July 1928. Britten was to become Head Boy, Victor Ludorum, and a member of the school cricket team in 1927 and 1928. The Sewells were near neighbours and family friends of the Brittens. Sewell was prompted to write to Britten in February 1948, following the publication of an article by Jason Brown in the *Lowestoft Journal* (31 January 1948), 'Benjamin Britten: the Lowestoft Man who thinks in sound':

I have a very vivid recollection of the evening when by appointment at your home I discussed with your father and mother the possibilities of your future. You had then been in the school a little while, although you were certainly not twelve years old. I felt it my duty to tell your father my estimate of the situation. At that time in my opinion, which I still hold, I had sufficient evidence that you could have been developed into a mathematical scholar. I was not advising this – far from it – but the prospects of a living and security in the world of music was not so assured, even for a genius, as to justify me in not putting the responsibility on your father, or at any rate letting him know that I felt you had other possibilities. You have made a wonderful success from the decision your father and mother took that evening. Of course, the fact was that I continued to facilitate in every possible way your special music lessons at Norwich and elsewhere, while ensuring your general education, so that you did get a good School Certificate immediately after going to Gresham's. I knew your father and mother fairly well, as you know, and I never remember any slightest indication that he doubted his wisdom in encouraging your obvious inclinations. Personally I always thought that he was absolutely right, but some men would have played for safety.

[. . .]

I think the shell which exploded so close in your babyhood came a million times nearer robbing the world of your genius than any thought of your father's could have done (if he <u>had</u> felt able to entertain one and carry it into effect).

See also EWB, pp. 35–6.

A fellow pupil of Britten's at South Lodge remembered the head-master was 'very good' at teaching maths and Greek but also, disturbingly, that he was 'sadistic', 'very fond of beating boys – which one didn't understand in those days . . . at that age. But obviously there must have been a little bit of a fixation.' Britten was in 'very good odour' with Mr Sewell; he was extremely good at maths and thus *persona grata*. Those less skilled in these subjects 'weren't quite so popular'. Was Black Bob in *The Little Sweep* a version of Mr Sewell? And how do we read the suffering of the Novice in Act I of *Billy Budd*?

We wonder if it was Mr Sewell who addressed Britten in class, 'Stand up the boy whose father voted Liberal!' This was an incident the composer himself remembered, a probable consequence of a Liberal success in a hitherto Tory seat. It throws light on his father's politics.

3 Duffer – perhaps Miss Hayes's dog.

4 Rose – one of the maids.

5 John Ward Pounder (b. 1915). He was at South Lodge at the same time as Britten, who was known to him as 'Little O'Cedar Mop'. (Britten's curly hair must have reminded his friend of the mop used with a famous brand of floor polish.) During their schooldays, Britten and Pounder collaborated in writing a play in six acts entitled 'The Precious Documents'. An incomplete manuscript survives in the Archive (see opposite page).

Pounder accompanied Britten on his trip to Florence in March–April 1934 (see Letter 46), and in 1938 lived for a time at Britten's and Pears's Nevern Square address. Britten's letters to Pounder, among the most revealing and informative of their period, amply testify to the warmth and closeness of an important early friendship. Pounder, who was to become a solicitor, remained in touch with Britten until the end of the composer's life.

6 A.J. Raffles, one of the most glamorous figures of crime fiction, was a character created by Ernest William Hornung (1866–1921). Raffles's adventures were published in four collections: *The Amateur Cracksman* (1899), *The Black Mask* (1901), *A Thief in the Night* (1905) and *Mr Justice Raffles* (1909). The '6d [Sixpenny] edition' was a cheap edition.

THE PRECIOUS DOCUMENTS

A PLAY IN 6 ACTS BY E.BB. & J.WP.

Act I.   In a room in Blondon's house
Act II. In a london cell [Day]
Act III In a London cell. [Night]
Act IV   on a sailing ship
Act V (sc. I) a room in Blondon's house
         (sc. II) Docks of Boulogne.
Act VI (sc. I) Judgement court. Boulogne.
         (sc. II) Drawing room of Blondon's
                                    [house.

Cast

Perceval Blondon.	J.W. Pounder.
Edourd. De Foi	E.B. Britten.
Vilarие De Despard.	E.B. Britten.
Warder.	{ E.B. Britten.
Mephistopheles	{ J.W. Pounder. J.W. Pounder.
Captain	J.W. Pounder
Judge	E.B. Britten.

The title page of *The Precious Documents* in Britten's hand (see note 5 to Letter 4)

7 Alice Walker (later Pratt), the family cook for fifteen years and sister of Nanny Scarce (née Walker) (see EWB, pp. 31–3). Mary was another maid.

8 Mrs Britten and her husband were visiting their elder son, Robert, who was at Oakham School, Oakham, Rutland, from 1921 to 1926.

9 'Littlen' = 'little one'. Britten sometimes thus addressed his mother (see Letter 12).

10 St John's Church, London Road, Lowestoft, where Britten was baptized, was the family church at this time. Now demolished.

5 To The British Broadcasting Company Ltd
From Mr R.V. Britten[1]

[21 Kirkley Cliff Road,
Lowestoft]
[before 14 July 1926]

This composition was written by a lad of 12 years, in nine days: written in his very few spare moments snatched from the hourly routine of his "Prep" school (in the very early mornings for instance). He has only an elementary knowledge of harmony. Has had no instruction of any kind in orchestration or counterpoint; a little in form. It is quite an original copy; no piano score written before. We thought it worth sending, if only for advice.

1 This fragment of a letter is pasted to the front cover of Britten's orchestral 'Ouverture', composed in June 1926. The manuscript full score (now in the Archive) was submitted to the BBC's '1926 Autumn Musical Festival Prize Competition' with Mr Britten's covering note. The pen name 'Never Unprepared' became something of a family motto in the Britten household: see Letter 277.

The entry form for the 1926 Autumn Musical Festival Prize Competition of the BBC: 'Never Unprepared' was the pen name of E.B. Britten (aged 12)

The first page of the 'Ouverture' by 'Never Unprepared' (see note 1 to Letter 5)

6 To Mrs Britten

Platt, Nr. Seven-oaks, Kent
August 28th [1926]

My darling Mummy,

I arrived here safely, worst luck, after a very dirty journey. I
found that Miss Peto[1] had travelled down by the same train but
I had not seen her. I came by the 5.20 instead of the 2.30, Miss
Peto wired just before dinner. It is miserable here, I suppose Miss
Peto is very nice, but she doesn't show it. By-the-way I hit my bad
finger on the train door getting out with my luggage so it is very
nasty, and it made me feel very sick. Yesterday in London I had
bad diherea(?), and felt very sick in the train, eventually I was
sick about 8 o'clock last night and went to bed. Then a lady who
is very kind and who is staying with them, her name I think is
Miss Perkins[2] or something woke me up about 11 o'clock at night
to give me some lequirus [liquorice] pills or something, she said
she give it me then so I should no[t] be disturbed in the night. That
made me feel worse than ever and I was rather sick about 2 or 3 hrs
afterwards. Eventually I went to sleep about 4 o'clock and woke at
7, and was sick again. I did not have any breakfast but lay and
read. (please excuse interval between words "have" and "any"
because I have just been sick again).

This room in which I am in is pested with <u>wapses</u>. It's terrible!
There are going to be some sports this afternoon, but I will not
be able to go, so I am dreading it for I shall be alone for I don't
know how long. I am very lonely now, because everybody's out.

Please Mum, persuade Daddy to come and fetch me soon because
it is too horrible and lonely for words here.

On Thursday night Barbara and Miss Hurst[3] and I went to the
Queens Hall. It was all modern music, and I have taken a great
like to modern <u>Orchestral</u> music.[4] We had Clara Butterworth[5] who
was a dreadfull Soprano, she swallowed all her words and you
could not hear one of them. And an awfully nice Baritone. Leslie
England[6] was the pianist, he played Schellings Suite Fantastique
for piano and orchestra,[7] it was only a show of tehnique(?) and he
did not put an atom of expression in partly because he couldn't
and partly because there was not any needed. The orchestral pieces
were a Delius piece called "Life's dance",[8] this was lovely; and
Holsts planets which were lovely. Especially the first, which had a
gorgeous rhythm in it.[9]

And a Saint-Sains Dances[10] and a Montague Phillip's Hillside Melody[11] which was very nice; and also there was some other thing which was lovely.

I must stop now because I have to write to Barbara. Please excuse the bad writing because I have not anything to write on.

With tons of love

from

BENI

Please give my love to Daddy, Beth, Bobby and the puss, and please persuade Daddy to come soon.

1 A resident of Oulton Broad, near Lowestoft, and known to the Britten family. She adopted Michael Halliday, one of Britten's South Lodge school friends (see note 1 to Diary for 10 November 1932). Britten's sister, Beth, suggested to us that her brother must have gone to Kent in the company of Miss Peto, and at her invitation, to stay at some kind of holiday home or boarding house.

2 Unidentified.

3 Helen Hurst (1887–1981), a social worker and Barbara's friend and lifelong companion. She was some fifteen years older than Barbara, whom she first met when Barbara came to work in Peckham, London, as a health visitor.

4 A Prom (Promenade) Concert given by the Queen's Hall Orchestra, conducted by Henry Wood.

5 Clara Butterworth, English soprano and wife of the composer Montague Phillips (1885–1969).

6 Leslie England (1902–1971), English pianist.

7 Ernest Schelling (1876–1939), American composer, conductor and pianist. His Suite was composed in 1905.

8 Delius's 'tone poem for orchestra' was composed in 1901 (revised 1912).

9 The first movement of Holst's *The Planets* (composed 1914–16) is 'Mars, the Bringer of War', the $\frac{5}{4}$ rhythm of which Britten correctly transcribes. The only other movements performed on this occasion were 'Venus, the Bringer of Peace' and 'Mercury, the Winged Messenger'. Britten was to record relatively few composers' deaths in his diary. An exception was Holst, a note of whose death is recorded on 25 May 1934.

10 The symphonic poem *Danse macabre*, Op. 40, later parodied by Saint-Saëns in his *Carnival of the Animals*.

11 Phillips's *A Hillside Melody* was composed in 1924.

7 To Mrs Kennard[1]
From Charles Macpherson

8, Amen Court, E.C. 4.
14th Dec: 1926

Dear Mrs Kennard

I am so sorry to have been so long. I had hoped to have a second look over the pieces, but now I must give you a hurried impression of my first 'Look over'.

The outlook is founded on the simpler classical; there is no counterpoint, or feeling in that direction. The work is of course remarkable for one so young, but there is as yet not much sign of individual outlook, or certainty in treatment. If unduly flattered I should say the spark would be quenched. It must grow undisturbed into flame; and for that reason let the boy develop naturally. If he wants to write he will still find the means of doing so. Let everyone be natural with him. If he is spoilt everything will go the wrong way. The next few years will be the real test.

He sounds nice & healthy tho', & if all goes well & he is willing to learn <u>and work</u>, he should certainly make a place for himself.

My love to Frank Durnford[2] & kindest remembrance to yourself.

E[ver] y[ours] v. sincerely
CHARLES MACPHERSON.

1 Mrs Kennard was the wife of the Rector of Sotterley, Wrentham, in Suffolk, and a friend of Mrs Britten, who had clearly asked her to approach Charles Macpherson (1870–1927), the organist of St Paul's, a composer, and professor at the Royal Academy of Music, for advice about her son's future. On the same day that Macpherson replied to Mrs Kennard he also wrote a note to Master Britten (see Letter 8). Mrs Kennard thought Macpherson's letter to Mrs Britten was ' "high praise" from a very cautious man'. There is further evidence to suggest that Mrs Britten was making similar approaches in search of advice. These Macpherson letters were in the possession of Britten's brother, Robert.

This was clearly a period when his parents were acutely conscious of their son's unusual talent. That they felt a need to monitor it, to keep it within bounds, is implicit in a remark of the father when writing to his wife, who was away visiting Robert, at the end of November: 'We've just had supper and I've let Beni write [i.e. compose] for 10 minutes while I write to you.' The boy's music and his volatile health were his parents' twin concerns. Towards the end of

this same letter, Mr Britten adds, 'Beni seems very well, but rather
blinky' ('When he was under strain [when young] Ben had a habit
of blinking his eyes with a sort of nervous tic' (EWB, p. 53)). In the
same year, in January, he had written to his wife, 'We found Ben
looking flushed and I thought rather bad – but now I know it was
because he had been reading over a roaring fire. He still has a bit of
a cold but [is] really much better.' In another, undated letter to Edith,
he expostulates, 'I'm so sorry Beni is bad, I hope it is only an exam
or something!!!' These are, of course, the trivia of family life and
domestic correspondence, but they were the start of the long series
of illnesses and bouts of ill-health that finally culminated in Britten's
fatal heart condition. These had their origins in the severe pneumonia
he contracted in infancy, which nearly carried him off. Hence his
parents' watchfulness.

2 Unidentified.

8 To Benjamin Britten
From Charles Macpherson

8, Amen Court, E.C. 4
14 Dec: 1926

Dear Master Britten

Here is your M.S. I hope you will go on writing whenever you
have the chance. Hear all the music you can, and when you begin
serious study you will find out a lot of things for yourself. Solving
your own difficulties in music, without slavish imitation of others,
or a too great insistence on some personal fancy or mannerism is
one of the best things to have for composing.

But, meanwhile, learn all your lessons, not forgetting to play
games!

I'm sure you will do well if you take things seriously. There is
nothing done without hard work; but I fancy you have this gift.

Yrs very sincerely
CHARLES MACPHERSON

Sunday, 17 June 1928[1]
[*Lowestoft*]

Am much better, go to the Colemans' to tea, I got up at 12 o'clock.
Have gramophone, and my Trio.[2] Rewrite some songs, written

on Friday and Saturday namely Dans les bois,[3] and begin to rewrite
Nuits de Juin.[4]

1 It was at the beginning of this year that Britten began to keep a
   pocket diary on a daily basis, a practice he maintained until 1939 and
   not beyond. Readers will notice the gap between the end of 1926
   and the first diary entry that we have chosen to reproduce from 1928.
   We have discovered no letters from the intervening year, 1927, nor
   any other documentation of particular interest or significance. The
   events of the period itself, however, are covered in the Chronology,
   e.g. Britten's first encounter with Frank Bridge.

2 Britten refers to his unpublished Trio in G minor, for violin, viola
   and piano, which he completed on 11 April. In his diary for that
   date we can read: 'With Mummy & Bobby, we try the trio. Hopeless
   failure!!'

3 An unpublished setting of Gérard de Nerval for soprano and piano.

4 The opening song from Britten's *Quatre Chansons Françaises*, settings
   of Hugo and Verlaine, composed for soprano and orchestra during
   June–September. The other songs were 'Sagesse', 'L'Enfance' (which
   makes dramatic use of the French folksong 'Biquette' in the orchestra)
   and 'Chanson d'Automne'. Britten selected his texts from *The Oxford
   Book of French Verse: XIIIth Century – XIXth Century*, chosen by St John
   Lucas, Oxford, Clarendon Press, 1924: this copy is in the Archive.
   The composer's diary documents some part of their composition: on
   26 August, 'I finish 3rd song of my french songs'; and on the 29th,
   'Begin another French song'. Britten dedicated the full score of the
   Quatre Chansons to his parents on the occasion of their twenty-seventh
   wedding anniversary, on 15 September. The songs make one final
   appearance in the diary, on 20 November, 'Ordinary work and walk,
   continue with transcribing my French songs for Pft, for Mr. Bridge',
   a task that was completed on 18 December. It was not until after
   Britten's death that these remarkable songs, which register the impact
   of Bridge's teaching on the youthful Britten, received their first performance, a broadcast given by Heather Harper and the English
   Chamber Orchestra, conducted by Steuart Bedford, on 30 March
   1980. *Quatre Chansons* were subsequently published (Faber Music,
   1982), and recorded by Jill Gomez, with the City of Birmingham
   Symphony Orchestra, conducted by Simon Rattle (EMI ASD 4177),
   with a sleeve note by Donald Mitchell. See also Christopher Mark,
   'Britten's *Quatre Chansons Françaises*', *Soundings*, 10, Summer 1983,
   pp. 23–35; Donald Mitchell, 'What do we know about Britten now?',
   in BC, pp. 26–7; and Christopher Palmer, 'Embalmer of the Midnight:
   the Orchestral Song-cycles', in BC, pp. 308–10.

9   To Mr and Mrs R.V. Britten

Farfield, Holt, Norfolk[1]
Sept. 21st, 1928.

My darling Mummy and Pop,

I am writing to tell you that I arrived safely, owing to the goodness of the chauffeur or chauffeurs.

I like this place quite, but I feel horribly strange and small.

We went to bed by 9 o'clock last night, and in breakfast by eight, this morning. I could not eat much breakfast. After that we got our study ready. I am in a Study with three other boys, by name of Meikeljohn (?), Marshall minor, and Savory.[2] They are quite nice, Meikeljohn is the nicest. Marshall, who is captain of the study, has a rotten old gramophone, on which he plays miserable jazz all the time!!

After you went last night I wandered about with Purdy[3] for about an hour, and then his study-mates came, and I was left alone, for about 20 mins. Then my 3 came. I feel rather an ass here, everyone stares, it is very nasty, but still it might be a lot worse. I had a letter from Beth and Laulie[4] waiting for me when I was alone, it was very nice. We had prayers about 8.0, taken by Mr. Fletcher,[5] whom I like very much, and then bed.

I did not sleep before 11 o'clock, but I went to sleep after that and slept soundly till about 7 o'clock. After Breakfast Meikeljohn showed me round the school, and at 10.30 we went into Chapel to a sort of glorified Morning Prayer. It is a high service, anyhow they sing plainsong, and in the Creed turn to the East and bow and nod etc.[6] There is a funny little chaplain, he seems rather nice.[7] I have not met Ouseley[8] yet or the Barrats.[9] They don't seem to try and find me. I have seen Comer,[10] who was at South Lodge, and he won't speak to me, although he has seen me a lot. He only said, the first time he saw me, that he knew me. That was all.

After chapel, we went into the school-hall, and the Head-master read out the form-orders etc. After that the Form-masters took their forms and read out the time-tables, I am in the 3b.[11] It is not at all a bad form, Pop, I am above Purdy, above his form and Dashwood[12] from Aldeburgh. After that we (i.e. the new boys) went to have our voices tried, and I am in the choir! I never have had a greater shock. After that, I went and found Mrs. Gaunt,[13] whom I had not seen yet, and asked her about some things, and then I came here, at 12.10 (mid-day), and went to my study, and am writing this letter.

Good-bye darlings, I am longing for November.[14]

Give my love to Bobby, sorry, Robert, and to Miss Hayes and the maids, Please.

Good-bye, good-bye, good-bye.

With tons of love, and kisses.

1 Britten entered Gresham's School, Holt, in September 1928 and left on 31 July 1930. 'Farfield' was his school house.

In her interview with Charles Ford (c. 1976/7), Beth recollected that her brother 'after he left prep school . . . wanted to go straight to London' to embark on his musical career:

> It was difficult for my parents, because they didn't quite know whether he was going to be able to make the grade. They were fluctuating . . . I think it was Barbara and Robert – obviously I had no say in it – I can remember them saying 'He *must* go to school. He must get at any rate his School Certificate . . . Because how do we know – you don't *know* he's going to be able to live by his music.' And so [our parents] said . . . 'All right, till he gets his School Certificate, then he can leave.' So he did that.

2 Matthew F.M. Meikeljohn (at Gresham's, 1927–31) and subsequently Professor of Italian at Glasgow University; Geoffrey C. Marshall (Marshall minor: 1927–31), for whose brother, Alan, Britten fagged briefly; and Philip H. Savory (1927–30), who was in the Lower Fourth at the same time (1929) as Britten. Britten's entry in his pocket diary for 21 September – the day on which this letter was written – reads: 'I am in a study [with] 3 boys, who might be worse, but might be better. They are full of swearing and vulgarity.' During his first term Britten fagged for Peter R. Wilson. ['Fagging' = a junior boy in the English public school system performing menial tasks for a senior boy.]

3 Thomas Purdy (1928–31). Britten would have known him from South Lodge, where he had also been a pupil (1926–8).

4 Miss Laulie (Mabel) Austin, a family friend and amateur musician, lived in Liverpool, and was one of Britten's godparents. She gave her godson numerous miniature scores as birthday and Christmas presents. Miss Austin was still in touch with the composer in 1945.

5 Basil A. Fletcher, Gresham's staff (1922–32). He was Britten's first housemaster (until November 1928) and form master of the Lower Fourth in 1929.

6 The character of chapel services at Gresham's would have struck Britten with special force because of his emphatically 'low church' upbringing, the consequence of his mother's (though not his father's)

church-going enthusiasm. The two music books used at Gresham's in services were *A Manual of Plainsong for Divine Service containing the Canticles noted, The Psalter noted to Gregorian tones, together with the Litany and Responses,* new edition by H.B. Briggs and W.H. Frere (London, Novello, 1902), and *The Public School Hymn Book with Tunes,* edited by a Committee of the Headmasters' Conference (London, Novello, n.d). Britten's copies – both inscribed 'Sept. 21st 1928 / E. Benjamin Britten / Farfield / Holt' – are in the Archive. This was Britten's first experience of plainsong, a form of music that was to become of increasing significance to him. See also GE, pp. 44–72, and Letter 76.

7 Revd F.G.E. Field, Gresham's staff (1905–30).

8 John A. Ouseley (1925–31).

9 John A.L. Barratt (1924–9) and his brother, Victor L. Barratt (1924–9).

10 John C. Comer (1925–8).

11 The Middle Third, whose form master was F.L. MacCarthy, Gresham's staff (1927–32).

12 John. H.C. Dashwood (1927–32). He was in the Lower Fourth at the same time (1929) as Britten.

13 School Matron? She left at the end of Britten's first term and was succeeded by Miss Gillett (see Letter 13).

14 From 9–10 November Britten was in London with his mother for a piano lesson with Harold Samuel (see note 1 to Letter 11) and a composition lesson with Frank Bridge (see note 2 to the same letter).
    His diary entries for these dates read:

9 November
Set off for London at 8.40 in morning by train, very slow. Mrs. Fletcher takes me to Sheringham in car. Meet Mummy at Ipswich. Get to Liverp. St. [Liverpool Street, London's N.E. Railway Terminus] at 1.20. Have dinner and go to H.S. [Harold Samuel]. Wonderful Lesson. Tea with Mrs. Bridge. With Barbara to dinner. Queen's hall absolutely wonderful (Hallé orch.)

Sir Hamilton Harty &
The Hallé Orchestra
Schubert – Symphony 8 in B min.
Beethoven – Symphony 7 in A maj.
Brahms – Symphony 4 in E min.

10 November
Lesson at 10.–11.30 With F. Bridge, very nice. Dinner at Slaters [a restaurant] with Barbara. Barbara takes me to King's Cross [railway station], Ruth takes Mummy to Liverp. St. I get to Holt feeling absolutely miserable, cold and hungry at 7.19.

10   **To Mrs Britten**
[*Incomplete*]

[Farfield, Holt, Norfolk]
[23 September 1928]

After nearly eight years of study, I had a very flimsy technick (?);
he[1] as good as said I had none at all. His words were, when I
finished playing, "And who taught you that?" Afterwards he made
out that it was hopeless for a boy of my age to play later Beethoven,
and that my love of Beethoven will soon die, as it does with
everyone! I afterwards played the Chopin polanaize.[2] You might
ask Bobby to look up and to tell me by letter whether the bars, 5–8,
you know   etc.

are marked p or f, I played them f, he said that they ought to
be pp practically, and then demonstrated how, playing with no
two notes together, and a gripping touch, and terrible tone. I
don't think much of his ~~technick~~ (oh I don't know) technich (?)!

After that he as good as said it would be no good whatsoever
for me to go into the musical profession. Music in this school is
now finished for me!

I did feel ~~funny~~ horrible when I went to bed last-night, but wasn't
the Daily Light[3] wonderful, just the one for me.

Last night they had the gramophone going here, Ole Man River[4]
and the other one:–[5]

or something like that. I did think of Bobby. Enough of that.

This school is not half as bad as I expected. I have been asked to
go to tea with Mrs. Gaunt this afternoon, it will be lovely, I expect.
Choir practise last night was great fun, I sing alto you know. The
numbers are like this:– Trebles about 30, Altos 8 (!!), Tenors 4,
Basses 14 approximately. Wonderful balance. You never hear the
altos. I had a lovely letter from Barbara, and enjoyed yours
thouroughly. Thanks awfully darling. I won't finish this letter yet,
in case I have more news after chapel.

We have had a very nice service in the Chapel from 10.30–11.15.
No sermon, but just plain simple Morning Prayer, with Plain
song, and three hymns, no hymns we know, but out of the Public
School Hymn Book.

Mr. Greatorex, who played the organ, does not play well. I am
sure it is bad never to play 2 notes together.

Well good-bye darling, I expect you are in St. Johns now, I do envy you. I wonder what you will do to-night, all by yourself, when the others are out. I say, ma-ma, I have had some horrible dreams lately about people being ill and dying, Mummy darling, please, please, if you or any one of the family in the house are ill, do send Bobby or Pop over in the car to fetch me.

Please do, Darling, promise that; oh! Darling do.

With Tons of love

BENJAMIN

1 Walter Greatorex, known as 'Gog' (1877–1949), Director of Music at Gresham's, 1911–36. He was a composer of hymn tunes, one of which, 'Woodlands', was named after a Gresham's school house. His predecessor, Geoffrey Shaw (1879–1943; Gresham's staff, 1902–10), had introduced the singing of plainsong in 1902, a tradition that Greatorex maintained.

Britten's attitude towards Greatorex was not to improve. He wrote in his diary for 1 February 1930:

Go to the most awful recital by Mr. Greatorex after tea; how ever the man got the job here I cannot imagine. His idea of rhythm, logic, tone, or the music is absolutely lacking in sanity. He played a Haydn & a Mozart Sonata & some tit bits to a small & scanty (no wonder) audience.

And on 16 February:

I completely lose my temper with Gog (luckily he wasn't present). He has now written the most abominable Benidicite which is performed in Chapel; unfortunately for everyone concerned I lost my temper on a piece of M.S. paper, & the most frightful bit of unplayable rubbish for pft. was the result.

And 22 May:

Greatorex seems to have taken offence to me lately. I really cannot be bothered about him any longer. He ought to have retired 50 years ago or better never have tried to teach music ever.

See also note 4 to Letter 18 and note 4 to Letter 19.

2 Polonaise in C sharp minor, Op. 26, No. 1.

3 An evangelical compilation, much favoured by Mrs Britten, which provided an exhortatory text for each day of the year. See also GE, pp. 7–8.

4 From *Show Boat* (1927) by Jerome Kern (1885–1945), words by Oscar Hammerstein II. For an admirable assessment of the position of *Showboat* in the history of American musical theatre, see Mark Steyn, 'A Shot of Southern Discomfort', *Independent*, 2 December 1989, p. 37.

5 'Can't help Lovin' dat man'. Britten's absolute pitch is already manifest: he transcribes the tune in its correct key! Basil Reeve, a boyhood
friend (see note 2 to Diary for 1 January 1931), remembers an amusing
incident which confirms the accuracy of Britten's ear. In the family
home, Reeve would strike the downstairs dinner gong, while upstairs
Britten would immediately locate the correct pitch on the keyboard.

11 To Mr and Mrs R.V. Britten

> Farfield, Holt, Norfolk.
> November 19th in evening. [1928]

My darling Mummy and Pop,

Thank you so much, Mummy for your letter, which I received
about half-an-hour ago.

I quite agree about the London business, and think it would be
nonsensical to go up next Monday, tho' I wouldn't have minded
it! Certainly it was horrible coming back, and it took quite a day to
recover. As it is I wouldn't have time to finish H.S.'s[1] work, or yet
Mr. Bridge's.[2] I cannot stop long as Prep is going to begin in a
minute or two.

I am awfully glad that you were all right in that gale, it really
was terrible here, I quite thought something was going to happen!

What an awful nuisance about the car; I bet you are tired after
that hectic night, what time did you get home?

One more thing darlings, I hope you don't mind, but you said
that when I needed jam, as I do now, I might ask you for some.
I was going to ask you to bring some to London, as I have absolutely
run out, and I have had to borrow some.

Well good night darlings,

Thank you so much for all your news and kindness; again thank
you for London, Pop, I know what it means to you, that little
time.

> With tons of love and thanks,
> your adoring son,
> BENJAMIN

P.S.   I just had to add a note, saying that I have had my hair
cut, or rather shawn.

It's awful, as short, shorter in fact, than the other boys! He first
of all cut it at the ordinary time, i.e. after prayers, quite short in
front, but shaved all up the back. This looked idiotic, of course! So

after I was in bed, and just going off to sleep, a boy came up and told me I was wanted. I went down, and he cut the rest off!

Don't worry darlings, it will soon grow!

P.[P.]S.   What about writing to H.S., will you please Mummy? If you think I ought to, will you write and say, and I will. What about going up from here about December 17th (Monday, we breakup on 19th), that is breaking up early? Just as you think however.[3]

1 Harold Samuel (1879–1937), English pianist. He taught at the Royal College of Music, London, and was noted as an interpreter of Bach and as an accompanist. Britten travelled to London for private lessons with Samuel from 9 November 1928 (the date of his first lesson) until 14 March 1930 (his last lesson). He had first met Samuel in Norwich on 14 May 1928, when Samuel was giving a recital with Audrey Alston, Britten's viola teacher (see note 3 to Diary for 16 February 1931). Britten wrote in his diary on the 14th:

VIOLIN AND PIANO RECITAL
STUART HALL, NORWICH
HAROLD SAMUEL
AUDREY ALSTON

SONATA (Piano) in A ♭ Op. 110	Beethoven
SONATA (Violin & Piano) in A major [BWV 1050]	Bach
SONATINE (Piano)	Ravel
SONATA (Violin & Piano) in G [Op. 78]	Brahms

(The Beethoven was especially lovely) Go to wonderful concert in Norwich. I turn over for H. Samuel. Very nerve-racking! I have a talk and some tea alone with him afterwards. Miss Astle comes with us.

He much admired Samuel's playing, writing in his pocket diary of a performance of Bach's D minor Piano Concerto on 13 August 1930: 'If I never again hear playing such as this I shall die happy.' When Samuel died in January 1937, Britten wrote on 18 January:

Long talks to Frank & E. Bridge. They are going to the memorial for Harold Samuel – who died last Friday – this afternoon. I am sorry not to be able to go to pay tribute to a great little man who was always so grand to me.

An obituary notice in the *Performing Right Gazette* (April 1937) reminded readers that Samuel

composed a good deal in his younger days including music for 'As You Like It' in 1907. This was followed by a comic opera, 'The Honourable Phil', which, however, only ran for seventy nights. His songs 'Diaphenia' and 'My Sweeting' are well known, but his greatest success was his wartime song 'Jogging along'.

Samuel and Bridge were not of the same mind when it came to recommending a composition teacher for their pupil (see note 1 to

Letter 23). It is not clear why, for the piano, Britten did not continue his studies at the College with Samuel but was instead assigned to Arthur Benjamin (see also note 1 to Letter 21 and note 6 to Letter 25). See also Howard Ferguson, 'People, Events and Influences', in *The Music of Howard Ferguson*, edited by Alan Ridout (London, Thames, 1989), pp. 8–11.

2 Frank Bridge (1879–1941), English composer and conductor and Britten's first and pre-eminent composition teacher. Britten was to become in effect a member of Bridge's family, a quasi-adopted son, and referred to as such in Bridge's letters (the Bridges had no children of their own). The boy first met Bridge at Norwich in 1927, where Bridge conducted the first performance of his Rhapsody for orchestra, *Enter Spring*, on 27 October (see note 3 to Diary for 31 March 1931). It was a work for which Britten had an unbounded and enduring admiration. He was introduced to Bridge by his viola teacher, Audrey Alston (Bridge too was a distinguished viola player). Bridge spent the next morning discussing Britten's compositions but the first lessons proper took place between 11 and 13 January 1928.

In an interview (at Aldeburgh, May/June 1960) with the Earl of Harewood, for a BBC radio programme, *People Today*, Britten very vividly recalled his first attempts at composition and his lessons with Bridge:

HAREWOOD: I'm sure you started to make music when you were very small, when you were a small child.

BRITTEN: Yes, I actually started – playing the piano, as one would expect, at a very early age. I started writing – music, I was going to say, but hesitated before, because it was really not much more than dots and dashes on a bit of paper; but that I did start at a curiously early age, about – when I was about five, I think, the story is. But it was much more the *look* of the thing on the paper which fascinated me.

HAREWOOD: You already wanted to write it down?

BRITTEN: Yes. In fact I was more interested in writing it down even than what it sounded like, but very soon, when I – for instance I got my mother to try and play these curious things I'd written down – I realized that one has to connect the notes with the sound, and that started, I suppose – I had a very good piano teacher, a local one – when I was about 8 – and then I started to write in a little more orderly fashion songs and counterpoint exercises, harmony exercises, and that went on all the time I was at my private school. I used to disconcert the other children by writing music in the dormitory and all that kind of thing; but my serious composition lessons started when I

was about twelve, I think it was, when I had the very good
fortune to meet Frank Bridge, who was the friend of my viola
teacher. I learnt the viola at an early age, and he took a great
interest in me and every holiday I used to go and stay with
him, either in his house in Sussex where he lived, or occasionally in London where he also had a house; and he taught me
an enormous amount. He taught me other things to think
about and gave me a broader horizon generally. I'm most
grateful for him having taught me [to] take infinite trouble
over getting every note quite right. He used to perform the
most terrible operations on the music I would rather confidently show him. He would play every passage slowly on the
piano and say, 'Now listen to this – is this what you meant?'
And of course I would start by defending it, but then one
would realize as one – as he went on playing this passage
over and over again – that one hadn't really thought enough
about it. And he really taught me to take as much trouble as
I possibly could over every passage, over every progression,
over every line and I'm most grateful to him for that . . .

Britten further documented his memories of Bridge and his composition lessons in an important and extensive article, 'Britten Looking
Back' (BBST), in which he concluded that:

Bridge never wanted to influence me too strongly too young; and yet he
knew he had to present something very firm for this stiff, naïve little boy to
react about. He had no other pupils, and it was a very touching relationship
across the thirty-four years separating us. In everything he did for me, there
were perhaps above all two cardinal principles. One was that you should
try to find yourself and be true to what you found. The other – obviously
connected with it – was his scrupulous attention to good technique, the
business of saying clearly what was in one's mind.

He gave me a sense of technical ambition. People sometimes seem to think
that, with a number of works now lying behind, one must be bursting with
confidence. It is not so at all. I haven't yet achieved the simplicity I should
like in my music, and I am enormously aware that I haven't yet come up to
the technical standards Bridge set me.

No less vivid memories of Bridge as teacher appear in 'Frank
Bridge: A Memory', by Daphne Oliver, a close friend of Marjorie
Fass, the artist, Aldeburgh Festival Programme Book, 1979, pp. 8–10:

Naturally there was much conversation about the young Benjamin Britten.
One day, after one of the A.M.O. [Audrey Melville Orchestra] concerts I
was bowled over by Frank's conducting of Ravel's *Bolero*, and tactlessly asked
next day: 'Will England never produce a composer of that stature?' 'Yes,' said
Ethel. 'You will hear of one, Benji Britten.' Of course there were sometimes
differences of opinion, especially as Benji grew older, and Marjorie once

wrote: 'As Frank got out of the car he muttered to me that never again would he help Benji over his work as some of the things he had pointed out the boy simply would not alter, so why waste his time and energy?' Another time he said to me apropos of Ben: 'You can't start a piano concerto with a drum-roll', but these were differences of opinion only; they were devoted to him, he was almost more to them than the child they never had.

It must have been in 1939 that Marjorie again wrote: 'Mr Brit came to give Benji a lesson on conducting his *Variations* (on a theme of Frank Bridge). We were all thoroughly tired except Mr Brit who was as fresh as a lark. His one-and-a-half-hour lesson to stiff, awkward little Benji nearly killed Benji with tiredness, but Frank with his wonderful arms like branches of trees in the wind full of power was as fresh when he stopped as when he began.'

3 In fact Britten had his lesson with Samuel on 14 December, and with Bridge on the following day.

OPUS	TITLE	INSTRUMENTS	KEY	DATE	Where composed
1.	Piano pieces:–	Pianoforte.			
	8 Waltzs.		Var	January 1925	Lowestoft.
	2 Scherzos		Eb maj, A maj,	Sept. 1925	London Lowestoft
	4 Scherzos		Eb maj, A maj, Db maj, C maj	aug – Sept 1925	Lowestoft.
	2 Waltzs		Ab maj, F min.	July – august 1925	Lowestoft
	2 Etudes		F maj	august 1925	Lowestoft
	4 Bourrées		D maj, C min, G maj, A maj	Sept – Oct 1925	Lowestoft.
	3 Fantasias		Ab maj	may 31st 1925, June 1925, Jan 13th 1926	Lowestoft
	Valse		E maj	October 1925	Lowestoft
	2 Fugue-fantasia		F min, E min	august – Sept 1925	Lowestoft
	Scherzo grand.		G maj	October 1925 1925	Lowestoft
	2 scherzo-tarantella		D min, D maj	October 15th 1925	Lowestoft

The first page of Britten's catalogue of his own compositions, made *c.*1927

12 To Mrs Britten

Farfield, Holt, Norfolk.
February 8th, 1929.

My darling Mummy,

Thank you everso much for the postal order, and the order about the oranges. You are a darling Mummy, taking so much trouble about me; please thank Daddy too.

As you realize, I now have my pen filled! I am down stairs, have been since mid-day Wednesday. But I've not gone out yet. I returned to the dormetry last night, for the first time and I was down to breakfast this morning. So you see I am progressing; I expect I shall be in school soon.[1]

Well darling little one, how are <u>you</u>? I do hope you are everso well and happy, also the rest of the family. The weather here is beautiful, and is doing everything to make <u>me</u> well, so I hope you are thriving in it!

Is it true that Mr. Inge[2] broke some boy's wrist in the playground? Please find out and let me know what boy it is, I do hope it is not Francis.[3]

By-the-way, I had another letter from Madeline[4] this morning; she asks me to write, and to be careful <u>not</u> to tell Francis, as he won't like it!

Please excuse me, if this letter smells of oranges; but you know how hard it is to get rid of the smell after two oranges 'a la Pop'!! It's the only way to eat them, I find, when you've got no sugur or knife & fork. So Pop is going to London, is he?[5] Is it for a meeting? I hope he will have a rest, and be refreshed. Please give him my best love when he returns.

I hope Beth enjoys the Lacrosse and that the people put her in her right position now. I wonder if she enjoyed the Dinner and the Lecture.[6]

Now, little one, it is post time. But tho' the letter goes I still think of you, every second of my life, and especially when I read my Daily Light, and realize that you will be reading it too. When are you coming over?

It's nearly four weeks now, and the "Feathers"[7] is waiting.

So farewell, angel of my heart,
Your adoring son,
BENJAMIN

Please give my love to Beth, of course.

Thank you ever so much for the quotation you sent, I will keep it and treasure it.

1 Britten fell ill on 24 January: 'Ordinary work up to break, and then I go to bed with my usual bilious complaint plus a nasty feverish cold', and was detained in the sanatorium until 6 February. The 'feverish cold', which in some cases developed into scarlet fever, appears to have afflicted many members of the school at this time. He was taken home on 23 February, returning to Holt on 12 March only to become immediately worse. He went back to Lowestoft on 26 March and was declared 'out of quarantine' on the 31st. Thus, for most of this term (which ended on 4 April) Britten was out of school. He suffered many bouts of ill health during his schooldays.

2 Perhaps the games master at South Lodge? He was also a musical friend of the family.

3 Francis C. Barton (b. 1916), a pupil at South Lodge from 1924 to 1929 and a friend of Britten's. His diary for 31 July 1928 – the 30th had been the last day of school for Britten at South Lodge – reads: 'Go and see some boys off. I am frightfully sorry to say good-bye to them, Francis Barton especially. He has been a ripping boy.' It was a warm friendship that extended beyond their schooldays. Barton had a successful career in the Royal Marines (1934–66), rising to the rank of Major-General. The 'Burlesque' from the *Three Divertimenti* for string quartet (1936: the revised version of three movements from the string quartet suite, 'Go play, boy, play', composed in 1933) was dedicated to Barton. In Britten's diary, on 24 May (Empire Day), he wrote about Barton: 'He is a great contrast to most of my friends – being in the Marines, a Tory, & conventional, but he is so charming & ingenuous, that he is decidedly bearable!'

There could be no better document of the friendship between Britten and Barton than that provided in a private communication written after the composer's death by Major-General Barton's sister, Mrs Joy Bowesman:

In 1928 Francis persuaded Ben to come & stay with us for a few days (we were part of a noisy, happy go lucky Rectory family), & his visit was a great joy to us. I was some years older than Ben, but I counted it a great honour to be allowed to play duets with this very shy, very delightful, very brilliant young pianist. (We still have the same Broadwood grand!) My father persuaded Ben to play at a party for his village parishioners – A 'Rondo Capriccioso' was greeted with respectful applause, but when he played 'God save the King' as an old fashioned gramophone 'running down' they felt he was a real musician!

After that, we kept in touch, on & off – occasionally Ben came to stay with us – & one day took Francis & me over to meet Frank Bridge, at Friston. Sometimes Francis went to him – & complained, in 1936, 'Ben can't talk about anything but the Spanish war!' As my brother was in the Royal Marines it was surprising that they remained friends!

We lost touch for a few years while Ben was in America, but both Francis

& I picked up our friendship with him later. (Years later, Ben wrote to me – about Francis, 'He meant a great deal to me in those very early days – His affection softened many blows.') And so the R.M. Commando & the pacifist remained on very friendly terms. My brothers were not very musical, & they used to express their opinions very freely about Ben's music! I can see my Mother now, leaning across the dinner table & saying in her kind voice, 'Ben – they're all <u>very</u> rude – don't take any notice –   But – I must admit <u>I</u> don't always <u>quite</u> understand your music!'

In 1954 our younger son, Dermot (a 'music-maniac'), having sung in the 'Ceremony of Carols' at his school, wrote to Ben saying how much he had enjoyed the work, & mentioned – as an afterthought – that he might remember our family. Ben wrote back saying that he had played duets with Dermot's mother! & and was kind enough to write to Dermot occasionally, mainly about music. (e.g. 'Sorry your family don't like the clarinet! but keep it up!' – this was a reference to the fact that we preferred him to practise in the Greenhouse!) [. . .]

In 1954 Ben invited Dermot for a weekend at Aldeburgh [. . .] I may say that one of our relatives expressed great concern at our allowing him to go 'to people like that'. We ignored it: I <u>knew</u> Ben. Dermot had a wonderful weekend, & Ben wrote me a long & most kind & understanding letter about the possibilities of a musical career for him.

In 1962 Dermot fell ill with cancer, & he died in September of that year. I have the two letters (amongst others) which Ben wrote me then. In 1964 (at the request of the Musical Director of Dermot's old school – <u>not</u> at ours) he & Peter spent the half of one Sunday coming down to Ramsgate & giving a recital to the school as a Memorial Concert for Dermot (for which they refused any fee) – knowing Ben, you would realise that <u>great</u> kindness to be completely 'in character', & you can imagine how much that evening meant to my husband & me, & to Francis who was also there.

The more famous Ben became, the less I felt we must 'push in' on him! But we continued our occasional correspondence, & in 1972 we, and Francis & his wife, spent a memorable day at Aldeburgh, with lunch at the Red House before going to 'Midsummer Night's Dream' at the Maltings. It was a very happy meal, with cricket stories from Peter, & the usual leg-pulling from Francis about Ben's music, to which he retorted, 'Well, <u>I</u> shan't be at this afternoon's performance, so you can <u>walk out when you like</u>!' I may add that I was completely enchanted with the 'Dream' & my 3 companions interested enough to stay the course!

And then Ben fell ill: I had a few more letters from him (& Peter also kindly wrote), & in 1976 my husband & I saw him at home – a few weeks before he died –   He was as friendly & affectionate as ever, but so very frail, & <u>so</u> sad   ('Joy – I've <u>tried</u> to write (music) with my left hand – but it just <u>won't</u>!') [. . .] I told him how much I liked 'Paul Bunyan', & it seemed that he was very glad it had been revived.

He tried to stand when we left, but I bent & kissed him, & he kissed my hand, smiled, & said, 'Dear Joy!' When I got to the hall, I turned, & he was still watching, & lifted his hand. We both knew it was 'Goodbye'.

Francis could not get to Suffolk till later in the month, & then Ben had become worse & could not see him, to Francis's great sadness. He & I went to the Memorial Service in the Abbey, & he said how amazed Ben would have been – as a small boy – to think that one day thousands of people would gather in such a place to do him honour.

4 Barton's sister.

5 One of Britten's childhood compositions had been entitled 'Do you no that my Daddy has gone to London today' (1919).

The first system of the first page of 'Do you no that my Daddy has gone to London today'

6 Beth was an enthusiastic team member of the Lowestoft Lacrosse
  Club, which she helped to found and for which she acted as secretary; perhaps the dinner and lecture were connected with this.

7 The Feathers Hotel, Holt, where Britten's parents stayed when visiting their son at Gresham's.

13   To Mrs Britten

Farfield, Holt, Norfolk.

Feb. 14th, 1929.

My darling Mama,

When I read your letter and Beth's and learnt that there was a
possibility of you coming over on Saturday, I was of course
absolutely mad with joy.

But as the snow has come, it is very deep here, and as I have
got another nasty cold and am not allowed to go out at all, are
you going to come? Surely Beth can't play Lax [Lacrosse] in this
weather, can she?

I am frightfully disappointed, of course, but please let it only be
postponed, not all together put off!

You will come, won't you darling, when the snow has gone and
when I am better and allowed to go out with you? Please, please,
do!

I am really writing to know if, when you do come, you could be
such an angel as to bring some things for me. They arn't, of
course, urgent and I can easily wait until you do come, which won't
be along time hence, I hope & pray!

I have run out of tooth paste, solely and completely and I would
be frightfully pleased, if, when the Crossley-Royce[1] comes gliding
up Farfield path, I could find one or two tubes of Kolynos nestling
in your pocket. As a matter-of-fact, Miss Gillett did notice that I
had run out, and without asking me, went out and bought me,
very kindly (!), a 1/6 tube of Kolynos![2] I couldn't do anything,
after her so-called kindness, but I have discovered a boy who will
want one in a few days time, and who is willing to buy it off me
so it's alright!

The second item, my darling pet, is some manuscript music
paper. I have completely run-out — —   Dinner (or rather Lunch)[3]
and I've rather alot to do for Franky [Frank Bridge]. Novilles
[Novellos: presumably how Britten had pronounced the name as

a child] have it, Augeners, 12–stave, paper <u>without</u> clefs. They will know.

And lastly darling pet, if you have stood all this, I want some of the last Musical Times. If possible about July–November 1928.[4]

My darling pet, I don't like asking for all this. Please excuse me doing so, as I feel a perfect beast, knowing all you have to do.

I must stop now darling, and go and lie down. By-the-way, Miss Gillett's ill, and Mrs. Thompson[5] is doing all her work. She's awfully nice.

Farewell, darling pet of my heart; please give my love to Pop and Beth. I'll write on Sunday giving you news.

With tons of love,
hoping & praying that you are absolutely well,
– as well as all the house (no pun intended)
your worshipping, adoring loving (etc.) son
BENJAMIN

Please excuse the writing and altogether this 'self'-ish letter.

1 The family car, upgraded by adding 'Royce'.

2 Britten used this brand of toothpaste until it disappeared from the market in the 1960s; see also Letter 284. Old currency: 1 shilling and 6 pence. There were 20 shillings in the £ and 12 pence in the shilling.

3 Britten had broken off writing his letter and resumed it after lunch: hence the interpolation.

4 In the 'Answers to Correspondents' section of the October 1928 issue of the *Musical Times*, p. 920, appear the answers to two questions put by 'E.B.B.' [Edward Benjamin Britten: his earliest music was inscribed 'E.B. Britten' or 'E. Benjamin Britten']. The first answer deals with the availability of published scores of Beethoven, the second with a query about an error observed by Britten in his copy of the Eulenburg edition of the *Missa Solemnis*. The accuracy of his observation is acknowledged (the identification of an entry of the chorus as distinct from the soloists) and his own annotation of it is to be found on p. 257 of his miniature score in the Archive.

5 The wife of G.R. Thompson, Britten's housemaster. He taught at Gresham's from 1912 to 1936 and led the second violins in the school orchestra.

14   To Mrs Britten

Farfield, Holt, Norfolk.
Monday, March 18th, 1929.

My angelic Mummy,

I am writing as you told me, beginning on Monday, to write a
little bit, each day and send it off on Tuesday. I do hope you are
everso well, and aren't anxious about me any longer, for I am just
this moment (about 3.30 p.m) |į *UP* !! and sitting in the chair in my
room. I am feeling better, but still rather sickyfied; but still that will
pass off in time. I am going quite "slowly" as you see, but it is
"surely" as well, and I shall be well enough, I know, to go home
on Saturday (!?). They all want it here, not actually want it but
advise it, so much so that Miss Gillett has given me instructions
not to put anything in the dirty-clothes basket, so to be ready by
then.

Mrs. Thompson came up and had a long talk with me last night,
just after tea; her nice, old, maid had just left, and she was very
sad about it. We had a long talk about maids etc.

Thank you darling for your dear, kind, sympathetic letter of this
morning. I did love having it, especially by the first post. The
Sponge cake and biscuits are absolutely "it", you were a pet to
send them. I am eating quite alot, but not too ravenously (how
in the world do you spell that? No wonder you talk about my
spelling!)

It was very nice of Dr. Evans[1] to ring up, anyway you were able
to tell him that I am past the "crisis"!

Miss Gillette came in for the letters in time yesterday afternoon,
so if they didn't arrive by first post they ought to have done,
anyhow it wasn't my* fault!

I suppose Barbara goes to-day, or at least has gone to-day. Her
stays are always too short, you must have enjoyed having her,
not that you would have much of her, by herself. How did she like
Marjorie?[2] I suppose Bobby is just as excited as ever. Did her
people come over? – More later, Mummy Darling.

It is now nearly 7 o'clock and I am back in bed, not feeling much
the worse for being up. I have the sickness feeling still, little one,
but it is a little better now; I felt, very naturally, rather wobbly and
dizzy, but I shall soon get over that.

I wonder what you are going to do, to-night darling. Some of

the boys here are going to Kenwyn's[3] House-play. I expect you will
all be sitting up in "heaven".[4] How I wish I could be with you; it
would indeed be "heaven" for me if I could be with you, but
Saturday night isn't far off, and then – !! Now I shall say goodnight, Mother-o'-mine. I do hope you & Pop will have a good
restful night, and will feel all the better for it in the morning. I
shall read the Daily Light and think of you doing it also. I must
just peep now and see what it's about . – it is very comforting,
and it has done me good to read it. Sleep in peace, Mother-o'-mine!

Tuesday morning. My pen is just about to run out, so soon I
shall have to change into pencil.

Well, darling, I do hope you and Pop slept well. I did quite,
infact better than usual; from about 1 o'clock I slept like I don't
know what. I am feeling better this morning, less of the sickness.
I have just had a good breakfast, which consisted of about 7 or 8
pieces of bread and butter and honey, and two cups of tea. I have
just (9 o'c) received your lovely letter and Beth's as well. You are
a darling to write so often. What is this about Breydon Water[5] that
Beth tells me? How many of you went, when? I do hope you
enjoyed yourselves.

I have just finished the grapes, darling, which were absolutely
ripping; You were an angel. Only one or two went bad, so up to
the very last they were a great pleasure. The honey too is excellent,
though I have not yet finished it. As for the flower, there are no
words to describe it; it brightens up the whole place. You are having
a busy day to-day, Mother-o'-mine. I do hope it will be a great
success and that you won't be too tired at the end of it. I am
yearning to hear the news of the Musical Society,[6] you will write
and tell me, won't you? or will you wait until Saturday? By the
way, if you haven't written about Saturday, do soon, won't you
darling? if those "business letters" that you mentioned in last
night's letter didn't refer to it. Excuse me being such a bother,
darling, won't you? especially as you are so frightfully busy.

I suppose Pop is having a very busy day to-day. I do hope he
won't be frightfully tired, and that his leg won't be atrocious. It's
too consience (however you spell it) -smiting for words, knowing
that he is slaving night and day, practically speaking, for us
children's good and upkeep, while we are enjoying ourselves; and
it's the same with your slaving, Mummy darling. Now I will put
this aside till later on in the day. Good-bye Mummy darling. Best
of luck in all the meetings (tho' it's little good me wishing it for

when you get this terrible scrawl it will all be over), a happy morning to you.

Approximately 2 o'clock. I have just had lunch Little One, a nice one of a poached (?) egg and some of the lovely biscuits that you sent me. I expect you are at Mrs. Evans[7] now, and I hope you are enjoying yourself. I had such a nice letter from Barbara this morning. Mr. Thompson brought it up to me, and we had quite a long talk together, and he told me he once, in 1917, stayed in Lowestoft, in Kirkley Cliff Road, presumably, from his description which was somewhat hazy, near Kitchener's Home.[8] Mrs. Thompson came up this morning, and brought me a Jig-saw puzzle,[9] which I spent the morning doing, and promised to bring me a gramophone up here, with some classical records, 2 she mentioned were Schubert's Overture to Rosamunde, and Unfinished Symphony. Unluckily when she went downstairs she found that the classical records would not fit on the gramophone which she was going to bring me; the only ones that would, being jazz.

I have been up since 11 o'clock to-day, feeling stronger, of course, than yesterday. Miss Gillette has very kindly brought me an easy chair from her room for me, so I am very comfortable sitting in a chair in front of the fire.

By-the-way, Williamson,[10] the boy who knows Freda[11] and who was out of school when you were here, has been fetched by his Mother home. You know, he was very slow in getting better, and had been out of school I think, 4 or 5 weeks. They didn't think it was worth sending [him] into school for the short time, and his Mother fetched him. He has got a very long journey, as he lives down in the New Forest.

There is a boy in the sick-room next door to me now. His name is Marris.[12] He doesn't seem very ill, tho', only just a cold I think. Anyway he spends his day gargling. He makes the most foul noise doing it, most disturbing for me, I can assure you. Miss Gillette has got a passion for gargling now. You know, Dr. Hendrie[13] is not much good. Miss Gillette does everything of her own accord, in the morning she gives him a brief summary of the previous day's events, while our noble Doctor gravely scratches his chin or nods his head. He just asks me how I'm feeling, for he has given up telling me to put my tongue out; Miss Gillette has to do that.

By-the-way, Mrs. Thompson said her mother wanted to come up and see me, so I am looking out for a frightful apparition at the door, any moment now. She will probably clash with Mr. Dacam (Brinney)[14] who wants to come, and to whom Mr. Thompson gave permission. I think I ought to have a special visitors' cloak-room, where they could wait until rung for, or somesuch thing.

Now, darling, I really must stop. I do hope you are not absolutely bored by the hopeless length of this epistle. Of course you will give my love to the various members of the family, including, naturally, Marjorie. Please thank Beth for her letter. Now farethee-way, Mother-o'-mine, don't worry.

With tons of love to You & Pop
Your adoring and grateful son,
BENJAMIN

P.S.   Miss Gillette sends her kind regards, and says she is ruling me with a rod of iron, <u>therefore</u> I am better!!!

P.[P.]S.   Reading this letter through, I find it's frightfully out of date, please excuse its outofdatiness. The notes at the bottom of the page are <u>Tuesday's</u>.

*I am relieved to hear from this morning's (Tuesday) letter that they did arrive in time.

1 Harold Muir Evans, the Brittens' family doctor, who lived in Turret House, Kirkley Cliff Road.

2 Helen Marjorie Goldson, fiancée and later wife of Britten's brother, Robert. See note 2 to Diary for 5 August 1931.

3 Kenwyn – one of Gresham's school houses. The others were Farfield, Woodlands and Howsons.

4 Family name for the upstairs drawing room. The ground floor was reserved for Mr Britten's dental practice.

5 Tidal mere at the mouth of the River Yare, near Great Yarmouth, Norfolk.

6 Mrs Britten was Secretary of the Lowestoft Musical Society. The Society had given a concert at the Marina Theatre, Lowestoft, on 14 March, with Bertha Steventon (soprano) and Leyland White (baritone) in a programme comprising Alec Rowley's *By the deep: 9*, a nautical fantasy for mixed voices (1928), and Bach's Peasant Cantata, 'Mer hahn en neue Oberkeet' (BWV 212).

7 The wife of Dr Evans (see note 1 above).

8 Lord Kitchener Memorial Hotel, a hostel for wounded or impoverished servicemen, at 10–11 Kirkley Cliff Road, where Mrs Britten from time to time undertook voluntary work.

The first page of 'Liebesfreude'

9 Britten never lost his liking for jigsaw puzzles. When recuperating from his heart operation in 1973, jigsaws were an occasional recreation. Wulff Scherchen remembers that jigsaws at the Old Mill at Snape were a means of relaxation after the bouts of intense concentration that were a feature of Britten's working life, and were to remain so. In the Mill, 'there was a succession of enormous jigsaws which lived literally on a huge table set aside just for this purpose', to which Britten would turn after quitting the studio in which he had incarcerated himself for hours, composing.

10 Alexander Robert Handley Williamson (b. 1914; Gresham's, 1928–33).

11 Freda Mary Britten Harmer, Britten's cousin. She was the daughter of Mr Britten's elder sister, Ellen Elizabeth ('Nellie') (1871–1945). Her father had been in partnership with Nellie's mother, Charlotte Britten (née Ginders), running a small dairy business in Maidenhead before he married Nellie, who is alleged to have fainted on the altar steps. Freda qualified as a doctor in 1933, but appears to have practised only from 1934 to 1937. She went to China to work, married, and had three children.

12 Charles William Suffield Marris (b. 1912; Gresham's, 1925–9).

13 A.S. Hendrie, school doctor and local general practitioner.

14 C. Brinney Dacam, on the staff of South Lodge, and a particular friend of Robert Britten's. In 1927 he wrote a poem, *Liebesfreude*, which Britten set for voice and piano, inscribing it in Dacam's autograph book.

15 To Oliver Berthoud[1]

[*Incomplete*]

[Farfield, Holt, Norfolk]
[?1929 or 1930]

. . . he or the agents forgot this engagement! I don't know to this day what happened.

I really must stop now. Excuse the terrible writing and horrible drivvle, but really one cannot talk or think when one has jazz booming in one's ears all the time.

Hoping you're absolutely well,

Yrs,

BENJAMIN BRITTEN

P.S.   about that Swiss melody; thanks awfully for it. I am thinking of making it into a concerto for muted horn, triangle played with drum sticks, and double-bass "col legno". Do you think it will be effective?!

It reminds me very much of one, a Swiss girl[2] taught me when staying with us.

P.T.O.

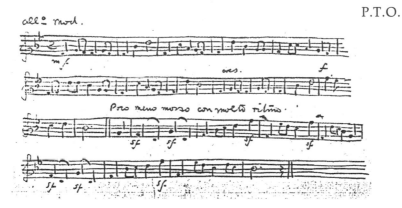

I think it's one of the most wonderfully stirring things I've ever met. The words to the 2nd half are: (excuse spelling; pronounced as in German with j's as y's); Ho, je --, je --, je --, derri di; Ho je derri di (twice); Ho je --, je --, je, derri di, Ho je derri di, derri da!

Next time I write or see you I will tell you some more, but I must really go now.

1 Oliver C. Berthoud (1911–1972), a Gresham's schoolfriend and musician (1924–9). Berthoud later became headmaster of Trinity School, Croydon, in which capacity he corresponded with Britten in connection with providing boy singers for the English Opera Group. Writing on 16 March 1971 Berthoud recalls their schooldays:

I remember our days together at Gresham's vividly. I recall quite clearly, for instance, the occasion when you and I and Christopher Eyres were playing the Mozart E flat trio [K. 563] in three different keys simultaneously, and Mr Greatorex marched in looking more than ever like the 'late' Beethoven. However, when he found it was not three rugger hearties wrecking the place but three of his right-hand boys in the music department, he retired baffled. I also remember your sight-reading at the piano the first few pages of the miniature score of the Schubert C major quintet [D. 956], which neither of us had heard but of which I was about to acquire the records. Your being able to do this struck me as positively miraculous.

2 Yvonne Clar, a Swiss *au pair* (see PFL, plate 43, and EWB, p. 78). The melody, which Britten reproduces, is a variant of the Swiss folksong 'Morge frueh, eh d'sunne lacht' ('Early in the morning before the sun is smiling').

16 To Mr R.V. Britten
From James Eccles
[*Typed*]

> Gresham's School, Holt, Norfolk.
> 30th September, 1929.

Dear Mr Britten,

It has just occurred to me that it is time I sent you the money for your boy's Exhibition, and I am very glad to enclose a cheque for £30. herewith for the year 1929–1930. When I say glad, I mean it, because all I have seen of your boy makes me very glad that I decided to take him last year. My only regret has been that his health was not too good during part of the year, but I hope, now that he has really settled down, he will have no further trouble in that way. I very much value his presence in the School from every point of view, and particularly his work and conduct, in addition to his music.

> With kind regards to your wife and yourself,
> I am,
> Yours sincerely,
> J. R. ECCLES

1 James Ronald Eccles MA (1874–1956), appointed to Gresham's in 1900, was second master from 1906 to 1919 and Headmaster from 1919 to 1935. He published a memoir, *My Life as a Public School Master* (n.d). See also Letter 23.

17 To Mr and Mrs R.V. Britten

> Farfield, Holt, Norfolk.
> October 6th, 1929.

My darling Parents,

What a marvellous Idea! It will be glorious to see you. I shall have the majority of the afternoon free and a little time after work, i.e. I shall be free from the end of dinner, 5 mins. to 2 approximately, until 4.15 and then from 5.55 (without having had tea) or 6.10 (having had tea) until five to seven, when prep starts. You are good to think of coming.

And so you are alone at home now. I bet you're enjoying yourselves, revelling in the silence of the house. Where is Beth going after she leaves Elinor Bond;[1] she's not staying there for three weeks, is she?

I had a glorious time last Friday. I made up my mind that I would
here that concert on the wireless,[2] by hook or by crook, and so I
arranged with a boy that if I could possibly get permission from
Mr. Thompson, I would go in to him and hear it. Well, I went to
Mr. Thompson, and he asked me to go into his drawing room and
hear it on his wireless! So I went in and heard it, in the greatest
of comfort, and enjoyed every moment except for a few
atmospherics and an occasional burst of conversation from Mrs.
Thompson.

The chorus in the symphony was simply superb, with perfect
high notes, especially that bit where they hold high A for, I think,
13 bars.[3] The violas came out marvellously in the bit you love, Pop;
with the roundest and fullest tone imaginable.

Enough of that. We are crowded with German boys here now.
Eleven and two masters have come to stay for a week at the
school, to promote, I suppose, friendly feelings between the
younger generations of England and Germany, corresponding to
the trip that our boys made to Germany. They, certainly, are a
funny looking lot, but they seem to be quite nice, and talk quite
alot of English, which is rather lucky, as there are not many
German-speaking people in the house.

They went to the Music Recital[4] last night, and what an opinion
they must have of the music of Gresham's School! It was the
worst Music recital on record – even the least critical boys say that.
It was silly, that is the only adjective which can qualify the
playing. All three of them, Gog [Greatorex], Mr. Taylor,[5] Miss
Chapman[6] (who played on a small viola, which sounded like a
cracked muted violin), sounded as if they were bad sight-readers,
had never seen the music before, and had never had an hour of
coaching.[7]

Well, I shan't bother you any more, with this twaddle; I'll tell
you the rest of the news when Tuesday comes, – ah, Tuesday!

Thank you ever so much for your letters Mummy, you are good
to write so much.

With ever so much love,
Your adoring and grateful son,
BENJAMIN

P.S.   I shall expect you at 2 o'clock on Tuesday, then, at Farfield?

1 A schoolfriend of Beth's.

2 The entry in Britten's diary for 4 October reads:

Spend most of a long and hard working day looking forward to Beethoven's 9th Symph. Mr. Thompson asked me to hear it on his wireless, when I asked him for permission to hear it on Willard's, & so I go in there from 8.30 (thereby missing approx. 40 bars as time was 8.25) until 9.45. The Chorus was simply magnificent as so were the soloists. Elsie Suddaby, Ethel Barklett, Tudor Davies, Roy Henderson (Men espe. good). Orchestra tired (end of Prom. season), but nevertheless good. A fine performance, but it didn't come over well.

The performance was conducted by Sir Henry Wood, with the National Chorus.

3 Britten refers to the finale, 'Freude, schöner Götterfunken', etc. The high A sustains the word 'Welt' ('der ganzen Welt!').

4 The programme was as follows: Mr Taylor (see note 5 below) played a Minuet and Allegro by Maurice Greene, a Gavotte and Allegro by Arne, a Gavotte by Boyce, and the Trumpet tune attributed to Purcell. Miss Chapman (see note 6 below) then performed Brahms's 'Cradle Song' and 'Le Basque' by Marais. Mr Greatorex contributed Paradies's Toccata, an Air and Gigue by Bach and Scarlatti's Sonata in C. Miss Chapman rounded off the occasion with an Air from Gluck's *Orfeo*, an Aria by Bach and a Rigaudon by Handel.

5 Hoult D.F. Taylor, ARCO (b. 1900), Gresham's music staff, 1928–43. When Britten left Gresham's in July 1930 Taylor gave him his own copy of Cecil Forsyth's *Orchestration* (London, Macmillan and Stainer and Bell, 1914), now in the Archive.

6 Joyce Chapman (Gresham's staff, 1925–54), who taught Britten the viola at school. She suffered from an undiagnosed progressive brain disease, which was responsible for the deteriorating quality of her playing. Britten could have had no knowledge of this tragic affliction at the time.

7 Britten had already observed in his diary on 6 October 1928, in the context of another musical occasion, that

It looked as if [Mr Greatorex] was a bad sight reader and as if he had never seen the music before; the way he stopped when he came to a hard passage and looked at it.

18 To Mr and Mrs R.V. Britten

Farfield, Holt, Norfolk
Jan. 19th, 1930

My darling Parents,

This is the first of eleven epistles to leave my hand, travel via M & G.N. [Midland & Great Northern Railway], pass through the

G.P.O. and be disposited on your doorstep at a quarter to eight
approximately on the following Monday morning,[1] in this
wickedest of terms. It is a pretty terrible thought, but I hope & pray
that the time will pass as quickly as did the time during these last
& much regretted-to-be-passed holidays.

Thank you ever so much for your letter Mama, & the parcel. I
simply cannot think how I left all those things behind; frightfully
sorry. I'm very glad that you had a good drive home, Pop, without
any mishaps; I suppose the light didn't fail again, did it? And so
the concert was a success after all, was it, Mummy? I should have
loved to have been there and have heard the monster Polypheme;[2]
Mr. Coleman[3] was right then about his voice.

You know, Pop, that Miss Gillett said that the term ended on
April 3rd; well, she was quite wrong, as officially it ends on the
9th which makes 12 weeks minus one day. Luckily, however,
several scholarships have been won, & to encourage the others
in the school to work and obtain a like reward, we have a few days
off the end of the term, & come home on the 5th, (a Saturday of
all days); and so 'taint so bad after all.

I didn't play hockey yesterday, as my clothes had not arrived,
but I expect I shall play on Monday – I am getting the very
cheapest of cheap things & only one of each, as really it isn't worth
getting more for only one term.

I hope the buoys are as good as ever, Pop, and just as regular.
I was reminded strongly of them the other night – there were two
boys snoring in bed next to me; one of them snored taking breath
both in and out, while the other only when breathing in. For
about five or even six times they agreed, & then gradually they got
out of time, & they took quite a time to get in again. It fascinated
me so much that I could not get to sleep.

Oh! How I envy you with a fire! When your hands are cold (as
mine are now) you can at least go to a fire and warm them, but at
this wretched place it makes them colder to put them on the pipes,
which are generally colder than the hands themselves; so at the
moment I'm sitting & shivering.

Gog seems to have meant what he said last term about
performing one of my bally works this term. He asked me for one
yesterday; and so I thrust the nicer modern one into his hands –
but he nearly choked & so I had to show him the silly small one,
and he even calls that one modern!!![4]

Please give my love to the various members of the family,
including Seizer,[5] who I hope is absolutely well – Give him a bone

for me. Thank Beth for doing up the nicely done-up parcel. I
suppose Bobby has returned from W.H.;[6] give <u>him</u> my love, and tell
him to be careful what essays he sets for his wretched pupils – I've
got one – "New Year Resolutions" – which makes me faint to
think of it. Also I suppose Laulie has gone, & so you can't give my
love to her; but you can to Auntie Queenie,[7] whose pictures are
progressing, I hope, very marvellously.

    And lastly there are your beloved selves; I hope you are frightfully
well, and not <u>too</u> tired.

With tons of love,
Your adoring & grateful son,
BENJAMIN

P.S.   Pop, have you heard from Franky [Frank Bridge] yet?

P.P.S.   Please tell Liza[8] that the Honey's marvellous. I think of
her, every mouthful of it I take.

1 The very theme of the documentary film, *Night Mail*, Britten was to
    create with W.H. Auden in 1935–6. See note 1 to Diary for 18 Novem-
    ber 1935.

2 A review from the *Lowestoft Journal*, 18 January 1930, of a performance
    of Handel's *Acis and Galatea* – 'last Thursday' – by the Lowestoft
    Musical Society:

    The palm is to be given to Mr Kenneth Ellis. He is a robust bass, powerful,
    and yet with a command of modulation which gives a marked effect to his
    singing. He was in the second part as Polyphemus, and he vocally did the
    roaring giant to the life. He disdained the book, sang note perfect, and it
    was evident that the audience was thrilled.

3 Charles Joseph Romaine Coleman (1879–1959), teacher of singing,
    piano and organ, a conductor and church organist. He held several
    professional posts during his long career: Nave Organist at Norwich
    Cathedral (1901–2) and later Assistant Organist; Organist and Choir-
    master at St John's, Lowestoft (1902–40); at Holy Trinity, Bristol
    (1940–42), and finally at St Peter Mancroft, Norwich (1942–59). While
    at his last post Coleman was influential in persuading Britten to
    compose the *Hymn to St Peter*, Op. 56a (1955), to mark the quincen-
    tenary of St Peter Mancroft Church. During his years in Lowestoft,
    Coleman conducted the Lowestoft Musical Society (of which Mrs
    Britten was Secretary), and in the activities of which Britten partici-
    pated. The Society gave the first performance of his Two Choral
    Songs, *A Hymn to the Virgin* and 'I saw three ships' (*The Sycamore
    Tree*) under Coleman's direction (see note 2 to Diary for 5 January
    1931). Britten's juvenile '6 Variations on "How bright these glorious

Spirits shine" (Revd J.B. Dykes)' for chorus, organ, piano and string quintet, was dedicated to, and inspired by, Mr C.J.R. Coleman. Britten and Coleman gave a joint recital (piano and organ) on 9 July 1934 at St John's, Lowestoft: see PFL, plate 69.

4 Britten had composed a Bagatelle for violin, viola and piano between 30 March 1929 and 25 January 1930. The manuscript is in the Archive. But it is not clear if this was the work – 'the nicer modern one' – that caused Mr Greatorex such distress or another work from Britten's portfolio. If the former, then Mr Greatorex conquered his antipathy sufficiently to take part in the first performance of the work on 1 March. See note 4 to Letter 19 and Letter 512, in which, from the vantage point of 1945, Britten refers to the 'mutual suspicion between Mr. Greatorex and myself'. EWB, p. 55, recounts that, on arrival at Gresham's, he was greeted by the music master with the words, 'So you are the boy who likes Stravinsky!' One of the reasons for the tension between master and pupil was probably the fact that Britten was not taking music lessons from Greatorex but from Bridge and Samuel. This may have been something of an affront to the school's head of music.

5 Caesar, the family dog, a Clumber spaniel. See also Letter 19.

6 West Hartlepool, the home of his fiancée, Marjorie. See note 2 to Letter 14.

7 Sarah Fanny Hockey (b. 1875, d. ?), Mrs Britten's younger sister, was an accomplished artist and achieved some success as a miniaturist, exhibiting at the Royal Academy, London. She painted portraits of all the Britten children, including Benjamin aged about nine; it is now in the possession of the National Portrait Gallery and is reproduced in PFL, plate 27. Aunt Queenie was later to develop a religious mania and to endure frequent periods of 'melancholia', when Mrs Britten was often summoned to look after her (see note 1 to Letter 50).

    A further portrait miniature by Aunt Queenie of Britten when young (perhaps not more than two years of age) is in the possession of the Archive, along with a portrait in oils of Britten's father. The miniature at one time was in the possession of Barbara, while the portrait of R.V. Britten was owned by Beth.

8 Unidentified.

19   To Mr and Mrs R.V. Britten

Farfield, Holt, Norfolk
Feb. 9th, 1930.

My darling Parents.

Do you know, I did something the other day, which will surprise you, nearly as much as it surprised me? I shot a goal in hockey, – I did really! I hit the ball (for once, I must admit) and after it had rebounded off about two of my opponents, it went, carefully avoiding the goal-keeper straight into the net. Don't you think it good? I could & would scarcely deign to touch another ball for the rest of the game.

Enough of that. Thank you ever so much for your letter, Mama. I am awfully sorry about Dr. Hutchinson;[1] but it must be a relief, as it had to come soon, hadn't it? That reminds me; you said in your letter, or rather, infered that Pop had written to me last Sunday. I have received nothing, and so presume that the letter was lost, or delayed, or something of the kind. I hope that there was nothing of vital importance in it, to be answered at once, on peril of my life so-to-speak; anyway I am frightfully fed up to have lost it, if there was such a letter.

Have you been having snow? I trust that there has been a warmer temperature in Lowestoft than here. We are simply being frozen out of house (& home?) here, and that is really the reason for my badness of writing and the untidiness of this letter – My hands are unfeelably cold and stiff.

We had two films, last night. One, a section out of the film, Napoleon Bonaparte,[2] and the second, the Epic of Everest.[3] The first was really ridiculous; the whole time nothing happened but people or soldiers, either marching into a town, or throwing bombs into the middle of a river, doing little or no damage to anyone. The second was, however, a great contrast, and the photography was marvellous.

I think that all the news has now been recorded, and there is nothing left to tell you. My trio[4] is progressing quite well, we are working quite hard at it; but the more I play it the less I like it, and the outlook, therefore, for the recital is anything but cheerful! Still, I am looking forward, yearning with all my heart to see you, and I hope that you will think it worth coming for.

Please give my love to Beth. I hope she is very well, and that her various duties are progressing in the very best manner possible.

And greet also Caesar (I see that you cannot drop that spelling of his name, and so I will use it also, though I prefer "Seizer" infinately) for me. I am very glad his manners in the street are good, and I hope that he doesn't make an excessive number of friends in the road.

Thank you ever so much for the socks, Mummy. They are beautiful. It was rather curious, but Miss Gillette said something to me, the day before about them; and said that she wanted some more for me. I said that you had promised them, & probably had not finished making them or toeing, heeling, or legging them, whatever you have been so angelic to do to them, and that as soon as they were ready, they would be sent. I said however that I would say quelquechose about them, when I next wrote.

And behold, the very next morning – there they were! Something for Psychologists or Telepathists or whatever they are called, to think about!

Now I must stop, as a walk I am off to go. Hoping & praying for your health and safety.

> You[r] very loving and adoring, likewise
> grateful son,
> BENJAMIN

1 Donald Henry Hutchinson, a local doctor (for some twenty years), magistrate, and prominent Lowestoft citizen, who lived in Kirkley Park Road. He had died after a long illness. He was an active member of the congregation at St John's.

2 *Napoleon*, the epic film written and directed by Abel Gance (1889–1981), and first shown in Paris in 1927. In its original form it lasted more than five hours, and employed three screens; what Britten saw was probably part of one of the drastically cut and re-edited versions distributed by MGM.

3 British film, released in 1924. Produced and photographed by Captain J.B.L. Noel.

4 The Bagatelle for violin, viola and piano was first performed at Gresham's on 1 March 1930, with Miss Chapman (violin), Britten (viola) and Mr Greatorex (piano). A review appeared in the school magazine, *The Gresham*, XII, October 1928–July 1930, p. 170:

We knew that Britten was a composer, but this was our first opportunity of hearing any of his work. He contributed a Pianoforte Trio in one movement called 'Bagatelle', in which he played the viola part. Written in a modern idiom, the Trio shows that Britten has already advanced a considerable distance in the technique of composition. He should go far and we take this opportunity of wishing him every success in the future.

20   To Beth Britten

Farfield, Holt, Norfolk.

Feb. 22nd, 1930.

My darling Beth,

Thank you everso much for your letter that has lain unanswered
for so long. It is practically a fortnight, I know, but I have been
so busy, & it is only now that I am able to write, being out of school
for a few days. I have been stopped writing music by the
screeching of the numberless gramophones bellowing along the
corridor, making such a din that I can hardly think what I am
writing (I hope therefore you will understand & forgive the
nonsensical character of this letter); and so I thought that I would
take up my pen, & throw a few words on paper for your benefit.

Oh, there is someone practising a clarinet along the passage!
There are no words to describe the screeching, bubbly, &
grotesque sounds that are proceeding from that comparatively small
bit of an instrument, – you never would believe that such a small
thing could be responsible for such a noise.

I suppose you have your sister Barbara with you now, how I
envy you all together! At least you are able to get warm, sitting
round a fire or somewhere. Here, I am just thawing, wrapped up
in a great coat & with fur gloves on (at least, on one hand – I
have to take one off my right hand because I cannot write with
furgloves on, & that accounts for the now freezing state of the
said hand). We never think of opening windows in this study; for
weeks not one inch of new air have we had; but it's still as cold
as ever!

I am sorry to hear of your sudden passion for the flicks; I hope
it's wearing off now, & that you aren't going so frequently now. I
think I described to you the two films we had here, of the "Epic of
Everest" & "Napoleon". We are going to have two more
educational ones, from Yankee land, that we have been asked to
try – namely Christopher Columbus,[1] & the Pilgrim Fathers;[2] they
are sure to be awful. It is a frightful nuisance that we have got to
have them, because that uses up the last free Saturday evening
in the term, & there is some ridiculous rule, which says that only
on Saturday evenings can films be shown to the school. Also there
was a thought that we were going to have a very good other film,
some comedy or other, done by the Cambridge amateur film

Society or something; and now we can't have it because of these
wretched Yankee films.

Do you know, I am getting quite a star at hockey now; quite
brilliant is the game I play now; my stick becomes raised above
my head less frequently, & less frequently, tho', I am sorry [to]
say, still quite often, does the ball completely evade contact with
the stick I use (your noble stick, a centenarian, I should think, by
now).

I am glad that you enjoyed your Lacrosse match against
somewhere, I forget where; anyhow it was the time the referee
(?umpire? I know that now you have umpires in hockey. What the
difference is I don't know – except that umpires don't run about,
& referees do – at least that is what I've been told, & it seems to
be true, for in hockey here, we have two such persons, one for
each end, who only walk up and down), to return to the sentance,
it was the time the referee played for your opponents.

How is Caesar? I hope's he's very well, & full of beans, & also
your self.

I must stop now to write to your parents.

Your very loving brothy,
BENJAMIN

I apologize for the lack of news – there ain't none at all.

1 Might this have been *Christophe Colombe*, a French film of 1910, produced by Louis Feuillade? We can find no record of an American
  film of the same title, but Britten is specific about the 'Yankee' origins
  of the films in question.
2 Unidentified. Might this have been *The Pilgrims*, American, 1924?

21 To Mr and Mrs R.V. Britten

Farfield, Holt, Norfolk
Feb. 23rd, 1930.

My darling Parents,

It seems hard to believe that in less than a week I shall be seeing
you. Lately the time has been going much faster, infinately faster
than at the beginning of the term, when every minute seemed
about a day.

I am still out of school, and swallowing with considerable
difficulty; but apart from that I am very well, free of any cold

worth speaking about or any like thing. I hope & pray that you are also free from such things.

I suppose that Barbara is with you now. Please give her my love ~~when~~ if she is still at 21 [Kirkley Cliff Rd.] when this arrives. If the ~~wheath~~ weather is anything the like (I am sorry about all these crossings-out but I cannot think straight to-day) it is here (need I say it is cold?!), she is having horribly hard luck.

Thank you ever so much both of you for your letters, and also you Mummy for the kind thought of the formalins. They are doing alot for my throat, I am sure, much more than this incessant gargling with Glycothymol or some such stuff, that I have to do to satisfy Miss Gillette.

I am writing to Harold Samuel, as you said, Mummy. It was a very difficult letter to write, & I hope it will not offend him for life when he sees it. I have not yet copied it out, but I have written a rough copy.[1] By-the-way, I got a notice from him of his change of address, (as before, we got one), and so it seems rather as if he is due home soon; he has not been advertised yet for any concerts, but I hope for the best. Did you have a card likewise, Mummy?

I am awfully glad about the wine, sorry, the "sac" and Frank Bridge, Pop. Did he seem pleased when he wrote? He jolly well ought to be. How stupid & ridiculous of the wine people not to have sent the wine before.[2]

I prophesy that I am going to have rather an unpleasant surprise to-morrow, when the second quarter's order is read. (a) and firstly, because I have not been able to do a thing right this quarter, & this last week I have been throwing away marks, left and right. (b) & secondly, the result of the last quarter was much to[o] surprising & lucky to last for long. And so I am hoping that my lucky star will not fail me too completely, & that next quarter will be slightly more successful.

I will get the afternoon off next Saturday, if you let me know when you arrive. I am looking forward very much to seeing the car in all its new glory & paint. How much did that woman (the woman who ran into you at Bungay, Miss White, was her name?) pay?

I must stop now, & write that letter to Harold Samuel, because I want to get it off by the post. The socks you sent, Mummy, (I am wearing them now), are simply spiffing; perfectly scruciatingly (<u>how</u> do you spell that word? I can't find it in the dictionary) warm.

Oh, I say, Pop. Have you read the "Bridge of San Luis Rey"?

(by Thornton Wilder). You must read it if you haven't, tho' I expect
you have. I read [it] yesterday, & I must say I enjoyed [it] very much.
        Hoping you are all very well, & longing for Saturday,
                        Your very loving & grateful son,
                                                    BENJAMIN

P.S. Looking back at the first two sides of this letter, in fact the
whole of it, I don't feel I ought to send it, so many are the crossings-
out etc. If I had not to write to H.S. I would copy it out again, but
I hope you will forgive me and excuse it.

1 Some problem, clearly, had arisen in connection with Britten's lessons with Samuel, perhaps to do with his availability. (It might have
   been that Samuel's other professional commitments made him an
   elusive teacher.) In Britten's diary for 11 March we find him writing:
   I have a letter from Mummy, saying write to H.S. & demand lesson on
   Friday as she has to see Auntie Queenie (why?). I see Thomson & Eccles,
   who say yes & in aft. I send a prepaid telegram to H.S., who answers in
   evening, saying yes on Friday aft. at 3. I have now all arranging to do; but
   what prospects!

2 Bridge wrote to Britten's father on 12 February:
   When we arrived home on Monday night we found that your wine had
   arrived. Most kind of you to send it. When I saw Benjamin last I hoped I
   had impressed on him the fact that your kind proposal should not materialize. Then your letter came saying you were sending the wine & it seems too
   late to tell you that I ought not to imbibe such things. However, here it is
   & thank you again. (Obviously, it will be entirely Benjamin's fault if I become
   a confirmed toper!) It gives me great pleasure to help your son. He has
   exceptional gifts & with sympathetic understanding from you people around
   him I think he is sure to achieve fine things. In any case I shall do what I
   can. A career in any art is always difficult at the beginning, as you know,
   but I am confident that Benjamin is made of the right stuff!

Monday, 7 April 1930
[*Lowestoft*]

Bobby arrives in aft. & Marjorie after tea. Go to Playhouse[1] with
Beth, for rather a poor (silent) film, "the 4 feathers", little
similarity to the book.[2] I go to a marvellous Schönberg concert on
the Billison's wireless.[3] Including "Chamber-Symp.", Suite of
[19]25 (pft.) & Pierrot Lunaire. I liked the last the most, & I thought
it most beautiful.[4] It was of course perfectly done.

1 A cinema in Lowestoft.

2 The Film (US, Paramount, 1929) was based on the famous novel of the same title (1902) by A.E.W. Mason (1865–1948).

3 Billison was Mr Britten's assistant in the dental practice, 1928–30, and he and his wife were family friends. The young composer was a frequent visitor to the Billison home because they possessed 'a marvellous moving coil wireless', on which he was able to hear many broadcast concerts.

4 A BBC Contemporary Concert 'held privately' at the Central Hall, Westminster, given by Erika Wagner (reciter), Eduard Steuermann (piano) and the Vienna 'Pierrot Lunaire' Ensemble, conducted by Erwin Stein (see note 9 to Letter 59). Schoenberg's Chamber Symphony was performed in the arrangement for reduced instrumentation by Webern. This marked the beginning of a period when Britten showed keen interest in and, on occasion, exceptional enthusiasm for Schoenberg's music. On the next day, he remarked in his diary, 'Schönberg got a terrible report in the D. Mail!!' On the 14th, he wrote,

Go in morning [. . .] to get my Schönberg (6 Short pieces), ordered on Friday [. . .] I am getting very fond of Schönberg, especially with study.

On 30 April, there was a 'modern music' evening at 21 Kirkley Cliff Road:

20 people including ourselves. All by contemporary composers (excluding 1 of Scriabin & a nocturne of Chopin (by request) played by myself.) Trio plays my bagatelle; pt. songs (2 of Holst); Mrs. Taylor & Mr. Coleman play J. Ireland VI. Son (no.1) complete, 6 pft. pieces (Schönberg).

At the end of the summer term Britten chose as school prizes, two volumes of John Drinkwater's plays, the *Oxford Book of English Verse*, Strauss's *Don Quixote* and five orchestral songs, Rimsky-Korsakov's suite from *The Golden Cockerel* and Schoenberg's *Pierrot lunaire*. Britten records these titles on 24 June and concludes the entry, 'Oh, I love my books!'

The story is often told that Britten, when a student, was unable to persuade the College to purchase the score of *Pierrot lunaire* for the library. But as his diary has made clear, he had his own copy in 1930, when still at school (since lost).

In 1933, Britten was to be introduced to Schoenberg in the interval of a BBC concert at the Queen's Hall on 8 February, when the composer conducted a performance of his *Variations for Orchestra*, Op. 31. Britten went in the company of the Bridges – 'Tickets from B.B.C. – front row dress circle – dinner jacket – top hat!' – and wrote in his diary about the work: 'What I could make of it owing to a skin-of-its teeth performance, was rather dull, but some good things in it.'

Later in 1933, on 24 November, Britten was impressed anew by a further performance of *Pierrot*:

After dinner (at 9.0) I go to B.B.C. Contemporary concert of Schönberg with Grace [Williams]. Meet there F.B. & Miss Fass. Steuerman plays superbly 2 sets of pft. pieces 3 longer ones, & 6 short ones I know. V. interesting & I enjoy the 2nd set. But the joy of the evening was Pierrot Lunaire, with Erika Wagner as a divine reciter (amazingly accurate) & Kolische [Rudolf Kolisch] & Heifits [Bernar Heifetz], Steuerman – [Robert] Murchie (flute), [Frederick] Thurston (cl.) & [Walter] Lear (BCl.) who almost came up to the standard of the rest. But what a work! The imagination & technique of it. I revelled in the romanticism of it.

And in 1937, on 12 March, he responded enthusiastically to Schoenberg's last quartet (No. 4): 'This is the work of a true master & some of it is marvellously beautiful.' See also note 2 to Letter 74; note 7 to Letter 77 and note 6 to Letter 90.

22   To Mr and Mrs R.V. Britten

Farfield, Holt, Norfolk.
May 11th, 1930.

My darling Parents,

Once more I take up my pen to begin the series of weekly epistles to travel to you in Lowestoft. This is the first of twelve, before I see the sunny shores (?) of Southern Lowestoft. Thank you all ever so much for your card, with its apt remarks; and you for your letter, Mama, and the most glorious of sweaters ever seen in this school. I am, in one way, very sorry to-day's Sunday, because I am unable to wear my sweater, and show it to the school. It arrived with the shoes (for which, receive my heartiest thanks, and apologies for being so slack as to forget them) just after the game of cricket yesterday (in which, needless to say I did brilliantly!); but luckily I had a net after tea in which to show off my new possession, and I was careful not to change back into my other dry-as-dust clothes until the latest possible moment, so as to give the rest of the school the pleasure of looking at it.

I am so glad that Elijah[1] fared well, I should have loved to have heard it. I cannot imagine Frank Phillips as Elijah, from what I can remember of him, but I expect he was very good. What like was the Soprano? An improvement I hope on her last performance with Sammons.[2]

Have you yet decided on what's going to happen about your

annual holiday; is Beth going to extend her London trip Aunt Julianne-ward?[3] I do hope that this half-hearted drizzle with interceptions of like-wise half-hearted sunshine will not continue, and that for once the proverb 'When Pop goes away, the rain it will stay; when homeward he fares, the Sun comes and glares', will prove incorrect.

I have no news to tell you, about my doings here, for literally I have done naught out of the way of first weeks of term. The dorm. is a gigantic improvement on the other hole, I am glad to hear; but oh! how I moan for my bed at "21". The wretched thing here is this shape:

with very hard and uncompressable springs. The result is that either I slip down into the hole on the wall side and give my elbow a bump on the wall, or I slip the other way, and all the clothes slip onto the floor, as shown in diagram.

I have not yet played tennis; the only time I arranged a game, of course, it rained. I hope for one in the near future (six weeks or so, I expect.); as I said before, I played cricket yesterday, but there was nothing extraordinary in that, except that I had one ball and made, two not out, which I consider rather bright for me.

But still I never play cricket, except I do well (!!!). Have you heard from our noble Headmaster yet, Pop? He began to say something about the letter (at least I presume it was going to be about your letter), but he saw someone else urgent and had to dash off.

Now I must stop and go and have dinner. I envy you two alone at "21". I yearn to be with you, but I expect you are enjoying the peace.

Please give my love to Alice, the honey is marvellous, tell her. Has Rose returned to leave yet? Also please give a bone to Caesar for me. I hope he's well.

And lastly, I hope [you] two are absolutely brimming over with health, and are enjoying a Sunday at Lowestoft; still, only 12 more weeks!

With tons of love & thanks,
Your loving son,
BENJAMIN

1　Britten's parents, an engagement photograph, 1900

2   Edith Rhoda Hockey, before her marriage to Robert Victor Britten

3 The wedding: St John's Smith Square, London SW1, 5 September 1901

4 R.V. Britten, 1909

5 Edith Britten, 1909

6b The first floor sitting room, known to the family – because of its upper location – as 'Heaven'

6a The family home, 21 Kirkley Cliff Road, Lowestoft, where Britten was born on 22 November 1913; Mr Britten's dental practice was on the ground floor

7   Beth; Edith Britten and her infant son, Benjamin; Barbara; Robert, 1914

8a Nursery theatricals; back row from left: Barbara; unidentified; Robert; Benjamin cross-legged in front row; Beth kneels on his right

8b Mrs Scarce, Nanny, with Benjamin, 1914

8c Benjamin, c.1915

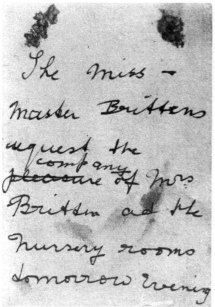

9a Invitation to the theatricals, probably   9b Benjamin and battleship, c.1916
in Nanny's hand

9c Beth and Benjamin, c.1916   9d Benjamin, c.1917

10a Benjamin in 'Heaven', seemingly playing from multiple parts, *c*.1921

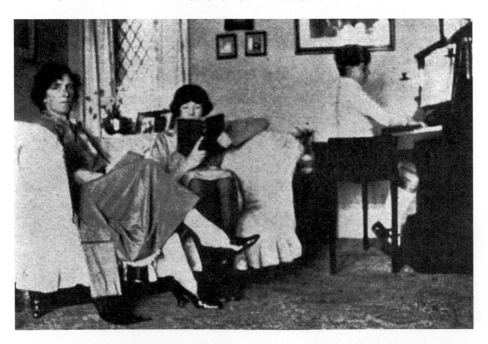

10b Benjamin plays to his mother and one of his sisters, *c*.1921

11a Edith Britten, 1918

11b Benjamin, c.1923, perhaps leaving for
school (South Lodge)

11c Edith Britten, 1922

12a South Lodge Preparatory School, Lowestoft

12b Benjamin and John Pounder in the front garden of 21 Kirkley Cliff Road, 1926

13 Benjamin in the garden, ?summer 1928

14a Gresham's, Holt (from a House photograph, summer 1929)

14b Gresham's, Holt (from a House photograph, summer 1930)

15a Gresham's, Holt, which Britten attended from 1928 to 1930: the School Chapel

15b Gresham's, Holt: Farfield House

16 Frank Bridge (1879–1941), whom Britten first met in 1927; the first recorded
lessons with Bridge took place in January 1928. Britten always kept this drawing of
Bridge by Marjorie Fass on the wall of his studio

P.S.   The eggs are lovely Mama; one got disfigured beyond all recognition on the journey, but all the rest are beautifully intact.
   I am glad you had a good journey home.

1 Mendelssohn's oratorio, *Elijah* (1846), was performed by the Lowestoft Musical Society at St John's Church, Lowestoft, with Nellie Palliser (soprano), Mary Cannell (alto), Emlyn Bebb (tenor), Frank Phillips (bass), conducted by C.J.R. Coleman.

2 Albert Sammons (1886–1957), English violinist, Nellie Palliser, and Mary Kendall (piano) gave a Lowestoft Musical Society Concert on 26 March 1930 at the Hippodrome, Lowestoft. Although Britten did not attend (he was still at Holt), he had evidently heard of the singer's poor performance.

3 Julianne Painter (née Britten; 1868–1946), Mr Britten's eldest surviving sister and Britten's godmother. With two of her sisters, Florence and Louise, Julianne started a girls' private school in Malvern, Worcestershire. In 1905 she married the Revd Sheldon Painter (d. 1936), whose family owned a drapery business in Malvern. After missionary work in Japan for twenty-seven years, he was appointed Rector of St Helen's Church, Worcester. He and his wife lived at the Rectory from 1929 until he died in August 1936. His wife survived him and in the 1940s lived in Malvern.

23 To Mrs Britten
From James Eccles

The Headmaster's, Holt, Norfolk.
June 21st, 1930.

Dear Mrs. Britten,

   We are <u>delighted</u> at your boy's fine success & I congratulate you very heartily![1] We feel some reflected glory & realise that's a great honour to the School! I am so very glad about it all. He is such a dear boy & so modest about all his brilliant performances![2]

Yours very sincerely,
J. R. ECCLES

I shall miss him <u>very</u> much.

1 Britten had won an open scholarship to the Royal College of Music, London. He sat for his scholarship on 19 June 1930 and wrote an account of the memorable day in his pocket diary:

I go to College at 10.0 & have a writing exam (Pt. song, Scherzo, modulations to write) from 10–3.0 with break for lunch at Barkers

[Department Store, Kensington High Street] with Mummy 1–2. & oral from 3–5.30 (I was in room with R.V. Williams, John Ireland, & Waddington (?) for about ½ hr.). After that I have surprise of winning comp. inspite of 2 brilliant others in final (5 altogether in it), including Alec Templeton a blind boy. In evening dinner with Barb. & Mummy at Hotel, & then with Mummy go to a marvellous performance of Hiawatha at Albert Hall. Perfectly glorious singing, staging, & ballet.

On 24 June Britten received a congratulatory letter from Harold Samuel:

> Arts Club,
> 40 Dover Street, W. 1
> Tel. No. 1452 Mayfair
>
> Dear Britten,
>   My heartiest congratulations! I should be glad to hear whom you are thinking of asking for, as a teacher of composition: I should advise you to try for R.O. Morris. I will help you about it, if you like [. . .].
>   Yours sincerely,
>   HAROLD SAMUEL

A few days later Britten received a congratulatory letter from Frank Bridge, which is both characteristically generous and an interesting document in its own right:

> Friston Field
> near Eastbourne
> Sussex
> June 25th 1930
>
> Dear Benjamin,
>   That's a splendid piece of news! <u>Congratulations</u>. So you are really going to finish with school this term. I had a vague sort of idea that you might try for a musical scholarship at Oxford some time or other, but with a scholarship at the Royal College you will be able to make a move with your piano work as well as composition. A very practical advantage besides being in touch with all kinds of people who are working in music. You must tell me more about the scholarship when we next meet. I am sure to be able to see you some time in the summer & before you actually begin at the R.C.M.
>   I think I might be able to get you under John Ireland for composition, but of this we can talk over later.
>   With every good wish & good luck.
>   Yours very sincerely,
>   FRANK BRIDGE

The conflicting advice offered by these two letters had to be resolved. In a later letter Bridge argued eloquently for John Ireland and it was this argument that prevailed. His marvellously wise letter to Britten on this subject deserves quotation in full:

Friston Field,
Near Eastbourne,
Sussex.
Aug. 13, 1930

Dear Benjamin,

It is, I fear unlikely that I shall be in London at all during August, &
possibly may not be there until the middle of September, so I don't see
much chance of talking to you about this problem of composition master at
the R.C.M.

Personally I think an institution only helps one to find one's feet, but as
the teacher you speak of & John Ireland are almost two different schools of
thought, that is if one can make any comparison when the first is not a
composer & the other is, it does appear necessary to get into touch with the
right influence in order to get the best out of your R.C.M. days.

I don't know whether a scholar has the right to say under whom he should
work, I fancy the authorities place him according to their own plans, but I
think it is essential that you express the wish to be with some particular
master, although it does not follow that the suggestion is accepted. But, if
you would ask yourself whether you want to be in touch with one whose
understanding must be, obviously, more firmly & mostly entrenched in the
past (all very sound, of course) than with one whose foundation of musical
technique is – let me say, equally classical, but who has been a creator of
music for many years, & furthermore, has the instinct of a fine musical
mind, (no one can make the reputation, such as John Ireland has, without
having an outstanding personality, whether all musicians agree about his
work or not) then I should say you would know almost at once which course
to take.

Your difficulty, at the moment, is that you have asked two people for
advice. If I were a young man I should plump for a live composer whose
activities are part of the present-day outlook with a heavy leaning towards
tomorrow's!

I think you may have to do a certain amount of work to sharpen up your
technique, which may appear to you, at first, as being a retrograde step, but
you know that this will be the first moment when serious study is to monopo-
lize your daily life, & possibly – il faut reculer pour mieux sauter! So now it
is not difficult for you to know what I think.

Whatever happens you know that I most heartily wish you a happy &
successful career during these musical school-days & then after — well. I
hope the Gods will be as kind to you as (I hope) they should be!

Love from Mrs Bridge
& Yours Ever
FRANK BRIDGE

Britten received a second letter from Samuel:

4, St. Leonards:
Newcastle. Co Down.
20th Aug: 1930

Dear Britten,

Forgive me for not answering you earlier. On the assumption that you had decided to take my advice, I had already fixed it for you to study with Mr. R.O. Morris. I sincerely ask your pardon, if I have been too precipitate about this, and hope you will feel disposed still, to agree to what has been arranged, as I feel that Mr Morris is the very man for you, and particularly calculated to supply you with what you need.

I am off to Canada tomorrow.

Meanwhile, the best of luck to you

Sincerely yours,
HAROLD SAMUEL

On 22 August Britten wrote in his diary,

Have an upsetting letter from H. Samuel, saying that he had already arranged for me to study under R.O. Morris, when we had arranged with Frank Bridge to go under John Ireland.

It was Bridge's advice that Britten finally took, and he began studying with Ireland the following month (see also note 14 to Letter 26). Perhaps it was Ireland who remarked, as reported in 'Opera's New Face', *Time*, 16 February 1948, p. 64, 'I've got a lad under me at the moment who has such an astonishing facility he makes one feel like an old duffer.'

2 However, in his last report from Gresham's, Miss Chapman wrote in the section devoted to Instrumental Music, 'When his intonation improves he will be a very useful viola player.'

24 To Mr and Mrs R.V. Britten

Farfield, Holt, Norfolk.
July 20th, 1930.

My darling Parents,

Isn't it simply marvellous – there are only ten days until the day when I return to Lowestoft. I am getting so excited that I don't know what to do. You are coming to fetch me, arn't you! You see I have such tons of things to bring – ranging from French grammars to sheets.

Nothing worth recording has happened since I last wrote, except rain. The rain here has been simply frightful, interspersed with patches of luke-warm sunshine. In the house matches yesterday, in the whole afternoon and two hours after tea, only one & a quarter hours of play were possible, and that, on a horrible wicket. By-the-way, I am playing for the first house XI – no, it <u>isn't</u> because hundreds of people are absent – there is only one boy who would have played, & even then I think I would have been in. I am frightfully bucked, because it is rather hard to get into the 1st XI of a house here, of a house of about fifty.

About the exam., I would rather not talk. I have done horribly badly in practically every paper, and have had the frightful mortification of hearing boys talk about the <u>easiness</u> of the papers! We are just half way through the exams., and have by far the hardest ones to come. However, in five days, it will all be over; although it will be ages before I have my fears confirmed by the result of the exam.[1]

I am going out to tea this afternoon with Miss Chapman, the violin mistress. I am going to play Vln. & Pft. sonatas with her, as I did once earlier on in the term. It is really great fun, as she is very good, and has an excellent technique, if not much else.

There is no more news, and so I will shut up now. I hope that everything is going well at Lowestoft – that you are having better weather than we, poor, soaked wretches here. I suppose that tennis, certainly on grass, is out of the question for Beth.

Please give my love to her, I hope she's well – oh, I'd forgotten she's gone away. I'm afraid I have not got time to write to her, so give her my love, when you next write, please.

I do hope you two are frightfully well.

Your very loving & grateful son,

BENJAMIN

P.S.   By-the-way, do you want me to bring my deck-chair home? It's in perfect condition, if that makes any difference.

1 Britten's diary for the period documents both his exams and his anxieties:

14 July
The School cert. exams. begin. We have Geography (world) to-day, 9.15–11.15. It is not as bad as I expected tho' I cannot hope to have passed. I have no more exams. to-day, but spend my time slaving at revision. [. . .]

15 July
[. . .] History exam in morning & German Comp & Story in evening, in which I do terribly. It appears that it was fairly moderate but I lost my head – and there's one pass gone bang!

16 July
I have only one exam to-day – English books (Chaucer (Pardoner's & Nun's Priests Tale, Shakespeare Richard II), from 2.30–5.0 It is not too bad tho' very long. [. . .]

17 July
I have 2 exams (Essay & German Trans [Translation] & Dict. [Dictation]) I come out of 1st about 10. mins before the end feeling frightfully giddy. In aft. I have temp of 99°, but I go into the German exam and don't do too badly. [. . .]

18 July
[. . .] I have another exam: French Dict & trans. I did not do well in it, but I hope that I scrape through (pass i.e.) [. . .]

21 July
Elementary Maths 11.0–1.0, French story & comp 2.30–4.45. I do frightfully badly in Elem. Maths, dizziness comes on badly in last ½ hr. I have given up hope even for a pass now. French not too bad. [. . .]

22 July
We have three exams today, European History, Elementary Maths II, Précis writing, at 8.30–10.30, 11.0–1.0, 2.30–4.0. respectively. I don't do too badly, tho' I don't like to think of the final result. [. . .]

23 July
Last exam that really matters Elementary Maths III, 11.0–1.0. I don't do too badly. There is only Geography now & I can't hope to pass in that. [. . .]

24 July
I have my last exam. in morning – Geography B in which I could scarcely do a thing. I dare not hope for a pass in the exam, although I have done better than I expected. [. . .]

25 July
There is only the General Knowledge Paper in the morning. [. . .]

His anxiety about failing the School Certificate was ill-founded:

4 September
I hear from Bazil [Basil Reeve, see note 2 to Diary for 1 January 1931], that I have passed my School cert. He saw it in the E.D.P. [*Eastern Daily Press*] besides seeing that he'd passed the higher. I'm relieved but I did not expect it in the least. [. . .]

5 September
I hear on a P.C. [postcard] from G.R.T. [Thompson] that I have passed School cert. with 5 credits. It is simply extraordinary the luck I am having now. [. . .]

College Years
1930–1933

Chronology: 1930–1933

Year	Events	Compositions
1930	*22 September*: Enters Royal College of Music. Composition lessons with John Ireland. Piano lessons with Arthur Benjamin. Lodges at 51 Prince's Square, Bayswater, London W2	
1931	*5 January*: First performance of *A Hymn to the Virgin* and 'I saw three ships', Lowestoft Musical Society *July*: Wins Ernest Farrar Prize for composition *September*: Moves to rooms at 173 Cromwell Road, SW5, with his sister Beth	*February–March*: *Thy King's Birthday*, for soprano, alto and chorus *April–May*: *Twelve Variations on a Theme*, for piano *May–June*: String Quartet in D
1932	*22 July*: Awarded the Cobbett Prize for *Phantasy* Quintet *12 December*: First performance of the Three Two-part Songs (Macnaghten–Lemare Concert)	*January*: Two Psalms (130 and 150), for chorus and orchestra *January–February*: *Phantasy* in F minor, for string quintet *February*: Three Two-part Songs (de la Mare), first published composition (OUP) *June–July*: *Sinfonietta*, Op. 1 *September–October*: *Phantasy*, Op. 2
1933	*31 January*: First performance of *Sinfonietta* (Macnaghten–Lemare Concert) *February*: Begins composition of *Alla Quartetto Serioso*: 'Go play, boy, play' (four out of five movements completed by December) *17 February*: First broadcast performance of the *Phantasy* Quintet by the Mangeot Ensemble *16 March*: Conducts the *Sinfonietta* at a College Chamber Concert	*February*: *Alla Marcia*, for string quartet *May*: *A Boy was Born*, Op. 3 *June*: Two Part-songs (G. Wither and R. Graves): Boosey & Hawkes publish Britten for the first time

Year	Events	Compositions
	July: BBC tries out *A Boy was Born*. Wins the Ernest Farrar composition prize for a second time *6 August*: First performance of the *Phantasy*, Op. 2 (BBC broadcast) *15 September*: BBC broadcast the *Sinfonietta* *11 December*: Three movements from *Alla Quartetto Serioso* and the Two Part-songs performed at a Macnaghten–Lemare Concert *13 December*: Passes ARCM examination and leaves the College. Returns to Lowestoft to live	

25 To Mr and Mrs R.V. Britten

51, Prince's Square, W.2.[1]
Sept. 24th, 1930.

Dearest and best-beloved Parents,

I don't know if you will receive this before you go. I am terribly sorry that I didn't write before to-day, but I was at the College the whole day except ½ hour for lunch.

This is a topping place to live in. Everyone is ever so nice, and with the two foreign men, it isn't at all dull. Miss Monday-Tuesday[2] is very nice & very kind. I hope that you arrived safely Mama, & had a good journey, also that, after the tiringness of the long journey, the Committee meeting was successful.

The concert was very nice last nice [night], with Howard Ferguson;[3] he is a very nice boy, and he payed for my ticket (3/-) not even allowing me to pay for the programme. We came out at half-time, and I wasn't very sorry (i) because the seats were very hard, and one of the works was very long (ii) the second part was all Elgar.

Miss Brock[4] is still going strong, Mummy. She means well, tho', and is very pleasant.

I have just come back (into the drawing room) from having a long talk on the telephone with your eldest daughter. She is very good and keeps on ringing up, and seeing how I am. I don't mind the telephone at all now, tho' when the dog begins barking, or the door is opened and the dulcet tones of the traffic come through, I find it hard to hear.

I must stop now, as Stein song[5] has been put on the German's gramophone, and I cannot write with that on.

Mr. Benjamin is very nice,[6] but says that if I wish to take Pft. seriously, I must practise 4 hrs. a day; – however we will discuss that on Friday.

Good-bye darlings, this is very nice here. Thank you very much for letting me come. I hope you are both as well as I am.

Your loving & grateful son,
BENJAMIN

P.S.   If you haven't left before this arrives, could you possibly bring my tennis racket and shoes? There is some possibility of tennis soon.

1 This boarding house, run by Miss Thurlow Prior, was Britten's first London address, to which he moved on 20 September 1930, for the start of his first term at the College on the 22nd. On the day of the move, a Saturday, he wrote in his diary, 'It is rather a nice place but rather full of old ladies. A respectable boarding house'. On the 22nd he added: 'Find out that a Miss Prior (who lives here) is a member of the National Chorus & knew Mummy at Lowestoft.'

2 Presumably Miss Prior.

3 Howard Ferguson (b. 1908, Belfast), British composer, pianist and musicologist. Harold Samuel was impressed by Ferguson's talent when aged thirteen and undertook his musical education. He studied at the College from 1925, where his composition teacher was R.O. Morris (this must have influenced Samuel's recommendation of Morris to Britten in 1930) and continued piano lessons with Samuel privately, whose executor he was to become. He was known to the Bridges (see PFL, plates 47 and 55) and it was probably through this circle of musicians that Britten came to know him. Britten wrote in his diary on 9 October, 'I go to dinner [. . .] with Howard Ferguson; jolly nice time. He plays me his Symphony, which I like immensely. Also go through Ravel trio & some of my things'. (See also Diary for 5 June 1931.) Ferguson and Britten remained friends. He later collaborated with Britten as a performer in the score Britten wrote for the GPO Film Unit's documentaries, *The King's Stamp* (1935), see note 1 to Letter 69, and *Coal Face* (1935), see note 2 to Letter 121, in which the piano-duet part was played by Ferguson and the composer. See also Alan Ridout (ed.), *The Music of Howard Ferguson*, (London, Thames, 1989).

The concert was a Prom at the Queen's Hall, London. The programme comprised Humperdinck's Introduction to Act II from *Königskinder* (1897); Mozart's Piano Concerto in B flat, K. 456 (Kathleen Long, piano); Mahler's Symphony No. 4 (Elsie Suddaby, soprano); Elgar's *Wand of Youth* Suite No. 1 (1907) and his arrangement (1923) of Handel's Overture in D minor, conducted by Henry Wood. It seems as if Britten's enthusiasm for Mahler at this stage was not sufficient to make him disregard the uncomfortable seats. 'Mahler 4th. Much too long, but beautiful in [?] parts' (Diary for 23 September).

4 A fellow lodger.

5 A drinking song (*Stein* = the large stoneware tankard from which beer is quaffed). The song to which Britten refers was quite probably the University of Maine's 'Stein Song' which Rudy Vallee, the celebrated crooner, made popular, written and composed by Emil Fenstead and Lincoln Colcord. In Ellery Queen's admirable thriller, *The Finishing Stroke* (Harmondsworth, Penguin Books, 1967), p. 177,

the song is introduced to provide a touch of authentic colour to an impromptu entertainment given (supposedly) on 5 January 1930: '[. . .] even Dr. Samson Dark performed, bringing down the house with an uncanny nasal imitation of Rudy Vallee singing the Maine "Stein Song".'

6 Arthur Benjamin (1893–1960), Australian–English composer and pianist. He joined the staff of the College in 1926 and was Britten's piano teacher 1930–33. Britten's *Holiday Diary*, Op. 5, for solo piano, was dedicated to Benjamin. (See also Letter 58.) From an entry in Britten's diary on 3 December, it seems clear that at this stage in his career he saw his prowess as a pianist earning him the livelihood he would need to support his commitment to composing: 'Benjamin although quite pleased, says that I am not built for a solo pianist – how I am going to make my pennies Heaven only knows.' The piano, not surprisingly, played a significant role in Britten's compositional efforts at this time. Two weeks after this letter was written he embarked, on 6 October, on sketching a Rondo Concertante for piano and strings (abandoned later in the month and left unfinished), the first subject of the first movement of which he took from an incomplete piece for two pianos that he had been working on in August.

26 To Mr and Mrs R.V. Britten

51, Prince's Square, W.2.
Oct. 26th, 1930.

My darling Parents,

   I am just back from a concert and am so mad that I can scarcely keep still. The cause is that there up above,[1] which was last on the programme (I shall not tell you the name of the culprit – you can tap the table & play the bit over on the piano, Mummy). I saw the marvellous programme of the concert (including a Brahm's Symphony) and I simply had to go this afternoon to the Albert Hall to hear the London Symphony Orchestra under Mengelberg.[2] The Hendersons[3] were going with me, but went out with a cousin at the last moment & so I went alone. I sat next to a foreign (sounded like Russian or something) woman, who talked to me at the end of some of the items. I think she is some famous dancer, because she said she'd danced with Ida Rubenstein who was mentioned in the programme. She annoyed me intensely, by saying that the Brahms was fit only for the seventeenth century. I replied by saying that it would be fit for the thirtieth. It was a marvellous concert – I wish you'd been there to hear the

Mummy. I ran across the park in record time after it.

After all that.

How are you both? I do hope you are as well as I am.

Barbara as I suppose you know is away for the week end. She is coming to a concert with me on next Tuesday – I have had 12/- tickets, front row, given me, by one of the Miss Atkinsons,[4] who is private secretary to some musical man. It is a violin recital – Balaković[5] or some name like that, and ought to be rather good.

I went to Church this morning and heard the Bish. of Kensington, who really was jolly fine. I went with the younger Henderson & May Prior, to St. Jame's(?) Paddington.

Thank you very much for your letter, the programme, & for returning the score so soon, Mummy. I am jolly glad you enjoyed the concert, and hope you enjoyed the Friday night as well.

I went to see Ruth[6] on Friday after tea, only she was out, and I haven't had time to go again since. However I was informed by the maid that Mrs. Hempson[7] was "going better", & that Pat was well. On the way back, I called on Mrs. Bridge. Frank had to postpone his voyage[8] for ten days or more, because of a bad knee. Now he is having the most magnificent reception, and everyone is thrilled with him!

Isn't it literally <u>wicked</u> that England's premier composer has to go out of the country (not only to U.S.A. but to Europe) to have any recognition what-so-jolly-well-ever?

Everyone is seething with excitement about the bye-election here.[9] I haven't been to any meetings but apparently they are very rough and extraordinarily noisy. The trouble is that no one knows who to vote for, there being 3 conservative candidates. In this little house, where every one is a die hard conservative (so much so that I feel I shall soon become a literal Bolshy), there are endless squabbles about it.

I went to the Theatre on Saturday afternoon with the Hendersons, and a Friend. We had meant to go to Kew, but so disgusting was the weather that we retreated to the gallery of the Appollo (Apollo?), to see the "Outsider".[10] It was magnificent – it is natural that I should say that, as every play I have seen is that; but experienced play-goers like Miss Prior say it's magnificent.

There is no mystery in how I got to know of the Carlyle thingumajigs,[11] and to Play. Barbara was asked when first there if she knew of anyone, but she kept discreetly silent, feeling that being new she wouldn't like to push. The next time there was still no one, and so I volunteered; so that's what happened, Mummy. They are very bad though; not a patch on the Madrigals,[12] who are really jolly good.

About next week end, I should adore to come; but shall I come on Saturday morning with your daughter or on Friday night alone? Anyway she's got to go back on Sunday night; and I can't do that, can I? What do you think?

I really must stop now. I hope that Mr. Sewell[13] will be satisfactory.

Please give my love to Beth. She'd better come up here and go to some concerts!! How's Caesar; give him my love. Ireland[14] & Benjamin are very nice still. The former is still terribly strict & I am plodding through Counterpoint & Palestrina at the moment. I played much better at my pft. lesson last week, thank heavens. He [Benjamin] was quite pleased, I think. By-the-way, I have spend 25/- on music (compulsory) since I came back a fortnight ago; isn't it frightful!

Also by-the-way (I shall never finish this letter) I have been let into the Madrigal Society for 10/6. Can I keep the extra 10/-, as I am terribly short because of the music?

Now really, I'm going to stop. I hope you are really absolutley well, in spite of this horribly cold weather. I am tiptop, in that respect.

Your very loving & grateful, & yearning-
for-next-week-end son,

BENJAMIN

1 Britten writes out the tune of Ravel's *Bolero*, the last item on the programme of the concert he had attended in the afternoon of the day on which he wrote this letter home. The rest of the programme consisted of Weber's *Freischütz* overture, Brahms's Third Symphony and Saint-Saëns's Second Piano Concerto.

2 Willem Mengelberg (1871–1951), conductor of the Concertgebouw Orchestra, Amsterdam.

3 Nora and 'Tumpty' Henderson were fellow lodgers.

4 Fellow lodgers at Prince's Square. The elder Miss Atkinson, the 'private secretary to some musical man', worked at Hill's, the famous violin dealers.

5 Zlatko Baloković, the Yugoslavian violinist. Britten's diary for 28 October gives us the details of the programme at the Queen's Hall:

> The recital was jolly good – the brilliant pieces (Paganini Concerto in D, & short modern pieces) far excelling in my mind the greater stuff (Tartini g min & Brahms D min Sonatas). V. enjoyable tho'.

6 Ruth Turner (née Hempson), a family friend from Lowestoft.

7 Ruth Turner's mother.

8 To the USA, for performances of his Piano Trio (1929) given under the auspices of the Coolidge Foundation. The work was published by Augener in 1930 and was dedicated to Elizabeth Sprague Coolidge. It had been first performed in London on 4 November 1929 by Antonio Brosa (see note 6 to Diary for 25 January 1931), Anthony Pini, and Harriet Cohen. It was given as part of the Coolidge Festival of Chamber Music, in Chicago, on 13 October 1930. The Coolidge and Brosa connections were later to become of much importance to Britten. See Letter 206 et seq.

9 A by-election was held in October 1930 in the constituency of Paddington South, following the death of the sitting Member, Commodore H. Douglas King. Vice-Admiral E.A. Taylor (Unionist) was elected.

10 A play by Dorothy Brandon, the first night of which had taken place on 3 October.

11 The Carlyle Singers, of which Barbara Britten was a member. Britten was asked 'to play' (i.e. to accompany) and had first attended a rehearsal of the group on 20 October.

12 The English Madrigal Choir, founded in 1929 and conducted until its demise in 1940 by Arnold Foster (1896–1963), English conductor, composer and educationalist. He was a pupil of Vaughan Williams at the College from whom he derived an interest in folksong. Between 1926 and 1961 he taught music at Westminster School, London; he was appointed director of music in 1939. It was this choir of which Britten (bass) and his sister Barbara (soprano) were members from 1930 to 1933.

13 Laurence Alleine Sewell LDS, RCS(Eng), became Mr Britten's assistant at the dental practice in November 1930. Britten recorded in his diary for 2 November: 'Mr. Sewell, new assistant to Pop, comes to supper at 8.0. He's quite nice.' By 1933 Sewell had become a partner. After Mr Britten's death in April 1934 (see Letters 46–8, and note 2

to Letter 136) Sewell bought the practice but retained the name of 'Britten and Sewell', an indication of Mr Britten's considerable reputation in Lowestoft.

14 John Ireland (1879–1962), English composer and teacher. He lived at 14a Gunter Grove, Chelsea, London SW10, after which the first of his piano pieces, 'Chelsea Reach', from *London Pieces*, 1917–20, was named. He taught composition at the College from 1923 to 1939; among his pupils were Alan Bush (see note 1 to Letter 87), E.J. Moeran (see note 6 to Letter 89) and Humphrey Searle. He was on the left of the political spectrum. An exercise Ireland required of Britten during his first term was a Mass in 4 parts in the style of Palestrina, which was begun on 4 October and completed on 16 January 1931. In a letter written on 23 March 1954, Ireland answered a question about his 'influence' as a teacher on Britten:

Although he is supposed to have studied with Frank Bridge, actually, Bridge told me he had not given him lessons [*sic*]. With me he spent a good deal of time over counterpoint, fugue & allied subjects before I let him loose, so to speak, to go his own way. I do not think he was influenced in matters of style by either Bridge or myself. He has had a most extraordinarily successful career, being now only about forty, at which age Elgar was only beginning to meet with recognition. But conditions have changed entirely since the days when Vaughan Williams, Holst, Bridge, myself and others were fellow students with Stanford . . .

From Britten's point of view, his studies with Ireland were not without difficulties (see, for example, Diary for 22 October 1931, 22 January 1932 and 12 February 1932). At one stage Bridge wrote about these problems to the Director of the College, Sir Hugh Allen, on his former pupil's behalf. Indeed, after suggesting that Britten's father ought to write a 'tactful letter' to Ireland rather than Allen, in December 1932, Bridge himself confronted Ireland with Britten's dissatisfaction about his teaching. A letter Bridge wrote to his former pupil on 4 January 1933 spells out the difficulties of the situation:

Telephone & J.I this morning – somewhere in the country – having just received the 'air-balloon' from Lowestoft. (I wouldn't have been surprised if he had said I had written the letter – but he didn't.) Sundry cross-questioning & other quasi-diplomatic conversations eventually led to the point of my saying that:– had I been in your shoes at the Ballet Club Concert [see Diary for 12 December 1932] I should have been as much hurt as you at not being spoken to. This produced protestations of all kinds. Then having decided that this was hardly enough to produce the 'air-balloon', I said that I had always thought it was objectionable for pupils at the R.C.M. being left for a whole fortnight whilst the prof. went off Ass. Boarding [examining for the Associated Board] but that this should be followed by another wk's lesson being thrown over for a rehearsal of a Violin Sonata was a fairly sickening experience. I tell you this because you should know what was said – plus this, or words to this effect, that we were your devoted friends & that it was obvious we should know of your major & minor problems whenever they arose. As you will see, I could hardly pretend that I knew of <u>nothing</u> which might have been objected to by you & so <u>that</u> much came out.

Britten's and Ireland's paths did not often cross in later years, but Wulff Scherchen recalled (in 1988) one encounter:

I am reminded of walking across a London square with Ben, and the two of us catching up with John Ireland, who was in the slough of despair because inspiration was failing him. With youthful incomprehension I later commented to Ben what a moaning misery he had been, only to be sharply taken to task for a lack of imagination and understanding.

A remark Britten made in later life to Joseph Cooper (who had worked alongside Britten at the GPO Film Unit) during a BBC broadcast, *The Composer Speaks*, suggests that Britten recognized in retrospect that he may have misunderstood Ireland's methods. Recalling his days at the College Britten remarked: 'They [Ireland and Benjamin] were both very kind to me and really nursed me very gently through a very, very difficult musical adolescence, which I was going through at that time.' (See Joseph Cooper, *Facing the Music: an autobiography* (London, Weidenfeld and Nicolson, 1979), p. 156.)

Thursday, 1 January 1931

[*Lowestoft*]

I to practise for Saturday (Bach 2ble Concerto) with Charles Coleman[1] & Bazil Reeve[2] at the Colemans at 9.15 as the C's go off to Norwich early. Then walk up to Morlings[3] with Bazil to try a pft. for Monday's concert.[4] Go with Beth (Bobby & Marjorie also go) to the pantomime (Aladdin) at the Marina[5] at the Chartres[6] invitation (26 there), & tea at Wallers[7] after. Back at 6.30. Bobby & M. go to Arnolds[8] after dinner. I finish my Sanctus for J. Ireland.

1 Charles Coleman (b. 1910), the son of C.J.R. Coleman, the organist of St John's Church, Lowestoft (see note 3 to Letter 18), and boyhood friend of Britten's. Coleman was a talented violinist, skilled enough, it seems, to have attempted one of the solo parts of Bach's Concerto in D minor for two violins (BWV 1043). On this occasion Britten took the other solo part, with Basil Reeve at the piano. Coleman was later ordained.

2 Basil Reeve (b. 1912), the son of Revd William Ernest Reeve, BD, Vicar of St John's (1925–36), who lived at 17 Esplanade, Lowestoft. Reeve, who became a skilful pianist, was Britten's closest friend during this period: they played a great quantity of music together.

In an interview (with Donald Mitchell, 3 October 1986, London;

Archive), Dr Reeve – a physician – remembers in some considerable detail his piano-playing sessions with Britten. He had no training himself, apart from three months' music lessons with Miss Astle –

. . . otherwise all the training I ever had was through this close association with Ben . . . I don't know how old he was. Maybe he was thirteen. He started playing the viola . . . he could transpose, and so at that time, maybe this was a year or so after we first met, we could play viola sonatas, cello sonatas, violin sonatas . . . Beethoven, Mozart a bit – funny, we never played Haydn, when we should've done, but we didn't. And then there was another boy, who . . . played the violin [Charles Coleman] and after maybe a year or so – somewhere quite early on – we started playing the Schubert Trios. Maybe we were fourteen, fifteen, something like that, and we used to spend a lot of time practising these and that wonderful B flat Trio, we played that quite a lot . . . Now then, also, somewhere about this time Ben . . . got interested in Brahms . . . Mrs Britten . . . started taking us up to Morlings and we could play two-piano music . . . Ben was absolutely mad about Brahms and he was incredibly interested, I remember . . . And he arranged the fourth movement – the last movement of the 4th symphony – for two pianos. [The beginning of the arrangement – 'Hard work, but experience' – is recorded in Britten's diary on 4 September 1930.] We used to go up and play that at Morlings.

It is significant that it was the passacaglia finale of the Brahms that fascinated the youth who was to become a distinctly passacaglia-minded composer. By June 1935, however, the symphony had become 'anathema' to him. See Diary for 20 April 1932.

Dr Reeve also recalled performances at two pianos of Beethoven's Third and 'Emperor' Piano Concertos and the play-through of Walton's Viola Concerto mentioned in the Diary for 15 September 1931, with Reeve at the piano: 'You see, *he* was a fantastic sight reader . . . I wasn't in his class, but because I had to, I became a very good sight reader.'

3   Ernest Jabez Morling, music retailer, 149 London Road North, Lowestoft. The shop also hired out pianos. In response to a letter from one of the daughters of the original proprietor, Miss M.E. Morling, Britten wrote in 1975:

I was most interested to read [your letter], and it reminded me again of the many times when I, as a child, walked from my home to play gramophone records of music which I wanted to hear, in your shop. Your father (?grandfather) was most helpful and long suffering with a probably very unreasonable little boy.

4   See Diary for 5 January 1931.

5   The Marina Theatre, Lowestoft, which later became a cinema and was destroyed by bombing during the Second World War.

6   The family of Frederick W.C. Chartres, Willingham St Mary, Beccles,

Suffolk. Chartres was Agent for the estates of Michael E. St John Barnes and Thomas Meakin Farmiloe.

7 Wallers, a small restaurant in Lowestoft.

8 Arnolds Ltd, drapers, 95, 97a and 100 London Road North, Lowestoft. The Arnolds were friends of the Britten family.

Saturday, 3 January 1931

Practise at 11.45 at the Colemans with Charles & Bazil. Musical Evening at 8.0. Chief Attraction – Mr. Voke's[1] singing. He sings esp. well Boris' Monologue (twice).[2] About 30 altogether came. We try my W.S. Blunt Song[3] for Sops. & Altos – utter failure. People terrified by accidentals and manuscript (copied by Aunt Q[4] – & self). Play Bach 2ble concerto. Mozart Sonata in D[5]

Merry Andrew,[6] etc.

1 Leon Charles Voke (b. 1900), American bass, who had shown Britten and his mother round the College on his first day there as a student on 22 September 1930. Voke studied at the College, 1927–31. He and his wife were friends of the Britten family and Mr Voke took part in the solo quartet in the first performance of *A Hymn to the Virgin* (see note 2 to Diary for 5 January 1931). The soprano soloist was Mrs Britten. Voke had also privately performed one of Britten's early settings of de la Mare, 'Vigil' (composed 23 December 1930), which the composer dedicated to him. Britten's diary for 28 December 1930 reads: '[. . .] Mr. V. sings my Vigil most beautifully. I like it now.'

2 'I have attained the highest power', from Act II of Mussorgsky's opera, *Boris Godunov*.

3 An unpublished setting of 'O fly not, Pleasure, pleasant-hearted Pleasure' (words by the English poet, Wilfred Scawen Blunt (1840–1922)) for two-part women's voices and piano. It was composed on 11 July 1930 in the sanatorium at Gresham's, when Britten was recovering from a feverish cold. The composition sketch and manuscript vocal parts (duplicated by the use of carbon paper) are in the Archive. In some manuscript vocal parts the Blunt setting is followed by 'I saw three witches' (Walter de la Mare), composed on 5 November 1930; Britten evidently thought of the settings as a pair.

4 Aunt Queenie.

5 K. 311.

6 John Ireland's piano piece, composed in 1918.

Monday, 5 January 1931

Do a good deal of counterp't in the morning, & walk with Beth afterwards. I go down to the church all the time practically in the afternoon, to go through the "Prayer",[1] & to arrange the chairs etc. Walk with Pop after tea. The concert goes quite well; my things are quite well done (the 2nd better than rehearsal) the Prayer also not too badly done – it's an absolute marvel. Rest of programme[2] – carols & very good organ solos by Mr. Coleman.

1   *A Prayer*, words by Thomas à Kempis, composed by Frank Bridge in March 1916, for chorus and orchestra. It was first performed in January 1919, in London, conducted by the composer. This performance by the Lowestoft Musical Society in St John's Church was accompanied by Britten (piano) and Ernest Tuttle (organ). Britten's annotated vocal score, formerly in the possession of Henry Boys, is now in the Archive.

2   The full programme of the 'Organ and Vocal Recital' was as follows:

1) Organ Solo	Toccata and Fugue in D minor	J.S. Bach
2) Carols	a) 'Past Three o'clock'	
	b) 'The Holly and the Ivy'	arr. Geoffrey Shaw
3) Organ Solo	Offertoire sur deux Noëls	Alexandre Guilmant
4) Two Choral Songs	a) 'A Hymn to the Virgin'	
	b) 'I saw three ships'	E. Benjamin Britten
5) Carol	'How far is it to Bethlehem?'	Geoffrey Shaw
6) Hymn	'Hark! the herald angels sing'	
7) 'A Prayer'		Frank Bridge
8) Organ Solo	Serenata	W. Wolstenholme
9) Carols	a) 'In dulci jubilo'	R.L. Pearsall
	b) 'The Carol of Bells on New Year's Eve'	A. M. Goodheart

These first performances of *A Hymn to the Virgin* and 'I saw three ships' were reported in the *Lowestoft Journal*, 10 January, p. 7:

The Lowestoft Musical Society presented a pleasing programme of carols and organ music at St. John's Church on Monday evening, and it was notable by reason of the fact that a young local composer, E. Benjamin Britten, aged 17, son of Mr. R.V. Britten, 21, Kirkley Cliff Road, South Lowestoft, provided the choral setting to two old carols. These were 'A Hymn to the Virgin' and the quaint 'I saw three ships'. The words of the first named are a mixture of Latin, and a kind of Chaucerian English, or something similar, and it was evident the pronunciation of some of the weird words puzzled the singers. The music of the composition was tuneful and pleasing, with a refined delicacy which demands careful treatment. In the other the spirit of the words is fully caught by delightful harmony. The Society's chorus did fairly well in both, and it is hoped that on another occasion more works will be heard from the pen of this young musician.

The performance was conducted by C.J.R. Coleman.

A Hymn to the Virgin was composed on 9 July 1930 during Britten's final term at Gresham's, and like the Wilfred Blunt setting (see note 3 to Diary for 3 January 1931) was written from bed in the school sanatorium. Britten made further adjustments to it in September of that year, and also composed a companion 'Choral song', 'I saw three ships'.

Britten revised the *Hymn* in April 1934, and it was published by Boosey & Hawkes (Winthrop Rogers Church Choral Series) in 1935. Also in April he attempted to revise 'I saw three ships' but without success. The carol was finally revised as *The Sycamore Tree* in November 1967 and first performed in its new version by the Ambrosian Singers, conducted by Philip Ledger, on 19 June 1968. It was published by Faber Music the same year.

Tuesday, 6 January 1931

The reporter of the E. Anglian Daily Times rings up to know about my songs! Scream!! Walk around the golf course with Aunt Q. while Beth has a golf lesson 12–1. Work at Agnus Dei II[1] (Canon) & cp't all the afternoon. Play 2 pft duets with Bazil at Morlings 5–6. It's ghastly to think of tomorrow – of course London's marvellous but home's so good.

1 See note 14 to Letter 26.

Wednesday, 7 January 1931

[*Lowestoft/London*]

I see the E. Anglian in morning: there is a long article & photo![1] Pack all the morning, or rather Beth does most of it. She takes me down to the station with Mummy in the car to catch the 2.31 to London. It is foul coming back – not to the College – but to this place – not really that I don't like it, but home is so beastly nice. Barbara meets me, & comes in taxi with me as far as Victoria.

Unpack all the evening. The Hendersons are still away, tho' Mr Skelton's[2] here.

1 The article, entitled 'Composer at 17 – Lowestoft Youth's Choral Songs' (*East Anglian Daily Times*, 7 January) is reproduced below. The photograph which accompanied this article, of Britten aged nine years and ten months, appears in PFL, plate 24.

2 A fellow lodger.

COMPOSER AT 17.

LOWESTOFT YOUTH'S CHORAL SONGS.

CAROL RECITAL BY MUSICAL SOCIETY MEMBERS.

Two choral-songs which form the basis of an extremely promising career, and to which music has been composed by E. Benjamin Britten, the 17-year-old son of Mr. R. V. Britten of 21, Kirkley Cliff Road, South Lowestoft, were heard by the public for the first time on Monday evening at St. John's Church, Lowestoft, when they were featured in the programme of an organ and vocal recital given by the members of the local Musical Society. Unfortunately, the chorus was rather disappointing in the renderings of the pieces, both of which, however, demand much from the singers, and require delicate treatment.

Last June, the young composer won the open composition scholarship of the Royal College of Music, and he has already written a large number of varied pieces, commencing at the early age of five years, and concentrating in particular on chamber music. He has studied under Frank Bridge, and is now being tutored by John Ireland.

Of the two songs heard on Monday, the first, "A hymn to the Virgin," was the better rendered, despite the difficulty occasioned the singers by reason of the quaint mingling of medieval English and Latin, as instanced in the lines:

All this world was for-lore Eva peccatrice,
Tyl our Lord was y-bore De te genetrice.

The solemnity of the composition was well interpreted, and, on the whole, the rendering was quite impressive, although much more might have been made of such a beautiful song.

"I saw three ships" provides a happy contrast with its joyful air, and was sung with organ accompaniment. But the attack of the chorus was ragged at times, and the rhythm was not sustained, with the result that the song was robbed of much of the charm it obviously possesses.

This was the first time that the Society, which has a fine record dating back over half-a-century, had included a number of carols in their programme, and St. John's Church thus provided a fitting setting to the recital. The members opened their evening's repertoire with Geoffrey Shaw's arrangement of "Past Three O'clock," in which they were at their best. Augmented by Mr. Leon C. Voke, who ably took the bass solos, the chorus proved itself to be well balanced, despite the preponderance of female voices which remains in the Society, and there was a pleasing blending of the various sections of the choir in a really creditable performance. Although hardly so confidently attacked, "The Holly and the Ivy" was nevertheless well worth hearing, while "How far is it to Bethlehem?" by the same composer, also gave delight to the good audience which filled the main body of the church.

With both pianoforte and organ accompaniment, the members next attempted "A Prayer" (Frank Bridge), but they were not particularly successful, opening well but afterwards losing much of their unity. However, in the two concluding carols "In Dulci Jubilo" (R. L. Pearsall) and "The Carol of Bells on New Year's Eve" (A. M. Goodheart), they were again heard to advantage, a nice conception of light and shade being evinced in the latter rendering, with plenty of tuneful vigour where necessary. On the whole, the recital, so far as the singers were concerned, was quite satisfactory, and thoroughly deserved the patronage accorded it.

Interspersing the vocal numbers were a number of beautifully-executed organ solos by Mr. C. J. R. Coleman, A.R.C.O., the popular conductor of the Society, who revealed much talent in his playing. W. Wolstenholme's Serenata was especially pleasing, while Bach's Toccata and Fugue in D minor was very sympathetically rendered, much pleasure also being given in the playing of "Offertoire Sur deux Noels" (Alex. Guilmant).

Mr. Ernest Tuttle provided the organ accompaniment, and Mr. Britten was at the piano. A collection was taken for the Society during the singing of the hymn, "Hark! the herald angels sing."

Next month "The Spectre's Bride" (Dvorak) is to be performed by the Society.

The Vicar (the Rev. W. F. Jones) presided, and at the conclusion recited special prayers for the Royal Family in its bereavement.

East Anglian Daily Times, 7 January 1931

Friday, 9 January 1931
[*London*]

Practise in morning & afternoon (11.30–12.20 & 2.15–4.15) –
Beethoven Sonata in G. (op. 49?).[1] L'st Movement & Schumann
"Pappillons".[2] Write up to 11.30. Go to Dinner with Barbara,
arriving at her flat at 6.0. Listen to the Wireless – especially to a
concert of contemporary music – Schönberg – Heaven only knows!!
I enjoyed his Bach "St Anne"; & quite liked his "Peace on earth"
for Chorus – but his "Erwartung" – ! I could not make head or tail
of it – even less than the "Peace on earth".[3] Back at 10.50.

1 Op. 49, No. 2.
2 Op. 2, for piano.
3 The concert was broadcast from the National Studio, London, by the
   BBC Symphony Orchestra conducted by the composer. Britten refers
   to Schoenberg's arrangement for orchestra of Bach's Prelude and
   Fugue in E flat (BWV 552, orch. 1928); *Friede auf Erden*, for chorus,
   Op. 13 (1907); and *Erwartung*, monodrama, Op. 17 (1909, but not
   performed until 1924). The soloist was the soprano Margot Hinnen-
   berg-Lefebre (1901–1981).

Monday, 12 January 1931

Usual writing & practise during the day. Writing 9.30 & 11.30; I
finish the Agnus Dei II moderately successfully, only looking over
I find hundreds of slips in partwriting (consecutive 5ths esp.). Do
some quite good work at pft. Go down to Augeners[1] to see about
the frame for my Brahms picture, after tea; only it costs 15/- & I
therefore don't get it. Write a small carol (Women's voices & alto)
"Sweet was the Song",[2] after Supper. Hendersons go to theatre.

1 The music publishers, whose London premises, at 18 Great Marlborough Street, included a music shop.
2 This ultimately formed the second movement of a five-movement
   'Christmas Suite' entitled *Thy King's Birthday*, for soprano and alto
   soloists and chorus, completed on 26 March. Britten's composition
   sketch details the chronology of its composition:
   1. 'Christ's Nativity' (Henry Vaughan), 2 March.
   2. 'Sweet was the Song' (William Ballet's 'Lute Book'), 13 January.
   3. 'Preparations' (Christ Church MS, ?17th century), 11 March.
   4. 'New Prince, New Pomp' (Scripture, Robert Southwell), 25 February.

5. 'The Carol of King Cnut' (Charles William Stubbs), 16 February.

Two volumes of poetry acted as the source for the texts: *Christmas Carols*, compiled by D.L. Kelleher, *The Augustan Books of Poetry*, second series, no. 18, London, Ernest Benn, n.d. (movements 1, 2, 4, 5); and *A Christmas Anthology*, *The Augustan Books of Poetry*, London, Ernest Benn, n.d. (movement 3). The former was given to Britten by his elder sister, Barbara, in November 1930; the latter was acquired on 5 March 1931. Both volumes are in the Archive.

In addition to Britten's composition sketch and ink fair-copy, there are a number of discarded sketch pages, including three incomplete movements: 'Thou Little Tiny Child' (1534), 'Be Merry' (*c.*1440), and 'What Cheer? Good Cheer!' (*c.*1500). These words are also to be found in the *Christmas Carols* volume.

Although *Thy King's Birthday* remained unpublished, Britten allowed 'New Prince, New Pomp' to be performed at the 1955 Aldeburgh Festival, by the Purcell Singers (soprano soloist: Rosamund Strode), conducted by Imogen Holst, on 24 June. In 1966 he revised his carol for women's voices, 'Sweet was the Song' (movement 2), and it received its first performance on 15 June 1966 by the Purcell Singers (alto soloist: Pauline Stevens), again conducted by Imogen Holst. The carol was published by Faber Music the same year.

Friday, 16 January 1931

I am writing songs now for Ireland – not necessarily in Palestrinian style.[1] I spend alot of my time this morning searching (for words) as yet unsuccessfully, although I have got some likely ones. Copy the Agnus Dei II out also, which finishes my Mass. Practise 11.30–12.45   2.15–3.30, & then go to College in an unsuccessful attempt to see the Bursar[2] about my extra pft. lesson, which the Director[3] said he'd see about, and about which, so far, nothing's been done. Work in evening. Henderson's out to theatre. Beastly wind.

1 Britten refers to his Mass in the style of Palestrina.

2 Edwin J.N. Polkinhorne (1879–1955), held this administrative post from 1923 until 1946.

3 The Director of the College from 1918 to 1937 was Sir Hugh Percy Allen (1869–1946), English organist, conductor and musical administrator. He was also Professor of Music in the University of Oxford from 1918 until his death in 1946. See note 8 to Letter 73, where Allen's attitude to Britten's wish to study with Berg is discussed.

Tuesday, 20 January 1931

I spend 2 hrs reading poetry solidly, & then write – in desperation – a very short song – "Sport"[1] of W.H. Davies. I don't like it; even less than usual. Practise 11.30–12.30, 2.15–4.15, 5.0–6.0 (the extra hour to make up for some of the time I've missed. I listen to Delius (1st Cuckoo & Summer Night)[2] on Miss Prior's wireless at 8.0 against a background of Jack Payne[4] – even then they were miraculous. He is a wizard.

1 William Henry Davies (1871–1940), English poet. Britten set Davies's anti-hunting poem 'Sport' for bass and piano. The text was taken from Davies's *A Poet's Calendar* (London, Cape, 1927). The poem so closely mirrors Britten's preoccupations that it is worth quoting in full:

> Hunters, hunters,
> Follow the Chase,
> I saw the Fox's eyes,
> Not in his face
> But on it, big with fright –
> Haste, hunters, haste!
>
> Say, hunters, say,
> Is it a noble sport?
> As rats that bite
> Babies in cradle, so,
> Such rats and men
> Take their delight.

In those two verses are not only laid out one of the most important themes of the early masterpiece, *Our Hunting Fathers* (see Letters 85, 86 and 88, and Diary for 20 July 1936), Britten was to write in 1936 with W.H. Auden – the relationship between men and animals – but also a clear reflection of the incident that closed his last term at South Lodge:

At the very last minute he got into disgrace. The subject of the end-of-term essay was 'Animals' and he seized hold of the opportunity to write a passionate protest, not only against hunting, but also against any form of organized cruelty, including war. The school authorities were shocked . . . Such a thing had never been known to happen, and he left South Lodge under a cloud of disapproval.

(See IHB, p. 20.)

2 *On Hearing the First Cuckoo in Spring* and *Summer Night on the River*, two pieces for small orchestra (1912), were broadcast on the London National Programme in a concert given by the BBC Orchestra, conducted by Julian Clifford. The programme also included Handel's

Concerto Grosso in D minor, Op. 6, No. 10; Betty Bannerman (alto) singing 'Malheureux, qu'ai-je fait' and 'Ah, j'ai perdu mon Eurydice' from Gluck's *Orfeo*, and French and Scottish folksongs; and Haydn's Symphony No. 101 in D ('The Clock').

3 Jack Payne and his Orchestra were broadcasting on the London Regional Programme at the same time as the orchestral concert. Clearly some of Britten's fellow lodgers preferred Payne to Delius. The well-known dance-band leader (1899–1969) directed the BBC Dance Orchestra, which was later billed as 'Jack Payne and his Orchestra'. Payne was a household name in the thirties, a decade that, in Albert McCarthy's words, represented

the golden years for the British dance bands, both economically and musically, and some of the leading groups benefited from the very inequalities that disturbed economists and sociologists. Amongst the general population economic distress might be widespread and unemployment figures reaching an all-time high, but the society clientèle who nightly wined, dined and danced at the leading London hotels and night-clubs, preferred to ignore such realities.

(McCarthy, *The Dance Band Era, The Dancing Decades from Ragtime to Swing: 1910–1950* (London, Spring Books, 1974), p. 76.) Payne's signature tune, known to all radio listeners, was 'Say it with Music'.

Britten was to put his experience of dance-band music to good use in the incidental music he wrote in 1939 for *Johnson over Jordan*, the play by J.B. Priestley, in which a central number is a big blues, 'The Spider and the Fly'. See also note 2 to Letter 160, and Letters 163 and 166.

Saturday, 24 January 1931

I go down to Harold Reeves,[1] about 11.30, to get a Mozart Symphony (E♭) that I hope to hear tomorrow. I also get Mahler's Wayfarer songs.[2]

The Hendersons go out to tea. I attempt to do some selecting of poetry (for songs & madrigals) but drop off to sleep, in afternoon! (The wind was terrific last night, & I didn't get much sleep.) Alter my madrigal[3] after tea. Play cards with Tumpty Henderson after tea.

1 A specialist music shop with premises at 210 Shaftesbury Avenue, London WC2. Reeves was also a publisher (on a small scale) of books on music.

2 The *Lieder eines fahrenden Gesellen* ('Songs of a Wayfarer').

3 'Love me not for comely grace' (Anon.) for SSAT, composed 23–4 January 1931.

Sunday, 25 January 1931

Church at 8.0 (Malcolm Sargent[1] takes collection) at St. Matthews, & 11.0 with Tumpty Henderson at Holy Trinity, Paddington. The Hendersons take Miss Gwynne[2] & me to L.S.O. Albert Hall concert & Mengelberg. Mendelssohn Midsummer's night's dream. Mozart Prague Symph [K.504]. Liszt 2nd pft concerto (Vronsky),[3] Wagner Prelude & Finale (Tristan). Quite good, very enjoyable. Go to supper at Bridges & then to B.B.C. Studio (at Waterloo) for Symphony concert which he [Frank Bridge] conducts. Marvellous show. Glinka (Russlan ov.), Mozart K.543 [Symphony in E flat, No. 39]. Miriam Licette[4] in Willow [Song] & Ave Maria (Otello – Verdi), Bridge Poem 2[5] – Magnificent – Tchaik. ov. Rom. & Juliet. Speak to Brosa[6] & Mrs, sit with them & Mrs Bridge. Back by Taxi at 11.30. It was terribly interesting to see everything. Orchestra very good – especially Lauri K.[7] & cellos. & Horns.

1 British conductor (1895–1967). He was to appear as conductor and narrator in *Instruments of the Orchestra* (1946), the original educational film version of Britten's *The Young Person's Guide to the Orchestra*, Op. 34. See also note 7 to Letter 514.

2 A fellow lodger.

3 Vitya (Victoria) Vronsky (b. 1909), Russian pianist. She married the pianist Victor Babin in 1933, and the partnership became a famous two-piano duo.

4 English soprano (1892–1969).

5 The second of two Poems for Orchestra (1915) after Richard Jefferies, *The Story of My Heart*, replacing the advertised Impression for small orchestra, *There is a willow grows aslant a brook* (1927). Paul Hindmarsh in his admirable PHFB, pp. 91–3, appears not to have known of this late change of programme.

6 The first mention in Britten's diary of Antonio Brosa (1894–1979), the Spanish virtuoso violinist, who was closely associated with Bridge and his circle. He had first met Bridge at the 1928 ISCM Festival in Siena and was later to become a close neighbour of the Bridges in Bedford Gardens, London. It was Bridge who brought Brosa and Britten together (see PFL, plates 52–4) and Brosa was to become an important figure in Britten's musical life. See Diary for 19 March 1931

and Letter 213, *passim*. See also Hubert Dawkes and John Tooze in conversation with Antonio Brosa, *R.C.M. Magazine*, 63/3, 1967, pp. 88–92, and 65/1 1969, pp. 8–12.

7 Lauri Kennedy, Australian cellist (b. 1898, d.?). He was a noted soloist and principal cellist in the BBC Symphony, London Philharmonic, and Covent Garden orchestras.

Tuesday, 27 January 1931

I finish my 2nd Madrigal[1] in morning, & start to copy it out after tea. I am more pleased with it than the 1st. Practising at usual times. Miss Prior, Miss Gwynne, & Miss Brock take the 2 Hendersons & me to Drury Lane in evening to see "The Song of the Drum".[2] [. . .] Bobby Howes[3] & his tall companion were absolutely sidesplitting. The dancing & scenary were stupendous. Back only by 12.0.

1 'To the Willow-tree' (Robert Herrick) for SATB, composed 26–7 January 1931. See also note 3 to Diary for 24 January 1931.

2 The musical play by the English librettists, Fred Thompson (1884–1949) and Guy Bolton (1884–1979), with music by Vivian Ellis (b. 1903), English composer (of celebrated musicals), and Hermann Finck (1872–1939).

3 Bobby (Robert William) Howes (1895–1972), English actor, singer and dancer, who starred in numerous musical comedies of the thirties. His 'tall companion' was Peter Haddon.

Wednesday, 28 January 1931

I finish copy of To the Willow-tree, & write a short, unsatisfactory song "Autumn".[1] This I copy out in spare moments, after lunch & tea. Go to College at 2.40 for Pft. lesson. Benjamin seems more pleased, although I play even more abominably than usual. Listen all the evening to Stravinsky concert.[2] Remarkable, puzzling. I quite enjoyed the pft. concerto. Sacre – bewildering & terrifying. I didn't really enjoy it, but I think it's incredibly marvellous & arresting.

1 A setting for voice and string quartet of Walter de la Mare's poem 'Autumn', which was first published in *Poems* (London, Murray, 1906). Britten's copy of the poem may be found in the series *The Augustan Books of Modern Poetry: Walter de la Mare* (London, Ernest

Benn, 1925–6). The volume is inscribed on the front cover: 'Benjamin Britten April 10th 1929.'

2 The programme of this Stravinsky concert, given by the BBC Symphony Orchestra, conducted by Ernest Ansermet, comprised the overture to *Mavra* (1922), Concerto for piano (1923–4), with the composer as soloist, *Apollon musagète* (1927–8), *Four Studies* for orchestra (1928, UK première) and *Le Sacre du printemps* (1911–13).

Saturday, 31 January 1931
[*Lowestoft*]

Write in the morning & then walk with Beth along cliffs; write most of afternoon & then walk with Mummy. Haircut at Priggs[1] at 5.30 & then walk with Pop down to Club.[2] I am writing a choral piece for 8–voices on a bit of Psalm.[3] It's jolly hard to write, & I am certain to find hundreds of consecutives when revising.

1 Bertie Horace Prigg, hairdresser, 261 and 263 London Road South, Lowestoft.
2 Mr Britten was a member of the Royal Norfolk and Suffolk Yacht Club, Royal Plain, Lowestoft. It was his custom to go there on Sundays. See EWB, p. 47.
3 The motet 'O Lord, forsake me not' (words compiled from Psalms 28, 38, 39 and 116) for double chorus, composed 31 January – 10 February 1931.

Friday, 6 February 1931
[*London*]

I practise as usual & write. Go to H. Reeves after tea to get Berlioz Sym. Fantas. Go to Magnificent Harty[1] Concert with Halle Orch. Handel Water Music – Brahm's 1st pft. Concerto (Backhaus)[2] literally thrilling. – What a marvel that first movement is. Berlioz Symphony Fant, which the orchestra played marvellously, it isnt much good as music, but a topping entertainment. Orchestral ensemble topping. Drummer superb. Backhaus was a bit unsympathetic in places, but he brought out the strength of the first movement marvellously. Incredible technique. Audience v. enthusiastic. Back at 11.5. Sat with interesting man (rather blind). Amateur & v. keen!

1 Sir Hamilton Harty (1879–1941), English composer and conductor of the Hallé Orchestra, 1920–33, in Manchester, but on this occasion visiting London. He was knighted in 1925. No doubt it was Harty's own famous arrangement of the Handel that was played.

2 Wilhelm Backhaus (1884–1969), German pianist and noted Beethoven interpreter.

Monday, 9 February 1931

Practise & write as usual. Sammons is practising & writing in the room next to mine in the afternoon.[1] I go to Queen's Hall to get tickets, & Augeners to get my Brahms picture framed after tea. Practise viola after supper, & then as I settle down to write, I notice in Radio Times[2] that Brahms quartet 3 is going to be broadcast by Hungarian S.Q.[3] So I borrow Miss Prior's wireless, & have marvellous $\frac{1}{2}$ hr listening to the purest music in the purest of possible forms. What a marvellous craze for the viola Brahms had! What a humorous theme the last movement has!

1 At the New School of Music which occupied the top floor of Westbourne Hall in Westbourne Grove, West London (the lower floors housed a dancing academy and billiard rooms), and was run by Mr Galsworthy, the son of a cousin of the novelist. It housed practice rooms for the College. Remo Lauricella (see note 1 to Diary for 11 February 1931) recalls Albert Sammons using the School as well as Paul Robeson (see note 3 to Diary for 3 August 1931).

2 The journal published weekly by the BBC which contained detailed advance information of forthcoming broadcasts on the Corporation's national and regional wavelengths. It has appeared virtually without interruption since 30 September 1923.

3 Hungarian String Quartet, not the eminent quartet founded in 1935 by Sándor Végh, but a predecessor of the same name, whose members were Emmerich Waldhuer (violin), Jean de Temesvary (violin), Tivadar Orazagh (viola) and Eugene de Kerpely (cello).

Wednesday, 11 February 1931

Lesson with Benjamin at 2.40. Meet an Italian (?) Violin Scholar[1] at College and arrange to practise duets with him. See Mabel Ritchie,[2] also, & she gives me her address. I listen to B.B.C. concert on Miss Prior's wireless. First half (Schumann, Manfred ov. –

marvellous work – Beethoven 4th concerto (Beautifully played by
Backhaus)) does not come through v. well. 2nd Half – Planets.[3]
These works arn't very much to my taste, but they are v. fine &
clever. Jupiter has some good tunes; Mars v. striking. Altogether,
too much, harp, celesta, Bells etc. Beginning of Saturn & end of
Neptune v. beautiful. Uranus great fun. I suppose they were well
played.

1 Remo Lauricella (b. 1912), English violinist and composer of Italian
   parentage. He won an open scholarship to the College, where he
   was a fellow student of Britten's and took private composition lessons
   from Bridge. Lauricella and Britten, when at the College, played
   together regularly on Tuesday afternoons and covered a wide repertory of violin music. He was a member of the London Philharmonic
   and London Symphony Orchestras for a number of years and also
   worked in South Africa. Britten composed Two Pieces for violin and
   piano for Lauricella. See note 1 to Diary for 7 May 1931, and also
   note 1 to Diary for 6 May 1932.
2 English soprano (1903–1969), who was later known professionally as
   Margaret Ritchie. She was to become a member of the English Opera
   Group and created the roles of Lucia in *The Rape of Lucretia* (1946)
   and Miss Wordsworth in *Albert Herring* (1947). Those roles, indeed,
   were created by Britten with her particular voice and character in
   mind. Britten realized Purcell's *The Blessed Virgin's Expostulation* for
   her and dedicated it to her. See also note 1 to Diary for 13 October
   1931.
3 A concert given by the BBC Symphony Orchestra, with the BBC
   Wireless Chorus, conducted by Adrian Boult, and broadcast from
   the Queen's Hall, London.

Monday, 16 February 1931

I finish my carol[1] in the morning, and also do acres of revision.
Practise at usual times. Go to see Mr. Bridge after tea. He offers
(and then refuses to let me do it, because of eyes) to let me correct
the copied out part of his Concerto Elegioso[2] ('Cello). I should have
loved to have done it. Spend about 1 hr & ¼ hr there. Mrs. Alston[3]
& Miss Fass (?)[4] were there. They are all going to hear Kreisler[5]
tonight. Lucky bounders! Practise Vla after dinner.

1 'The Carol of King Cnut'. See note 2 to Diary for 12 January 1931.
2 *Concerto Elegiaco* was the subtitle of Bridge's *Oration* for cello and
   orchestra, composed in 1929–30 and first performed (a broadcast) on

17 January 1936 (a BBC Contemporary Music Concert) by Florence Hooton (cello) with the BBC Symphony Orchestra conducted by the composer. According to the soloist, Bridge had changed the title of his cello concerto from *Concerto Elegiaco* to *Oration* because it was an outcry against the futility of war (see PHFB, p. 179).

Britten wrote on the occasion of the first performance in his 1936 diary:

> I meet Basil Wright, Basil Reeve & Henry Boys at BBC. at 10.20 for Contemporary concert at which F.B.'s 1930 Oration for 'Cello (Florence Hooton – splendid, young as yet & perhaps abit immature but, with lovely technique & control) & orchestra is played.

3 Audey Alston (1883–1966), English violinist and viola-player, and wife of the Rector of Framingham Earl, near Norwich. She studied at the College (1900–06) where she became a friend of Frank Bridge. Beth Britten writes in EWB, p. 48:

> My mother had a friend, Audrey Alston, who was the wife of a Norfolk parson. She was a very good musician and involved with the musical life in Norwich, where my mother met her. Audrey also had a son John, the same age as Ben, who was a gifted pianist and at eight years old was playing the organ in his father's church, and this was a bond between the mothers. Audrey came to Lowestoft with John, and the two little boys played duets together, each mother thinking her son the better. Ben wanted to learn a string instrument and as Audrey was a professional viola player she started to teach him.

Mrs Alston was a member of the Norwich String Quartet (Leader: André Mangeot) whose concerts Britten attended, and occasionally gave recitals (see note 1 to Letter 11). It was Audrey Alston who first introduced Britten to Bridge, and to whom Britten dedicated his *Simple Symphony*. After being widowed in 1926, she married Mr Lincolne Sutton.

4 Marjorie Fass (1884–1968), a close friend and neighbour of the Bridges in Sussex, who was also a gifted amateur artist and musician. She studied piano, violin and art in Brussels, and singing in Italy. We are indebted to her for her many drawings of the Bridges, the youthful Britten, and Brosa. (See PFL, plates 50, 51 and 54.) Over two hundred letters from Frank and Ethel Bridge to Marjorie Fass, written between 1918 and 1939, are in the Archive (gift of Daphne Oliver). See Letters 71 and 73 and the many quotations from the letters of Marjorie Fass to Daphne Oliver.

5 Fritz Kreisler (1875–1962), American virtuoso violinist and composer of Austrian birth.

Thursday, 19 February 1931

I go to Ireland's studio for my composition Lesson. It is, I suppose, a very good one, but certainly not a cheering one! I am now "getting it" for variety of styles in my carol – it is quite right, but that doesn't make it any the more pleasant! Meet Barbara at Selfridges[1] as usual at 5.0 & then to Madrigals.

1 The department store in Oxford Street, London.

Wednesday, 25 February 1931

Write & practise in morning as usual. V. good pft. lesson (instructive i.e.) in afternoon, after which I go with Remo Lauricella to the London University Library, which I am going to join. See Mrs. Bridge after tea, about some concerts that F. is conducting soon. Finish my slow movement in evening,[1] & also listen to Mossolov's[2] Music of Machines; it comes through badly. It is v. interesting & fiendishly clever. But, is it music?

1 'New Prince, New Pomp'. See note 2 to Diary for 12 January 1931.
2 Alexander Mossolov (1900–1973). His *Music of the Machines* (1927) – here given its UK première – was a famous example of supposedly 'realistic' Soviet music. The concert, given by the BBC Symphony Orchestra under Adrian Boult from the Queen's Hall, also included Berlioz's *Les francs Juges* overture, Elgar's Violin Concerto, and Beethoven's 'Eroica' Symphony.

Thursday, 26 February 1931

Composition lesson at 10.0. Ireland is quite pleased with my latest carol.[1] Go to Augeners & Chesters[2] for Brahms op. 21 Variations & Prokofiev op. 12 prelude for pft. Study. Practise in afternoon. No madrigals. Walk with Hendersons after tea. Go to Chamber Concert at R.C.M. 8.15. In a long programme Helen Perkin[3] (Ireland's star & best comp. pupil) plays her own Ballade for pft. V. competant with only about 1 bit of original work. Too long, I thought, for material. Beethoven A min (op. 132) quartet, tolerably played. Divine work! as also is Brahms G. maj Vln sonata.[4]

1 See note 2 to Diary for 12 January 1931.

2 J. & W. Chester, the music publishers, whose offices and shop in 1931, like those of Messrs Augener, were located in Great Marlborough Street, London W1, at Nos. 11 and 18 respectively.

3 Helen Craddock Perkin (b. 1909), English pianist and composition pupil of Ireland at the College, 1926–33, where she was awarded an Octavia Hill Travelling Scholarship to study with Webern in Vienna. After giving a remarkable performance of Prokofiev's Third Piano Concerto at a College concert, Miss Perkin became Ireland's protégée, amid much gossip. Ireland entrusted to her the first performance of his Piano Concerto (1930), which he dedicated to her, and she established herself as an authoritative interpreter of his music. For a more detailed account of Ireland's relationship with her see Muriel V. Searle, *John Ireland: The Man and his Music* (Tunbridge Wells, Midas Books, 1979), pp. 76–8.

4 Apart from the works cited, the programme also included: Duparc's 'Chanson triste', Fauré's 'Claire de lune', Loeillet's Trio in D minor for flute, oboe and piano, Korngold's 'Mariettas Lied', and Medtner's 'Winternacht'.

Wednesday, 4 March 1931

Walk after breakfast for about ¼ hr. as is now the rule. Usual writing (continual unsuccessful attempts at new carol)[1] & practising. Lesson with Benjamin at 2.40, & then go to University Library to get some books with Lauricella. Get Stravinsky Sacre; Brahms Vln Concerto; Franck Symphony (Min scores) & Beethoven: Impressions of contemporaries.[2] Walk with Tumpty after tea. Work (again unsuccessfully) after dinner. Little Viola practise.

1 Probably one of the incomplete settings from *Thy King's Birthday*. See note 2 to Diary for 12 January 1931.

2 *Beethoven: Impressions by His Contemporaries*, by O.G. Sonneck (New York, 1926).

Thursday, 5 March 1931

Ireland rings up in morning & says that I'm to go to my lesson at 10.30 instead of 10.0. I have a v. good one, tho' short. He is quite pleased with bits of my carol. Practise as usual in afternoon, go to Bumpus'[1] to look for new carols to set (get Christmas Anthology),[2] before meeting Barbara at Selfridges at 4.45; shopping with her & Madrigals. Practise Vla a bit after dinner.

1 J. Bumpus & Son, the famous London bookshop, which did not long survive the Second World War.
2 See note 2 to Diary for 12 January 1931.

Sunday, 8 March 1931

Go to church at 11.0 with Miss Prior at St. Mark's.[1] Have v. fine sermon by Bish. of London,[2] & v. fine anthem "Many Waters"[3] of Ireland v. well sung. Walk with Miss Prior after dinner. Write letters for rest of afternoon & evening until supper at the Bridges at 7.30. Go to BBC Studio for concert[4] which Mr. B. conducts with Mrs. B. & Miss Fass (?). Revel in Haydn (Symp. 104), & Bridge 2 Tagore Songs[5] – marvellous Creations, not superbly sung by Astra Desmond.[6] P. Herrman[7] plays Schumann Vlc Concerto poorly, R-Korsakov Cap. Espagnol, marvellously played by the orchestra as was every item, the B.B.C. Orch is awfully fine, but discipline (owing to No. of conductors) faulty. Wind – excellent; L. Kennedy & F. Thurston[8] (clar.) simply superb. Bridge conducted marvellously. Back by taxi at 11.10.

1 St Mark's Church, North Audley Street, London W1. See also note 1 to Letter 43.
2 Arthur Foley Winnington-Ingram (1858–1946), Bishop of London, 1901–39.
3 Motet (1912) for treble, baritone, chorus and organ, entitled 'Greater Love Hath No Man' but sometimes known as 'Many Waters Cannot Quench Love'.
4 Given by the BBC Symphony Orchestra.
5 Bridge's Tagore Songs for voice and piano or orchestra, of which there are three, were composed between 1922 and 1925. The two songs heard on this occasion were 'Day after Day' and 'Speak to me my Love'.
6 English alto (1893–1973).
7 Paul Herrman.
8 Frederick Thurston (1901–1953), English clarinettist. Principal clarinettist in the BBC Symphony Orchestra, 1930–46.

Friday, 13 March 1931

Begin completely re-writing 'Christ's Nativity'.[1] Practise
11.45–12.45. Go to College in a fruitless effort to find out about
R.C.M. Union.[2] I practise 3.30–4.30. Go to quite a good concert
(British Women's Symphony Orch)[3] at Queen's Hall with Barbara
(tickets given by Miss Atkinson). They play Sibelius' beautiful
En Saga, quite well, & also (with Emilo Columbo)[4] Max Bruch's
G min. Vln concerto. C. plays some pifling little solos (including
Debussy's charming fille aux chevaux de lin)[5] competantly. To
finish with Bantock's[6] Hebridean Symphony – mediocre stuff!

1 See note 2 to Diary for 12 January 1931. Britten evidently retained
  the original date of composition of this movement, 2 March, despite
  later revisions.

2 The society of past and present College students founded in 1905.

3 Reginald Pound, in *Sir Henry Wood* (London, Cassell, 1969), p. 229,
  writes: 'Formed in 1922, and often languishing thereafter, the British
  Women's Symphony Orchestra was said to have graduated, or "come
  out", under the aboundingly energetic Malcolm Sargent in 1929.'
  Sargent conducted this concert.

4 *recte* Emilio Colombo, violinist.

5 'La Fille aux cheveux de lin', from Book 1 of Debussy's Twelve
  Preludes for piano (1910), arranged for violin and piano. The
  accompanist was the English pianist Gerald Moore (1899–1986).

6 Granville Bantock (1869–1946), English composer. His *Hebridean Symphony* (1915) was first performed in 1917. He was knighted in 1930.

Saturday, 14 March 1931

I go to the Leicester galleries[1] (starting before 10) to see Epstein's[2]
new sculptures & Southal's[3] paintings. The latter are quite
beautiful. Some of the former are entrancingly delightfull (esp. Joan
Greenwood).[4] Re. Genesis, I do not know; altho' I spent ages looking
at it, I do not understand it. It's very marvellous & amazing. Do
some music shopping on way home H. Reeves Dvorak Cello
Concerto (B min) & MS. (Augeners). Go to concert – Maud Randall[5]
in afternoon – with Miss Bicknell the lady-cook here – who was
at school at St. Anne's, & afterwards tea at Maison Lyons[6] with
her. There was nothing striking abt. the concert – only competant

playing. – Schumann Symph. Etudes, Group of modern pieces & Chopin B. min. sonata.

1 The Leicester Galleries, in Leicester Square, were particularly well known for their exhibitions of contemporary painting and sculpture.

2 Jacob Epstein (1880–1959), American-born sculptor. His *Genesis*, which Britten mentions, was one of his most controversial sculptures. It generated much (ill-informed) debate in the thirties about the legitimacy of 'modern' art. Kenneth McLeish, compiler of the *Penguin Companion to the Arts in the Twentieth Century* (Harmondsworth, Penguin, 1986), remarks (p. 396) that perhaps Epstein's 'challenge to accepted ideas constituted his main "idea" '. Also exhibited were Epstein's *Putti*, *Esther*, *La Belle Juive* and *Rebecca*. He was knighted in 1954.

3 Joseph Edward Southall (1861–1944), English artist and designer, and one of the 'Birmingham Group' of artists active in the early years of the century. His exhibition of 'Paintings and Drawings' was held at the Leicester Galleries during March and April 1931.

At the 1975 Aldeburgh Festival examples of Southall's work were included in an exhibition of the Birmingham Group entitled *The Earthly Paradise*. It was on this occasion that Britten purchased two watercolours by Southall – of sailing barges at Walberswick, Suffolk – to give to Peter Pears on his sixty-fifth birthday. The paintings are now owned by the Britten–Pears Foundation.

4 A portrait bust of the actress and theatre director (1921–1987), when a child.

5 English pianist, a pupil of Myra Hess.

6 The Lyons Corner Houses and teashops, with their waitresses, 'nippies', were popular centres for eating and meeting in the thirties. When first launched, they were described as 'the operation of a revolutionary concept of mass catering'. In his 'Letter to William Coldstream, Esq.' (in *Letters from Iceland* (London, Faber and Faber, 1937), p. 218), Auden recalls how 'poet and painter sneaked out for coffee'; and of course their destination was

> Upstairs in the Corner House, in the hall with the phallic pillars
> And before the band had finished a pot pourri from Wagner
> We'd scrapped Significant Form, and voted for Subject [. . .]

Tuesday, 17 March 1931

Go to John Ireland's via the College at 10.30. Have v. good lesson. I think he quite likes "Preparations".[1] Practise 12.15–12.45 & all

aft. Lauricella doesn't turn up as arranged. Go to recital[2] with
Tumpty by Sheridan Russell (Vcl), assisted by var others. All
English programme – some old music,[3] well played by Russell, &
v. interesting suite of L. Berkeley[4] for Vlc & Oboe (H. Gaskell).[5]
Rather dull Idyllic Fantasy of C. Scott[6] for Voice (Dorothy Moulton),[7]
vlc & ob. New Sonatina (pleasant & competant) for vlc & pft of Ben
Burrows;[8] nothing striking or original at all.

1 See note 2 to Diary for 12 January 1931.

2 At the Grotrian Hall, Wigmore Street, London W1.

3 Transcribed by Harold Craxton (1885–1971), English pianist and
teacher, who published many such editions of early English music.

4 Berkeley's five-movement *Petite Suite* (1927), revived in a BBC Radio 3
concert on the occasion of the composer's eighty-fifth birthday, 12
May 1988. See Peter Dickinson, *The Music of Lennox Berkeley* (London,
Thames, 1988), pp. 23, 34.

5 Helen Gaskell (b. 1906), English oboist, a member of the BBC Symphony Orchestra, 1932–66.

6 Cyril Scott (1879–1970), English composer and pianist. His *Idyllic
Fantasy* was first published in 1921.

7 Dorothy Moulton (1886–1974), English soprano, a noted exponent of
contemporary music during the 1920s and 1930s. She married (Sir)
Robert Mayer, in 1919.

8 Benjamin Burrows (1891–1966), English composer. His Sonatina for
cello and piano was composed in 1930 and published by Augener in
1931.

Wednesday, 18 March 1931

Lesson at 2.40. Mummy arrives at 4.0 by bus from Lowestoft.
Barbara comes to dinner. Go with Mummy to BBC. Beethoven
concert, conducted by Oskar Fried.[1] Fidelio, 4th & 9th Symphonys.
The first two were played beautifully. But Fried seemed to frighten
the orchestra in the 9th. He altered scoring right and left. 1st
movement, impressive, 2nd mov. too fast; the 3rd too slow. Last
movement was notable for fine singing of Nat. chorus[2] & soloists.
All considering it was rather a disappointing performance – of the
conductor's. He was raging all the way through the 9th – there is
no reason why he should blame the whole orch & choir for the
slips of the 4th Horn (C♭ scale (3rd mov.) & Timpani (2nd mov.)

1 German conductor (1871–1941), and noted Mahler disciple, which might account for his extensive retouchings of the Ninth.

2 The National Chorus, formed by the BBC in 1928 for the first perform-ance of Granville Bantock's oratorio *The Pilgrim's Progress*. The choir was renamed the BBC Chorus in 1932, became the BBC Choral Society in 1935, and from 1977 has been known as the BBC Symphony Chorus. During their early years the chorus gave a number of im-portant performances, including Mahler's Eighth Symphony (UK première 15 April 1930), Beethoven's *Missa Solemnis* (December 1930), Walton's *Belshazzar's Feast* (25 November 1931), and Stravinsky's *Symphony of Psalms* (27 January 1932). The soloists in the Ninth Symphony were Isobel Baillie (1895–1983), Scottish soprano; Astra Desmond; Walter Widdop (1892–1949), English tenor; and Keith Falkner (see note 6 to Diary for 22 March 1931).

Thursday, 19 March 1931

Quite good lesson with Ireland in Chelsea at 10.0. Practise afternoon. Tea with Barbara & Mummy at Selfridges at 4.45. Go with Mummy (with tickets from Mrs. Brosa via. Mrs Bridge) to topping recital by Antonio Brosa.[1] He is simply superb. Incredible technique, with beautiful interpretation. His Bach Chaconne was great. Prokofiev op. 16 Vln. Concerto didnt contain much music, but was rather like a compendium of School for Virtuosity vln exersises. He played it toppingly; A great violinist.

1 Brosa's recital took place at the Wigmore Hall, London. His accompanist was the English pianist, George Reeves (1895–1960). Apart from the Bach and Prokofiev, Brosa also played Veracini's Sonata in A minor.

Sunday, 22 March 1931

Get up early & go to St. Matthews with Mummy at 8.0. Spend all morning (11.0–1.0) & afternoon (2.30–4.45) – with lunch back here – at Bach Choir, St. Matthew Passion, cond. A. Boult,[1] with D. Silk,[2] M. Balfour,[3] S. Wilson,[4] H. Eisdle,[5] K. Falkner[6] and A. Cranmer.[7] A very good performance on the whole. & very moving. Keith Falkner & St. Wilson were great & Dorothy Silk also. Choir quite good – oh, it's a great work! Tea with Barbara; back here for supper. Write to Pop afterwards. Early bed, by 10.0.

1 Adrian Boult (1889–1983), English conductor. Boult for a time taught
   at the College (from 1919) and succeeded Stanford as conductor of
   the College orchestra. In 1930, after serving for six years as conductor
   of the City of Birmingham Orchestra, he was appointed Musical
   Director of the BBC and became Chief Conductor of the BBC Symphony Orchestra from 1930 to 1950, when he was succeeded in
   this post by Sargent. Britten's persistently negative view of Boult's
   conducting was undoubtedly fuelled in part by his own passionate
   advocacy of Frank Bridge as a conductor and musician and by his
   conviction that Bridge should have had the job that was offered
   to Boult. In addition, Britten, we think, was suspicious of Boult's
   'university' training, as distinct from Bridge's, who had had much
   practical experience as a performer. (This was a scepticism that Britten throughout his life never totally abandoned.) It would be a mistake to explain his misgiving about Boult wholly in terms of rival
   personalities. He was not alone in finding Boult's performances inadequate (featureless) from time to time, but he was surely unique in
   finding them quite so consistently bad. It is only for this performance
   of Bach's *St Matthew Passion* under Boult that his hostile tone is
   momentarily modified. The relationship was never a warm one, and
   there was further friction in connection with the performance of the
   Occasional Overture in C, commissioned for the opening of the BBC
   Third Programme and given its first broadcast performance by the
   BBC Symphony Orchestra under Boult on 29 September 1946. However, in later years the two men exchanged occasional (and polite)
   letters about relatively marginal matters. We must conclude that
   Britten's was a somewhat partial view, especially in view of Boult's
   remarkable record with regard to performances of twentieth-century
   music. Boult, it must be added, never showed any very special
   enthusiasm for conducting Britten's works, though that perhaps was
   not so surprising, given the composer's views (of which Boult must
   surely have had an inkling). However, it was Boult who conducted
   the second performance of *Our Hunting Fathers* in a BBC Contemporary Concert on 30 April 1937, when Britten recorded in his diary:

   I have a rehearsal with Boult [. . .] it goes quite well, tho' he doesn't
   really grasp the work – tho' he is marvellously painstaking [. . .] They
   do my Hunting Fathers very creditably – I am awfully pleased with it too,
   I'm afraid.

   Boult was also to conduct one of the early performances of the
   Piano Concerto (with Britten as soloist: see note 1 to Letter 162); the
   first broadcast of *Les Illuminations* on 12 April 1940; the 'Four Sea
   Interludes' from *Peter Grimes*, at the Proms in 1945 (and again in
   1947); *Sinfonia da Requiem* in December 1945 and in Vienna, with the
   Vienna Symphony Orchestra, in 1948; and the Violin Concerto (with

Theo Olof as soloist) in 1947. He was knighted in 1937. See also
Michael Kennedy, *Adrian Boult* (London, Hamish Hamilton, 1987),
pp. 156–7 and 206–7.

2 Dorothy Silk (1883–1942), English soprano.

3 Margaret Balfour (b. ? , d. 1961), English alto.

4 Steuart Wilson (1889–1966), English tenor. He was a founder member
   of the English Singers and a famous Evangelist in Bach's *St Matthew
   Passion* and Gerontius in Elgar's oratorio. He was Music Director of
   the Arts Council of Great Britain during the crucial post-war period
   1945–8 and then Head of Music at the BBC, 1948–9. He was knighted
   in 1948. Pears and Wilson were distantly related.

5 Hubert Eisdell (1882–1948), English tenor.

6 Keith Falkner (b. 1900), English bass-baritone. He was particularly
   well known as a soloist in oratorio. After retiring, he worked for the
   British Council in Italy, 1946–50. He was later to become Director of
   the Royal College of Music, 1960–74. He was knighted in 1967.

7 Arthur Cranmer (1885–1954), English baritone. His outstanding role
   was Christus in the Bach Passions.

Monday, 30 March 1931

Write some more var.[1] in morning & stick my "Thy King's Birthday"
together. Usual practise, go to R.C.M. at 3.30 to see Miss Darnell,
Lady Superintendant[2] about oculist. Go to see "Tell England"[3] in
evening (with some complimentary tickets of Louis Lederer)[4] at
Palace Theatre with Tumpty. It is a simply amazing film, not much
like the book. Terribly realistic and too harrowing really to be
enjoyable. Exhilarating in a way, to see all those lives given up, –
but for nothing. Parts very well played.

1 The *Twelve Variations on a Theme* for solo piano, composed 27 March
   – 1 April 1931, and revised 27 April – 6 May 1931. They were apparently never played during Britten's lifetime, and were given their
   first performance by Murray Perahia at the Maltings, Snape, on 22
   June 1986, as part of the 39th Aldeburgh Festival. They were published by Faber Music the same year.

2 A. Beatrix Darnell (1873–1970), Lady Superintendent at the College,
   1919–39. The general welfare of students was her particular responsibility.

3 The British film released in 1931 about a group of schoolfriends who
   join up in 1914 and perish at Gallipoli. The screenplay was by

Anthony Asquith, after the novel by Ernest Raymond. It was directed by Anthony Asquith and Gerald Barkas.

4 A friend of the Hendersons.

Tuesday, 31 March 1931

Practise & write as usual. Play with Lauricella in afternoon. Go to lunch with Laulie[1] in morning at Mackies[2] – she is staying up here for a day or two. Go to Waterloo Studio (B.B.C.) to hear contemporary concert, with Bridges. He conducts B.B.C. orch "Enter Spring"[3] & "Willow aslant a Brook" (Bridge) rather badly played, but magnificent, inspired works. Brosa St. quart.[4] plays with orch concerto by Conrad Beck.[5] Interesting, but that's all, incredibly played. And to end up with an absurd Concerto Grosso by Igor Markievitch.[6] Intolerably difficult, & consequently only mod. played by the orch. This must have been written with the composer's tongue in his cheek.

1 See note 4 to Letter 9.

2 Mackies, a manufacturer of bread and biscuits, and owners of a café and shop at 11–12 Marble Arch, London W2.

3 Bridge's Rhapsody for orchestra, *Enter Spring*, was composed 1926–7 and first performed at Norwich on 27 October 1927. Britten (aged 13) was in the audience and in later years recalled how profoundly impressed he was by the 'riot of melodic and harmonic richness' the work represented. This was the occasion when Britten was introduced to Bridge through the good offices of Mrs Alston (see note 3 to Diary for 16 February 1931), and in Britten's own words, 'We got on splendidly, and I spent the next morning with him going over some of my music [. . .] From that moment I used to go regularly to him, staying with him in Eastbourne or in London, in the holidays' (BBST). Following its Norwich première in 1927, *Enter Spring* was heard on four further occasions: at a Promenade Concert in 1930; BBC studio performances in 1931 and 1932, and a Queen's Hall Concert later that same year (see Diary for 26 October 1932). This was its last performance until Britten revived the work at a concert in the Royal Festival Hall, London, on 9 April 1967, when he conducted the New Philharmonia Orchestra. He repeated *Enter Spring* at the 1967 Aldeburgh Festival, conducting the New Philharmonia once again, in a concert at the Snape Maltings on 18 June. His final illness prevented him from fulfilling his intention to record both *Enter Spring* and *The Sea*. The manuscript full score of *Enter Spring* is now in the Archive.

4 The Brosa String Quartet, founded by Antonio Brosa. The Quartet was to have a marked influence on the standard of ensemble playing.

5 Conrad Beck (1901–1989), Swiss composer. The work to which Britten refers was Beck's Symphony No. 4 for string orchestra, composed in 1929, and also known as 'Concerto for Orchestra'.

6 Igor Markevitch (1912–1983), Russian-born composer. His Concerto Grosso was first performed in Paris on 8 December 1930.

Saturday, 18 April 1931
[*Lowestoft*]

Practise Rondo[1] in morning at Colemans. Should have played tennis with Mr. Sewell & Mrs Rogers[2] 3–4, 5–6, but it rains all aft. Tea with them at Hatfield.[3] Musical Evening (all Beethoven) at 8.0. 2 Owles, Dr. Mead, 3 Colemans, 2 Phillips, 2 Boyds, Mrs & John Nicholson, Mrs. Taylor, Miss Goldsmith.[4] Sing a good many Rounds & Canons. Mrs. Taylor plays 5th Sonata (F maj) with Mr. Coleman (rather wonky intonation).[5] I play op. 10 no. 3 (D maj) sonata. Mummy sings Klächen's 1st song from Egmont (with pft. duet acc. Mr. Coleman & Me).[6] I also play Brahms (Hungarian Song) variations[7] as a last resource as I have no more Beethoven at the moment. Everyone seems to enjoy themselves, especially singing the Rounds.

1 Britten's arrangement for violin, viola and piano of Beethoven's *Rondo a capriccio*, Op. 129, transcribed 7–9 April, in which Britten took the viola part, Charles Coleman the violin, and C.J.R. Coleman the piano.

2 The fiancée of Laurence Sewell. She had a son by her first marriage, Edward (Teddy).

3 The Hatfield House Hotel, Esplanade, Lowestoft.

4 '2 Owles': Mr and Mrs Sydney Owles of 41 Corton Road, Lowestoft. Mr Owles was the Manager of Barclays Bank, 1 and 2 Commercial Road, Lowestoft. Dr John C. Mead was in practice with Dr Hutchinson and Dr Goldsmith. '3 Colemans': Mr and Mrs Charles Coleman and their son, Charles. '2 Phillips': The Revd and Mrs Richmond W. Phillips, Hartside, Victoria Mansions, Kirkley Cliff Road, Lowestoft. He was a Licensed Preacher within the Norwich Diocese and had preceded T.J.E. Sewell as Headmaster of South Lodge. '2 Boyds': neighbours at 22 Kirkley Cliff Road. Mrs and John Nicholson, the wife and son of Joseph Arthur Nicholson, the Britten family solicitor,

who lived at 4 Gunton Cliff, Lowestoft. John (1914–1975) was a fellow pupil at South Lodge (1923–8). He and his family remained lifelong friends of the composer. Mrs Taylor: wife of Sydney Taylor, solicitor, Hillingdon, Gunton Cliff, Lowestoft. She was an amateur violinist who had played in a domestic performance of Britten's *Miniature Suite* (1929) for string quartet. (Mrs Taylor's manuscript first violin part is in the Archive.) Miss Goldsmith: presumably the daughter of Edmund Onslow Goldsmith, MA, 44 Marine Parade, Lowestoft, of Hutchinson, Mead and Goldsmith, physicians and surgeons.

5 The 'Spring' Sonata, Op. 24, for violin and piano. Patricia Nicholson, John Nicholson's widow, recollected in 1985 an account of another performance:

> Ben used to have to play, either at his mother's musical evenings or [Mrs Taylor's] . . . and he found her absolutely appalling to play with. There was one occasion when he got into trouble because he was playing the Beethoven 'Spring' Sonata and she simply could not get the scherzo right . . . and he was in complete disgrace because he banged the lid down, and walked upstairs and wouldn't continue.

6 Klärchen's song 'Die Trommel gerühret' from Beethoven's incidental music for the play by Goethe. This song had been arranged for voice and piano (four hands) by Britten on 13 April in readiness for this Beethoven soirée on the 18th; he also translated the text into English. The event speaks for the youthful Britten's enthusiasm for Beethoven. On his writing desk at this time stood a small plaster bust of the revered composer (see PFL, plate 70).

7 The *Thirteen Variations on a Hungarian Song*, Op. 21.

Tuesday, 28 April 1931

Practise pft all morning until 12.0 when I go to have my photo taken at Boughtens.[1] Wretched Agony![2] Mummy walks there & back (+ Beth) with me. Cut Back lawn grass in afternoon. Do a good bit more of Variations[3] (copying & rewriting). Anne Arnold comes to tea & goes to Brownies[4] with Beth after. Walk with Pop after tea & before supper. South Lodge boys return.[5]

1 Thomas Boughton, photographer, 54 London Road North, Lowestoft. See also PFL, plate 40. This might well be the photograph to which Britten refers, in which case it belongs to a slightly later date than the caption suggests.

2 Britten was never to overcome his dislike of having his photograph taken, much photographed though he was.

3 See note 1 to Diary for 30 March 1931.

4 The junior section of the Girl Guides. Beth was evidently one of the adult helpers.

5 The end of the Easter holidays.

Wednesday, 29 April 1931

Shave in morning; I shave once every 2 days now with a Cut throat,[1] which Pop has taught me to use. Practise all morning until 12.15, when I walk with Mummy. Play tennis in afternoon (3–4.15) with Beth, Mrs. Black[2] & a Nephew (?). Not by any means excellent tennis, but great fun! Miss Bradley[3] & Dr Mawson (of St. Luke's) come to tea. Cut Front Lawn before tennis & after tea. Beth goes to cinema with Blacks in evening. Walk with Pop to Club after dinner.

1 A razor with open blade, now largely supplanted by the 'safety' razor.

2 The wife of James Alexander Black, 28 Kirkley Cliff Road.

3 Annie Bradley, matron of St Luke's Hospital (Metropolitan Asylums Board), Kirkley Cliff Road.

Tuesday, 5 May 1931
[London]

I finish my rewritten Variation in morning & after lunch. Practise 11.30–12.45, & 2.15–4.15 with Lauricella, with whom I play Greig G min. Sonata & Mov. 1 of Dvorak's Vln Concerto (A min) which he plays magnificently. Go to H. Reeves after tea & get Saint Saën's 4th Pft Concerto, soiled (where, I know not!) for 3/- instead of 4/-. Play cards (Rummy)[1] with Mr Gates & Mr Summers 2 of the new people[2] here. Barbara rings up.

1 A popular card game.

2 New lodgers.

Wednesday, 6 May 1931

Have my hair cut before 9.30 at Whiteleys.[1] Revise my Variations until 11.0. Practise 11.0–12.0. Go to College to make various business arrangements, & have lesson with Benjamin 12.40–1.0.

Practise all aft. 2.15–4.15. Practise viola after tea. V. hot day, for this time of year. Dinner early at 6.45 & go to Queen's Hall to B.B.C. Concert.[2]

1 The department store in Queensway, Bayswater. It has recently been refurbished as a shopping mall after being closed for a number of years.

2 Given by the BBC Symphony Orchestra, conducted by Adrian Boult. The programme comprised: Weber's overture to *Euryanthe*; Vaughan Williams's *Fantasia on a Theme by Thomas Tallis* (1910); Saint-Saëns's Piano Concerto No. 4 in C minor, Op. 44 (played by the French pianist, Alfred Cortot (1877–1962)); Mahler's *Lieder eines fahrenden Gesellen* (sung by the German mezzo-soprano, Maria Olczewska (1892–1969)); and Elgar's *Engima Variations*.

On a supplementary page added to his diary entry, Britten wrote a detailed account of the concert:

[. . .] Euryanthe ov. (Weber), beastly bit of music, mauled about by Boult (2nd Subject more than 2^{ce} as slow as 1st Sub.). Bad slips on part of orch. V. Williams Tallis Fantasia. v. beautiful (wonderfully scored), but over long. well played. Cortot in Saint-Saëns 4th Con; very wonderful playing in spite of many wrong notes, which one didn't mind. Encored, playing (marvellously heavenlily) a Chopin Walse (C♯ min). Mahler's Lieder eines Fahrenden Gesellen (Maria Olszewska, wonderful singing). Lovely little pieces, exquisitely scored – a lesson to all the Elgars & Strausses in the world. Enigma Variations, a terrible contrast to these little wonders. I listened with an open mind, but cannot say that I was less annoyed by them, than usual. Of course there must be alot in them, but that type of sonorous orchestration (especially in Var. V, IX, XII, (which seem exactly alike to me)), cloys very soon. Of course there are lovely moments (Dorabella is good, but is spoilt by trite ending. Var. XIII is very effective. on the whole I think Isobel's the best) but oh! no. XIV!! The orchestra played their exacting, but effective parts very well, & Adrian Boult was a sympathetic conductor, I suppose. I suppose it's my fault, and there is something lacking in me, that I am absolutely incapable of enjoying Elgar, for more than 2 minutes.

Thursday, 7 May 1931

Go to College after beginning an unsatisfactory piece for violin & pft,[1] for aural training with Mr. Allchin[2] at 11.0–12.0. Back for lunch. Practise 2.15–4.10. Meet Barbara at Selfridges at 5.0 after having gone to the Aeolian Hall[3] for some music. The Madrigal choir is bigger than before, & is I think v. good. Back to dinner at the flat with Barbara. Have wireless; Harold Williams (?)[4] singing

'Going down Hill on a Bicycle: a Boy's Song' (after H.C. Beeching), for violin and piano: the first page of Britten's pencil sketch

Somerville's[5] 'pleasant' Maud suite. And a few Chopin preludes, exquisitely played by Cortot.[6]

1 Probably Britten's first attempt at the Two Pieces for violin and piano, 'Going down Hill on a Bicycle (after H.C. Beeching)' and 'By the

Moon we sport and play (after Shelley)', composed for Remo Lauricella, 29–30 June 1931. Britten recorded their composition in his diary
on 29 June: 'I write in morning & evening a piece for Vln & Pft (going
down hill on a Bicycle – after H.C. Beeching).'

On 30 June:

I write a Vln & Pft piece, "Moon", in morning – more satisfactory than the
Bicycle one. Copy parts out, & Lauricella plays them in aft. He's going
to practise them, but plays them already well.

There is no evidence that the pieces were ever performed publicly;
they remain in the Archive.

2 Basil Charles Allchin (1878–1957), taught at the College, 1920–47,
and was Registrar, 1935–9.

3 A small concert hall situated in Bond Street, London W1, and particularly suited to chamber music and recitals.

4 Harold Williams (b. 1893, d. ?), Australian bass and leading oratorio
singer. He was joined by an unidentified accompanist.

5 Arthur Somervell (1863–1937), English composer. His best-known
song-cycle, *Maud* (settings of Tennyson), was composed in 1898.

6 Alfred Cortot performed Chopin's Twenty-four Preludes, Op. 28. In
the same programme he accompanied Maggie Teyte.

Friday, 8 May 1931

Begin last movement of a St. Quartet[1] in morning, before going to
1st comp lesson with Ireland. He is quite pleased with My fugues,[2]
more especially with the last. I practise all afternoon. See Mr & Mrs
Bridge after tea. Have long talk with them, & do a bit of correcting
of proofs of his marvellous opera "Christmas Rose".[3]

Walk with Mr Summers + Gates (two new men here) after
dinner.

1 String Quartet in D major, composed 8 May – 2 June 1931. Britten
revised this work in 1974 for publication in 1975 (London, Faber
Music) and for its first public performance in the same year at the
28th Aldeburgh Festival by the Gabrieli String Quartet on 7 June.
The Prefatory Note to the score, provided by the composer, is of
particular interest, spelling out as it does the context in which the
work was composed and certain musical influences on it which
derived from a pursuit that Britten so often mentions in these diaries,
madrigal singing:

Another of my extra-mural activities was singing in a choir conducted by
Arnold Foster and madrigals became a great passion; the influence of them

can perhaps be seen in this work. I remember well that when I showed the quartet to Bridge, he complained that the counterpoint in it was too vocal. Maybe, particularly in the case of the first two movements, he was right, though John Ireland did not agree.

2 The *Three Fugues* for piano, written as an exercise for Ireland, 14–24 April 1931.

3 Bridge's opera in three scenes, *The Christmas Rose*, with a libretto based on a play for children by Margaret Kemp-Welch and Constance Cotterell, was composed 1919–29. A vocal score was published by Augener in 1931. See also note 2 to Diary for 4 and 8 December 1931. Three performances of the work were given at the Parry Opera Theatre of the College, in a student production, conducted by Frank Bridge in December 1931, the first on the 8th (see Diary for that date). No further performances took place during the composer's lifetime.

Friday, 15 May 1931

Begin Slow Move. of quartet before going to Coll. at 11.45 to find my comp. lesson has been moved to Thursdays, only the Coll. has not informed me of this, so that I miss a lesson this week. This Establishment! Practise 2.15–4.0 Go st[raight]. to Barbara's flat where Beth is, having travelled up from Lowestoft by Bus arr. 3.30. Walk with her before dinner (all 3 of us there). Go to "Stand up and Sing"[1] (3/6 seats at Hippodrome) – Jack Buchanan, Elsie Randolph,[2] Anton Dolin,[3] 7 Hindustans[4] (marvellous gymnastic feats) in a perfectly topping, side-splitting rolicking good show. Back at 12.0.

1 *Stand Up and Sing*, musical play written by Douglas Furber (1885–1961), with music by Philip Charig (1902–1960) and Vivian Ellis. This was the show's first production.

2 Jack Buchanan (1891–1957) and Elsie Randolph (1904–1982) were a famous musical-comedy partnership in the thirties.

3 Anton Dolin (1904–1983), the British dancer and choreographer. He studied with Nijinsky and subsequently joined the Diaghilev Company. In 1930 he co-founded the Camargo Society (see note 4 to Diary for 15 November 1931) for which he created the role of Satan in Ninette de Valois's *Job* (music by Vaughan Williams) in 1931. During this same period Dolin also appeared in a number of revues, including *Stand Up and Sing*. He writes in his *Autobiography* (London, Oldbourne, 1960), p. 54:

When the Old Vic gave its first evening of ballet on September 22nd 1931, they gave also the first public performance of *Job*. I was now appearing in *Stand Up and Sing*, at the London Hippodrome, starring Jack Buchanan. Jack, with his ever-gracious manner, gave me permission to dance for Lilian Baylis. I would dash over to the Old Vic to dance Satan, and then get back to my musical show. When I took my call at the end of *Job*, I took it dressed in evening trousers and patent leather shoes, half ready for my appearance in the finale of *Stand Up and Sing* at the Hippodrome.

From 1931 to 1935 he appeared with the Vic–Wells Ballet, and in 1935 founded with Alicia Markova the Markova–Dolin Ballet. He danced in New York with the Ballet Theater from 1940 to 1946, and in 1944 he choreographed Stravinsky's *Scènes de ballet*. He was knighted in 1981.

4 This must have been one of the earliest – if not the first – of Britten's encounters with non-Western performers. On 6 May 1933, he was to attend a concert of Indian music and dancing at the Ambassadors Theatre and was greatly impressed:

I haven't seen anything for ages which has thrilled me more. Marvellously intellectual and perfectly wrought dancing [. . .] music, full of variety, rhythmically & tonally.

(See also Donald Mitchell, 'What do we know about Britten now?' in BC, p. 40, note 23.)

Wednesday, 27 May 1931

Pop, Mum, & Beth go to Gloucester by car from Lowestoft, to stay.[1] Go to Covent Garden after breakfast in an unsuccessful attempt to get campstools to put in a queue. Have my hair cut at Whiteleys, before practising (11.0–12.0) & v. good pft. lesson 12.40. Practise in aft. & then meet Barbara & Miss Hurst, have dinner at Eustace Miles,[2] & then go & sit in queue for Cov. Garden op. Lohengrin[3] at 7.30. Op. very well done; orch moderate. Elsa v. good actress only distressing wobble (E. Teshermacher). Loh. (Willi Wörle) excellent; best of all Olkzewska as Ortrud. What a voice! The opera is (except for one or two banal bits) exceedingly beautiful – no wonder its so popular.

1 They were probably visiting Britten's aunt, his father's elder sister, Florence Hay Britten (1875–1956), who lived at Cresswell Cottage, Whiteshill, near Stroud, Gloucestershire. She took a BA degree at the University of London and became a teacher, first at the private school founded by herself and her sisters Louise and Julianne. Florence was later to become headmistress of the Girls' High School in

Bridgetown, Barbados, in which capacity she was once introduced to the Prince of Wales (later Edward VIII). This event was dramatized by the seven-year-old Britten in his domestic entertainment, *The Royal Falily* (reproduced in PFL, plate 19). Aunt Florence retired in 1923 to Gloucestershire and finally, owing to deteriorating health, lived in a nursing home in Great Malvern.

2 A health-food manufacturer who had a restaurant at 40–42 Chandos Street, London W1.

3 The cast in Wagner's opera: Elsa, Marguerite Teschemacher (1903–1959), German soprano, who later created the title role in Strauss's *Daphne* (1938); Tetramund, Herbert Janssen (1895–1965), German baritone; and Ortrud, Maria Olczewska, who was the leading mezzo-soprano in Wagner repertory at Covent Garden during the mid-twenties and early thirties.

   The performance was conducted by Robert Heger (1886–1978), German conductor and composer, who appeared often at Covent Garden between 1925 and 1935.

Sunday, 31 May 1931

Go to Church with Summers to St. Marks, N. Audley St, at 11.0. V. nice service altho' it is too high for my liking. Miss Prior brings us back in her Austin 7. Go to Madrigal Practice at Cecil Sharpe House,[1] meeting Barbara at Hyde park Corner, having walked across park, & progressing by bus. Tea with her at an A.B.C.[2] in Oxford st, & walking by myself back here. Practice Viola a bit after dinner.

1 The home of the English Folk Song and Dance Society (2 Regent's Park Road, NW1), named after its founder, Cecil Sharp (1859–1924), the collector of folksongs and dances.

2 ABC = Aerated Bread Company, a chain of tea shops very popular in the thirties, perhaps a notch or two below Lyons in quality and status.

Tuesday, 2 June 1931

Finish (after one or two attempts) the Slow movement of My quart. I am quite pleased with it. Practise as usual, in aft. with Lauricella. Go to sing (in evening dress) at the Cecil Sharp house, at a Folk song, & Folk-dance concert at 8.30. Patuffy Kennedy Fraser[1] also

sings, quite charmingly, some Hebridean Songs with harp. We sing
a group of Madrigals, & a group of Folk song arrangements.
Interspersed with these are many & monotonous (I am heretic
enough to say!) folk dances, tho' some were beautiful. Barbara,
of course, sings, & Miss Hurst also goes. Back at 11.15.

1 Helen Patuffa Kennedy-Fraser (Mrs Hood) (1889–1967), Scottish
   pianist and singer – daughter of Marjorie Kennedy-Fraser
   (1857–1930), the Scots singer and collector of folksongs. She toured
   with her mother in America and Canada, and visited Paris, Amsterdam, Vienna, The Hague and nearly every town in Scotland and
   England, giving recitals of the songs of the Hebrides.

Friday, 5 June 1931

Write a bit in morning & then to Patron's Fund[1] rehearsal in
morning. Only new work is Howard Ferguson's Short Symphony
in D minor.[2] V. fine work not too well played by N[ational]. Symph.
Orch under Sargent. Schumann's ineffective Vlc conc. (Audrey
Piggott),[3] Chausson's Chanson Perpétuelle[4] (well sung by Veronica
Mansfield)[5] & Strauss's v. long & meandering Burlesque for Pft &
Orch. Practise in aft. Go to R.C.M. chamber concert with Tumpty
in evening, at 8.15. V. dull show. Sibelius, Voces intimae, [string]
quart.[6] well played but blurred out of all recognition by the hall.
Ravel's delicious Int. & Allegro, (Harp etc.), quite well played,
made the concert worth going to.

1 The Patron's Fund was founded by Ernest Palmer in 1903 to provide
   the opportunity for 'open rehearsals with professional orchestras in
   the hands of experienced conductors' and charged them with the
   'important task of bringing young British composers and performers
   to the public ear'. (See H.C. Colles and John Cruft, *The Royal College
   of Music: a Centenary Record 1883–1983*, London, Prince Consort Foundation, 1982.)
2 The *Short Symphony* is not listed among Ferguson's published works.
   In *The Music of Howard Ferguson*, edited by Alan Ridout (London,
   Thames, 1989), p. 16, Nigel Scarfe writes, 'This work was later sup-
   pressed, although the opening of the second movement formed the
   basis of the third movement of the Octet [1933].'
3 Audrey Piggott (b. 1906), English cellist and star student at the College at this period.
4 For voice and string quartet, Op. 37, a setting of the poem by Charles
   Cros (1842–1888).

5 Veronica Mansfield (b. 1904), Australian-born mezzo-soprano who later taught at the College.

6 In addition to Sibelius's *Voces Intimae* quartet (in which Bernard Richards's sisters, Irene and Olive, were first violin and cello, respectively) and Ravel's *Introduction and Allegro* for harp, string quartet, flute and clarinet (1905), the programme included three songs by Richard Strauss, the Sonata in E flat for violin and piano by the blind Welsh pianist and composer Alec Templeton (1909–1963; see note 1 to Letter 23), a group of Brahms *Lieder* and Liszt's *Prelude and Fugue on the Name of Bach*. The Ravel was a work greatly admired by Britten throughout his life.

Friday, 12 June 1931

Write much more of Vln Part[1] in morning. usual practise. Walk after tea with Tumpty, Gates, & Summers in the park. After dinner go to marvellous B.B.C. Concert[2] (at 9.45) at Studio, with Bridges. Wagner Faust ov. & Strauss Don Juan. Marvellous works, thrilling & moving. Glazunov's dry & academic 6th symphony. I have never heard the orch. play better; they were enthusiastic about his conducting, & I don't wonder! He introduced me to Harry Barlow,[3] the world's greatest Tuba player, who showed me alot about the instrument, & also told us a little about his life's study of the instrument, which is treated so badly in the orch. – the yard-dog of the orch. as he puts it.

1 Britten began copying out the parts for his String Quartet in D major on 11 June, completed violin I on the 13th; violin II was finished by the 16th. The viola part was begun on 17 June, continued on the 22nd and finally completed four days later, on the 26th. The cello part was copied out 1–7 July. These original parts, with a few small adjustments, were used by the Gabrieli Quartet more than forty years later, for a play-through of the work when Britten was revising it in 1974.

2 A studio concert given by the BBC Orchestra (leader: Arthur Catterall), conducted by Frank Bridge and broadcast on the National Programme.

3 Henry (Harry) Barlow (1870–1932), principal tuba player with the BBC Symphony Orchestra, 1930–32. Britten was to redress the tuba's fortunes, not only in his last opera, *Death in Venice*, but in earlier works and perhaps especially in *Our Hunting Fathers* (see DMBA, p. 37). Britten clearly took Barlow's espousal of the instrument to heart.

Wednesday, 17 June 1931

Begin Viola part. Usual Practise. Walk with Gates after tea. Frank
Bridge rings up at dinner to know whether I can go to Russ[ian].
Ballet (at Lyceum)[1] instead of Mrs Bridge who's not well with
toothache. So I go with him & Miss Fass. See De Falla's El Amor
Brujo[2] – Wonderful. Glinka Ratmir's Dream,[3] mod[?erate]. & most
glorious of all Petrushka;[4] this is an inspiration from beginning to
end. Wonderful dancing esp. Voizikowsky[5] as P. Finish with a
rolicking Danses Polovtsiennes[6] (Borodin – P. Igor). I have never
even imagined there could be such dancing.

1 A season at the Lyceum Theatre, Wellington Street, Covent Garden,
London, where ballet was often given. The Ballets Russes proper
was founded in 1909 by the Russian impresario, Sergei Diaghilev
(1872–1929), whose influence on European ballet was far-reaching.
Diaghilev engaged the most prominent writers, composers and painters of the day, not to mention a brilliant ensemble of dancers and
choreographers. After Diaghilev's death his company disbanded,
though many of his original team formed various 'Russian ballet'
ensembles, exploiting the name. In 1932 the remnants of Diaghilev's
company reformed themselves as the Ballets Russes de Monte Carlo,
the immediate predecessor of which had given the season at the
Lyceum. At least two of the ballets mentioned by Britten – the Borodin
and the Stravinsky – were Diaghilev creations.
2 Manuel de Falla's one-act ballet, composed 1914–15. See also note 3
to Diary for 1 June 1932.
3 Adapted from his opera *Ruslan and Lyudmila*.
4 Stravinsky's 'burlesque' in four scenes, choreographed by Fokine,
and first performed by the Ballets Russes de Diaghilev in Paris on
13 June 1911.
5 Leon Woizikorsky (originally Wojcikowski; 1899–1975), Polish dancer,
ballet-master and teacher, who joined the Ballets Russes in 1916.
6 The 'Polovtsian Dances' from *Prince Igor*, choreographed by Fokine
for the Ballets Russes in 1909 for their opening season.

Thursday, 18 June 1931

Go to Ireland for good comp. lesson at 10.0. Come back via R.C.M.
with Lauricella. Play tennis 4–5 with Gates; play v. badly. Go to
opera (Lyceum) with Miss Hurst & Barbara (B. & I take Miss H.)

to see Sadko.[1] v. well done – voices all good, save for excessive wobble. Music v. pretty, tuneful, but v. thin. Opera a mass of spectacular scenes; not really an opera. Scenery v. good. Chorus good; orchestra mod. not as good as last night (under E. Goossens[2] both nights – v. fine). Orchestration wonderful of course. Back about 12.0.

1 The British stage première of the opera-legend in seven scenes by Rimsky-Korsakov.
2 Eugene Goossens (1893–1962), English conductor, brother of Leon Goossens (1897–1988), who first performed Britten's *Phantasy* oboe quartet, and the harpists Marie and Sidonie Goossens. In 1940 Britten was to meet Goossens in the United States, when he was conductor of the Cincinnati Symphony Orchestra. It was there, on 28 November 1941, that Goossens conducted the first performance of Britten's *Scottish Ballad*, Op. 26, with Ethel Bartlett and Rae Robertson as soloists. (See note 1 to Letter 336.) In 1954 Goossens conducted the New Symphony Orchestra in a recording (Decca LXT 2941) of *Les Illuminations* and *Serenade* with Peter Pears and Dennis Brain as soloists.

Saturday, 20 June 1931
[*London/Friston*]

I have early breakfast & go to Victoria[1] & catch 9.20 to Eastbourne, where Mrs. Bridge meets me in Miss Fass's car (a friend of theirs who lives v. near & is with them most of the day) & motors me to their lovely cottage in Friston.[2] I play tennis all afternoon & after tea with Mr. Bridge who is really very good, & amazingly steady. Great fun. Miss Fass is here to tea & dinner, & Mr. B. & I go to her house & listen, after supper, to a bit of Carmen, on her wireless from Rome. The country around here is too superb for words. No one about at all – lovely!

1 The Southern Railway terminus serving the south of England and the Continent. Eastbourne is on the south coast and provided the nearest rail link to Friston when travelling from London.
2 Friston Field, the Bridges' country home built for them in 1923. The house still stands today. See PFL, plates 47–8.

Sunday, 21 June 1931
[*Friston*]

After breakfast at 9.30 I go for a long walk over the Downs with Mrs. Bridge. After that Mr. Bridge looks at my choral work (Thy K's B.)[1] – he is mod[erately]. pleased with my progress. Lunch with Miss Fass. Play tennis abit in afternoon with Mr. Bridge, & again after tea – he really is remarkably good. Tea at Miss Fass' & dinner (the 3 of us) back here. Listen to a Stratton Quartet[2] concert on wireless at Miss Fass's. She lends me some madrigals.

1 *Thy King's Birthday*; see note 2 to Diary for 12 January 1931.
2 The Stratton Quartet replaced the advertised ensemble, the Roth String Quartet, sharing the recital with the baritone Robert Maitland.
   The Stratton String Quartet (1927–42), leader George Stratton (1897–1954), was prominent in the thirties. It was later to give the first performance of Britten's *Three Divertimenti* at the Wigmore Hall on 25 February 1936. The other members of the Quartet were William Manuel, violin; Lawrence Leonard, viola; and John Moore, cello. The Quartet was later renamed the Aeolian String Quartet.
   Stratton was leader of the London Symphony Orchestra from 1933 to 1952.

Friday, 26 June 1931
[*London*]

Finish Viola part in morning. Practise 11.0 till lunch. Go to First Orch rehearsal at College, for pt. of afternoon. Then go on to Arthur Benjamin for tea at his house. See more of his very clever & amusing opera "Devil Take her".[1] He also looks at my songs & quartet[2] which he seems to like. Go on to Barbara's for dinner at 7.15. Back at 10.30 by bus.

1 *The Devil take her*, Benjamin's one-act comic opera, was first performed at the College on 1 December 1931 (see Diary for that date). The first professional production was given at the Old Vic on 30 November 1932, conducted by Sir Thomas Beecham.
2 The *Three Small Songs* for soprano and small orchestra: 'Love is a Sickness' (Samuel Daniel), 'Aspatia's Song' (John Fletcher), and 'Hymn to Pan' (John Fletcher), were composed in a voice and piano version 8–15 June, and orchestrated 19–24 June 1931. They remained unpublished and unperformed during Britten's lifetime. They were

first performed, in the voice and piano version, on 6 October 1986
by Louise Camens and Stephen Ralls as part of a Britten Symposium
held at the Britten–Pears School for Advanced Musical Studies,
Snape. The quartet was the work Britten had been composing in
May and June. See also Diary for 31 May 1932.

Friday, 10 July 1931

Write a good deal more of my Psalm[1] in morning. Practise as usual.
Walk with Tumpty after tea in park, and across park with
Summers after dinner. I see his father for a bit. Nora Henderson is
an absolute revelation to me, in how awful a person can be.

1 Britten composed his setting of Psalm 130, 'Out of the depths have
  I cried unto Thee, O Lord', 8–19 July 1931, scoring the work for
  chorus, brass, percussion and strings, 28 September – 3 October. The
  Psalm was reorchestrated, this time with the addition of woodwind,
  30 December 1931 – 19 January 1932.
      As a companion to Psalm 130, Britten also composed a setting of
  Psalm 150, 'Praise ye the Lord', during October 1931, scoring it in
  December. As with the earlier psalm setting, Britten revised his
  orchestral version, incorporating corrections and revisions probably
  suggested by John Ireland.
      The two Psalms remained unheard during Britten's lifetime in spite
  of Vaughan Williams's efforts to secure a performance in 1932 (see
  Diary for 10 February 1932 and 22 June 1932). In 1962 Britten returned
  to the text of Psalm 150, making a new setting for two-part children's
  voices and instruments (Op. 67), first performed at the 1963 Aldeburgh Festival on 24 June.

Saturday, 11 July 1931

Walk with Tumpty & Summers in morning. Go to Barbara's in
afternoon. We sit in Ranelagh (?) Gdns[1] before tea, have tea at
her flat; walk part of way back here where she has dinner & a bath
afterwards.
    I have a sudden passion for writing limericks in morning. Write
about a dozen on people in this house.[2]

1 The pleasure gardens in south-west London famous for musical
  entertainments in the eighteenth century.
2 No examples of these, alas, seem to have survived. Perhaps this

burst of literary activity (which might have told us a lot about the household at Prince's Square) was stimulated by Britten's unflattering observations, the day before, on one of his fellow lodgers. Wulff Scherchen, recollecting Britten in 1989, wrote: '[Ben] loved punning, clerihews and limericks. At times, when in an exuberant mood, he would continue making up puns till I was weak with laughter and had to beg him to stop.' This was a memory from the thirties, from the pre-war years at the Old Mill at Snape. The same infectious high spiritedness was to be part of domestic life in Stanton Cottage, Amityville, on Long Island, when Britten and Pears joined the Mayer family in 1939.

Sunday, 12 July 1931

Church at 8.0 at St. Matthews with Tumpty & (alas) Nora, & also at 11.0 at St. Marks with Miss Prior. Go to tea with Barbara, & walk to Trafalgar Sq. with her & take a bus back here. (She has to go to Char[ing]. X to meet Miss Hurst). Walk with Summers after supper.
    Write about ten more limericks.

Monday, 13 July 1931

Write more Psalm, practise 11–12, lesson (to make up for last Wed.) with Benjamin 12.40. Practise in afternoon. Walk after tea with Miss Alford,[1] a great collector of Folk songs & dances, writer of books & novelist who is staying here. She is amazingly interesting & knows tons about ballet, & proposes that I should write music to one of her ballet "books".[2]

1 Violet Alford (1881–1972), one of the most widely known and respected authorities on the folklore of the traditional dances and dance customs of western Europe. She was among those who shared in the pioneering work of Cecil Sharp on the folk dances of England, but she was to become an expert on the traditional dancing of the Basque region. In 1927 Miss Alford organized the first visit of an English dance team to the Basque Festival at Bayonne; one of those who went was another enthusiast, Imogen Holst. She published over a hundred books and articles from 1923 onwards, mostly concerned with the folk dancing of the Basque region.

2 To kindle Britten's enthusiasm, Miss Alford took him the next day to see Ida Rubinstein (1885–1960), the Russian dancer, at Covent

The first page of the scenario for *Plymouth Town* in Violet Alford's hand

Garden in a programme that included Honegger's *Les Noces de l'amour et de Psyche* (after Bach, 1928); *David*, by Henri Sauget (b. 1901), and Ravel's *Ma Mère l'oye* (1912) and *Bolero* (1928), which was written for Rubinstein. Britten recorded his impressions in his diary:

Don't think much of Rub. but scenery & Corps de ballet – Wonderful. Bach v. beautiful (quite brilliantly arranged by Honegger) tho' long. David, dramatic but music poor. Bolero taken very slowly; interesting but not exhilerating.

On 31 July Miss Alford sent Britten her scenario for a ballet entitled *Plymouth Town* (an excerpt from which is reproduced on p. 189, complete with a verse from the sea song 'A-Roving' ('In Plymouth Town there lived a maid') on which Britten based his score. It provides an interesting musical precedent for *The Golden Vanity*, Op. 78. Britten purchased a copy of the folksong on 10 August, and sketched the work in Lowestoft, 12–28 August. He scored it 19 October – 22 November, and submitted it to the Camargo Society (see note 3 to Diary for 15 November 1931) for consideration on 6 December 1931. *Plymouth Town* is one of the longest of Britten's works from this period, and one of the few scored for orchestra. Its theme – one of innocence corrupted – is typical of Britten in later years; and it is equally typical that the theme should have surfaced so early in his compositional career. *Plymouth Town* was not taken up by the Camargo Society, but in spite of this Britten embarked on a second, untitled ballet with Violet Alford based on a Basque scenario in June 1932. See note 1 to Diary for 15 June 1932. Already, on 5 August 1930, Britten had written in his diary, 'Am considering writing of a Ballet. I am searching Anderson [Hans Andersen].' Two pages from the MS full score of *Plymouth Town* are reproduced on pp. 192–3.

Wednesday, 22 July 1931

I go to comp[osition]. exam. at Coll. at 12.0. Absolute Farce. Examiners – V. Williams,[1] Waddington,[2] Edgar Bainton[3] (not, unfortunately, Ireland). I have $\frac{1}{2}$ hrs exam on all the work done this year! Of course they look at the wrong things & make me play the wrong things out of the hundreds of things I take them! I don't practise in afternoon, but lie on my bed, as my feet are v. red & swollen. Write to Gates after dinner.

1 Ralph Vaughan Williams (1872–1958), English composer. He joined the teaching staff of the College after the end of the First World War, a post he retained until 1939, although he undertook occasional deputizing for colleagues for several years afterwards. Britten's relationship with Vaughan Williams (and to his music) was never an easy one. He had no great enthusiasm for his senior's works and remembered what he took to be a generally unsympathetic attitude on Vaughan Williams's part during his student years, although he and Pears, with the Zorian String Quartet, were occasionally to perform Vaughan Williams's song-cycle, *On Wenlock Edge*, and in 1948 recorded the work for Decca (M 585–7). Christopher Headington remembers being told by Pears that it was he who persuaded Britten to perform a work 'he didn't much like because – doubtless among

other things – "badly scored" '. (On the other hand, as note 2 to Diary for 6 May 1931 has revealed, Britten, in earlier days, had thought the Tallis Fantasia 'v. beautiful' and 'wonderfully scored'.)

On 4 December 1930, Vaughan Williams had conducted Britten (a member of the Carlyle Singers) in a performance of the *Fantasia on Christmas Carols*, as part of the Kensington Festival: 'R.V.W. Xmas Fantasia thrilling to sing,' Britten wrote in his diary, '& I should think to listen to. V. beautiful', an opinion he did not maintain.

Later, on 16 June 1933, he attended (with Grace Williams) a production at the College of Vaughan Williams's opera, *Hugh the Drover*:

It needs a larger stage, of course – even so the First Act was very exciting & the rest was a dreadful anti climax. V.W. had shown in places apt use of chorus, in other dreadful disregard of natural movements. The music was full of folk-songs (if you like that sort of thing) – it was best so – when not (as between Scenes in Act II) it was dreadful.

It was probably on the occasion of the 1931 award of the Farrar Composition Prize (see note 1 to Diary for 24 July 1931) that Vaughan Williams is said by one source to have remarked, 'Very clever but beastly music.' (See, however, Letter 28.) We cannot be absolutely sure of the occasion but the comment itself is well attested; whether it was Vaughan Williams's or another's, there can be little doubt that it rather accurately reflected the kind of testy, disbelieving, dismissive impatience that was all too often the stock reaction to the student Britten's gifts. One is reminded of a somewhat similar comment on a different occasion recalled by John Ireland in an interview with Arthur Jacobs (BBC Radio, 11 August 1959):

He was the most highly talented and brilliant pupil I've ever had [. . .] I remember quite well at the examination for the scholarship, I was one of the three who were present to adjudicate these scholarships. And Britten was then about sixteen, I think, if that [. . .] of course, we were astonished, and one of the examiners, who is now dead – *not* Vaughan Williams – said, 'Well, I don't think it's decent that a public schoolboy [. . .] of that age should be writing this kind of music.'

Vaughan Williams, in any event, was to show a generous, sympathetic and, one might think, altogether more characteristic attitude with regard to Britten's early Psalms, of which he tried (unsuccessfully) to secure a performance: see note 1 to Diary for 10 July 1931 and note 1 to Diary for 22 June 1932.

2 Sydney Peine Waddington (1869–1953), English composer and teacher of harmony at the College from 1905. He was a close and influential friend of Vaughan Williams. For further information see RVW's 'Obituary – Sydney Waddington', *R.C.M. Magazine*, 49/3, 1953, pp. 79–80.

3 Edgar Bainton (1880–1956), English composer, pianist and teacher, who was director of the Music School in Newcastle upon Tyne, 1912–33.

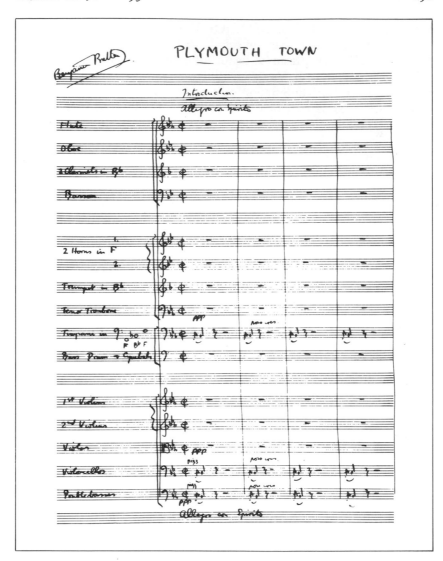

Pages 1 and 91 of the MS full score of *Plymouth Town*; the inscription at the end reads: '*Fine/Benjamin Britten /Nov. 22nd 1931./173 Cromwell Rd.,/S.W.5./& 21 Kirkley Cliff Rd.,/Lowestoft*'

The trumpets of the Marine Patrol are heard "off"
Trumpet "off" (senza sord.)
marcato

Friday, 24 July 1931

I hear from Lauricella that I have won the Farrar Comp[1] prize, &
go to College soon after breakfast to confirm this. I pack all the
rest of the day, with breaks for meals, 1 hrs. Practise, 11.45–12.45,
1 hrs. v. enjoyable & quite good tennis with Mrs Johnson[2] at Hotel
Commodore, 4–5. Barbara comes after dinner to help me in my
packing. Go to say good-bye to Mr. Bridge abt. 10. & don't get
home till abt. 12.30. V. interesting talk; he's been to international
festival at Oxford.[3].

1 The Ernest Farrar Composition Prize. Farrar was a composer and
  organist (1885–1918; killed in action). He was a student at the College,
  1905–9, and a friend of Frank Bridge. The prize was founded in his
  memory but is now amalgamated with the Sullivan Prize. Britten
  was to win the prize again in 1933.
2 The parlour maid at Britten's lodgings.
3 This was the ninth annual festival of the ISCM (International Society
  for Contemporary Music) held in London and Oxford.
      At future ISCM Festivals, in 1934 (Florence), 1936 (Barcelona), 1938
  (London) and 1941 (New York), important performances were to be
  given of early works by Britten.

Sunday, 26 July 1931
[*Lowestoft*]

Church with Mum & Aunt Janie at St Johns, at 11.0. Terrible hymns,
tho' quite a fine sermon by Rev ? Stanley.[1] Barbara goes back to
town by 5.10 unfortunately. Mummy goes to station with her. Walk
with Pop (& Caesar) both before supper & bed. I am finishing
Maurois' marvellous Disraeli.[2] Play innumerable Beethoven Sonatas
at various hours of the day.

1 The Revd Thomas Henry Stanley, MA, BD, was the Canadian-trained
  curate at St John's, from February 1931. The incumbent, the Revd
  William Reeve, was away in Blankenberghe, Belgium, during the
  month of July.
2 *La Vie de Disraeli* (1927), the biography of Disraeli by André Maurois.
  It first appeared in an English translation by Hamish Miles: *Disraeli:
  A Picture of the Victorian Age* (London, John Lane, 1927).

ROYAL COLLEGE OF MUSIC.

TEACHERS' TERMINAL REPORT, MIDSUMMER TERM, 1931.

Pupil's Name **Britten, Edward. B.**

	Regularity, Punctuality, and Industry	Progress and General Remarks	Teacher's Signature
PRINCIPAL STUDY *Composition*	*remarkable*	*has produced a great deal of very able & interesting work, there considerable grasp of form & technique.*	*J.I.*
SECOND STUDY *Piano*	*Has a natural aptitude & is truly musical.*		*AB*
PAPER WORK			
AURAL TRAINING			

The Christmas Term commences on Monday, 21st September, 1931.

I hear the best news of him from V.W. (all the rest) I have not forgotten the letter.

July, 1931. Mr Britten will be ... **Hugh P. Allen** Director.

Britten's Terminal Report at the College for the midsummer term, 1931

27 To Remo Lauricella

21, Kirkley Cliff Road,
Lowestoft.
July 29th 1931

Dear Remo,

Thank you everso much for your letter which arrived on Friday. I am so sorry I haven't answered it before, but I came away on Saturday & have been very busy since I arrived.

I was so sorry that I didn't see you on the Thursday; I meant to come to the College, but I wasn't frightfully well, and unable to go.

Heartiest congrats. on winning the fiddle prize[1] – of course I knew you couldn't help it. I was so surprised when I got your letter to find I'd got a composition prize that I had to go to the College at once to find out whether it was true or not. I am very bucked about it, especially because I shall be able to get an expensive new tennis racquet.[2] I don't think that I shall be coming up to town these holidays at all, and so I shall have to wait until next term to see you. I must stop now & post this – Please excuse it's brevity.

Hoping you are well,

Yours very sincerely,

BENJAMIN BRITTEN

1 Lauricella had been awarded the Alfred and Catherine Howard prize for violinists.
2 See Diary for 30 July 1931.

Thursday, 30 July 1931

Usual playing, but walk with Beth, going to Molls[1] & buying a new tennis racquet with prize money – Austin[2] – 75/- (paying 70/-) a superb one. I play tennis 5–7 on court opposite (too wet for grass) with sometime Beth & sometime Mr Sewell, but even this racquet cannot raise my play above the most execrable standard. Walk with Pop before bed.

1 Moll's Sports House, athletic outfitters, 173 London Road South, Lowestoft.
2 Tennis racquet named after 'Bunny' Austin (1906–1990), English tennis champion. See also note 2 to Letter 292.

Friday, 31 July 1931

Walk with Beth in morning; after playing Viola with Aunt. Go to Meads to tennis at 3.0, playing on Mrs Woodger's[1] court. Just Kathleen Mead, Beth, Tommy Pedder,[2] & I. We have some quite good tennis on the whole. Get back rather late, at 7.30. Miss Alford sends me a libretto for a ballet – it looks amusing but will be dashed difficult to cope with.

1 The Woodgers lived at North Lodge, 10 Yarmouth Road, Lowestoft.
2 Tommy Pedder, a childhood friend of the Brittens and the Meads.

Sunday, 2 August 1931

Walk with Pop in morning after which I play Beethoven's Diabelli
Var. [Op. 120] all through – what an incredibly marvellous work!
Willcock,[1] who has been on the broads, comes to see me in the
afternoon & we walk together. Walk with Pop, Beth & Rosemary[2]
after tea, & with Pop before bed. Begin reading Long Road of John
Oxenham.[3] So far jolly good.

1 See note 1 to Letter 482.
2 Rosemary Pollard, a schoolfriend of Beth's who lived in Norwich.
  She occasionally stayed with the Brittens in Lowestoft.
3 John Oxenham (1855–1941), English novelist and poet, whose name
  was originally William Arthur Dunkerley. His novel, *The Long Road*,
  was first published by Methuen in 1907.

28 To Mrs Britten
From Sir Hugh Allen
[*Typed*]

Royal College of Music
Prince Consort Road, South Kensington,
London, S.W.7.
3rd. August, 1931.

Dear Mrs. Britten,

I was delighted to hear from Vaughan Williams who examined
at the end of the term for the Composition how highly he thought
of your boy's work. I will do my best next year to give him as much
assistance as is possible for I have a high opinion of his ability
and would desire to do everything to help him. Is there any
possibility of making application to the County Council Education
Authorities of your district.[1] It rather depends upon the place in
which he was born, but if you would let me know, I would see
if it were possible to do anything in that direction.

Yours sincerely,
HUGH P. ALLEN

1 To the best of our knowledge, Britten did not receive any funding
  from the Suffolk County Council to support his studies at the College.

Monday, 3 August 1931 (Bank Holiday)

We all, except Pop (who stays to play golf) go out for lunch & tea
to a lovely spot near Covehithe,[1] near the sea. Picnicing is very
nice. Back at 6.0. Go to Sparrows Nest[2] in evening (including Pop
this time) to hear Paul Robeson[3] & a Vaudeville company. He has
a remarkable organ, but didn't seem able to use it. I am not an
enthusiast of the Negro Spirituals. The rest of show tame, except
a man called Halls[4] v. funny & clever, & a clown[5] & acrobats.[6]

1 A village between Southwold and Lowestoft.

2 The following description appears in *Kelly's Directory for Suffolk* (1929
   edition):

   Sparrow's Nest Park, sometimes called 'Victoria Park' was purchased by the
   Corporation in 1897, and laid out in such a manner as to preserve the natural
   beauties of the site; about one-third of the total area consists of well-wooded
   grassy slopes, in which is a spring of mineral water; at the foot of these
   slopes is Sparrow's Nest House.

   The theatre was in the grounds of the park. In 1919 Britten and his
   mother took part in a dramatic performance of Charles Kingsley's
   The Water Babies at the Sparrow's Nest Theatre: see PFL, plate 15.

3 The American bass (1898–1976), the legendary black singer of his
   time, who was celebrated for his rendering of Negro spirituals,
   appeared in Lowestoft on 2 and 3 August. He was also a striking
   actor, in the theatre (*Show Boat*) and films (*Sanders of the River*). Remo
   Lauricella tells us that Robeson sometimes made use of the studios
   at the New School of Music which he and Britten used for practising.
   His career in the United States stopped abruptly in the 1940s after
   his espousal of communism. See also Martin Bauml Duberman, *Paul
   Robeson* (London, The Bodley Head, 1989) and Murray Kempton's
   review, 'The Fate of Paul Robeson', *New York Review of Books*, 27
   April 1989, pp. 3–7.
       It was Robeson who made famous Earl Robinson's *Ballad for Ameri-
   cans*, with words by John Latouche, the broadcast of which in November 1939 created a sensation and provided Auden with a model
   against which he was to react in *Paul Bunyan*, although at the same
   time the *Ballad* may be said to have left its mark on Auden's and
   Britten's 1941 operetta. For a full account of the impact made by
   Robinson's *Ballad*, see Duberman, pp. 235–7, and DMPB, p. 107. The
   original recording of *Ballad for Americans*, with Paul Robeson, the
   American People's Chorus and the Victor Symphony Orchestra, conducted by Nathaniel Shilkret, was reissued on Vanguard VSD 57/58.
   A photograph of John Latouche appears in Christopher Sawyer-
   Lançanno, *An Invisible Spectator: A Biography of Paul Bowles* (London,

Bloomsbury, 1989). This is a still from a 1936 film, *145 W. 21.*, for which Bowles wrote the music, and in which Aaron Copland also had a role. In 1943, on 28 and 29 September, Robinson's *Ballad for Americans* was heard in London at the Royal Albert Hall in a pair of concerts sponsored by Lord Beaverbook's *Daily Express*, symbolizing the Anglo-American alliance and celebrating the contribution of blacks to the war effort – hence the presence of a black chorus, though the soloist was white (Kenneth Cantril). In the preparation of this event, Marc Blitzstein was prominent.

4 Alec Halls.

5 Clown Argo, who undertook bird and animal impersonations.

6 The acrobatic duo, Christopher and Columbus.

Wednesday, 5 August 1931

Bathe with Beth & Rosemary before lunch – Mummy has a Care of Girls committee meeting,[1] & with Mummy, Beth, Rosemary, Mr & Clive Chartres before tea. Mr & Mrs, Jean, & Clive come to tea on Beach. Bobby arrives by 6.53 from West Hartlepool. His marriage to Marjorie (Alas) is arranged now.[2] Go to Palace[3] to see Talkie film Charlie's Aunt,[4] with Beth & Rosemary in evening. Screemingly funny.

1 One of Mrs Britten's social welfare activities.

2 The marriage was to take place at West Hartlepool on 3 September.

3 Palace Cinema (E.V. Barr Ltd), London Road South, Lowestoft.

4 Sound film version of *Charlie's Aunt*, an American film adaptation (Columbia Pictures, 1930) of Brandon Thomas's riotously funny stage play with Charles Ruggles (1886–1970) in the title role, directed by Al Christie.

Monday, 10 August 1931

Practise Viola & Piano in morning, & walk with Mummy in morning. Go up to Morlings with Bobby in aft, to get "A-Roving" (Plymouth Town),[1] on which Miss Alford's Ballet (which I am going to set to Music) is based. Mr. Horne (& his wife)[2] come in after Supper. He used to dig[3] with Pop in Ipswich when they were young.

1 See note 2 to Diary for 13 July 1931. This copy of the sea shanty seems not to have survived.

2 Ernest Horne, dental surgeon of 10 Station Road, Beccles. Mr Britten had known Horne from his early days as an assistant to Mr Pennaren, dental surgeon of Fonnerau Road, Ipswich.

3 To share lodgings.

Wednesday, 12 August 1931

Begin an introduction to my Ballet in morning. Walk with Bobby & Caesar before lunch. After lunch Beth drives Mum. over to Normanshurst[1] for a Care of Girls Bridge drive.[2] Play tennis here with Beth, Bobby Margaret & Joan Stewart,[3] & Barbara Spashet.[4] Not Super tennis. Go on Pier with Beth & Bobby after dinner.

1 The home of Mrs H.R. Tamplin in Normanston Drive, Lowestoft.

2 'Drive': communal game of Bridge, in this instance a fund-raising activity for one of Mrs Britten's good causes in Lowestoft.

3 Friends of the Brittens who lived at Bungay.

4 Daughter of George Spashett (Vice-Consul of Sweden, Latvia and Germany), Langdale, Cotmer Road, Oulton Broad, Lowestoft.

Saturday, 22 August 1931

Walk with Bobby up to Morlings, after breakfast to get Ravel's Introduction & All° (played by Cockerill, Virtuosos, Murchie & Draper)[1] & Bridge Novellette no 3 (Virtuosos) on 2 Records.[2] Absolutely thrilling!

Go to Chartres with Beth in car at 3.30 for tennis; have only rather feeble tennis on a very wet court.

1 John Cockerill, English harpist; Robert Murchie, English flautist; Charles Draper, English clarinettist. The members of the Virtuoso String Quartet were Marjorie Hayward, violin; Raymond Jeremy, violin; Edwin Virgo, viola; and Cedric Sharpe, cello.

2 Bridge's three *Novelletten* for string quartet were composed and first performed in 1904 and published in 1915. The recording of the Ravel and the Bridge was released in May 1929 on HMV c1662–3. Britten's set of records is in the Archive.

Tuesday, 25 August 1931

We all have rather filthly colds – Bobby is in bed all day with one. Don't do anything special all day – stuck with Ballet (being saturated in Ravel!). Walk with Caesar twice in morning; & with Pop after tea & dinner.

Friday, 28 August 1931

I finish my ballet "Plymouth Town", at which I work morning & evening. I am quite pleased with it. Go to Arnold's to tennis in afternoon with Beth, by bus. There is quite a crowd there (in all abt. 10). Mod. tennis, good & bad in spots. Cut lawn after coming back, & also take Caesar for walk. Pop isn't at all well in evening.

Wednesday, 9 September 1931

A car runs away down hill in morning, & hits a woman & child, by our gate.

I get W. Walton's Viola Concerto from O.U.P.[1] It's a fine work but difficult. Walk with Beth before lunch. Go with Beth & 4 Chartres (– Gordon) to "Hell's Angels"[2] at Marina in aft. Marvellous photography spoilt by slop. stuff. Listen on a hired wireless to Brahms prom.[3] Rhapsody [Op. 53] – wonderful work, spoilt completely by atmospherics, as was rest of concert. D'ble Concerto [in A minor, for violin, cello and orchestra] Arthur Catteral,[4] good, L. Kennedy wonderful – tone comparable to Casals.[5] Magnificent 4th Symph to wind up with.

1 William Walton (1902–1983), English composer, whose music was published by Oxford University Press (who were to be Britten's first publishers: see Diary for 29 February 1932). Walton's Viola Concerto was first performed on 3 October 1929, with Hindemith as soloist. Britten ordered the piano score (published in 1930) from London, perhaps to prepare himself for the concert next day (see Diary for 10 September 1931). This score, signed and dated by Britten, is in the Archive. Britten was later given a copy of the miniature score, published in 1938, inscribed: 'To Benjamin from William'. The two men were to become friends, though the relationship was not without its frictions. As Susana Walton, the composer's widow, recounts in her memoir of her husband (*William Walton: Behind the Façade*, Oxford, Oxford University Press, 1988), pp. 122–3, 'William considered

[Britten] a rival.' She described an incident that shows how the jealousy of which Britten was conscious, and to which he sometimes would refer, could manifest itself in unexpected ways and locations:

By chance, Ben Britten's new opera *Peter Grimes* was being premièred at the Lucerne Opera House, and the window of the music shop was full of scores by Britten [. . .] A large photograph of Britten was propped on a chair. Without looking to right or to left, William, clutching his quire of paper and his pencils, reached into the window of the shop, picked up the photograph, and put it neatly on the chair seat, face down. Then he dusted off his hands with satisfaction and left.

But one should not dwell on the tensions. In fact, Walton's letters to Britten reveal a generous and admiring response to the younger man's music from the pre-war years onwards. For example, on hearing an early performance of the *Bridge Variations*, conducted by Constant Lambert, Walton scribbled an undated pencil note, 'Having just listened to your "Variations" I should like you to know how very excellent I thought them. It is really a fine work.' He appeared as a witness on Britten's behalf at his conscientious objector's Tribunal in 1942 (see Letter 397), a gesture Britten was warmly to acknowledge in 1963, in a letter to Walton: 'I've never forgotten your noble and generous support of me in a very low moment in the War.' He wrote in the same letter (16 December):

I don't know if I ever told you, but hearing your Viola Concerto & Portsmouth Point (works which I still love dearly) was a great turning point in my musical life. I'd got in a muddle; poor old John Ireland wasn't much help, & I couldn't get on with the 12–tone idea (still can't) – & you showed me the way of being relaxed & fresh, & intensely personal & yet still with the terms of reference which I had to have. It comes, I'm sure, because the ideas were fine & clear, which is all that matters – [. . .]

In 1953 Walton was a contributing composer to the *Variations on an Elizabethan Theme (Sellinger's Round)*, first heard at the Aldeburgh Festival in that year; and his one-act opera, *The Bear* (after Chekhov), a story brought to his attention by Peter Pears (see Susana Walton, op. cit., pp. 197–202) was first performed at the 1967 Aldeburgh Festival. His *Improvisations on an Impromptu of Benjamin Britten*, for orchestra, was first performed at San Francisco on 14 January 1970. The theme was taken from the (revised) slow movement of Britten's Piano Concerto. But perhaps the strength of Walton's admiration found its best expression in the remarkable letter he wrote to Britten on 23 November 1963, a day after Britten's fiftieth birthday. It is a letter that puts into perspective the two composers' friendship and renders any human failings insignificant:

You must almost by now be suffering from a surfeit of adulation & praise, so I won't add to it. All the same I should like to tell you, that I celebrated your birthday in my own way by playing my favourite works – Spring

Symphony – Nocturne & War Requiem – each in its different way a master-
work, particularly the latter – a non-stop masterpiece without blemish – in
fact, on a par with the two great Requiems of the 19th century, or for that
matter, any other century.

In the last years your music has come to mean more & more to me – it
shines out as a beacon (how banal I'm becoming!) in, to me at least, a chaotic
& barren musical world & I am sure it does for thousands of others as well.
I know that I should understand what is going [on], but I suppose it is a
matter [of] age – old age maybe; but there it is – I don't. But I do understand,
appreciate & love, I hope, nearly everything about your music, not only the
ingenuity & technique but the emotional depth of feeling, & above all the
originality & beauty of sound which permeates these works. The War
Requiem is worth 100s of Lord Russells & Aldermaston marches & it will
surely have the effect which you, possibly subconsciously, have striven for,
for you have made articulate the wishes of numberless inarticulate masses.

Britten responded in wholly characteristic terms which at the same
time, showed how genuinely moved he was by Walton's fine words
(again his letter of 16 December 1963):

I am most grateful to you for having written so warmly & generously for
my birthday. I had already been so pleased to get the telegram from you
& Su, & then was overwhelmed, to get the letter as well. It was a wonderful
tribute from a colleague, & you know, I think, how much this kind of thing
means – especially in those (very frequent!) moments of depression when
one can't find the right notes, & also loathes every thing one has ever done.
(I don't think any composer has ever felt less confident than I – especially
somehow when the public praise seems to have got rather out of hand!)
I do thank you most warmly.

See also MKWW.

2 The celebrated early 'talkie' about two Americans who become fliers
  in World War I, also noted for its use of monochrome and colour
  photography. Released in the United States in 1930, *Hell's Angels* was
  directed by Howard Hughes (1904–1976), with music composed by
  Hugo Reisenfeld (1879–1939).

3 Given by the BBC Symphony Orchestra conducted by Henry Wood.
  Muriel Brunskill (1899–1980), the English alto, who had studied with
  Wood, was the soloist in the *Alto Rhapsody*.

4 Arthur Catterall (1883–1943), English violinist. He was leader of the
  Hallé Orchestra and BBC Symphony Orchestra and founded and led
  his own string quartet, the Catterall String Quartet.

5 Pablo (Pau) Casals (1876–1973), the Spanish cellist.

Thursday, 10 September 1931

Go in car up town in morning with Mum & Beth, & walk back with Caesar. Play tennis, 3.30–4.30, 5.30–7.30 on court opp. with Beth, K. Mead, Mr. Amery,[1] Mrs Sewell, Teddy Rogers & after tea Mr. Sewell. Listen to Prom. after dinner; British Composers' Night.[2] Walton's wonderful Vla Concerto (beautifully played by Tertis)[3] stood out as a work of genius. Lambert's[4] Rio Grande very interesting, & beautiful, as was Holst's Ballet from Perfect Fool,[5] & Warlock's[6] Capriol Suite. Boughton's[7] 2 songs (beautifully sung by Trefor Jones)[8] amusing, quite delightful. Smyth's songs[9] Chrysella, & the Dance – the reverse – despicable!

1 Probably George R. Amory, of 19 Wellington Esplanade, Lowestoft.

2 Given by the BBC Symphony Orchestra, conducted by Henry Wood at the Queen's Hall, London. The composers Dame Ethel Smyth, Constant Lambert and William Walton conducted their own compositions. Apart from the works Britten mentions in his diary entry, the programme also included the *Four Conceits*, Op. 20 (1917, orchestrated 1921), by Eugene Goossens.

3 Lionel Tertis (1876–1975), English viola player.

4 Constant Lambert (1905–1951), English composer, conductor and writer. He was a pupil of Vaughan Williams at the College. *The Rio Grande* was composed in 1927 and first performed in 1929. Lambert was conductor of the Camargo Society's ballet productions (see note 4 to Diary for 15 November 1931) and Music Director of the Vic–Wells ballet, from 1931 to 1947. The piano soloist in *The Rio Grande* was the English pianist, Angus Morrison (b. 1902), a close friend of both Walton and Lambert. Britten and Lambert were never close friends or colleagues but their careers touched at various points. In the pre-war years there was a ballet proposal discussed with Lambert (see note 2 to Letter 120) and, post-war, another idea for a ballet was mooted (see note 3 to Letter 415). Lambert had written about Britten's Piano Concerto, in 1938 (see note 1 to Letter 145), and in April, a year later, conducted the first performance of *Ballad of Heroes* (see note 4 to Letter 167). After Britten's return to England in 1942, Lambert conducted a performance of *Sinfonia da Requiem* in December (see note 9 to Letter 397). See Richard Shead, *Constant Lambert* (London, Simon Publications, 1973) and Andrew Motion, *The Lamberts: George, Constant and Kit* (London, Chatto and Windus, 1986).

5 *The Perfect Fool* was first performed at Covent Garden on 14 May 1923.

6 Peter Warlock (Philip Heseltine) (1894–1930), English composer, principally of songs and vocal chamber music, editor and writer. His
  Capriol Suite for string orchestra was composed in 1926.

7 Rutland Boughton (1878–1960), English composer, principally of
  opera. The 'two songs' to which Britten refers were taken from
  Boughton's most successful opera *The Immortal Hour*, composed
  1912–13 and first performed at Glastonbury, 1914: 'Song of Creation'
  and 'Faery Song' ('How beautiful they are, the lordly ones'). See also
  Addenda 3 and 4.

8 Trefor Jones (1901–1965), Welsh tenor.

9 Ethel Mary Smyth (1858–1944), English composer, conductor and
  pioneering feminist. She was created a DBE in 1922. 'Chrysella' and
  'The Dance', both of them songs with chamber music (or piano)
  accompaniment, were composed in 1909. The songs were sung by
  the English baritone, Herbert Heyner (1881–1954).

Friday, 11 September 1931

Finish an arrangement of Haydn's D maj. 'cello concerto[1] in
morning for viola, & practise it. Walk with Beth also, & in
afternoon. Play tennis with her 5.30–6.30 on court opposite. Listen
to a section of Beethoven Prom;[2] Marvellous Leonora no 2. (In many
ways I prefer this to no. 3; there is no anticlimax); concerto no. 2,
beautifully, & joyously played by Cyril Smith.[3] "Thou Monstrous
Fiend" (Fidelio)[4] sung by Stiles Allen;[5] – a wonderful organ, naught
else. At this moment we were cut off for a wretched babble from
Snowdon.[6]

1 Only the viola part of the first movement, *Allegro moderato*, survives
  in the Archive. Presumably the piano part was the printed copy from
  which Britten worked: the Peters edition, edited by Julius Klengel.
  In 1960 Britten conducted a performance of the Haydn D major Cello
  Concerto, with the French cellist, Maurice Gendron (see note 1 to
  Letter 499), and the Aldeburgh Festival Orchestra, in Orford Church,
  on 26 June. In 1964 Britten provided cadenzas for Haydn's recently
  discovered C major Cello Concerto; these were written for Mstislav
  Rostropovich, who first performed them, under Britten, on 18 June
  at the 1964 Aldeburgh Festival.

2 Given by the BBC Symphony Orchestra, conducted by Henry Wood,
  at the Queen's Hall, London. Apart from the works Britten mentions
  in his diary the programme also included Symphony No. 7.

3 Cyril Smith (1909–1974), English pianist.

4 Leonore's great Act I recitative and aria, 'Abscheulicher, wo lebst du hin'.
5 Lilian Stiles-Allen (1896–1982), English soprano.
6 Viscount Snowden (1864–1937), Chancellor of the Exchequer in the Labour government (1929–1931), and in the ensuing 'National' government led by Ramsay MacDonald. Snowden presented his crisis budget to Parliament on 10 September. What Britten heard on the 11th was Snowden's explication of it to the nation, in a BBC broadcast, a tradition that is sustained to this day. He resigned in September 1932, when he was Lord Privy Seal.

Tuesday, 15 September 1931

Bazil Reeve comes in morning; play a bit of Walton Concerto with him.[1] Walk up town with him & Beth. Play tennis 3.0–4.30; with K. Mead & Beth & Mr. Poole (late Master at South Lodge)[2] & after tea 6.0–7.0 with Mr. Poole.

1 Reeve playing the piano reduction, with Britten at the viola.
2 Probably Sydney Poole of 14 Cleveland Road, Lowestoft.

Tuesday, 22 September 1931
[*London*]

Walk & shop (Harrods)[1] with Mum & Pop in morning. Go to Liverpool St. to see them & Barbara off to Lowestoft by 3.10. Tea here. Walk after. Go to Prom.[2] after early dinner (6.30). Volga Boatman's Song (blatently arranged). Song of Flea (Moussorgsky)[3] – Harold Williams excellently sung – very amusing. Rachmaninov's terrible – vulgar, old-fashioned 2nd Pft. Concerto (Solomon).[4] Mossolov's Factory – amusing – nothing more. Tchaikovsky's 4th Symphony – which makes one long for chamber music & Mozart, & makes one deplore the discovery of "Fate".[5] Rather ragged orchestral playing. I prom, only till $\frac{1}{2}$ time.

1 The department store in Knightsbridge, London. On the day before, Britten and Beth had moved to a new address, 173 Cromwell Road, SW5.
2 Given by the BBC Symphony Orchestra, conducted by Henry Wood, at the Queen's Hall, London. Apart from the works mentioned by Britten in his diary, the programme also included an orchestral version of the Volga Boatman's Song, Rimsky-Korsakov's overture to

Ivan the Terrible, and the Scherzo and March from Prokofiev's opera, *The Love for Three Oranges* (1919).

3 Mussorgsky: 'Mephistopheles's Song of the Flea' (text from Goethe).

4 Professional name used by Solomon Cutner (1902–1988), English pianist, who was to suffer an incapacitating stroke in 1956. Solomon was the soloist in the first performance of Bliss's Piano Concerto when it was given at the World's Fair, New York, in 1939.

5 Britten refers here to the identification of the 'motto' theme of the opening bars of the symphony's first movement with 'Fate' (cf. Beethoven's Fifth Symphony, whose 'motto' was similarly attributed).

Thursday, 24 September 1931

Go up to Harrods in morning to see abt a Pft for Pop to give to Bobby.[1] Practise in Lounge[2] 11–1.0. Practise in N. School of M. 2.40–3.40. Go to Madrigals at 6.0; general meeting as well as singing. Get back for dinner at 8.0, & listen afterwards, on wireless in Lounge to Prom[3] – Ireland's Pft Concerto & Holst's Planets. I still think the first very loosely put together, & second too sugary (celesta); both have v. fine & beautiful moments; but I feel no music of that generation can be compared to works like Walton's Viola Concerto.

1 Britten's brother, Robert, not only played the violin but also the piano. The boys formed a violin and piano duo, and a favourite piece was the César Franck Sonata. On occasion, the brothers – when boys at home – had competed for the family instrument's use (with the younger brother usually coming off best). Perhaps the intention of Britten's parents was to remedy an old grievance by giving Robert a piano of his own in celebration of his wedding on 3 September.

2 At his digs.

3 From the Queen's Hall, given by the BBC Symphony Orchestra, conducted by Henry Wood and Gustav Holst.

Tuesday, 29 September 1931

More scoring in morning & evening.[1] Practise as usual only 2.30–4.0 with Lauricella in N.S.M. [New School of Music.] We do the Beethoven Vln Concerto, which he plays in evening really very well. Listen in on a rather poor wireless, to Mozart's Jupiter

Symphony. Even then it was magnificent, especially the
exhilerating & gorgeous last movement. What a marvellous man
Mozart is! (It was from the Prom).[2]

1 Of Psalm 130.
2 Given by the BBC Symphony Orchestra conducted by Henry Wood,
   at the Queen's Hall, London. The programme also included Haydn's
   Symphony No. 7 in C, 'Le Midi', Mozart's Piano Concerto in A (K.
   488), with Frank Merrick as soloist, and arias from Haydn's *The
   Seasons*, with Clara Serena (alto) as soloist.

Wednesday, 30 September 1931

V. good lesson with Benjamin 12.20–1.0. Practise in afternoon at
N.S. of M. & go afterwards to Augeners to get music. Go to Prom
(Bach) with Mollie Floud[1] at 8.0. V. long programme to stand for.
Sarabande, Andante & Bourree (strings), v. good & well played.
Murchie in B minor Flute Suite (delightful playing). 2 Conc[erto]s
(C & C min), 2 pianos (Ethel Bartlett & Rae Robinson)[2] –
wonderfully played. Thalben Ball[3] in B min Prelude & Fugue; only
bit of organ music I've ever really enjoyed. Also arias by Stuart
Robertson[4] (excellent) & Gladys Ripley[5] (not so good). Also Suite
no. 6 Bach–Wood[6] – Even Wood's garish orchestration could not
spoil some of this music. Back at 11.25.

1 Mollie Floud (b. 1911), the daughter of Sir Francis and Lady Floud.
   She studied the piano at the Academy and was later a pupil of
   Clifford Curzon's. Her twin brother, Peter (d. 1960), was at Gresham's from 1924 (went up to Oxford in 1930) and thus was senior to
   Britten. Britten and Floud became friends and sustained their friendship in London, particularly during Britten's post-College years. An
   authority on William Morris, Peter Floud was Keeper of Circulation
   at the Victoria and Albert Museum, London, at the time of his death.
2 See note 1 to Letter 261.
3 George Thalben-Ball (1896–1987), Australian-born British organist.
   He was appointed Organist and Director of the Choir at the Temple
   Church, London, from 1923 to 1981. He was knighted in 1982.
4 (Herbert) Stuart Robertson (1901–1958), English bass-baritone.
5 Gladys Ripley (1908–1955), English alto, particularly noted as a singer
   in oratorio.
6 This should not be confused with any one of Bach's four orchestral
   suites. Henry Wood compiled his own suites of music by Bach which

he orchestrated himself. His sixth suite was first introduced at a Prom in the 1916 season. Wood (1869–1944), English conductor, was founder of the Promenade Concerts, 'the Proms', and their moving spirit, 1895–1944. A work of Britten's – *Soirées Musicales*, Op. 9 – was included for the first time in the Proms in 1937, on 10 August, when the BBC Symphony Orchestra was conducted by Wood (see note 2 to Letter 100), who was also to conduct the first performance of Britten's Piano Concerto, with the composer as soloist, on 18 August 1938 (see note 3 to Letter 143).

He published an autobiographical memoir, *My Life of Music* (London, Gollancz), in 1938.

Thursday, 1 October 1931

V. long but extremely interesting lesson with Ireland at his Studio – 10.0–1.0! Practise in afternoon & walk home. Madrigals at 6.0–7.30; very amusing & enjoyable. Play cards with Diana May[1] after a late dinner.

1 A fellow lodger at the boarding house (see Diary for 13 January 1932).

Friday, 9 October 1931
[*London/Lowestoft*]

Write, until 11.0 (a new piano version of 3 Orch. Songs,[1] begun yesterday). Pack, & then practise till 1.0. Catch 3.10 from Liverpool St home. Travel all way with Elizabeth Nicholson.[2] Fairly quick journey. Pop & Beth meet me in car. – Mummy being in middle of tea party. Our new Erard (or rather 2nd hand) has arrived, & the Kemmler gone to Bobby.[3] The Erard is superior in touch (& in case) but inferior in tone. It is a full grand (6'8").

1 See note 2 to Diary for 26 June 1931. The 'new piano version' seems not to have survived.

2 Elizabeth Nicholson (1909–1987), the sister of Britten's South Lodge schoolfriend, John Nicholson.

3 Perhaps rather typically, Britten found himself in possession of the 'new' Erard, while the cast-off Kemmler boudoir grand went to Robert. Robert was teaching at the Elms School, Colwall, near Malvern, at this time. The struggle for occupancy of the piano stool was graphically described in *Time*, 16 February 1948, p. 64:

At two Benjy was calling himself 'Dear', demanding to be put at the piano by squawking 'Dear pay pano' [. . .] His elder brother and two sisters liked to play the piano, too, but the young composer managed to wrest it from them by announcing that he 'had a thought', a line that soon became a household gag.

Tuesday, 13 October 1931
[*Lowestoft/London*]

Mabel Ritchie[1] sings my 3 songs before going off by train at 9.48. Walk with Mummy, Beth, & Caesar, & pack in morning. Catch 2.31 to London. Mum & Pop bring me to station in car. Pretty good journey, on time. Meet Barbara, by accident, in Metropolitan,[2] at Nottinghill Gate. Attempt to write in evening, but am driven to desperation by a loud wireless on landing outside.

1 Margaret Ritchie had stayed overnight with the Brittens, having given a concert with Frederick Woodhouse, English bass, in St Margaret's Institute (attached to St Margaret's Church, the ancient parish church of Lowestoft), under the auspices of the Lowestoft Musical Society.

2 The Metropolitan and District Railway Station, now merged with the Notting Hill Gate station of the London Underground.

Thursday, 15 October 1931
[*London*]

Amazingly good, & frightfully instructive lesson from Ireland in Chelsea at 10.0. Mainly on orchestration of Psalm 130. Practise all afternoon, here, as I wanted to get more than 1 hr's work done. Tea at Selfridges with Barbara at 4.45, & Madrigals afterwards. Great fun. Get back for dinner at 8.0.

Wednesday, 21 October 1931

Score, practise, & then good pft lesson at 12.40 at Col. Practise & hair cut in aft (Whiteley's). Go to B.B.C. Concert[1] (1st half – Area,[2] 2nd half – Stalls with Bridges). Strauss[3] – conducting Mozart E♭ Symphony, his own three Hölderlin Prayers[4] (beautifully sung by Margarete Teschemacher) & Domestic Symphony.[5] Dull & annoying Mozart – can it be he who wrote Don Juan?[6] Hölderlin songs; boring & monotonous Straussian sounds. Domestic; amusing, & annoying by turns; but with some lovely bits. Orch. as good as could be with such a conductor (or rather beater). Come home by bus, via Bridges, by 11.5.

1 Given by the BBC Symphony Orchestra, Queen's Hall, London.
2 The Area at the Queen's Hall was the seatless, low-priced central part of the auditorium, at ground-floor level, where the 'Promenaders' gathered. It seems probable that Britten encountered Frank Bridge at this concert and joined him after the interval in the stalls, where there was conventional seating.
3 Richard Strauss (1864–1949), German composer and conductor.
4 *Drei Hymnen von Friedrich Hölderlin*, Op. 71, for voice and orchestra (1921). This performance was their British première.
5 *Symphonia domestica*, Op. 53 (1902–3).
6 Strauss's tone poem, Op. 20 (1888–9).

Thursday, 22 October 1931

Have lesson at 8.45 p.m. with Ireland, instead of 10.0 a.m. (owing to some muddle at R.C.M.) – not a good one, which was not improved by the fact that he was quite drunk most of the time – foully so. Lunch with Mr. & Mrs. Bridge (at their house). I am doing some copying (Pft part of Pft & orch. rhapsody)[1] for him. Practise in afternoon here, a bit. Tea with Barbara, Selfridges at 4.45. Madrigals afterwards.

1 Bridge's *Phantasm*, for piano and orchestra, was composed in 1930–31 and first performed on 10 January 1934 at the Queen's Hall, during the BBC's British Music Festival, with Kathleen Long as soloist and the composer conducting the BBC Symphony Orchestra. Britten wrote in his diary: 'F.B. conducts his own Phantasm which K. Long plays brilliantly (I turn for her). Audience seems to like it very much.' He adds next day: 'F.B. had execrable notices of <u>Phantasm</u> in <u>every paper</u>.'
   The work received only one performance between 1940 and 1970. A fragment of Britten's copying exists in the Archive.

Friday, 23 October 1931

Bit more scoring in morning, & practise. Go to College in afternoon, to listen to orchestral (first) rehearsal. Sibelius symphony (?).[1] V. Dramatic, but rather fine. Slackly rehearsed (no details) by Malcolm Sargent. Practise a bit after tea. Barbara rings up after dinner.

1 That Britten had apparently forgotten which Sibelius symphony was rehearsed is indicative of his ambivalent feelings about the Finnish composer.

Tuesday, 27 October 1931

Do usual scoring & practising in morning. Very foggy day. Practise with Lauricella in afternoon. Do alot more copying of Bridge Phantasm after supper – staying up until 11.15 partly to listen to some General Election[1] (which is today) results on Wireless – so far only a long list of Conservative successes.

1 Ramsay MacDonald (1866–1937) had formed a second Labour administration in 1929. In the 1931 General Election, the consequence of MacDonald's desire to establish a coalition government, a split Labour party led to its defeat at the polls. MacDonald remained as Prime Minister of a 'National' government (1931–5) in which Stanley Baldwin (1867–1947), his Conservative opponent, served as Lord President of the Council.

Wednesday, 28 October 1931

No lesson in morning so score & practise instead. Play tennis in afternoon 3–4 with Miss Gillespie[1] on Lincoln's Inn Fields.[2] She is very good, & we have marvellous fun. Back for tea. Listen to B.B.C. Symp. concert[3] on wireless in evening. Henry Wood. Beethoven – Coriolan; "Der Frist ist um" (Flying Dutchman)[4] – well sung by Herb. Janasen[5] (wobbly intonation occasionally tho'). Sibelius 1st Symphony – amazingly fine – rather Brahm's like. He does some very commonplace things tho'. Har. Bauer[6] in G maj Beethoven Concerto. 1st & 2nd mov.s magnificent. 3rd too fast, & rather ragged. To end – Liszt's brilliant & amazing Mephisto Walser [–Waltz].

1 Dr Helen Gillespie, a fellow lodger.

2 Lincoln's Inn Fields, London WC2, the site of one of the ancient Inns of Court where barristers still have their chambers and where there are still public tennis courts.

3 Given at the Queen's Hall, London.

4 *recte* 'Die Frist ist um': Britten refers to the Dutchman's aria in Act 1 of Wagner's opera.

5 Herbert Janssen (1895–1965), German baritone. He was famous for his Wagnerian roles.

6 Harold Bauer (1873–1951), pianist of Anglo-German parentage, finally resident in the USA.

Wednesday, 4 November 1931

Pft lesson 12. to – [omission] I play (2nd pft) Franck Symp. Var. [*Variations symphoniques* for piano and orchestra] with Benjamin (1st pft. V. good. Play tennis with Miss Gillespie, 3–4 Lincoln's Inn Fields – great fun. Bath before early dinner (6.50) & go to B.B.C. concert[1] – ½ time Area & ½ time Circle with F. B. Adrian Boult (terrible execrable conductor) leads the show. Elgar Intro. & All⁰[2] – nice spots but terrible – "Toselli's Serenata"![3] H. Samuel in Brahms 2nd [Piano] Conc. – v. disappointing reading tho' excellent technically – too pompous & slow. Schumann 1st delightful symphony – indifferently played. Go home with F.B. & Brosas (Mr. & Mrs.), for lemonade, back here 11.15.

1 Given by the BBC Symphony Orchestra at the Queen's Hall, London.

2 *Introduction and Allegro*, Op. 47, for string quartet and string orchestra. On this occasion the quartet part was played by the Catterall String Quartet.

3 Enrico Toselli (1883–1926), Italian pianist and composer. He wrote a number of songs, one of which – 'Serenata' – became an immensely popular item. Britten refers to it here to emphasize his dislike of the Elgar. His opinion however was to change. He conducted several highly successful performances of the *Introduction and Allegro* during the late 1960s and recorded the work in 1969 (Decca SXL 6405). At the 1971 Aldeburgh Festival, he conducted a performance of *The Dream of Gerontius* with Pears as Gerontius on 9 June. Britten and Pears subsequently recorded the work (Decca SET 525–6).

Friday, 6 November 1931

Bit of scoring before going to RCM. to see Herbert Howells[1] – show him Psalm 130 – he is very encouraging & nice. Meet a pupil of his – Lord (Howard de ?) Waldon.[2] Go to Orchestral (in part vocal) rehearsal of Benjamin's opera – Devil Take her, in opera theatre. It's very amusing, & in places quite beautiful. Go for a walk after tea with Diana. Play Bridge with her & her grandmother, & Mrs. Fairley[3] after dinner.

1 Herbert Howells (1892–1983), English composer. He was a pupil of Parry and Stanford at the College and taught there from 1920, until his death.
2 Lord Howard de Walden (1880–1946). He was benefactor and first President of the British Music Society, founded in 1918 and disbanded in 1933, and generous patron of the arts. He was a friend of the English composer, Josef Holbrooke (1878–1958), for whose operatic trilogy, *The Cauldron of Annwyn*, Walden wrote the libretto.
3 A fellow lodger.

Saturday, 14 November 1931

Walk (to various Libraries – Boots[1] & Public) in morning, 10.0. with Diana. Practise Pft & Vla a bit after that. Go to take pts of my quartet to Mr. Howard-Jones[2] (to whom Mr. Ireland has shown my score) – as there is a faint chance of some quartet playing it over. Diana & her grandm. have a Mr. Jonas (cousin) to dinner, & I sit with them & afterwards. Walk with him (& D.) a little way to his home at 9.30.

1 The Nottingham firm of pharmacists, who from 1899 to 1966 ran a subscription lending library in their chemist shops all over the country. The Public Library service on the other hand was a free, public amenity (and remains so).
2 In the preface to the published score of the D major Quartet Britten wrote: 'Mr. Howard-Jones (Evelyn Howard-Jones, the pianist and friend of Delius) arranged for it to be played through by the Stratton Quartet.' See also Diary for 16 March 1932.
   Howard-Jones (1877–1951) had been a scholar and teacher at the College. He gave the first performance of Delius's Three Preludes for piano (1923), the first of which is dedicated to him, on 4 September 1924, and a month later, on 7 October, gave the first performance, with Albert Sammons, of Delius's Second Violin Sonata (1923).

Sunday, 15 November 1931

Church at St. Judes[1] at 11.0. After that walk to Marble Arch & back with Diana – to get some exercise! Go to tea with the Montague Nathans[2] at 4.0 – many people there including Miss Farquhar.[3] He looks at My ballet [*Plymouth Town*] & says I am to send it to the committee of the Camargo Society[4] (of which he is secretary) for consideration. Write letters after supper.

1 St Jude's Church, Collingham Road, London SW5.
2 Montagu Montagu-Nathan (1877–1958), English violinist and writer on music. He specialized in Russian music and wrote several general historical studies and composer biographies, including *Glinka* (1916), *Moussorgsky* (1916) and *Rimsky-Korsakov* (1916). Montagu-Nathan acted as Secretary for numerous musical and other organizations in London, most notably the Camargo Ballet Society (see also note 4 below).
3 A fellow lodger. In his diary for 13 November Britten had written:

   Aft. supper go in to a Miss Farquar's niece's flat (Miss F. is living here) to meet alot of nieces & nephews & people – including Mr. Mrs & Miss Montague Nathan [. . .] They are awfully nice.

4 The Camargo Society, founded in 1930 in the wake of the death of Diaghilev in 1929. The Society, which enlisted the talents of those as various and distinctive as Frederick Ashton, Anton Dolin, Maynard and Geoffrey Keynes, Constant Lambert, Lydia Lopokova, Ninette de Valois, *et al.*, successfully organized a number of productions which led to the formation of the Vic–Wells Ballet and eventually the Royal Ballet (based at the Royal Opera House, Covent Garden). Among the Society's notable achievements was the production of Vaughan Williams's *Job*, first danced in London in 1931 under the Society's auspices. In 1932 the Society mounted a ballet – a short choreographic poem – based on Frank Bridge's orchestral work, *There is a willow grows aslant a brook*. Andrew Motion (*The Lamberts: George, Constant and Kit* (London, Chatto & Windus, 1986), pp. 183–92), argues convincingly for recognition of Constant's central role in the foundation and development of English ballet, from the Camargo Society to the Royal Ballet of the present day.

Wednesday, 18 November 1931

Lesson with Benjamin at 12.20. Practise with Lauricella at N.S.M. all afternoon. Go (Frank Bridge takes me) to Q.H. [Queen's Hall] to B.B.C. Symp. Concert at 8.15. Locattelli's[1] Concerto di Camera

in E♭. Gieseking[2] in Bach D min (not at all a good performance –
dull & heavy) Schönberg 5 orch. pieces[3] (some quite fine – better
than I expected – Colours – no. 3 – marvellous) & a Dull &
unscholastic (especially in treatment of grace notes in 2nd mov.)
perf. of Beethoven's marvellous 7th symph. Orch. as before –
material marvellous – but badly trained in ensemble & everything
by that worst of all conductors (?) Adrian Boult.

1 Pietro Antonio Locatelli (1695–1764), Italian composer.

2 Walter Gieseking (1895–1956), German pianist.

3 *Fünf Orchester-Stücke*, Op. 16 (1909), the third of which, 'Farben',
   Britten refers to specifically.

Sunday, 22 November 1931
[*Lowestoft*]

Birthday.[1] Presents – Fur gloves (Mum & Pop) & choice of records
– Stravinsky & Delius (ditto). Books – (Beth, Barbara, Bobby, Lazy)
– M.S. Paper (Maids & Nanny) – Money (Miss Turner[2] 6/6). Church
with Mum at 11.0 – St. Johns. Finishing scoring of "Plymouth
Town" in aft. Miss Turner comes to tea – & Mum & I walk home
with her after. Walk with Pop after dinner; also play gramophone
records – the Stravinsky "Oiseau de feu" & Delius "Brigg Fair".[3]

1 Britten was eighteen.

2 Perhaps related to Ruth Turner mentioned in Letter 26.

3 Stravinsky's ballet, *The Firebird* (1910) (Columbia L 2279–82), released
   in August 1929, conducted by Stravinsky, and Delius's *Brigg Fair:
   An English Rhapsody* (1907) (Columbia L 2294–5), released in 1930,
   conducted by Sir Thomas Beecham. Britten's copies of these discs
   have not survived.

Monday, 23 November 1931

Play golf (Beth ordinary, while I chuck) before lunch. Only Three
holes (2½; Beth's ball being lost at 3rd) – winning 1st, all squ. 2nd.
Walk with Beth up to Morlings to order Honnegger Pac. 231[1]
(gramophone record) (Birthday Present), in aft. Walk with Pop
after tea; after that Miss Ethel[2] comes in. Play Bridge after dinner;
& walk with Pop before bed.

1 Honegger's *Pacific 231*, for orchestra, was first performed in 1924. In
  1931 two recordings were available, both conducted by the composer:
  by the Grand Symphony Orchestra on Parlophone R 11296; and by
  the Continental Symphony Orchestra on Victor 9276. Whichever
  copy Britten possessed has not survived.

2 Ethel Astle.

Wednesday, 25 November 1931
[*London*]

No lesson with Benjamin. Go to O.U.P. to get Walton's Belshazzar's
Feast[1] – & to Langham St. (Cranz) to get Delius Serenade.[2] Practise
with Lauricella in aft. Have tea with F.B. afterwards – he gives me
the score of his 6tet.[3] Go to B.B.C. Symph. Concert at 8.15.[4] Sit
first in area – Haydn Symphony 88 (G) & Mozart Symph.
Concertante (Sammons & Tertis (2nd rather disappointing)) – both
played with over 60 strings!! Rather ragged & uninspired playing
under Boult. 2nd Half in stalls with Bridges (speak to V. Williams,
Howells & Bliss). Holst's – Hammersmith[5] – interesting, but not H.
at his best. Walton's Belshazzar's Feast (National Chorus – mod.
good) – very moving & brilliant (especially 1st half) – but over long
– & to[o] continuously loud – I felt. Back via Bridges at 12.0.

1 Walton's cantata for baritone solo, chorus and orchestra (text selected
  by Osbert Sitwell (1892–1969)) had been first performed on 8 October
  at Leeds. The vocal score was also published in 1931. Britten was
  preparing himself for the first London performance of the work
  which took place later that day, with Stuart Robertson as soloist. His
  copy of the score is missing.

2 The 'Serenade' from Delius's incidental music to *Hassan* (1920–21),
  the five-act play by James Elroy Flecker (1884–1915), produced in
  London at His Majesty's Theatre on 20 September 1923. Eugene
  Goossens conducted and Basil Dean (1888–1978) directed. The popular 'Serenade' from Act I scene 2 was published by Universal Edition
  in three separate arrangements, all available by 1931: for piano (1923),
  arranged by Philip Heseltine; for viola and piano (1923), arranged by
  Lionel Tertis; and for cello and piano (1931), arranged by Delius's
  amanuensis and friend, Eric Fenby. The copy Britten purchased (perhaps of the Tertis transcription) is missing.

3 String Sextet (1906–12). The score was published by Augener in 1920.

4 At the Queen's Hall, London.

5 Prelude and Scherzo for orchestra, Op. 52, the version Holst made

in 1931 of a work originally written for military band. The performance that Britten heard of *Hammersmith* was the first of the work in its new format.

Sunday, 29 November 1931

Leave here at 11.30 to go to Harold Samuel at Hampstead for lunch & tea. Have marvellous time – he plays Partita in E min [BWV 830] to me (magnificent) & also I play (ugh!) some Schubert duets with him. Isolde Menges[1] & Ivor James[2] come into tea with him & to rehearse afterwards – but I go immediately after tea. It's frightfully foggy. Barbara comes to supper. After she goes I begin some variations (sop. cont. Vln. Vla. Pft) on a French Carol.[3]

1 Isolde Menges (1893–1976), English violinist, sister of Herbert Menges (1902–1972), the conductor. Isolde founded the Menges String Quartet in 1931 and in the same year joined the staff of the College, where she taught for many years.

2 Ivor James (1882–1963), English cellist. A former Royal College student and Professor of cello and chamber music from 1919 to 1953. He was a member of the English String Quartet (1909–25), the quartet in which Frank Bridge also played (see also note 1 to Diary for 3 February 1932). He was also a member of the Menges Quartet.

3 The *Variations on a French Carol* (Carol of the Deanery of Sainte Ménehould) for women's voices, violin, viola and piano, composed 29 November – 1 December 1931. Britten prepared the parts and wrote out the fair copy of the score 5–17 December (see also note 3 to Diary for 9 January 1932).

Monday, 30 November 1931

I finish (only the end is to be altered) my variations, in morning. Can only get a short bit of practise owing to people (Capt. Courfield – ugh – above all) in house objecting. Still I do abt 1½ hrs good work in Westbourne Grove in aft.[1] Hair-cut after. Walk with Diana after tea & write letters after dinner.

1 At the New School of Music.

Tuesday, 1 December 1931

Can only get 1 hrs. practise in morning & $\frac{1}{4}$ hr in aft. rest of time writing. Go to R.C.M. at 4.0 for Pianoforte Technique exam (act. 4.45) – exam. Mr. Whitehead[1] – scales & arpeggios – pretty mouldy. Go with Mr. & Mrs. Bridge to first performance of R.C.M. opera – Holst – Savatri[2] (rather dull, but beautiful in a way) & Benjamin's op. "Devil Take Her". Brilliantly done. Marvellous little work – every note comes off – charming & witty to a degree. The College students in it were not put in the shade by Trefor Jones (Poet) or Sarah Fischer[3] (Wife) – excellent as they were – which is saying alot. Enthusiastic reception.

1 Percy Algernon Whitehead (1875–1953), a member of the piano teaching staff at the College from 1920 to 1938.
2 *Savitri*, Op. 25, Holst's chamber opera in one act (1908–9). The cast at this performance was as follows: Satyavan: Howard Hemming; Savitri: Eugenie Walmsley; Death: Roderick Lloyd. The production was by Clive Carey (1883–1968), and it was conducted by Sir Thomas Beecham.
3 Sarah Fischer (1898–1975), French Canadian soprano, who sang in the 1920s and 1930s with the British National Opera Company and at Covent Garden.

Wednesday, 2 December 1931

Practise for abt. $\frac{3}{4}$ hr. in morning, – score, – then lesson, v. good with Benjamin. Practise with Lauricella all aft. & walk with Diana after tea. Write letters & bath after dinner. More rows about my practising – people threaten to leave if it doesn't stop! It is all so stupid, because it could be perfectly simple if people could say straight out to <u>me</u> – "not today thank you", instead of going & moaning round Miss Wrist.[1] As it is they tell <u>me</u> they don't mind it. The av[erage]. person seems to be a dishonest fool.

1 Miss Wrist, a fellow lodger at Burleigh House. Beth Welford recalls that she and Britten

made friends with an old lady called Miss Wrist, who had a top-floor room. She probably was not very old but she seemed so to us. She wore very thick glasses which magnified her eyes and made her look very old, but she was great fun and came to stay with us in Lowestoft several times.

(EWB, p. 64)

Friday, 4 December 1931

No lesson with Ireland again which I find out after tramping to the R.C.M. Finish Bridge copying[1] after lunch, & take it to him after practising 2.45–4.30 at N.S.M. Have tea with Mrs. Bridge. Then he looks at the end of my score of Plymouth Town – which has to be sent in soon to the Camargo Ballet. He also gives me the vocal score of the "Christmas Rose"[2] – marvellous thing. Read after dinner.

1 Of *Phantasm*.
2 Britten's copy of the newly published vocal score is now in the Archive.

Tuesday, 8 December 1931

Not v. satisfactory lesson with Ireland at 11.10. Practice all afternoon at N.S.M. More copying out of carol after tea. After dinner I go with Barbara to R.C.M. to operas (sitting with Mrs. Bridge & Miss Fass) – Christmas Rose & Blue Peter (Armstrong Gibbs).[1] The performance vocally quite good (Miriam[2] excellent) orchestrally bad. C. Rose may not be an excellent opera from the stage point of view, but when there is little action the music is always sublime – & that is O.K. for me! The Blue Peter was an amusing little thing – merely Musical Comedy – clever in its way – but as different as anything from the adorable C. Rose.

1 Armstrong Gibbs (1889–1960), English composer. A pupil at the College of Charles Wood and Vaughan Williams and on the staff there 1921–39. His comic opera in one act, *The Blue Peter* (libretto by A.P. Herbert), was first performed at the College in 1929. Gibbs was a prolific song-writer and especially successful in his settings of Walter de la Mare. A large collection of his manuscripts forms part of the Britten–Pears Library.
2 Miriam, one of the principal characters. This soprano role was undertaken by Eugenie Walmsley. The other members of the cast were: Reuben: Joyce McGlashan; Shepherd I: Morgan Jones, who later played the role of Bob Boles in the first performance of *Peter Grimes* (1945); Shepherd II: Howard Hemming; Shepherd III: Roderick Lloyd. The opera was produced by John B. Gordon and conducted by the composer.

Thursday, 10 December 1931

Score in morning & pack[1] in afternoon. Go at 6.15 to dinner with Bridges & then to Northampton Polytechnic Institute (Clerkenwell)[2] for concert for poor people by Audry Chapman Orchestra[3] cond. by F. B. Amateur strings (marvellous) & prof. wind (quite good). They play Brahms Tragic ov., Schubert B. min. Symp.. Dvorak Serenade for Strings (rubbish) & Tchaikovsky's adorable Romeo and Juliet. Harold Williams sings Non pìu Andrai (Figaro)[4] not too well, but Song of the Flea (Moussorgsky) marvellously so that it has to be repeated. The orch is magnificent althro' [all through], & F. B. of course superb. The performance of the Tchaikovsky drives me potty.[5] Supper at Bridges & back by 12.0.

1 Britten was returning home to Lowestoft for the Christmas holidays on 12 December.

2 Northampton Polytechnic Institute, Clerkenwell, a Technical College in St John's Street, London EC1. It was founded in 1896 and specialized in courses of engineering, physical science and opthalmic optics. It now forms part of the City University.

3 According to PHFB, p. xvii, this was 'a semi-professional ladies orchestra' later known as the Melville Orchestra 'which gave concerts in poorer London suburbs'. Bridge began conducting it in the mid-1920s. In his *The City University: A History* (London, City University, 1980), p. 155, John Teagre writes that the Audrey Chapman Orchestra concerts were

very well attended from the first ones given in 1923–4 and the practice was for Audrey Chapman (Mrs Melville) and her husband to contribute financially, e.g. £109 towards the £200, the cost of the first three concerts. The Finsbury Borough Council paid for printing the publicity material and the programmes and the College gave free accommodation. There was a series of musical education talks in association with the concerts. All very much part of the Polytechnic concept. 'The management desire to continue the propaganda of musical education in Clerkenwell.' The series continued for several years.

Daphne Oliver remembers that it was at one of these concerts that she met Britten for the first time: 'He, little more than a boy, was playing the cymbals'.

4 Figaro's aria from Act I of Mozart's opera, *Le Nozze di Figaro*.

5 It remained a favourite work of Britten's. At the 1968 Aldeburgh Festival he accompanied Galina Vishnevskaya and Peter Pears in the duet from the opera, *Romeo and Juliet*, which Tchaikovsky never

completed, the music of which is identical with the overture's 'love' music. Those who heard that performance will remember Britten's piano accompaniment which magically evoked the full range of colours of Tchaikovsky's orchestration, familiar from the overture. Nothing could have spoken more eloquently for Britten's intimacy with and admiration of the piece. In PPTMS Pears recalled Britten's piano-playing:

[. . .] he had an extraordinary perception between his brain and his heart and the tips of his fingers. You could watch Ben holding his hands over the piano preparatory to playing a slow movement, a soft, soft chord – and you could see his fingers alert, alive, really sometimes even quivering with intensity [. . .] it was amazing what colours he could get. He thought a colour and he could do it.

Britten also arranged the overture to *Romeo and Juliet* for organ in April 1934, presumably for the joint organ and piano recital he gave with C.J.R. Coleman on 9 July 1934 at St John's Church, Lowestoft. However it was abandoned in favour of an arrangement of the first movement of Tchaikovsky's First Piano Concerto (see PFL, plate 69).

Sunday, 13 December 1931
[*Lowestoft*]

I go to church at 8.0 at St Johns with Mum. Walk with Pop in morning. Read in afternoon. Mr. Roberts (South Lodge Master) comes to tea at 4.15. Mum. sings & I play before supper. Walk with Pop before bed – foul toothache.

Monday, 14 December 1931

Walk with Beth before lunch; do some writing – score of variations before that. Pop takes out a tooth for me in afternoon by injection, & it bleeds somewhat until evening. Walk with Mum after tea. Gramophone & read after dinner. Pop has a masonic 'do'.[1]

1 'do' = social event. Britten's father was a Mason, i.e. a member of the Freemasons, an international body organized in 'lodges' and using elaborate ritual as part of their proceedings. Various benevolent activities are pursued. Perhaps Mr Britten's Masonic participation complemented the social activities his wife engaged in through her church.

Tuesday, 22 December 1931

Frank Bridge sends me – for Xmas – the score (& pts) of his new Trio.[1] I am very bucked as it is a most interesting & beautiful work. Score practically all morning & before dinner. Beth & I go to Badminton Club – run by Meads – at St. Margaret's Institute: there are practically no people there who can play at all. Fun in a way.

1 On its first performance on 4 November 1929, Bridge's Piano Trio was again ill-received by the English critics on account of its alien Continental 'modernity' , 'owing a great deal to Scriabin and Schönberg [. . .] he can no longer be regarded as a "Young British composer" ' (Herbert Hughes in the *Daily Telegraph*, 5 November), and 'It seems that he had made common cause with the advocates of modernity [. . .] My impression is that he is bartering a noble birthright for less than a mess of pottage' (*Musical Times*, May 1930, p. 42). The coupling of Skryabin and Schoenberg has its own fascination. Clearly Skryabin was perceived (in England, at least) as an apostle of modernity. Mr Greatorex, the music master at Gresham's, was thought by some to be unusually adventurous and 'advanced' because of his taste for Skryabin (a recollection of another Gresham's old boy, Stephen Spender). Britten's tremendous enthusiasm for Bridge's newly published work led him to work extremely hard on it, with Lauricella and Richards, during 1932.

Spender was to contribute a kind of prose poem entitled 'Greatorex' to a special issue of the school magazine, the *Grasshopper*, published in 1955 to mark the 400th anniversary of the founding of the school, which includes a graphic description of this legendary personality at the piano:

Greatorex!
When he appeared the ice unfroze and the boys were boys – that is to say, frogs croaking round a pond,
Round his piano, where they croaked. Between tunes they whispered:
'Is Greatorex the eighth or the ninth greatest musician in England? A great king, why has he come down among us?'
Greatorex has a domed, bald head, Beethoven's patent sour expression, curls glued to the back of his skull.
I look and look and long to have a round, bald head, with, at the back, crinkled curls.
Teaching the piano, he says, 'You will never learn to play the piano.'

This issue of the *Grasshopper* also included Britten's musical salutation, 'Farfield (1928–30)', the setting of lines from the Testament of John Lydgate, for solo voice and piano, and contributions from John Pudney and W.H. Auden. Mr Greatorex was remembered by Auden in *The Old School, Essays by Diverse Hands*, edited by Graham Greene (London, Cape, 1934), pp. 5–6, in the chapter on Gresham's entitled 'Honour', where he wrote:

to [Greatorex] I owe not only such knowledge of music as I possess, but my first friendship with a grown-up person, with all that that means. As a musician he was in the first rank. I do not think it was only partiality that made me feel, when later I heard Schweitzer play Bach on the organ, that he played no better.

As a person he was what the ideal schoolmaster should be, ready to be a friend and not a beak, to give the adolescent all the comfort and stimulus of a personal relation, without at the same time making any demands for himself in return, a temptation which must assail all those who are capable of attracting and influencing their juniors. He was in the best sense of the word indifferent, and if the whole of the rest of my schooldays had been hateful, which they weren't, his existence alone would make me recall them with pleasure.

Mr Greatorex made a strong impression on all his pupils, but the estimate of his musicianship by Auden and Britten was radically different.

Wednesday, 23 December 1931

Score in morning & then shop with Mum & Beth & car. All of us (including Mum. & Pop who go on to Southwold[1] but are back to C's for tea) go in afternoon to Sotterly in car to Chartres; for holly picking. Get quite alot. Tea at Chartres: back by six. More scoring before dinner. After dinner Beth & I sing carols up this Road (from Wellington Esplanade) with Guild of Fellowship.[2] 8.30–11.0 (with food at Reeves). Get quite alot of money – quite fun – tho' I'm hoarse now!

1 Town on the Suffolk coast, once an important port, twelve miles south of Lowestoft, where Mr Britten held a weekly surgery.
2 Of St John's Church, which met for devotional and social activities.

Friday, 25 December 1931 (Christmas Day)

Church (St John's) 8.0 (with Mum, Barb. Beth) & 11.0 with Mum. Marvellous presents. inc. Petroushka[1] & Minnie Maylow (John Masefield)[2] – Mum & Pop: Pencil, Beth – Mozart Vl. Vla. Symph[3] – Laulie: Ride of Valkyrie[4] – Maids, Barbara gives me Monthly Musical Record[5] every month. Beth & I prepare for evening in afternoon. Mr & Mrs Sewell (Laurence & Fernande) & Teddy Rogers come to Xmas dinner. We have quite fun afterwards. Bed 12.30.

1 Britten's copy of the miniature score, published in Berlin by Edition Russe de Musique, survives.

2 John Masefield (1878–1967), English poet, playwright and novelist, created Poet Laureate in 1930. *Minnie Maylow's Story, and Other Tales and Scenes* was first published in 1931.

3 Britten's copy of the Eulenburg edition of the miniature score of Mozart's *Sinfonia concertante* in E flat (K. 364), survives, inscribed in Britten's hand 'Xmas 1931' and numbered '126' in his sequence of scores. It was a favourite work.

4 Prelude to Act III of Wagner's *Die Walküre*. This copy survives (Philharmonia Edition, n.d.) and is signed and inscribed by the recipient: 'Dec. 1931. From Nanny. Alice, Ruby, Phyllis No. 125'. Alice Pratt was the cook, and sister of Nanny (Annie) Walker, the Britten family nanny until 1921. See also EWB, pp. 29–33.

5 The *Monthly Musical Record*, a monthly periodical published from 1871 to 1960 by Augener. The first editor was Ebenezer Prout.

Saturday, 26 December 1931 (Boxing Day)

Score more after breakfast at 9.30 & before dinner. I finish the scoring of 150th Ps. [Psalm] & am quite pleased – now for no. 130. Walk with Pop at 11.0 until lunch. Beth & I should have played Hockey in afternoon (arr. by Bill Arnold) but we have to stain the dining-room floor for Tuesday's dance & there is no other time. This we do & move various bits of furniture in aft. & after tea a bit. Mum & Barbara sing abit after dinner. Usual walk – bed.

Tuesday, 29 December 1931

Walk with Beth up town in morning to Morlings to choose records (to hire) to play on hired Radiogram[1] for to-night. Various odd jobs – final movings for dance in aft. & after tea. Dance 8–1.0 in dining room. Abt. 33 people come. I think it goes pretty well.[2] After they have gone we put back majority of furniture getting to bed at 2.30 abt.

1 A combined radio and gramophone, an instrument found in many
   homes in the thirties and forties but not, it seems, in the Britten
   household. Britten writes in his diary for 20 December 1932: 'Morling
   comes in morning & aft to fix up our new Wireless (Echo-[?]Superhet.
   built into H.M.V. Gram pick-up.) – absolutely superb.'

2 Britten showed little enthusiasm for dancing and even less skill. He
   was, Paul Wright confirms, 'a hopeless dancer'.

Thursday, 31 December 1931

Play gramophone a bit in morning before it goes back to Morlings.
Walk with Beth before lunch. Barbara goes away by 2.28. Mum
& I go to station with her. Walk to Miss Turner's with Beth before
tea to return a book. Go to Amorys with Beth in evening to play
games. Abt. 10 there. Quite amusing, back by 11.30. End of Year.
    What for next?

Friday, 1 January 1932

More Scoring of Psalm 130 in morning. Beth & I go to Badminton
Holiday Club in aft. (about 12 there). Quite fun but not excellent
badminton. Pop, Mum, Beth & I go to St. Luke's[1] dance for Nurses
in evening at 8.0.
    I come away and go to Phillips at 9.35 to listen on wireless to
concert. F. Bridge is conducting[2] – marvellous – Rimsky-Korsakov
Scheherazade – brilliant. Sach's Monologues & extracts from Act III
Meistersinger.[3] What a conductor that man is – what tone he gets
from his strings. After that the dance seemed deadly dull. But don't
leave till 12.30.

1 St Luke's Hospital (Metropolitan Asylums Board), Kirkley Cliff Road,
   Lowestoft, an isolation hospital.

2 The BBC Studio Orchestra with Arthur Fear (baritone).

3 Sach's Monologues: 'Was duftet' and 'Wahn! Wahn!'. The excerpts
   from Act III comprised the Prelude, Dance of the Apprentices, Procession of the Masters, and Homage to Sachs.

Thursday, 7 January 1932

Practice with Charles Coleman, chez lui, 10.0–10.45 for Sat. Hair cut at Priggs at 11.15. Go up to Morlings with Aunt Q before lunch to get 2 records of Petrouchka, marvellous music – playing quite good. L.S.O. Coates.[1] Go to tea with John Nicholson at 3.0 for his gramophone & records. Hear Beethoven B♭ (op 90 odd) Trio (Cortot, Thibaud,[2] Casals.) Superb music & playing. Also Mendelssohn Concerto (Kreisler)[3] – of course efficiently played. Back at 7.10. Bridge in evening. Walk with Pop – bed.

1 Albert Coates (1882–1953), English conductor and composer. Britten's copy of Coates's 1929 HMV recording of the complete ballet (HMV D1521–D1524) is in the Archive. He apparently bought the set of four records in two batches, completing his purchase of the recording on 13 February.

2 Jacques Thibaud (1880–1953), French violinist. The Cortot–Thibaud–Casals Trio was founded in 1905 and it immediately became one of the most widely admired ensembles of the day. With the advent of electrical recording techniques they committed many exemplary performances to disc, including Beethoven's 'Archduke' Trio, Op. 97 (HMV DB1223–DB1227). Britten's copy of this 1929 recording is in the Archive. In his scheme for a gramophone records recital in 1973, Britten intended to include a performance of Brahms's Double Concerto, with Thibaud and Casals as soloists: 'We had this recording at Gresham's, and I used to devize methods of getting hold of it.' See Introduction, note 12, p. 64.

3 Kreisler's recording of the Mendelssohn Concerto, with the Berlin State Opera Orchestra conducted by Leo Blech (1871–1958), was released in 1927 on HMV DB997–DB1000.

Saturday, 9 January 1932

Beth & Mum do most of my packing (I help) before 11.30. Practice with Charles Coleman at his house for evening. 11.30. Walk with Mummy up town at 12.30–1.30. Practice with Mr. Coleman as well as Charles at their house 2.15–3.15. Walk with Caesar before tea. Go & see Miss Ethel after & practice pft abit.

<u>Musical Evening</u>

at 8.0   Besides ourselves 3 Colemans, Mrs. & John Nicholson. Mr. & Mrs. Back[1] (who both sing) Mr. & Mrs. Owles. Mrs. & Miss

Phillips. 2 Miss Boyds. 2 Miss Astles (Miss Ethel plays). Miss Banks.[2] Miss Goldsmith. Sing alot of Part Songs including My variations[3] – quite good. I play Ravel Jeux d'eau & Debussy "Reflets" & Franck Symp. Variations. Mum sings Ireland "12 Oxen" & Armstrong Gibbs "To one who passed Whistling". Quite a success. They go about 11.45.

1 The family business was Backs Ltd. (Wine & Spirit Merchants), Bevan Street, Lowestoft.
2 Presumably the daughter of Ernest Banks, MA [?schoolmaster], 20 Corton Road, Lowestoft.
3 *Variations on a French Carol*. This was the first performance. There had been a rehearsal on 6 January when Britten wrote:

We do [. . .] my Variations on a French Carol, which really go v. well considering lack of balance, difficulty of reading French, & strangeness with any idiom except that of "I passed by your window" [popular drawing room ballad by M.H. Brahe] & Tosti's "good-bye".

Tosti (1844–1916), Italian composer and singing teacher who taught the British royal family and was knighted in 1908. 'Good-bye' was his best-known song.

Sunday, 10 January 1932

Walk with Pop & Beth in morning. Mum doesn't go out as her leg is bad. Read in afternoon (finish Appel Cart[1] – marvellous) & gramophone (Petrouchka). Mum & I finish packing after tea. Walk with Pop before bed. Beastly to be the last day.

1 The play, *The Apple Cart* (1929), by George Bernard Shaw (1856–1950).

Tuesday, 12 January 1932
[*London*]

I am to stay in this room & so I unpack all morning, and arrange about Piano & what not.[1].
   Go to R.C.M. in afternoon at 2.15 & play with Lauricella until about 5.0 (Brahms [Violin] Concerto mov 1. & bits of Bridge [Piano] Trio which we are going to play). Go to see Mr. & Mrs. Bridge after dinner – talk alot he lends me his Piano Trio Fantasy[2] & gives me 2 pft pieces "Hidden Fires" & "Graziella".[3] Magnificent. Get back before 11.0.

1 Britten had moved from a boarding house at 51 Prince's Square, London W2, to Burleigh House, 173 Cromwell Road, London SW5, where he and his sister Beth rented rooms from 21 September 1931.

2 Bridge's *Phantasy* in C minor for piano trio, composed (according to PHFB) 'after 1907' and published by Novello in 1909. The *Phantasy* was written for the second Cobbett Musical Competition: it was awarded the first prize of £50 – John Ireland and James Friskin came second and third respectively – and received its first performance by the London Piano Trio on 27 April 1909. The arch-shape form of the *Phantasy*, including exposition and recapitulation linked by a developmental andante and scherzo, was taken as the basic model for Britten's own phantasies, i.e. the *Phantasy* in F minor for string quartet (1932; see note 1 to Diary for 27 January 1932) and *Phantasy*, Op. 2 (1932), for oboe and string trio. It is interesting to observe that in choosing F minor as the key of his string quintet Britten was also following the precedent set by Bridge in *his* string quintet *Phantasie* of 1905, which was Bridge's entry for the first Cobbett Musical Competition, held in that year. It was awarded second prize.

3 For solo piano, composed in 1926 and published by Winthrop Rogers in 1927. Britten's copies of both pieces are in the Archive.

Wednesday, 13 January 1932

My piano is brought in the morning. It fits in the room quite well. Score abit before going to R.C.M. for Lesson with Benjamin (pft). Have a talk with him & Howells (& play Psalm 150). In afternoon go to Augeners to get Brahms Pft. Sonata 1 & Rachmaninoff Preludes (op. 32)[1] – 10/5!!! Walk all the way back by 3.30. Practise abit before & after tea & score abit before dinner. Afterwards play card games with Mrs. Jonas & Diana May (her grand-daughter). Early bed.

1 Britten's copies of the Brahms and Rakhmaninov are in the Archive.

Friday, 15 January 1932

Score abit before I go to R.C.M. for lesson with Ireland at 10.35. The piano tuner comes here at 10.0. V. good lesson with Ireland – most instructive.

In afternoon 2–3.15 I go dashing all over the shop to try & get tickets for Mum & Pop for Cavalcade[1] on Monday aft. Eventually get what I am sure are wrong ones. Practise until tea time & abit afterwards; don't touch viola, more scoring (alterations of 150th Psalm) 6–7. Play cards with Diana May after dinner.

1 The patriotic play of 1931 by Noël Coward (1899–1973), which celebrated British history during the first thirty years of the century.
Michael Denison writes that

Cavalcade was [Coward's] most ambitious production, suggested to his ever
fertile mind by a photograph of a troop ship leaving for the Boer War. It
gave him the opportunity to proclaim in a brilliant mixture of pageantry and
understatement his intense patriotism, coupled with a warning that 'this
country of ours which we love so much' was losing its way. His enemies
found it obscene that the author of The Vortex should treat such a subject.
The nation and the English-speaking world responded differently.
                    ('Sir Noël Peirce Coward', in DNB, 1971–80, pp. 186–9)

Tuesday, 19 January 1932

Mum & Pop leave by car at 10.30. I go with them as far as Baker
St. to help them on their way. It's beastly that they've got to go.
Return & finish scoring of Psalm 130. In afternoon I go to R.C.M.
& play with Lauricella until 4.0 & then play trio (Bridge – Phantasy
C min.) with addition of a 'Cellist – Richards,[1] who is nice & very
good. Great fun. We mean to do this regularly. Barbara comes in
in the evening, to have a talk with us. Sit in Beth's room (no. 26)
all evening.

1 Bernard Rowland Richards (b. 1913), English cellist, who studied at
the College, 1930–36. He first encountered Britten in September 1930,
on the occasion of the College entrance examination, when Richards
recalls that Britten finished his theory examination after only twenty-
five minutes, and, on handing it in, was sent back by the incredulous
invigilator and made to check it again. In 1932 Britten and Richards
formed a piano trio with Remo Lauricella, and the following year
Richards played double-bass in a performance of the Sinfonietta conducted by the composer (see note 2 to Letter 32). The two men had
occasional contact after Britten left the College: with one of Richards's
sisters, Irene (a violinist), they formed 'The 1935 Trio' to give a single
concert in Lowestoft on 30 January 1936. Britten's diary entry for that
date reads:

Meet Bernard & Irene at Liverpool St. & catch with them 12–25 to
Lowestoft. Lunch on train – write for amusement to words of menu a
canon (to be read upside down – table music) which we sing with gusto.
Mr. Coleman meets us in his car. They are staying with us. After tea
with Mum we walk on beach & along fish-market. Then to Royal Hotel for

rehearsal – waste much time in getting platform arranged – organisers forgetting that fiddlers and 'cellist have to bow (boh). Eventually home by 7.10 – hurried change – I have a quick run thro of Fun Fair [*Holiday Diary*] on pft. as I have been suddenly asked for a solo – gulp some food & and we are down at Royal on stroke of 8. Play Schubert B♭ (we are terribly nervous & it doesn't go too well – nothing serious, but unsteady) – Beethoven Op. 11 & Bridge Phant. go as well as we have ever played them & we really enjoy them.

Richards also played for several GPO film music recording sessions, including *Night Mail*. He was later a member of the RAF Orchestra, the Boyd Neel and Jacques String Orchestras, and the English Chamber Orchestra where he was once again in touch with Britten (see PFL, plate 345), in addition to pursuing a career as a chamber music player.

Friday, 22 January 1932

Have about ¼ hrs. lesson with Ireland at (nominally) 10.35–11.50. He spends the rest of the time telephoning, finishing someone else's lesson & talking about his concerto.[1]

Practise Pft. all afternoon & after tea.

In evening Beth & I go to Bridges to listen to the Busoni concert on wireless. Very wretched Music (Violin Concerto & Turandot Sweet).[2] Back by 10.15.

1 His Piano Concerto.
2 The full programme of this Busoni concert, the third of the 1931–2 season of BBC Contemporary Music Concerts, was *A Comedy Overture*, Op. 38 (1897–1904); the Violin Concerto in D, Op. 35a (1896–7), with Joseph Szigeti (violin), and *Turandot – Orchestral Suite from the Music to Gozzi's Drama*, Op. 41 (1911), with the BBC Orchestra (Section D) (Leader: Arthur Catterall), conducted by Adrian Boult.

Wednesday, 27 January 1932

Lesson with Benjamin 11.40. Practise before that. Write more Phantasy[1] in aft. Go to dinner with Bridges at 6.20 & to concert afterwards with them (Mr. Bridge coming at half time). Ansermet[2] (Queen's Hall) conducting B.B.C. Eroica [Beethoven], badly played under not inspired conducting. Stravinsky, Capriccio for Pft. (Strav. himself) & Orch. Amusing but not much more. Marvellous Symphony of Psalms (Strav.) tho'. Bits of it laboured I thought but the end was truly inspired. Chorus, not too bad (National)[3] & orch. better in 2nd half of programme.[4] The

performance left much to be desired tho' Ansermet was good. Back
at 11.15.

1 *Phantasy* Quintet in F minor for 2 violins, 2 violas and cello, composed
20 January–11 February. It was awarded the Cobbett Prize for 1932
and received its first performance on 22 July at the College. See also
notes 1 to Diary for 18 July and 13 September (when the work
underwent revision) and 12 December 1932.

2 Ernest Ansermet (1883–1969), Swiss conductor, who was to become
an outstanding Britten interpreter and advocate. He was to conduct
two important premières, *The Rape of Lucretia* (Glyndebourne, 1946)
and *Cantata Misericordium*, Op. 69 (Geneva, 1963). Britten presented
Ansermet with the composition sketch of *Lucretia*, which came into
the possession of the Conservatoire de Musique, Geneva, after the
conductor's death. The manuscript is now held on deposit at the
Bibliotheca Bodmeriana, Geneva.

3 The BBC's National Chorus.

4 The concert also included Handel's Overture to *Agrippina*.

Friday, 29 January 1932

Do a bit of writing (Phantasy) before going to R.C.M. for lesson
with Ireland at 10.35.

Do some vocal scoring of Psalms to send R.V. Williams to look
at. Practise Pft & more writing in aft. Go to tea with Mr. & Mrs.
Laurance Sewell (up for a holiday) at Lyon's Popular at 5.0. Play
Bridge with Diana & her Grandmother & Beth after dinner; don't
feel too well so go early to bed with bath.

Sunday, 31 January 1932

Go to the Zoo with Beth & Diana, leaving at 10.30 & getting back
at 1.45. V. interesting & a lovely day. Go with Lauricella to a
L.S.O. [London Symphony Orchestra] concert at Albert Hall –
Beecham.[1] Hansel & Gretel ov. [Humperdinck] – charming.
Haydn's delightful 3rd Symp. [No. 99 in E flat] v. well played.
Delius Pft. Conc. (Katherine Goodson).[2] Don't like the work – Liszt
& Tchaikovsky, not much Delius. Beethoven Symp. 2 very well
played. V. spirited under Beecham only first mov. too fast.
Barbara comes to supper. Listen to Tchaikovsky's marvellous
Romeo & J.[3] on wireless at 9.15.

1 Sir Thomas Beecham (1879–1961), English conductor. As a conductor
  he was self-taught. He formed the Beecham Opera Company (in
  1915; subsequently the British National Opera Company); the
  London Philharmonic Orchestra (in 1932); and the Royal Philharmonic Orchestra (in 1946). A champion of the music of Sibelius and
  Delius, he mounted two important and influential festivals of the
  latter's music, in 1929 and 1946. He was much admired as an
  interpreter of Haydn and Mozart. His relationship, however, with
  Britten's music was never a warm one. He conducted a performance
  of the Violin Concerto with Bronislaw Gimpel as soloist in December
  1951 in the composer's presence (see PFL, plate 248). For Britten's
  typically adverse reaction to a performance of *Tristan*, Act I, under
  Beecham, see Diary for 11 May 1932; and five years later, on 14
  October 1937, his critical tone had not changed:

  Peter & I go to the Beecham show (with the very fine Leeds Festival chorus)
  of the Mass in D [Beethoven] – & it is a tremendous disappointment –
  not that one really expected anything really good from that irresponsible
  man. Every speed was just wrong – the work is obviously alien to the vandal
  – the Crucifixus was scandalous. Even then the work stood out as one of
  the supreme masterpieces of all time.

  Beecham wrote an early volume of autobiography, *A Mingled Chime*
  (London, Hutchinson, 1944).
2 Katherine Goodson (1872–1958), English pianist.
3 Tchaikovsky fantasy overture, *Romeo and Juliet*, was performed by
  the BBC Orchestra (Section B), conducted by Nikolai Malko.

Tuesday, 2 February 1932

I write more of the slow mov. of my Phantasy & also practise piano
in morning after walking a good way with Beth towards her
academy.[1]
  Go to practise with Lauricella at R.C.M. in aft. & have great
difficulty in finding a room. We have some quite good practise at
the Bridge trio – it's less Greek than before now. Practise pft. a bit
before supper & do more vocal scoring in evening. I have just
finished reading David Copperfield again. It is an absolutely <u>first</u>
rate book – inspired from beginning to end.[2]

1 The Paris Academy of Dressmaking and Design in Bond Street. See
  EWB, pp. 62–3.
2 Britten's admiration for the novels of Dickens was lifelong. In an
  interview with Charles Osborne (*London Magazine*, October 1963,
  p. 95) Britten responded to a question about 'writing a Dickens

opera': 'I am a great reader and lover of Dickens, but although many of the scenes I could think of operatically, I would find the overall shape almost impossible to cope with. One, however, I have thought about seriously.' The novel in question was undoubtedly *David Copperfield* (much of it set on the East Coast) which he constantly re-read. In his conversation with Murray Schafer, in *British Composers in Interview* (London, Faber and Faber, 1963) pp. 113–24, he remarked, 'I am very fond of Dickens and I try to read at least one of his novels a year' (p. 122).

Wednesday, 3 February 1932

Practise before going to R.C.M. at 11.40 for v. good & instructive Pft lesson with Benjamin. Beth stays here all day to do stitching or something. I write more vocal score all aft. & abit after tea finishing Psalm 130 before bed in evening. Go to see Bridges at 6.0 & stay to dinner coming home at 8.30 tho' to find Beth at Barbara's. Mr. Bridge plays the viola absolutely marvellously. What the world has lost by him not playing anymore in public![1]

1 Bridge swiftly acquired a reputation as a conductor and chamber music player during the early 1900s. He was a founder member of the English String Quartet – one of the finest quartets of its generation – playing the viola in it from 1902 until the 1920s. Britten, too, was a viola-player and on his departure for the United States in May 1939 Bridge gave him his own instrument as a farewell present. See note 1 to Letter 172.

Sunday, 7 February 1932

Rather late breakfast. Go to church at St. Jude's with Beth at 11.0. In afternoon Mr. & Mrs. Bridge take me to Albert Hall to Berlin Phil. Orch. (Fürtwängler).[1] Hackneyed Programme. Haydn London Symp; Wagner, Siegfried Id. [Idyll] & Flying Dutchman ov.; Tschaikovsky's Pathetic Symp. F's readings were exaggerated & sentimentalised (esp. so in last item – no wonder a member of the audience was sick!! The orch. is a magnificent body, tho' slightly off colour to-day (e.g. wind intonation, 1st clar. & 1st Horn). Strings are marvellous. Timpanist great. Marvellous ensemble & discipline.

Go to tea with Barbara (also Beth) at her flat.

Back, walking, by supper.

1 Wilhelm Furtwängler (1886–1954), German conductor.

Wednesday, 10 February 1932

Go to College after finishing Vocal score & practising at 11.40 for
lesson (v. good) with Benjamin & to give vocal score of both Psalms
to R.V. Williams (teaching there). Go up to Augeners in aft. to get
some music. Listen to Ireland's Pft. conc. from Bournemouth
before tea. Practise Pft. after tea. Go to B.B.C. concert Queen's Hall
(area). Beethoven's miserable King Stephen ov. miserably played
under Boult. Brahms Vln conc. (Busch[1] – marvellous technically but
as hard as nails with little feeling for music). Ireland's magnificent
Mai-Dun[2] – quite well played for the B.B.C. orch. Bax's new Winter
Legends[3] (Harriet Cohen)[4] longwinded rambling boring stuff – so
feeble and dull after the Ireland. Orchestra <u>bad</u> all evening; Boult
worse. Come back via Bridges at 11.15.

1 Adolf Busch (1891–1952), German violinist and composer, brother of
the conductor Fritz Busch (1890–1951).

2 Symphonic rhapsody for orchestra, composed 1920–21.

3 Arnold Bax (1883–1953), English composer. He was knighted in 1937
and appointed Master of the King's Music in 1942. *Winter Legends*,
his Sinfonia concertante for piano and orchestra, was completed in
April 1930 and given its first performance at this BBC concert. See
also Lewis Foreman, *Bax – A Composer and His Times* (London, Scolar
Press, 1983), pp. 257–9.
  Britten was rarely in touch with Bax – the first occasion was in
1938 – but he made an approach in 1943, in connection with Michael
Tippett's appearance before a Tribunal for Conscientious Objectors,
for which Bax agreed to write a testimonial.

4 Harriet Cohen (1895–1967), English pianist, studied at the Academy.
She was a noted interpreter of the music of Bach and of English
music of her time, particularly that of Bax, her close friend. She was
chosen by Elgar to record his Piano Quintet in A minor, Op. 84
(1918–19), and gave the first performance of some works by Bridge.
Cohen wrote a performance handbook entitled *Music's Handmaid*
(London, Faber and Faber, 1936), and a volume of memoirs, *A Bundle
of Time* (London, Faber and Faber, 1969).
  After Bax's death Cohen gave Britten and Pears several Bax manuscripts, including Two Songs for voice and string quartet ('My Eyes
for Beauty Pine' (1920) and 'O Mistress Mine' (1916)) and 'Wild
Almond' (1924) for voice and piano. They are now in the Archive.

Thursday, 11 February 1932

Walk with Beth as usual a bit in morning. Finish Phantasy, &
practise the rest of day. Go to Bridges for supper at 6.30 and then
F.B. [Frank Bridge], E.B. [Ethel Bridge], Miss Fass, & I go to Audrey
Chapman Orch. at Northampton Institute, Clerkenwell. F.B.
conducts the most marvellous musical thrill of my life yet.
Beethoven, ov. Coriolan, 9th Symphony (1st 3 movs.), Elgar
Serenade Strings (rather dull), Mozart Symp. Conc. Vln Vla (Isolde
Menges & Bernard Shore[1] – only moderate) & Beethoven Egmont
ov. The strings (all amateurs) were the best I have <u>ever</u> heard. The
2nd class professional wind were quite good (3rd & 4th Horns
especially in slow mov. of 9th). The Beethoven overtures were
electric; but as for the 9th Symph. – !!
   Back via Bridges, for supper, at 11.45. Beth waits up & we have
some tea.

1 Bernard Shore (1896–1985), English viola player.

Friday, 12 February 1932
[*London/Lowestoft*]

Go to R.C.M. after packing at 10.35 for c [composition] lesson with
Ireland. He arrives at 11.0. I spend ½ lesson correcting the proofs
of his Pft. Concerto. The rest of the lesson he spends telephoning
– so I don't get much out of that! I catch 3.10 from Liverpool St.
home arrv. after a long & rather cold journey at 6.10. Met by Mum:
Jolly good to be back. Walk with Pop before bed.

Sunday, 14 February 1932
[*Lowestoft*]

Church at 8.0 at St. Johns with Mummy. She goes at 11.0 too whilst
I go for a long walk in country with Pop & Caesar. Read more
Barnaby Rudge [Dickens] begun last holidays & alot of Petroushka
(gramophone) in afternoon.
   Walk with Pop & Mum before supper. Read after supper – usual
walk & bed.

Monday, 15 February 1932

I write two part songs, one in morning & one in afternoon – one tripe t'other less rotten (Ride-by-Nights).[1] Jeffreson Schilling[2] comes to see us (home from Mauritius) before Mum & I go out for a walk with Caesar at 12.30. After tea Pop takes Mum, Caesar and me for drive in car – marvellous in country. Read more Barnaby after supper.

Walk – bed.

1 'The Ride-by-Nights' ultimately formed the first of the Three Two-part Songs (de la Mare) for boys' or women's voices and piano, subtitled 'Three Studies in Canon'. The second and third were 'The Rainbow' (composed 17 February 1932) and 'The Ship of Rio' (composed 18–20 February 1932). The songs were published by Oxford University Press in 1932 (see Diary for 29 February and Letter 29, pp. 251–2), and first performed by the Carlyle Singers conducted by Iris Lemare, with Britten at the piano, on 12 December. (See also letter 31.) Presumably the unsuccessful part-song was discarded.

2 Probably the son [*recte* Jefferson] of George Schilling, LMSSA Lond., physician and surgeon of Kessingland, Lowestoft. Britten occasionally played piano duets with Jefferson's sister, Molly.

Tuesday, 16 February 1932
[*Lowestoft/London*]

I finish Barnaby after breakfast & have Petrouchka all the way through. Pack & go for a walk with Mummy. She comes with me to station & I catch the 2.31 back arr at Burleigh House at 6.45 to find Beth in bed with a temperature of 101. Probably 'flu. At anyrate Barbara comes round after dinner and manages her.

Wednesday, 17 February 1932
[*London*]

Practise all morning. R.C.M. rings up to say no lesson with Benjamin. Beth is still in bed, but abit better. Write a part song (canon) 'Rainbow' in aft. Walk with Diana after tea. Go (area) to B.B.C. concert at 8.15 Queen's Hall. Henry Wood Mozart Flute [Overture to *The Magic Flute*] (typical up-to-date Mozart – presto & fff). Strauss's masterpiece of Characterisation Don Quixote.[1] Cassado[2] solo 'cello. Quite good but not perfect. This work is too diff. for performance under modern conditions. 20 rehearsals are needed. Hindemith's Konzertmusic (Brass & Strings).[3] Some magnificent stuff & lovely scoring quite well played. In 1st ½ Maggie Teyte[4] sang Ravel's Scheherazade marvellously gems of songs as they are; to end Concerto in G. min (Wood–Handel(!))[5] – Marcel Dupré.[6] I suppose his playing was good.

1 *Don Quixote*, Strauss's fantastic variations on a theme of knightly character for cello and orchestra, composed 1896–7.

2 Gaspar Cassado (1897–1966), Spanish cellist and composer.

3 *Konzertmusik*, Op. 50 (1930), for brass and strings; this was its first performance in England.

4 Maggie Teyte (1888–1976), English soprano. In January 1948 she recorded Britten's *Les Illuminations* with John Ranck (piano), released in 1978 on Desonar GHP 4003. See also note 4 to Letter 398.

5 Wood was an enthusiastic arranger of other composers' music. This Concerto (Set 2, No. 5) for organ and orchestra was rescored by Wood for the larger resources of the symphony orchestra.

6 Marcel Dupré (1886–1971), French organist, composer and teacher. In 1945 Britten was to provide the organist with two themes, on which he improvised a prelude and fugue, on 24 July, at an event promoted by the BBC.

Thursday, 25 February 1932

I finish copying Phantasy in afternoon working most of aft. & morning when I'm not practising. Go out for a walk 12–1 with Beth. Go to Madrigals (meeting Barb. for tea at Selfridges) alone – Barb. has cold. Go on afterwards to Phil. concert (Queen's Hall) – Malcolm Sargent – Idomeneo ov.[1] & Surprise Symphony – tepid performances – rather bad in detail. Ravel's new pft. concerto[2] which I cannot take seriously. Brilliantly played by Marguerite Long[3] & inefficiently conducted by Ravel. The slow movement is piffle! Léon [Goossens] plays Eugene Goosen's attractive Oboe Conc.[4] superbly as can only he. De Falla's El Amor Brujo, which wears very well, to end an interesting concert. Sargent not too bad in modern works seemed out of place in the classical.

1 Britten was to conduct memorable performances of Mozart's opera (with Pears as Idomeneo) at the Aldeburgh Festivals of 1969 and 1970.

2 Ravel's G major Concerto, composed 1929–32; this was its first performance in England.

3 Marguerite Long (1874–1966), French pianist, who gave the first performance of the concerto and to whom it was dedicated.

4 Op. 45, composed in 1927.

Monday, 29 February 1932

I finish my copy of the 3 pt. songs in morning, before going to lunch with Hubert Foss[1] at the Oxford University Press (Amen House) at 1.0. He looks at a good many of my things and keeps the part songs. I come back via the R.C.M. giving in my Phantasy for the Cobbett competition.[2] Go to the Bridges for tea & a talk, & to Barbara after supper until 10.15.

1 Hubert James Foss (1889–1953), who founded the music publishing division of Oxford University Press in 1925. He was responsible for bringing Britten into the Oxford list but lost him to Ralph Hawkes and Boosey & Hawkes in 1934.

2 In a sleeve note to *Benjamin Britten: Early Chamber Music* (Unicorn-Kanchana DKP 9020, 1983), Donald Mitchell and John Evans write:

Britten was stimulated to compose the 'Phantasy' form by the requirements of the Cobbett Chamber Music Prize, established in 1905 by W.W. Cobbett, the lexicographer and chamber-music patron. Cobbett's aim was to revive a specifically English brand of chamber music, based on the model of the episodic, single-movement form of the early seventeenth-century Fancy. The competition rules laid down that the twentieth-century counterpart should also be in one continuous movement, of no longer than twelve minutes' duration, and would show a comparable interest in the part-writing [. . .]. Perhaps, however, the most interesting result of Cobbett's initiative was not a form that acknowledged the Fancy but the somewhat unexpected making of common cause with the idea of the continuous one-movement form, traversing in one compressed scheme all the ground normally covered in a four-movement sonata or symphonic form, which in Europe in the first half of the twentieth century was one of the most influential and significant formal innovations.

Tuesday, 1 March 1932

Lesson with Ireland at 10.35: have nothing to show him, except orchestration of Psalms, as I have been copying over the weekend. Go to R.C.M. via Augeners (to get Debussy quart.)[1] at 3.0 to practise trio until 4.30. Do some quite good work at Bridge –

lovely work.[2] I go to a concert at the Y.W.C.A. [Young Women's Christian Association] (Gt. Russell St.) with Mrs. Bridge (actually go with Mr & Mrs. Brosa[3] in taxi as well) Brosa Quartet – Haydn Emperor, Beethoven C♯ (Miracle) & Debussy G min. They played superbly (except for a slip on part of new 'cellist – Manucci – in Beethoven). Brosa is, of course superb. Go back to a Mrs. Pember(?) in Sussex Gardens, after for supper. A whole crowd goes including Bridges (+ Mr.) Brosas & a very nice Miss Bowes-Lyons.[4]
    Back before 2.0.

1 Debussy's String Quartet in G minor, composed 1893. Britten's copy of the miniature score is in the Archive.
2 Probably Bridge's 1929 Piano Trio.
3 Peggy Brosa, wife of the violinist, Antonio Brosa.
4 A member of the Bowes-Lyon family to which the Duchess of York, later Queen Elizabeth, the consort of King George VI, belonged.

Thursday, 3 March 1932

I go and arrange with Mrs. Borrett (who has the piano now) about Mrs. Melville's[1] piano being brought here to-morrow. Go to the R.C.M. at 12.0 to have a little trio practice. I have a bad day for writing – beginning many things but only writing 1 bad small pft. piece.[2] Usual Madrigals & tea at Selfridges with Barbara.

1 Probably Audrey Melville of the Ladies' Orchestra that Frank Bridge conducted. Mrs Borrett remains unidentified.
2 Unidentified, probably lost.

Friday, 4 March 1932

Mrs. Melville's pft. is brought here & my other taken away between 10.15–11.15. Spend along time sorting out room – there really is quite alot of room in my room now surprisingly enough.
    Practise Pft in afternoon – also write home. Walk to R.C.M. after tea with Diana to see if anything from V. Williams.[1]
    Listen to Bartok concert[2] broadcast 9–10.30. Suite no. 1 contained some charming moments, but meandered 'a la Liszt' & Strauss much. Rhapsody (with composer at piano) more striking & the "Amazing Mandarin" most original of all. I cannot say I <u>love</u> this music but it is amazingly clever & descriptive.

1 Probably in connection with the possible performance of Britten's Two Psalms.

2 Given by the BBC Orchestra (Section D) conducted by Henry Wood, at the Queen's Hall. The programme comprised: Suite No. 1 (1905), rev. *c*. 1920); *Rhapsody* for piano and orchestra (?1904); and the suite compiled from *The Miraculous Mandarin*, pantomime in one act (1918–19).

Sunday, 6 March 1932

Church at St. Judes with Mrs. Jonas & D. [Diana] at 11.0. Do some writing in aft. var. on a theme of Bridge.[1] Barbara comes to tea – in Drawing room. Go to supper with Bridges & then (+ Brosas) to B.B.C. Studio for orch. concert (F.B. conducting). Brahms 3rd Symp. Orchestra rather poor. Isolde Menges in A min. Bach conc. – very good but not my Bach – finally F.B. magnificent & lovely Enter Spring which the orch. played quite well. Beth comes back by 5.25–9.15. Barbara's here to meet her, but gone when I get back at 11.15.

1 An incomplete set of variations for solo piano using the same theme – from Bridge's *Idyll No. 2* for string quartet – that Britten was later to use for his *Variations on a Theme of Frank Bridge*, Op. 10. (See note 3 to Letter 106.)

Wednesday, 9 March 1932

Practise Pft. before going to R.C.M. for a v. good lesson on Bach. Chromatic Fant. & Fugue with Benjamin at 11.40. In aft. I write one or two feeble variations, & begin a Violin & Viola concerto.[1] Also write after tea & a bit after dinner. Then, I also write home & listen to a bit of a B.B.C. concert.[2] Lamond[3] playing Tsch. Bb min. conc. what appeared to be rather clumsily, also Berlioz's Carnival Romane.

1 Concerto in B minor for violin, viola and orchestra, composed 9 March – 4 May 1932. Britten revised the slow movement of the concerto in June 1932. There is a complete composition sketch of the concerto in the Archive, with some indication of orchestration. No full score was made.

2 A broadcast relay from the Queen's Hall, London, with the BBC Symphony Orchestra conducted by Henry Wood.

3 Frederic Lamond (1868–1948), Scottish pianist and composer.

Thursday, 10 March 1932

I finish the first movement of my 2ble concerto in evening having
written alot – all morning until 12.0 – when I go to R.C.M. to
practise Trio but cannot find a room vacant – all aft. until 3.30–4.30
pft. practise and after dinner.

Meet Barb. & Beth at Selfridges at 5.10 & go to Madrigals at 6.0
with former. Back for dinner at 8.15.

Friday, 11 March 1932

Lesson with Ireland at R.C.M. at 10.35 – he is pretty pleased with
my concerto so far. Practise pft. all afternoon, after lunch for a bit
and after tea I scan through a book "Early Closing" by Wynne
Willson[1] – the best school book I've ever read. Listen to wireless
– mediocre Vaudeville[2] in evening.

1 Dorothy Wynne Willson (1909–1932), English author. Her novel,
  Early Closing, was first published London, Constable, 1931. Miss
  Wynne Willson's father had taught Britten at Gresham's.
2 A 'special Vaudeville programme of Street Pavement Artistes',
  including Duncan Ross, the Dines Spoon Troupe, William Ross and
  Violet Martin.

Sunday, 13 March 1932
[*Friston*]

Long talk with Mr. Bridge in his studio in morning. Also walk with
Mr. & Mrs. B. – Mr. Graves (oculist) & secretary before lunch. Go
to Miss Fass' in afternoon over the downs & tea at her house. Also
play darts after tea. She comes to supper. We all listen to B.B.C.
concert[1] – Malcolm Sargent conducting ordinary performances of
De Falla's 3–Cornered Hat – L'apres-Midi – Rachmaninoff 2nd
concerto (Solomon v. good) & Stravinsky – L'Oiseau de Feu. After
lunch Mr. Bridge plays alot of his things – including bits of his
[omission: illegible] beautiful Piano Sonata.[2]

1 A studio 'Sunday Orchestral Concert' given by the BBC Orchestra
  (Section B).

2 The Sonata, composed 1923–4, was dedicated to the memory of the composer Ernest Bristow Farrar (see note 1 to Diary for 24 July 1931).

Tuesday, 15 March 1932
[*Friston/London*]

Up early at 7.0. Breakfast at 7.25; Mr. Bridge & I are driven in Miss Fass' car by John (Chauffeur) to Eastbourne to catch 8.10 to Victoria. Mrs. Bridge comes up in evening. Practise for rest of morning, & go to R.C.M. for long practice of Trio with Lauricella & Richards. Listen to wireless after dinner – new B.B.C. dance band (Henry Hall)[1] – seems v. good.
    Also write letters. Beth goes to Barbara's to try on dresses.

1 Henry Hall (1898–1989), English band-leader. He succeeded Jack Payne as director of dance music for the BBC from 1932 to 1937. Hall's signature tune was 'Here's to the Next Time'. This broadcast was the début of the BBC Dance Orchestra.

HENRY HALL'S Greatest
Arrangement
"LOVE TALES" Selection
Containing : Love, Here is my Heart ; Speak to me of Love; A Bachelor Gay ; I Love Thee ; Frasquita Serenade ; If Winter Comes ; Drink to Me Only ; God send you back to me ; Love Will find a Way; Whisper and I shall hear ; If you were the only girl.

F.O. (not including P.C.), 7/6 ; S.O. (not including P.C.), 6/- ; P.C., 2/· ; Extras, 8d. ; Piano Solo, 2/6.

Wednesday, 16 March 1932
[*London*]

Practise pft. before going to R.C.M. at 11.40 to find Benjamin away examining. Go to Bridges for lunch to listen to broadcast performance of his Phantasy Quart. (Pft. – F♯)[1]
    Go to Queen's Hall after to get rid of a ticket for Weingartner[2] B.B.C. concert tonight. Go to Howard-Jones' after dinner. He has got the Stratton Quartet to try over my St. quart.[3] and one by a

Mr. Cox.[4] Considering it was sight-reading it was very good. I am
v. pleased with it – it sounds more or less as I intended it. Back
by 11.45.

1 Bridge's *Phantasy* in F sharp minor for violin, viola, cello and piano,
   composed in 1910 and first performed on 21 January 1911 by the
   Henkel Piano Quartet. The performers in the broadcast from Brad-
   ford to which Britten refers were Norman Rouse (violin), Sydney
   Errington (viola), Douglas Bentley (cello) and Edgar Knight (piano).
2 Felix Weingartner (1863–1942), Austrian conductor, composer and
   author. Britten was to meet Weingartner in 1934: see Letter 58.
3 The String Quartet in D major.
4 Probably David Cox (b. 1916), English composer and writer on music,
   and later External Services Music Organizer for the BBC, 1956–76.

Friday, 18 March 1932

Write an unsatisfactory beginning to a slow movement of my
concerto in morning. Also practise pft. Miss Alford comes in
afternoon at 2.30–3.30 to see me – she wrote the book of my ballet
[*Plymouth Town*]. Go to R.C.M. at 5.0–6.0 to rehearse with
Richards & Lauricella.

   Listen to concert on wireless in evening Anne Thursfield,[1] &
Huberman[2] (first excellent – 2nd only good in spots) Barbara &
Miss Hurst come round to see Beth about dresses in evening. I also
write letters.

1 Anne Thursfield (1885–1945), English mezzo-soprano.
2 Bronislaw Huberman (1882–1947), Polish violinist.

Sunday, 20 March 1932

Go for a walk in morning in Hyde Park with Beth & Elinor Bond
– school friend of hers. Listen to Wireless in aft. – Matthew Pass.
part I from York Minister.[1] Not by any means 1st rate performance
– but what music it is! Also write 2 letters. Kathleen Carter,
another school friend of Beth's comes to tea in B's room. Beth & I
go to church at St. Judes at 6.30 & go to Barbara's after supper.

1 Conducted by Dr Edward Bairstow, with Astra Desmond (alto), Steuart Wilson (tenor) and Arthur Cranmer (bass).

Monday, 21 March 1932

Spent practically whole day writing a fatuous slow movement for
my concerto – only ⅔rds of it. Practise pft. abit in aft. Walk with
Diana after tea. Listen to wireless abit after supper.

Tuesday, 29 March 1932
[*Lowestoft/London*]

Write more of last mov. of Concerto in morning – I shall tear <u>that</u>
up soon. Also practise Pft. a bit. Pack suitcase. Walk with Beth
Mum & Barb. Catch 2.31 back to London with Barb. Taxi to Sloane
Sq. with her – tube here. Place v. empty only abt. 10 people.
Write letters & listen to wireless abit[1] before early bed.

1 Britten would have heard either a programme of chamber music
  (Mozart and Brahms string quartets and Wolf songs) or a concert of
  light orchestral music conducted by Joseph Lewis.

Monday, 11 April 1932
[*Worcester*][1]

Rain most of day. Uncle S. [Sheldon] is in bed until tea with bad
cold, & without a voice. Read (or rather finish) the Hill – by H.A.
Vachell[2] – v. good, if too full of Harrow & Sentimentality. Walk (by
self) to station before lunch, & along river before tea. Most of the
odd moments of the week-end have been spent in helping to do
an enormous jig saw puzzle. Bed at 10.0.

1 Britten had gone to Worcester to visit his aunt Julianne and her
  husband, the Revd Sheldon Painter. Apparently he did not stay with
  the Painters at St Helen's Rectory, 4 College Yard, but at a nearby
  boarding house.
2 Horace Annesley Vachell (1861–1955), English novelist. His novel *The
  Hill*, a school story set at Harrow, was first published in 1905, and
  touched unusually for its time on 'passionate' schoolboy relationships.

Wednesday, 20 April 1932
[*Lowestoft*]

Practise with Bazil & Charles [Coleman] in morning, after finishing
Slow mov. Go with Bazil up to Morlings for 2 piano duets all aft.
3–5. Do Cesar Franck Symp. Var.; Brahms D min. conc. (1st mov.)
Schumann Var. [Andante and Variations in B flat, Op. 46] (2 Pft.).
Beethoven 2nd Conc. (1st & 3rd mov.). My arrangements of Bridge
Sea Suite (mov. 1 & 3)[1] & Brahms 4th Sym. mov. 1.[2] Back to
Reeves for tea. Play in garden aft. V. rainy day in spots. Pop goes
to Masonic. Mum to Flick [cinema] with Miss Haes [Hayes] in
evening.

1 Britten had first heard Bridge's orchestral suite, *The Sea* (1910–11), at
the 1924 Norwich Triennial Festival conducted by the composer. He
made the arrangements of 'Seascape' (movement 1) and 'Moonlight'
(movement 3) played on this occasion, in December 1930, recording
in his diary on the 15th:

I arrange the Sea Foam [movement 2] from the Sea Suite for 2 pfts,
beginning in the morning & working in afternoon & evening. I finish it
but there is plenty to alter.

16 December
I work, continuing the alteration & arrangement of the Bridge (I begin the
1st movement) in morning [. . .]

22 December
Practise viola & then write (finish Moonlight – from Sea Suite) until lunch.

Four years later, in May 1934, Britten undertook a second arrangement of 'Sea Foam' and 'Moonlight', this time for piano and organ.
'Moonlight' was performed in a concert at St John's Church, Lowestoft, on 9 July 1934 by Britten and Mr C.J.R. Coleman. (For a copy
of the programme see PFL, plate 69). All these arrangements are in
the Archive. In later life Britten conducted a performance of *The Sea*,
on 23 June 1971 at Snape Maltings, as part of the Aldeburgh Festival.

2 The manuscript of this arrangement seems not to have survived.

Saturday, 23 April 1932

Get by post, the min. score of L'Apprenti Sorcier[1] from Harold
Reeves. Walk with Beth & Caesar before lunch. Mum & Pop go
to Ipswich by car to see Aunt Janie in aft. Beth & I go too, & take
Alice to see her mother at Farnham.[2] Beth & I have tea at
Restaurant. I borrow vocal scores of Elektra[3] & Otello[4] (which used
to belong to Uncle Willie).
    Arrive home abt. 8.30. Walk with Pop – bed.

1 Britten's copy of the miniature score is in the Archive.

2 Near Stratford St Andrew, Suffolk.

3 Strauss's fourth opera, *Elektra* (Hofmannsthal), 1906–8. Britten's copy of the vocal score – the first edition, Otto Singer, Berlin, Fürstner, 1908 – was inscribed by him later in life: 'Given to BB by his Uncle William Hockey c. 1922 whilst he was staying with him in Berners Street Ipswich'. This diary entry makes clear that Britten misremembered the date and the occasion of acquiring the scores. Uncle Willie had already given his composer–nephew a copy of John Stainer's and W.A. Barrett's *A Dictionary of Musical Terms*, 4th edition (London, Novello, 1889), in 1922.

4 Verdi's opera, greatly admired by Britten.

Wednesday, 4 May 1932
[*London*]

Finish last mov. of my concerto before going to R.C.M. for Pft. lesson with Benjamin, but I expect I shall scrap it all. I find out that I have won the Cobbett prize – £13.13s. to the better! Go to O.U.P. to get some music in aft. & come home & practise. Walk with Diana after tea. Listen to B.B.C. concert on wireless after dinner. Rather a shaky performance by Nat. Chorus of Jesu, Joy & Treasure motet. They certainly made a loud if not a joyful noise in the 9th Symphony (Beethoven). Boult conducts an uninspired performance. Some instrument parts played v. well; but on whole v. ragged considering amnt. of rehearsal. Boult is beginning to fool abt. with things – he has dropped his so-called 'letting the music speak for itself'.[1]

1 A live relay from the Queen's Hall. In the Ninth, the BBC Symphony Orchestra and BBC National Chorus, with Isobel Baillie, Muriel Brunswick, Walter Widdop and Horace Stevens as soloists, were conducted by Adrian Boult. The performance was the first given in Sir George Henschel's English translation. The Bach motet was *Jesu meine Freude* (BWV 227).

Friday, 6 May 1932

Begin new trio[1] after breakfast – I'm putting my Concerto away for a bit. Before breakfast at 8.0 I go for a short walk in park. Go to

R.C.M. to see Lauricella before lunch. Practise pft. all aft. Walk with Diana after dinner.

1 The *Phantasy-Scherzo* for piano trio, subsequently retitled *Introduction and Allegro*, was composed 6–20 May 1932. It was dedicated to Britten's College friends, Remo Lauricella and Bernard Richards. Never publicly performed during the composer's lifetime, it received its first performance on 22 November 1986 by Marcia Crayford (violin), Christopher van Kampen (cello) and Ian Brown (piano) at the Wigmore Hall, London. It remains unpublished. See also Diary for 24 July 1932.

Sunday, 8 May 1932

I catch 12.10 from Marylebone [railway terminus, north London] to Gerrards X [Gerrards Cross, Buckinghamshire], where Sir Leonard Hill[1] meets me & takes me to Chalfont St. Peter where his family lives – & Lady Hill & Nannett Hill. Have lunch & tea – with games of Badminton in garden in between & return by 5.58–6.20 with Nannett. Listen to B.B.C. concert after supper.[2] Fogg[3] – Bassoon concerto. Tho' well played by Archie Campden[4] – I hate a whole work for Bassoon – anyhow there wasn't much music in it. Dvorak's 5th Symphony ['From the New World'] – which I really enjoyed in spite of it being so hackneyed & some v. ragged playing. But Dvorak does things so well.

1 Leonard Erskine Hill (1886–1952), English physiologist, and his wife, Janet. He was knighted in 1930. Hill and his family owned a cottage at Corton, near Lowestoft, and knew Mr Britten well. The youngest daughter was Nanette (Nan).
2 Given by the BBC Orchestra (Section B) conducted by Henry Wood.
3 Eric Fogg (1903–1939), English composer. His Bassoon Concerto in D, composed in 1930, was the best known of his later works.
4 Archie Camden (1888–1979), English bassoonist, for whom Fogg composed his concerto.

Tuesday, 10 May 1932

Lesson with Ireland, instead of last Friday, at 10.35. In the aft. Lauricella & Richards come to my room, to practise Bridge Trio at 2.30 (I go to fetch them) – 4.0. Finish cutting back lawn & play tennis against wall with Mrs. Fairly after tea. Go to dinner at 7.30 with Bridges, back from Friston for 2 days. He looks at some of my things (Phantasy & 3 Canons)[1] & lends me Meistersingers. Back before 12.

1 The *Phantasy* Quintet in F minor and the Three Two-part Songs.

Wednesday, 11 May 1932

Practise Pft. before going to R.C.M. for lesson with Benjamin at 11.40. Bit of Pft practise & Viola practise in aft. Rain most of day until aft. Roll lawn after tea. Go to Cinema (Kensington) with Diana after dinner – & see some utter tosh – Strictly Dishonorable.[1] Listen to Prelude to Tristan from Covent Garden, before dinner, under Beecham – Disgraceful![2]

1 The 1931 American film based on Brock Pemberton's stage play telling the story of a young girl who accepts the offer of a man's apartment and then is piqued because he leaves her alone. Produced by Universal, it was directed by John M. Stahl.

2 Act I only of *Tristan* was relayed by the BBC, with Frida Leider (Isolde), Maria Olczewska (Brangäne), Herbert Janssen (Kurwenal) and Lauritz Melchior (Tristan).

Friday, 20 May 1932
[*Lowestoft*]

See about ordering my new suit with prize money from Masterson[1] in morning. Also do alot more of Trio which I finish in aft. Mum & Beth have tea party with tennis. Mrs. & Miss Enraght,[2] friend & Mrs. MacNab.[3] I play one set with them. Play after tea, no play before because of rain. Putrid tennis.

   Walk with Caesar before bed. Pop isn't so well & is in bed all day.[4]

1 Frederic Masterson, tailor, 164 London Road South, Lowestoft.
2 The wife and eldest daughter, Evelyn, of Revd Canon Hawtrey J. Enraght, MA (1871–1938), Rector of Lowestoft (1931–8).
3 The wife of Alexander MacNab, Kildonan, London Road South, Lowestoft, a local doctor.
4 The onset of the illness that was eventually to lead to Mr Britten's

death on 6 April 1934. See also note 1 to Letter 47 and EWB, pp. 63–4.
An earlier illness in August–September 1931 had prevented Mr Britten from attending Robert's wedding in Hartlepool.

Monday, 23 May 1932
[*London*]

Copy out Cello part of Scherzo [*Phantasy-Scherzo*] in morning, also
bit of pft. practise. Go to R.C.M. in aft. to see people & on to
Oxford Circus etc. to get music. Pft. practise after tea. After dinner
go with Hall[1] to marvellous but terrible film, Kamaradschaft.[2]
Enough to make one dream for ages.

1 E.B. Hall, a former pupil of South Lodge.
2 *Kameradschaft* (*Comradeship*), important and influential German film
(Nerofilm, 1931) directed by G.W. Pabst, about the rescue of a group
of entombed French miners on the Franco-German border by fellow
workers from Germany.

Tuesday, 24 May 1932 (Empire Day)

Copy out Violin part of Trio [*Phantasy-Scherzo*] in morning also
practice Pft. abit. Lauricella & Richards come in aft. & do some
work at Bridge Trio (Scherzo – terribly difficult) & also read through
mine, which is difficult but will be effective I think.
    Go to Liverpool St. to meet Beth on 5.59 from Lowestoft. Taxi
back. Barbara comes to see us in evening.

Thursday, 26 May 1932

Mum has big League of Pity[1] show at Sparrow's Nest. Rewrite
Part song no. 2 ['The Rainbow'][2] in morning before Lauricella &
Richards come at 12.30 to practise for an hour. Pft. practise in aft.
Meet Beth at 5.0 & go up to Reeves where I pick up a second hand
min. score of Tristan – marvellous work![3] Beth & I go to
Kamaradschaft again in evening; even more impressed than
before – if poss.

1 A charitable organization that flourished between the wars and subsequently. 'Fortunate' children were enrolled by their earnest parents

to raise money for the poor. They wore an enamel badge with the emblem depicting a blue bird.

2 Britten had submitted his three Two-part Songs (see note 1 to Letter 29) to Oxford University Press.

3 The youthful Britten was a fervent admirer of Wagner. Apart from this miniature score of *Tristan und Isolde*, his collection of scores included *Tannhäuser* (a gift from his parents on his thirteenth birthday, 22 November 1926), the 'Venusberg' music from *Tannhäuser* (1926), the 'Good Friday' music from *Parsifal* (October 1927), 'Forest Murmurs' from *Siegfried* (January 1927), the *Faust Overture* (January 1928), 'Siegfried's Funeral March' from *Götterdämmerung* (22 November 1929) and 'The Ride of the Valkyries' from *Die Walküre* (Christmas 1931). Britten's Wagner scores represent his largest collection of any single composer, Beethoven apart.

29 To Hubert Foss
Oxford University Press

173, Cromwell Rd., S.W. 5.
May 28th 1932

Dear Mr. Foss,

Here are the revised part-songs. I hope the alterations will meet with your approval.[1]

You will notice that I have dropped the title "Studies in Canon", as I think it sounds too fearsome. I think the titles of the poems themselves are enough.

Yours sincerely,
BENJAMIN BRITTEN

1 Foss had written to Britten on 29 April:

I have had a very enthusiastic letter about your <u>Three Studies in Canon</u> from the editor of the series, Dr W. Gillies Whittaker. He quite rightly points out that the accompaniments are rather difficult, particularly No. 3, and that would hamper their sale. Also he goes on to say as follows:

'I don't feel quite comfortable about the compass. Will you ask the composer if he thinks a tone lower would be possible for the first? The second I certainly think ought to be a tone lower. From the vocal point of view the music falls between two stools. If it is for young people's voices, say secondary school girls, F sharp and G are too high for the lower. It would cause strain.'

[. . .] I should like very much to recommend these for publication, subject to your agreeing to Dr Whittaker's points.

Whittaker (1876–1944), was the English scholar, conductor and composer, and friend of Gustav Holst.

Britten evidently consulted Bridge about Whittaker's and Foss's criticisms of the songs. Bridge wrote to Britten on 7 July with thoughtful advice:

In these early days of your musical pilgrimage the factions of Dr Wh. & thingumyjig F. [. . .] & J. I. [John Ireland] must be tactfully considered. It can't be helped. It is the way the world wags. So lose no time. Find out at the offices of Associated Board of R.C.M. & R.A.M. where J. I. is. Write to him & enclose partsong. Ask him the identical question & see what he says. I think the answer will be the same as you expected from me. At least the advantage of you doing this would be seen when, or if even, Dr Wh. or F [. . .] should mention the point later to J.I. & then the road would be 'all clear'.

The Three Two-part Songs were published in 1932 by Oxford University Press. In a letter from Mr Britten to Robert, on 28 August 1933, he wrote: '[Ben] has had his first "Royalty" today 15/- from the Oxford U. Press & they have sold about £1000 [sic] copies of his Songs (the short ones) here & in the United States.'

Tuesday, 31 May 1932

Send off my entries for Mendelssohn Schol.[1] in morning (2 Psalms – score: Phantasy 5tet – Cobbett: & 3 Sop. Songs – Vocal Score).[2] Practise Pft. after that. Lauricella & Richards came in aft. We practise my Phantasy Scherzo all time. Listen to Act I of Mastersingers on wireless after dinner.[3] What struck me most is what little attention anyone paid to the written music. Beckmesser v. good – Habich;[4] & Schorr[5] as Sachs & Lehmann[6] as Eva – what little I heard of them.

1 The history of Britten's relationship with the Mendelssohn Scholarship Foundation and his unsuccessful attempts to secure election as a scholar is of an extraordinary fascination, revealing what must surely seem to us a surprising resistance to the acknowledging of the young composer's evident gifts. Small wonder that in retrospect Britten felt his College years to have been somewhat thin in encouragement of him as a composer.

We are indebted to Miss Pamela Harwood, the Honorary Secretary of the Mendelssohn Scholarship Foundation, for the following detailed account of the events of 1932 and 1933 which finally led to Britten's pained letter of 1 December 1934 (Letter 62) declining the proposed award. Editorial interpolations are enclosed within square brackets:

The Mendelssohn Scholarship was thrown open for competition in February 1932 and forty candidates entered, each submitting three works under *noms de plume* according to the rules. These were in due course inspected and reported on and in July the Foundation's Committee met to interview the short-listed candidates and to award the Scholarship. Unfortunately, opinions were divided as to the relative merits of the candidates. None of the work submitted was thought to be so good as to make the choice obvious. Of the two candidates who eventually emerged as the most likely winners, Ivor Walsworth, aged twenty-two and in his third year at the RAM as a pupil of William Alwyn, appeared to be more immediately accomplished; the other contender, Benjamin Britten, a pupil of Ireland at the RCM and then aged eighteen and a half, though showing considerable originality of thought and imagination, seemed not by then to have acquired the technical expertise to make the most convincing use of his undoubted talent. The decision was deferred until November 1932, when the two candidates were interviewed by the members of the Committee. Britten played to them on the piano portions of two of his works – the *Phantasy* for String Quintet [which had won the Cobbett Prize in May] and a setting of Psalm 130 for chorus and orchestra [composed 1931, unpublished].

Finally it was agreed to elect Ivor Walsworth to the Scholarship (valued at £150) for one year, and to award Britten a maintenance grant of £50, a sum which would not imperil the £40 a year RCM Scholarship which he held.

It was also agreed that both Walsworth and Britten should be asked to submit more recent work for performance at a Committee meeting in June 1933. This performance duly took place on 2 June and the work of Britten's which was played was the *Phantasy Quartet*, Op. 2, for oboe, violin, viola and cello, played by students at the RCM [viz. Natalie Caine (oboe), Remo Lauricella (violin), Frederick Riddle (viola) and Bernard Richards (cello)].

[Britten's Diary for 2 June 1933 reads:

At 4.0 the Quartet [. . .] go to Academy to play my Phant. to the Mendelssohn Schol. Committee. Unfortunately it goes v. badly once again. Of course they are only students, but Laurie [the violinist] made in both performances some unforgivable howlers – lack of experience of course.]

The Committee was not on the whole favourably impressed with it and Mr Theodore Holland observed that it was not nearly so good as the *Phantasy String Quintet* which had recently been broadcast by the BBC. Nevertheless, it was agreed that a further £50 maintenance grant be awarded to Britten for the academic year beginning September 1933 [and he was so informed by the Secretary on 3 June].

The following November the Mendelssohn Committee heard three movements of a new String Quartet played by RCM students, but on this occasion no opinion of the work was recorded. [These were three movements from the projected *Alla Quartetto Serioso*, 'Go play, boy, play', composed in 1933 and revised in 1936 as *Three Divertimenti*.]

In November 1934, after hearing of Britten's successful work during the year (broadcast of *A Boy was Born*, Op. 3, in February; the performance of the *Phantasy Quartet*, Op. 2, at the Florence ISCM Festival in April, and the second broadcast of the *Sinfonietta*, Op. 1, in July) the Committee also listened to a performance by George Loughlin of four of Britten's piano pieces –

'Early Morning Bathe', 'Yachting', 'Fun-Fair' and 'Night' [*Holiday Diary*, Op. 5].

It was agreed that he should be appointed Mendelssohn Scholar for a period of 6 months from 1 September 1935 and that the emolument should be £100.

On 7 February 1935 the Secretary of the Foundation reported with regret the contents of Britten's letter of refusal dated 1 December 1934 [Letter 62].

2 The *Three Small Songs* for soprano and small orchestra.

3 Act I only was relayed from the Royal Opera House, Covent Garden, conducted by Sir Thomas Beecham.

4 Edward Habich (1880–1960), German baritone.

5 Friedrich Schorr (1888–1953), Hungarian (later American) bass-baritone. He was thought to be the finest Wagnerian bass-baritone of his time, a noted interpreter of the roles of Wotan and Hans Sachs.

6 Lotte Lehmann (1888–1976), German (later American) soprano.

Wednesday, 1 June 1932

Practise Pft. before lesson with Benj. [Benjamin] at 11.40. He gives me Walton Symph. Conc. & Schumann Phantasy to work at.[1]
Begin a partsong (I loved a lass) in aft.[2] After tea I go to Augeners & Chesters to get music (De Falla – El Amor Brujo)[3] – walk back thro' park – marvellous day. More pt. song after dinner. Also listen to wireless – Saint-Saëns Carnival des Animaux – and a wonderful, impressive but terribly eerie & scarey play "The Turn of the Screw" by Henry James.[4]

1 Walton's *Sinfonia concertante* for orchestra and piano obbligato, composed in 1927. Britten had purchased a copy of the piano score on 24 September 1930 with school prize money (for mathematics). His copy of the Schumann *Phantasy* in C, Op. 17, is inscribed 'June 1932'. Both scores are in the Archive.

2 This setting of George Wither forms the first of the Two Part-Songs, the other being Robert Graves's 'Lift Boy'. (See also Diary for 18 July 1932.) Both songs were originally entitled 'Two Antithetical Part-Songs' for boys' or female voices and piano, and first performed at a Macnaghten–Lemare concert, Ballet Club (Mercury Theatre), London on 11 December 1933, by an unnamed chorus conducted by Iris Lemare. Britten writes of the performance in his diary: 'My 2 part songs (which I accompany) go quite well – esp. Lift Boy. But really think there isn't a singer in the lot of them.'

Britten recomposed the songs in June 1933 for the more conventional SATB chorus, in which form they were published by Boosey

& Hawkes (see also note 3 to Letter 49 and note 1 to Letter 51). The original – and odd – title of the pair of songs may have derived from their strongly contrasted protagonists, a 'Lass' on the one hand and a 'Lift Boy', on the other.

3 Britten's copy of the miniature score – inscribed 'Cobbett Prize 1932' – was lent by him to Henry Boys (see note 2 to Letter 103), with whom it remained until 1986; it is now in the Archive, which also possesses a modern edition of the miniature score containing Britten's pencil conducting marks. Forty years on, he conducted a performance of *El Amor brujo* at the 25th Aldeburgh Festival, on 19 June 1972, with Anna Reynolds (mezzo-soprano), Steuart Bedford (piano) and the English Chamber Orchestra.

4 This dramatized version of James's novel was adapted and produced by E.J. King Bull, with incidental music by Gerald Williams, conducted by Leslie Woodgate. Britten read the story itself for the first time in January 1933, writing in his diary on the 6th, 'Read more of James' glorious & eerie "Turn of the Screw" ', and on the 7th, 'Finish the "Screw". An incredible masterpiece.' After twenty-one years' germination, his opera *The Turn of the Screw*, based on James's story with a libretto by Myfanwy Piper, was first performed by the English Opera Group on 14 September 1954 at La Fenice, Venice, as part of the Venice Biennale. His copy of *The Turn of the Screw* dating from this period has not survived.

Thursday, 2 June 1932

Finish "I loved a lass" in morning – quite pleased with it. Trio practise here at 12.20–1.30 with Lauricella & Richards – work at my Scherzo all time. Pft. in aft. Walk with Diana in aft. (Her parents have gone to Lowestoft). Listen to Act I of Tannhauser in evening[1] – tolerable, but bad singing of Tannhauser[2] & Das Hirt (why not a boy for this?)[3]

1 Relayed from the Royal Opera House, Covent Garden, and conducted by Charles Webber (1875–1954) who replaced Beecham, with Josephine Wray (Venus), Heinrich Tessmer (Walter) and Herbert Janssen (Wolfram).

2 Sung by Kurt Taucher (1885–1954), German tenor, noted for his roles in Wagner.

3 Sung by the soprano Norah Gruhn. The part of the young shepherd boy has traditionally been a 'trouser' role, but Britten's suggestion that a boy might sing it is far from impractical: it is a small

unaccompanied part at the beginning of Act I scene 3, and well within the range of a boy's voice.

Friday, 3 June 1932

Go to R.C.M. at 10.00 & Lauricella & Richards & I play my trio to Ireland who is pleased with it. Have lesson with him 11.0–12.0. In aft. pft. & walk after tea with Beth. In evening listen to wireless – a very amuzing Musical Comedy skit – the Pride of the Regiment by Walter Leigh.[1]

1 Walter Leigh (1905–1942; killed in action), English composer, and his collaborator V.C. Clinton-Baddeley (1900–1970), the English writer, did much to raise the standards of light music on the London stage during the early 1930s, with their musical, *Aladdin, or Love will find out the Way* (1931) and their very successful comic opera, *Jolly Roger, or The Admiral's Daughter* (1933); *The Pride of the Regiment, or Cashiered for his Country* was first produced at St Martin's Theatre in 1932.
   It was probably Leigh's gifts for stage music of all kinds that led him to compose film scores for the GPO Film Unit from 1933, of which the most accomplished and inventive was *Song of Ceylon* (1934). Britten himself was later to become a colleague at the Unit in 1935–6, and thus would have had access to Leigh's experience.

Thursday, 9 June 1932

Rotten day for writing. Only write a putrid song[1] after tea. Trio practise 11.30–1.30 (Lauricella alone for 1 hr). Good work at Bridge Scherzo. I practise Pft. abit in aft.
   Barbara, Beth, & I go to His Majesty's [Theatre][2] to see "Dubarry"[3] at 8.15. V. spectacular Musical Comedy. V. entertaining but not exactly intellegent. Anny Ahlers[4] is most attractive & Heddle Nash[5] sings well. Back by 11.30.

1 Unidentified.
2 Haymarket, London SW1.
3 *The Dubarry*, comic opera by Carl Millöcker (1842–1899), Austrian composer, first performed in its revised version with new lyrics by Paul Knepler and J. Williminski, at His Majesty's Theatre on 14 April 1932.
4 Annie Ahlers (1906–1933), German-born singing actress who played the title role.

5 Heddle Nash (1896–1961), English tenor, who took the part of René Lavallery. He had made a sensational operatic début as the Duke in Verdi's *Rigoletto* at the Old Vic in 1925, and subsequently worked with the British National Opera Company.

Wednesday, 15 June 1932

Pft. practise before going to R.C.M. for lesson, v. good, with Benjamin at 11.40.

In aft. I start, unsatisfactorily, a new Ballet (by Miss Alford) but can't make much head way with it.[1]

Walk with Beth after tea.

1 Britten had already completed one ballet – *Plymouth Town* – to a scenario by Violet Alford. Two scenes of this new ballet exist; they were drafted on 15–16 June. Although without a title, a description of the stage events, transcribed from Britten's composition sketch, gives us an inkling of its character:

Introduction
Scene – A Sunday afternoon. A Basque Village Pelote ground. The Fountain or Wall is against the Church. Basque houses on either side. Mountains in the distance.

Sheep bells are heard. The shepherd leads his flock into the village. He whistles to them. They come to him at the trough to drink. He begins to fold them into a bergerie underneath one of the houses (ground level). The sheep break away and run all over the pelote ground, jumping up the tiered seats. He pursues them. The shepherd gets them into order. He shuts them in the bergerie. The Church doors open and the congregation comes out. A lively ram jumps right over the half-door of the bergerie. The shepherd in pursuit. He takes the ram back into the bergerie.

[Scene II]
The young men and girls form into couples, fours and sixes, and begin a Fandango with endless repeats. The shepherd leaps over the half-door of the bergerie, pushes out the young man dancing in front of the captain's daughter and takes his place.

Britten gives no reasons for discontinuing the project, but he clearly showed excellent sense in abandoning it.

Thursday, 16 June 1932

Write all morning & a bit of aft. & abit late in evening, re-starting ballet – not satisfactorily bother it all. Practise Pft. in aft. Go to Whiteley's for hair cut after tea; Beth & I go to Bridges to fetch some things Mrs. Bridge had brought for me in her car from Friston. Stay abt. an hour.

Friday, 17 June 1932

Go to R.C.M. to find Ireland not there at 10.0. Return, after listening to a bit of a Patron's Fund Rehearsal,[1] to pft. practise. Bit more of that in aft. & also read much poetry (on roof – on acct. of marvellous weather) on off chance of finding something to set to music. Beth & I go up to Oxford St. for her to shop aft. tea. Getting some stalls thro' Lauricella, Beth & I go to "Hiawatha"[2] at Albert Hall. Taxis both way, as we change. An amazing show. V. impressive.

1 The works Britten might have heard in rehearsal were: Mozart's concert aria, 'Mia speranza adorata' (K. 416) and his Clarinet Concerto in A (K. 622); Saint-Saëns: Piano Concerto No. 2 in G minor; and Schumann: Piano Concerto in A minor, Op. 54.

2 The three-part 'Indian' Cantata (1898–1900) by Samuel Coleridge-Taylor (1875–1912), English composer, based on Longfellow's poem. During the 1920s and 1930s *Hiawatha* was frequently performed as a pageant at the Royal Albert Hall, on this occasion produced by T.C. Fairburn, and sung by the Royal Choral Society, with Horace Stevens and Harold Williams sharing the title role, and Elsa Macfarlane, Elsie Suddaby and Flora Woodman sharing the role of Minnehaha, conducted by Malcolm Sargent. Other soloists included Lilian Stiles-Allen, Trefor Jones and Henry Wendon. The choreography was by Eupham Maclaren.

Monday, 20 June 1932

I begin a movement which might be a bit of a Chamber symphony[1] in morning. Practise Pft. in aft. Go up to Hawkes[2] after tea & get Kodály's Psalmus Hungaricus[3] – marvellous work. Beth goes to Hampstead to play tennis with Kathleen Mead after tea. I listen to a Vaudeville on wireless and write letters after dinner. Too full of Psalmus to write music!

1 The *Sinfonietta*, Op. 1, for chamber orchestra, composed 20 June – 9 July 1932 (sketch) and scored 11–16 July. Britten dedicated the piece to Bridge. See also note 2 to Letter 32.

2 The music publishers and retailers, Boosey & Hawkes, 295 Regent

Street, London W1, who were later to become Britten's publishers, 1934–63.

3 *Psalmus hungaricus*, Op. 13 (1923). In 1965 Britten invited Kodály to the Aldeburgh Festival, during which a number of his works were performed. On 19 June, in this same Festival, the first performance of Britten's *Gemini Variations* ('Twelve Variations and Fugue on an Epigram of Kodály'), Op. 73, was given by the two young Hungarian musicians to whom the work was dedicated, the Jeney twins, Zoltán and Gábor.

Wednesday, 22 June 1932

Practise Pft. before going to R.C.M. for Pft. lesson at 11.40. Hear from R.V. Williams that he can't get my Psalms done anywhere.[1] Write more Symph. in afternoon. Walk with Beth after tea. Go to R.C.M. with her at 8.15 for part of chamber concert, Stravinsky's 3 pieces for Str. Quartet (marvellous works) are creditably (not more) played by a quartet including Richards. Then a dismal, disgraceful in technique & musicianship, performance of "La Folia"[2] by R.C. Onley.[3] A dull cantata ("Non sa che sia dolore" – but it might have been in Sanscrit) by Bach followed. After that we fled.

1 Vaughan Williams had written to Sir Ivor Atkins (1869–1953), organist at Worcester Cathedral and Director of the Three Choirs Festival from 1898–1948, about Britten's Psalms:

I am sending you herewith the 2 Psalms by the young composer Britten aged 18 [. . .] I should be obliged if you will look at it and give me your opinion [. . .] I've been through the Psalm – I think it is rather good & well written for the voice. Of course it wd never have been written except for the 'Symphonie des Psaumes' [Stravinsky] but is no worse for that [. . .]

Vaughan Williams wrote with similar generosity in the same year to Anne Macnaghten recommending that she should 'get into touch with Benjamin Britten – I believe he has a string 4tet ['Go play, boy, play']. I don't know it – but his orchestral & choral things are fine.'

2 A set of variations for violin and piano by Corelli, arranged by Fritz Kreisler.

3 Ronald Charles Onley (b. 1912), a violin exhibitioner at the College, 1928–34.

Thursday, 23 June 1932

I write more of Symph. in morning, before Richards & Lauricella
come at 12.30–1.30 to rehearse. Do the Bridge Pft. Quartet
Phantasy,[1] (without viola) marvellous work. Finish first mov. of
symph. in aft. Walk with Beth after tea.
   Write letters, read & do abit of revision after dinner.

1 *Phantasy* in F sharp minor.

Monday, 27 June 1932

Too hot to do much work – nevertheless I start the slow movement
of my Symph. Practise Pft. before lunch & tea. Mum & Pop come
to stay the night on the way home from Stroud.[1] They arr. in car
abt. 6.30. Pop is better but not at all well yet. Barbara comes after
dinner.

1 They had been visiting Mr Britten's sister, Florence.

Thursday, 30 June 1932

Write more of slow mov. in morning, afternoon & after dinner
practically finishing it. Lauricella & Richards come 12.30–2.0.
Good work at Bridge. Meiklejohn of Gresham's comes to see me
after tea – very pleased to see him. Austin beats Satoh[1] at
Wimbledon, thus being in final – greater rejoicings!
   Rain at last, tho' still hot.

1 Jiri Satoh, Japanese tennis player.

Monday, 4 July 1932
[*Lowestoft*]

Pop still the same with aches and pains. Write more of last mov.
of symph. in morning, & Beth & Diana & I bathe from hut at
12.0. Walk with Beth & Caesar up town in aft. After tea Beth gives
me some lessons in driving the car the other side of Carlton[1] after
that we bathe (Diana as well) at 6.0. Cold but fun. Bridge abit after
dinner.

1 Carlton Colville, south of Lowestoft.

Thursday, 7 July 1932
[*London*]

Write more of last mov. in morning & aft. Lauricella & Richards
come to practise 11.15–1.30. Do good work. Beth & I go to Booseys
after tea to see abt. a presentation Baton from Lowestoft Musical
Soc. to Mr. Coleman.[1] Write home & listen to wireless after
supper. Prokofiev's attractive overture on Yiddish Themes,[2] a Bax
carol,[3] Elizabeth Maconchy's[4] ordinary Pft. concerto (Kathleen
Long)[5] some amazing Beggar Songs of Hermann Reutter.[6] Pft. solos
of Bartok[7] & Walton's Delightful & attractive Facade.[8] Performances
on the whole inadequate under Stanford Robinson[9] – except for the
Wireless Singers[10] who sang brilliantly.

1 The Lowestoft Musical Society presented him on 12 July with a silver-
mounted ebony baton, in celebration of his thirty years as a leading
musician in the town.

2 *Overture on Hebrew Themes* for chamber ensemble (1919). The concert
was given by the BBC Orchestra (Section C), and the Wireless Singers, conducted by Stanford Robinson.

3 'Of a Rose I sing a Song', carol for small choir, harp, cello and double-
bass, composed 1920.

4 Elizabeth Maconchy (b. 1907), English composer. She studied at the
College 1923–9 with Charles Wood (1866–1926) and Vaughan Williams, and later in Prague where her Piano Concertino (which Britten
refers to as a concerto) was performed in 1930. Works by Maconchy
have occasionally been performed at the Aldeburgh Festival and the
two composers remained cordial friends. She was created DBE in
1987.

5 Kathleen Long (1896–1968), English pianist.

6 Hermann Reutter (b. 1900), German composer.

7 The Romanian Dance No. 1 (1915), Burlesque No. 1 (1908) and *Allegro
barbaro* (1911).

8 *Façade*: the first suite for orchestra (1926), not the original entertainment with poems by Edith Sitwell of 1922.

9 Stanford Robinson (1904–1984), English conductor, a member of the
BBC Music Staff, 1924–66.

10 The BBC's resident professional vocal octet, formed in 1927 by Stanford Robinson. In 1934 another eight voices were added, thus forming two groups of eight singers, known as the BBC Singers 'A' and
'B'. Peter Pears was a member of the BBC Singers, 1934–7.

Saturday, 9 July 1932

Writing all aft. & after tea I finish my Symphonietta for 10
instruments. Beth & I go to Clapham Common[1] to play tennis
(practice) 11.0–12.30. V. Hot. We go in the Gallery of the New
Theatre[2] to see Twelfth Night in evening 8.30. Marvellous show
– very funny, & superbly acted – Jean Forbes-Robertson[3] (Viola) &
Phyllis Neilson-Terry[4] (Olivia) & Arthur Wontner[5] (Malvolio)
being especially good.

1 London SW4.

2 St Martin's Lane, London WC2; now known as the Albery.

3 Jean Forbes-Robertson (1905–1962), English actress. As well as being
  a noted Viola she is chiefly remembered for playing Peter Pan in
  James Barrie's play for children, for eight consecutive Christmas
  seasons, from 1927 to 1934. Her second husband, André van
  Gyseghem (1906–1979), directed the Left Theatre production of
  Montagu Slater's *Easter 1916*, for which Britten composed the incidental music in 1935. (See note 1 to Letter 98.)

4 Phyllis Neilson-Terry (1892–1977), English actress.

5 Arthur Wontner (1875–1960), English actor–manager.

Monday, 11 July 1932

Begin to score my Symphonietta in morning. V. Hot day with
Thunderstorms. Practise Pft. in aft. Go to R.A.M. Marylebone
Rd.[1] at 5.0 to hear result of Mendelssohn Scholarship with 2 others
(inc. Grace Williams[2] & a Mr. Baxter[3]). Complete fiasco. Owing to
a muddle at beginning between Mr. Sargent[4] & Walton O'Donall[5]
the proceedings have to start from begining again, so we wont
hear until September. Marvellously efficient!! Beth & I go to dinner
with Hanworth[6] at Temple[7] at 7.0. Great time. Dr. (Mrs) Hanworth
& Mr. Hanworth & Dr's sister Dr. Wallace[8] there. Back by 11.30.

1 Royal Academy of Music, Marylebone Road, London NW1.

2 The Welsh composer, Grace Williams (1906–1977). She was a pupil
  of Vaughan Williams at the College and studied with Egon Wellesz
  (see note 1 to Diary for 25 November 1932). Williams was eight years
  older than Britten and thus their College paths did not cross. It was,
  however, at the College that Britten first heard Williams's music on
  1 July: 'Listen to a Patron's Fund Rehearsal. Grace Williams' 2 Psalms

– incompetent music [. . .].' From this unpromising start grew an important friendship which was strengthened by their association with the Macnaghten–Lemare concerts (see note 2 to Diary for 16 July 1932), where on one occasion a work by each of them was given its first performance: Britten's *Sinfonietta* and a withdrawn Movement for trumpet and chamber orchestra by Williams. (See PFL, plate 63, where the programme is reproduced and Letter 40, the first of Britten's letters to Williams.) The two composers were to remain in touch during the post-war period, and in November 1950 Pears and members of the London Harpsichord Ensemble were to give the first performance of Williams's arrangement of Three Traditional Welsh Ballads. See also Malcolm Boyd, *Grace Williams* (University of Wales, Welsh Arts Council, 1980).

3 A composition student at the Academy.

4 Malcolm Sargent, the conductor.

5 Walton O'Donnell (b. ? , d. 1939), member of the teaching staff at the Academy.

6 Dr Honoria Josephine Hanworth, 41 Hurlingham Court, Fulham, London SW6.

7 The Temple Bar restaurant, 227–8 Strand, London WC2.

8 Hygenia Leigh Josephine Wallace, MRCS (Eng), LRCP (London), 3 Plowden Buildings, Temple, London EC4.

Tuesday, 12 July 1932

Still very hot – RCM for lesson with Ireland. He's very pleased with my Sinfonietta. Write home before lunch. Trio practice here in aft. Do more scoring of my Sinf. after dinner.

Wednesday, 13 July 1932

Pft. lesson after pft. practise in morning at 11.40 at RCM with Benjamin. In it I also play B. & Herbert Howells my sinfonietta, of which they approve. Spend rest of day copying out Sinf., except after dinner when I go & see the Bridges, back in town for a few days. Beth goes to Barbara.

Saturday, 16 July 1932

Ring up Anne Macnaghten[1] abt. the concerts of British Work at which they're probably going to do my Sinfonietta.[2] I finish copying this in morning, aft. & after tea. Beth & I meet Barbara at Selfridges for some iced elevenses. I buy a Vol. of Graves'[3] marvellous poetry. Barbara comes in evening. Beth is out to dinner, with Elinor Bond.

1 Anne Catherine Macnaghten (b. 1908), English violinist. Among her teachers were Brosa and André Mangeot (see also note 1 to Letter 35). She founded a women's quartet, the Macnaghten String Quartet, which made its début in London in 1932. The Macnaghten–Lemare concerts were founded in December 1931 (with Iris Lemare and Elisabeth Lutyens) with the express aim of presenting 'concerts of contemporary music of differing trends in which British music predominates and discovering and encouraging composers of British nationality'. It was the Macnaghten concerts that gave Britten his first public platform. See Anne Macnaghten, 'The Story of the Macnaghten Concerts', *Musical Times*, September 1959, and 'The First Fifty Years' (with an afterword by Ian Horsbrugh), in the programme book for the New Macnaghten Concerts – '50 Years of New Music, 1931–81', pp. 4–5. For Lutyens's role in founding the concerts, see Merion and Susie Harries, *A Pilgrim Soul: The Life and Work of Elisabeth Lutyens* (London, Michael Joseph, 1989), pp. 66–9. Lutyens was not an admirer of Britten's music: 'A brilliant journalist', she called him, 'able to produce an instant effect at first hearing, understandable to all. Each repeated hearing yields less – or so I find.' She was also unsympathetic to his homosexuality – and his success.

2 The first public performance of the *Sinfonietta* was given at a Macnaghten–Lemare Concert on 31 January 1933 by the Macnaghten String Quartet with Adolf Lotter (double-bass), and the English Wind Players conducted by Iris Lemare. (See also note 2 to Letter 32.)

3 Robert Graves (1895–1985), English poet and novelist. The volume of poetry – *Poems 1926–1930* (London, Heinemann, 1931) – contained 'Lift Boy' which Britten set shortly after buying the book. (See Diary for 18 July 1932.)

In 1960 Graves invited Britten to compose music for his musical play, *A Song for Sheba*, a project that never materialized. For a full account see Martin Seymour-Smith, *Robert Graves: His Life and Work* (London, Hutchinson, 1982), pp. 486–9.

Monday, 18 July 1932

Walk abit of the way with Beth to her academy in morning. I finish "I lov'd a lass", & write a new part song to go with it "The Lift Boy" – R. Graves. Anne Macnaghten comes to see me before lunch

– she is going to do either my Quartet (1931) or the phantasy quintet.[1]

Practise Pft. in afternoon. Walk after tea. Copy out Elizabeth Ann[2] after dinner.

1 The first public performance of the *Phantasy* Quintet in F minor was given at a lunchtime concert on 12 December 1932 at the church of All Hallows-by-the-Tower, Barking, London, by the Macnaghten String Quartet: Anne Macnaghten (violin 1), Elise Desprez (violin 2), Beryl Scawen-Blunt (viola), Mary Goodchild (cello), with Nora Wilson (viola). Later the same day the work was included in the third Macnaghten–Lemare concert at the Ballet Club (Mercury Theatre), London. In the same programme was the first performance of Britten's settings of Walter de la Mare, the Three Two-part Songs, given by the Carlyle Singers conducted by Iris Lemare with Britten at the piano.

2 An unpublished setting for voice and piano of John Drinkwater's 'Elizabeth Ann' ('This is the tale of Elizabeth Ann') had been rewritten on 17 July. It was most probably first composed earlier in the year; the surviving manuscripts, a composition sketch and an ink fair copy, date from the time of the July revisions.

Wednesday, 20 July 1932

Go to College at 11.0 for comp. exam. Examiners R.V. Williams, S.P. Waddington & Ed Bainton. Richards, Lauricella & I play my Intro. & Allo to them, & they see my Ballet [*Plymouth Town*], Sinfonietta, 2 latest pt. songs, etc. Seemed quite pleased. Go to H.M.V. Regent St.[1] to get gram. records in aft. intending to get Till Eulenspiegle. I get Stravinsky's great Psalm Symphony.[2] Come back via hair cut at Whiteleys. Rewrite bit of old Quart.[3] after dinner.

1 His Master's Voice gramophone record shop.

2 Stravinsky's *Symphony of Psalms*, performed by the Walter Straram Orchestra (Paris) and the Alexander Vlassoff Choir conducted by the composer, was released on the Columbia label (LX 147–9) in 1932. Britten's copy is in the Archive.

3 Probably the String Quartet in D major (1931), perhaps prompted by a hope that the Macnaghten Quartet might perform it, though in fact they never did.

Thursday, 21 July 1932

Practise Pft. before the Trio comes at 11.30 to practise until 1.30.
We do Bridge Quintet[1] & Mozart Pft. Quart. (G min.). I pack all
afternoon. After tea I go for Second Study Pft. exam (examiners –
Benjamin – Bainton & another – horrors!) at 4.30. Come back via
Anne Macnaghten's, where I leave my old Quartet. I find that I
have won the Sullivan prize[2] (£10) cheers! Pack after dinner &
write letters.

1 Quintet in D minor for 2 violins, viola, cello and piano, composed
originally in 1904–5, and substantially revised in 1912. It was first
performed by the English String Quartet, with Harold Samuel
(piano), in May 1912. Britten, Lauricella and Richards were preparing
the piece before playing it with Frank and Ethel Bridge (see Diary
for 23 July 1932).

2 One of the College's annual prizes for composition founded in 1900
by Miss H. Pole in memory of the composer Sir Arthur Sullivan
(1842–1900), who was himself the first holder of the Mendelssohn
Scholarship at the Academy in 1856.

Friday, 22 July 1932
[London/Friston]

Go to RCM at 10.30, after finishing packing etc. to hear competition
Cobbett prize – performance of my 5tet – bad – but I expected
worse. Ivor James & Waddington there – including Cobbett himself.
The Trio (Lauricella & Richards) & Beth & I set off for Friston at
1.0 from 173, C.R. [Cromwell Road] in Richards car (Beth helped
him with the driving) arr. after good journey at 5.0. We 3 stay at
Miss Fass' & Beth with B's. Tennis after tea, & games after supper.

Saturday, 23 July 1932
[Friston]

Practise Trio from 9.30–11.30 & tennis at B's after that. We all picnic
at Wilmington[1] at David (giant) for lunch. Come back & Mr. B.,
Miss Fass & Beth, Bernard & I bathe in sea. Tennis after tea (with
Mr. B., Beth, Miss Fass & Bernard). After supper at Miss Fass'
we play (with F.B. as a superb Vla. 1 & Mrs. B. as Vl. 2) Mozart
Pft. quartet in G min & Bridge Pft. Quintet – marvellous fun.

1 A village six miles north-west of Eastbourne, and close to Friston, the Bridges' Sussex home. Wilmington is famous for the 226–foot-high figure, known as the Long Man of Wilmington (and locally referred to as 'David'), cut into the chalky soil of the South Downs.

Sunday, 24 July 1932

Pelting with rain & wind all day. We practise my Phant. Quintet (me playing Vla. 2!!) in morning. Lunch at B's play about in garden in rain in aft. with Bernard. Mr. Graves[1] & Miss [illegible] come over after tea. After supper & tea more playing – my Intro. & All$\underline{o}$ for Trio, Bridge Phant Quintet (Pft) & his marvellous trio[2] in which he coaches us.

Late bed.

1 A friend of the Bridges, not the poet.
2 Probably the Piano Trio (1929).

Tuesday, 26 July 1932
[*Lowestoft*]

Unpack in morning & practise abit, also listen to Stravinsky's marvellous Psalm Symph., on gram. Walk with Mum, shopping, before lunch; walk with Caesar to the May's in aft.[1] They come to tea at house with Ping-pong after. Rain stops us going to hut to bathe. Begin to copy out parts of Sinfonietta before dinner. Write letters after, & go to post – all of us.

1 On their return from India, Diana May's parents rented a house in Lowestoft.

Saturday, 30 July 1932

I have vocal score of Stravinsky's great Psalm Symph. sent from Chesters. More copying of Horn part of Sinf. in morning. Walk with Beth, before. Bathe with her & Mum at 12.30. In aft. Beth & I go to tennis party at Mrs. Dance's.[1] Not v. excellent tennis. Among those present is Mrs. Owles. John[2] cries alot in evening.

Walk with Pop before bed.

1 Wife of Charles Dance, Ascona, Gunton Cliff, Lowestoft.

2 Britten's nephew, John Robert Marsh, had been born on 23 June. Robert and his family had arrived the previous day.

Sunday, 31 July 1932

I go down at 10.0 with Ethel Boyd to play hymns (piano) for Children's Country Holiday Fund[1] in St. Johns. Quite fun – nice kids. Church there afterward with Mum at 11.0. Finish Horn part in afternoon. Walk after tea with Pop, Beth & Bobby. Write letters after supper & goodnight walk with Pop.

1 A charity run by the Church Army (see Diary for 7 August) which organized seaside holidays for deprived children.

Sunday, 7 August 1932

I go to help Ethel Boyd at St. Johns at 10.0 with the Children's Holiday Fund, as last Sunday. Not nearly as good tho', as the service was taken in a sentemental exaggerated, Sankey & Moodeyish manner by the Church Army.[1] Church after at 11.0 with Mum. Bazil Reeve comes in afterwards to hear Strav.'s Psalm Symph. Read more 'Grub St.'[2] & bit more copying in aft. Walk with Pop, Bobby, & Beth after tea to club. Grub St. in evening & walk with Pop.

1 The largest evangelical lay society in the Church of England, founded in 1882 (four years after the Salvation Army) by Wilson Carlile (1847–1942). Sankey and Moody were the joint American compilers of hymn-tune collections which were particularly popular in the Victorian period. The Salvation Army has made their hymn tunes familiar throughout the world.

2 *New Grub Street*, a novel by George Gissing (1857–1903), first published in 1891.

Tuesday, 9 August 1932

Finish 2nd Fiddle part in morning (only 2 more, thank heaven!), & practise Pft. Bathe with Bazil Reeve, & Mum & Beth before lunch. Also bathe with Chartres (Mr., Clive & Jean) when they (+ Mrs.) come over to tea down at hut. Pop takes Mum, Beth & me to

Sparrow's Nest to see "Mr. Cinders"[1] – musical comedy. Very amusing & principal parts, very good.

1 A musical comedy in two acts by Clifford Grey and Greatrex Newman with music by Vivian Ellis and Richard Myers, which was brought from the Adelphi Theatre, London, to Lowestoft for the week beginning 8 August. The hit number in the show was Ellis's 'Spread a Little Happiness'.

Thursday, 11 August 1932

Laurence is ill & Pop has his work to do.

V. hot day. Have 4 strenuous sets of tennis with John Nicholson in morning on his court. Go st. down to huts after to bathe with Beth & Kathleen Mead – v. warm, at 12.30. Beth & I go to tennis in car, at Chartres (Sotterley) at 3.30. Have quite good tennis. Back by 7.25. After dinner I run into Boyd's to hear F.B.'s 'Blow out you Bugles'[1] (sung by Frank Titterton,[2] very well), from Promenade Concert – conducted by him. Seemed very fine. More copying afterwards, & walk with Pop.

Get Walton's Portsmouth Point, ov., on gram record.[3] Disappointed. Ineffective & apparently bad & careless workmanship.

1 A setting of Rupert Brooke's poem 'The Dead' for tenor and orchestra (or piano), with optional trumpet, composed in 1918.
2 Frank Titterton (1891–1956), English tenor.
3 This recording (the first of *Portsmouth Point*) was made by the New English Symphony Orchestra conducted by Anthony Bernard (1891–1963), and released in January 1930 on Decca M 94. Britten's copy is in the Archive. He was to express a quite different view of the overture to Walton in 1963: see note 1 to Diary for 9 September 1931.

Tuesday, 16 August 1932

Practise Pft. & Viola in morning & bathe with Mum & Beth before lunch. In aft. Beth & I go to Normanston Park[1] to help the Boyds entertain the slum children from town (see previous Sundays) [31 July]. Play cricket with them, & arrange races for them. Quite fun. They are nice children. Back by 7.0. Write letters after dinner.

1 On the outskirts of Lowestoft.

Friday, 19 August 1932

Walk before breakfast as usual with Caesar – this time with Ethel, David & John Boyd[1] as well. Go up town in morning to Boots, Morlings, & Public Library,[2] where I pick up 2 books of Lyrics (Elizabethan & 17th Cent.)[3] for 2/6 instead of 10/6 each! Bathe with Beth & Cyril Reeve.[4] V. rough but fun. V. hot day as yesterday. I go to tea with Reeves to meet a Christopher Gledhill[5] from Oriel (Bazil's college) [Oxford]. Go to "Mata Hari"[6] at Palace with Beth to see Greta Garbo.[7] She is most attractive, I suppose, but what slop!

1 In 1930 Britten composed three pieces for piano solo – 'John', 'Daphne' and 'Michael' – depicting three Lowestoft friends, the first of which was inspired by John Boyd (16 September), the nephew of the Brittens' neighbours, the others by Daphne Black (4 October) and Michael Tyler (27 December). The third piece makes a quotation from 'Ragamuffin', the second of Ireland's *Three London Pieces*, which was obviously intended as a salute to Britten's teacher. The *Three Character Pieces* were first performed by Sarah Briggs at the Chester Summer Music Festival, on 28 July 1989, and published by Faber Music in the same year.

2 The Carnegie Public Library and Museum, Clapham Road, Lowestoft.

3 *Elizabethan Lyrics* and *Seventeenth Century Lyrics*, chosen, edited and arranged by Norman Ault, (London, Longman, 1925 and 1928). Britten's copy of the latter volume has survived, inscribed: '(Sullivan Prize 1932)/Benjamin Britten/August 1932'.

4 Edward Cyril Reynold Reeve (b. 1913; South Lodge, 1925–7), Basil's brother.

5 Christopher Gledhill (b. 1912), son of the vicar of Bungay and a gifted musician (pianist) in his own right whom Britten met occasionally between 1934 and 1936. They played music together and early in 1935 Gledhill helped Britten with proof reading. He was connected with the Bungay Orchestra.

6 The 1931 Metro-Goldwyn-Mayer film based on the story of the World War I spy, directed by George Fitzmaurice.

7 Greta Garbo (1905–1990), Swedish-born film actress, and great heart-throb of the 1930s.

Monday, 22 August, 1932

Yacht-club regatta week

Pft. practise before going to Bungay[1] in car with Beth at 12.0. We play Tennis Tournament.[2] Our Handicap Singles take place to-day; Both of us lose. Beth (playing v. well) to Elizabeth Nicholson 7/5 – 6/2 & I (playing atrociously) to a Mr. Watts[3] 6/4 – 6/4. Quite fun tho'. Back by 5.0. Go up to Morlings after tea. Walk with Pop before bed.

1 A small market town 16 miles west of Lowestoft on the Suffolk–Norfolk border.
2 The 22nd Waveney Valley Championship, held at Bungay. Britten was occupied with the tournament for the remainder of the week, reaching the doubles' final. He wrote in his diary for 27 August: 'I play my final with John, losing to Eardley Todd & Parry Evans 6/3 4/6 6/3 (?) – playing v. badly.'
3 Unidentified.

Friday, 26 August 1932

Walk before breakfast as usual with Caesar. I go to Bungay with John Nicholson & Elizabeth & Barbara Spashett. They pick me up in car, at 10.15. I play Doubles with John against 2 Hughes[1] & win 1–6, 6–[omission] 8–6, at 11 o'clock, & after lunch with N's & Spashetts, play against 2 Seagos[2] & win 6/2. 6/2, & after tea win against 2 Gorsts[3], 3/6, 6/4, 6/2. Truly a day of luck! The N's win all theirs except one. Back with them by 7.30.

1 Unidentified.
2 Edward Seago, the artist, was to be among those who attended the première of Our Hunting Fathers at Norwich in 1936. This entry must refer to him and his brother, John. See also Jean Goodman, Edward Seago: the other side of the canvas, new edition (Norwich, Jarrold, 1990), pp. 30–31.
3 Unidentified.

Tuesday, 30 August 1932

Practise Pft. & long walk with Caesar – to do some thinking[1] – in morning. Lady Hill, Nan, Maurice & wife come over to bathe & tea on Beach in afternoon. John Nicholson comes too.

Thundery showers, but mainly fine. Barb. Beth, Bobby & Marjorie go to Laurence & Fernande for coffee. Walk with Pop before bed.

1 It became an established habit of Britten's to think about his current compositional projects while walking. These long walks came to be an essential part of the actual process of his composing.

Wednesday, 31 August 1932

Bobby, Marjorie and John catch 8.18 back to Prestatyn in morning. Beth takes them to station in car. Practise Pft. & bathe with Mum, Beth, Barbara before an early lunch at 1.0. Beth & I go to a tennis tournament given in the Back's garden at Oulton for Oulton Church funds. Quite fun inspite of rain, 1.30–7.0. After dinner Pop takes us all to see Sunshine Susie[1] at Hippodrome.[2] Utter piffle, but Jack Hulbert[3] is very amusing.

1 The 1931 Gainsborough film, directed by Victor Saville, the story of a banker who pretends to be a clerk in order to court a typist.

2 Hippodrome Theatre (and cinema), Battery Green Road, Lowestoft.

3 Jack Hulbert (1892–1978), English actor, singer, librettist, choreographer and director who, with his wife Cicely Courtneidge (1893–1980), appeared in thirteen London musicals and many films.

Thursday, 1 September 1932

My records of "Sacre du P."[1] arrived yesterday. They are magnificently played in spots, but the speed seems unreasonable in places, e.g. The Dance of the Earth, where the 8 Horns are left high & dry struggling. To-day Mum, Barb., Beth (driving), & I go to the Priests[2] at Harleston,[3] at 12.30. We have lunch up the river & tea in the house – owing to rain. Back by 7.0. Bathe before dinner. Right thro' the "Sacre" after.

1 This recording of Stravinsky's 1913 ballet Le Sacre du printemps was performed by L'orchestre symphonique de Paris conducted by the composer. It was released on Columbia LX 119–23 in 1931. Britten's copy has not survived.

2 Friends of the Britten family who also had a house in London near the Bridges. Beth Welford remembered that they gave wonderful tennis parties.

3 A small market town in Norfolk, 22 miles west of Lowestoft.

Friday, 2 September 1932

Go up to Morlings & Library after pft. practice in morning. At former I pay for the World's Wonder (Sacre – 24/-) & at the latter, I get some Ravel pft. music. In afternoon John & David Boyd come to tea on beach. Mum, Barb. Beth & I bathe.

Saturday, 3 September 1932

Practise Pft. in morning & walk with Caesar and (pt. way) David Boyd. We were going over to Hills in afternoon but there is bad weather & we don't go. Read instead starting "Good Bye to all that".[1] Bathe after tea with Barb. & Beth. Mum, Barb, Beth go to see "Good Night, Vienna"[2] (film) at Palace after dinner. Read & walk with Pop.

Pencil because of lost fountain pen.[3]

1 The autobiographical memoir of the First World War by Robert Graves, first published London, Jonathan Cape, 1929.
2 The film version of the musical, originally composed for radio by Eric Maschwitz and George Posford.
3 Britten went over this entry in ink later.

Monday, 5 September 1932

Barbara goes off to town by 9.55 in morning. Beth (driving) Mum & I go to station with her. She goes for fortnight to Lakes[1] tomorrow. Bathe with Mum & Beth before lunch. Walks with Caesar before tea, & with Pop & with Mum after. Read & gramophone (more "wonder") in evening.

1 The Lake District, NW England.

Friday, 9 September 1932

Masterson is making me some Tails (bought with my Sullivan Prize) & I have them fitted in the morning. Begin abit of a new Phantasy[1] (doubtful) & Bathe with Mum & Beth before lunch. In afternoon we have a tennis party – up at the tennis club at 3.0 – 6.30. Barbara Spashett, Mrs. Speak[2] & T.J.E. Sewell come. Have tea up there. Marvellous day after pelting rain until 10.30 a.m.

1 Probably Britten's first thoughts for his *Phantasy*, Op. 2, for oboe and string trio. See also Diary for 20 September 1932.
2 Wife of Arthur Speak, Aitchison, Home Close, Pakefield, Lowestoft.

Saturday, 10 September 1932

Mum goes to Ipswich to see Aunt Janie's[1] new house, by bus starting 9.45 arr. back 6.30. Go up town before lunch to libraries. From the public I get Cecil Gray's Contemporary Music.[2] Very fine, but I don't altogether agree with everything he says. Read this & walk with Caesar in afternoon. Pop goes to the Hospital to be X-rayed after tea at 5.0. Beth & I go with him in car.

1 Mrs. Britten's sister-in-law, Jane Hockey, had moved from 88 Berners Street, Ipswich, to 14 Fonnereau Road. This remained the Hockey family home until the death of Aunt Janie's daughter, Elsie, in February 1984.
2 Cecil Gray (1895–1951), Scots composer and critic. *A Survey of Contemporary Music* (London, Oxford University Press, 1924).

Tuesday, 13 September 1932

I spend most of day copying out a revised version of 5tet Phant.[1] to send to Mendelssohn Schol. Committee (I had the 1st copy away for Cobbett comp.) Bathe (fearfully cold) with Mum & Beth before lunch. Walk with Pop before dinner. Write to Bridges as well as copying & playing after dinner.

1 These were only minor revisions, a result of the composer hearing the work twice at the Cobbett Prize performance on 22 July 1932.

Thursday, 15 September 1932

Send off my Phant. in morning & Pft. practise before a walk with Mum & Bathe also with Beth before lunch. Do some altering of parts of revised Phant. in aft. Tea in garden & Bathe with Beth before dinner.

Sunday, 18 September 1932

Walk with Pop & Caesar in morning. Beth, Mum go to St. Johns.
Bazil Reeve comes to tea & bathe before with Beth & me. Have
gramophone & pft. – including the complete "Sacre" etc. Pack
before supper.

Monday, 19 September 1932
[*Lowestoft/London*]

Catch 8.30 to town. Beth takes me to station in car & Mum to see
me off. Arr. 11.30. Go to R.C.M. for Allen's termly address at 1.0
See Lauricella. Unpack all afternoon. After tea I go shopping with
Mrs. Millar.[1] Listen to a Wagner Prom[2] after dinner on a very bad
wireless. Mastersinger ov. Bachanale [*Tannhäuser*], Siegfried Idyll.
Hagen's Songs[3] (Norman Allin).[4] Funeral March & finale from
Götterdämmerung (Florence Austral)[5] – orchestral playing rough,
but some good wind playing.

1 A fellow lodger.

2 Broadcast from the Queen's Hall, London, given by the BBC Symphony Orchestra conducted by Sir Henry Wood.

3 Hagen's Watch ('Hier sitz ich zur wacht' (Act I)) and Hagen's call
  ('Hoi-ho' (Act II)), from *Götterdämmerung*.

4 Norman Allin (1884–1973), English bass.

5 Florence Austral (1894–1986), Australian soprano, a notable Isolde
  and Brünnhilde.

Tuesday, 20 September 1932
[*London*]

I write more of my Oboe Phantasy[1] in morning & practise. Bernard
Richards & Lauricella come in afternoon & we read through
Ravel's Trio. Walk with Lauri after tea. After dinner I listen to prom
on wireless – British Programme.[2] Delius' marvellously beautiful
tho' meandering & too long, Song of the High Hills, completely
dwarfs the rest of the aenemic programme – Cyril Scott's dismal
Noel,[3] Elgar's typical Sea Pictures & Ethel Smyth's "Aubrey Brain"
Vl & Hrn. Concerto.[4]

1 *Phantasy*, Op. 2, for oboe and string trio, composed 20 September –
  20 October 1932. See also note 1 Letter 35.

2 Broadcast from the Queen's Hall, London, given by the BBC Symphony Orchestra and a section of the BBC Chorus, conducted by Sir
  Henry Wood, with Enid Cruickshank (*Sea Pictures*), and Isobel Baillie
  and Eric Greene (*Song of the High Hills*).

3 His *Christmas Overture* for orchestra, with the optional 'Nativity
  Hymn' for chorus and orchestra to Crashaw's words, was composed
  in 1913.

4 Smyth's Concerto for Violin, Horn and Orchestra (1927) was composed for the English horn-player Aubrey Brain (1893–1955; father of
  Denis Brain) and the Anglo-French violinist Jean Pougnet
  (1907–1968), both of whom were the soloists at this Promenade Concert.

Thursday, 22 September 1932

Practise Pft. before going to R.C.M. for a rehearsal of my Sinfonietta
at 11.0 in Mr. Buesst's[1] class. I have never heard such an appalling
row! However when we have a flute & a 'cello & when the players
have looked at their parts, I think it will be all right. Another fruitless
attempt to continue the Phantasy in the afternoon. Walk after tea
round about the place. Beth & I go to Barbara after dinner.

1 Aylmer Buesst (1883–1970), Australian conductor. These rehearsals
  took place almost weekly throughout the autumn and winter terms,
  though almost always with missing instruments and different players, culminating in a performance of the work at a College Chamber
  Concert on 16 March 1933, conducted by the composer (see note 2
  to Letter 32).

Friday, 23 September 1932

Lesson with Ireland at 10.35. Practise Pft. in afternoon. Ring up
Hubert Foss about the Agreement re my pt. songs. Walk with Beth
after tea. Listen to Beethoven Prom[1] on the atrocious wireless here.
Beethoven's 1st & 8th Symphonies played without care or
thought. Ria Ginster[2] sings the 2 "Egmont" songs, & Myra Hess[3]
plays the 4th Conc. Write letters also.

1 A broadcast from the Queen's Hall, London, given by the BBC Symphony Orchestra conducted by Sir Henry Wood.

2 Ria Ginster (b. 1898), German soprano.

3 Myra Hess (1890–1965), English pianist. During the Second World War she founded and administered the series of lunchtime recitals at the National Gallery, London, in which Britten and Pears were to appear, and where they gave a number of memorable recitals.

Saturday, 24 September 1932

Bit of Pft. practise in morning & walk – shopping – with Beth. After lunch we go on a river trip, with Mrs. Millar, down to Greenwich[1] from Westminster.[2] Very int. all thro' docks. Start at 2.30, back by 4.45 with 45 mins walk at Greenwich. Walk back from West. via the Tate Gallery.[3] See a marvellous picture of a "Dead Boy", by Alfred Stevens (?). [4] Go to Barbara after dinner, hear bit of Prom. concert.[5]

1 A popular river and sight-seeing trip on the Thames.

2 Westminster Bridge, where the river boats were boarded.

3 Millbank, London SW1.

4 Alfred Stevens (1818–1875), English artist and sculptor.

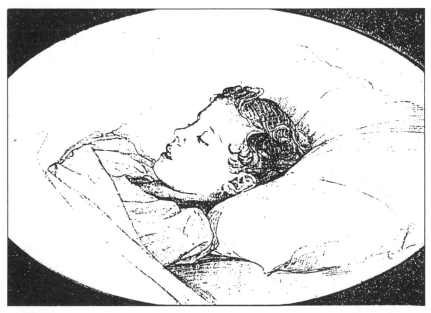

Alfred Stevens's 'Dead Boy' (by kind permission of the Trustees of the Tate Gallery, London)

5 A broadcast of the first part of the Promenade Concert from the Queen's Hall, London, given by the BBC Symphony Orchestra conducted by Sir Henry Wood. The programme was: Lalo's Overture *Le Roi d'Ys*; excerpts from Verdi's *Otello* sung by Thea Phillips and Walter Widdop; Schubert's Entr'actes in B minor and B flat from *Rosamunde*; Liszt's Piano Concerto No. 1 in E flat with Egon Petri (piano); Honegger's *Mouvement symphonique, Pacific 231*; and Bach's Toccata and Fugue in D minor orchestrated by Paul Klenovsky.

Tuesday, 27 September 1932

Practise Pft. in morning. I go to R.C.M. at 11.30 to play abit of the Dvorak 'cello concerto for Bernard in a lesson from Mr. Whitehouse.[1] Write a bit more of Phantasy in aft. & evening – I seem to have got thoroughly stuck with the Scherzo. After tea I go out with Mrs. Millar to get a second-hand bookshelf from a place near Church St. for 5/-.

1 William E. Whitehouse (1859–1935), English cellist.

Thursday, 29 September 1932

I go to R.C.M. at 11.0 for the most execrable rehearsal of my Sinfonietta without proper Dblbass & flute this time. In afternoon I practise with Lauri & Bernard at Ravel [Piano Trio] at R.C.M. 3–4.30. Meet Barbara at Selfridges & then go to Madrigals with her. Whole lot of new stuff. Back for dinner at 8.0. Beth has Elinor Bond to dinner.

Thursday, 6 October 1932

Begin a filthy cold. Rehearsal of Sinfonietta at 11.0 – minus doublebass & oboe! Not much sign of improvement. Rehearse in aft. at 3.0 with Bernard & Lauri. after which I meet Barb. & Beth at Selfridges for tea – & Barb. & I go & Madrigal. Write abit more Phant. after dinner.

Saturday, 8 October 1932

My proofs for my 3 2–part songs arrive in morning. I correct tons
of mistakes. Spend rest of morning & afternoon – walking, talking –
& beginning to paint stand for my bookshelves. Beth goes to tea at
Roehampton[1] & to theatre afterwards. Barbara comes to dinner.
Hall comes in afterwards.

1 Beth was visiting a friend at the Froebel Institute, founded in 1892
to train teachers in the methods and philosophy of Friedrich Wilhelm
August Froebel, the pioneer of kindergarten education.

Monday, 10 October 1932

Go to Ireland at 10.0 to get his advice about proofs. Stay all morning
talking etc. Correct the proofs in afternoon. Also finish my Oboe
Phant. in aft. & after tea. More or less satisfactory – sometimes I
think it is my best work – sometimes my worst. Walk with Beth
before dinner. Don't go to choral practice because of foul cold. My
attempt to listen to Brosa's[1] on wireless is frustrated by the said
[battery] wireless running out!

1 The Brosa String Quartet (Antonio Brosa (violin 1), David Wise (violin
2), Leonard Rubens (viola), Livio Mannucci (cello)), performed
Beethoven's String Quartet in A minor, Op. 132, and Borodin's String
Quartet in D. Tatiana Makushina (soprano) sang songs by Chausson,
Fourdrain, Fauré, Tchaikovsky and Rimsky-Korsakov.

Wednesday, 12 October 1932

Practise Pft. before going to R.C.M. for lesson with Benjamin at
11.40. Hubert Foss (of O.U.P.) comes to lunch at 1.0. Play him
my Oboe Phant. after & show him my Antithetical Songs. Begin to
copy out my Intro. & Allº for trio in afternoon & after dinner.
Walk with Beth before dinner.

Thursday, 13 October 1932

More copying before going to R.C.M. in morning for the most
atrocious of all rehearsals of my Sinfonietta. Only 8 inst. out of
the 10 (& of these 3 new!). What an institution. Rehearse there in

aft. with Bernard & Remo. Meet Barb. & Beth at Selfridges – tea –
Madrigals with Barb. at 6.0 – Dinner with Bridges with moaning
about R.C.M. Back by 10.30.

Friday, 14 October 1932

Lesson with Ireland at 10.35 – v. good & after we go & see Mr.
Waddington & new arrangements are made that my Sinf. should
sound less like aenemic cats. Copy out in afternoon until 3.15 when
I go to Whiteleys to have my hair cut. After tea write home. Go
to Bridges at 7.0 & with Miss Fass we go to B.B.C. Studio at
Waterloo Bridge,[1] where at 8.0 F. B. conducts a concert.[2] Frank
Titterton with a magnificent voice sings two F. B. Songs – Adoration
& Love went a-r. [a-riding] – heavenly things, & the Prize Song.[3]
Leonora 3 (taken slower than usual – with gain in effect) Borodin
Symph. no. 2 (not particularly impressing as a work but the
playing was, in spots delightful) & an exuberant perf. of Rimsky's
Wedding March from Coq d'Or. Back to 4 B.G's[4] for supper until
11.45.

1 An adapted warehouse on the south bank of the River Thames which
   functioned as an overspill studio. When the BBC moved from Savoy
   Hill to Broadcasting House, Portland Place, London W1, the Waterloo
   Studio was retained.
2 A relay given by the BBC Orchestra (Section D) led by Laurence
   Turner.
3 From Act III of Wagner's *Meistersinger*.
4 4 Bedford Gardens, W8, the Bridges' London home.

Sunday, 16 October 1932

Walk with Beth before catching 1.0 train to Rickmansworth[1] with
Alan Frank[2] (colleague of H. F. [Hubert Foss]). I have lunch with
Mr. & Mrs. Foss. Play something of mine to them in aft. Catch 5.21
back after tea. After supper write letters, & listen to Spencer Dyke
Quart.[3] playing Beethoven F min. quart. (sure a wonder of the
world) & Bridge 3 Idylls (marvels in another way). Even the
quartet's murderous playing couldn't murder them.

1 In Hertfordshire, 20 miles north-west of central London.
2 Alan Frank (b. 1910), English publisher, editor, writer and clarinettist.

He joined Oxford University Press in 1927 as assistant music editor, and became music editor in 1948 and head of the music department, 1954–75. He played the clarinet in a number of Britten's film scores, including *The King's Stamp* (1935). He contributed occasional music criticism, to the *Listener*, for example, and sometimes chose a work of Britten's as his topic. His wife was Phyllis Tate, the composer.

3 The Spencer Dyke Quartet (Spencer Dyke (violin 1), Tate Gilder (violin 2), Bernard Shore (viola), Cedric Sharpe (cello)). Their concert also included songs by Franz and Jensen sung by the mezzo-soprano, Lily Zaehner, and John McEwen's Sixth String Quartet ('Biscay').

Thursday, 20 October 1932

Go to R.C.M. after revision of my Phant. at 11.0 for rehearsal of my Sinfonietta. Much better owing to better attendance (although there was no doublebass) & three new players. Trio practise there in afternoon – good work at Ravel. Meet Barb. & Beth at Selfridges & then Madrigals with Barbara. Early bed.

Tuesday, 25 October 1932

Copying all morning, I finish score of Phant. A long job. Now for parts! Bernard & Lauri come in afternoon. Ber. stays until 6.0 to do the Bridge Vlc. Sonata[1] lovely work. Go to Bridges to dinner at 7.15 & listen to a performance of Act II of Tristan on wireless. Beecham spoils it by hurrying & there is only a very poor orchestra.[2] Florence Austral & Walter Widdop[3] (Isolde & T.) very good. The rest rather poor. Even they couldn't spoil this wonder of the world. Back by 11.30.

1 Sonata for cello and piano, 1913–17. Britten retained an affection for the piece for the rest of his life, and gave memorable performances of it with Mstislav Rostropovich (b. 1927), with whom he recorded the work in July 1968 (Decca sxl 6426).

2 The performance, given by the Covent Garden Opera Company, was relayed by the BBC from the Theatre Royal, Glasgow.

3 Widdop was noted for his singing of the *Heldentenor* roles of Siegmund and Tristan. He was to sing the solo tenor part in the first performance of Britten's *Ballad of Heroes*, Op. 14, on 5 April 1939.

Wednesday, 26 October 1932

Practise Pft. before Benjamin at 11.40. Copy out ob. part of Phant. in aft. Go for walk after tea. May[1] comes to see me before tea. After dinner B.B.C. Symphony Concert[2] with Bridges. Bantock's ghastly Sappho ov. Bridge's heavenly Enter Spring. Tchaikovsky's Violin Concerto – atrocious work (Mischa Elman[3] – superb fiddler but impossible musician), & Franck's symphony lovely in spots. Boults speeds were wrong almost without exception. There is magnificent material in the orchestra but it's tired out. Back to Bridges until 12.30 & back for a bit of copying.

1 Frederick May (1911–1985), Irish composer and a contemporary of Britten's at the College.
2 Given at the Queen's Hall, London, and conducted by Adrian Boult.
3 Mischa Elman (1891–1967), Russian-born American violinist.

Thursday, 27 October 1932

Finish Oboe part before going to College for rehearsal of my Sinfonietta; a great improvement – although no doublebass!! Trio in afternoon, Bernard to stay to do Bridge sonata after. Go to dinner with Nan Hill at her club (New Victorian) & to the Ballet Club[1] after. See L'après midi [d'un faune, by Debussy] – quite good, only with piano tho'. Lord Berners'[2] – Le foyer de danse, very amusing. Markova[3] was very fine. Filthy night.

1 At the Mercury Theatre, Notting Hill Gate, London, W11.
2 Lord Berners: Gerald Hugh Tyrwhitt-Wilson (1883–1950), English composer, painter, author and diplomat. His early works appeared under the name of Gerald Tyrwhitt. He wrote several witty and distinguished ballets of which the best known are *The Triumph of Neptune* (1926) and *Wedding Bouquet* (after a play by Gertrude Stein) (1936). *Le Foyer de Danse* (1932) was derived from three movements originally belonging to *The Triumph of Neptune*, and choreographed by Frederick Ashton.
3 Alicia Markova (b. 1910), who danced with the Rambert Ballet Club, 1931–3.

Wednesday, 2 November 1932

Every single spare moment of day is spent in a feverish attempt to get a score of my Sinf. done by Sat.[1] Lesson with Benjamin at 11.0. Go to B.B.C. concert at 8.15 (area).[2] Inc. H. Samuel playing well (but not perfectly) Bach's D min Concerto. Not as good as I have heard him. Ireland's beautiful Forgotten Rite[3] & a by no means perfect performance of Belshazzar's Feast by B.B.C. Chorus. Denis Noble[4] is v. fine singer. It is amazingly clever & effective music, with some great moments, I feel.

Back at Bridges until 11.30 & then an hour's copying.

1 Britten submitted his *Sinfonietta* and *Phantasy* Quintet (for strings) in F minor to the selection committee of the 1933 ISCM Festival held that year in Amsterdam. They were both rejected, though he was to succeed a year later with the *Phantasy* Quartet, which was performed at the 1934 Festival in Florence.
2 Given at the Queen's Hall, London, by the BBC Symphony Orchestra, conducted by Adrian Boult.
3 Prelude for Orchestra, composed in 1913.
4 Denis Noble (1899–1966), English baritone. Noble had been the soloist at the first performance of *Belshazzar's Feast* at Leeds in 1931.

Friday, 4 November 1932

Copying before & after lesson with Ireland at 10.35 & after lunch & tea, I get my copy of Sinf. finished, thank God! The Committee of the Mendelssohn Scholarship meet at R.C.M. Ivor Walsworth[1] is the Scholar this time. (See July 11th). He wasn't even in the original trio. Apparently as he was at the R.A.M. an R.C.M. person got it last time, so it must needs be an R.A.M. this time. So much for an Anonymous exam! However they give me a grant of £50 so as not to discourage me in composing!!!!!! Beth & I go to dinner at the Bridges & all of us to the Corona Cinema[2] after. See Thark[3] (R. Lynn, T. Walls & Claude Hulbert).[4] v. funny.

1 English composer (1909–1978). He was a student at the Academy and again awarded the Mendelssohn Scholarship in 1933. Walsworth had a distinguished career with the BBC, holding several key appointments including, finally, that of Music Organiser for the Transcription Service.
2 Coronet Cinema, Notting Hill Gate, London, W11.
3 The cinematic adaptation of Ben Travers's farce about the heir to an

old mansion who spends a night in it to prove that it is not haunted. Directed by Tom Walls and released in 1932. See also Ben Travers, *Vale of Laughter, An Autobiography* (London, Geoffrey Bles, 1957).

4 Ralph Lynn (1882–1962) and Tom Walls (1883–1949), English actors noted for their appearances in popular Aldwych farces of the period. Claude Hulbert (1900–1964), actor brother of Jack.

Saturday, 5 November 1932
[London/Lowestoft]

Pack my suitcase & time my entries for the International Festival (Sinf. & 5tet Phantasy) before taking them to O.U.P.

Catch 3.10 from Liverpool St. Home. Met by Mum & Pop in car. Wireless in evening. Walks with Pop before dinner & before bed.

Wednesday, 9 November 1932
[London]

Go to Ireland at 9.45 to run through Heldenleben[1] on his gramophone. Lesson with Benjamin at R.C.M. at 11.40. Alter some parts in afternoon. Go to B.B.C. Concert (area) at 8.15.[2] Henry Wood. Myra Hess plays the Beethoven G maj. after rather a ragged Brandenburg no. 6. She plays it technically v. well, but ridiculous cadenzas, & she & Wood have no idea of the 2nd Movement – it's Andante not Adagiossississimo. A fine performance of Strauss' Heldenleben to finish with. It contains some marvellous things, & some great scoring, but the common-place harmony of alot of it kills me. The programme is vile I think.

1 *Ein Heldenleben*, Op. 40, tone poem (1897–8) by Richard Strauss. Britten possessed the recording made by the New York Philharmonic conducted by Willem Mengelberg on HMV LGD 1711–5. One of the records from the set has survived and is in the Archive.

2 Given by the BBC Symphony Orchestra at the Queen's Hall, London.

Thursday, 10 November 1932

Rehearsal of Sinf. at R.C.M. at 11.0. Back to old style of rehearsal, only 8 people & 2 new!! However – See Grace Williams after. In afternoon, bit of pft. practise & Michael Halliday[1] (late of South Lodge & now in Mercantile Marine)[2] comes to tea & walk with him after across park, when I go to Madrigals & after to Bridges (up for day & night) for dinner & he [Halliday] goes to Theatre. He stays the night here, however.

1 South Lodge, 1923–7. Halliday was killed in action during the Second World War, and was one of the friends to whose memory Britten dedicated his *War Requiem*.
2 Merchant Navy.

Saturday, 12 November 1932

Go to Whiteley's in morning to have hair cut, & then on to St. Martin's Lane to Chatto & Windus¹ to get a copy of Ancient English Carols.² I am setting some in a work for Chorus soon, I expect.³ Read & practise Pft. in aft. Beth goes to a theatre with some old St. Anne's girls. Go to see Grace Williams after tea. Read in smoke-room after dinner.

1 The London publishers.
2 *Ancient English Christmas Carols* MCCCC–MDCC, collected and arranged by Edith Rickert (London, Chatto & Windus, 1928). Britten's copy, in which he was able to find most of the texts for *A Boy was Born*, is in the Archive.
3 *A Boy was Born*, Choral variations, *a cappella*, was composed November 1932–May 1933.

Monday, 14 November 1932

Pft. practice all morning. The afternoon I spend in reading carol after carol. Walk with Beth after tea – After dinner I go to 25 Rosary Gardens, for a Carlyle Singers rehearsal. They do my three songs,¹ quite well. Back, in Betty Lutyen's² car, at 10.20.

1 The Three Two-part Songs.
2 Elisabeth Lutyens (1906–1983), English composer and wife of Edward Clark: see note 9 to Letter 36. She was the daughter of the architect, Sir Edwin Lutyens (1869–1944). See also note 1 to Diary for 16 July 1932.

Wednesday, 16 November 1932

Lesson with Mr. Benbow¹ in morning (deputising for Benjamin – examining) at 11.40. Practise before that & in afternoon. Also write letters & read carols. Walk after tea. Go to B.B.C. concert (in area) at Queen's Hall at 8.15. Ansermet conducts a poor perf. of Der Freischütz, & a not too thrilling one of Debussy's incomparable Nocturnes. Eliz. Schuman[2] sings 3 delightful Mahler songs[3] & Et incarnatus (C min. Mass) of Mozart marvellously. A competant performance of the all astounding Sacre to finish with. Back with Grace Williams to Bridges.

1 Charles Edwin Benbow (1904–1967), English composer and pianist, who taught at the College from 1929 to 1967. See also note 1 to Letter 41.

2 Elisabeth Schumann (1885–1952), German soprano whom Britten particularly admired during the 1930s.

3 'Rheinlegendchen', 'Ich atmet' einen Linden Duft' and 'Wer hat dies Liedlein erdacht?'.

Thursday, 17 November 1932

Rehearsal at R.C.M. Buesst. Full team for first time (with 2 doublebasses!!). Quite an improvement to-day. Lunch with Bridges. John Alston[1] was there too. Bernard & I rehearse F.B. Vlc. Son. 3.30–4.30. Meet Barb. & Beth at Selfridges at 5.15 & Madrigal with Barb. until 7.30. Do nothing until an early bed.

1 John Alston (b. 1914), the son of Britten's viola teacher, Audrey Alston (later Mrs Lincolne Sutton). He was to become Director of Music at Lancing College, Sussex (1948–74). His brother, Christopher, appears in a group photograph at Friston on the occasion of Bridge's birthday in 1933: see PFL, plate 53.

The Alston and Britten families were close and sometimes spent holidays together, as John Alston remembers:

I got to know Ben quite well. We were the same age. He was – what – six months older – five months older than I was, that's about all. We used to spend a lot of holidays – we had a bungalow near Bacton. He used to come over there. D'you know the famous 'Chaos and Cosmos' story? [. . .] That happened there. [. . .] At our bungalow [. . .] Ben must have been about what – nine? ten? Discovered writing furiously on manuscript paper one morning. My mother said to him, 'What are you writing, Ben?' And he said, 'Oh, it's a symphonic poem, "Chaos and Cosmos" ' [. . .] We used to play duets together occasionally; I remember doing that and we used to play games. He was very good at ping-pong. He used to beat me easily always, and tennis, too. He was a very, very good sportsman.

(Interview with Donald Mitchell, 20 June 1988, Aldeburgh; Archive)

Tuesday, 22 November 1932

Practise Pft. & more sketching of Xmas work [*A Boy was Born*] in morning. Bernard comes in aft. & work at F.B. Sonata. Beth arrives back by bus at 4.0. Tea with her & B. [Bernard] in her room with my birthday[1] cake. Walk with her afterwards. Barb. comes to dinner; cards after & with Miss Wheatley.[2] Write to Mum & Pop after that.

    For my birthday I have: Gold Watch from Mum & Pop: Come Hither[3] (W. de la Mare) from Beth & Barb. Letters & sweets from Bobby: 6/- from Aunt Nellie: 6/- & sweets from Miss Turner. M.S. paper from the maids.

1 Britten's nineteenth birthday.
2 Probably a fellow lodger.
3 An anthology of 'rhymes and poems for the young of all ages' (London, Constable, 1923; new revised edition, 1928). Britten's copy is in the Archive.

Thursday, 24 November 1932

F. B. gives me a copy of his Pft. Sonata.[1]
    Usual style of R.C.M. rehearsal at 11.0 – with 3 new people – only with 10 altogether – rather a wonder! After lunch I see Allen about Schols. etc.[2] Rehearsal with Ber. (Sonata) & then + Lauricella (Trio – F.B.). Walk to Selfridges, & then to Madrigals with Barb. New Bass in Madrigals – Paul Wright[3] – very nice. I have imported him from the Carlyle [Singers]. Beth & I go back to dinner with the Bridges. Listen to a faked perf. of Petroushka by Beecham[4] – within an inch of collapse all the time. Back by 11.30.

1 The copy is in the Archive and inscribed: 'For Benjamin at 19!!/Nov. 22. 1932/ From F. B.'
2 See Letter 30.
3 Paul Herré Giraud Wright (b. 1915), British diplomat, and friend of Britten from the 1930s. His autobiography contains a brief, though illuminating, recollection of his friendship with the composer: see *A Brittle Glory* (London, Weidenfeld and Nicolson, 1986), pp. 15–16. Wright's memories include the discussion with Britten of an idea for a ballet in which dancers were to impersonate the instruments of the orchestra. He also recalls him improvising at the piano in his Cromwell Road lodgings and in particular a brilliant rendering of the

medieval carol, 'Unto us is born a Son', and its last verse 'O and A, and A and O'. Wright confesses to disliking the improvisation at the time, a form of musical expression Britten described as a means of 'expurgation'. (It was of this very carol that Britten was to make an arrangement (unpublished): see Diary for 23 December 1932.) Wright was a shrewd observer of Britten during his student years in London. He recalls that there were some things 'one didn't joke about with Ben', those that 'touched on his deepest musicality and musical instinct'. Even at this early age he was 'a formidable character: his charisma was already evident'. He showed a notable capacity for disapproval 'if one put a foot wrong'.

In these pre-war years, Wright was employed by the John Lewis Partnership, where he organized musical events for the staff, for example the annual John Lewis Revue, which satirized the management, among other targets, and for which Wright wrote the music and lyrics. Britten was among the audience. But there was also a John Lewis Choral Society in which Wright was involved, and it was to a 'terrible performance of Parry's *Blest Pair of Sirens'* (or an equivalent) that Britten was invited *by mistake*. To this day, Wright remembers Britten's agonized face, out in the auditorium.

Wright himself at one stage aspired to be a professional horn-player. His musical gifts allowed him to 'fool about' at the piano with Britten, for example finding out what 'we could make of turning "Three Blind Mice" upside down (or something of the sort)'.

Wright found it hard to accept Britten's departure for the States and argued against it. This led to a rift which was never quite healed. But he 'rejoices in the memory of a precious friendship'.

4 Given by the London Philharmonic Orchestra and broadcast from the Queen's Hall by the BBC.

Friday, 25 November 1932

I write the theme of my choral variations in morning. Write letters in aft & walk. Mrs. Miller comes to tea in Beth's room. Go to Grace Williams at 5.0 meet Dr. Wellesz[1] from Vienna. Walk with Beth after. After dinner go to Broadcasting House for a Van Dieren[2] concert at 9.0 with Bridges (ticket from Gerald Finzi).[3] Quite the most dull, dismal & boring music ever written. Megan Foster's singing was the only bright spot.

1 Egon Wellesz (1885–1974), Austrian composer, musicologist and teacher. He was a pupil of Schoenberg's and the author of the first monograph (1921) on his teacher. In 1932, the University of Oxford gave him an honorary D. Mus., which was no doubt the reason for

his visit to England. He left Vienna after the Anschluss and settled in England. In 1939 he was appointed Reader in Byzantine music at Oxford, and stayed there for the rest of his life.

Wellesz was the first of those significant links between Britten and Vienna, the world of Mahler and the younger generation of Viennese composers. The association was reinforced by Britten's trip to Vienna in November 1934, which led to his first encounter with Erwin Stein (see note 9 to Letter 59).

2 Bernard van Dieren (1887–1936), English composer and writer, of Dutch birth.

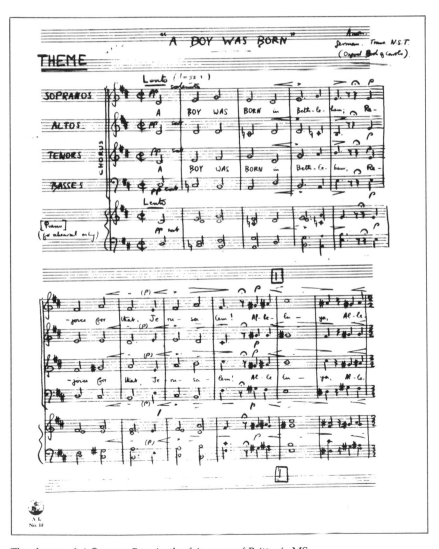

The theme of *A Boy was Born* in the fair copy of Britten's MS

This broadcast concert, from the Concert Hall at Broadcasting House, was the first in a series devoted to music by van Dieren. His String Quartet No. 5 (1931) played by the International String Quartet; a group of songs sung by the soprano Megan Foster (b. 1898), with Frida Kindler, his wife, piano; *Tema con Variazione* for solo piano; and a setting of Psalm 62, performed by the Wireless Singers conducted by Stanford Robinson.

3 Gerald Finzi (1901–1956), English composer who taught at the Academy from 1930 to 1939. Finzi and Britten first met in 1931. See also Letter 32. Finzi remembered in later life that he had employed the youthful Britten as a copyist. This must have been, Christopher Finzi informs us, 'between when Britten came to London and the latter part of 1933 when my father married and left London'.

30 To Benjamin Britten
From Mr R.V. Britten

Nov 27–32
21, Kirkley Cliff Road,
Lowestoft.
Telephone: Lowestoft 112

My dear Son Benjamin

My love to you!
Now then! When you have these great Items of news to impart write 'em backwards or in Italics or Underline them or anything to make them stand out; also Explain them properly. Here we have to rush round (or "Mum" does) borrowing books and all that to find out what the "Octavia" Scholarship is![1] So I'll tell you as you dont seem to know!! It's a Compo Scholarship for the Education and Maintenance (It doesn't say whether it's £1 a week or £5) abroad of a Student for –

<u>3 years</u>
What do you think of that my young fellow? Why it's better than the Mendleshon [*sic*] – Bar the Abroad Eh! I wonder if <u>they</u> arrange where – I don't suppose they just let you go where you like do you?

So you saw Hughie[2]? I hope you wore a pair of Trousers with a big hole in the Knee! "Mum" & I of course are all for the Octavia and we Congratulate you most heartily dear Boy. As a matter of fact I expect old Hughie will do anything to escape another letter from me!!

It's Sunday night and has been a perfect day; beautiful Morning – bitter cold wind tho – and a pouring wet afternoon. I took Caesar this morning and went the long walk – you know over the fields as well as Golf Links –   He got fully dirty in the first ditches but somewhat cleaner after hours in the pond on the Kessingland Road.

I very nearly bought a car on Friday a "Wolsey Hornet" 12 horse, six cylinder; two months old. The man wanted £160 for her and I got to the state of offering £150. Then some blighter gave him £170. I hope you are having a nice week end –   Pay my compliments to the "Bridges" when you see them again. I dont know how you are off for Money for I am trusting to you to let me know, all this going about mopps it up I know. I hope the watch is keeping good time – it's now 4 minutes to 9 p.m. just see if it's right as I set it by Mine Benjamin.

"Mum" sends her dear love to her "darling boy"   She didn't Actually say that but I know that is exactly what she feels; She is up in Heaven – writing letter I expect – as I dont hear the Box of Tricks[3] going.

I don't see why you cant have (1) as well as (2).[4] I must write again to Hughie. We should want the £50 for new clothes and things.

So long my dear Son

Courage and a Straight purpose will take a Man anywhere.

I've got rather a good book – Ghost stories! Some are really good and give one a real "cold" feeling.

Do you want me to bring Dress things for the 12th.[5] Wont my new Blue do?

Goodnight Benjamin My son. Good luck to you

Yours as always "Pop"

R. V. BRITTEN

1 The Octavia Hill travelling scholarship. See note 2 to Letter 39.
2 The Director of the College.
3 The wireless.
4 The Octavia Hill *and* Mendelssohn scholarships.
5 See Diary for 12 December 1932, from which it appears that Mr Britten did not attend the concert.

Tuesday, 29 November 1932

Go for lesson with Ireland at R.C.M. at 10.35. Bernard comes & we play Vlc. Sonatas all afternoon. Beth & I meet Victor Clark[1] at 6.30 at Savoy Theatre[2] – have a meal – & (having queued for Pit) see Mikado.[3] A first rate show. The performance was excellent, tho' not perfectly perfect. Lytton[4] was outstandingly funny. What heavenly shows these operas are!

1 Unidentified.
2 The theatre in the Strand, London WC2, was built for the Gilbert and Sullivan operas.
3 Operetta in two acts by Arthur Sullivan (1842–1900), and W.S. Gilbert (1836–1911).
4 Sir Henry Lytton (1867–1936), English singer and prominent member of the D'Oyly Carte Opera Company. He retired from the stage in 1934.

Wednesday, 7 December 1932

I finish the 1st variation[1] before going to lesson with Benj. [Benjamin] at 11.0. After lunch I go to Bridges to acc. Lauri. [Lauricella] playing Tchaikov. concerto to F.B., who gives him a lesson on it. Come back to tea, to which Howard Ferguson comes; talk & play.

   Listen to Elgar concert after dinner.[2] The Intro. & Allᵒ makes some nice sounds, but the form seems so unsatisfactory & bits of Toselli's Serenata & the fugetta annoy me. So does most of the Enigma Var. & all of the Second Symph.

1 'Lullay, Jesu', the first variation of *A Boy was Born*.
2 The second of three concerts given by the BBC Symphony Orchestra to celebrate the seventy-fifth birthday of Elgar (1857–1934), broadcast from the Queen's Hall, London. Adrian Boult conducted the first half of the programme – *Introduction and Allegro*, Op. 47, for strings, and the *Enigma Variations*, Op. 36 – while the composer himself conducted the second part, a performance of the Second Symphony, Op. 63.

Sunday, 11 December 1932

Beth's not frightfully well. Walk with her abit in park – with foul weather as yesterday – in morning. Rest of morning & afternoon – besides writing letters – I begin a transcription of F.B.s lovely Willow for Viola & Pft.[1] Grace Williams & Barbara come to tea. Walk with Beth before supper. Listen to wireless after – inc. Elgar's Falstaff which contains some v. fine stuff – also some . . . . .!!!²

1 Bridge's *Impression* for small orchestra: *There is a willow grows aslant a brook* (1927). During December 1932, the Camargo Ballet company staged a choreographic version of the work. Britten attended a performance on 4 December and wrote in his diary:

> Go to Camargo Ballet after supper with Bridges and Miss Fass. Pretty dismal show except for Wendy Toye's magnificent dance in F.B.'s "Willow". There were things I didn't like about her choreography tho'.

It was no doubt this occasion which sparked off the making of the transcription. Britten completed it on 13 December, and it is now in the Archive. The arrangement for viola and piano was published by Thames in 1991. He later made a reduced orchestral version of the *Impression* (with the permission of Ethel Bridge) for performance at the first Aldeburgh Festival, on 13 June 1948.

2 The concert was given by the BBC Orchestra (Section D) conducted by Adrian Boult. The other works in the programme were Walton's overture, *Portsmouth Point*, and Tchaikovsky's Piano Concerto No. 1, performed by Solomon.

Monday, 12 December 1932

More transcribing before meeting Mum at Liverpool St. at 11.25 – she's not frightfully well. After lunch the Bridges come here for a bit & I do a bit more transcribing. Walk with Beth & Mum before changing. Barb. comes to dinner. No. III of Lemare MacN. Concerts at Ballet Club. Choral & string programme. Arnold Foster[1] – 3 Manx [Folk] Songs. Lillian Harriss[2] – Phantasy Trio. Jane Joseph[3] – a little Child – Female voices & St. Quint. My 2–pt. Songs (3 – Oxford Press – W. de la Mare) – sung v. well. I accompany. They go down well. Helen Perkin plays a suite of Christian Darnton[4] (I turn over). Betty Lutyens – 5 Os. [Osbert] Sitwell Poems for chorus & Vls. CB. Hrn, Trpt. & Pft.[5] My String Quintet Phant. v. badly played by Anne MacN's quart. + Vla. Worse, by far, than rehearsals. 3 Three Madrigals.[6] The choir was poor. I sang bass & Barbara Soprano, Iris Lemare[7] conducted, quite well. I go to Lady MacN's[8] for a party afterwards – but not for long. I collect Beth & Mum from B's [Barbara's] after & we were back soon after 12.

1 Foster's *Three Manx Folksongs*, arranged for mixed choir, comprising 'The Sea Invocation', 'Manx Courting Song' and 'Love of my heart' ('Graith my Curee'), were composed in 1927–8.

2 Lillian Harris, a Foley exhibitioner at the College and one of Britten's

fellow students. She was awarded a Cobbett Prize for her *Phantasy Trio*, which was given its first concert performance at this Macnaghten–Lemare concert.

3 Jane M. Joseph (1894–1929), a composition pupil of Gustav Holst. She acted as his amanuensis in the preparation of the full score of *The Planets*. Britten refers to her *Christmas Song*: 'A little Childe there is iborn'.

4 Christian Darnton (1905–1981), English composer, writer and educator, of left-wing sympathies. During the 1930s and 1940s he achieved some national and international success: for the last twenty years of his life, however, he composed little. From 1930 to 1934 he was assistant editor of the *Music Lover*, in which capacity he reviewed this concert. With Britten, he was a member of the committee advising Adolph Hallis on his contemporary music series (see note 8 to Letter 248), occasions (and company) that Britten did not much enjoy. See note 4 to Letter 31, and LFBML, pp. 227–8, 243–5 and 248–9: the last includes a page from Darnton's *Ballad of Freedom*, for tenor solo, chorus, brass, percussion and strings, composed in 1942, which bears a resemblance to Britten's earlier *Ballad of Heroes*.

5 The first performance of Nos. 1, 3, 8, 10 and 7 of Lutyens's song-cycle, *Winter the Huntsman*. Grace Williams was the pianist.

6 'Hey ho, chill go to plough no more' by Mundy; 'Love me not for comely grace' by Wilbye; and 'Though Amarylis dance in green' by Byrd.

7 Iris Lemare (b. 1903), English conductor, teacher and administrator, and co-founder of the Macnaghten–Lemare Concerts. An early and important advocate of Britten's music, she conducted the first public performance of *A Boy was Born* on 17 December 1934 in a later Macnaghten–Lemare concert at the Mercury Theatre. Britten's diary entry for that date reads:

Dash off – with Bridges – to the Mercury Theatre where Iris Lemare conducts a show of my 'Boy'. Mostly very poor I'm afraid – Herod being esp. wobbly. I came out after it, not being able to stand the strain!

8 Lady Macnaghten (Antonia Mary, née Booth) (1872–1952), Anne Macnaghten's mother and wife of the High Court Judge, the Rt Hon. Sir Malcolm Macnaghten (1869–1955)

Friday, 16 December 1932

[*Lowestoft*]

Do alot of work at F.B. Pft. sonata in morning before walk with Caesar (& Mum for abit) before lunch. Walk with C. also after lunch & before dinner. Mum has a singing aft. – they do my songs[1] &

some Beethoven canons. Only Mrs. Owles, Mrs. Back & Miss Newsum[2] come tho'.

Play some viola with Mum before a walk with her & Caesar in evening.

1 Probably the Three Two-part Songs.

2 Unidentified.

31 To Anne Macnaghten

21, Kirkley Cliff Road, Lowestoft.

Dec. 22nd, 1932.

Dear Anne,

Thank you so much for sending on the letter about Walter de la Mare.[1] It was very kind of E.C.[2] to take the trouble of writing to your mother, who was very kind in sending it to you, who were very kind in sending it to me, who received it with many thanks. Please thank all those concerned.

I now return it in case you want to keep the signature or something.

Oh – of course, thank you <u>so much</u> for <u>your</u> letter. It was very rude, but quite polite for you. I am relieved beyond all words about your New Year's resolution (about age . . . . lack of . . . in B . . . B . . . .), and I hope to see a definite improvement in you when I return to London next January. (After all there isn't so much "lack of" now – thank Heaven!)

I got all my packing done splendidly (done by my mother), & caught the train in good time (also . . ditto . . ditto . .). I am now in the thros (throws, throes??) of sending off calendars, handkerchiefs, & whatnots to unheard-of relations. That's why I haven't acknowledged your esteimed epistle of the 15th ult. before this.

I saw the Times Criticism[3] – upon which I pass no comment – & am slowly recovering. Needless to say I shall continue to compose – I might even compose a quartet. I haven't seen the Music Lover[4] yet – but I have ordered a copy. .... ????? !!!!!

Are you in London still? Or are you gracing Ireland with your thrilling, shining personality? I should loathe to be in town for Christmas.

Do you know we are going to sing carols at 12 a.m. (no p.m. on

Saturday – Sunday – you know in the evening & morning. (Midnight). About eight or more of our Spartan selves are going to parade up and down outside friends' houses (friends up to this i.e.) singing about a certain Wenceslas who looked out etc. etc.

Brave – what?

I am spending a good deal of time getting down some of my surplus fat, playing badminton and running with our hound along the beach. I am a perfect sylph now.

I must stop now & write some more letters to aunts, etc.

My father says that he is sorry that he couldn't meet you; he realises that he has lost a great deal thereby, & also thinks that you have lost something – for he ain't a bad chap (he says that – I don't).

Have a good Christmas. Don't eat too much.

I shall – I can guarantee. (plum pudding)

Fare well.

BENJAMIN

1 Walter de la Mare (1873–1956), English poet. Britten much admired de la Mare's poetry, settings of which are extant from his very early years (see *Tit for Tat*, a volume of five early de la Mare songs published in 1968 and dedicated to the poet's son, Richard). Britten's three part-songs for two-part boys' or women's voices and piano were settings of 'The-Ride-by-Nights', 'The Rainbow' and 'The Ship of Rio'.

2 Edward Clark. See note 9 to Letter 36.

3 The notice in *The Times* (16 December 1932), ended with this comment:

A string quintet by Benjamin Britten, who also contributed a group of attractive two-part songs, contained many good ideas and a beautiful coda, but did not build up into a satisfying whole. This was well played by Miss Macnaghten's Quintet.

The notice was unsigned (the normal *Times* practice) but was probably written by Frank Howes (1891–1974), then an assistant music critic of *The Times*, who contributed a signed review to the *Musical Times* for January 1933, which made much the same points in slightly different words.

4 The review in the *Music Lover* of 17 December was contributed by C.D., Christian Darnton, the composer, one of whose own works, his First Piano Suite (1930), was included in the programme. Darnton commented that the settings of de la Mare's poems were 'good from one who, I believe, is only 19; even though they were reminiscent in a quite peculiar degree of Walton's latest songs which were heard recently elsewhere'. As for the string quintet, Britten was not identified by name but was put down in no uncertain terms:

[. . .] whether it be spelt Phantasy, Fantasie or plain Fantasy, the fact usually remains [. . .] that the licences in construction which the title implies only cover up a deficiency of technique.

Thursday, 22 December 1932

See Bazil after breakfast & arrange Carols for Sat. Hair cut & walk with Pop before lunch. Practise Vl. & Vla. with Charles Coleman in aft. probably for Saturday. Shop abit after tea, & walk with Pop.

Write letters after dinner & also listen to beginning of Hely-Hutchinson's Carol Symphony[1] – utter bilge.

1 Victor Hely-Hutchinson (1901–1947), South African-born composer, conductor, pianist and administrator. His best-known work is the *Carol Symphony*, based on traditional English Christmas carols. He was a member of the BBC staff from 1926, and while Director of Music, from 1944 to 1947, commissioned from Britten the *Occasional Overture* in C, for the opening of the Third Programme in September 1946. In a BBC internal memorandum, dated 19 June 1933, Hely-Hutchinson wrote:

I do whole-heartedly subscribe to the general opinion that Mr Britten is the most interesting new arrival since Walton, and I feel we should watch his work very carefully.

(LFBML, p. 164)

Friday, 23 December 1932

I arrange "Unto us a boy is born" for tomorrow night.[1] Also shop & post parcels. Go to the Mead's Badminton at St. Marg's Institute at 3.0. Only 6 there (Kathleen M. [Mead], Audrey Enraght & 2 Reeves). Nicholson's dance at their office at 8.30 (John fetches us – Beth & me). Only about 15 couples. Quite fun – for a dance. Michael Pank (of South Lodge) was there. Back by 1.30.

1 The arrangement is in the Archive.

Saturday, 24 December 1932

Post parcels & shop in morning before Aunt Flo takes Beth & me
to Sotterly to get some holly. Barbara arrives in aft. by 3.24 – &
goes straight to bed with a feverish cold. Have a rehearsal at 5.30
for to-night. Shop with Beth after. Listen to Yeoman of the Guard[1]
after dinner, do up parcels & decorate. Go carol-singing, starting
here at 12.0. Marg. & Connie Phillips, 2 Boyds, 2 Reeves, Laurence
Sewell & Charles Coleman & Miss Goldsmith & Beth & I. Sing
about 8 carols in all. Go to 12 places singing about 3 at each. In
parts (so-called!) of course. All old carols including my arr. of
"Unto us a boy". At 2.0 a.m. they come into kitchen for
refreshments. Beth & I wash up & we go to bed by 3.30.

1 Operetta (1888) by Gilbert and Sullivan, broadcast by the BBC from
the Savoy Theatre.

Sunday, 25 December 1932 (Christmas Day)

Church at 8.0 at St. Johns with Mum, Beth, & Aunt Flo. Walk with
Pop in morning. Read in aft. Walk with Pop & Beth before supper.
Xmas dinner mid-day. Presents include marvellous Swan "Eternal
Pen"[1] from parents. F.B. sends me score of [Tchaikovsky's]
Francesca da Rimini.[2]

1 A fountain pen.
2 This score of a work much admired by Bridge is in the Archive. It
was also a favourite work of Britten's, who conducted a performance
of it at the 1971 Aldeburgh Festival on 13 June.

Monday, 26 December 1932 (Boxing Day)

Up late by ten. Walk with Pop before lunch. Go to tea at Sewells
– Fernande, Laurence & Teddy & Bobby (son) there – with Aunt
Flo & Beth at 4.15. Christmas dinner at 7.15. Afterwards the maids
come up & we act Cinderella[1] (Beth, Aunt Flo & I) & various
charades.

1 A domestic pantomime was a traditional event in the Britten household.

32   To Gerald Finzi
[*Postcard*]

173, Cromwell Road, S.W. 5.
[Postmarked 15 March 1933]

If you aren't doing anything to-morrow evening (Thursday), and
you feel inclined, you might drop into the College hall and hear
a show of my Sinfonietta which I shall be trying to conduct.[1]
  I suddenly thought that you might like to know.

BENJAMIN BRITTEN

1 The 'show' to which Britten refers was a College Chamber Concert
the next day, 16 March, when he conducted a performance of his
Sinfonietta, Op. 1, for ten instruments, the result of weekly
rehearsals over two terms.

THURSDAY, 16th MARCH (Chamber)

QUARTET for Strings, in C sharp minor, Op. 131 ..   .. *Beethoven*
    FREDERICK RIDDLE, A.R.C.M. (Gowland Harrison Exhibitioner),
    ELSIE STINTON (Heywood Lonsdale Scholar), NORA WILSON (Exhibitioner),
    JAMES WHITEHEAD (Morley Scholar).
RECITATIVE AND AIR .. In truth, to bear the Cross }
                 Come, healing Cross .. } (*St. Matthew Passion*) .. *Bach*
    VICTOR HARDING, A.R.C.M. (S. Ernest Palmer Operatic Exhibitioner).
    Violoncello obbligato : JAMES WHITEHEAD (Scholar),
    Accompanist : LANCELOT HARDY.
SONATA for Violin and Pianoforte, in D minor, No. 1 .. .. *F. Delius*
    ELIZABETH MACLURE, A.R.C.M. (Exhibitioner), HELENA HUNTER-TOD.
PIANOFORTE SOLO .. Fantasia in C major, Op. 17 (First movement) .. .. *Schumann*
    FREDERICK MAY (Octavia Scholar).
SINFONIETTA for Ten Instruments .. .. *Benjamin Britten* (Scholar)
    WINIFRED GASKELL, A.R.C.M. (Scholarship Exhibitioner), NATALIE CAINE (Scholar),
    STEPHEN WATERS (Scholar), JASON LEWKOWITSCH (Scholarship Exhibitioner),
    JOHN DENISON (Scholarship Exhibitioner).
    GERALD EMMS, A.R.C.M. (Gowland Harrison Exhibitioner), VIOLET PALMER, A.R.C.M.,
    FREDERICK RIDDLE, A.R.C.M. (Gowland Harrison Exhibitioner),
    MARGUERITE SLOANE, A.R.C.M., BERNARD RICHARDS (Scholar).

The Calendar of College Concerts for 1933, showing the performance of the *Sinfonietta*
on 16 March

Britten recorded in his diary the events of the day:

Go to R.C.M. at 11.0 for final rehearsal of Sinf. It goes v. well. Pft. practice
abit before going to R.C.M. for Trio rehearsal 4–5.30. After dinner R.C.M.
Chamber concert at 8.15. Mum & Beth go. Bridges & Brosas also there.
Beethoven C♯ min quart competantly but dully played; an atrocious perf.
of Delius Vl. Sonata No. 1.   F. May plays bit of Phantasy of Schumann,
& I conduct a show of my Sinfonietta which goes quite well.

This performance, however, was not the première of the *Sinfonietta*:
the first public performance had been given, not at the College, but
at a Macnaghten–Lemare Concert on 31 January, conducted by Iris
Lemare. The diary entry reads:

Go to last of series of Lemare–MacNaghten concerts at 8.30 at Ballet Club. [H. K.] Andrews, Oboe Conc. (Sylvia Spencer). My Sinfonietta; Jacob Wind 5tet, Finzi Introit (Anne M.), Grace Williams – Tr. [Trumpet] & orch. [soloist, Richard] (Walton). Considering amt. of rehearsal & nature of same, my work went quite well – but oh!

The *Sinfonietta* and *Phantasy* Quintet were the only works by Britten to be performed in public at the College while he was a student. No doubt this was partly responsible for the composer's negative feelings towards the College at the time, and in later life. The reception of the work after its first public performance included a strikingly positive review by Christian Darnton in the *Music Lover*, 4 February:

A Sinfonietta for ten instruments – flute, oboe, clarinet, bassoon, horn and string quintet – by Benjamin Britten was a really outstanding work. When one is still nineteen events move fast. And this was a great advance on the two other works heard at the last of these concerts on December 12. The Sinfonietta contained some exceedingly stimulating musical thought, considerable constructive power and surprising technical skill. Mr. Britten is a credit to his teacher, John Ireland.

The *Daily Telegraph* critic (1 February) was less enthusiastic:

Mr Benjamin Britten in a Sinfonietta for ten instruments showed that he can be as provocative as any of the foreign exponents of the catch-as-catch-can style of composition.

For the *Times* review, see note 2 to Letter 53.

33 To Mr and Mrs R.V. Britten

173 Cromwell Road, S.W. 5.
May 10th, 1933.

My darling Parents,

I can't write much to-night, but I thought that I'd write and tell you that I had done something about a piano. I have actually a piano in my room, now, a nice bright red one. It is hired from Cramers.[1] Don't be annoyed yet, tho. Study these nicely balanced accounts.[2]

CHARGES ON Pft. BORROWED (without charge).

		£.	s.	d.
Carrage	(possibly)	.. 10	.. 0	..
Tuning	(quite)	7	.. 6	..
Charge on retaining room during long vacation	(at least)	8	.. 0	.. 0 ..
Total (minimum)		8	.. 17	.. 6 ..

P.T.O.

CHARGES ON Pft. HIRED.

	£.	s.	d.
(Hire of Pft. per term £3 .. 3 .. 0s. [sic])			
Hire of Pft. for 2 terms.	6 ..	6 .. 0 ..	
see: Carriage of Pft. (both hither & thither)			
		Nil.	
Tuning of Pft.		nothing.	
Owing to having no pft. in room during long vac.			
Charge for retaining room		nix.	
Total (maximum)	6 ..	6 .. 0 ..	
	8 ..	17 .. 6	
Balance.	6 ..	6 .. 0	
	£2 ..	11 .. 6 ..	

Therefore you will see why I now have this bright red piano in my
room.

You will read in the papers all about yesterday's do at college.[3]
My comments are.

1) Deadly dull. I shouldn't have gone but for the fact that I wanted
   to see George & Mary.
2) I didn't see George & Mary owing to fact that position of my
   seat was too far in rear to permit view of these esteemed
   personages.
3) The faint Elizabeth Aveling,[4] tho' pitiable, was probably a very
   clever bit of stage manageing. She was singing execrably (not
   to say badly); and probably realising this fact

. . . . ⌃ ⌃ .⁙. .   Whereupon –
thunders of applause at drama of gallant fainter. Whereas, in
ordinary course of events, normal thunders of applause at dismal
singer ("biting sarcasm", in case you didn't realise it).

I must stop, as I have to write to Nan Hill, before going to Covent
Garden at 10.15 p.m. with Grace to place stools for tomorrow's
performance of Tristan.[5] (10.15 p.m. I may point out is $\frac{1}{4}$ hour
ahead, so I must accelerato).

As you may see, I am having the busiest of lives up here, in
contrast to your lazy life in Worcester. However, I am glad that
you are enjoying yourselves. Thank Aunt Julianne, & Uncle Sheldon
for being so nice to you. My love to 'em, I hope they're well.

Take care of yourselves. Look after both cough & ankle.

Beth sends love.

So do I.

Tons of it.

Your loving & hasty,

son,

BENJAMIN

1 The music dealers, 99 St Martin's Lane, London WC2.

2 £1 in 1933 would purchase the equivalent of £33.70 in 1990, a figure based on changes of food prices over the period 1933–90.

3 1933 was the Jubilee Year of the Royal College of Music, celebrating the fifty years since its establishment in 1883. A Jubilee Concert was organized on 9 May, at which both King George V and Queen Mary were present (they were Patrons of the College).

A full account of the concert was contributed to the *R.C.M. Magazine*, 29/3, 1933, pp. 68–9, by H.C. Colles, who wrote, 'Who could have foreseen that the singer would have swooned on the platform?', an event that it seems the London evening press made much of: 'Singer faints at Royal concert'. The programme included music by Arthur Bliss, Holst, Ireland, Parry, Stanford, Vaughan Williams and Charles Wood. At the end of his long review Colles quotes a question put to him by a member of the audience: 'A very interesting concert, but which of the composers the College has produced comes up to the two who produced the College?' The founding fathers of the College were Parry and Stanford. Colles found this an 'awkward' question to answer. That the question could be put, and found 'awkward', allows a glimpse of the taste and judgement current in Britten's College days.

4 Senior Pupil and Scholar at the College and daughter of Claude Aveling, the College Registrar. Her 'swoon' was vividly described by Colles. 'The Conductor struggled on, Miss Aveling struggled up from her fainting posture, but the affair was disintegrating to say the least of it, and the success of the subsequent numbers was imperilled.'

5 Britten's diary for Thursday, 11 May, reads:

Go on to Covent Garden and meet Beth and Grace before 6.0. Tristan begins at 7. Good seats (3rd row of gallery – 3rd for preference). Fride Leider suddenly [in]disposed, Henny Trundt is rushed from Cologne in the aft. V. good; rather ungainly but sings and acts well. A mild Isolde, who is most impressive at the end. Melchior is simply superb. What a voice! The subtlety of his movements is incredible. Olezeweska & Janssen (Bran. & Kurn.) were worthy of themselves – colossal & moving achievements. Beecham & orchestra only blots on the marvellous show. Cor Anglais v. good. But what music! Dwarfs every other art creation save perhaps [Beethoven] 9th. The glorious shape of the whole, the perfect orchestration: sublime idea of it & the gigantic realisation of the idea. He is the master of us all.

On the next day, the 12th, Britten writes, 'Tristan has left me somewhat dazed, so I can't do much work.' He adds a note on Leider's absence: 'Since heard that Beecham was vilely rude to Leider who refused to sing in morning. I am not surprised.'

34 To J.F.R. Stainer[1]
Mendelssohn Foundation[2]

173, Cromwell Rd., S.W.5.
May 13th, 1933.

Dear Mr. Stainer,

Thank you for your letter. As I have not been to the Royal College for a few days I have only just received it.

I have been waiting for a letter from Mr. Walsworth all this time, before making any arrangements for June 1st [*recte* 2 June]. This is very unfortunate as I have been engaged on a large choral work [*A Boy was Born*] ever since the beginning of the Christmas term, and, even though it <u>could</u> be performed by nine soloists, there is of course no time to prepare it for June 1st. I have another work, a quartet for Oboe and Strings, which I have finished, since the award of the Mendelssohn Scholarship,[3] of which I could arrange a performance; but I think it is only fair to myself to say that it is by no means up to the standard of the choral work. I suppose you could not communicate this fact to the committee?

Would you wish for any other work besides the Oboe quartet, which lasts about 15 minutes? I have two part-songs,[4] written last July, of which I might arrange a scratch performance.

I should be very pleased if I could have an answer to this very soon, as parts have to be copied, performers to be found, and much to be arranged.

Yours sincerely,
BENJAMIN BRITTEN

---

1 The son of John Stainer (1840–1901), the composer of the oratorio, *The Crucifixion* (1887).

2 A fund to endow a scholarship for composers and performers. It was launched in 1848 and the first scholarship was awarded in 1856, to Arthur Sullivan. The fund was restricted to composers in 1890. It still exists today.

3 Britten had been awarded a maintenance grant of £50. Walsworth was the elected Scholar.

4 The part-songs did not form part of Britten's submission to the Mendelssohn Scholarship Committee.

35 To Mr and Mrs R.V. Britten

173, Cromwell Road, S.W. 5.
June 22nd, 1933.

My darling Parents,

I thought that I would put a note into Beth's, as she was writing, as I don't know whether I'll have time to write over the week-end.

I am not definitely certain whether I am going away tomorrow as I haven't heard a word from the Bridges. But I expect it's all right. I hope I'll go, as the weather is so unpleasant up here.

Some good news. The broadcast is all fixed up as you know.[1] Goossens is probably going to play – he seems to want to, if the B.B.C. will ask him. I have had a nice letter from Norman Stone[2] of the English singers,[3] and my part-songs go along when copied out. Arthur Bliss[4] is giving some chamber concerts in town next Winter (Grotrian or Wigmore Hall), & I hear from very reliable quarters that he is going to do my oboe quartet.[5] Of course they are agitating for stuff for the Ballet Club concerts.[6] And last – but definitely not least!! Hermann Scherchen[7] the very well known German conductor is going to do my Sinfonietta in Strasbourg in early August – the parts have gone off to-day. I don't know details, but I think it's definite. I must stop now as Beth's letter is to go. I do hope that your Alexandra Day[8] was a success, Mum. I bought a rose but it wasn't much use for you. I hope that you found your way easily back, Pop. I thought of you hard.

Hope you are both as well as possible, Wish you were coming up this week-end.

BENJAMIN

I had some excellent tennis with Mangeot & his two sons out at Cobham on Tuesday. Not very much of it as we didn't arrive until 3.45, But they are all very good & one of them positively brilliant.

1 The first broadcast performance by the BBC of the *Phantasy* Quartet,
   Op. 2, was given on 6 August. This was also the first professional
   performance of the work. The celebrated oboist was Leon Goossens,
   to whom the work is dedicated, who played with members of the
   International String Quartet (André Mangeot, Eric Bray, Jack Shine-
   bourne). Britten remarked in his diary for that day:

   Goossens does his part splendidly. The rest – altho' they are intelligent
   players, aren't really first class instrumentalists.

   The first *public* performance of the Quartet was given on 21 November by the same performers at St John's Institute, Westminster, under
   the auspices of the Music Society, in a programme that also included
   Berg's Piano Sonata (played by Helen Perkin), a string quartet by
   Perkin, and Ireland's Piano Trio No. 2 (1917). The same performers
   repeated the work at a 'Concert of Old and New Chamber Music' at
   31 Tite Street, Chelsea, London, on 27 November. Of the St John's
   Institute performance of the *Phantasy* the *Monthly Musical Record*,
   December 1933, wrote:

   Benjamin Britten's oboe quartet aroused considerable interest, being uncannily stylish, inventive and securely poised for a composer reported to be still
   in his teens.

   The Times, 25 November, found 'Britten's oboe quartet' to be

   the most original. Its material, though not in the least far-fetched, is arresting
   and his treatment of the oboe as a kind of melodic marginal comment on
   the main argument sustained by the strings is also original, but again quite
   natural and unforced. By comparison John Ireland's 15–year-old pianoforte
   trio sounded old-fashioned [. . .]

   The work was also heard at the ISCM Festival held in Florence in
   1934, on 5 April, played by Goossens and members of the Griller
   String Quartet. The multiplicity of performances of a quartet that
   had just been rejected by the Mendelssohn Scholarship Committee
   makes its own ironic point.
      Christopher Isherwood (1904–1986), the novelist and playwright,
   who was to become a friend of Britten's in the thirties, was for a
   year secretary to André Mangeot, the leader of the International
   String Quartet. For an account of his employment (in 1925–6), see
   Jonathan Fryer, *Isherwood* (New York, Doubleday, 1977), pp. 79–82,
   and Brian Finney, *Christopher Isherwood, A Critical Biography* (London,
   Faber, 1979), pp. 56–8; Isherwood's *Lions and Shadows* (London,
   Hogarth Press, 1938); *Kathleen and Frank* (London, Methuen, 1971);
   Christopher and His Kind (New York, Farrar, Straus, Giroux, 1976);
   and *People One Ought to Know, Nonsense Poems*, illustrated by Sylvain
   Mangeot (London, Macmillan, 1982).

2 English tenor (1890–1967) and editor of early music (e.g. Schütz and
   Schein).

3 A vocal sextet, which Stone joined in 1924 four years after the original group – dating from the 1900s – had been reconstituted. In October 1932 the group was again re-formed as the New English Singers. Peter Pears was a member, 1936–8.

4 English composer of American descent (1891–1975). Director of Music at the BBC, 1942–4. Master of the Queen's Music, 1953–75. His autobiography, *As I Remember*, was published in 1970 (London, Faber and Faber).

5 We have not been able to trace this performance, if indeed it happened. The Grotrian Hall, closed in 1938, damaged in the war and demolished, was previously the Steinway Hall, with a capacity of 400. The Wigmore Hall, still in existence, was previously known as the Bechstein Hall and opened in 1901. The London branch of Bechstein's was compulsorily wound up in 1916 and the hall sold. It reopened in 1917 under its new name. Its capacity in the thirties was 540. It was – and remains – the traditional platform on which aspiring young performers make their London début.

6 The Macnaghten–Lemare concerts.

7 German conductor (1891–1966) with a particular and distinguished reputation for his pioneering performances of and enthusiasm for twentieth-century music. In a tribute to Scherchen in 1966, Pierre Boulez wrote:

> Scherchen showed himself to be one of those rare personalities naturally at home with novelty, something he needed for the full expansion of his vital powers, and for the expenditure of his superfluous energy.
>
> (*Orientations* (London, Faber and Faber, 1986), p. 499)

He was an early continental admirer of Britten's, whom he was to meet at the Florence ISCM Festival of 1934, where the *Phantasy Quartet*, Op. 2, was performed. Some doubt attaches to the performance of the *Sinfonietta* mentioned by Britten in this letter. His diary for 7 August reads:

> My Sinfonietta was down to be broadcast under Scherchen from Strasbourg at 8.30; but the programmes seem all altered & we can get nothing.

The earliest mention of Scherchen occurs in Britten's diary on 17 December 1930, when he wrote:

> Go to B.B.C. Symph concert at St Luke's Hospital – Mr. Colvin's Wireless. Why they gave this Mass in D to Scherchen – Heaven only knows. Of course there were beautiful bits – Sanctus & Benedictus & Kyrie – but the end of the Credo was incredibly scrambled. Chorus good – seemed to me that all their work was wasted. Soloists – tenor – not too bad – Soprano – dreadful. Orchestra respectable – what I could hear of it – it didn't come through too well – I thought.

See *Hermann Scherchen 1891–1966, Ein Lesebuch*, compiled by Hansjörg Pauli and Dagmar Wünsche (Berlin, Akademie der Künste/ Edition Hentrich, 1986). See also LFBML, p. 212.

8 Queen Alexandra (1844–1925), the consort of Edward VII. An annual national flag day (with emblems in the shape of pink wild roses), was held each June in aid of the organizations in which she took a special interest. There was intense competition in Lowestoft to sell the most 'Alexandra' roses.

36 To Mr and Mrs R.V. Britten

173, Cromwell Road, S.W. 5.
July 2nd, 1933.

My darling Parents,

Happy month to you. May the end of it be happier than the beginning of it, because on July 23rd or thereabouts you will have your youngest bright spark with you again; that's to say if everything goes well, for at the present moment it looks as if I shall never get my work done. For – before then I have got to: copy out 9 parts of my Christmas work (each of at least 14 closely written pages) (to be tried over by the Wireless singers[1] on to-morrow week); rewrite a good deal of my Oboe quartet[2] to be broadcast on August 6th; write three quartet pieces for Anne MacNaghten[3] (this only if I have time); to say nothing of practising piano for A.R.C.M.[4]

However – it seems rather silly to say that we have had time to go to Wimbledon yesterday after all that; nevertheless we did, and had a very hot time. It was frantically crowded & we spent practically all the time queueing. We queued for the bus to take us to the ground; we queued for practically ½ hour for admission; spent our time queuing for standing room from which to get a glimpse of the players; queued for ages for a bus to take us to the station; & at the station we queued for about 10 mins. to discover that we needn't have queued at all. So it wasn't particularly exhilarating until soon after 5.30 when a complete stranger came up and presented us with two glorious seats for the centre-court; so we had over an hour of complete bliss seeing Cochet, Hughes & the marvellous Helen Wills.[5]

I expect that Beth has told you all about Covent Garden ballet.[6] We had excellent seats – Beth & Grace actually better than the Bridges & myself. She [Beth] wants to know if you saw her photo

in the Daily Mail (for Friday) among the delegates & MacDonald –
because she swears she was taken. However it was probably for
the Daily Herald or Lowestoft Journal.

I go to lunch with the B.B.C. chorus master[7] to-morrow. I daren't
hope, but I'm afraid it won't be a Queen's Hall show[8] this year.
Scherchen got hold of my Sinfonietta for Strasbourg either through
Foss or Clark[9] of B.B.C.

I really must stop now. I am sorry if this letter has seemed rather
drunk & stupid; reasons are that Barbara is here & is chattering
hard with Beth; also that it is frightfully hot, & also I am pretty
dead, after yesterday, & after a long walk in park this morning,
much work this afternoon, a sun bath after tea in the garden, & a
45 mins sermon by Elliot[10] this evening.

I am sorry that Alexandra Day wasn't a success, Mum, but if you
will have it when I am away what can you expect? Don't bother
about hurrying over the pull-over – it's too hot to think about such
things at the moment. Do something for John in the meantime.

Well now I must post this & escort Barbara to the underground
– we both have our dogs. Pop! I am glad that you're feeling better.
Keep it up.

Hope you're neither of you working too hard.

Your very loving & grateful son,
BENJAMIN

Love from both your female offspring.

P.S.   What is Laurence bothering about? I thought it was decided
that I would play with him (unless he has great objections), & the
entrance form hasn't got to go in until about Aug. 15th.[11]

1 The Wireless Singers were the forerunners of the present day BBC
   Singers, a group of forty professional singers directed during this
   period by Leslie Woodgate (see note 1 to Letter 42). On 10 July there
   was a run-through of *A Boy was Born* with one voice per part for the
   benefit of the BBC music staff. Britten had already played the work
   over to Victor Hely-Hutchinson and two other BBC colleagues on 16
   June, along with the *Phantasy* Quartet (by which Hely-Hutchinson
   was also much impressed). It had originally been intended to broadcast the work for the first time in November but eventually this was
   rescheduled to take place in February 1934 (see Letter 42). The vocal
   parts Britten copied out are now in the British Library, Add. MSS
   59798.

2 The *Phantasy* Quartet was frequently revised between October 1932 and November 1933.

3 The three movements from the projected string quartet suite, 'Go play, boy, play' (a quotation from Act I of Shakespeare's *The Winter's Tale*), were first performed by the Macnaghten String Quartet on 4 December at All Hallows Barking (an ancient City church now known as All Hallows-by-the-Tower), and subsequently on 11 December at the Mercury Theatre as part of a Macnaghten–Lemare Concert. Britten wrote in his diary for 11 December: 'Anne did her best with my "Go play, Boy, Play" – but again, I want 1st class instrumentalists besides enthusiasm.' *The Times* critic wrote:

[. . .] an unfinished string quartet in three movements by Benjamin Britten, with the motto 'Go play, boy, play', [. . .] was played not, indeed, by boys, but by the all-female Macnaghten String Quartet with a ruthless efficiency well suited to the music, showed fertility in ideas and an assured touch in handling an instrumental medium.

4 Britten passed his ARCM (Associate of the Royal College of Music, Pianoforte (Solo Performance)) on 13 December 1933, after which he left the College. A reproduction of the postcard announcing his success appears in PFL, plate 67.

5 Henri Cochet (France), George Patrick Hughes (UK) and Helen Wills (USA), the tennis stars of Wimbledon in 1933.

6 One of two gala performances in honour of the delegates of the World Monetary and Economic Conference by the Camargo Ballet and the Vic–Wells Company on 29 June. The programme included *Coppelia*, Act I, conducted by Constant Lambert, and *España* and *Swan Lake* with Dolin and Markova. The Conference had opened on 12 June and ended 'in total failure' on 23 July: 'No consensus was reached on any issue.'

7 Cyril Dalmaine (1904–1986), composer, conductor and broadcaster, was chorus master of the BBC Chorus from July 1932 until 1933.

8 A reference to the projected performance of *A Boy was Born*.

9 Edward Clark (1888–1962), English conductor, husband of the composer Elisabeth Lutyens. A Schoenberg pupil, Clark (like Scherchen) was an outstanding advocate of twentieth-century music, never more so than when he worked at the BBC, from 1923 until 1936. He was elected President of the ISCM in 1947. A first-class account of Clark appears in the biography of Lutyens, by Merion and Susie Harries, *A Pilgrim Soul: The Life and Work of Elisabeth Lutyens* (London, Michael Joseph, 1989), 'The European-looking Gentleman', pp. 72–86. In 1950, when Clark had fallen on very hard times, Britten was among the signatories of an appeal on his behalf to the BBC, which was reluctant to employ him. See note 1 to Letter 69.

10 The Revd Wallace Harold Elliot was incumbent of St Michael's Church, Chester Square, London SW1.

11 Britten refers to the Bungay (Suffolk) Tennis Tournament which took place in August and September 1933.

37 To Benjamin Britten
From Mr R.V. Britten

21, Kirkley Cliff Road,
Lowestoft.
Telephone   Lowestoft 112
July 11 – 33

My dear Son Benjamin.

Hearty congratulations! over and over again and also envy & jealousy.

Oh! Ben my boy what does it feel like to hear your own creation?[1] Didn't you want to get up and shout – It's mine! It's mine! I understand your feeling that – "you don't care a cuss whether they do it or not now."

What a break to get a crowd who could really do it as you want it. I want to cry!

Thanks for letting us know so soon we were all on edge to hear.

Go on my son

Your very loving & admiring
Pop
R. V. BRITTEN

1 Britten had communicated good news of the run-through on the 10th of *A Boy was Born* to his parents.

38 To Edward Clark
BBC

[LFBML, *pp. 165–6, incomplete*]

21, Kirkley Cliff Road, Lowestoft.
13th August, 1933.

Dear Mr. Clark,

I have received a letter from the BBC asking for scores, and parts of my Sinfonietta for performance on September 15th.[1] Since Mrs. Waterman[2] has erroneously asked for 3 first violin parts, 2 second etc., I presume that it is intended to be placed in an orchestral

concert. I wonder if there is any possible chance of this being
altered. I should so much prefer it being put in a chamber concert,
where the listeners are tuned up to Chamber Music, and have not
been listening to full orchestral sounds. It will certainly sound
thin after any orchestral piece. I happen to know that the Brosa
String Quartet are keen to do the string parts and if you could
get the principals of the woodwind section, I am sure there would
be a more satisfactory result. I believe that it would be financially
not so easy, but I am sure it is worth the change. Also I should
think that rehearsing would be easier. They wouldn't be tied
down to one or two hours, which is not nearly enough, as you
must feel yourself. This might mean putting the work off to a
much later date, but I am sure that that is no objection. Please
consider these points as I do feel it essential that a chamber work
be played in a chamber concert.[3]

Have you one score of the work yourself? I know there is one
somewhere at the BBC which I would like sent to the above
address as soon as possible as I have one or two important
alterations to be made. If it isn't in your possession could you
please take steps to see this is done?

I do hope you were able to listen in to Leon Goosens beautiful
programme of my oboe Phantasy.

Hoping you are well.

Yours sincerely,
BENJAMIN BRITTEN

P.S.   If you cannot see your way to accepting my proposals as to
change of date, as I sincerely hope you can, could you possibly see
that the work is announced correctly in the Radio Times – Sinfonietta,
<u>for ten Instruments</u>.[4]

1 The *Sinfonietta* was given its first broadcast performance on 15 September at 10.30 pm, conducted by Clark. Britten wrote in his diary
for that date: 'V. rushed in places and obviously thoroughly under-
rehearsed. Some of the soloists were good.' An earlier performance
under Clark had been planned by the BBC and the work was
rehearsed on 5 February. But the work was withdrawn from the
programme. Britten's diary for 5 February gives the reasons:

Go to Broadcasting House at 11.30 for a rehearsal of my Sinfonietta with
Clark. He only has time to do ¾ hrs at it, which of course, isn't nearly
enough. So we agree to withdraw it from this afternoon's (4.15)
programme; and it is announced then to be done in the near future.

Bridge (to whom the *Sinfonietta* was dedicated) congratulated
Britten in a letter dated 19 September, written in Bridge's typically

humorous manner: 'I haven't told you that it was a <u>marveallious</u> perf. of your Seamfonnyetta. Herr Klark is Marveallious too – in the words of a celebrated, female Shakespeare – he is Deevine.'

A further broadcast performance took place on 29 June 1934, also conducted by Edward Clark (see Letter 52).

2 Probably a BBC employee.

3 Clark replied that he could not alter the arrangements for 15 September. He would bear the Brosa Quartet in mind if the programme were to be repeated.

4 This designation was dropped, however, when the work came to be published. In the complete catalogue of Britten's works first published in 1963 by Boosey & Hawkes, in which the composer took a lively interest, the description of the resources – 'for chamber orchestra' – allows for the additional strings which are an authorized option ('small String Orchestra').

39 To J.F.R. Stainer
Mendelssohn Foundation

173, Cromwell Road, S.W. 5.
Oct. 4th, 1933.

Dear Mr. Stainer,

Thank you for your letter. I am at present writing a quartet,[1] which I expect will be finished shortly. I will arrange for a performance of this on Nov. 3rd at 4 pm. if you wish.

I am glad you were able to hear the broadcast performance of my Sinfonietta. I believe it is to be repeated in the near future. The B.B.C. also are going to perform a larger choral work of mine, at present in the press, soon after Christmas.

If possible, can you tell me when I am to receive my Grant from the Committee?[2] I should be grateful if it could be as soon as possible.

Yours sincerely,
BENJAMIN BRITTEN

1 Britten refers to the 'Go play, boy, play' string quartet suite. The suite, as originally conceived, was never completed.

2 In a letter to Paul Benecke, Mendelssohn's grandson and (?) Treasurer of the Mendelssohn Foundation, Britten writes on 9 October:

I wonder if, under the special circumstances, it would be possible to pay me the whole sum at a near future date. I am to receive a grant from another source (Octavia Hill travelling Scholarship) after Christmas, and as my financial position is becoming rather serious, it would ease matters enormously if you could do as I suggest.

The scholarship mentioned was one of the College bursaries. It was probably with this grant that Britten hoped to study with Berg in Vienna. See note 8 to Letter 73 and note 1 to Diary for 23 August 1937.

Sunday, 31 December 1933
[*Lowestoft*]

Go for a drive in car (last day of Humber)[1] with Barb. & Beth, & then for short one with Mum. Read in aft. – finish Barrie's little wonder – 'The Little White Bird'.[2] Walk with Barb. before tea. See her off at Station with Bobby, back to town at 5.28. Walk with Bobby before bed. Pop's pretty bad in evening – sick with cough.

I'm not sorry this year is over, tho' in many ways it's been a good year. Beth has started building up what looks as if it's going to be a fine business.[3] Bobby's school is progressing, slowly though surely.[4] I have had a good deal of publicity – Broadcasts & D. Telegraph especially. But the slur on the whole has been Pop's dreadful illness. I know that every one of us would give all we have to see him well & fit again. Mum's nursing & pluck has been the only bright spot in the whole dreadful time. – So, farewell 1933. Let us see whether 1934 can give us back what seems to us the impossible – Pop's health.

1 The family's motor car. Britten wrote in his diary for 14 December 1932: 'Arrive [at Lowestoft] after good journey with tea, at 5.59 – Met by Pop in marvellous new car – Humber Snipe – 2nd hand bought with Dr Blackburn's money.'

2 J.M. Barrie (1860–1937), Scots dramatist and writer whose most popular work remains *Peter Pan*. *The Little White Bird* was first published in 1902.

3 Elspeth Beide, the dress-making establishment at 559 Finchley Road, Hampstead, which Beth ran with her friend Lilian Wolff. See EWB, pp. 67–9.

4 Robert ran a preparatory school – Clive House – at Prestatyn, North Wales. See also Letter 48.

A Working Life
1934–1939

Chronology: 1934–1939

Year	Events	Compositions
1934	*23 February*: First performance of *A Boy was Born* (BBC broadcast) *6 March*: First performance of *Simple Symphony* at Norwich *5 April*: *Phantasy*, Op. 2, played at International Society for Contemporary Music (ISCM) Festival, in Florence, which Britten attends, accompanied by John Pounder *6 April*: Britten's father dies in Lowestoft after a long illness *October–November*: Travels in Europe with his mother. In Vienna meets Erwin Stein and Hans Heinsheimer, and begins work on the Suite, Op. 6, for violin and piano *30 November*: First performance of *Holiday Diary* *17 December*: First performance of three movements from the Suite, Op. 6	*February*: *Simple Symphony*, Op. 4 *July*: *Te Deum* in C *August*: *Jubilate Deo* in E flat *October*: *Holiday Diary*, Op. 5
1935	*May*: Begins his association with GPO Film Unit writing incidental music for documentary films *5 July*: Meets W.H. Auden *October–November*: Begins his association with Group Theatre *November*: Moves to Flat No. 2, West Cottage Road, West End Green, NW6, with Beth	*April*: *Two Insect Pieces*, for oboe and piano *Friday Afternoons*, Op. 7 *May*: GPO Film: *The King's Stamp* *June*: GPO: *Coal Face* (with Auden) Suite, Op. 6 *July*: GPO: *The Tocher*, *C.T.O.* and *Telegram Abstract* *September*: Gas Association Films: *Men behind the Meters*, *Dinner Hour* and *How Gas is Made* GPO: *How the Dial Works*, *Conquering Space*, *Sorting Office*, *The Savings Bank* and *The New Operator* GPO: *Negroes* (with Auden)

Year	Events	Compositions
		Group Theatre: *Timon of Athens*
		December: Left Theatre: *Easter 1916* (Montagu Slater)
1936	*January*: Signs exclusive publishing contract with Boosey & Hawkes, London. Revises *Alla Quartetto Serioso* as *Three Divertimenti*	*January*: GPO: *Night Mail* (with Auden)
	25 February: *Three Divertimenti* performed by Stratton Quartet	*March*: *Russian Funeral* (March for brass and percussion)
	March: Joins permanent staff of GPO Film Unit	Strand Films: *Peace of Britain*
	April: To Barcelona for ISCM Festival where Antonio Brosa plays Suite, Op. 6. Attends first performance of Berg's Violin Concerto on 19th	*May*: Left Theatre: *Stay Down Miner* (Slater)
		May–June: *Our Hunting Fathers*, Op. 8 (with Auden)
		Soirées Musicales, Op. 9
	25 September: First performance of *Our Hunting Fathers* in Norwich, with Sophie Wyss (soprano) and LPO conducted by the composer	*September–November*: GPO: *Calendar of the Year, Men of the Alps, The Saving of Bill Blewitt, Line to the Tschierva Hut, Message from Geneva* and *Four Barriers*
		TIDA Film: *Around the Village Green*
	October: Moves to 559 Finchley Road, NW3, with Beth	Capitol Films: *Love from a Stranger*
		Group Theatre: *The Agamemnon of Aeschylus*
		November: *Two Ballads*: 'Mother Comfort' (Slater) and 'Underneath the abject willow' (Auden)
		December: Strand Films: *The Way to the Sea* (with Auden)
		Temporal Variations, for oboe and piano
1937	*31 January*: Britten's mother dies in London	*February*: Group Theatre: *The Ascent of F6* (Auden and Isherwood)
	May: Friendship with Peter Pears begins	Left Theatre: *Pageant of Empire* (Slater)
	August: Purchases the Old Mill, Snape	*March*: *Reveille*, for violin and piano
	27 August: *Bridge Variations* performed at the Salzburg Festival, conducted by Boyd Neel; Pears present	*April*: BBC: *King Arthur* (D.G. Bridson)
		May: Cabaret Songs (Auden)
	October: Rents a room at 38 Upper Park Road, NW3, but lives mainly at Peasenhall,	*June*: BBC: *Up the Garden Path* (with Auden)
		July: *Variations on a Theme of*

Year	Events	Compositions
	Suffolk, while awaiting the restoration of Old Mill *19 November*: First performance of *On this Island* (BBC broadcast)	*Frank Bridge*, Op. 10 *September*: BBC: *The Company of Heaven* (R. Ellis Roberts) *October*: *On this Island*, Op. 11 (Auden) *November*: BBC: *Hadrian's Wall* (with Auden) *December*: Group Theatre: *Out of the Picture* (Louis MacNeice) *Mont Juic*, Op. 12 (with Lennox Berkeley)
1938	*22 January*: Beth marries Kit Welford *March*: Moves to new London flat at 43 Nevern Square, SW5, which he shares with Pears *April*: Moves into the Old Mill, Snape, which he shares with Lennox Berkeley *June*: Attends ISCM Festival in London where he meets Aaron Copland *18 August*: First performance of Piano Concerto at Proms with composer as soloist	*January*: BBC: *Lines on the Map* (series of four programmes) *May*: BBC: *The Chartists' March* (J.H. Miller) BBC: *The World of the Spirit* (R. Ellis Roberts) Theatre: *Spain* (Slater/Binyon Puppets) *July*: Piano Concerto, Op. 13 *November*: Group Theatre: *On the Frontier* (Auden and Isherwood) Theatre: *They Walk Alone* (Max Catto) *Advance Democracy* (Randall Swingler), for chorus
1939	*February*: Moves to new London address with Pears, 67 Hallam Street, W1 *5 April*: First performance of *Ballad of Heroes*, conducted by Constant Lambert *21 April*: BBC broadcasts first complete concert of Britten's music which includes first performance of 'Being Beauteous' and 'Marine' sung by Sophie Wyss *29 April*: Britten leaves UK with Pears on SS *Ausonia* bound for N. America	Realist Film Unit: *Advance Democracy* *February*: Theatre: *Johnson over Jordan* (J.B. Priestley) *March*: 'Being Beauteous' and 'Marine' (Rimbaud) *Ballad of Heroes*, Op. 14 (Swingler and Auden)

40 To Grace Williams

[*Boyd, pp. 9–10¹*]

21, Kirkley Cliff Road, Lowestoft.

Jan. 3rd, 1934.

My dear Grace,

Thank you very much indeed for your very rude present [an eraser]. I have never in my life had an insinuatinger one. However, I cannot help agreeing with you. I am awfully sorry that I didn't send you a Christmas card or anything seasonable like that; as a matter of fact I usually send about three Christmas cards, but this year I have sent none at all – partly because I couldn't find a decent one – and party because I loathe the things. However, I wish I had sent you a really nice Calender, with a text for each day, and a beautiful picture on it – holly, bells and all the rest.

As a matter of fact your present is even more necessary now than ever. You should see what I am writing. I cannot write a single note of anything respectable at the moment, and so – on the off chance of making some money – I am dishing up some very old stuff (written, some of it, over ten years ago) as a dear little school suite for strings² – You see what I have come to – I can't even concoct school songs now!³

Considering the ghastly circumstances⁴ we haven't had too bad a Christmas. My brother came, wifeless, for a few days after Christmas and it was very nice to have all the family together. Pop is really pretty bad now, I'm afraid, and he is suffering a bit; the trouble also is that everyone hear knows all about it – and more – so much so that when one goes out, one is stared at as if one is a blinking museum specimen, and everyone speaks in a hushed and awed kind of voice to one (excuse sentence).

However 'it's an ill wind', and we are not going out at all in the evenings – consequently no dances for me – which is a decided blessing.

I hope you had a good time at Christmas with a decent lot of presents. I came off pretty well. F.B. [Frank Bridge] sent me a colossal box of chocolates, and Mrs. Bridge⁵ a sort of hammer-tool contraption.

I have just got a superb record of Furtwängler and the Berlin Phil. doing the Tristan prelude – all for 4/-. There is a slight wobble at the end, and the last few bars of the prelude are missing – owing to the fact that it's on two sides only I suppose[6] – but even then it's a thrill, and the playing's superb.

Have you heard any decent music from abroad? I have been listening a frightful little, owing to Pop.

I really must go and wash for dinner now. Write some time. Do you see that Emil's[7] on again in town? I have to go up on the 10th for a few days, and I hope I'll see it then.[8]

Many thanks indeed for the rubber. It really was frightfully decent of you to send it.

Yours,
BENJAMIN

Mr. Benjamin Britten.

21 Kirkley Cliff Road.
Lowestoft.

Visiting card

1 Published in *Welsh Music*, 6/6, Winter 1980–81: see 'Benjamin Britten and Grace Williams: Chronicle of a Friendship' by Malcolm Boyd, pp. 7–38 (hereafter 'Boyd').

2 Britten's *Simple Symphony*, Op. 4, composed December 1933 – February 1934 and first performed on 6 March at the Stuart Hall, Norwich, when the Norwich String Orchestra was conducted by the composer. The work was dedicated to his first viola teacher, Audrey Alston (Mrs Lincolne Sutton). Britten writes in his diary for 6 March:

Charles and Mrs. C. [Coleman] call for me at 9.30 to go to Norwich in their car. Arr. 10.30 at Stuart Hall for rehearsal. Meet Peter Bevan at 11.11 from London – he is a friend of Ber's [Bernard Richards] & is helping us in the 'cello department. Lunch with him and Mrs. Chamberlain. At 2.45 show starts at Stuart Hall. Mangeot (Cond. Moeran) plays 2 concerti (Vivaldi & Haydn) with orch. – v. badly. I conduct my 'Simple Symphony' which doesn't go too badly – except for a serious [?error] in the Saraband. A Scratch Quartet scrambles through 2 movs. of Mozart G maj K. 387.

'W.L.', in the *Eastern Daily Press*, 7 March wrote:

The other orchestral item in the programme was a first performance of 'A Simple Symphony for Strings,' written by the lad of ten years of age and

now 'arranged' and conducted by the young man whose future as a composer seems to be exceptionally rich in promise. The 'Simple Symphony' has
the customary four movements but they are unconventionally labelled –
'Boisterous Bourrée', 'Playful Pizzicato', 'Sentimental Saraband', and 'Frolic-
some Finale' – thus calling in alliteration's artful aid to help in the understanding of a composition that could be best described as artless in the sense
that it has all the virtues of spontaneity and a quite unusual lavishness in
its prodigality of ingenious ideas. Perhaps naturally it was happier in its
expression of the jolly exuberance of youth in the boisterousness and the
playfulness than in the languorous sentiments of the saraband. But it is
rather more than the remarkable specimen of juvenile precocity which its
author seems to regard it even in the form it has now taken when he has
brought riper experience to its arrangement in its present form. Mr Britten
conducted it apparently with almost as much enjoyment as the orchestra
played it and the audience appreciated it.

  [. . .]

Those comparatively few who were present yesterday will not need to be
reminded, but those who unaccountably were absent may be glad to know,
that the next Audrey Alston concerts will take place on the afternoon and
evening of April 5th, with a programme of piano quartets, in which Mr John
Alston will be the pianist.

Audrey Alston and E.J. Moeran were apparently the moving spirits
behind the concert and were first in touch about it on 17 February.
The parts for the performance were copied by the composer.

3 *Friday Afternoons*, Op. 7, composed at various times between 1933
  and 1935. They were written for the boys of Clive House School,
  Prestatyn, North Wales, where Robert Britten was Headmaster.

4 'Ghastly circumstances': the illness of his father, which he goes on
  to describe in the rest of the paragraph. See note 6 to Letter 46 and
  note 1 to Letter 47.

5 Ethel, Frank Bridge's wife (1881–1960), was Australian (née Sinclair).
  She was an accomplished musician in her own right and had studied
  the violin at the College, where she met Bridge. They were married
  in 1908.

6 HMV DB 3419. As Boyd, p. 10, n. 4, points out, the Prelude was
  continued on DB 3420 which also included the 'Liebestod'.

7 *Emil und die Detektive*: the 1931 UFA film version of the immensely
  popular children's book by the German poet and writer Erich Kästner
  (1899–1974), directed by Gerhard Lamprecht. Britten first saw the
  film on 28 March 1933 in the company of his sister, Beth, and Grace
  Williams. The exuberance of Kästner's story – the hero of which is
  a small boy – impressed itself fully upon the youthful Britten. On 28
  March he wrote in his diary that *Emil* was

  the most perfect & satisfying film I have ever seen or ever hope to see.
  Acting as natural & fine as possible – magnificent & subtle photography
  – plot very amusing & imaginative – a collosal achievement.

Three days after seeing the film Britten purchased a copy of Kästner's novel (the German text, now held in the Archive), and by 3 April 1933 he was planning a suite based on the *Emil* story. An *Alla Marcia* for string quartet, composed in February 1933, was first conceived as the first movement of the projected five-movement suite *Alla Quartetto Serioso* ('Go play, boy, play'). It was dropped from that scheme and conscripted for possible service in the envisaged 'Emil' suite. Later still, it formed the basis of the song 'Parade' in *Les Illuminations*.

In spite of Britten's initial enthusiasm, the notion of an 'Emil' suite faded as other projects assumed greater importance. One might have expected the 'Emil' idea to resurface when Britten saw the film again on 10 January and after listening to a BBC radio adaptation in February, but rather surprisingly it did not. However, the pleasure Britten took in Kästner's novel did not diminish. The seminal *Alla Marcia* was recorded by the Gabrieli String Quartet in 1982 (Unicorn-Kanchana, DKP 9020, with a sleeve note on Britten's early chamber music by Donald Mitchell and John Evans).

8 At the Cinema House, Oxford Circus.

The first performance of *Simple Symphony* by E.B. Britten (arr. B.B.)

41 **To Edwin Benbow**[1]
BBC

21, Kirkley Cliff Road, Lowestoft.
Jan. 24th 1934.

Dear Mr. Benbow,

Could you please let me know whether anything has yet been fixed about the broadcast of my 'Boy was Born'? I have heard through the Oxford Press that Feb. 23rd has been proposed. If this is so, I should think that arrangements with the boys ought to be made, for though the part for them is not difficult, it probably is not much like what they are accustomed to sing. Copies are available by now I should think, if you could ring up the Oxford Press and tell them you are wanting them.

I am very keen that you should let Frank Bridge conduct the work. I feel that he would do the work splendidly, and I know he is willing to do it.[2]

I think I spoke to you about the augmentation of the Wireless Chorus[3] for the work. When the work was accepted for performance by the B.B.C. it was decided that it was essential to have at least 60 or 70 singers, with about 10 boys.

If by any chance you are not concerned with this branch of business at the moment, could you please pass this on to the authorities who are. I am sorry to bother you like this but I feel that the time for preparation is getting very short, & I am rather worried – having heard nothing from you.[4]

I shall be at the above address for a good time now, with periodic visits to town. I shall probably be in town for a bit next week.

Yours sincerely,
BENJAMIN BRITTEN

1 Benbow was assistant chorus master of the BBC Singers, 1933–5. He had been one of Britten's ARCM examiners at the College, in December 1933.

2 However, Bridge was not invited to conduct, nor did he conduct the work on any future occasion. The chosen conductor was Leslie Woodgate. See Letter 42.

3 The chorus could be divided into smaller sections according to the nature of the work to be performed.

4 It seems that Britten had heard nothing from the BBC since September 1933, when he had been informed through his publisher (Hubert Foss of OUP) that the proposed November 1933 performance was to be postponed to February 1934, at the earliest.

42 To Leslie Woodgate[1]
BBC

21, Kirkley Cliff Road, Lowestoft.
Feb. 10th 1934.

Dear Mr. Woodgate,

You said, when I last saw you, that you would be rehearsing my choral work some time this week, and would like me to be there. I am free to come to town any time, although I should prefer to be back here by Friday. If you want me before Wednesday morning, please ring me up or send a telegram here, as early as possible tomorrow.

I am very keen indeed to attend as many rehearsals[2] as possible, & also to see that the boys are going the way they ought to – ![3]

Hope all is going well,
Yours sincerely
BENJAMIN BRITTEN

1 English conductor and chorus master (1902–1961). He joined the BBC in 1928 and was chorus master of the BBC Choral Society from 1934–1961. Woodgate's association with Britten's music was an important one. He was later to conduct the first performances of *Hymn to St Cecilia*, Op. 27 (BBC Singers, 22 November 1942), and *Saint Nicolas*, Op. 42 (1948 Aldeburgh Festival). He also conducted some of Britten's incidental music for radio, notably, *The Sword in the Stone* (1939) and *A Poet's Christmas* (1944).

2 Britten's diary reads as follows:

15 February [London]
Go to rehearsal of my 'Boy etc' at B.B.C. at 11.0–1.0 under Woodgate. It really goes promisingly well. Everyone is very decent about it.

16 February
At 5.0 go to St. Marks. N. Audley St. for a rehearsal of the Boys for my choral work. They sing like angels – for this stage of rehearsal.

22 February
I go to rehearsal at B.B.C. at 11.0–1.15. Rather disappointing, tho' the Wireless Singers (Leaders) are all away. The Boys' intonation, after being impeccable at their own hall, is very bad.[. . .] Go to rehearsal of Boys at St. Marks at 6.0, & they sing excellently – after being so bad at the B.B.C.

23 February
Elgar dies.
F.B. comes with me to rehearsal at 11.0. Better than yesterday but not good. Back to late lunch here, to which Julian Herbage comes. In aft. go back to see Mr. Goodwin (Radio Times) at B.B.C., back to tea here, then

go up to rehearse Boys again at St. Marks. Bath & dinner at 7.30, then Mr. and Mrs. B. take me up to Broadcasting house for contemporary concert. My 'Boy was Born' goes infinitely better than rehearsals, some of it really going well. It goes down pretty well. Cyril Scott plays 2nd pft sonata; 4 Choral songs of Rubbra (1st 2 very sensitive) & a Motet of Woodgate (conductor) for a rousing (not much more!) finish. Whole lot of us (Mr. & Mrs. B., Mr. & Mrs. Brosa, D. Wadham, John Alston, Harold Samuel & friend) meet at MM [Mainly Musicians] Club for supper.

   Bad fog; We (Mr. Mrs. B. & I) drive H. Samuel back to Hampstead arr. here [Cromwell Road] at 1.40.

(Rubbra had contributed an article about *A Boy was Born* to the *Radio Times*, 16 February 1934, p. 450.)

3 Britten is thinking here about his preference for the raw, vibrant tone of boys' voices as distinct from the cultivated purity of the Anglican Cathedral tradition.

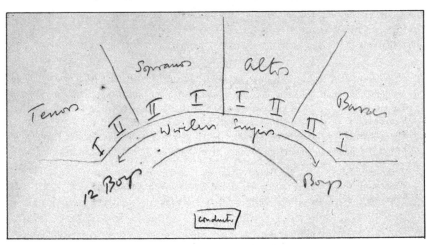

A Boy was Born: scheme for onstage disposition of performers

43 To Leslie Woodgate
BBC

21, Kirkley Cliff Road, Lowestoft.
Feb. 18th 1934.

Dear Mr. Woodgate,

   I heard the boys at St. Marks[1] on Friday. I don't think that you'll have much trouble with them, as they know it quite well already. They had some rather wonderful ideas of some of the tempi, and were occasionally somewhat on the lumbering side; but I think I have put most of that right.

In one or two places I have instructed some of them to drop out (the head boy will give you details of this) & I have, provisionally, instructed two only to sing Var III.[2] If you don't find this enough, you had better put one or two more in, but I think it ought to be ample.

I hope the rehearsal to-morrow goes well. I'm sorry I can't be with you.

Yours sincerely,
BENJAMIN BRITTEN

P.S.   Please don't let the boys drag the beginning & end of Var I. It <u>mustn't</u> be too slow.

1   The first performance of *A Boy was Born* brought Britten into closer contact with the church, its choir, and its choirmaster, Maurice Vinden (1894–1968). Later in 1934, in July, he wrote for them a *Te Deum* in C, and in August a *Jubilate Deo* in E flat, published posthumously in 1984. The orchestral version of the *Te Deum* was first performed at the Mercury Theatre on 27 January 1936. In his diary Britten writes:

Auden comes for a meal – & after Beth, he & I trail up to Mercury Theatre, for Iris Lemare's concert – a dismal concoction of odds & ends, played in an amateur way. This is the last year of my connection with these shows! I play viola in Reginald Goodall's quite competant show of <u>Te Deum</u> – which goes to show attitudes of these concerts! Auden flees at interval, & Beth & I soon after – having heard some quite promising Essays for Pft. by W. E. Glasspool. I should have had broadcast of my 'Lift-Boy' and 'Lov'd a Lass' but – 'decency forbids'!!!

The orchestral version of the *Te Deum* was commissioned by the BBC who broadcast a performance given by the St Michael's, Cornhill, conducted by Harold Darke, on 28 February 1936. (Darke had already performed the organ version on 13 November 1935.) Britten wrote in his diary for the 28th:

[. . .] at 11.0 odd listen to Harold Darke & his Michael singers doing my Te Deum with B.B.C. orchestra. They don't sing it badly – tho' May Bartlett is a very clumsy soloist. The scoring seemed abit too subtile – but that was only the placing of the microphone. But it made some delicious sounds! which I am not ashamed of – !!

Reginald Goodall was later to conduct the historic first performance of *Peter Grimes* at Sadler's Wells in 1945 and alternate with Ernest Ansermet in conducting the first performances of *The Rape of Lucretia* at Glyndebourne in 1946. Twenty years later he emerged as a Wagner conductor of the first rank.

2   'Jesu, as thou art our Saviour'. The published score of the work allots this line to a solo boy's voice. In both the composition sketch and manuscript fair copy Britten had indicated the use of a semi-chorus of boys for this same passage. The final version reflects the experience of the rehearsals.

44   To Grace Williams

[*Boyd, pp. 16–18*]

21, Kirkley Cliff Road, Lowestoft.

Feb. 26th, 1934.

Dear Grace,

Thank you for your letter.[1]

(a).   I should imagine that the cymbal trill with finger tips would be inaudible in your example. I should think knuckles would be better. But do you really want a trill? Wouldn't a smite on one cymbal with a side-drum stick be better? They can get a really good fp>pp, I should imagine – or even a trill with side-drum sticks? Sorry, I am not much help in this.

(b).   I should be inclined to double the appogiatura (?acciacc— — —tura?) on the 1st oboe at the end with any wind possible. I think it would sound a mistake as it stands – if you heard it at all, because the side-drum – even tho' marked 'mf' – will make a good row. What's wrong with 2 oboes, & 2 clars. doing

? Flutes 8ᵛᵃ??

Thank you for your searching comments on my 'Boy'. I am afraid I haven't time to answer them fully at the moment, as I want to get this off to you. You are right about some things, but I feel convinced (& always have done) that Var. I is the best music of the lot. Of course on Friday, Woodgate had to play absolutely for safety & stick to rigid 'tempo'; the boys also, poor little devils, were nervous & upset – you should have heard them in their own hall & with a piano – they sang like angels – and consequently the music suffered. Herod was certainly tame, and here again Woodgate was playing for safety. I wish you had heard the rehearsals – then you would have said that the show was a miracle!

I'll talk about the finale later. Meanwhile I am up to my eyes in copying parts – I am conducting a string orchestra in a suite[2] which I have recently concocted (for something to do) from stuff I wrote at the age of 9–12. You would love this!

I'm sorry to hear about Iris' contretemps.[3] Give her my sympathies & wish her the best of luck for to-morrow when you see her, please.

I rang you up on Sat. morning, hoping you'd be free to come & choose some records with me. But you were out. I am glad that Parry Jones' songs[4] are progressing. Write something for the wireless chorus.

Yours,

BENJAMIN

I am going to Italy.[5]

1 Grace Williams's letter, written on the day of the broadcast of *A Boy was Born* or the day after, is reproduced and fully annotated in Boyd, p. 10 *et seq*. Her technical queries relate to a Concert Overture she was submitting for a *Daily Telegraph* competition, which had been announced in October 1933. Britten's 1934 diary shows that he too had thought of participating: but in the light of the entry for 5 February – 'Try & struggle a bit with an overture in the morning; 2 pages of sketch result' – it is perhaps not surprising that he seems to have abandoned the attempt. The two sketch pages remain unidentified. Williams's overture did not win the prize (though it was highly commended). Frank Bridge was one of the adjudicators of the competition. He wrote to Britten on 24 April, after the announcement of the results:

I ought to receive a free copy of D.T. daily for life, although I will never again burst into song about competitors or competitions. Of course one can readily burst into flames or tears! You may believe it – or not – but I have forgotten everything I saw in the way of scores & blessed if I can remember what G.Ws work was like – which was only known by a mottoe. Anyway – you saw there was an academy professor in the "also ran". Serves some of them – which is it? – right? or wrong?

See also Letter 48.

2 The *Simple Symphony*.

3 The 'contretemps' surrounded the first performance of Gordon Jacob's oboe concerto (No. 1, 1933), which after a good deal of to-ing and fro-ing was finally given under Iris Lemare with Evelyn Rothwell as soloist at a Macnaghten–Lemare concert on 27 February.

4 Three settings of Byron and D.H. Lawrence for voice and orchestra composed by Grace Williams between 1929 and 1934 for Parry Jones (1891–1963), the Welsh tenor. See also note 1 to Letter 55.

5 To attend the ISCM Festival, with his friend, John Pounder. See Letter 46.

45   To Leslie Woodgate
BBC

21, Kirkley Cliff Road, Lowestoft.
Feb. 28th 1934.

Dear Mr. Woodgate,

I haven't seen a single paper in which there has been any notice at all of all the hard work you put in, and time you gave up in preparing my choral work for last Friday.[1] I think you did wonders considering the limitation of time you had for rehearsal, and I think the critics might have had the justice to give you some thanks.

But, I suppose it is the way – if you had been preparing 'Elijah' praise would have been showered on your head.

I have had a large number of letters, and practically everywhere it seems to have come over well. People seem to have liked it; which is rather surprising – however that is only a tribute to your and the chorus' prowess.

Please thank the chorus, and especially the Wireless Singers, for all the hard work they put in for me.

I only hope that you and they will collaborate again in some more things of mine some day.

Yours sincerely,
BENJAMIN BRITTEN

P.S.   Please remember me to your wife. I hope she didn't make her cold worse by coming out that night.

1   Ferruccio Bonavia, in the *Daily Telegraph*, 24 February, wrote:

The first work played was entitled 'A Boy was Born', a set of choral variations by Benjamin Britten, a young man hardly out of his 'teens. Understand "variations" in the modern, broad interpretation of the word. Not all the variations are equally successful, though all are interesting and resourceful. The ingenuity of the writing is striking, even when, as in the first variation, the effect of surprise begins to wear thin before the end is reached.

The simpler variations produced the deepest impression last night, and the third variation, 'Jesu, as Thou art our Saviour', is a remarkably beautiful and poetic thing. Here modern harmony comes to a fine point, and hints at possibilities that are, as yet, unexplored.

'S.G.' [Scott Goddard] wrote in the *Morning Post*, 24 February:

To appreciate fully the creative ingenuity displayed in Mr. Britten's 6 Choral Variations on the Theme, 'A Boy was Born', one would have needed to follow from score. But cleverness of craft never overweighed aesthetic beauty, though there was some unevenness in the disposal of it. The form is new – and challenging.

It is a question whether voices, lacking the individual characteristics of instruments, can support the weight of a long, unaccompanied work in this style. Mr Britten handled them to produce the maximum of variety, and he was not afraid of mingling classical harmony with modern when it suited him.

M.D. Calvocoressi, in *Musical Opinion*, April 1934, wrote:

[. . .] it seems to me that now and then he avails himself of his technical efficiency a trifle ostentatiously. The first, second and fifth variations gave me the impression that he had thought of instrumental colour effects, and revelled in artfully achieving equivalents of them. I wonder whether this is fair criticism: maybe, if there had been musical critics in Jannequin's time, they would have found an excess of tone-colour display in his 'Bataille de Marignan' and 'La Chasse du Cerf'. And if one pays no undue share of attention to the technical artifices, one will find, no doubt, as good music in these three variations as in the admirably telling third and fourth.

46 To Mr and Mrs R.V. Britten

Pension Balestri, Piazza Mentana 5, Firenze.

[30 March 1934]

My darling Parents,

Well, here we are! I am sorry we didn't send our joint telegram last night as soon as we arrived, but the train was pretty late, and we had somewhat of a bother about rooms – however more of that anon.

I was jolly glad to get good news of the day (Tuesday) from your two daughters, and it sent me off in good spirits. I hope you got the card from the Wilton[1] – they did us very well, but were rather expensive; we had some sandwiches cut (John [Pounder] 4, me 2), and they charged 4/6! However it was nice to have everything done well, nicely to time, and conveniently, and we had no bother about getting good seats in the train to Newhaven. Mrs. Bridge turned up unexpectedly at Victoria to see us off. We met some people on the train – an English man and wife (Swiss-French) & child – who helped us a good deal. The journey to Newhaven was uneventful, and incidents began after that. The channel was very choppy and an enormous number of people succombed to it. There was a good roll which seemed to upset them. Of course I was not of their number, but I must say that seeing so many people ill made me feel squeamish once or twice – especially as people would run to the windy side in their dire need! However we cleaned ourselves up before we landed. We got to Paris at about 6.0 p.m. – in good style although the train was packed – the

French porteurs seeing our friends had a child packed us all through
the 1st class department of the ship, and we got to the train very
quickly. Paris was marvellous. We had a superb ride through on
the omnibus provided by the tour – included in our tickets – right
across Paris before it got dark, seeing tons of interesting things –
Place de la Concord, Tour Eiffel, Nôtre Dame. We left our friends
here, and picked up another one Miss Cherry, a schoolmistress –
rather prim, but very amusing. We eat at the Buffet of Gare du
Lyons, and had a good meal – amusing the people around by our
orders to the waiters. We didn't have much difficulty in this, even
though the school-mistress' French wasn't as good as ours! We got
to the 8.50 train in good time and got quite good seats – only one
other in the train [compartment] besides us three. It was dark of
course and we pulled down the blinds and after a time turned off
the light and tried to sleep. Everyone else seemed to sleep very
well – although John was awake a good deal early on – but I simply
couldn't get a wink at all. Whether it was the motion, or the
awkwardness of the position – the seats wern't too long, tho' they
were comfortable enough – I don't know, but I passed a pretty
miserable night. However it didn't last long, and by five it was
quite light. The scenery from there to Turin, where we arrived at
11.0 was incredible. Snow everywhere – lakes, mountains galore, I
have never seen anything like it. The light was so superb – very
sunny, with occasional clouds – and it made the colouring very
brilliant. As you notice, I cannot describe it. Customs weren't very
difficult – much more in Italy than in France. They came round just
after a most colossal tunnel (I don't know its name) after Modane –
and just looked through our luggage, an inspector followed by
armed Police. However we were tactful and didn't mention
'Marmalade' or anything to do with it, and got through. It was here
we met a third lot of friends, one Arthur Cook,[2] friend of Dent,
the president of the Festival,[3] and a man and sister coming to
Florence for a few weeks, of the name Pierce[4] – he was at
Charterhouse[5] to John's delight. After Turin, we got a bit tired of
traveling – the trains were still crammed and until Genoa (about
3.30, Italian summer time) we had to sit on our luggage in the
corridor. The journey from here onwards was marvellous – if it
hadn't been for the incredible amount of tunnels – quite 70% of the
way we were actually in the cliffs. You see, the railway runs for
about 100 miles right along the coast of the Mediterranian. When
we saw the sea it was superb – lovely and still and blue, absolutely
transparent. It was also getting pretty hot, and the scenary with

palms and all that was quite tropical. We got to Pisa – saw the
good old tower – and changed there – with some difficulties, none
of us knowing a word of the language – and took about two hours
to Florence. This was by far the worst bit of the journey – crowded,
hot, in a carriage with three gross perspiring (and playing cards)
Italians – and as we hadn't any of us slept much, if at all, we were
dead tired – Our school-mistress left us at Pisa, by-the-way. Of
course it wouldn't have been bad if we could have come straight
to a decent hotel, had a bath, eaten and gone to bed, but that
didn't happen.

Look here, this has got to be posted, I will continue in our next
– don't worry about what happened, because now we look back
on it it seems quite funny, and it certainly ended well, as this place
seems everything one could want – comfortable, and cheap, and
the two Pearces are here too, to help in matters. We are both happy,
well, and are going to enjoy ourselves, if we know that things are
going as well as possible with you. I hope Nurse Bessie[6] is a real
help, and that you will have quite a cheerful Easter with your
children – although you are sonless and daughterful.

Much love to you all. Courage, Pop. We are thinking of you alot,
and certainly wish you were here with us.

I'll write again soon.

Much love,

BENJAMIN

1 Probably a hotel close to Victoria Station.

2 *recte* Arnold Cooke (b. 1906), English composer, pupil of E.J. Dent
and Hindemith. In 1934 he was teaching at the Royal Manchester
College of Music. Cooke's *This Worldes Joie* for solo tenor, written for
Peter Pears, was performed at the 1955 and 1967 Aldeburgh Festivals.

3 Edward J. Dent (1876–1957), who was elected the first President of
the newly formed ISCM in 1922. Britten was to come closer to him
and his circle of friends in later years, in part through his encounter
in Florence with Wulff, the son of the conductor Hermann Scherchen.
See Letter 136. In a letter to Herbert Thompson written on 4 April,
Dent described the Festival:

I am at Florence for the International Festival. We have had endless worry
over it, and have been obliged to change things at the last moment; but it
is going very well, and so far we have had excellent audiences and good
programmes. The weather is pleasant and Florence always makes everyone
feel happy. I created much amusement at the opening ceremony by making
a speech (in answer to the Prefect of Florence, who made the usual oration
all about Mussolini) in which I emphasized the dangers of nationalism and

the necessity of free thought and speech for the artist. It was the sort of thing no Italian would dare to say now, but I gathered that they were all enormously pleased to hear someone else say it! I carried it off by paying all sorts of compliments to Italy and Florence as the homes of music, and watched my audience getting nervous as I brought out all sorts of dangerous words like 'revolution' and then qualified them with the adjective 'musical'. The Germans all liked it very much, but I expect it would have been more risky to make such a speech in Germany itself. Our German section is in a state of suspended animation and we don't yet know what will happen to it. For the moment it is standing aloof and sending no representatives; but Dr Holl of the Frankfurter Zeitung is here. Otherwise the Germans are all Jews and alleged Communists; Scherchen is conducting and will have a great reception to-night, I expect – he is popular in Italy. But of course the orthodox Nazis will be furious at that. [. . .]

The most enjoyable thing is the number of young musicians from different countries, many of them here for the first time in their lives, like Benjamin Britten. They make friends with each other as far as languages permit, and all seem very happy together.

For the complete text, see LFBML, pp. 172–3.

Scherchen's concert (4 April) included Ravel's Concerto for Piano (left hand) and Orchestra, in which the soloist was Paul Wittgenstein, who had commissioned the work and was to commission Britten's (left-hand) *Diversions* in 1940 in the USA, where both the composer and the pianist were then living.

4 J. Allan Pearce, a solicitor, whose recollections (in 1988) of the Pension Balestri included a memory of a staircase

down which John Pounder came tripping, very nimbly for such a tall man, watched by Ben seated at the elderly upright piano in the hall, who vividly described his descent on the keys. The four of us, Ben, my sister, myself and John were joining up to make an expedition [. . .]

Apart from that, the only other real memory I have of Ben was standing with him on the Ponte Vecchio and admiring the moonlight on the Arno [. . .] But it was a delightful holiday, four young English people together . . .

John Pounder, I remember much better, as he was a great extrovert, not retiring like Ben, and was, as it were, the 'life and soul' of the party. I also well remember Professor Dent and his fatherly manner.

The staircase incident inevitably calls to mind the 'running down-stairs' music Britten was to write a year later for the GPO film, *The King's Stamp*. (See also PR, pp. 58–9.) In 1988, the hotel (no longer a Pension) looked much as it did in 1934 and the staircase was there, leading into the hall, but not the piano. The building has since been extensively renovated.

5 John Pounder's public school, at Godalming, Surrey.

6 Nurse Bessie was engaged to help Mrs Britten look after her husband who died at the age of fifty-seven while his son was in Florence, on

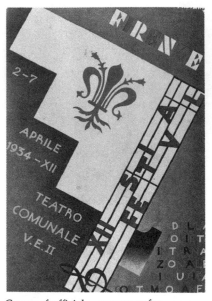

Teatrino del Teatro Comunale V. E.

Giovedì 5 Aprile 1934-XII · alle ore 21

Secondo Concerto da Camera
della S. I. M. C.

PROGRAMMA

I°	Fantasia per Oboe, violino, viola e violoncello	BENJAMIN BRITTEN (Inghilterra)
II°	Trio per pianoforte, violino e violoncello	HENRIK NEUGEBOREN (Ungheria)
III°	Cantata per mezzosoprano, flauto, oboe d'amore, liuto, viola d'amore viola da gamba e violoncello	RICHARD STURZENEGGER (Svizzera)
IV°	Quartettino per archi	LEOPOLD SPINNER (Austria)
V°	Sonata per pianoforte e violino	JAROSLAV JEZEK (Cecoslovacchia)
VI°	Cinque liriche per una voce e pianoforte	H. E. APOSTEL (Austria)
VII°	Sinfonietta per archi	LARS ERIK LARSSON (Svezia)

Cover of official programme for
ISCM Festival, Florence, 1934

Programme of concert including
Britten's *Phantasy* Quartet, Op. 2

6 April, of a cerebral haemorrhage, in the final stages of lymphadi-
noma. Britten had been summoned home on the 7th by telegram,
'Come today, Pop not so well', but arrived on the 9th to find his
father already dead. 'A great man with one of the finest brains I have
ever come across & what a father!', he wrote in his diary. This letter
was the last from Britten to contain words addressed to his father:
'Courage, Pop.' The course of Mr Britten's illness is set out in note
1 to Letter 47.

47 To J.F.R. Stainer
Mendelssohn Foundation

> 21, Kirkley Cliff Road, Lowestoft.
> April 15th, 1934.

Dear Mr. Stainer,

It was very nice of you to write to me about my Choral Variations
and about the Florence Festival. I went to Florence for it, and had a
very enjoyable time there until I was suddenly called away home,
to find that my father had died. It has been rather a terrible shock,
for although he has been ill for a long time he seemed to be holding
his own.[1] Of course this has left us in somewhat straitened
circumstances,[2] and at the expiration of my last grant from the

Mendelssohn Scholarship I shall be compelled to find a job. I suppose you don't know of any further financial help that I could obtain? If there is any possible chance anywhere I should be infinitely grateful if you could tell me of it.

Thanking you again for your letter.

Yours sincerely,
BENJAMIN BRITTEN

1 The course of Mr Britten's illness is fully documented in Britten's diaries, from May 1932 until the end. In 1933 there are twenty-seven entries about his father's worsening condition, e.g. 'We have to live from day to day now' (8 October); 'Pop's cough is dreadful: why in the world cant something be done for it?' (11 October); 'It's imposs-ibly ghastly leaving home with Pop like this' (12 October). The year 1934 opened badly – 'Pop's cough is frantic, after dinner; he's also suffering a good deal all the time. His birthday today.' (4 January); and, as it progressed, the entries grow ever more anguished: 'a positively night-mare of a day. Spend most of morning, aft & after

XII° FESTIVAL

DELLA

SOCIETÀ INTERNAZIONALE

DI

MUSICA CONTEMPORANEA

Sotto l'Alto Patronato di
S. E. BENITO MUSSOLINI

The patron of the ISCM Festival, Florence, 1934

tea sitting with Pop whose chest is unbearably painful. [. . .] More morphia at night' (7 March); 'Doctor Evans comes in every day now. Long talk with Pop in evening on finance.' (13 March); 'Pop has a good night, but is in dreadful agony most of the day' (26 March); and the final entry while Mr Britten was still alive: 'Pop brightens a bit to say "goodbye" to me' – Britten was to leave that day (27 March) for the ISCM Festival at Florence – 'but doesn't seem too well.'

The funeral took place in Lowestoft on 11 April, in the afternoon. Britten and his brother Robert had chosen the music: the 'last number of Matt. Pass. and Var. iii of my "boy" [Jesu, as Thou art our Saviour]. Mum is being marvellously brave' (10 April). The service was conducted by Basil Reeve's father and Britten's Uncle Sheldon: 'a very simple and lovely service [. . .] Mum is a perfect marvel, even when we go up to Kirkley cemetary after she has control of herself.' See also EWB, pp. 70–76.

2 'Straitened circumstances' was the first reaction to the shock of his father's death. In his Will, Mr Britten bequeathed £100 to each of his four children, £50 to his grandson, John, and all his real and personal estate (including his dental practice) to his wife, Edith. Robert Britten recollected his father leaving £15,000. His was a prosperous dental practice and he enjoyed a considerable reputation. Three servants were part of the family establishment. Mrs Britten was the principal beneficiary who herself, on her death, was to leave £12,000. (Source: Robert Britten, Conversation with Donald Mitchell, 16 November 1977, London; Archive.)

48   To Grace Williams

[*Boyd, pp. 19–20*]

Clive House, Prestatyn, N. Wales.[1]

April 22nd, 1934.

My dear Grace,

First and foremost – heartiest congratulations on getting a mention in the Telegraph. I am very sick that you didn't get a prize – but don't be disheartened, as a mention in the previous competition was chosen for the International festival this year![2] Seriously – it is jolly good, and I suppose you'll get good shows all over the place, now. Good advertisement. What you must think of me all this time I daren't think. Actually so much has happened that when I'll have time to tell you all, I can't imagine. However first of all, many thanks for your last helpful letter – about last March I think – I am sorry I haven't answered it before, but things were in such a muddle just before I left for Florence that I didn't have a moment – and even if I had had time I couldn't have told you what my plans were. So I just went to Florence. I had a very good time – met alot of decent people – Scherchen[3] is very nice – Goossens & the Grillers played my Quartet very well, and it was very well received, and alot of people said they liked it. There was some pretty poor music played – but I'll tell you about that some other time. I received a cable on the Saturday from home – last day of Festival – and I had to leave at once. I got to Lowestoft on Monday morning after a pretty filthy journey – spending two nights travelling and not knowing what I was going to meet at the end of it. However, the worst happened, and my father had died a few days before. It was rather a shock, as he had seemed to be holding his own pretty well – getting, perhaps, abit worse, but not seriously. Luckily for him it was quite sudden, and he was unconscious the whole time.

Since then it has been rather confused. Mum had had a very bad time, so I brought her here for a few weeks – to my brother's school. She seems to be picking up abit now. We spent two days in London on the way here, but you weren't back then. By-the-way, if you would like to see Beth – I know she'd like to see you – her number is Hampstead 6695 – Elspeth Beide.

So, Grace, here we are. I have to come up to town on May 22nd. Perhaps we shall be able to meet then. I hope you'll have a good time, & that everything will go swimmingly.

Best of luck. Let me hear from you sometime.

Yours,
BENJAMIN B

1 After his father's death, Britten and his mother went to stay with Robert at Clive House.

2 Britten refers here to his own *Phantasy* Quartet which had just been performed at the Florence session of the ISCM, when the *Morning Post*, 10 April, reported that: 'Everyone liked this fresh and pleasing work, which had a charming woodland and pastoral flavour.' The music critic of *The Times*, 9 April, wrote:

> The Fantasia Quartet [*sic*] was warmly received, as it deserved to be. It is original in design and at the same time unpretentious. Its colloquies between the oboe and the strings stamp it as music which belongs inherently to the instruments for which it is scored, which is more than can be said of all the works heard at the Florence Festival.

Britten had submitted the work for the 1933 *Daily Telegraph* competition on 29 October 1932. 'Alter bits of May's 1st fiddle part, before practising & catching 12.45 to Croydon, via Daily Telegraph, where

I leave my entries for comp.' The results were declared on 13 March 1933. Britten was not the winner (Edric Cundell was placed first, Armstrong Gibbs second and Elizabeth Maconchy third), but his quartet was 'highly commended'.

3 On 7 April, the day he left Florence to return home, Britten writes 'leave score for Scherchen'. This might have been a copyist's score of the *Sinfonietta*, but was most probably a published copy of *A Boy was Born* (Oxford University Press, 1934), which Britten certainly had with him in Italy.

49   To Leslie Woodgate
BBC

Clive House, Prestatyn, Flintshire.
May 8th 1934.

Dear Mr. Woodgate,

You said recently that you would be so angelic as to run through my two part-songs (4 part, with piano).[1] I think you said May 22nd. Could you let me know definitely, and also what hour? I have to travel from Wales so it would be infinitely more convenient if it were the afternoon. But of course, I shall have to fit in with your arrangements.

I will let you have the score for parts to be copied later this week. I am afraid print is out of the question at the moment, but a publisher (Mr. Ralph Hawkes)[2] may be induced to come and listen if it is in order.[3]

Hoping you are well. This is a lovely spot, but somewhat shut off from the rest of the world.

Yours sincerely,
BENJAMIN BRITTEN

1 'I lov'd a lass' and 'Lift Boy'.

2 Ralph Hawkes (1898–1950), a director of the music publishers, Boosey & Hawkes Ltd, of which the Chairman was Leslie Boosey. It was Hawkes who was to encourage Britten during the early stages of his career. He was to offer him an exclusive publishing contract with his firm on 25 November 1935. Hawkes's belief in the young composer remained undiminished even when Britten's early music was slow to establish itself. In grateful response, Britten in 1936 dedicated to him his song-cycle, *Our Hunting Fathers*. He remained an influential friend and adviser, not only in London but also in New York, where he was head of the Boosey & Hawkes office.

In an interview with Donald Mitchell (April 1977, Toronto; Archive) a publishing colleague from North America, Bailey Bird, remembered Hawkes:

As far as I know he was not musically educated, but he had an exceptional ear and appreciation of contemporary music. I always think of this man with Britten, being responsible for taking him to Boosey & Hawkes and getting him a retainer there in his early days so that he could work [. . .]

After the great success of *Peter Grimes*, Hawkes

had just come from England after the annual meeting of the Boosey & Hawkes Directors, and he was in very good spirits and during a meal with me he told me that he had a very amusing experience this year [c.1946] because for years and years, when he attended the annual meetings, at the end of the meeting the Chairman usually turned to him and said, 'Well, Mr Ralph, I see we have spent so much money on Britten so far; when are we going to start getting some of this back? Do you have a report on Mr Britten?'

On this occasion, however, it came to the end of the meeting and nothing happened, and the Chairman said, 'Well, if there's no other business the meeting will be adjourned.' So [Hawkes] said: 'Just a minute, Mr Chairman. I haven't received my usual questions about Mr Britten this year.'

Hawkes concluded by saying to me: 'At last I'm vindicated.' He was certain that this man was going to be the saviour of British music or whatever you want to call it. He was so convinced about this man's talent – there was no question; there was just no question. It was just a case of waiting, you know. He had the patience. He had the patience to wait and wait – till it happened.

A vivid description of the dynamic Hawkes in New York appears in a volume of autobiography by Hans W. Heinsheimer, *Best Regards to Aida* (New York, Knopf, 1968), pp. 181 *et seq*. In 1947 he was invited to become one of the founding directors of the English Opera Group. See also Letter 160, in which Britten pays tribute to Hawkes, and Ernst Roth, 'The Vision of Ralph Hawkes', *Tempo*, 78, supplement, Autumn 1966, pp. 6–8.

3 Later in 1934 Boosey & Hawkes published the Two Part-songs and took over the *Sinfonietta* and *Phantasy* Quartet from Oxford University Press, with whom Britten had agreements for these two works, though OUP had published, i.e. printed, neither score. Up to this date his principal publishing affiliations had been with OUP. It seems, however, that they had shown no particular interest in these part-songs. Hence, no doubt, his hope that Ralph Hawkes might be persuaded to come along to the run-through. In a letter from Woodgate to Britten of 10 May, the conductor mentions that Harvey Grace, of Novello, had also expressed an interest in the works (Novello specialized in choral items). Clearly there was a flurry of interest on the part of publishers at this time in Britten's potentialities.

50   To Mrs Britten

Clive House, Prestatyn, Flintshire.
May 11th, 1934.

My darling Mum,

I want just to let you have a note for the week-end – and to tell you that you have my thoughts all the time – not that you need telling <u>that</u> I hope!

I was very glad to get your letter, and to hear your news.[1] So Queenie is not too bad, and you are making progress? I hope the place is still nice – although everywhere is lovely in this weather. It has been positively grilling here to-day – in fact I have 'cast a clout' – my pull-over, in other words. It's been a lazy day too, the kind of day on which to do nothing as I have all day – except for writing a song. But it's a pretty rotten one – just one of the school songs.[2]

I got alot of things off to the B.B.C. this morning – the scores of the part songs they are going to try over. I heard from Leslie Woodgate, & he gave me a choice of times. Tuesday (22nd) morning, or Wednesday (23rd) afternoon. So I plumped for the Wednesday time, so I shall be able to travel up with Beth in the morning. F.B. conducts a show that night,[3] & we go down to Friston the next day. He comes to Aberystwythpgfflly (however you spell it) on Wednesday next. I suppose that he & Mrs. B. won't be able to come over here, but I'm going to write & ask them.

I miss you most terribly, my dear, although these two are very good. Ryle[4] is sleeping in your room – it was fixed when I got back – I suppose <u>he</u> is wakened up by my light arrangement now – I wish it were you instead! Still I hope you have better nights now, & that the beds are nice & soft.

Excuse this rambly letter – I can't think straight to-night – too hot.

Mr Holgate[5] is coming in to-night – but wild elephants couldn't stop me listening to Don Quixote to-night – except the wireless running out of course.[6] To-morrow the Woods come – & on Monday we go to the Browns.[7] Sickening but I suppose I've got to go through it for Robert's sake.

John yelled Gwaddy[8] going past your room to-day. Robert asked him where you had gone – & he said Liverpool.

If Marjory hasn't done anything about your business yet I'll remind her – but she's been very busy to-day.

Much love to you, my sweet.

Keep a brave heart – we all need to.

See you soon. Your loving admirer

BENJAMIN

Love to Queenie

1 Mrs Britten had been sent for by Aunt Queenie who was in the middle of an attack of 'melancholia' on 7 May 1934.

2 No. 7 of *Friday Afternoons*: 'There was a man of Newington'.

3 A BBC concert. Britten wrote in his diary on the day (23 May):

V. sensitive performance of Mozart E♭ Symph.. Franz Osborn [1905–1955, British pianist of German birth] plays Franck Symph. Var. – very hard – & insensitive. F.B.'s charming Summer and a riotous perf. of Dvorak Carnival make up rest.

4 A junior master at Clive House School.

5 Britten wrote in his diary for 17 May:

Mr Holgate fetches Robert & me & takes us in his car to Mostyn Iron Works (of which he is works manager). Shows us all over it & we see a cast taken at 11.0. It is extremely interesting & thrilling, & the colours & shadows of the flames were incredible – Kolossal!

6 Strauss's symphonic poem formed part of a concert given by the BBC Symphony Orchestra conducted by Bruno Walter (1876–1962), broadcast by the BBC from the Queen's Hall, London. Britten wrote in his diary:

Listen to bit of B.B.C. concert under Walter (on very good newly hired wireless). Schubert 7th [9th] Symphony was spoilt by exxaggeration & lack of taste. Don Quixote (with Feuermann as a first-rate soloist) was very good indeed, but not inspired – the wind variation wasn't successful, tho' the end was extremely beautiful. What lovely music most of this is – the introduction & end esp.

7 The Browns and Woods were friends of Robert's.

8 Presumably a conflation of 'Granny' and 'Daddy'.

51 To Leslie Woodgate
BBC

Clive House, Prestatyn, Flintshire.
May 11th 1934.

Dear Mr. Woodgate,

Thank you so much for your letter. May 23rd (Wednesday) at 14.30 will suit me perfectly.

Here are the scores – I hope you find them legible. I have a copy of the piano part, so don't bother to have that copied. By-the-way, I suppose I shall be allowed to manipulate that instrument myself?[1]

No, I haven't tried Novello's yet, and if nothing comes of the present negotiations with Hawkes I will send them there.

Thanking you so much,
Yours sincerely,
BENJAMIN BRITTEN

1 Britten played the piano, and his diary for 23 May confirms that a representative of Boosey & Hawkes (though not, it would seem, Ralph Hawkes himself) was present: 'run through of my 2 pt-songs [. . .] go pretty well and I meet a man from Hawkes who likes them???'. The songs were indeed taken on by Boosey & Hawkes, though Britten was asked to simplify the piano part of 'Lift Boy', an item about which Leslie Boosey (see note 1 to Letter 110), the head of the music-publishing firm, had reservations: would it be successful with amateur choral societies in the provinces? Britten however insisted that the two part-songs should be published simultaneously. He considered making a version of the songs for strings and percussion, but this was never carried through.

52 To Edward Clark

21, Kirkley Cliff Road, Lowestoft.
Telephone: Lowestoft 112
June 20th 1934

Dear Mr. Clark,

I see from a programme sent me that you are going to broadcast my Sinfonietta next Friday week. I am very anxious to be present at one or two rehearsals, and I am planning to come to town on either the Wednesday or Thursday of that week. Could you let me know when you are rehearsing?[1]

I hope you are well and that everything is going as it should with you. I enjoyed myself no end in Florence at Easter, and I wish I had seen more of you.[2]

Yours sincerely,

BENJAMIN BRITTEN

1 The first rehearsal of the *Sinfonietta* Britten attended was on Thursday, 28 June, when he wrote in his diary:

> Go (at 4.30) to a rehearsal at B.B.C. (St. George's Hall) with Clark of Sinfonietta. Not good – he doesn't know the work.

The next day (the day of the performance) he was at the rehearsal preceding the concert: 'Clark does the work better.' He continues:

> Show at 9.0 – Contemporary concert. Van Dieren [*Diaphonia*] (v. long) – Lucas Partita (welcome after the V.D. but not much in itself – tho' Sarabande is quite lovely) & my Sinfonietta – which the orchestra plays quite well considering all. Quite well received. Personally I am bucked with it.

Van Dieren's *Diaphonia* (unpublished) for baritone and orchestra was composed in 1916 and comprises a sequence of three Shakespeare sonnets linked by instrumental interludes. One of the sonnets Van Dieren chose, 'When most I wink', Britten was to set himself in 1958 in his *Nocturne*, Op. 60. An unrealized late project of Britten's was a sequence of Shakespeare sonnets which would be linked by instrumental interludes.

Leighton Lucas (1903–1982), English composer and conductor. His *Partita* (1934) was scored for piano and chamber orchestra.

On 12 July Britten wrote to Clark:

> It was very good of you to take such trouble over my 'Sinfonietta' the other night. It was by far the best performance it has ever had, and it has done me a lot of good in many ways!

2 Clark had attended the ISCM Festival at Florence.

53 To J.F.R. Stainer
Mendelssohn Foundation

21, Kirkley Cliff Road, Lowestoft.

July 19th, 1934.

Dear Mr. Stainer,

Thank you for your letter. If humanly possible I will arrange for a chamber work performance on Nov. 5th. So far this year I have not written anything in that line, but I expect something will materialise before then.[1]

I was glad you were able to listen to the Contemporary concert the other night. I was quite pleased with the performance of my Sinfonietta. As the Times have once given me a very flattering notice for this work,[2] I suppose they feel that they have done their duty by it, and can in future ignore it! I must say that I feel it was an injustice of their part to ignore the Lucas Partita; as I thought it very interesting, if slightly immature, and certainly much better shape than the long rambling 'Diaphonia', which I am afraid irritated me beyond all measure. Much as I should like to like this van Dieran work, I found that, even after careful listening at two long rehearsals, I was unable to appreciate it.

Thank you very much for writing,

> Yours sincerely,
> BENJAMIN BRITTEN

1 *Holiday Diary*, suite for piano, was to be composed later in the year. See Letter 56.

2 *The Times* (3 February 1933) had reviewed the first performance of the *Sinfonietta* on 31 January:

> Mr Benjamin Britten, after taking something from Hindemith, seems to be striking out on a path of his own. His *Sinfonietta* for 10 instruments (five strings, four wood-wind, and horn), shows that he possesses a power of invention apart from the efficiency with which he handles his material. The work, which is in three movements (*Poco presto – Andante – Tarantella*) is throughout strongly rhythmical; in fact the last movement which grows into a frenzy that completely suggests the traditional origin of the dance, is built out of rhythmic figures rather than purely musical themes. On this occasion Mr Britten permits himself to indulge effects of barbarism, which at least hold the attention. He has already enough to say for himself to excuse his independence of tradition.

54 To Hubert Foss
Oxford University Press

> 21, Kirkley Cliff Road, Lowestoft.
> August 2nd, 1934.

Dear Mr. Foss,

Thank you for your letter. I am very glad that you have decided to publish my 'Simple Symphony'. I quite agree to all the terms, and I certainly think the sooner the job is put in hand the better – to catch the beginning of the school year.

I have thought alot about the title – hence this delay – & I see your adviser's point. But I have searched the dictionary in vain, & I can find nothing else suitable. After all – no one can pretend that the material is not simple, & technically it certainly is not difficult.

However I suppose at the moment it is not vital, & I will bear it in mind for a bit.

The school songs are well in hand, & will be ready to come to you in a few weeks' time. I have also concocted a Te Deum (Choir and Organ). Does this interest you?[1] I am coming to town in August sometime; perhaps you might like to have a look at it.

Excuse the scribble, but I want to get this off to-day.

I hope your holiday in Dorset was a success, & that all the family is thriving after it.

Yours sincerely

BENJAMIN BRITTEN

1 The *Te Deum* was published by Oxford University Press in 1935. *Friday Afternoons*, on the other hand, went to Boosey & Hawkes. See Letter 64.

55 To Grace Williams

[*Boyd, pp. 20–21*]

21, Kirkley Cliff Road, Lowestoft.

Sept. 25th, 1934.

My dear Grace,

What a good show! I have never known the West Regional behave better. Except for a slight wobble at the end of the 'Service', it was perfect althrough.[1] Parry Jones was miles better than I expected, & except for one high B♭ (B♮ ?) (in the 1st, I think), acquitted himself with credit. I should never have thought that such a 'Tristan' could have done it.

I like the first song the least of the three, though the climax thrilled me. I am not sure whether the opening bars are strongly enough scored; the effect was tame compared to what you obviously intend it to be. Perhaps the players hadn't got hold of it by then. If I remember rightly, I felt also that P.J.'s first phrase in that song didn't hit me enough. It didn't carry conviction. Perhaps it's too low for him – anyhow, you will get few tenors with a reasonable high B♭ to do it satisfactorily.

No. 2 was by far the best of the three. The middle section is beautiful & touching – really.

I love the opening bars of the 'Service', but do you want it as fast as that? It didn't sound nearly spacious or solemn enough – only just uncomfortable. The end puzzles me. It seemed too long & indefinite. The wireless behaved rather badly here, consequently it is hard to judge. But from what I remember from looking at the score, the end isn't as satisfactorily managed as I feel it might be.

I was thrilled with the folk-song arrangements – they are by far the best arrangements of any folk-songs I know.[2] We <u>must</u> get someone to print them. Until you get them translated, though, I am afraid that few publishers will look at them. Why not have a shot yourself? I marked off Brecon as being the one that was most immediately attractive; and the last Ogmore has a query against it, for I think that St. Althan would make the most satisfactory concluding one if you issued them as a group. (Of course a high & loud ending revolts you

but an audience would love it!!)

Mari Cwyd is a lovely song, & I will die in the effort to see it in print somewhere. What does Parry J. say? Can he suggest a likely publisher whom he might influence? Perhaps if he was asked nicely he might go and sing them for you at Boosey's. Write & say if you are willing for me to communicate with them.

Finally the composer at the piano lent distinction to the evening (((But the end of the last song sounded as if the train to Wales had been late!!!)))

Excuse the awful scribble but I'm writing against time.

Many thanks for telling Fred May to write to me.

The weather has been lovely here to-day; I thought of you basking in Wales.

Once again – hearty congrats.,

Yours,
BENJAMIN

1 Britten refers here to the broadcast of the 'Parry Jones' songs by Grace Williams given by Jones with the Western Studio Orchestra conducted by Reginald Redman on the BBC West Region station on 24 September. Tristan was among Parry Jones's many operatic roles

which included Boles in *Peter Grimes*. 'Service' was the third song, a setting of D.H. Lawrence's 'Service of All the Dead'. See also Boyd, pp. 20–22.

2 Six of the folksong arrangements Britten heard were published by Boosey's in 1937 as *Six Welsh Oxen Songs*. In this letter Grace Williams joins the select company of folksong arrangers admired by Britten. He had already praised Percy Grainger's arrangements in his diary for 3 March 1933:

two brilliant folk-song arrangements of Percy Grainger [. . .] knocking all the V. Williams and R.O. Morris arrangements into a cocked-hat.

In 1943, Vaughan Williams published *his* view of the first volume of Britten's folksong arrangements in the *Journal of the English Folk Dance and Song Society*, 4/4, December:

Are we old fogeys of the Folk-song movement getting into a rut? If so, it is very good for us to be pulled out of it by such fiery young steeds as Benjamin Britten and Herbert Murrill. We see one side of a folk-song, they see the other. They probably think our point of view hopelessly dull and stodgy, but that is no excuse for us to label them self-conscious or deliberately freakish.

Personally I am delighted to see these rockettings come to a sound *terra firma* from which I believe all flights of fancy must take off – beautiful melody, spontaneous melody, melody which belongs essentially to us.

The tune's the thing with which we'll catch the conscience of the composer. Do these settings spring from a love of the tune? Then, whatever our personal reaction may be we must respect them. [. . .]

Welcome, then the younger generation who will push along the highway, turning now to the right, now to the left, each divagation balancing the other so that in the end the straight line is kept intact.

Five years later, in the same journal, Frank Howes – not the most sympathetic of critics – was to write in much the same spirit, of the famous HMV recording (DA 1873) of 'The Foggy, Foggy Dew' by Pears and Britten (5/3, December):

In nothing does Benjamin Britten show his originality and fertility – it would be wrong to call anything so spontaneous ingenuity – as in the figuration which almost any words will produce from him for their accompaniment. One gasps with delighted astonishment at what he does with 'Newcastle', so unheard of, yet so pat. The suggestion of a guitar gives a raffish air to 'The Foggy Dew' and makes it more salacious. 'The Plough Boy' is set to a brazenly simple figure of repeated chords with a tinkle now and again in the treble. The merit of these arrangements is that the music arises straight out of the song, from the words rather than from the tune, yet not offending against the tune. That they are not like Sharp or Vaughan Williams or Moeran merely shows that we have come to the next generation to whom folksong once more reveals new life. The songs are sung by Peter Pears who makes every word intelligible, with Britten at the piano.

However, in *Grove V* (1954), Howes changed his tune:

[Britten] has never immersed himself in folksong, as Bartók and Vaughan Williams did, and his actual settings are unequal just because his acquaintance with it is comparatively superficial – perhaps the quickness of his mind is a snare. His *Scottish Ballad* (Op. 26) for two pianofortes and orchestra is an ugly perversion on the psalm-tune 'Dundee'. The collections of English folksong for solo voice and pianoforte contain some strained examples, but others show once again that extraordinary mixture of sophisticated ingenuity with simplicity of effect.

56 To J.F.R. Stainer
Mendelssohn Foundation

Parkweg 18, Basle, Switzerland.[1]

Oct. 20th, 1934.

Dear Mr. Stainer,

I am sorry not to have answered your letter before this, but I have been in considerable doubt as to what I could get played to you on November 5th at the Academy. I have written nothing in the chamber music line since you last met. However, Messrs. Boosey & Hawkes are just publishing four, as yet unnamed, piano pieces which I have written for them about a fortnight ago.[2] So I have asked Mr. Arthur Benjamin to arrange for a good pupil of his to play them to you, for I was not in the position to pay a professional pianist. As you see I am abroad, and so I shall be unable to play them myself, as I should have liked. I am travelling on the continent until Christmas.

If there are any alterations in arrangements, could you communicate with Mr. Benjamin at 66, Carlton Hill, N.W. 8.?

Yours sincerely,

BENJAMIN BRITTEN

1 Britten, accompanied by his mother, was travelling in Europe during the autumn of 1934. They left England on 16 October and visited Basel (17–28 October), Salzburg (29–31 October), Vienna (1–20 November), Munich (21–6 November) and Paris (27–8 November), returning to London on 29 November.

2 *Holiday Diary*, composed 3–12 October. The work's first title, 'Holiday Tales', was probably suggested by the dedicatee, Arthur Benjamin. In 1944, when the piano suite was performed by Clifford Curzon, Britten wrote the following programme note:

These little pieces were written just ten years ago, and they are (subjective) impressions of a boy's seaside holiday, in pre-war days.

I   Early morning bathe: There is, as might be expected, a somewhat

characteristic opening, before the main, rhythmic & flowing, section begins.
II   Sailing: descriptive of the varying moods that can occur in small-boat sailing.
III Fun-fair: a lively & care-free rondo, with several side-shows.
IV   Night: a cool, starry, seascape – the day & its excitements are nearly forgotten.

This document is in the British Library. It was among the pianist's papers.

57   To Barbara Britten

[EWB, *pp. 78–80*]

Hotel Hapsburg, Salzburg, Austria.
Oct. 30th 1934

My dearest Barbara,

I am awfully sorry not to have written before this – if only to answer all your numerous letters you have so kindly sent me. It was a pity that they all were lost in the post. I suppose Sloane Square station pillar-box is continually being robbed. Nevertheless – as Mum is writing this morning I thought I would therein put a letter, and save the colossal expense incurred in sending Briefe[1] to England. I suppose that Mum has told you what a gap it leaves in our monies when we post letters – why, it is cheaper to travel first-class to London than to send a letter there – or nearly.

You must forgive any little foreign idioms that occasionally spring into this letter. I have been talking so much German that it is with much effort that I can write in English. My German is nearly as good as your Swiss was – but can you say: 'Der Metzger wetzt das Metzgemesser!?'

We had a great time in Basel, as Mum will have you told. I think it is a good place, and the people are too awfully hospitable. They simply wouldn't let us do anything ourselves – they almost wanted to feed us. And the food. Ooh the food, the hors d'oeuvres were so good that I invariably had to stop after it, & see delicious soufflés, Florellen, Bombes glacés, whisked away from our very noses.

I agree with you about the Kauffman–Meyer couple. Flausi only turned up for Saturday & Sunday before we left. But Bethley we saw practically every day. I think she's a saint. Just a saint. And Lisel is an awful dear – her husband & child are most amusing. Peterli is the most rampageous kid ever known – but we got on well together, & he taught me alot of bad german.

This is a funny place – quite nice in spots. But the sheets are only as wide as the mattress & (tell it not in Gath) there was last night no paper (Sshh!) in the ((aunt)) – To Resume in loud tones – it will be nice to see the place and see where Mozart was born etc.[2]

Of course the journey yesterday was almost silly it was so lovely – all through the south of Switzerland, and the whole length of the Tyrol.

At first we were springing up all the time & shreiking wildly at each hill – but at the end we were blasé, and murmured – 'not a bad glacier over there – what!' But, I have never seen anything like it.

We go to Wien on Thursday, & then duty starts. I shall have to go round introducing myself to crowds of people, who will never have heard of English music (don't blame them), and who don't speak English.

By-the-way, I shall probably have to come back to London for Nov. 30th & come out to Paris for a few weeks after – as I have a first performance at Wigmore Hall, & even if I don't hear the show, I must see that Betty Humby (pianist) plays the pieces properly.[3] So keep the date.

I hope the job is going well, & that you are settling down more. Bethley sent her love, & we all drank your health on Sunday at her flat – in the presence of Bethley, Flausi, Mde Eisinger, Rosemary same, & a friend. I don't think the Reinharts were there. By-the-way, if you can possibly see Kati Eisinger who is staying in London (have you her address) it would be nice – as they were so good to us.

Tell Beth I'll write when Mum writes – as I can't afford the stamp.

Much love

BENJAMIN

1 A pre-stamped airmail proforma supplied by the post office.

2 Britten was to write to Beth on 4 November, 'It was very interesting seeing where Mozart was born, wrote and lived and all that sort of thing.'

3 English pianist (1908–1958), the second wife of Sir Thomas Beecham, whom she met in the USA during the war. Britten wrote in his diary on 30 November:

Go to Betty Humbys at 10.30 & she really plays the 'Tales' splendidly [. . .] I dash to the Wigmore Hall at 8.45 to hear Betty H. play my pieces well, but the audience doesn't like them very much.

Nor, it seems, did Mr Stainer of the Mendelssohn Foundation, who had heard them earlier on 5 November. See note 1 to Letter 62.

58 To Arthur Benjamin

Hotel Regina, Wien IX, Freiheitsplatz.
Nov. 4th, 1934.

Dear Mr. Benjamin,

I am so sorry not to have written to you before this, but I simply haven't known ever what my address would be for longer than two or three days. I am staying here for about a fortnight.

I do hope that you have not had any bother about those pieces of mine, and that you found a pianist who would play them.[1] He or she cannot have had any bother over them because they are very simple, really. Is it too much to hope that sometime you might play them yourself? If you approve, I should rather like to dedicate them to you, as they are my first real attempt (and probably last!) at piano writing. Betty Humby is playing them at the Wigmore Hall on November 30th, so I have to be back in England for a few days then.

I spent about ten lovely days in Basel, with various friends.[2] The country was simply superb all round and we spent alot of time motoring round about. Musically too the place was interesting – there is a first-rate orchestra, & very good opera too. I met Weingartner,[3] who was very charming, but not very interested in modern music, I felt.

Have you ever been by train from Basel or Zürich to Vienna? I have never known such glorious scenery – right through the Tyrol. We broke our journey at Salzburg, and stayed there for three days before coming on here. I heard a glorious show last night – a really good introduction to Viennese opera – 'Die Fledermaus' really superbly played & sung & acted.[4] Don't be surprised if I write nothing but Vienna Waltzes from now onwards![5] After that, I could only be merely blasé when I heard the Vienna Philharmonic at the top of its form this morning.[6]

I hope you are well. Infinite thanks for what you are doing & have done for me.

Yours sincerely,
BENJAMIN BRITTEN

P.S.   Could you please see that that copy of the piano pieces is sent straightaway to Boosey & Hawkes? Have you thought of a decent title for them? – I am absolutely stuck!

1 George Loughlin played Britten's suite to the Mendelssohn Scholarship Committee on 5 November.

2 On 17 October, the day of his arrival in Basel, Britten records in his diary that he and his mother were met by Bethley Kaufmann-Meyer and her stepfather, Herr Reinhart: 'We are staying with B's parents at Parkweg 18.'

3 In 1934 Weingartner was Director of the Basle Conservatoire and conductor of the concerts of the Allgemeine Musikgesellschaft there. In a letter to Beth of the same day, Britten wrote:

> Weingartner was very nice, but not much help. He was very busy and couldn't (or wouldn't) give me the introductions I wanted; but he gave me a ticket for the rehearsal of a show he was conducting, which was very interesting.

(See EWB, pp. 80–81, for full text)

Mrs Britten, in a postscript (25 October) to a letter to Beth of 24 October, wrote: 'Benjamin has gone for an interview with Weingartner who will advise us where to go and whom to see.' Mrs Britten was clearly in charge of her son's itinerary. Her letters are extensively quoted in EWB, and include many references to the friends encountered on the visits to Basel, Salzburg and Vienna, some of whom were acquaintances made by Britten's parents when on holiday in Europe in previous years. See PFL, plate 42.

4 Britten writes of the performance in his diary:

> [. . .] we go to opera at 7.0 to see Fledermaus (J. Strauss). Superb show – never have I heard an orchestra play like that – incredible rhythm, precision & eagerness. And the singers too. Everything was worthy of the inimitable, delightful work – inspired from the beginning to the end. A marvellous introduction to the Wiener Oper.

5 Cf. the fourth movement of Britten's violin and piano Suite, Op. 6 (1934–5), which is a waltz, and the sixth, 'Wiener Waltzer', variation of the *Bridge Variations*, Op. 10 (1937).

6 Britten's diary for 3 November tells us that he hears 'a rather uninteresting Sinfonia of J.C. Bach [. . .] but it is very beautifully & crisply played' and on 4 November, 'Beethoven's lovely Pastoral Symphony', in which Willem Mengelberg, the conductor, 'rescores [it] in places almost out of recognition', and Mahler's Fourth. Even Mahler, according to Britten, was adjusted by Mengelberg – 'M. of all people knew to the nth degree what he wanted.' None the less Britten 'enjoyed this work enormously – I know it's long – but not too long (except perhaps the 3rd movement) for me. Elizabeth Schumann sings the lovely solo incomparably.' Britten purchased a miniature score of the symphony at this time, and wrote on the flyleaf, 'Benjamin Britten, Wien 1934'. Many years later he corrected it to correspond to Mahler's final version of the work, in preparation for his

performance of the work at the 1961 Aldeburgh Festival. In his 1963
conversation with Murray Schafer, *British Composers in Interview*
(London, Faber and Faber, 1963), p. 119, Britten remarked, 'My
experience of conducting the fourth symphony at Aldeburgh showed
me what a master of form he is, particularly in the first movement
of that great work.'

59 To Grace Williams

[*Boyd, pp. 22–4*]

Hotel Regina, Vienna.
Nov. 8th, 1934.

Meine liebe Grace,

This won't be a very long letter I'm afraid, as I haven't got too
much time for writing – can one ever find time in this place? Well,
we are here, & I hope you arn't too jealous – after all you've been
here an awful lot,[1] & this is my first visit. I am probably not living
the life here that you would enjoy very much – but I am loving
every moment now – and hate the idea of leaving. The friends
we stayed with in Basel were such dears & treated us so well – I've
never had such a time – everyone seems to be wealthy there –
wonderful houses, marvellous food, & they took us everywhere in
glorious cars. Musically too – very good. There is an excellent
opera – I heard four operas very well done, a simply lovely show
of Zauberflöte.[2] One of the people I stayed with knew Weingartner
(who lives there) & I had a very long talk with him & found him
nice & helpful, tho' not interested in modern music at all – in fact
I went to a rehearsal & show of a concert of [Richard] Strauss he
conducted & it was VERY BAD – but the orchestra was first-rate,
& oh – Elizabeth Schumann was a dream.[3] But I am all E.S. mad
now – I heard her here on Sunday – but more of that later. We
stayed in Basel – (talking plenty of German as they speak very little
English) – just a fortnight, & then spent 3 days in lovely Salzburg
on the way here. Of course, after Zauberflöte I was thrilled with
the Mozart relics, & there are many of those there.

You will laugh when you know that we are going to stay on here
for the rest of our stay in Wien – we went round & looked at
pensions, & found out terms – & this Hotel took us for the same
amount as the pensions would – & it is a lovely place, just off the
Ring as you said. Food excellent, & nice quite [*sic*] room to work
in, (& I am working alot)[4] & awfully nice people.

Music:- 3 times to the opera so far – Fledermaus on Saturday,

'Cav. & Pag' (this was substituted for something else at the last
moment), & Falstaff last night.[5] Vienna went mad over this last –
it was a new production & the applause lasted for nearly a quarter
of an hour – Prohaska[6] (from Berlin) & Krauss[7] coming back time
after time. Grace – you must admit that this is great stuff – I don't
expect you to accept early Verdi – but the Requiem, Otello, & this,
you must like – especially when done as it was last night – it was
thrilling. Of course the orchestra – it was the full number last
night – is unsurpassable. I went to a show at the Konzerthaus on
Sunday, & sat next to an awfully nice young Viennese, who told
me lots about everything. Mengelberg, who wasn't too good – his
Pastoral was BAD – conducted. Oh – but the orchestra, it nearly
drove me potty!! Never such tone, & precision, & spirit – the first
horn – well, all the horns – the orchestra played as if it wanted to
play – I felt sorry for you with those London orchestras! Much as
I want to like them, & do admire alot of their playing – it's nothing
like this. However you know it already.

I met a very nice man from the Universal Edition – introduction
from Foss – one Dr. Heinsheimer.[8] I had a long talk with him, in
broken English & German, and he has kept some of my stuff to
show to Erwin Stein whom I am to meet on Saturday.[9]

Of course the Viennese themselves are lovely people. I love going
into shops just to talk to them – to ask how much things cost. I
think they are the kindest, cheerfulest, people I've ever met. And
they are going through pretty dreadful times too, but it doesn't
seem so by their expressions.

And the tragedy now is that we have to leave in less than a
fortnight. Betty Humby is playing those piano pieces of mine at
the Wigmore on Nov. 30th, & though I don't want to hear the
show particularly I must see that she plays them as I want them.
So I've got to be back on Nov. 29th or before – and, having
especially got some travellers' marks for Germany we have got to
go there to Munich – for at least a week. If we don't use these
marks we have to sell them at a great loss. However – I shall
either go by self to Paris for about 10 days before Xmas, to see a
young composer I met in Florence[10] – or save what money I've
got left, & come here again next year – travelling 3rd [class], &
living on nothing when I get here.

Adieu, Grace. I hope everything's going well. Are those Welsh
translations done yet?[11] I hope you're well, & working alot.

                                               Herzliche Grüsse,
                                               BENJAMIN

P.S. I didn't say that the concert on Sunday included the Mahler 4th of which I bought the score. It really is a most lovely work – & was beautifully played – Elizabeth Schumann singing the last lovely solo like a dream. I am longing for chances to hear more Mahler.

1 Grace Williams had spent a year post-College studying with Egon Wellesz on an Octavia Hill Travelling Scholarship (1930–31).

2 On Thursday, 25 October:

Delightful staging & orch. playing quite good. Of course nothing can be said abt. the music. It is just great from beginning to end. Heil, Mozart!

3 The concert, on Saturday 27 October, included Strauss's *Macbeth*, *Ein Heldenleben*, and seven songs in which Elisabeth Schumann was the soloist.

4 While in Basel (on 22 October) Britten began work on a Magnificat for boys' voices, an incomplete sketch of which survives in the Archive, and his Suite, for violin and piano, on 5 November. The final version of the Suite was not to be achieved until June 1935.

5 'Cav. & Pag' [Mascagni's *Cavalleria Rusticana* and Leoncavallo's *Pagliacci*] followed on the 6th:

very fine operas – but after the other things I have seen lately I couldn't make myself thrilled, though I enjoyed them. I fancy the orchestra felt that way too.

And on the 7th, the first night of an enthusiastically received new production of *Falstaff*:

But the greatest honours go to great old Verdi – for his glorious score – humour, tenderness abounding, & the glorious fugue to end. Hats off, Gentlemen!!

6 Jaro Prohaska (1891–1965), Austrian baritone. He sang the title role in *Falstaff*.

7 Clemens Krauss (1893–1954), Austrian conductor. He was Director of the Vienna Opera from 1929 to 1934 and again from 1947 to 1954. He was a close friend and outstanding interpreter of Richard Strauss.

8 Hans W. Heinsheimer (b. 1900), German-born publisher and writer on music, now an American citizen. He was head of the opera department of Universal Edition, the great Viennese publishing house, at the time Britten was visiting Vienna. Britten met Heinsheimer on 5 November: 'He is very nice indeed.' Heinsheimer emigrated to the USA in 1938 and was first employed by Boosey, Hawkes, Belwin, Inc., New York, and then later by G. Schirmer, Inc., where he became director of the symphonic and operatic repertory. In both these capacities Britten was to encounter Heinsheimer again, in New York, when the composer was resident in the USA from 1934 to 1942, and also in later years. Heinsheimer published

three volumes of autobiography: *Menagerie in F sharp* (New York, Doubleday, 1947), *Fanfare for 2 Pigeons* (New York, Garrett Publications, 1949), and *Best Regards to Aida* (New York, Knopf, 1968).

9 The visit to 'Dr. Stein' took place on 10 November: 'He is very nice & interesting.' They met again on the 18th.

Stein was the Austrian-born conductor, editor, publisher and writer (1885–1958). A pupil of Schoenberg, Stein worked for Universal Edition, Vienna, as an editor from 1924 to 1938. He moved to London in 1938 after the Anschluss, to work as an editor at Boosey & Hawkes and became a British citizen, although in 1940 he was for a time interned as an enemy alien on the Isle of Man (see LFBML, pp. 234–7). There was not only a strong professional relationship with Stein, who was to become one of Britten's closest colleagues and influential musical advisers; when Britten and Pears returned to England from America, they formed a very close relationship with Erwin and Sophie Stein and their daughter, Marion, a family relationship, indeed, that reflected some of the qualities of the 'family' that the two men had left behind them in the States (the Mayers) and which doubtless met some of the same needs. (See Introduction, p. 39 and Letter 430.) When, in 1944, a fire destroyed the Steins' flat, Britten and Pears invited them to share their London home at 45A St John's Wood High Street from November 1944 to summer 1946. It was a move that consolidated the personal and professional links and led, in the post-war period, to a continued sharing of London homes. It was Erwin Stein who prepared the vocal scores of *Serenade*, *Peter Grimes* and *Billy Budd*. *The Rape of Lucretia* is dedicated to him and it was probably for Stein's sixtieth birthday, in November 1945, that Britten composed his unpublished song, 'Birthday Song for Erwin', with words by Ronald Duncan. See also the Earl of Harewood, 'In memoriam: Erwin Stein 1885–1958', in TBB, pp. 160–64.

10 Rudolph Holzmann (b. 1910), German-born composer, who had studied with Hermann Scherchen in 1933. Britten had attended a performance of Holzmann's Suite for piano, trumpet, saxophone and bass clarinet at the ISCM Festival at Florence on 3 April. (The saxophonist was Sigurd Rascher, whose path was to cross Britten's in America, in 1939.) Britten and Holzmann met on 28 November when Britten was in Paris on his return home: 'Rudolph Holzman comes to see me – he is a young composer I met in Florence.' For political reasons, Holzmann was described in the Festival programme as 'Tedesco indipendente' – 'independent German'.

11 Perhaps of Williams's *Welsh Oxen Songs*.

60 To G.H. Hatchman[1]
Performing Right Society

Hotel Regina, Wien IX, Freiheitsplatz.
Nov. 18th, 1934.

Dear Sir,

I am sorry I have not sent the receipt of the Certificate of
Membership, sent me in October in Basel, before this.[2]   I have
been waiting until I was able to give you further particulars of
works of mine. I am afraid that I forgot to bring forms to use in
notifying you of works of mine to be controlled by the Performing
Right Society; but the following are the particulars:

Suite for Pianoforte Solo. 'Holiday Tales'.

Pieces included: (1) Early Morning Bathe. (2) Yachting. (3) Fun
Fair (4) Night. Time in performance of each piece respectively
(1) 2 mins., (2) 4–5 mins., (3) 2–3 mins., (4) 6–7 mins. Publisher
is Messrs. Boosey & Hawkes.

I send you details now as I think there is a performance of this
work at the Wigmore Hall on Nov. 30th, & it is not certain whether
I'll be in England by that time.

Yours truly,
BENJAMIN BRITTEN

1 G.H. Hatchman (1892–1952), Secretary of the Performing Right
Society from 1929, and General Manager from 1951.
2 Britten had been admitted to membership of the PRS on 13 September. His name appeared in a list of new members in the *Performing
Right Gazette*, October 1934 (see p. 428).

61 To Grace Williams
[*Picture postcard: Vienna; Vienna Opera House
Boyd, p. 25*]

Hotel Regina
[19 November 1934]

This is just to make you jealous. I have seen Robert & his friend,
& found them awfully nice.[1] I spent yesterday afternoon with them
& family in the Holzhauslein, if you remember it – they all send
viele Grüsse to you. We've got to leave here on Wednesday, &
am sick abt. it. But I'm coming back – soon & oft. Meistersinger,

Siegfried, last week & Götterdämmerung to-night!!!² So glad about your overture & B.B.C.³ See you soon – keep Nov. 30th evening.⁴

BENJAMIN

We go to Pension Romana, Romana Akadamiestr. 7, Munich, on Wed.

1 Robert Hille, 'a friend of Grace', and 'an American friend of his', were first met by Britten on Saturday, 17 November. (Not 'Lille' as Boyd has it, p. 25, note 18.)

2 Britten saw *Götterdämmerung* on 19 November: 'The scenery was fine, tho the end was distinctly lame for the music, but then what wouldn't be?' On the 15th, *Siegfried*: 'A lovely show . . . And the music. . . . . !!!!' On the 13th, *Meistersinger*: 'The five hours of the music didn't seem as many minutes; the incredible vitality, modernity, richness in lovely melody, humour, pathos in fact every favourable quality.'

3 See Boyd, p. 25, note 20. It seems that the Concert Overture that Williams had submitted for the *Daily Telegraph* competition in 1933 had been accepted for performance by the BBC.

4 When Britten's piano suite, *Holiday Tales*, was to be performed at the Wigmore Hall.

62 To J.F.R. Stainer
Mendelssohn Foundation

173, Cromwell Road, S.W. 5.

Dec. 1st, 1934.

Dear Mr. Stainer,

Thank you for your letter, which I am sorry I have not been able to answer before this, having only just returned from the continent.

I am afraid it causes me some embarrassment. Had I been fortunate enough to have been awarded the Scholarship, it would have given me great pleasure to be known as the 'Mendelssohn Scholar'. But it would appear that the Committee has overlooked the unpleasant circumstances of the 1932 Competition. And although I have gladly accepted the small sums, kindly granted to me, I do feel that the title 'Mendelssohn Scholar' should go only to the recipient of the full award of £150 a year. If my acceptance of the title is to be made a condition of the next grant, I am afraid that I must respectfully refuse it. I trust you will understand this.

I need scarcely add how much I regret that you found, as you say, my pieces outside your comprehension. But perhaps you will be glad to know that, when they were played at the Wigmore Hall last Friday, the audience seemed appreciative.[1]

Yours sincerely,
BENJAMIN BRITTEN

1 Britten refers to the first public performance of his *Holiday Tales* on 30 November, which Stainer and his colleagues had had played to them on 5 November. The critic in *The Times*, 4 December, commented:

in the appreciation of period and style, [Miss Humby] showed born intelligence and feeling. Britten's clever pieces have as their titles 'Early Morning Bathe', 'Yachting', 'Fun Fair' and 'Night' which, with the possible exception of No. 2, they live up to as good illustrations. As music they are well founded in that they avoid formulae and yet have a sturdy unity and structure of their own.

63 To G.H. Hatchman
Performing Right Society

21, Kirkley Cliff Road, Lowestoft.
Jan. 1st, 1935.

Dear Mr. Hatchman,

I am in somewhat of an awkward position as regards to the Oxford Press and performing rights.

Before I was elected to be a member of the P.R.S. this autumn, I had submitted a work to the O.U.P. Since then Mr. Foss has decided to accept it. I have explained to him the position, and have expressed my wish to retain all performing, broadcasting & mechanical rights – no agreement being signed yet of course. He has refused my request as regards to the broadcasting and mechanical rights.

If I take the work away from him of course there is the possibility of not being able to find another publisher – although there is a chance of the contrary. On the other hand the works are only school songs, or songs suitable for smaller choirs[1] – so I don't think that the mechanical rights or even broadcasting rights would enter much into it.

But I should very much like to know what you advise, if you

could be so good. Mr. Frank Bridge advised me to write to you.[2]
Thanking you in anticipation,

Yours sincerely,
BENJAMIN BRITTEN

1 Britten refers to his *Friday Afternoons*.

   Hatchman's reply has not survived, though Britten's diary for 8
January 1935 indicates the advice he received:

write to Foss – deciding to let him have my 12 School songs – but this is
my last work outside the P.R.S. – the O.U.P. not being members.

2 Bridge was a prominent member of the PRS Council.

64 To Hubert Foss
Oxford University Press

21, Kirkley Cliff Road, Lowestoft.
Jan. 8th 1935.

Dear Mr. Foss,

I am sorry not to have answered your letter, about my school
songs, before this, but this is not the kind of question to be settled
in a day.[1]

What I have come to the conclusion is, that I must make up my
mind about the principle of performing rights at an early age. I
have cast my lot with the P.R.S., and I feel it right to stick to them.[2]

But, as I had submitted these songs to you before I actually
became a member of the society, and as I should very much like
to have them in your catalogue I have decided to leave them with
you, together with all the performing rights. It is a great mistake
to separate performing and broadcasting rights, I feel, especially as
the P.R.S. make no such distinction between them.

In future, however, I must have all my works controlled by the
P.R.S. as a matter of principle. I appreciate enormously the
interest you have shown in producing my work; although I feel
compelled to say that the rumours I have heard of your great
disappointment in the way that the 'Boy was born', was going,
have rather hurt me.[3]   After all, it hasn't been out a year yet –
and I notice that it isn't even advertised on the back of my 'Simple
Symphony' among the other O.U.P. choral works. But I hope that
the long article on the work in a recent 'Observer'[4] will do some
good.

I have thought much about the title of the songs. 'Friday Afternoons' I think may stand, but I see your point about the sub-title. The trouble is that 'school-songs' is what they really are! The only other thing I can think of is 'Choral Songs' (but that might put the solo singers off) or 'Twelve youthful songs' – or something like that. When would be the earliest to get them out? The earlier the better I feel, especially as they have been hanging about so long.

I shall be sending back the first proofs of the 'Te Deum' very soon. Have you fixed anything about a show of that, yet? I like the idea of St. Pauls, as you once suggested.

I hope you are well, and have had a good Christmas. We have had rather a quiet one – but good on the whole.

How is the family?

Yours sincerely,
BENJAMIN BRITTEN

P.S.   When does the Simple Symphony come out? Have you fixed any performance of that?

1 Foss had written on 19 December 1934:

We are going ahead with your Twelve Songs for Schools, and propose to experiment by issuing them in piano book at 3/- [shillings] with voice parts at 9d. [old pence] We proposed to pay you a royalty of $12\frac{1}{2}$%.

In this same letter, Foss included a report on the songs by W.G. Whittaker who presumably advised OUP on their choral publications. He reported on *Friday Afternoons* as follows:

These are very jolly and I think your idea of a complete volume for a start is good. But I think the title will restrict their sale. Some are not particularly good for schools. You won't find many teachers willing to use those crunching discords which occur in some. Moreover, bodies like girls' clubs, Women's Institutes, and women's choirs generally, would not use them if they were labelled 'school'. Why not another title?

2 It was not until January 1936 that the *Performing Right Gazette* (then the official organ of the Performing Right Society) was able to announce that OUP had been elected to membership. In the same issue (5/7) it was announced that among the new members who had joined the Society since July 1934 was 'Mr Edward B. Britten (Composer)' (along with Mr Arthur L. Benjamin, Noël Coward and E. J. Moeran). It was almost two decades before the Society was able to convince some major publishers to make common cause with the composers and other publishing colleagues who had already acknowledged the importance of the Society's control of the perform-

ing right in the works of its members. 'The new elections', said the Editorial in the *Gazette*,

will be a matter of considerable satisfaction to the existing composer and author members who have works published by firms belonging to the incoming group. Hitherto these composers and authors have for the most part been unable to secure any income from general performing rights in respect of such works, since they had in many cases assigned the rights to the publishers, whose policy was to allow performances (other than broadcasting) to be given free.

It is important to spell out this bit of PRS history, without which it is difficult to understand the points Britten – already a committed PRS member – is making to Foss. As the letter shows, Britten was ready to compromise in the case of *Friday Afternoons*, but thereafter 'I must have all my works controlled by the P.R.S. as a matter of principle.' This seems to have been unacceptable to Foss who wrote in reply on 23 January:

And now about 'Friday Afternoons'. I believe in them and I want to publish them but I am nervous that they will not immediately find a market, for none of these outstanding new things do. Now, owing to this performing right situation I am faced with the possibility of bearing a loss on these songs which I can never recover on other works of yours. In other words, by publishing them I should really be helping your future publishers and that hardly seems fair to us.

The cards are all on the table now, and I think that you must choose for I stick to my original offer and will put them through if you really want me to.

I am leaving for Scotland. If you decide to take the songs away, and it seems the logical thing to do, my secretary will send you the MSS back on your instruction.

Friday Afternoons was eventually published, in 1936, by Boosey & Hawkes, with whom Britten was to conclude a publishing agreement on 3 January 1936. There can be little doubt that the difference of opinion with OUP about the 'performing right situation', as Foss described it, must have contributed to the youthful composer's decision finally to look elsewhere for a publisher. See also Cyril Ehrlich, *Harmonious Alliance, A History of the Performing Right Society* (Oxford, Oxford University Press, 1989). Plate I in his study reproduces Britten's application for membership.

3 To this Foss replied in his letter of 23 January:

You mustn't on any account imagine that I am disappointed with you or the work because 'The Boy' has not sold. My railings are against the public and the musicians, and I am still unable to understand why an event of the importance of its creation should leave the practising musicians unmoved.

4 A considered review of the first concert performance of *A Boy was Born* on 17 December 1934 by A.H. Fox Strangways appeared in the *Observer*, 23 December. The review was reprinted under the title

'Christmas' in *Music Observed*, edited by Steuart Wilson (London, Methuen, 1936). Fox Strangways concludes his article:

And a word about the composer: not his personality, of which I know nothing, but his music, which tells us all we need to know. It has one mark of mastery – endless invention and facility. He takes what he wants, and does not trouble about what other people have thought well to take. He rivets attention from the first note onwards: without knowing in the least what is coming, one feels instinctively that this is music it behoves one to listen to, and each successive moment strengthens that feeling. He inspires confidence; there is no wondering what is coming next: whatever that may be, and whether we 'like' it or not, we shall agree with it.

65   To Grace Williams
[*Boyd, pp. 25–7*]

21 Kirkley Cliff Road, Lowestoft.
Jan. 16th, 1935.

Meine liebe Grace,

Es tut mir sehr leid, dass ich nicht vorher geschrieben habe.[1] But I have really been very busy – and so have you, by Jove! I am really getting quite tired of the name G.W. in the Radio Times. I heard your first show[2] – stayed in especially to hear it – and also the Suite[3] from the W. [West] Regional, in sections; but really the thing came over so badly that I can't attempt to judge it – all I seem to remember, between grunts and whistles and shrieks is the diminished fifth B–F – But I remember some exciting wind passages in the last movement. It is going to be done at Iris Lemare's show? When? I must definitely come along to hear it.[4]

Re – the first concert – R.V.W. I know is a very nice man, but he shouldn't conduct. It was <u>hopeless</u>. The concert came over quite well; it wasn't the wireless's fault. But, oh, the ragged entries, the half-hearted & doubtful playing – and the beastly tone. I know I have heard the Vienna Phil; but I was also listening to the Basel Symphony to-night – under some quite unknown man – and it was <u>streets</u> ahead of that show. I know that you'll fly at me – but I loathed the Machonchy work. It may have been badly played – but it wasn't only that. I was bored stiff with it, and it hasn't left any impression on me save that of boredom. Sorry! I'm probably wrong, & I am anyway awfully pleased that the Int. Festival [ISCM] have chosen a work of hers. Will she be able to go? What is this work like, if you know it?[5]

Anyhow after her business, your two Psalms were a great relief.

I know they arn't your best work, but they (no. 1 especially) contain some good stuff. I must borrow the orch. score when I come to town. There are things I want to know. After you of course the music in the programme was finished. I struggled for about three or four minutes with R.O. Morris & then switched off. I tried to be politely interested in Robin Milford, but failed utterly. The fifteen biblical songs[6] of R.V.W. finished me entirely; that 'pi' and artificial mysticism combined with, what seems to me, technical incompetence, sends me crazy. I have never felt more depressed for English music than after that programme – putting your effort aside – especially when I felt that that is what the public – no, <u>not</u> the public, the critics love and praise.

— — —

I was terribly sorry to have to miss the Overture[7] last night. I always have to go to an orchestra in Bungay near here on Wednesday evenings,[8] and at that time we were actually stranded in a car without any water, and in a thick fog. How did it go? Charles W.[9] is at least a musician, whether he can conduct or not.

And now – when is your next show? What kind of a Christmas did you have? Ours was pretty quiet, rather naturally. Now I am waiting for Adrian Boult to return so I can be examined to see if I can be any use on the B.B.C.[10]   Until then I seem to be spending my whole time correcting proofs – and what a job! I am dead sick of it – after four long works to be done.[11] And much more of it in sight, too.

You'll have to excuse this letter. I am writing on my knee, and the wireless is making a distracting noise in my ear. But it is warm in here, and the other rooms in the house are draughty to say the least of it, in this wind.

O for Wien! But I have a lovely record of Elizabeth Schumann in some Fledermaus solos.[12]

How goes life with you?

BENJAMIN B

1 'I am very sorry that I have not written to you before.'

2 A broadcast on 28 December, when the BBC Symphony Orchestra and Wireless Chorus had been conducted by Vaughan Williams. The programme included Elizabeth Maconchy's *Comedy Overture*, Grace Williams's Two Psalms for soprano and chamber orchestra (Megan Thomas – soprano), R.O. Morris's Concertino, Robin Milford's Two Pieces for orchestra, 'Prelude on St Columba' and 'May in the Green-

wood', and Vaughan Williams's *Five Mystical Songs* (with Roy Henderson – baritone). (See Boyd, p. 26.)

3 Williams's Suite for chamber orchestra, broadcast on 14 January by the BBC Western Studio Orchestra, conducted by Reginald Redman, in a programme of unpublished works by Welsh musicians.

4 The work was performed at a Macnaghten–Lemare Concert at the Mercury Theatre on 4 February under Iris Lemare, in a programme which included *Fra Lippo Lippi* (1934) for tenor and chamber orchestra by Alan Rawsthorne, and Elizabeth Maconchy's *Great Agrippa* (1933), a ballet for fourteen instruments and percussion. Britten writes in his diary:

Grace Williams comes to dinner at Burleigh House where I am staying, & after we both go to the Mercury Theatre to the Iris Lemare concert. Orch. Nothing of much interest, except a Suite of Grace, which has some good things in – esp. 1st & 2nd mov. & a ballet on an amusing subject – Great Agrippa [. . .].

5 Maconchy's *Prelude, Interlude and Fugue* for two violins was performed at the 1935 ISCM Festival.

6 A mischievous multiplication which registers Britten's disapprobation of the work.

7 The broadcast of Williams's Concert Overture on 16 January. Either Britten misdated this letter or, as Boyd suggests, interrupted the writing of it and continued the next day, the 17th.

8 An amateur orchestra at nearby Bungay with which Britten rehearsed once a week on Wednesdays. This was an appointment that had probably come about through Mr Coleman, the organist at St John's, Lowestoft. Britten's diary for 15 January records:

Spend most of morning, aft, & evening arranging Strauss Dui Du Waltz [from *Die Fledermaus*] for the B.B.B.B. (Benj. Britten Bungay Band, alias the Hag's Band).

The occasion itself on the 16th seems to have been a disappointment and thwarted by fog:

Charles Coleman takes me over to Bungay rehearsal at 5.30. Owing to fog very few are there – 9 only – and the playing is execrable. It is no use trying to rehearse them – the only advice worth giving them is 'Go away & learn your instruments.' Dreadful journey back – running out of water, in the thick fog. However a good dinner, and the Mahler gram. records (Kindertotenlieder) restore my faith in life.

These Wednesdays were not shining musical events but Britten consoled himself with the thought that they gave him experience of conducting.

9 Charles Woodhouse (1879–1939), English violinist, orchestral leader

and versatile musician, who evidently conducted Williams's Overture.

10 Britten was exploring the possibilities of employment at the BBC. His leaving the College and the death of his father the previous April obviously combined to make the seeking of employment an urgent matter. Nothing finally came of the approach to the BBC, but there is a certain irony that it had to be made through the conductor about whom Britten had such unambiguously hostile feelings. On 8 February Britten had an interview at the BBC with Owen Mase and, his diary records, a 'short one with A. Boult & L. Woodgate. There is a probability of me coming there for a whole time job! Ugh!' On 25 April Britten met Owen Mase again at the BBC, and left, it seems with a negative impression: '[. . .] I shan't be there for a while, I fear.' But in May his fortunes were to change (see Letter 69).

11 Among them proofs of the *Sinfonietta*, the *Phantasy* oboe quartet and *Holiday Tales* [*Diary*].

12 'Mein Herr Marquis' (Act II) and 'Spiel' ich die Unschuld vom Lande' (Act III) from Strauss's operetta, recorded by Elisabeth Schumann and the Vienna State Opera Orchestra conducted by Karl Alwin on HMV E 545. Britten's copy of the gramophone record is in the Archive.

Sunday, 20 January 1935

[. . .] Usual Sunday, long walk with Beth in morning. Wireless, reading, letters, work at other times of day. F.B. conducts a lovely B.B.C. Orch. concert at 9.20. Haydn 99 Symphony – v. beautifully played – Schönberg's lovely Verklärte Nacht – which the strings played splendidly. A rousing show of his own thrilling Enter Spring with the heavenly tune in it. And a brisk finale in Coq D'or Wedding March. Act.[ually] the hall's a bit too resonant, but otherwise it was a fabulous concert.

These silhouettes of Bridge rehearsing the studio (Maida Vale) concert Britten
describes in his diary (above) were done by Marjorie Fass on 21 January, from line
drawings made the day before and now in the Archive

66 To Leslie Woodgate
BBC

21, Kirkley Cliff Road, Lowestoft.
Feb. 25th 1935.

Dear Mr. Woodgate,

I wonder if you could let me know the date on which you propose
to do my two part songs 'I lovd a [lass]' & 'Lift Boy'?[1] I have to
make some arrangements & it would simplify matters a bit if you
could let me know when you want me to come and smite the
piano – rehearsals too I suppose??

Nothing fixed I suppose about a 'Boy was born'?[2]

Boosey & Hawkes are bringing out a very simple 8 part song –
that I wrote ages ago in my youth – which might amuse you. But
as you set it yourself, I believe (A Hymn to the Virgin) you will
hate it.[3] Still I'll bring it along some time.

How are you? Working abit I suppose.

Best wishes,
BENJAMIN BRITTEN

1 Britten (at the piano) rehearsed the Two Part-songs with Woodgate and the Wireless Singers at the BBC on 27 March, in a programme of contemporary British composers which included Ireland's 'Twilight Night', Vaughan Williams's 'Fain would I change that note'' and Whittaker's 'Old Skinflint'.

2 See note 6 to Letter 73.

3 Britten's *A Hymn to the Virgin* had been composed in 1930 (while at school at Gresham's) and revised in 1934. Woodgate himself had composed a setting of the same text for baritone, men's voices, strings, piano and organ (published in 1923 by Stainer and Bell). On 14 October Britten writes in his diary:

Dash back to B.B.C. in time to hear Leslie Woodgate do my Hymn to the Virgin – with 2nd choir singing thro' echo room – which really sounds lovely.

67 To J.F.R. Stainer
Mendelssohn Foundation

21, Kirkley Cliff Road, Lowestoft.
March 3rd, 1935

Dear Mr. Stainer,

I have just received a further cheque for £25 from Mr. Benecke. This, and the fact that I have heard nothing further from the committee, leads me to think that there is no objection to my last letter to you, so I am forthwith paying it into the bank, together with the previous cheque which I have held over since writing to you. If there is any objection to this, could you please let me know forthwith?[1]

I am very grateful indeed to the committee for their generous grant, and I hope you will convey my great thanks to them.

Yours sincerely,
BENJAMIN BRITTEN

1 The Committee's response led Britten to write in his diary on 6 March:

Mendelssohn Committee have capitulated completely – I now need not be called Mend. Scholar, can keep my £50 – & am requested to 'let bygones be bygones' and try again for the Schol. in June – I don't know yet.

Britten was to make no further submissions.

68   To Sylvia Spencer[1]

Clive House School, Prestatyn, N. Wales.
After to-day (17th) until Monday (22nd)
c/o Frank Bridge, Esq., Friston Field, Nr. Eastbourne, Sussex.
Monday (22nd) – Wednesday (24th)
at Elphinstone House, Hastings, Sussex.[2]
April 17th, 1935

My dear Sylvia,

Of course you are nothing but a waster of other people's valuable time. Talk of dashing a piece off in five minutes! I have spent at least three weeks worrying [at] the blessed thing – with the result that I have written two insect pieces[3] – sketched three more – sketched the scoring for accompaniment of string orchestra. In fact out of a simple little piece for oboe & piano has grown (or is growing) a large and elaborate suite for oboe & strings.[4] It is all your fault, of course; I didn't want to write the blessed thing – I am supposed to be (a) finishing a string quartet[5] (b) finishing a violin & piano suite (c) writing an orchestral work for Norwich Festival 1936[6] (d) writing an orchestral work for Robert Mayer . . . [7]

Anyhow, here are the oboe parts of the two completed pieces – I'll send along the piano parts when they are copied out nicely. Choose which you want to do at Peckham or Clapham or wherever you are playing. If you choose the 'Grasshopper' – you might look at the other one sometime – because I shall want you to play the whole lot sometime if you will. In this second one (Wasp) the notes don't matter nearly as much as the speed – which must be pretty hectic. I don't think the 'g-h' [Grasshopper] will bother you at all – unless I have written some impossible things in the 'più animato' (in the middle).[8]

Look here – I shall be in town from Thursday to Saturday (25th-27th) – can you spare me an afternoon with your oboe to go through the things & alter what is necessary? If you can let me have a card at one of the above addresses, we perhaps can fix something. I'll bring the piano parts along then.

Have a good Easter. Are you going away?

Yours,
BENJAMIN BRITTEN

1 Sylvia Spencer (1909–1978), English oboist, studied at the College, 1923–30. Spencer, with members of the Griller Quartet, gave an early

performance of the *Phantasy* Quartet on 4 December 1934. Britten recorded the occasion in his diary:

[. . .] go to concert of Contemporary Music Society. Sylvia Spencer & the Grillers play my Oboe quartet very beautifully, not perfectly, but with imagination and spirit. It goes down well.

She also played for Britten in some of the film recording sessions at the GPO Film Unit in 1935.

2 Britten was staying with his old friend from South Lodge days, Francis Barton.

3 'Wasp' (completed 13 April) and 'Grasshopper' (15 April). These were first performed at the Royal Northern College of Music, Manchester, as part of a Sylvia Spencer Commemoration Concert, on 7 March 1979, by Janet Craxton and Margot Wright. A performance by Spencer herself remains untraced, although she and the composer did rehearse the pieces, as Britten's diary entry for 26 April 1935 tells us: '3.0 to Brechin Place to rehearse Grasshopper & Wasp with Sylvia Spencer – she is fine & I am very pleased with the little pieces.' These were posthumously published in 1980 (London, Faber Music). The sketches for the 'three more' mentioned by Britten have not survived.

4 This did not materialize, nor do any sketches exist. Britten's *Temporal Variations* (1936) for oboe and piano (see note 1 to Letter 96 and note 8 to Letter 248) was originally entitled 'Temporal Suite'. Was *Temporal Variations* the eventual product of the composer planning, in April 1935, 'a large & elaborate suite for oboe & strings'?

5 This was the wholesale revision of the earlier and incomplete 'Go play, boy, play' string quartet suite (1933), three movements of which were performed in 1936 as *Three Divertimenti* and posthumously published in 1983 (London, Faber Music). Britten began work on his revision on 30 March at Lowestoft and the *Divertimenti* were given their first performance by the Stratton String Quartet at the Wigmore Hall on 25 February 1936, when Britten wrote in his diary:

The show of quartet is at Wigmore Hall at 5.30 in a so-called Patron's Fund Festival. The Stratton play my pieces, a quintet of Bax & a Brahms – which I do not stay to hear, feeling as I do about Brahms at the moment. The pieces don't go nearly as well as in the morning, and are a dismal failure. Received with sniggers & pretty cold silence. Why, I don't know. Perhaps they are worse than I had hoped. They are not great music – but I did feel that they are interesting & quite brilliant. Perhaps even now they need a little more boiling – but it may be best if they hop right into the fire! very depressing [. . .]

The next day Britten wrote:

As I expected the Telegraph (J.A. Westrup) gives me a stinking notice on quartet & on my works in general. Tho' Edwin Evans is nice in the Daily

Mail – I feel so depressed – in spite of myself – that working on the Russian Funeral March for Alan Bush is almost impossible. I feel like a spanked school-boy – exactly as I used to feel after a jaw – I remember perfectly. It's all silly, as I don't usually care a jot for critics least of all J.A.W.

J.A. Westrup (see note 4 to Letter 118) wrote in the *Daily Telegraph* of 26 February:

Benjamin Britten's 'Three Divertimenti' for string quartet, played by the Stratton Quartet, were depressing rather than diverting. As in some other works from the same pen, there was much play with technical devices, but little solid matter to justify the escapades. Mr Britten will have proved his worth as a composer when he succeeds in writing music that relies less on superficial effect.

The critic of *The Times*, 28 February, took a similar line:

The first of the Tuesday evening concerts of chamber music sponsored by the Royal College of Music Patron's Fund included the first performance of three divertimenti for string quartet by Benjamin Britten and four pastorales for tenor voice and pianoforte by Herbert Murrill.

Britten's three movements are slight by definition – a march, a valse and a burlesque. Indeed the title of the last might have been equally well applied to the other two. The composer shows at the beginning his admiration for Bartók's string quartets, and there is a great deal of clever writing, especially in the ghost of a valse. The divertimenti were admirably played by the Stratton Quartet [. . .].

Westrup's notice stayed with Britten as a leading example of the adverse criticism by which he was discouraged as a young composer. Edwin Evans, however, described the *Three Divertimenti* as 'clever, brittle music with a vein of parody'.

6 What Britten eventually composed for this occasion was the orchestral song-cycle, *Our Hunting Fathers*.

7 German-born patron and benefactor of music (1879–1985). He founded the Robert Mayer Children's Concerts and later the organization 'Youth and Music'. He was knighted in 1939. The orchestral work Britten mentions never materialized nor do any sketches survive. In 1939 Mayer was to approach Britten again about the possibility of writing 'a short work for the Children's Concert movement'; see Letter 180. This proposal also came to nothing.

8 A rapid, staccato passage including some low and technically more demanding tessitura.

Monday, 6 May 1935
[*Lowestoft*]

The Jubilee[1] is frightfully lucky in having such a heavenly day. We listen to broadcasts of a bit of the procession & service, but it's not thrilling. I am up pretty early, trying to think – but no luck all day. Mum hires a car for us, & we all three take out lunch to Sotterly – & lie baking in the sun. In aft. we go to Chartres – have some tennis with Beth & after tea with Clive C. Only see Clive & Mrs. C. – the others jubilating in the park with the villagers. Back (me driving part of way) by 7.30. Latish supper. Talk & late bed after packing & a 'phone talk with Kerstie.[2]

1 The anniversary of the accession to the throne of King George V in 1910. On 4 May Britten had written in his diary: 'We're having fights about decorating our house for Jubilee (as everyone else); at present I don't think its right – too nationalistic'; and on the 5th, 'After helping Beth decorate house a bit with flags – (under duress); she & I have a walk with John Pounder up fish market.'

2 Mrs Kersty Chamberlain, one of the founders of the Bungay Orchestra which Britten had conducted in 1934.

69 To Grace Williams
[*Postcard: Boyd, p. 30*]

173, Cromwell Rd., S.W.5.
[15 May 1935]

Sorry I didn't have time to 'phone you. I worked night & day from Tuesday to Thursday – music arrived from your copyist yesterday at 1.45 (he was v. good) & we started recording at Blackheath abt. 3.30–9.30. It was good fun tho' & went pretty well – you must see the film when it comes out![1] I am going to Lowestoft to-day until Thursday next. I'll 'phone then. Give my love to Furtwängler on Monday.[2] Many thanks for restoring my confidence on Tuesday! & also for getting Percy Rowe[3] for me.

BENJAMIN

1 Britten's search for employment ended with the beginning of his association with the GPO Film Unit, the studios of which were at Blackheath. The composer was brought to the attention of the Unit's resident sound-expert, Alberto Cavalcanti (1897–1982), by Edward Clark. According to his secretary, Clark was pestered by Bridge to help Britten (see also DMBA, p. 94, n. 1). The film to which he refers was *The King's Stamp*, directed by William Coldstream (see note 1 to Letter 73), the artist who enjoyed a brief flirtation with documentary films during the mid-thirties. *The King's Stamp* concerned the design

and printing of the King George V Silver Jubilee commemorative postage stamp, and featured the stamp's designer, Barnett Friedmann. See PR pp. 48–69 and 434–8.

Britten recalled his days at the GPO Film Unit in a 1946 Schools' Broadcast, *How to become a composer*, subsequently published in the *Listener*, 7 November 1946:

When I was nineteen I had to set about earning my living. I was determined to do it through composition: it was the only thing I cared about and I was sure it was possible. My first opportunity was the chance of working in a film company. This was much to my taste although it meant a great deal of hard work. I had to work quickly, to force myself to work when I didn't want to, and to get used to working in all kinds of circumstances. The film company I was working for was not a big commercial one: it was a documentary company and had little money. I had to write scores not for large orchestras but for not more than six or seven players, and to make these instruments make all the effects that each film demanded. I also had to be ingenious and try to imitate, not necessarily by musical instruments, but in the studio, the natural sounds of everyday life. I well remember the mess we made in the studio one day when trying to fit an appropriate sound to shots of a large ship unloading in a dock. We had pails of water which we slopped everywhere, drain pipes with coal slipping down them, model railways, whistles and every kind of paraphernalia we could think of.

As well as music for films I discovered that radio and theatres sometimes wanted incidental music for their plays. It was also extremely good practice for me as a young composer to take exact instructions from the directors and producers of the plays and to try and please them.

2 *Tristan* was to be conducted by Furtwängler that evening at Covent Garden.

3 The copyist referred to earlier in this letter, and recommended to Britten by Williams.

70 To Remo Lauricella

21, Kirkley Cliff Road,
Lowestoft.
August 1st 1935

Dear Remo,

I wonder if you remember saying, not long ago, that if you had the chance you would come down here and give a joint recital with me – for expenses only.[1] I have just been asked to give a short one (from one hour to an hour & a half) on October 4th this year – for expenses only – and I wonder if the idea appeals to you. Of course it is good advertisement – & if everything went well, I am sure you would be asked down again for the normal fee. Can you let me know what you feel about it?

If you like the idea – & it might be quite amusing – we could meet in August sometime and discuss the programme. What I suggest would be – some classical sonata (duet), some shorter modern work for violin and piano (actually one or two movements from my new suite would fit in), then a group of solos from you, and then ditto from me.[2]

I shall be coming to town somewhere about August 20th for a few days, and then I come to town permanently again in September when we could rehearse.

Please let me know as soon as possible, as I must make other arrangements if this isn't attractive to you.

Antonio Brosa is playing my suite marvellously – we played it to Eugene Goossens the other day. We are going to broadcast it very soon, I think.[3] Boosey & Hawkes are publishing it.[4]

Let me know soon about Oct. 4th.

Yours,
BENJAMIN BRITTEN

1 A concert at the Royal Hotel, Lowestoft, on 29 November (not 4 October), in aid of the Lowestoft Association for the Care of Girls (one of Mrs Britten's good causes).

2 Lauricella and Britten played jointly the Sonata in A by Handel, three movements from Britten's Suite, Op. 6 – the March, Lullaby and Waltz – and Nardini's Concerto in E minor. Britten's solos were Beethoven's Six Variations in F; Ravel's *Jeux d'eau*; Chopin's Nocturne in F sharp and 'Funfair', from Britten's *Holiday Diary*. Lauricella contributed solos by Dvořák–Kreisler, Brahms–Hochstein and Kreisler. As encores, Britten played a polka and waltz by Johann Strauss, and Lauricella, Kreisler's arrangement of a number from de Falla's *La Vida breve*. Britten wrote in his diary: 'Over 100 there – & it goes really well, tho' personally I suffer badly from nerves esp. in my solos [. . .]'. The next day, 'Spend most of day walking (& talking Violin!) & showing R.L. the town, fish markets, sea and beach.' Lauricella vividly remembers this tour which started before dawn, and in numbing cold, in order to watch the return of the fishing fleets to harbour, an event that Britten insisted his friend should witness.

Among Lauricella's personal memories of Britten is a vivid one of the youthful composer riding on public transport with a roll of manuscript paper in his pocket, on which from time to time he would scribble down any musical ideas that came to him.

> BENJAMIN   BRITTEN   (Piano)
>
> and
>
> REMO   LAURICELLA   (Violin)
>
> *November 29th, 1935.*

3 The broadcast was given on 13 March 1936 on the BBC National
Programme (see PFL, plate 78). See also note 1 to Letter 76.

4 Britten was correcting proofs of the Suite on the day before the
concert was given, as his diary entry for 28 November makes clear.

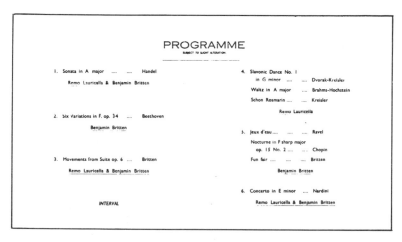

The Lowestoft recital, 29 November 1935

Friday, 2 August 1935

Final version of boys song in morning.[1] Before a bathe & read
(Fascism, by Palme Dutt)[2] in sun on Beach. [. . .] Letters after
dinner, & try to talk communism with Mum, but it is impossible
to say anything to anyone brought up in the old order without
severe ruptions. The trouble is that fundamentally she agrees with
me & won't admit it.

1 'Begone, dull care', the first song from *Friday Afternoons* which Britten
had begun to compose on 30 July – 'I sketch yet another school song
in morning – a fraction more successful if anything – this in morning
and aft.' – and had continued the following day – 'do abit more to
school song – I think it'll do'.

2 (Rajini) Palme Dutt (1896–1974) was a well-known communist analyst and propagandist. He has been described by Hugh Thomas as the 'outstanding English communist intellectual' of his generation. His book on fascism was published in 1934. It is significant to note that whereas up to this date Britten's diaries have been innocent of political comment or indeed observations on international events – almost the only exception is his recording the R.101 (dirigible) disaster on 5 October 1930 – from this point onwards politics and international events increasingly impinge. This must reflect the influence of Britten's new politically minded and politically aware friends with whom he was working at the GPO Film Unit, Auden especially (see note 3 to Letter 71).

Thursday, 3 October 1935
[*London*]

After having appealed to the League of Nations since January – Abyssinia is to-day attacked by Italy.[1] Great indignation & excitement in London – Evening newspapers doing a roaring trade.

Go up to Soho Square [offices of GPO Film Unit] in morning & work with Auden & Coldstream on Negroes – much of which has to be altered for Grierson,[2] as being too 'flippant' & subjective. Lunch with them & work again in afternoon, this time with Legg[3] on other films. Meet Beth & tea with her & Auden after which she & I flat hunt without success. I eat with David Green & two friends of his – Taylors – nice people,[4] after which we go to Ballets Jooss which are very good in spots – Big City & Green Table[5] – having lovely things in them – poorer music, but some good dancing & lighting.

1 Subsequent diary entries trace the course of the Abyssinian crisis:

4 October
The War continues, enormous number of casualties – Abyssinian reverses – to general sorrow. No sign of League activity as yet. Still enormous excitement – esp. round Soho.

6 October
The Abyssinian war continues apace! Adowa apparently being captured, tho' the general opinion is that Italy will get the worst of it. The League meanwhile falters & hum's & ha's. Will meet again on Wed. to decide who is the agressor!

8 October
The Italians begin to use poison gas in their 'civilisation' of Abyssinia.

Five months later Britten was to sum up the international political scene as he perceived it on 7 March 1936:

The International situation now is ludicrously complicated – Germany now discards Locarno & Versailles & occupies Rhine territory – Italian successes on Abyssinian front continue in spite of financial difficulties – Japan owing to the shooting of her statesmen in last week's revolt is more milataristic than ever [the military *coup d'état* on 26 February] – & Russia is pressed on the other side as well by Germany & Poland. Central Europe is a hot bed of intrigue – and our re-armament plans mount up & up – etc. etc.!!!!

2 John Grierson (1898–1972). His pioneering role in the history of the documentary film has been well summarized by Elizabeth Sussex in her Introduction to the Post Office Video Catalogue of GPO Film Unit productions:

John Grierson, the son of a Scottish schoolmaster, first got the documentary idea when he saw Flaherty's *Nanook of the North* as an undergraduate in Glasgow, and he developed it while studying the communications media on a Rockefeller research fellowship in Chicago in the 1920s.

In London in 1927 he got himself appointed films officer to a government department, the Empire Marketing Board, set up the previous year by public relations pioneer Stephen Tallents, and two years later made a huge impression with his first film *Drifters*. As a consequence he was able to set up a film unit and gradually recruit the team of young tyros who would forever be associated with his movement – Basil Wright, John Taylor, Arthur Elton, Edgar Anstey, Stuart Legg, Harry Watt, Evelyn Spice [. . .] But then, in 1933, the EMB closed down. At this point, very luckily, Sir Kingsley Wood (then Postmaster General) appointed Sir Stephen Tallents (he had been knighted in 1932) to the new post of public relations officer at the GPO, and Tallents contrived to take Grierson and the whole film unit with him to the Post Office. Thus was the GPO Film Unit born.

See also *Grierson on Documentary*, edited by Forsyth Hardy (London, Faber, 1979); Forsyth Hardy, *John Grierson: A Documentary Biography* (London, Faber and Faber, 1979); Paul Rotha, *Documentary Film*, 3rd edition (London, Faber and Faber, 1952) and *Documentary Diary: An Informal History of the British Documentary Film, 1928–39* (London, Secker & Warburg, 1973); and 'John Grierson' in *Film Dope*, edited by David Badder and Bob Baker, 21 October 1980, pp. 17–33.

3 Stuart Legg recorded Auden's text for *Night Mail*.

4 Nice, but unidentified.

5 *The Green Table*, given its première in Paris in 1932, was the *chef d'oeuvre* of the Ballets Jooss. Its choreographer was Kurt Jooss and the scenario was highly topical and anti-militaristic: it showed the interminable rounds of international diplomacy finally resulting in the very consequences all the paralysing discussion was supposed to avoid – the outbreak of war. The composer was Fritz Cohen, who had earlier written the music for *The Blue Angel*, in which Marlene Dietrich starred, along with Cohen's hit number, 'Falling in love again'.

71 To Marjorie Fass

173, Cromwell Road, S.W. 5.
Actually from G.P.O. Film Unit, Soho Square.[1]
Oct. 23rd [recte 24th, 1935]

Dear Marj,

Here is a very belated birthday present. I am sorry I couldn't manage to get it sent before this, but I have had just a horrible amount of stuff to get done – this complicated by a worrying advent of a wisdom tooth – I thought one had finished with tooth-cutting ages ago!

I hope you will enjoy this book[2] – I haven't read by anymeans all of it, and I feel horribly tempted to keep it for a few days now & read it all. But I mustn't make it any later. I know you would like W.H.A.[3] very much. He is a very startling personality – but absolutely sincere and very brilliant. He has a very wide knowledge, not only of course of literature, but of every branch of art, and especially of politics; this last in the direction that I can't help feeling every serious person, and artists especially, must have. Strong opposition in every direction to Facism, which of course restricts all freedom of thought.

Perhaps you will lend me the book when you've finished with it.

I saw John Alston yesterday. He said you were much better. You know how glad I am about that. It has been [a] nightmare for all of us.[4]

Auden came with me to the B.B.C. Symphony concert with dear Boult last night.[5] I expect you listened, but with the incomparable advantage of being near the saving knob! I much prefer the Berg in the original form, don't you? Even given a sympathetic conductor who knows the work it is so much less intimate and flexible – though some lovely sounds were there. Of course the performance was execrable – it seemed to me as if A.B. had said to himself (if he were capable of forming opinions of anything) 'This is a clever work, but perhaps a little too free – after all one doesn't talk of or mention these things in public, does one? One must make it as decent & clean as possible!' And he did, didn't he? Practically every speed was wrong – the Estatico too slow, by half, the Adagio too fast – to prevent it becoming too sensuous – no doubt. What would he do with Tristan, I wonder!!

As for Flesch,[6] to me he seemed to play like the solid old German professor he looked. And the orchestra accompanied like a suet-pudding – & one of those nasty heavy & sticky ones, too.

Sorry, Marj. dear, to let you in for these effusions. It helps me to get it off my chest, and you needn't read it!

I have a rather free morning at Soho Square waiting for some films to come from the studio – stuff we recorded on Saturday.[7] 3 hours doing a film of less than 3 minutes! Great trouble in getting the words across. I am also having a rather amusing time – negotiating with a firm of obvious film crooks – or maniacs. They have proposed that I should do the music to a large film – say they have engaged the London Phil. [London Philharmonic Orchestra] for a whole week to do the recording (the L.P.O. secretary knows nothing of it – I 'phoned him). No one knows anything of him – that he ever has made a film – inspite of his long stories of Hollywood, Soviet Russia & Lubitsch etc.[8] An interesting experience, but one must go warily!

Beth & I are planning to move into a new flat.[9] A dreadful business when one has so much work to do, because all the furniture has to be procured. However, anything to get away from Boarding Houses.

Hope you like the book
Much love to you all
BENJAMIN

P.S.   Please could you tell Mr. & Mrs. Brit[10] how much I am enjoying the piano at 4 B.G.'s.[11] I am rehearsing a trio there this afternoon. Until I get my flat working, I am stuck for a piano. I should write myself – but at the moment have less than no time.

1 The London address of the GPO Film Unit was 21 Soho Square, W1; the studios were in Blackheath.

2 Probably the anthology *The Poet's Tongue*, which Auden had edited with John Garrett and was first published in June 1935 and twice reprinted in that year. This title seems the most likely candidate.

3 Wystan Hugh Auden, poet (1907–1973) and – Pears apart – the most profoundly influential of Britten's close friends. As Basil Wright, who was close to both men, was to write in a private communication (1948), 'It may well be that it was Wystan who first awoke Ben's real imaginative and emotional life.' There is scarcely need here for a conventional biographical note. Auden's achievements are public knowledge, while the history of his relationship with Britten, both

creative and personal, is woven into the texture of the ensuing letters and accompanying documentation, not merely in these volumes but in volumes yet to come. But it may be helpful to bear in mind one or two general observations: for a start, the likely impact made on the provincial youth from Lowestoft by the eccentric though endearing Auden, who must certainly have been the first Bohemian that Britten had encountered (and Auden's Bohemianism was not assumed but fundamental to his character and thus all the more powerful). A remarkably vivid portrait of Auden in 1936 by Isherwood – a year after Britten's first meeting with him – allows us to estimate the probable shock on the reserved and outwardly conventional young composer:

Wystan hasn't changed in the least. His clothes are still out at the elbows, his stubby nail-bitten fingers still dirty and sticky with nicotine; he still drinks a dozen cups of tea a day, has to have a hot bath every night, piles his bed with blankets, overcoats, carpets and rugs; he still eats ravenously – though not as much as he once did – and nearly sheds tears if the food isn't to his taste; he still smokes like a factory chimney and pockets all the matches in the house. But although I found myself glancing nervously whenever he picked up a book, fiddled with the electric light cord or shovelled food into his mouth while reading at meals; although I was often very much annoyed by his fussing and by the mess he made – still I never for one moment was more than annoyed. I never felt opposed to him in my deepest being – as I sometimes feel opposed to almost everyone I know. We are, after all, of the same sort.

(*Christopher and His Kind* (London, Eyre Methuen, 1977), p. 180)

Britten's very first meeting with Auden took place on 5 July 1935, at the Downs School, where Auden was teaching. It was the beginning of their collaboration at the GPO Film Unit:

[. . .] Basil Wright calls for me in his car at 10.0 & takes me down to Colwall near Malvern. [. . .] We come here to talk over matters for films with Wystan Auden (who is a master at the Downs School here [. . .]) Auden is the most amazing man, a very brilliant & attractive personality – he was at Farfield, Greshams, but before my time. Work with him in aft. [. . .]

The tone of that entry is sustained in the present letter. But of course, there had been many meetings in the interim, all of them faithfully recorded in Britten's diary. Three entries, at least, are of particular interest:

4 September
I go, after some 'phone calls, to Unit at 11.0 and work there, & in bookshops, gramophone shops (Levy – Whitechapel) & elsewhere with Auden at the Negroes Film. He is a remarkably fine brain. [. . .]

17 September
Spend day with Coldstream & Auden in Soho Sq. & British Museum etc. Doing work for Negroes. I always feel very young & stupid when with

these brains – I mostly sit silent when they hold forth about subjects in general. What brains! [. . .]

5 October
[. . .] See Rupert Doone's production of T.S. Eliot's Sweeney Agonistes & W.H. Auden's 'Dance of Death'. Both very exhilerating & interesting shows, splendidly put on (Decor & very lovely masks by Robert Medley) & acted. A's play is a very serious contribution to literature. [. . .]

The theme of Auden's (and his friends') overwhelmingly articulate and intellectual capacities as compared with Britten's perception of himself as a muted and inarticulate musician was to prove a leading theme in more senses than one. He was never entirely to rid himself of a lack of self-confidence and feelings of inferiority. It was a deep-seated uncertainty which may well have made its own contribution to the eventual disintegration of the friendship in the post-war years.

All the odder this, as in one respect, at least, Britten and Auden were astonishingly well matched: each possessed a prodigious technical virtuosity which enabled him to turn his hand virtually to any form of verse or music. Whether it was popular song, parody, or the most elaborate and complex of inventions (whether the linguistic means were words or notes), both Britten and Auden, seemingly at the drop of a hat, could summon up the appropriate 'voice'. They were brilliant ventriloquists, both, a feature that distinguishes their early work (and we are not necessarily thinking of their joint works) and singles them out as exceptional creators in the history of twentieth-century English letters and music. It was a gift that gave rise to a mortifying suspicion in thirties England, in which the amateur tradition and disdain for 'showing off' were prized virtues.

Quite apart from their professionalism, the very commitment of Britten and Auden to their respective professions was another bond. Indeed, the idea of total commitment was hard to get across. There is a well-known story that tells how at a tennis party Britten was asked what he intended to be when he grew up (EWB, p. 37): ' "A composer", was the prompt response. "Yes, but what *else*?" ' History, of course, was to come up with the answer: nothing else. (See BBAA, p. 15.)

This story has its counterpart in an exchange between Auden and his tutor, Nevill Coghill, at Oxford, recounted by Geoffrey Grigson in his *Recollections, Mainly of Artists and Writers* (London, Chatto & Windus, The Hogarth Press, 1984), p. 67:

Tutor: 'And what are you going to do, Mr Auden, when you leave the university?'
Auden: 'I am going to be a poet.'
Tutor: (since something must be said) 'Well, in – in that case you should find it very useful to have read English.'
Auden: (after a silence) 'You don't understand, I am going to be a great poet.'

This unshakeable sense of vocation, serviced by a superb professionalism, was characteristic of both men; and itself made possible
the period of fertile collaboration between 1935 and 1942: 1936, which
saw the composition of *Our Hunting Fathers* (see DMBA), and 1941,
which saw the first performance in New York of *Paul Bunyan* (see
DMPB), were key years.

In the Introduction (see pp. 16–23), we have touched on Britten's
evident difficulty in freeing his feelings sufficiently to allow him to
give physical expression to his sexuality. Auden, who had no such
problem, clearly led the attempt to 'unfreeze' the young composer,
to argue him into accepting his own sexual constitution, and more
importantly, perhaps, to learn to love and to give himself as part of
that experience. Auden made the point in a poem, 'Underneath the
abject willow', written for – and about – Britten:

> [. . .]
> Your unique and moping station
>   Prove you cold;
>   Stand up and fold
> Your map of desolation.

> [. . .]
> Coldest love will warm to action,
>   Walk then, come,
>   No longer numb,
> Into your satisfaction.

That was a poem written in March 1936, and strangely, one might
think, set as a duet for voices and piano by Britten in the same year.
He must surely have realized that it was not only addressed to him
but also quite specifically critical of his reluctance or inability to enter
into that 'satisfaction' which only physical consummation can bring?
(Interestingly, an adaptation and revision of the duet into a solo
voice format (with Pears in mind?) was made later by Britten in the
USA. It remains unpublished.)

If there was an invitation built into the poem – and one does not
doubt that Auden would have happily collaborated in warming Britten into life and love: 'Coldest love will warm to action' – it was not
accepted. But this seems less a rejection of Auden, than the continuing manifestation, as we see now, of Britten's suspended or frozen
sexuality, which was not to be released until later, perhaps not until
1939, in North America, when Pears we must suppose, achieved
what Auden could not – he persuaded Britten to walk into his 'satisfaction'.

It is not surprising, then, that Pears was certain that 'there was no
love affair' (see HCWHA, p. 188), a view supported by Isherwood
(ibid.): 'If there was sex between Auden and Britten, I remember

nothing of it. My guess would be No. Nothing between Britten and me, either.'

Was Auden in some sense an unsuccessful suitor? It has been suggested that poems from 1936 and 1937, two of them inscribed to Britten ('Underneath the abject willow' and 'Night covers up the rigid land' (both written in March 1936)) offer evidence of Britten's 'rejection' of Auden. John Evans, for example, in his sleeve note for an EMI recording which includes two unpublished Auden settings (EL 27 0653 1) writes of Auden harbouring 'an unreciprocated passion'; but one of the two poems in question, 'To lie flat on the back with the knees flexed', formed part of a sonnet sequence written in 1933, long before the two men had met. (Other unpublished Auden settings, of 'The sun shines down' and 'What's in your mind, my dove, my coney' (complete) and 'O what is that sound' (incomplete), are likewise of texts from 1930 32.) As for the other, 'Night covers up the rigid land', there is an ambiguity there in what in any event is an ambiguous poem – that is, the personal experience it might seem to describe does not match up with what we know of the personal histories of Britten and Auden at the time the poem was written (the *song* was not composed until 27 October 1937). Auden's emotions were largely centred elsewhere, while we have no knowledge of a commitment on Britten's part that would have led Auden to believe he was rejected in favour of another. Britten and Pears had not met when the poem was written; and it was after they had embarked on their friendship that the song was composed.

We cannot, perhaps, arrive at a clear-cut answer, the more so since Auden, as 'Underneath the abject willow' so clearly shows, had appointed himself as Britten's sexual mentor and therapist, an advisory role he was to sustain in later years (see note 1 to Letter 144). There was, too, the inscription published in Auden's and MacNeice's *Letters from Iceland* (London, Faber and Faber, 1937), which was also an injunction: 'For my friend Benjamin Britten, composer, I beg/That fortune send him soon a passionate affair.' But, as Edward Mendelson has remarked (in *Early Auden* (New York, Viking, 1981), p. 193), it was during the early months of 1936 that Auden 'wrote more love poems than in any comparable period in his career'. Among these 'offerings to Eros' were some other marvellous love lyrics that Britten set, e.g. 'Let the florid music praise', which was to open *On this Island*, and 'Fish in the unruffled lakes', and some, e.g. 'Dear, though the night is gone', which Britten did not set and where the subject (object?) of the poem was certainly not the composer. All of these texts belong to February and March 1936, like 'Night covers up the rigid land'.

There can be little doubt that 'Underneath the abject willow' and 'Night covers up' combine personal statement, exhortation, obser-

vation and experience, and also, most importantly, the poetic intention to make a good poem which is something entirely different from
autobiography masquerading as poetry. It is unwise (or at any rate,
unsafe) to assume that a poem's I and You are identical with the I
and You we think we know. In short, we should be cautious of too
literal an interpretation of 'Night covers up' and its inscription, and
read it, rather, in the context of the lyrical outpouring that was
characteristic of Auden's poetry in these months. Odd enough, as
we have remarked, that Britten set Auden's minatory comment on
his numbness: odder still, if 'Night covers up' were indeed a frustrated lover's plaint, to make a setting of that too. But either way,
these fascinatingly enigmatic texts tell us something direct, unequivo-
cal and sharply illuminating about Britten's personal history and
psychology in the mid-thirties, no matter what conclusions we may
draw with regard to Auden's role in the relationship at this time.

'Love' itself is capable of infinite definition. To define it – 'O tell
me the truth about love' – was one of Auden's preoccupations. How
we care to use that word in connection with Britten and Auden calls
for delicate judgement; but the storm of tears with which the composer reacted to the news of Auden's sudden death in 1973 was
eloquent, even after the long years of estrangement, of the depths of
the early friendship. There was nothing numb about Britten's grief.

In a broadcast interview with Lord Harewood ('People today', BBC
Radio, May/June 1960), Britten replied to a question about poetry:

[. . .] the person, I think, who developed my love was the poet, Auden,
whom I met, I think, in the late teens. We collaborated over music and verse
for a film, and he had an enormous influence on me for quite a considerable
period. He showed me many things. I remember, for instance, he it was
who introduced me to the works of Rimbaud, who was only a name to me
then; and he showed me the different periods in verse. I remember he
showed me Chaucer for the first time. I'd always imagined that was a kind
of foreign language, but as he read it, which was very well, I understood
almost immediately what it meant, and I find now that it isn't so difficult to
read – one must just have confidence and read ahead and then the meaning
comes very strongly, very easily.

A later reference to Auden was made by Britten in the course of
an interview (Charles Osborne, *London Magazine*, 3/7, October 1963),
when he remarked, 'I was certainly greatly influenced by Auden
personally, but never musically'; and added, in reply to a question
about *Paul Bunyan* and the possibility of further collaboration:

I should consider it an honour if Auden wanted to collaborate with me again,
but I don't know how it would work now. *Paul Bunyan* would need too
much working on to make it acceptable generally, and I don't know that
either he or I would have the interest to do this.

See also note 2 to Letter 397.

4 Marjorie Fass had been seriously ill.

5 The concert at the Queen's Hall, London, comprised the Sinfonia from Bach's Cantata No. 174, 'Ich liebe den Höchsten von ganzem Gemüte', Berg's *Lyric Suite* in the composer's arrangement of three movements (Nos. 2–4) for string orchestra (its UK concert première), Beethoven's Violin Concerto and Brahms's First Symphony.

6 Carl Flesch (1873–1944), Hungarian violinist and distinguished teacher. The prize named after him has been awarded since 1945.

7 Britten composed his score for an unidentified film simply known as 'Telegram Abstract' in July 1935, recording it on 20 July 1935. The music is scored for boys' voices and a small instrumental ensemble. The first recording proved to be technically inferior, thus a second recording session was undertaken on 19 October. Britten records the occasion in his diary:

> [. . .] down to Blackheath by 9.30 to give us some practical help in the new recording of Telegram Abstract film (Fl, Ob, Cl, Xyl. & Glock, Perc. & Pft) with Cooper's lads – one of which Harold [omission] does all the talking & very efficiently & dramatically too. This takes all the morning.

Britten was alleged to have composed music for the GPO animated film *H.P.O.*, sometimes known as *6d Telegram* (see Eric Walter White, in DMHK, p. 313). However, the *H.P.O.* film (released in 1938) credits the music to Brian Easdale (see note 1 to Letter 148). 'Cooper' referred to by Britten in the diary entry is Joseph Cooper (b. 1912), English pianist and broadcaster, who in 1935 was organist and choirmaster at a church in Blackheath, near the GPO Film Unit's studio. He joined the Unit as a composer shortly after this recording session. For his memories of the Unit's activities, including Britten's and Auden's work together, see Cooper, *Facing the Music: An Autobiography*, (London, Weidenfeld and Nicolson, 1979), pp. 75–7. See also note 1 to Letter 121 and PR, p. 443.

8 Britten writes in his diary:

> *22 October*
> [. . .] meet at Oddenino's [the restaurant] a Mr. Lortorov for whom I am probably going to do some music soon – films again.

> *23 October*
> Spend morning at Unit – talking over many things – finding incidentally that Lortorov, with whom I am negotiating, is probably nothing but a crook!

9 Flat 2, West Cottage Road, West End Green, London NW6. The flat was over the rear of the Carlton Garage, West End Lane. Telephone: Hampstead 4818.

10 Pet name used by close friends of the Bridges.

11 Bedford Gardens, the Bridges' London home.

72 To Henri Temianka[1]

Flat no. 2,
West Cottage Road,
West End Green, N.W.6.
Nov. 15th 1935.

Dear Mr. Temianka,

I am very sorry that we are not able to meet and try my Suite[2] this week before you left. I 'phoned yesterday morning, but you were already out. I had imagined that you were here all this week.

The printed copy of the work should be ready at the end of next week. I hear that you will call on Sunday at Maida Vale. Perhaps you will leave an address where I could send it on to you, as I certainly want you to have a copy at once.

Hoping you will have a most successful tour – I envy you most terribly going to Russia![3]

Yours sincerely,
BENJAMIN BRITTEN

1 American violinist and conductor (b. 1906), of Polish–Jewish parents. He emigrated to the USA in 1926, settling finally in Los Angeles. In 1946 he founded, and became the leader of, the Paganini Quartet. He published a volume of memoirs, *Facing the Music: an Irreverent Close-up of the Real Concert World* (New York, David McKay, 1973). In 1950 the Paganini String Quartet led by Temianka made a recording of Britten's First String Quartet on Liberty Records, SWL 15000. A copy is in the Archive, inscribed by Temianka: 'For Benjamin Britten, in the hope that this recording will convey the devotion and love with which it was made.'

2 Three movements of the Suite (March, Lullaby and Waltz) had been given their first performance by Temianka and Betty Humby on 17 December 1934 at the Wigmore Hall. Britten had now completed the Suite (in June 1935) and published copies were just about to be made available. He was clearly anxious that Temianka, who had launched the work, should be among the first to receive a copy.

Temianka recalled his first meeting with Britten and the première of three movements from the Suite in his memoir (pp. 244–5):

Some time after my concert with Vaughan Williams, I received a telephone call from a beautiful young blond pianist, Betty Humby [. . .] She wanted me to meet a brilliant but unknown young composer–pianist, Benjamin Britten. We were introduced and he proceeded to write a suite for Betty and me, of which we gave the first performance in London. [. . .] I received

the music from him only two days before the performance. As if to justify
the delay, Britten had peppered the piece with fiendishly difficult passages.
Taking my first peek at the completed score, I saw barbed-wire entangle-
ments winding their way from beginning to end. To complicate matters
further, I had a longstanding commitment to give a concert somewhere
in Lancashire the day before the London première. I reserved an entire
compartment on the train and spent six hours practicing Britten's piece while
traveling north to the concert, six more hours traveling back to London, and
then I practiced about ten hours non-stop on the day of the première itself.

The première went surprisingly well. Performers are able to summon
massive reserves of adrenalin when disaster seems imminent. Britten joined
us on the stage afterward, warmly shook hands, and shared in the applause.

Britten wrote of the performance in his diary for 17 December:

Rehearse abit with Betty Humby in morning at Wigmore Hall [. . .] Beth
& I have dinner with Barbara and Helen, & we all go off to Wigmore
Hall to hear Betty Humby play my 3 pieces with Temianka – considering
that they've only had them such a short time, they go excellently (T. being
esp. good).

On the same evening *A Boy was Born* received its concert première.
The diary continues:

Dash off – with Bridges – to the Mercury Theatre where Iris Lemare
conducts a show of my 'Boy'. Mostly very poor I'm afraid – Herod being
esp. wobbly. I came out after it, not being able to stand the strain.

3 A remark that revealingly reflects the enthusiasm for Russia – the
   idea of Russia – common among members of Britten's generation in
   the thirties. In his diary for 23 December 1935, we find him writing
   at home in Lowestoft:

Write a long letter to Mrs. Chamberlain (Kersty) in defence of Communism
– not a difficult letter to write! It has shocked alot of people that I am
interested in the subject!

(See Paul Hollander, *Political Pilgrims: Travels of Western Intellectuals
to the Soviet Union, China and Cuba* (New York, Oxford University
Press, 1981), and particularly Chapter 4, 'The Appeals of Soviet
Society: The First Pilgrimage'; and Valentine Cunningham, *British
Writers of the Thirties* (Oxford, Oxford University Press, 1988), p. 396
et seq.)

Monday, 18 November 1935

I start work at G.P.O. Films again to-day. Work – first at Soho
Square at 10.15 & then later at Blackheath on a new film T.P.O.
(Railway Post)[1] with Cavalcanti & Watt. Meet Herbert Murrill[2] at
4.30 & go instrument (harpsichord or like)–hunting until 6.45 without
success, with the result that at 8.0 (after a meal with Mr & Mrs M.)
with dress rehearsal ready to start we have no instrument![3]

However a brain wave of H.M. saves situation – we stick drawing pins into the hammers of the theatre piano & result – a fine harpsichord of considerable power & volume! The rehearsal doesn't go badly – as rehearsals go. Back here by 12.0.

1 'T.P.O.' (Travelling Post Office) was the working title of the GPO Film Unit's most famous production, *Night Mail* (1936), directed by Harry Watt (1906–1987) and Basil Wright (see note 1 to Diary for January 1936). In a private communication, Mrs Walter Leigh recalled (in 1981) her husband's involvement in the project:

Actually Walter Leigh had been asked to do it but even though he agreed, he had finally to accept some theatre work which was infinitely more lucrative. I clearly recall him setting out to see Grierson (or Wright or who?) to tell him that he could not do the job. He did not feel he was letting them down as he was going to recommend a most brilliant and talented young man, Britten in fact.

Britten worked on the film's sound-track during November and December 1935, and composed his music, including the novel setting of Auden's poem 'This is the night mail crossing the border', in January 1936, a text specially devised for the film. It tells the story of the Mail Express train collecting, sorting and dispatching the mail during its overnight journey from London to Scotland. The first showing of the film took place on 4 February 1936, as part of the opening programme of the Arts Cinema, Cambridge. The programme also included 'a fanfare specially composed [. . .] by Walter Leigh and recorded by members of the London Symphony Orchestra'. For a detailed account of the chronology of the composition of *Night Mail*: see DMBA, pp. 80–85, and PR, pp. 466–8. See also Hans Keller, 'Film Music: Britten', *Music Survey*, 2/4, Spring 1950, pp. 250–51, and EMWHA, pp. 442–3 and 666–9.

Watt went on to direct several notable documentary films made by the GPO Film Unit's wartime successor, the Crown Film Unit, led by Ian Dalrymple (1903–1989), including *London Can Take It* (with Humphrey Jennings) and *Target for Tonight*.

2 English composer (1909–1952) and musical director of the Group Theatre, 1933–6, for which Murrill composed incidental music for Auden's *The Dance of Death* (1934) and Auden's and Isherwood's *The Dog beneath the Skin* (1936). Murrill joined the BBC in 1936 and became Head of Music from 1950 until his death.

3 Britten refers to the dress rehearsal of the Group Theatre production of Shakespeare's *Timon of Athens*, the first play for which he composed incidental music. See Diary for 19 November; PFL, plate 99 (which shows Doone dancing in one of the ballets Britten wrote for the play), and PR, pp. 494–8.

Tuesday, 19 November 1935

To Soho & Blackheath during morning & early aft. to work on
T.P.O – but very little is done as yet. Back here by 5.0 to rehearse
a little Vl. & pft with Lauricella. Beth comes with me at 8.30 to 1st
night of Group Theatre production Timon of Athens at Westminster
theatre[1] – Nugent Monck[2] production Ernest Milton[3] – Timon (very
fine esp. in 2nd half) Harcourt Williams[4] as Apemantus. Ballet by
Rupert Doone[5], very lovely decor by Robert Medley[6], music by me
– played by Sylvia Spencer, Miss Mellier (Oboes & Cor Anglais),
Miss Murrill (Piano – harpsichord!), Tony Spergeon (percussion)
under Herbert Murrill – it goes very well – Beth & I don't stay
long at party after – so as to catch last bus home.

1 Ivor Brown reviewed the first night in the *Observer*, 24 November:

'Great plays are great only for the moment in which they are received:
because we believe that the ideology of "Timon of Athens" is relevant to
the present, we believe that its revival has a logical place in our programme.'
   So they tell us at the Westminster. The first remark is total nonsense. The
second is completely contradicted later on by the description of the piece as
'Shakespeare's comment on a world which then was beginning, and now is
at an end.' The confusion of thought in this programme-note has been
equalled by the confusion of styles in the production. Mr Monck had lit the
stage cleverly, and it was not his fault, I suppose, that Mr Robert Medley's
decoration gave an air of miminy-piminy charade to the whole business, or
that Mr Rupert Doone's ballet suggested nothing whatever of Attic shape or
Jacobean masque, and was just Fifth-Georgian Goings-on, for which, I think,
the Greeks would have had several words, and the Jacobeans even more.
The maids of Athens were made to wear hooped skirts and bounced about
as though ruined. Timon's plaint was another 'Beggar's Opera', whose scene
Shakespeare had set round a blasted Macheath. Lest we should nod, Mr
Nugent Monck suddenly discharged a cry of players to pursue each other
round the stalls with much clashing and slashing of swords. 'Timon' is only
semi-Shakespeare, but it is not so feeble as to need this kind of antic on its
side.
   The Group Theatre must pull itself together and take a dose of common
sense. Whatever you may do about 'Timon of Athens', leave it on the shelf
or take it to the stage, the one fatal method of approach is preciosity and
Chelsea caperings. You may deem the play mad or majestic, or both at once,
but you must not give the impression that a high-brow clique has been
saying 'Isn't this fun?'

2 English theatre director and producer (1878–1958), noted for his
Shakespeare productions.

3 English actor (1890–1974), who was later to play the role of the
Guidanto in *On the Frontier*.

4 English actor and producer (1880–1957).

5 Rupert Doone, English dancer, choreographer and producer – real name Ernest Reginald Woodfield (1903–1966). Doone began his career in the theatre as a dancer during the early 1920s, appearing in 1929 with Diaghilev's Ballets Russes. He was a founder member of the Group Theatre and between 1934 and 1939 was the principal figure in guiding its artistic policy. He directed the Group Theatre's first production in 1932 – Vanbrugh's *The Provok'd Wife* – and went on to direct the majority of its repertoire, including Auden's and Isherwood's *The Ascent of F6* (1937) and *On the Frontier* (1938), *The Agamemnon of Aeschylus* (1936) in MacNeice's translation, and MacNeice's own *Out of the Picture* (1937). See also note 2 to Letter 89. After the Group Theatre's activities had ceased in 1939 Doone undertook the direction of the theatre school at Morley College, London, in 1940, where he remained until ill-health forced him to retire. In 1950 he initiated a revival of the Group Theatre which continued until 1956. See Robert Medley, *Drawn from a Life: A Memoir* (London, Faber and Faber, 1983), and Michael Sidnell, *Dances of Death: The Group Theatre of London in the Thirties* (London, Faber and Faber, 1984).

6 English painter and stage designer (b. 1905). He was chief designer for the Group Theatre when Britten was musical director and resident composer, and responsible, among other productions, for the costume designs of *Agamemnon* and the décor of *The Ascent of F6*. See PFL, plates 98 and 100–02, and Gordon Hargreaves, 'Robert Medley: From the life', Aldeburgh Festival 1985 exhibition catalogue.

73 To Marjorie Fass

Flat 2,
West Cottage Road,
West End Green, N.W. 6.
Dec. 30th, 1935.

My dear Marge,

What a lovely present arrived from you the other day! You shouldn't have bothered to do it as you weren't feeling fit – but it is very sweet of you. I think the lino-cut is <u>fine</u>! My dear Marge you are a genius – if you can work like that with conditions as they are, what will you stop at when everything goes well? By-the-by, a very good artist – who actually now is film-directing,[1] & who was a great friend of Roger Fry,[2] was here the other night and much admired your picture of 'David'[3] – which is hanging in state in our living room.

I haven't had time to read much of the Auden yet[4] – but I feel
that most of it is definitely going to be for me – knowing him as
I do, & feeling quite alot in sympathy with his ideals. I am working
with him on various projects outside films[5] – it is a treat to have
someone of his calibre to think with!

I hope you managed to pick up some of last night's musical
treats![6] It was sickening that they were so close together – I had
to miss practically all the orchestral concert – but, tell it not in Gath,
I am not a lover of May Blyth. I am now enjoying very much the
recording of my work[7] – I have had it done by the same firm as
Mr. Brit had his lament – & it really is excellent. The show was
80% fine, though the last movement is a disappointment – everyone
felt that.

I am afraid that Christmas was practically spoilt for me by the
news of Berg's death.[8] I feel it is a real & terrible tragedy – one
from which the world will take long to recover from. The real
musicians are so few & far between, arn't they? Apart from the
Bergs, Stravinsksys, Schönbergs & Bridges one is a bit stumped for
names, isn't one? Markievitch may be – but personally I feel that
he's not got there yet. Shostakovitch – perhaps – possibly.

I am glad to hear last night that you were feeling abit better. You
are having the most awful time, my poor dear – but remember
that not long ago you were feeling better – & il faut se reculer etc.
(Don't follow my example, who seem to have spent my life mentally
reculing, & the mieux sauter doesn't seem to arrive! But one feels
like this sometimes!)

I am looking forward to the time when you can come up & look
at this flat – see my pictures & hear my records. And I am <u>sure</u>
it will be soon.

Thank you Marge dear for the very nice present, & now oblige
my by presenting me with a fine New Year's present – in being
completely fit again.

The very best wishes, as ever,
Yours,
BENJAMIN

1 William Coldstream (1908–1987), the distinguished painter, with
whom Britten became acquainted at the GPO Film Unit, where Coldstream was working as an assistant to John Grierson, the head of the
Unit. Coldstream was educated at the Slade School of Art, London (of
which he was to become head from 1949 to 1975). Coldstream was
drawn to films because he felt it to be a 'contemporary medium' and

while with the Unit he participated in the making of three films with music by Britten: *The King's Stamp* (1935), *Coal Face* (1935) and *Negroes* (1935). Auden played a leading creative role in both *Coal Face* and *Negroes*, although the latter project was abandoned in its original form and revived in 1937/8 in a revised, less experimental version (see PR, pp. 102–18, and EMWHA, pp. 424–8 and 669–70). Coldstream (in a conversation with Donald Mitchell, 18 November 1978; Archive) vividly recalled Auden as 'one of Nature's governesses', the voice of Nanny. He remembers Britten as naïve, charming and unsophisticated, 'an ordinary schoolboy', with no intellectual friends. But at the same time he was aware of something exceptional behind the schoolboyish façade. Interestingly, he identified the GPO films, when talking about them in general terms, as 'leftwing propaganda'. See also DMBA and Bruce Laughton, *The Euston Road School: A Study in Objective Painting* (Aldershot, Scolar Press, 1986), pp. 109–26. Coldstream was knighted in 1956. See Addenda, pp. 1337–80.

2 The art critic and artist (1866–1934), and member of the Bloomsbury group. Virginia Woolf wrote a biography of Fry in 1940.

3 Probably a painting by Marjorie Fass based on Michelangelo's *David*, which she much admired and had sketched during a visit to Florence.

4 Evidently Marjorie Fass had returned the Auden volume to Britten, for which he had asked in Letter 71.

5 The only Britten–Auden collaboration at this period outside the film studio was *Our Hunting Fathers*. Britten writes in his diary for 2 January 1936:

Auden comes back here for a meal at 7.30. We talk amongst many things of a new Song Cycle (probably on Animals) that I may write. Very nice and interesting & pleasant evening.

An undated note of Auden's to Britten shows the gradual evolution of the new work's title, which was finally taken from an existing Auden poem.

Dear Benjamin
    Many thanks for letter. No, I dont think Auden and

$$\begin{matrix} \text{on} \\ \text{or} \\ \text{versus} \end{matrix} \quad \text{Animals}$$

is a good title. The only thing I can think of is "The $\frac{two}{other}$ Kingdom(s)". I'll have a stab at modernising Rats a little and send it you in a day or so. I am my own agent in these two poems (Our hunting fathers has been published in the Listener) so $\frac{get}{give}$ me the best terms you can. If I think you're cheating me, I'll send them to Curtis Brown.

                                                        Love,
                                                        WYSTAN

6 Britten refers to two concerts broadcast by the BBC: *A Boy was Born*, with the BBC Chorus and the boys of St Alban the Martyr, Holborn, London EC1, conducted by Leslie Woodgate; and a BBC Orchestra concert conducted by Frank Bridge. Britten wrote of his own work in his diary:

Apart from a contretemps in Finale it goes well – beginning fine & some very exciting. I can't help but like this work as I feel it is genuinely musical. Woodgate takes us after to Maida Vale where F.B. conducts a concert.

Bridge's programme comprised the Overture to *The Barber of Seville* by Rossini, his *Lament* (1915) for string orchestra, Mozart's Symphony No. 31, Liszt's song 'The Loreley' and Gluck's 'Ye Gods, see me humbled before ye' (from *Alceste*) in which May Blyth (1899–1985), was the soloist. She was noted for her interpretations of contemporary music and sang in the first English performances of *Wozzeck* (Marie) and Busoni's *Doktor Faust*. The performance of Berg's opera took place on 14 March 1934:

Listen to broadcast of concert performance of Wozzeck (1st in England) from Q.H. – by B.B.C. orch and Adrian Boult with Bitterauf as Wozzeck (superb) & May Blyth as Marie (seemed excellent) & a large & efficient cast. It wasn't very satisfactory as a broadcast – voices too loud & blurring. Only the third Act (& bits of second) were intelligible. The music of this is extraordinarily striking without the action, while that of the first isn't – except for the exciting march & beautiful little lullaby. The hand of Tristan is over alot of the intense emotion, but Berg emerges a definite personality.

In 1948, in a letter to Peter Pears dated 22 October, Britten recalls his impressions of another broadcast of *Wozzeck* (from Hamburg) which he heard in the company of Arthur Oldham:

The reception last night was hopeless, & Arthur got a very strange impression of the work. Actually the performance was very poor, only Wozzeck having any idea of character or pitch. We were lucky if Marie was within a fourth of her notes! You must get us to imitate the small boy singing "hop-hop" at the end. Arthur was quite bewildered even with the score (perhaps because of it, because really it makes the simplest passages look like Chinese). I alternated between mad irritation at the ridiculous excesses of it, with the ludicrous, hideous, & impossible vocal writing, and being moved to tears by the incredible haunting beauty of lots of bits of it. If only he could relax in the relaxed bits!

7 A private recording of the broadcast performance of *A Boy was Born* made by the Marguerite Sound Studios in Hendon. The recording would have been taken direct from the broadcast and transcribed onto acetate discs. As the letter tells us, this was the studio used by Bridge for recording the performance of his *Lament* broadcast the same evening. He had written to Britten earlier in the month, making a characteristically generous gesture:

In a moment of enthusiasm for automobiles I thought a secondhand Rolls Royce might be a nuisance, especially in a flat [. . .] And so, this is to command (neither beg nor implore!) your Royal Highness not to spend any cash on Xmas. 'anythings'. On us, that is! We would both like to add those unnecessary personal expenses – as you should wish – to the cost of any bit of mech.[anical] recording of your choral work that you want. See? So just to partly swell the fund [. . .] please add the enclosed and I hope some of the recording will be good.

8 Berg had died on 24 December. He was one of the two living idols of Britten's youth – his only rival was Frank Bridge – and the admiration remained constant throughout his life. (As late as 1972, when Britten was working on his last opera, *Death in Venice*, in Germany, he made a point of attending a performance of *Wozzeck* at Darmstadt.) Britten was clearly aware of the Austrian composer's serious illness, and wrote on 23 December: 'Go for a very long & mysterious walk – 10.30–11.30 [p.m.]. Think alot about Alban Berg.'
The next day he wrote:

Hear that Alban Berg dies. This makes me very miserable as I feel he is one of the most important men writing to-day. And we could do with many successors to Wozzeck, Lulu & Lyric Suite. A very great man.

Berg was one of the composers whom Britten had 'discovered' and explored with Henry Boys (see note 2 to Letter 74), and so it was only natural that he should have been in touch with his friend, then living at St Albans, after news of the composer's death had reached him. Boys remembers still the telephone call Britten made on 28 December in which he gave vent to his 'absolute desolation' and described his 'mysterious walk' of the 23rd.
The day after the phone call – it seems as if Britten had some difficulty in locating Boys – the two friends met and walked together in London and once again Berg was clearly uppermost in their minds:

After much housework for me Henry Boys arrives at 11.30 & we then go for a very long walk to Hendon where Bridges tell me the Marguerite recording studios are. Eat at Hendon & bus back here & spend afternoon talking (Berg), gramophoning (Mahler, Kindertotenlieder) & playing (Berg – Wozzeck).

The music-making, listening and talking which followed the walk – later that night Britten and Boys attended the broadcast performance of *A Boy was Born* at the BBC – seems almost to have taken on the shape of a wake for Berg: the choice of the Mahler song-cycle speaks for itself.
In his 1963 interview with Murray Schafer, *British Composers in Interview* (London, Faber and Faber, 1963), p. 114, Britten thought that it was at Frank Bridge's suggestion that he should 'leave England and experience a different musical climate'. His desire to study with

Berg, and its frustration, he later recorded in his own words in BBST, 17 November 1963:

I'd finished at the College with a small travelling scholarship and wanted to go to Vienna [. . .] But when the College was told, coolness arose. I think, but can't be sure, that the director, Sir Hugh Allen, put a spike in the wheel. At any rate, when I said at home during the holidays, 'I *am* going to study with Berg, aren't I?' the answer was a firm 'No, dear.' Pressed, my mother said, 'He's not a good influence', which I suspect came from Allen.

There was at that time an almost moral prejudice against serial music – which makes one smile today! I think also that there was some confusion in my parent's minds – thinking that 'not a good influence' meant morally, not musically. They had been disturbed by traits of rebelliousness and unconventionality which I had shown in my later school days.

Britten may have been right about Allen's opinion, which makes all the odder a comment by the Director, added in his own hand to the midsummer report for 1933, Britten's penultimate term at the College. Allen wrote: 'I hear fine news of his work. After next term he will get a new experience abroad.' This sounds as if some post-College arrangement for study abroad had already been set up. If with Berg, or with Berg in mind, what was it that caused Allen – if he did – to 'put a spike in the wheel'? (See also note 1 to Diary for 23 August 1937.)

It had certainly been Britten's hope that he would be able to meet Berg when, with the help of his scholarship, he visited Vienna with his mother in the autumn of 1934 – but by a stroke of singular ill-fortune Berg was out of Vienna at that time, composing. It was Erwin Stein, then working for Berg's publishers and himself a close friend of the composer, who 'stood in' for Berg and with whom Britten expected to discuss some of his own compositions, as Letter 59 indicates. That Berg's death followed so soon after the disappointment of the Vienna visit was a cruel blow. Boys was luckier. He had met Berg in January 1931 at Cambridge, when the composer was adjudicating works submitted to the ISCM under the chairmanship of E.J. Dent. For a photograph of that occasion, see Mosco Carner, *Alban Berg: The Man and The Work* (London, Duckworth, 1975), plate 11. In a letter to Schoenberg about an earlier ISCM meeting in 1928, Berg wrote about his support for the choice of Zemlinsky's Third String Quartet:

Apparently not all of the gentlemen of the jury were aware that Zemlinsky's Quartet writing isn't much worse than that of, say, Bridge, that his powers of invention are not much poorer than, say, Bloch, and that he is scarcely less modern than, say Alfano –.

Bridge's Third String Quartet was among the works selected. See *The Berg–Schoenberg Correspondence*, edited by Julianne Brand, Christopher Hailey and Donald Harris (London, Macmillan, 1987), pp. 366–7.

74 To Mrs Britten

Fl. 2. [West Cottage Rd.,
West End Green, N.W.6.]
[30 December 1935]

Just a tiny note Mum, because I want to get back to my records.[1] I
have had the work done – found the man's private address &
Henry Boys[2] & I tramped out to Hendon yesterday morning to
see him. They seem very good reproductions – and the show was
90% good, I thought – tho' the end was bad. Henry & I went
back to the Bridges after – had a very nice party with them and the
Brosi – & weren't back here too early, I can tell you![3]

To-day I wasn't too punctual at the GPO [Film Unit] – there was
alot to get tidied – but I was the complete house-maid! Made the
beds, got the breakfast, did the laundry, & the shopping when I
bought a fine joint!

Had a busy day at the G.P.O. – working with Auden.[4] Back here
for a nice meal, & my records!

To-morrow I go to the Prom to hear Toni B[rosa] play the
Tschaikovsky concerto[5] – why not listen?

Now, ma cherie, take care of yourself. You must, for our sakes,
& everyone's sakes. We can't spare you – and if you go on working
like this, well you'll have a compulsory rest, & you won't like that
– have to postpone the moving & all. No Biltmore[6] yet – think of
that! I am not worrying about you (said he lying) – because I know
you will be sensible – so don't disappoint me!

Much love, my darling,
Love to all the rest,
BENJY

P.S.   Tell Bobby that I will meet him with Beth if I possibly can
on Thursday – but can't promise anything. Beth says – tell him ten
to one – it will give us more time.

A most successful New Year to you, my sweet –

1 Britten adds in his diary for 30 December:

'I have records of my "Boy" & they are lovely. Better than I thought.
Terribly exciting.'

2 [Claude E.] Henry Boys (b. 1910), English critic, composer and
teacher. He read English at Cambridge, but involved himself passion-
ately in musical pursuits, in which he was guided by E.J. Dent. Boys
was also a student at the College (from 1929 to 1933), and it was

there that he met Britten for the first time on 17 July 1933. It was a day on which Britten had played through *A Boy was Born* to Herbert Howells and later that same day to Boys. Boys further recollects his enthusiasm on being shown a score of the work by Arthur Benjamin, Britten's piano teacher at the College: 'I was absolutely thrilled [. . .] It seemed so different from the ordinary, choral tradition, although it crosses the English choral tradition. It was tradition, not traditionalism!' According to Boys, it was the excitement generated by his encounter with the 'Choral Variations' that led to the visit to Lowestoft for a fortnight in August and September 1934, the year in which Britten's father had died, in April.

I took a tennis racquet because he was a very keen player [. . .] and we used to do music in the morning and either show off on the front with our excellent tennis or go to [. . .] his friends [. . .] for tennis in the afternoon. [. . .] He used to play the viola sometimes, trying to go through cello sonatas of Beethoven in that week [. . .] and he showed me a lot of Frank Bridge and other things that I didn't know very well, or at all, and I took *Oedipus Rex* and Three Pieces from *Wozzeck*, I remember. [. . .] And he was well acquainted (I suppose through Frank Bridge, because he wouldn't have got that at the Royal College of Music) [. . .] with Schoenberg [. . .] with some Schoenberg, anyway. [. . .] We played through and sometimes he would pick up his viola and [. . .] I can remember him once playing a piece he liked very much and very beautifully – 'Night and Day'! [. . .] I found [Mrs Britten] a little intimidating. She was a newly made widow, as it were. [. . .] We were left alone in the front room overlooking the sea with the piano, and [Britten] was writing then *Holiday Tales* [*Holiday Diary*] – he'd nearly finished; and Jack Moeran came over to see us and tried to convert us to Sibelius, which we didn't want to think about then.

Britten's 1934 diary allows precise documentation of Boys's visit and Britten's response to it. Boys arrived in Lowestoft on 27 August. On the 28th:

Also play some Vla and Pft with Boys – Walton Concerto althrough [. . .] In aft we play a four at tennis (Kit, Beth, Boys, I) [. . .]

29 August
[. . .] 11.25 to Moeran's where we lunch. He comes back with us [Mrs Britten and Beth] & bathes & has tea + H. Boys.

[This must have been the occasion when Sibelius was discussed. In 1936, on 13 October, Britten was to write in his diary:

After dinner Jack Moeran comes with his new Symphony [G minor, first performed 1938] – it has some excellent things in it, but terribly under the Sibelius influence – mood, ideas & technique. This is going to be almost as bad as the Brahms influence on English music I fear.]

4 September
[. . .] long Vla & Pft. playing with Henry Boys [. . .] H.B. comes to dinner – have much int. talk & gramophone after – esp. Stravinsky Symphonie des Psaumes and Beethoven Mass in D – both incredible masterpieces.

6 September
[. . .] Henry comes to do some Vla & pft. Go all through F.B's Vln sonata
(with Bazil beating time hard).

7 September
Go out shopping up town immediately after breakfast. See H.B. on way
back, change & have a work at F.B. Sonata with him before John Alston
fetches Mum, him & me over to his step-father (Lincoln Sutton)'s house
at Framingham. [See also PFL, plate 74.]

8 September
Work a bit, play a bit & walk a bit with H.B. – morning [. . .] Have bath
before dinner after which H.B. comes and we talk, talk, talk.

9 September
H.B. comes for a long walk & bathe [. . .] He stays to tea & supper, in
between which we play, gramophone & talk, talk, talk as usual.

14 September
H.B. comes rather early, & we have a final run though of F.B.'s Vln. sonata
– it is a great work to play. Go down to station to see H.B. off by 3.33.

These excerpts from Britten's diary give the flavour of this remarkable
encounter, remarkable perhaps not so much for the repertory scrutinized – Boys, an early and passionate advocate of Stravinsky, was
delighted to find that he and Britten shared the same enthusiasms
and 'the same sort of explorative instinct' – but for the protracted
'talk, talk, talk' about music that was a feature of this Lowestoft
fortnight. It provides an instance of, one guesses, lively and articulate
discussion which was rare in later years, when Britten became so
suspicious of 'intellectualizing' about music.

Out of this successful and stimulating first meeting developed the
friendship between the thoughtful, articulate and cosmopolitan Boys
and the younger composer whom he thought 'a genius [. . .] the
most versatile musician I've ever met. [. . .] I think there are lots
of musicians, excellent musicians, who can write music; but I think
Ben [. . .] was a *real* composer.' (And here Boys referred to the
relationship of Erwin Stein to Berg and Schoenberg: as accomplished
a musician as Stein was, it soon became clear to him that he did not
have 'this thing that they had', and which Britten had.)

The friendship continued in London and was characterized by the
same 'explorative instinct' and much debate. On 11 October 1936,
for example, Britten wrote in his diary, 'Henry comes back to supper
[. . .] & we talk & talk music etc (mostly pro-Mahler & anti-Brahms),
& play Wozzeck. I should work but this is good'; and later the same
month on the 30th:

I go out immediately after dinner to Wigmore Hall – concert by the Boyd
Neel Str. Orchestra. I sit with Toni Brosa & Henry Boys. They play a
mixed programme inc. my Simple Symphony (which goes swimmingly &
gets a rousing reception!) & the wonderful new Suite of Schönberg [the
Suite for string orchestra, 1924] – a miracle in every way – very striking &

full of deep passion & content. It goes down very badly, but H.B. & I have coffee out after still raving over it!

Boys, when still a schoolboy, had been introduced to Mahler's music (see also letter 103) by Norman Demuth (1898–1968), English composer and writer. Boys remembers the thirties as a period when 'Walter Legge and Ernest Newman and Ben and I were about the only enthusiasts' for Mahler. It was Boys who wrote a note to accompany the publication of the Mahler Society recording of the Ninth Symphony, with the Vienna Philharmonic Orchestra con-ducted by Bruno Walter (HMV DB 3613–22), released in 1938 and instigated by Legge.

Boys wrote one of the earliest and most important articles on Britten (see note 2 to Letter 128) and contributed a 'Musico-dramatic analysis' to the symposium edited by Eric Crozier on *The Rape of Lucretia* (London, The Bodley Head, 1948). In 1939 Britten dedicated his Violin Concerto, Op. 15, to him. After Britten's return from America in 1942, he re-established contact with Boys through Ronald Duncan, and in 1947 Boys was designated Musical Assistant to the English Opera Group. He was responsible for making the vocal scores of *Lucretia* and *Albert Herring*.

Around the time of the composition of *Peter Grimes* Boys had met Britten

in Oxford Street [. . .] and we went into a pub to have a Guinness (he loved Guinness) and he talked and said one very impressive thing: 'I think I have all the technique to do anything. I must *be* more!' And that next work was *Peter Grimes*.

The comment – highly significant in itself – and that it was made to Boys – seems to embody the spirit of an altogether unusual relation-ship in Britten's life. Let his diary entry for 23 May 1936 have the last word:

[Tennis] until 7.30 when we eat a meal, sit over it alot, come back here for a bit & then walk back to Golders Green where [Boys] catches his bus – still talking 19 to the dozen tho' I must say he has a startling brain – makes me feel about ten, tho' I get on splendidly with him & always I am exhilerated & stimulated by his talkings [. . .]

3 1.45 am according to Britten's diary for 29 December.

4 Diary, 30 December: 'I am working on T.P.O. sound with Auden with whom I spend complete day – at Soho Sq. & Blackheath.'

5 Diary, 31 December:

I got to Prom. concert at Queen's Hall [. . .] for Tschaikovsky evening, in which Toni Brosa plays the Vln Concerto – Qua violin, marvellously – the slow movement being a miracle of beauty – but excessive virtuosity & speed robbed the music of something in places. The rest of the programme was popular Tsch. but very great & lovely. This man is of course maligned and scoffed at out of all reason now. So it is really rather fun admiring him so – more than their 'National' Moussoursky – the Vaughan Williams in excelsis (tho' of course of infinitely more value!).

Brosa's 'excessive virtuosity' was to raise its problematic head in later years, in connection with Britten's own Violin Concerto (1939), of which Brosa gave the first performance and the violin part of which he 'edited', along lines that the composer came to dislike. The accretions were eventually removed, when Britten revised the concerto in 1958.

Britten's last diary entry for 1935 concludes:

I refuse the pressure of the Brosas to go and be merry at the M.M. Club – because I hate these shows. Instead I come back here & listen to alittle of my Boy records in bliss. Outside people seem very merry & bright – but only surely because 1935 is departing – much reason for rejoicing.

6 'Biltmore' was the name of the house at Pole Barn Lane, Frinton-on-Sea, Essex, into which Mrs Britten moved in February 1936 after the sale of the dental practice and family home at Lowestoft in 1935, following her husband's death. Britten wrote in his diary on 28 February 1936, the occasion of his first weekend visit to Frinton:

It is strange indeed to come back to 'home' here. But pleasant on the whole & the house is really very charming & cosy. Definitely good.

Biltmore also provided at least one further attraction for the composer:

It is enormously more pleasant that we have not now to be out of dining-room by 9.0 – for 'practice' waiting-room reasons – so we take advantage of this & breakfast at 9.0.

The house no longer stands, having been bombed during the Second World War.

January 1936
[DMBA, *p. 18*]

1936 finds me infinitely better off in all ways than did the beginning of 1935; it finds me earning my living – with occasionally something to spare – at the G.P.O. film Unit under John Grierson & Cavalcanti, writing music & supervising sounds for films (this one T.P.O. Night Mail) at the rate of £5 per week, but owing to the fact I can claim no performing rights (it being Crown property) with the possibility of it being increased to £10 per week or £2 per day; writing very little, but with the possibility & ideas for writing alot of original music, as I am going under an agreement with Boosey & Hawkes for a £3 a week guarantee of royalties;[1] having a lot of success but not a staggering amount of performances, tho' reputation (even for bad) growing steadily; having a bad inferiority complex in company of brains like Basil Wright,[2] Wystan Auden & William Coldstream; being fortunate in friends like Mr & Mrs Frank Bridge, Henry Boys, Basil Reeve (& young Piers Dunkerley[3] – tell it not in Gath) and afar off Francis Barton; being comfortably settled in a pleasant, tho' cold, flat in West Hampstead with Beth, with whom I get on very well; doing much housework but with prospect of having a woman in more than twice a week in evenings & once in mornings. So for 1936.

1 Britten's £8.00 per week in 1935 (£5 + £3) was just over twice the national average earnings figure that year. In 1989 that same proportion (double the national earnings) would amount to an annual income of around £25,000. He was indeed managing to earn his living 'with occasionally something to spare'.

2 Basil Wright (1907–1987), English documentary film-maker and producer. After studying at Cambridge, Wright joined John Grierson at the Empire Marketing Board Film Unit in December 1929. Wright's role developed and in 1934 he made one of his most celebrated films, *Song of Ceylon*, with music by Walter Leigh. At the GPO Film Unit he was one of a team responsible for *Night Mail*, and it was he who brought Auden and Britten together for the first time. (See Charles Osborne, *W.H. Auden: The Life of a Poet*, (London, Eyre Methuen, 1980), pp. 108–9; HCWA, pp. 177–8; and Wright's own memoir 'Britten and Documentary', *Musical Times*, 104 November 1963, pp. 779–80.) In 1936 Wright had had an idea for a ballet in which he could collaborate with Britten: see note 2 to Letter 120.

   In 1937 he founded the Realist Film Unit, producing *Advance Democracy* with music by Britten, and during the Second World War was a producer for the Ministry of Information. Between 1945 and 1946 he worked as producer-in-charge at the Crown Film Unit, during which time Britten composed his educational film, *Instruments of the Orchestra* (see note 7 to Letter 514). He wrote an authoritative history of the cinema entitled *The Long View* (London, Secker & Warburg, 1974).

3 Piers Montague Dunkerley (1921–1959). He was a pupil at South Lodge from 1930 to 1934 and then attended Bloxham School, Banbury, Oxfordshire. There was extensive correspondence between Dunkerley and Britten while Piers was at school; and it seems that it was to Britten that Dunkerley turned for advice. Britten writes in his diary on 7 April 1936:

Long walk in park [with Piers] [. . .] he needs some help poor lad. Bloxham seems a queer school, & it makes one sick that they can't leave a nice lad like Piers alone – but it is understandable – good heavens!

During the war he served as a Captain in the Royal Marines. He was wounded and taken prisoner in June 1944. The *Bloxhamist* (school magazine, No. 455, April 1945) contained the following news item:

Lieutenant P.M. Dunkerley, Royal Marines Commando, was reported missing some time after 'D-Day', but we are thankful that he has now recovered from his wounds and appears to be alive and well in Germany. We have just received a card from him in which he says: 'I hope to call on you on my way to Japan.'

At the end of the war he continued his service career and remained intermittently in touch with Britten: we know that he was present at the first performance of *Billy Budd* in 1951. Later in the 1950s he returned to civilian life, to which, however, he found it difficult to adjust. Dunkerley was engaged to be married and invited Britten to be best man at his wedding, an invitation Britten's composing commitments did not permit him to accept. But Dunkerley's marriage plans fell through and it was this disappointment, perhaps, coupled with the struggle to accommodate himself to a civilian job (he was employed by a large firm of coal merchants in London), that led to his suicide on 8 June 1959.

Britten had first met Dunkerley in 1934. He makes his first appearance in the diary for that year on 18 March, at Lowestoft. Britten had seen his sister Barbara off at the railway station, after which, he wrote, 'Walk abit back with Dunkerley of S. Lodge.' Thereafter, there developed a firm friendship between Britten, aged twenty-one, and Dunkerley, aged thirteen, which expressed itself in many meetings – in 1935 alone there are twenty-two diary entries – and a voluminous exchange of letters, in the late 1950s. While Dunkerley's letters were all carefully kept by Britten and are now in the Archive, we have been able to locate only a small part of the composer's side of the correspondence.

The friendship with Dunkerley – which began, one may think, with particular appropriateness in a week when Britten was sketching out ideas for a work based on Jules Renard's famous novel of childhood, *Poile de Carotte* (Britten was a passionate admirer of Duvivier's film) – provides us with a model example of Britten's schoolboy relationships: these were friendships in which he could play the role of counsellor and proxy father (Dunkerley, as it happened, was fatherless) and which at the same time embodied a kind of idealized senior–junior boy comradeship, an extension of the hierarchies and friendships of school. These were all potent factors in Britten's emotional life.

His diary shows unequivocally the importance of such relationships, though in fact that may not be the right word to describe what Britten already recognized in himself as a fundamental need: there is a particularly interesting diary entry for 15 April 1936:

[. . .] meet Piers at 3.0 at Piccadilly & go to Tatler for Disney Season. Some lovely, witty, Silly Symphonies. Adored by all ages & classes. A large tea after (since I missed lunch) & walk & ping-pong with the lad after. He is a nice thing and I am very fond of him – thank heaven not sexually, but I am getting to such a condition that I am lost without some children (of either sex) near me.

In this same year, Auden played the role of Father Christmas in the GPO film, *Calendar of the Year*, for which Britten wrote the music. In the Christmas party scene, among the children assembled as 'extras', were Piers Dunkerley and his sister, Daphne. A still from this scene is reproduced in *Film Dope*, 21, October 1980, p. 29. Britten wrote in his diary on 10 January:

I leave at 5.30 – & go up to Piccadilly to meet Piers & Daphne – collect twelve chairs & take them all up to Coldstream where Auden & he shoot a sequence for Miss Spice's film 'Calendar of the Year' – this being a New Year's party of a typical respectable upper middle class family. Beth, Lilian Wolff, & brother, the 2 Romilly's* are among the sixteen or so. It is amusing to watch & to talk to Olive Mangeot† – also there, watching – although I feel Auden has made some mistakes in choice   some being definitely Bohemian! Over by 11.30 – tho' I dispatch Piers & Daphne (who make a success) by 10.45. Piers makes friends with Giles Romilly – not too great, I hope, tho' Giles seems nice, & may broaden Piers mind alot – which he needs – but he is a nice lad for all that.

---

* The '2 Romilly's' = Esmond (1918–1941), who married Jessica Mitford, and Giles (1916–1967; suicide), nephews of Mrs Winston Churchill. Both Esmond and Giles participated in the Spanish Civil War and as pacifist schoolboys published a magazine, *Out of Bounds*, 'against Reaction, Militarism and Fascism in the Public Schools'. The brothers subsequently collaborated in a book, also called *Out of Bounds*, which Britten was reading in 1935. In an Appendix in Julian Symons, *The Thirties, A Dream Revolved* (London, Faber and Faber, 1975), pp.154–6, the reactions of a number of public schools to *Out of Bounds*, culled from the first two issues of the magazine, are reprinted. Among them is this report from Gresham's:

At a recent debate a motion that 'In the opinion of this House a Fascist Dictatorship is preferable to Socialism' was carried by ninety-nine votes to fifty-four.

Considerable interest in politics is taken, and John Strachey's *Coming Struggle For Power* has been read by the upper forms.

A portrait of Giles, disguised as Gavin Blair Summers, appears in T.C. Worsley's *roman à clef, Fellow Travellers*, new edition (London, Gay Modern Classics, 1984). See also Worsley's autobiography, *Flannelled Fool: A Slice of Life in the Thirties* (London, Alan Ross, 1967), pp. 97–100; Valentine Cunningham, *British Writers of the Thirties* (Oxford, Oxford University Press, 1988); and the obituary of Giles which appeared in *The Times*, 14 August 1967.

By a strange coincidence, Giles Romilly was one of the small band of prisoners, 'with illustrious connections', held captive in Colditz in 1944–5, along with the then Viscount Lascelles (later the Earl of Harewood), who post-war was to become a close friend of Britten's. See Harewood, *The Tongs and the Bones: The Memoirs of Lord Harewood* (London, Weidenfeld and Nicolson, 1981), p. 55 *et seq*.

† Olive Mangeot = the first wife of André, the violinist.

Back by train to find Mum waiting up patiently & with a meal for us – which we don't want, having 'snacked' steadily all the evening.

That a landscape, whether interior or exterior, was somehow incomplete for Britten without children, and boys in particular, is clear from the diaries: observation of boys as part of the furnishing of his private landscape (rarely other than that) runs like a subtheme through many entries across the years, not to excess but certainly often enough to draw one's attention. A litany addressed by Pears to an anxious Britten in 1945 seems to paint that very landscape. 'So don't worry', he was to write, 'and remember there are lovely things in the world still – children, boys, sunshine, the sea, Mozart, you and me.' But the 1936 entry, from which we quote above, also strikes an emphatically self-defensive note, 'I'm very fond of him – thank heaven not sexually.' In an earlier entry, on 3 February, we find an observation combined with self-defence, Britten as it were defending himself *to* himself. He had just travelled by train to London from Lowestoft:

Have some tea on the journey & some buns, but rather because of the very nice little restaurant-boy who brings it along & talks abit, Quel horreur!! But I swear there is no harm in it! Dinner here [. . .] & spend after in writing letters (to Piers, (my protégé) & Francis Barton – this is getting bad!) & telephoning.

One notes the guilty tension ('Quel horreur!! But I swear there's no harm in it!') between children as necessary adjuncts – 'I am lost without some children [. . .] near me' – and as objects of desire. But without it, would we have had *The Turn of the Screw*, say, or *Death in Venice*? The diary entry of 3 February touches on one of the mainsprings of Britten's creativity.

Although Dunkerley did not die on active service, Britten regarded him none the less as a war casualty, or perhaps better, as a casualty of the war; and it was for that reason that he included Piers among the dedicatees of *War Requiem*. But the dedication must also have reflected the many years of a friendship which had its origins in a stroll back from Lowestoft railway station with a boy in 1934.

The Dunkerley story was to end, we think, with an extraordinary, long-postponed coda. In 1970 Britten was in Australia for the English Opera Group tour of the Church Parables. He was able to do a certain amount of sight-seeing, often in the company of Sir Sidney Nolan, the Australian artist, a close friend. In a conversation with Donald Mitchell, 11 June 1990, Jubilee Hall, Aldeburgh (as part of the 43rd Festival), Sir Sidney recollected a journey to the Barrier Reef. We reproduce his memory virtually *verbatim*:

SN: [. . .] we flew to Brisbane on the way, which is quite a long way from Sydney, it's about 600 miles flight and it was quite a long flight, and we came to a place called Townsville, which is half an hour away from Brisbane you see and we landed.

Well, this was the place where my young brother, who drowned in the war, was buried. So I got out of the aeroplane and I went over – it was only a short stop – and I went over to a corner of the sort of compound where they had some wire round, and I stood there in very hot sun and Ben came over and said, you know, 'Why are you standing here like that?'

And I said, 'Well, my young brother's buried here.' And he said, 'Do you mind if I stand with you?' Once again we did the same thing, we stood for about ten minutes in silence, then we got back on to the aeroplane; and then comes something which is rather complicated to explain.

But he then told me about a kind of ballet that he would plan to do for Covent Garden. He'd decided not to do an opera but he would do a ballet and it would be on Australia, and he wanted me to work out something to do with the Aboriginals; and he had a story of a friend of his who tragically hanged himself on the morning of his wedding. I think it was at Oxford – I don't know, he didn't tell me who it was, but it was quite a deep thing in him; and he was going to combine these two ways – because he had the feeling that Western civilization wasn't bringing up its children properly, and he felt that the Aboriginals in the past had. [. . .] they reared their children to deal with life and be at one with it, and we hadn't done that. We'd got it more kind of complicated and more difficult. And he was going to try and show on the stage the two things simultaneously – the life of the boy growing up in the Australian Aboriginal tribe, and the life of a boy growing up and going to Oxford and everything else – in other words, having an English thing – and have the simultaneous thing: the tragic ending on the one hand, of the English boy, and the kind of ordeal of fire and water the Aboriginals have, a kind of *Magic Flute* ending for the Aboriginal thing.

But in the telling of it he became very . . . and this is the difficult part for me to explain . . . he became very boyish and very kind of happy and [. . .] very approachable and you know, well, like a brother – just completely easy, and it was a side of him that I had actually never seen. And it lasted for about an hour and a half – had about three brandies – and . . . I was kind of overwhelmed by this revelation of his identity, of his character. And then we were due to land at Cairns for the Barrier Reef in about twenty minutes, and he suddenly said, 'Well, that's the end of that. Now', he said, 'When we get back to England I won't be like that any more.' He said, 'My destiny is to be in harness and to die in harness.' So he said, 'There won't be any more of that.' [. . .] what I'm trying to explain, I think, is that the task of a creative artist in Ben's position is so immense, so overwhelming, that it takes over all of his life and perhaps hid this other boyish, open, very touching thing.

[. . .]

DM: The work, alas, never got written, though it was certainly something that Ben gave a lot of thought to, the Australian ballet, but like other projects at the end of his life, it didn't materialize.

SN: No, there just wasn't enough time. I prepared a kind of synopsis, and between us we worked it all out, and it led to my doing an enormous series of flower paintings called 'Snake', which is a panel of 1,500 paintings – it was 120 feet long and 20 feet high – and it more or less consists of all the wild flowers that can come up in the desert in central Australia. There's kind of paradise. When it rains there these flowers come up, some of which have been dormant for 50 years, the seeds have been there. [. . .] I started on them and I did 30 or 40 of them and Ben came to dinner and we went upstairs and he looked at them and he said, 'They're very silent.' Well, I took that as a great compliment; as the greatest compliment. The man with the most wonderful ear in the world was able to hear the silence of the paintings. I was terribly thrilled about that. And then he asked me to do a painting –

DM: Yes, tell us about the Aboriginal boy –

SN: Well, he asked me to do something, because he had the feeling that our civilization, the European one, was going through a big crisis and was very complex and in some respects a tragic destiny, and he had the feeling that the Aboriginals, which is quite true, had for 40,000 years kept a harmony with the continent and kept a discipline and hadn't gone to war or anything like that and he just wanted me to do a boy as a memory of the ones he'd seen at Alice Springs, and to do something else to indicate the nature of it; and so I did that, I did the boy with the boomerang painted on him.

[. . .]

DM: All of us will regret the ballet never happened. But what you have told us gives us an extraordinary insight, I think, into Britten. This tragic death of the friend who committed suicide, that again, clearly, is an example of a hidden experience, within Britten; and yet when he went to Australia and had the Australian experience, that was a way of unlocking that experience in just the way we've been talking about earlier; and it would have found expression and perhaps mitigation through the writing of the ballet.

SN: Well, he wanted to say it, and then he instantly wanted to have it locked back again.

DM: – to have it locked back again, yes.

SN: And that was the end of that. It could only be discussed again in the context of a work of art.

DM: Exactly; that's exactly what I mean – a work of art would have exteriorized it and pacified the tragedy of it.

There can be little doubt, in our view, that the friend who was in Britten's mind when he stood by the grave of Nolan's brother was Piers Dunkerley. There are discrepancies. Dunkerley committed suicide in Poole, not Oxford, and he did not hang himself but died by self-administered seconal poisoning, not on his wedding day but in his fiancée's home after a 'heated discussion about the future and their plan to marry' in August. Reports of his death appeared in the *Daily Sketch*, *News Chronicle* and *Daily Telegraph* of 11 June 1959.

Nolan himself, as is evident from his memory of the occasion, was uncertain about Oxford: it is likely, it seems to us, that this particular location came up as part of a discussion of the contrast between the 'English thing' – for which Oxford might have stood as a convenient symbol – and the Aboriginal way of rearing their young.

As for the remaining discrepancies – the mode of Piers's suicide, that it took place in the context of a row about the wedding, not on the wedding day itself – these seem to us to be explained by a mis-remembering of the details of the event either by Britten or Nolan or by both of them; and perhaps the wedding-day catastrophe by hanging was the shape the incident would have taken in the ballet's scenario.

A last point: had there been another case of a friend's suicide which made a comparable impact, those close to Britten and Pears would surely have known of it. Our investigations have drawn a blank. There was indeed the tragic suicide of Noel Mewton-Wood in 1953, but the event was entirely unlike the circumstances of Dunkerley's death in all other respects; nor, yet more significantly, had Britten himself known Mewton-Wood as a young boy. It was Piers's trials and tribulations with which he had identified himself during the boy's adolescence.

Dunkerley, we believe, was at the heart of the proposed ballet, was its inspiration one might almost say. For Britten it might have been – among other things – an expurgation: this particular wheel would have turned full circle.

See also Brian Adams, *Sidney Nolan: Such is Life* (Hutchinson, 1987), pp. 203–4, where the ballet, its design and content, is described in further detail:

One suggestion was for these [flower] designs to be flashed onto the stage during the action to fuse the constrasting Aboriginal and European elements of the story so that Oxford choristers and a tribal circumcision ceremony might merge at the climax when the young Englishman and his bride-to-be underwent the rites of fire, water and sexual initiation similar to that experienced by Tamino and Pamina towards the end of *The Magic Flute*.

The painting of the Aboriginal boy, inscribed 'Ben & Peter/with love/Sidney & Cynthia/19 Sept 1971', is in the possession of the Britten-Pears Foundation.

Monday, 20 January 1936

To Blackheath all day until 6.0 when I eat out & come back here to work for the evening. Beth is back from Lowestoft, where she found Mum not too well – very highly strung – obviously from over-work. She (B.) is out for evening tho'. Very dramatic announcement from B.B.C. at 9.38 – 'King dying'. All stations close down except for an impromptu service Ps. [Psalm] 23, a colossal prayer. Further announcement at 9.45 – when Bulletin is repeated – Stuart Hibbert[1] getting more awed & quavery than ever – ditto at 10.0 – 10.15 – 10.30 – 10.45 (feelings are now working off a bit) – 11.0 – 11.15 (definitely cool now, tho' Hibbert still emotional) – 11.30, – 11.45, – 12.0 (really this King <u>won't</u> die') so I switch off & continue my work till 1.45 (finishing score, thank God!).[12]

1 Stuart Hibberd, the BBC's Chief Announcer, whose voice was closely identified with State occasions: 'The King's life is moving peacefully towards its close' is what he actually said.

2 While Britten was completing the orchestral version of his *Te Deum*, the life of George V came to an end. He wrote in his diary on the next day:

Apparently the King, obviously considering the feelings of the B.B.C. announcers & engineers, died at 11.55 last night. Great excitement – black round papers – tremendous eulogies – flapping black ties in buses & tubes. I can't feel any emotion – never having had any contact with the man – & disagreeing with Royalty on account of propoganda in Imperial & National directions. He may be a good man, & he certainly was very busy all his life – still he was well paid! Any how now – long live Edward VIIIth!

At the time of the King's death, Hindemith (1895–1963) was in London; and in an article 'At the service of music' (*Independent*, 15 May 1990), Bayan Northcott vividly describes the circumstances of his being commissioned to write an instant commemorative piece:

When the news of the death of George V broke early on 21 January 1936, there was panic in the Music Department of the BBC. Clearly, it would be unsuitable for the BBC Symphony Orchestra to go ahead with its scheduled programme for the following day, which was to include the British première of a rather jolly new viola concerto by the 40-year-old German composer, Paul Hindemith. Only one person refused to be fussed; shutting himself away in a studio at 11pm, Hindemith emerged at five o'clock the next morning with a brand-new six-minute score for viola and strings. The parts were hastily copied, the piece rehearsed under the immensely relieved baton of Dr Adrian Boult and on the evening of 22 January, with the composer himself as soloist, his gravely beautiful *Funeral Music* was broadcast to the world.

Britten heard the broadcast, and wrote in his diary at the end of the day:

Lovely laze in evening – listening to what little Broadcasting there is (owing to King's death) – only a very dull concert of BB.C. orch. under Boult – a vilely bad show of Egmont. Ov. – a meditation of Hindemith (concocted since the death of king) on a Bach Chorale – very dull.

Wednesday 18 March 1936

[. . .] go straight to Queen's Hall [. . .] for Shostakovitch's Lady MacBeth opera in concert form.[1] Coates conducts – capably (in so far as the ensemble was good) but unintelligently as regards speeds. Slobodskaya sings beautifully as Katerina, Parry Jones fine as husband and Macklin good as Sergei – passable rest of cast. Of course it is idle to pretend that this is great music throughout – it is stage music and as such must be considered. There is some terrific music in the entr'acts. But I will defend it through thick & thin against these charges of 'lack of style'. People will not diferentiate between style & manner. It is the composer's heritage to take what he wants from where he wants – & to write music. There is a consistency of style & method throughout. The satire is biting & brilliant. It is never boring for a second – even in this form. Some of the vocal writing is extravagant. But he may have special singers in view. After – can't resist temptation of ping-pong with Toni Brosa. John Alston brings me back in his car. The 'eminent English Renaissance' composers sniggering in the stalls was typical. There is more music in a page of MacBeth than in the whole of their 'elegant' output!

1 See illustration on p. 411, which offers full details of the performers, among them Peter Pears in the role of the Second Foreman. Britten and Pears were not to meet until 1937. It is of some special interest that Britten was so much impressed by the orchestral interludes in the opera. These surely exerted an influence on the 'Dance of Death'

in *Our Hunting Fathers* and the interludes in *Peter Grimes*. See also Donald Mitchell, 'Britten on *Oedipus Rex* and *Lady Macbeth*', *Tempo*, 120, March 1977, pp. 10–12. Britten's comments on *Lady Macbeth* were written (for *World Film News*) in advance of the performance. At the end of these he hoped 'that the critics will give this work a better welcome than they gave to "Oedipus Rex" '. He cannot have been much encouraged by the response of the 'eminent English Renaissance' composers he reports in his diary.

Britten's admiration for Shostakovich and *Lady Macbeth* were life-long. The two composers first met during September 1960 at the London première of Shostakovich's First Cello Concerto (given by Mistislav Rostropovich). Three years later, folowing the British pre-mière of the revised version of *Lady Macbeth*, now retitled *Katerina Izmaylova*, Britten was to write to Shostakovich:

> The Red House,
> Aldeburgh,
> Suffolk.
> December 26th 1963

My dear Dmitri Shostakovich,

Our good friend Slava [Rostropovich] has been with us for 2 days here & will bring this note to you from me – to thank you most warmly for your wonderful letter. I was deeply sad not to be able to greet you with thousands of other English people at the performance of 'Katerina'. I hear from all sides what a reception you had, & how this great work is loved & admired. You know how much I love this opera myself, & rejoice that it has made so many friends here. I am also happy that you had a chance to see how people here cherish you as composer & personality. I would have loved to have been able again publicly to show how I, personally, admire & cherish your work. For years now your work & life have been an example to me – of courage, integrity, & human sympathy, and of wonderful invention & clear vision. I must say that there is no one composing to-day who has an equal influence on me. That you find pleasure in my own works, had time to see Grimes while you were here, & liked it, is for me a great thrill & honour. My dear friend, & generous colleague – I look forward to meeeting you soon again & in the meantime I send by our beloved Mercury my warmest wishes for a happy & in every way successful New Year.

With renewed thanks, & warmest good wishes to you & your wife,

> Your devoted
> BENJAMIN BRITTEN

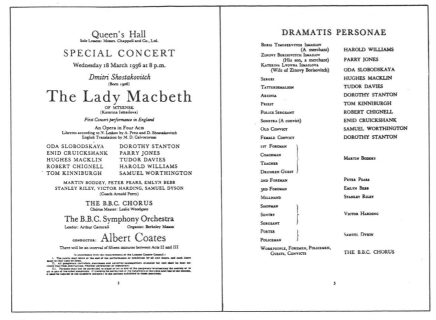

The first concert performance in England of Shostakovich's *Lady Macbeth*, 1936

75 To Grace Williams

[*Boyd, pp. 30–31*]

Flat no. 2,
West Cottage Road,
West End Green, N.W. 6.
April 6th, 1936.

My dear Grace,

Thank you very much for your letter and card – <u>and</u> for getting the tickets.[1] I enclose a cheque for what I make the sum you spent – these things always take money you know!

I met Donald Taylor[2] the managing director of Strand Film Co. this morning & he was very pleased with your stuff for the film – not that it means much but he <u>does</u> know what is suitable & comes off as <u>film</u> sound – not necessarily music, which we all know you can write. So I am jolly glad about it. I am certain that you will get alot of jobs from them now, & I'll try to get you a G.P.O. job too.[3]

Now – as to my long silence. I went down to Bournemouth

(Stravinsky's son is a very good pianist)[4] and then straight to Frinton & to bed where I stayed till Thursday – and I couldn't write any letters. So I was relieved to get your card saying you didn't want me last Friday. It wasn't sheer neglect!

Now I have had a severe blow. The film I gave yours up for, and on which I have worked night & day since Thursday & which was to be recorded on the 9th is indefinitely postponed. In other words it probably will never now be made.[5] The question is now whether I can get the money I am owed for time. Oh, this film racket! – you were daft ever to come into it.

I am going to Paris by air (& thence to Barcelona)[6] on either the Tuesday or Friday after Easter. Is either of these any good for you? It would be lovely if you could come.

No more now – bed calls. I am <u>very</u> glad about the film, & not surprised.

I go to Frinton on Thursday.

Love,
BENJAMIN

1 For the performance of *Parsifal* at Covent Garden on 4 May when Britten was accompanied by Grace Williams, who in fact made him a gift of the tickets. The diary reads:

> It is not Wagner at his best & there are dull passages – but a lot of the last two acts are splendid [. . .] Production pretty lousy. Some of the settings impressive, but the flower maidens in Victorian Bathing dresses with paper caps & none too slim either, were a slight for the Gods!

2 Donald Taylor (b. 1911), had worked for Grierson at the Empire Marketing Board and GPO Film Units. In 1935 Taylor and Ralph Keene founded Strand Films, the first company to undertake the production of documentaries exclusively on a commissioned basis. The eminent film-maker and historian, Paul Rotha (1907–1984), joined Strand as Director of Productions in 1936. See also *Paul Rotha*, BFI Dossier No. 16, edited by Paul Marris (London, British Film Institute, 1982).

3 The Strand film for which Williams composed music cannot be identified, but it was undoubtedly through Britten's connection at this time with Rotha and Strand – he had composed incidental music for the pacifist film, *Peace of Britain*, in March 1936 (see DMBA, pp. 60–67, and PR, pp. 472–4) – that he was able to help Williams. Evidently Taylor had approached Britten who declined the invitation in favour of a different project (see note 5 below). Williams never received a commission from the GPO Film Unit.

4 Soulima Stravinsky (b. 1910). His father wrote the Concerto for 2 solo pianos (1931–5) for Soulima and himself to perform. On this occasion, 27 March, he played, under his father's direction, the *Capriccio* for piano and orchestra (1928–9) with the then Bournemouth Municipal Orchestra: 'He plays it excellently – with just his father's style – it is an engaging work.' The programme also included *Pulcinella* and the *Firebird* suite. 'A great man is Stravinksy – sans doute,' Britten concludes.

5 *Around the Village Green*, a Travel and Industrial Development Association (TIDA) documentary co-produced and co-directed by Marion Grierson (sister of John Grierson) and Evelyn Spice. It scrutinized rural life falling under the shadow of industrial Britain. Although Britten began work on his music in April 1936, TIDA imposed financial restraints which postponed the project until the autumn. The score comprises arrangements of folk tunes and traditional melodies, including 'Early One Morning' and 'The Plough Boy' which were subsequently included among Britten's voice and piano folksong arrangements. See also note 3 to Letter 90 and PR, pp. 119 34 and 474–5.

6 Britten was to attend the 1936 ISCM Festival in Barcelona, at which he was to perform his Suite for violin and piano with Brosa. He had written in his diary on 11 January:

See in the Telegraph that the International Jury (including Webern & Ansermet) have chosen my Violin Suite for performance in the Barcelona (Contemporary Music) Festival this April. Very pleasing.

76   To Robert Britten

Biltmore, Pole Barn Lane, Frinton
April 10th 1936

My dear brother Robert,

Sorry for this long silence. Very dilatory & slack I agree – still I have a morsel of excuse as business has been very pressing & my business usually increases in the evenings my only letter writing time. My only letters for the past month seem to have been cheques – but still you being a family man, will realise what that's like. Thank you for your letters. I am glad you liked the broadcast – I certainly enjoyed it – funnily enough, I wasn't the slightest bit nervous. Toni is a marvel to play with, and everything went so much better than at rehearsals. I personally like the Suite – but that may be a purely a foible![1]

I go to Barcelona on Friday week (17th) so I shall miss your visits
to London & here. A pity, but still you must repeat them in the
Summer. Can't you find a conference or something? Schoolmasters
are always having conferi. I am to Barcelona by air. With a clear
conscience too! I have too much to do to leave before, & I must be
there by the Friday. Nice and quick – what: – leave London itself
8.0 a.m – in Barc. at 3.55 p.m. same day. I am going Air France
which will add an element of thrrill!

About your pageant.[2] I haven't really the slightest idea what you
want. But, apart from concocting a whole oratorio, I expect I could
manage something. After all, I have so much to do (including one,
possibly two) films, music to two new plays,[3] a long orchestral &
vocal work for Norwich Fest. etc.) that one little thing extra won't
make much difference. I can't gather what type of thing you want.
Something to scare picts or scots wasn't it? Is it sung intentionally
to scare them, or do they happen to over-hear them singing it?
Taking into consideration it is:– medieval tunes, sung by simple
folk, possibly highly religious – I should think some plain-song
chant sung by all al'unisono, best, such as:

I started it, so decided to finish it. Do you want that sort of thing? Sung absolutely without accompaniment. In the last line you see the voices divide. In which case (if you want to divide – they could sing it all unison if you want) sopranos & tenors together sing top parts, altos & basses together sing bottom ones. So you always have men & women on each part. You may only want men to sing it – in which case it's simple to divide. If it's too high transpose it.

I must go now – post. Have a good Easter. My love to my nephew. I hope you're all well.

What price Naziland?

Love & kisses
BENJAMIN

1 Britten wrote in his diary for 13 March, the day of the broadcast:

[. . .] go to B.B.C. at 9.30 for balance & control test & then start broadcast at 10.20. All nervousness forsakes me, thank heaven, & all goes as well as possible. There are points in the Beethoven that we can't agree about (op. 30 no. 3) – but it goes much better than at rehearsals. Sophie Wyss sings some Mahler divinely – my Birds (which I play for her) very sweetly & some Walton as well as the accompaniment let her. My Suite goes perfectly – Toni playing like the God of a fiddler he is!

This performance of the Suite was in fact the première of the full, five-movement version of the work – Introduction, March, Moto perpetuo, Lullaby, Waltz – in which form it was subsequently heard at the 1936 ISCM Festival, and published by Boosey & Hawkes. In 1976, the final year of the composer's life, Britten gave permission for the publication and performance of a three-movement version of the Suite – March, Lullaby, Waltz – while asking that the five-movement version should continue to be made available. The abbreviated version was entitled 'Three Pieces from Suite, Op. 6' for violin and piano, and the original opus number retained.

2 Presumably mounted at Robert's school in Prestatyn. Britten's instant provision of a unison melody must represent the earliest manifestation of plainsong in his music, albeit that the chant is of his own making.

3 One of the plays for which Britten had written incidental music was Montagu Slater's *Stay Down Miner*, first performed on 10 May at the Westminster Theatre, London, in a production by Wilfred Walter for the Left Theatre. His diary for 10 May reads:

[. . .] in aft. after letters etc. go to Westminster theatre at 4.30. A short run thro with the band of bits of the stuff then a show of 'Stay down Miner' at 5.15 & one at 8.15. Beth & various friends come to the 2nd. Considering the state of the dress rehearsal the shows are marvellous. Margaret Yarde is superb & the whole cast is fine. The music doesn't go badly – little as there is of it. I think the play is really good – very dry &

terse, with a strong sense of comedy. The last scene needs to be tightened.
A meal in between with Montagu S. & another man.

A notice of the production appeared in *The Times*, 12 May, 1936:

'Extraordinarily complicated!' So ended the eleventh scene of *Stay Down Miner*, by Montagu Slater, presented by the Left Theatre at the Westminster on Sunday night. The line won an instant response from an audience who had racked their brains with laudable but unprofitable patience to disentangle the obscure relationships and obscurer schemes of a Welsh village that seemed to live by and for strikes. Only a specialist in revolution could hope to grasp the subtle shade of policy dividing a stay-down strike from a hunger strike, or the fine distinction of principle between wrecking the 'scabs' train with dynamite and rolling rocks upon it from above. It would have been easier to take an interest in the play if some indication had been given of the nature of the grievance against which the principal characters were striking. No doubt there are audiences (in Bloomsbury, if not in the Welsh Valleys) to whom a strike is a good thing in itself, needing no justification; but a play that is intelligible only to one political school is not the best drama, and rhetoric that is persuasive only to the converted is poor propaganda.

L.A. Butt, in *Left Review*, 2/9, June 1936, wrote:

The Left Theatre production of Montagu Slater's *Stay Down Miner* at the Westminster Theatre on May 10th was a very enjoyable show. It was, at moments, more than that, when the drama of class-struggle broke through the rather confusing relationships between the characters. For in several respects the play was confusing, both politically and emotionally. On the question of direct action, for instance. In the first scene we see Bronwen Jones banging nails into a wooden contraption which is to puncture the tyres of a bus bringing blacklegs to the pit-head, a tactic which is a complete failure; and later she harangues the crowd that wants to obstruct the blacklegs' train – the argument being, quite rightly, that the railmen down the line should have taken action through their branch to stop it. As this actually happened during the stay-down strike last autumn, it seems a pity that history was not made use of on the right side for once. And I would welcome an explanation of the emotional tangle in the cottage scene between the black-leg's wife, the manager's wife, and the sweetheart of the volunteer striker.

What we are not made to feel, except very momentarily, is the sense that this is a mass thing, that these few characters are the selected symbols of a whole community, and beyond that, a class. For instance, in the scene down the pit, the interest was concentrated on three individuals, who, as far as I remember, behave without any indication of the fact that they belonged to a shift of a hundred men. We don't get the mass feeling as we did in Slater's reportage of the strike. We don't get the small shopkeepers, or the bus drivers, or any of the other sections who must have clustered round the mining village. I know that the cast had to be kept small, and that their influence or presence would have had to be indicated obliquely, but it could have been done, and it would have added to the convincingness of the play as well as to the political moral (as drawn in the reportage before mentioned).

To create the drama of social forces, of which Slater gave so fine an example in *Easter 1916*, is the urgent need of the moment, and in the dramatic knitting together of the scenes I think this play shows a technical advance.

A photograph of the stage set for *Stay Down Miner* (1936) which accompanied L.A. Butt's review of Slater's play

A little more explanatory matter, a somewhat greater explicitness, would clear up these uncertainties, and make this play a contribution of really first-rate value to the working-class drama.

See also note 1 to Letter 98 and PR, pp. 228–38 and 500–03.

We cannot be sure of the title of the second play. Had Britten already been invited to compose incidental music for the forthcoming Group Theatre production of *The Agamemnon* (translated by Louis MacNeice), first performed on 1 November?

77 To John Pounder

I am becoming regular music correspondent to World Film News[1] now. I think it's a <u>lousy</u> paper.

Biltmore, Pole Barn Lane, Frinton-on-Sea
April 14th 1936.

My dear John,

Thank you for your voluminous letter. I received it on a bed of sickness – stricken with 'flu of a sort. Since then I have been as overworked as usual, & it is only on these holiday times that one can find time to write letters.

Excuse the pencil (it is a new one, Easter present – real silver – very bourgeois) – but I write this sitting in front of our hut on the beach in glorious sun. My pen is run out & I don't want to miss the last bit of sun before it goes in, by returning to the house to refil(l) same.

Well, mon cher, I go to bonny Barcelona on Friday – going by air as time is so short & I can't go before. Extravagence peut-être, but I have a pretty clear conscience as I am abominably busy.

Anyhow, I shall probably crash – & even a hot death like that will probably be more pleasant than a slow one in mustard gas! What price Naziland? Apropos of that – I met my good looking, aristocratic, acme of ideal manhood, friend David Layton[2] (son of Sir W. same of News Chronicle ownership) on Friday, & he knows the dickens of a lot about foreign affairs – especially economic. Luckily we had the same views on the subject (he is pinker than his father) as it would have been <u>very</u> difficult to argue with him. The great question seems to be: if Great Britain had taken a firm stand with France, Russia, Belgium etc. from the <u>beginning</u>, would the effect have been in Germany (a) the fall of Hitler i.e. disillusioned (however you spell it) Germany kicking out a failure, or (b) a united Germany including Communists & Roman Caths. standing behind Hitler for the sake of Der Vaterland? Rudolph Holzman is certain of (a). Many people fear (b). What is thine opinion? I favour (a). Anyhow one must do something – not flounder about like the dear Nat Gov [National Government]. The trouble is that so many people believe the danger of war now passed – living in a fool's Paradise (or Garden of <u>Eden</u>,[3] what!)

I am glad you enjoyed the broadcasts. I enjoyed the Suite, I must say. Toni played like a God. I hope it will go as well at Barc. . I wish you were coming. It would have been pleasant.

This is a nice place you know. A strange mixture of thoroughly good taste – the front is beautiful – a lovely green sward running right along – and appallingly bad villas – not two alike the <u>whole</u> mile's length of front! The people are extraordinarily aristocratic & rich (mostly latter). I don't think I've seen one interesting face the whole week-end. Amazingly dull.

This is not personal John, tu sais, but it <u>is</u> pleasant to go out & meet no one who had known you since you were a curly headed little boy – '<u>that</u> high!!' I adore it. Of course we do know some people – one especially very charming (& delightfully coarse) too. But Frinton is quite a large place. The house is nice. I have a delightful attic room. This hut is also very pleasant – lovely beach in front – and my pleasure is added to by some very attractive _____ no, I mustn't say it. This is (unfortunately) a civilised country.

I have developed an Anatole France[4] passion. Just finished 'Elm Tree on the Mall' which is glorious, and The Merrie Tales of Toumbrock (?) which are even better. Little bits of heaven. Otherwise I've read far nichts. I've too much to do. I am now working on the Norwich Festival work – Auden has done me some

glorious words for it. Real stunners. He has also asked me to do
the music for his new play with Chris. Isherwood.[5]   I am doing the
music for Slater's new play to be produced on May 10th. All about
a stay down mine-strike in S. Wales. Very fine too.

I must stop now. I hope you can read some of this.

My foster child Piers D. is doing well. I had a long talk with him
the other day which was a great strain on me ("the normal
functions" etc. etc). You can't imagine how delightfully paternal I
can be!

My regards, respects etc to your parents. I hope they are well.

Some time this summer you must come over by car for the week-
end. It's <u>very</u> lovely. We must fix it.

The Chaplin film is <u>fine</u>.[6] I adored it. Will you have listened to-
night to the sins of my youth?[7]

Love
BENJAMIN

1 *World Film News and Television Progress*, into which *Cinema Quarterly*
was incorporated. The first issue appeared in the month of this letter.
In the October issue Britten wrote about Walton's score for Paul
Czinner's film of *As You Like It*:

> That the Directors of 20th Century Fox Film Corporation should have invited
> one of the 20th century stars of British music to write for one of its biggest
> productions is very creditable indeed. But the invitation seems to have
> exhausted their enterprise. His name, perhaps symbolically, is absent from
> the programme, and the opportunities he has had for writing serious film
> music seem negligible.
>
> There is, of course, the Grand Introduction over the credit titles – pompous
> and heraldic in the traditional manner. There is a Grand Oratorio Finale with
> full orchestra, based on Elizabethan songs, in which a bunch of Albert Hall
> contralti is very prominent. Both these are written with great competence,
> and indeed Walton is incapable of any sort of inefficiency.
>
> But apart from suitable *Waldweben* noises at the beginning of each
> sequence, which tactfully fade out as the action starts, that is the whole of
> Walton's contribution to *As You Like It*.
>
> One cannot feel that the microphone has entered very deeply into Walton's
> scoring soul. A large orchestra in which strings are very prominent has
> been used, and in the accompanying pastoral music one is conscious of the
> energetic ranks of the London Philharmonic sweating away behind the three-
> ply trees.
>
> As far as he is allowed, Walton makes one or two musically apt sugges-
> tions. The introduction is very neatly dovetailed into the chicken-yard, and
> Leon Goossens on the oboe mixes very creditably with the Wynadottes
> [farmyard fowls]. Also a neat and poetic use of the leitmotiv *Rosalind* is to
> be noted.

But the music for *As You Like It* is not the advance on *Escape Me Never* which we all expected.

In the same issue it was announced that Capitol Films had 'signed Benjamin Britten to write the music for their new film *Love from a Stranger*, starring Anne Harding'.

2   An old schoolfriend (b. 1914; Gresham's, 1928–33), to whom Britten dedicated the *Alla Marcia*, 'P.T.' (Physical Training), the first movement of the 'Go play, boy, play' string quartet suite. He was the son of Sir Walter Thomas Layton (1884–1966), economist, editor and newspaper proprietor. In a private communication dated 18 October 1982, Layton recalled:

We both, I think, came to Holt the same term and were in the same form – 3C (?). He came top and I came second in the first term. He got a double remove to 3A and I only got one to 3B – most annoying – and of course it meant that I saw less of him thereafter.

He did not join the Officers Training Corp (OTC) nor did I. My family didn't believe in military training for schoolboys, though we were not Quakers. For this reason perhaps I saw more of him than might otherwise be expected, for we were in different houses – he was in Farfield and I at Woodlands. What mattered was that not being in the OTC put us both in a rather special category. We were outside the ordinary system and when the OTC was parading or doing what it felt it had to do we played cricket in the nets or went for runs.

I can tell you where the bugle theme in Noye's Fludde came from. We used to play in the cricket nets at the bottom of the cricket field when the OTC band practised in front of the cricket pavilion about 200 yards away. As a result, we used to get a grand echo from the main school building, which was about 100 yards away also in a different direction. When the platoon marched in line across the field if they came anywhere near our net it used to be our ambition to drive the ball between the two files. Yes, humour as well as seriousness, he liked fun. [. . .]

We got on rather well, I think, and we were quite good friends. There were no problems of understanding and we talked about everything. [. . .] I [. . .] very vividly remember discussing with him his problem of deciding what kind of music he wanted to write. I don't know on what occasion this took place, but I remember him telling me very clearly that he had such facility in imitating the other composers that he didn't know which way to turn. He didn't know which way to find himself. I am a musical illiterate but have a good musical appreciation and so was deeply disturbed. I suppose that's the right word but it's a little difficult to explain. If you have that sort of ability it seemed terrible not to know what you were trying to do.

Sometime after leaving school I remember visiting him in his flat with Peter Pears, and then he [. . .] illustrated just what I have been writing. He converted Good King Wenceslas first of all into Mozart and then into Delius, or something of the kind.

See also note 3 to Diary for 24 November 1932.

3   Britten punningly refers to the then Foreign Secretary, Anthony Eden

(1897–1977), who replaced Sir Samuel Hoare in 1935 and was to become Prime Minister in 1955.

4 The French novelist, critic and essayist (1844–1926). His *L'Orme du mail* was published in 1897. *The Merry Tales of Jacques Tournebroche*, translated by Alfred Allinson, was published in 1923.

5 *The Ascent of F6*: see note 1 to Letter 100.

6 *Modern Times* (1935), which Britten had seen in the company of Piers Dunkerley on 7 April. He comments:

Much maligned, but I enjoyed it no end. Perhaps the silence is aggravating, but the material is endless, & makes one think too – although it is very 'defeatist' throughout. But what an actor! Paulette Godard is very charming too.

7 A broadcast performance of the *Simple Symphony*, conducted by Boyd Neel. In the same programme was Schoenberg's Suite in G, for strings. 'It is a delightful work to listen to', Britten wrote in his diary,

& I should imagine a good deal more. It might be a Hommage to Mahler both in matter & manner – but that doesn't detract from its value – rather adds to it. This seems an unexpected development for Schönberg – but quite natural.

78 To Mrs Britten

[*Picture Postcard: Rambla de Canaletes, Barcelona*]

Hotel Falcon, Barcelona
[Postmarked 21 April 1936]

Did you get my wah [wire]? We had a fine journey – very exciting & extremely quick. A long way by Flying Boat over Mediterranean. Brosas met us.[1] I am staying at the above address – so please write <u>there</u>. Every thing points to a fine time. People very pleasant. Meeting crowds, of course. I'll write a letter later. Hope you're having a good weekend in town with Beth. Love to Robert. Hope he's well. Wish you were here, but the journey was <u>very</u> bumpy!

Love
BENJAMIN

1 Britten was travelling with Dorothy Wadham (Mrs Hubert Foss) and Hubert Foss. They left London (Croydon Airport) on Friday 17 April and arrived in Barcelona the same day, via Paris, Lyons and Marseilles, where they joined a flying boat for the last stage of their journey. During his first hours in Barcelona Britten met Edward Clark, Lennox Berkeley (see note 2 to Letter 86), Basil Wright and John Taylor, John Grierson's brother-in-law and a member of the GPO Film Unit.

The programme book cover for the ISCM Festival, Barcelona, 1936, and schedule of programmes

79 To John Pounder

[*Picture postcard: Temple de la Sagrada Familia, Barcelona*]

Hotel Falcon, Barcelona.
[21 April 1936]

This half-finished wonder, the glory of the Catalans, looking like a disbanded Holywood set, we saw yesterday & plan to see again. The town is full of other masterpieces of different types by the same man – Gaudi[1] a religious maniac – it seems.

This is otherwise a very pleasant place – people delightful – concerts good on the whole (a wonderful Berg one). We had a fine tho' exciting air journey here.

BENJAMIN

1 Antoni Gaudí (1852–1926), the Catalan architect who worked in Barcelona where he produced irregular and often fantastic buildings, as much sculpture as architecture. His most famous work is the church of the Sagrada Familia, begun in 1883 which remains unfinished.

80   To Mrs Britten

Hotel Falcon, Ramblas, Barcelona.
April 21st, 1936.

My darling,

I shan't be able to finish this to-day – but I have five minutes
before I go off to rehearsal with Toni [Brosa] for to-night's show.[1]
Every minute of the day is occupied & I am really enjoying it. There
are lots of nice & very friendly people here – always meeting
more. I decided to stay on here, & it is worth it to be near all the
other English crowd.[2]

It is a lovely place – warm, tho' not hot so far, and yesterday
there was a great deal of rain – a pity because we went out for
an excursion up a mountain nearby & could see very little.

This is no use – there is no time at all for letter writing – this is
Thursday morning now – I haven't had a second since I finished
on Tuesday afternoon. Apologies my darling, but I can tell you all
the news when I get back – it will improve with the keeping. The
concert went very well – Toni played like a God, & tho' I was very
nervous nothing went wrong in my part! It went down
surprisingly well, considering the kind of music it was up against[3]
& we were re-called three times. People seem to approve of it.

Now the next event is that I am to broadcast with André Mangeot
on Friday evening 10.20 p.m. (incidentally the other concert was
broadcast). It is no use you trying to listen, I'm afraid, (a) because
it is only from Barcelona, a weak station (b) because you won't
know in time! It was to have been Saturday – but at the last moment
it has been postponed. Anyhow it is only small sonatas with
André & you know what that'll be like![4]

I have just got your letter. Many thanks indeed for writing such
a long nice one. You seem to have had a busy week-end – two
theatres & goodness knows what else! I hope you didn't get tired,
& that now you are enjoying the peace & quiet of Biltmore. It
seems funny to think of it here, in all this sunshine. It has been
heavenly & very warm the last two days. Toni & Peggy are dears
and I'm seeing alot of them.

Lor! I must go – I'm late allready for André's Rehearsal – I must
take a taxi – but luckily it is very cheap.

It's no use – ma petite – I shall never finish this. I return on

Tuesday afternoon[5] & I shall 'phone you about seven – if arrived.

Much love – I'm enjoying myself alot.

BENJAMIN

Take care of yourself.

1 The performance took place at 6 pm at the (?) Casal des Metges. The rehearsal in the afternoon had gone well but Britten's diary (unusually) is blank when it comes to the performance. See however the continuation of this letter for a report of the event.

2 Apart from his travelling companions, the Brosas, and those he met on his first day, Britten encountered Arnold Cooke, Peter Burra, Egon Wellesz, and Jack Gordon (a producer at the Sadler's Wells Company who was responsible for repertory and casting). In a letter to Pears from Barcelona, dated 1 May, Burra was to write, 'The Festival itself was terrific fun, and I made a lot of friends, – especially Lennox Berkeley who was having a work done [Overture, Op. 8], & is adorable. Will you be singing in his "Jonah" next month? Benjamin Britten is a very good person too.' This letter of course was written before Pears and Britten had themselves met. (See also PFL, plate 83, where the identification of Gordon and Burra in the caption should be reversed.) Burra was in Barcelona as a special correspondent for *The Times*. A report of the 'Music Festival at Barcelona' was published in the paper on 21 April, the opening paragraph of which ran as follows:

The fourteenth annual festival of the International Society for Contemporary Music, which began on Saturday at Barcelona, promises to be the most interesting as well as the most brilliant that the Society has held. In a tottering Europe, in which contracts are not always fulfilled and any form of international co-operation is becoming increasingly difficult, the organizers of the festival felt that, whatever else happened, Spanish honour would never let them down and that Barcelona would stand by its signature. As it turned out, recent developments in Spanish politics have decidedly helped the cause of music. Catalonia has got back its President and its extremely musical 'Counsellor for Culture', while the Central Government in Madrid is playing up handsomely by sending both of its orchestras to take part in the festival.

3 The programme contained among other works Walter Piston's Flute Sonata (1930), Egon Wellesz's *Sonnette der Elisabeth Barrett-Browning* (translated Rilke), Op. 52 (1934), for soprano and string quartet, and Bartók's Fifth String Quartet.

4 Britten's diary records that the broadcast planned for Friday, 24 April, though rehearsed on the 23rd, was cancelled in the studio at the very last minute 'because of a political speech (Presidential elections) which won't end'. In early April, it should be remembered, Spain (which in any case was in a state of political turmoil) was gripped

by a constitutional crisis over the Presidency. In July there was a
revolution and, following it, the Civil War. The broadcast, however,
was reinstated and finally given on Sunday, 26 April, at 12.30 p.m.
when Britten and Mangeot were heard in sonatas by Purcell,
(?Henry) Eccles and Michael Festing. 'Pretty bad', wrote Britten, 'and
very under rehearsed.'

5 28 April.

81 To Grace Williams

[*Picture Postcard: Barcelona, Spain
Boyd, pp. 32–3*]

[26 April 1936]

Thank you for your card. I was going to send you a card but
Wellesz, who is here, was going to sign this as well, & I can't
find him; so I won't wait any longer. This is really a lovely spot,
and the festival has been beautifully organised – not too much music,
good excursions (Montserrat[1] is uncanny) – & great dancing – the
whole town turns out to dance Sardanas on the slightest
provocation![2]   Oh – this native music! The new Berg concerto is
great[3] – Best of the festival. Back by air on Thursday.

BENJ

1 The famous mountain monastery near Barcelona. Diary, 24 April:

It is a heavenly spot – unlike anything around, with its incredible fingers
of stone. It is difficult not to believe in the supernatural when in a place
like this, especially as we go to a concert of old church music in the chapel,
beautifully sung (a lovely Vittoria canon) in semi-darkness. Lunch there,
& after go up in the funicular to the top – where the wonders increase.

2 On Saturday 25 April Britten attended a festival of folk dances at
Mont Juic, with Lennox Berkeley and Peter Burra. In 1937, Britten
and Berkeley were jointly to compose a Suite of Catalan Dances for
orchestra entitled *Mont Juic*, Op. 12. See note 2 to Letter 122.

3 On Sunday, 19 April, the world première was given of Berg's Violin
Concerto, with Louis Krasner (b. 1903) as soloist. Curious circumstances attended the performance, as Egon Wellesz recounts in his
article, 'E.J. Dent and the International Society for Contemporary
Music', *Music Review*, 7, 1946, pp. 205–8:

Anton Webern, who was to conduct the first performance of Berg's Violin
Concerto and three fragments from Ernst Křenek's opera *Charles V* had a
nervous breakdown during the rehearsal on Saturday morning. The perform-

ance was arranged for Sunday evening, and Dent was faced with the possibility of having to cancel the Berg and the Křenek, since the last rehearsal was arranged for the early afternoon. It was mid-day when, after a short discussion with Dent, I went to Hermann Scherchen and said, 'Here is the score of Berg's Violin Concerto, you can have a rehearsal in the afternoon and one in the evening. Can you do it?' Scherchen, who was looking at the score for the first time, hesitated, but after a while he said he would try if he could get through it with the orchestra. In the meantime Dent had asked Ansermet to take over Křenek's 'Three Fragments' [. . .] On Sunday Scherchen gave a perfect performance of the Concerto, and Ansermet of the 'Three Fragments'. No one would have believed that the two conductors had only known the scores for a single day.

Britten wrote in his diary:

The first half of programme (Borck, Gerhardt, Krenek) is completely swamped by a show of Berg's last work Violin Concerto (just shattering – very simple & touching) & the Wozzeck pieces – which always leave me like a wet rag. [. . .] There is a Mayoral Banquet which we [Britten and Arnold Cooke] cut. You can't be polite after Berg!

The other works in the programme, apart from the Berg concerto, were: Prelude and Fugue, Op. 10 (1934) for orchestra by the German composer, Edmund von Borck (1906–1944; killed in action); the first performance of the ballet suite *Ariel* (1936) by Roberto Gerhard (1896–1970), Spanish composer of Franco-Swiss descent, who was to become a British citizen; and fragments from the opera, *Karl V* (1930–33), by Ernst Křenek (b. 1900), Austrian composer who was to settle in the USA in 1937.

Britten missed no opportunities to hear further performances of the Berg concerto. He was present (with Bridge) on 1 May at a memorial concert for Berg given by the BBC:

Von Webern conducts – not good at all – & orchestra definitely B.B.C.-ish. Two pieces from Lyric Suite – very moving, but less intimate than the quartet version. Then Crasner plays the Violin Concerto – the show not a patch on the Barcelona one – which is again a very moving experience. It certainly is a very great work, & at the end I feel pretty wet with anger about losing a genius like this. Then of course the British spirit becomes uppermost & they play with great gusto 'God save the King' (as if it mattered compared with the other loss). It took an English institution to do that. [George V had died on 15 January.]

On 30 November Britten confesses, 'I become very extravagant & buy the full score of Berg's miraculous Violin concerto. My God what a sublime work'; and on 9 December he hears the work again at Queen's Hall, again with Krasner but this time with the BBC orchestra conducted by Wood ('both lousy and haphazard'): 'It is a grand work – & has an extremely moving effect on me like no other stuff. It is so vital & so intellectually emotional.'

82 To Mr Harold Walter[1]
Performing Right Society

Biltmore, Frinton-on-Sea. [Essex]
June 5th, 1936.

Dear Mr. Walter,

I enclose details of works of mine published by the O.U.P. & Year Book Press,[2] which you said you wanted. I have included the choral work 'Boy was Born' merely because separate numbers of that are now published which I believe would come under your regulations – as 'part-songs'.[3]

The rather cryptic composer & arranger of the Simple Symphony is caused by the fact that it is based on very early works (when I called myself E.B. Britten) and arranged by me more recently; so I have called it by "E. B. Britten" (arr. "B.B."). It is sometimes called by Benjamin Britten by mistake, though.[4]

I hope this is clear.

Yours faithfully,
BENJAMIN BRITTEN

1 Harold Leonard Walter (1895–1985), Assistant Secretary of the PRS from 1932. He succeeded G.H. Hatchman as Secretary in 1938 and General Manager in 1952, retiring in 1964.

2 These were Three Two-part Songs (Oxford University Press, 1932); *A Boy was Born* (OUP, 1934); *Simple Symphony* (OUP, 1934); and *May*, unison song with piano accompaniment (1934), published by the Year Book Press, Ascherberg, Hopwood and Crew (originally A. & C. Black) in 1935.

3 The Theme, and Variations 3 and 4.

4 *Simple Symphony* was published as the work of 'E.B. Britten (arranged B.B.)'. Britten insisted on this odd nomenclature because he wished to make it clear that the work was not an entirely new composition. In later life, however, the composer relinquished his original stipulation, attributing the *Simple Symphony* to 'Benjamin Britten'.

> ### New Members.
>
> THE following Composers, Authors and Publishers have been elected to Membership of the Society since the publication of the last list in our July, 1934, issue. The total number of members of the Society at the present date is 1,128.
>
> Mr. Jack Beaver (Composer and Arranger).
> Mr. Arthur L. Benjamin (Composer).
> British and Dominions Music Co. (Publishers).
> Mr. Edward B. Britten (Composer).
> Mr. Auguste Chevalier (Composer).
> Mr. Albert H. Coates (Composer).
> Mr. Noel Coward (Composer and Author).
> Mr. Herman Darewski (Composer and Author).
> Baron Frederic d'Erlanger (Composer).
> Mr. James Dyrenforth (Author).
> Mr. A. P. Herbert (Author).
> Mr. Eric J. Honour (Composer and Author).
> Mr. Mark H. Lubbock (Composer).
> Mr. E. J. Moeran (Composer).
> Mr. Michael Mullinar (Composer).
> Dr. Solomon Rowsowsky (Composer).
> Mr. Mena D. Silas (Composer and Author).
> Vivian Campbell and Co., Ltd. (Publishers).
> Mr. George L. Zalva (Arranger).

From the *Performing Right Gazette*, October, 1934: the list of new members

83 To John Pounder

Biltmore, Pole Barn Lane, Frinton-on-Sea.
June 23rd 1936

My dear John,

The King's birthday – so naturally I had to write to you. On second thoughts it is my nephew's birthday – perhaps more important.

I have just read your letter, & I have decided not to answer it in detail (a) because I have been working hard all day & I can't think lucidly at the moment (b) because there is too much to answer (c) for I should certainly throw myself over the cliffs on to the very respectable châlets below if I did. What do I think of the League's (or rather our) efforts – Schusnigg – Thomas . . . – I ask you![1]

I have been here working hard for the whole of June. I had hoped to be able to ask you over, but I have had so much to get done that I daren't to – realising the amount of work I should do if you came. Now it will have to wait until September (Mum is leaving Frinton for July & August – letting the house).

I have been working all the time on the work I'm to do for the

Norwich Festival. Words are partly written & scheme devised by
Wystan Auden – and it's pretty good – very satirical, and likely
to cause a good amount of comment – especially the prayer to God
to rid the house of rats. It has always puzzled me to think what
the rats opinion must be of God (naturally the same God – vide
the Bible & sparrows etc.) when being poisoned in the name of
the Lord. Consequently you can imagine the setting isn't exactly
reverent – words are lovely – Anglo Saxon modernised by
W.H.A.[2] The rest is similar – a lament for a dead Monkey & a
Hunting Song[3] – I enjoyed <u>that</u> one!

Thank you for sending the publisher of Golden Asse. I have
ordered it since, but had to pay 5/- for it – still it was worth it.
After all I think we are only doing the Cupid & Psyche bit of it –
we, that is Basil Wright & me. It is heavenly stuff, isn't it. I'm
sick that Ravel got in first with Daphnis [*Daphnis et Chloé*, 1909–12]
– because I think that is the loveliest love story ever. But Cupid
is good & has I think a greater range. As well as this ballet with
B.W., I am supposed to be doing another with Montagu Slater (a
quasi-political one based on Gulliver – have you read the original
Gulliver? If not do so at <u>once</u> – it is incredibly superb) – and one
based on the Auden work with Rupert Doone.[4] I am also doing
two films or so – so I shall have a busy enough Autumn.[5] Talking
of Communism – I did the music to Slater's last Left Theatre play
– Stay down miner – a <u>very</u> good play, inspite of the Telegraph.[6]

I refuse to talk of politics, it is so depressing – especially at the
moment. It is a faint hope that the Socialists will have done
anything to-day in Parliament.[7]

How did your exam go in town? I am sorry I wasn't in town to
give you my moral support, or to hinder you in your preparation
for it.

How is Lowestoft? Frinton is pleasant, in that it is very quiet &
work-able in. I don't like the people, though – not at all. Some
perhaps. But not most.

I had a great time at Covent Garden this year – Flagstad is a
miracle, and must be heard to be believed.[8]

I am going to Cornwall for July & August. By myself in a hut for
a month, and with family for the rest. Ought to be good.

How goes the C.P.? I am very glad you have taken the plunge.[9]
Very courageous.

Are you well?

Love
BENJAMIN

1 Kurt von Schuschnigg (1897–1977), Austrian Chancellor, 1934–8, years that culminated in the annexation of Austria by Germany; J.H. Thomas (1874–1949), trade union leader and Labour politician. He had been obliged to resign on 22 May from Baldwin's National Government over a supposed Budget 'leak'.

2 The first song, 'Rats Away!', in *Our Hunting Fathers*.

3 The second song, 'Messalina', and the third, 'Dance of Death (Hawking for the Partridge)'.

4 For a composite note on these projects and another unrealized ballet mooted in 1938, see note 2 to Letter 120.

5 Probably *Love from a Stranger*, along with a number of GPO documentaries.

6 W.A. Darlington's unfavourable notice appeared in the *Daily Telegraph*, 11 May:

> I have a very solid respect, founded on personal acquaintance, for Montagu Slater's intellectual gifts. But I do wish that when he writes for the theatre he would avoid the Hyde Park orator's habit of wrapping himself up in a fog of words, so that you can sometimes find out what his subject is but seldom what he is trying to say about it. Clarity is a dramatist's first virtue.
>
> For the greater part of Mr Slater's play, 'Stay Down Miner', presented at the Westminster by the Left Theatre last night, I found it quite impossible to discover what he was driving at. It was vaguely to be apprehended that the theme was a 'stay-down strike' in a coal-mine – but did Mr Slater approve of the strike weapon or didn't he, and if not, why so?
>
> However, in the last act Mr Slater introduced the character of a very stupid police-court magistrate who had to have everything explained to him. With a sigh of relief I identified myself with this gentleman, and at last learnt, that Mr Slater, while deploring violence in general, believes in 'direct action' on occasion.
>
> Even the characters were left vague, with the result that the players spent most of their time struggling to find something to act. Wilfrid Walter, Margaret Yarde, Arthur Goullet and Eadie Palfrey as my friend the magistrate were luckiest in this respect.

7 On the 15th, Britain had abandoned sanctions against Italy, originally imposed in connection with the war in Ethiopia. On the day this letter was written, Clement Attlee called for a vote of censure on the government for its irresponsible foreign policy. The motion was defeated by 214 votes.

8 Britten had heard Kirsten Flagstad (1895–1962), Norwegian soprano, at Covent Garden on a number of occasions in May, and his response was always admiring. On 2 June, he heard her in a broadcast of *Tristan*, Act III, and wrote in his diary,

> a really wonderful show [. . .] with Melchior & Flagstad right on the top of their lovely forms. True I missed Leider, but what a voice this Isolde had, & what serenity in the Liebestod. Jannsen is superb of course. But

what music! It gives me such an inferiority complex & yet makes life worth living with such art – words as well as the incredible music.

9 For a brief time Pounder was a member of the Communist Party, like so many young men of his generation. 'This was the time of Hitler and the Spanish Civil War', he writes, 'and we were all very Left-wing.'

84 To Beth Britten
[EWB, *pp. 95–6*]

Quarryfield, Crantock, Newquay, Cornwall.[1]
July 9th 1936

My dear Beth,

I hope you got my card announcing my arrival the other day. I am sorry I didn't write yesterday but I had to write to Mum & the Bridges & there didn't seem much time besides.

The journey down was very thrilling. The Cornish Riviera is a terrific train and extremely rapid. I had some difficulty in meeting her Nettleship at the station as I had been told the wrong time of arrival & had to wait for her to turn up. She is somewhat strange and unconventional – as you might gather from her letters – but is very kind, not that I see very much of her, though.

The place is very lovely – and beautifully quiet. You can see lots of houses from my window but they are miles across the valley. The coast is very rocky & tempestuous and just as one imagines it to be. Considering all the frightful stories one hears about tragedies in the sea (Miss N. lost a nephew last year – Augustus John's son – here) I don't feel inclined to bathe in a hurry. But the weather has been foul so far – beastly rain all yesterday & a nasty wind to-day – so there hasn't been much temptation.

My woman who is 'doing' for me is very nice & quite a good cook – but it is not going to be exactly cheap – £1 per week for hut, 12/6 for woman, & goodness knows what for food and infinite extras. However I expect I shall manage somehow – but don't send me lots of enormous bills for the Lagonda, will you!

Let me have a card saying how you got back from Lewis'[2] etc. I was very worried about you, inspite of the fact you drove so beautifully to Paddington for me! I should use it alot about town if you want to. Saves fares.

I am enjoying myself alot here really. It is lovely to be able to work with absolutely no interruptions. I have alot of good books & lots of lovely walks. But I daresay after a month I shall be pleased to see you.

I must take this to post. Love to Barbara when you see her, & Kathleen.[3] I hope she gets a job. Isn't it good about Mum letting Biltmore for 2 weeks?[4] Any luck about your flat yet?[5] Perhaps when the summer's over –

Much love,
BENJAMIN

1 Britten left for Cornwall on 7 July. He was met at Newquay by Miss Ethel Nettleship,

who takes me out to Crantock, where I am to live in a hut in her grounds. It is perfectly glorious country – a glorious little village – and, o, the sea view! – so I can foresee a pretty pleasant month – working at <u>Hunting Fathers</u> – reading a lot & walking the neighbourhood.

His current work on the song-cycle commenced the next day, 8 July, when he completed the scoring of the Prologue, and for relaxation 'was pouring over Mahler symphonies & Beethoven later Quartets & there is a tremendous amount in common in them I feel'.

Ethel Nettleship and her sister Ursula (see note 1 to Letter 118) were two of the daughters of the pre-Raphaelite painter Jack Nettleship; another sister, Ida, was the wife of Augustus John (1878–1961), English painter, and died in 1907. Much information about the Nettleship family is to be found in Michael Holroyd's biography of Augustus John (Harmondsworth, Penguin, 1976), in which, on pp. 671–2, there appears an account of the drawing of Ursula's nephew, Henry, to which Britten refers. See also EWB, pp. 94–100.

2 The department store in Oxford Street, London W1.

3 Kathleen Mead, who shared the London flat with Britten and Beth. See EWB, pp. 98 *et seq.*

4 While Mrs Britten was herself away on holiday.

5 Britten had written in his diary on 15 April:

Poor Beth has many worries – whether to continue at Finchley Road at the end of the lease (June) – if so for how long, whom with & can she let her upstairs portion.

85 To Grace Williams
[*Picture postcard: Newquay, Cornwall*
Boyd, p. 34]

Quarryfield, Crantock, Newquay, Cornwall
[July 1936]

The work is going very excitingly at the moment,[1] and what with the country & the solitude I am feeling very blissful. The bathing is so good – too.

How is London? When does the Pirates come off?[2] Best of luck
for it. How's the ballet?[3]

BENJAMIN

1 Britten refers to *Our Hunting Fathers* which had been the subject of
a long and characteristically thoughtful letter from Bridge, on 9 July:

Yes, I think the Fathers <u>should</u> be hunting in public before appearing at
Norwich. Not too long before – 10 days or so. [. . .]

The point is that you must make sure of the music, & if you wanted to
rescore any bit it matters to nobody – but not to <u>rewrite</u> any of it after
printing. If you have any doubt at all – including voice part queries, although
I can't imagine there will be any – then I should withhold publication.
Adequate reduction for piano is essential. [. . .]

Don't even touch the music once it is printed!

I haven't seen this work – except the opening chord – but if you think the
actual performance will make you wish things were different then I should
postpone publication. Precisely what is in your mind about being "sure there
will be a good many alterations" may even now point to revision <u>before</u> the
first taste at the rehearsal. You look into it <u>now</u>!! Avoid the experiment.

Bridge was to write again to the composer about the work, after
attending the studio broadcast given by Sophie Wyss, with the BBC
Symphony Orchestra conducted by Adrian Boult, on 30 April 1937:

It is an odd thing that music has to have really the right approach in order
to make its own mark. I felt rather a lot in sympathy for you about Friday
night's performance. Beyond 'Our hunting fathers' I heard almost no other
words & this left everybody wondering precisely what it was all about. Even
Marj. <u>'over the air'</u> didn't hear the words. But, both Ethel & I got much
more of your work at Norwich with all its short-comings & bad conditions
of rehearsal etc. The quintescence of disappointment on your young face
was so marked that had I had a few minutes alone with you, I might have
consoled you with the fact 'that many a good work has begun its public life
in much the same indifferent way.' It is extremely hard to bear, but one
<u>must</u> & I suppose <u>does</u>, anyway. Of course, a real blot on the prog., having
a further display of xylophone colour immediately [Leighton Lucas's *Sinfonia
Brevis* for horn and eleven instruments, which incorporated Javanese game-
lan effects], was perfectly sickening for me. And surely for you too. You'll
have to reconcile yourself about even the smaller public getting to know
your work. Opportunities are not likely to be many.

2 Grace Williams was teaching at Camden High School for Girls and
this was probably a school production of Gilbert and Sullivan's *The
Pirates of Penzance* in which she was involved.

3 Williams's unpublished ballet, *Theseus and Ariadne* (1935).

Monday, 20 July 1936
[*Crantock*]

I work hard at scoring – nearing the end of Hawking – & very
excited – do 13 pages to-day – working, morning, aft., & after
dinner.[1] The weather is execrable to start with, but afternoon &
evening are superb. Have a good bathe after tea with Miss N –
surfing with a board for the first time – & good it is, too.
Incidentally, Lennox Berkeley writing this morning (saying he's
coming here on Sat) tells me to listen to J. Françaix's Piano
Concertino[2] this evening (not specifying time). Which of course,
as I have no wireless – nor know anyone here who has, is
impossible. However – coming back thro village after a heavenly
beach-walk at 10.45 – I hear a wireless, stop & listen, hear
announcer say – 'You will now hear a concertino by J.F. . . .' &
so hear whole thing. It is very charming & what with wind in trees
& cool of Summer evening it makes a delicious effect. Perhaps
too much like the other works I know of his (Trio, Vln Conc.)[3] –
but nevertheless – musical.

Spanish revolution – those bloody fascists trying to get back into
power. However it seems as tho the Government & people have
the situation in hand.[4]

1 Britten was working on the full score of *Our Hunting Fathers*. 'Hawking' = 'Dance of Death' in the published version.

2 Jean Françaix, French composer (b. 1912). His Concertino was written
in 1932.

3 There is no violin concerto. Britten must have been thinking of the
1934 *Suite concertante*, for violin and orchestra.

4 On 18 July a military rebellion led by Franco against the Spanish
government marked the beginning of the Spanish Civil War. Britten's
diary for 22 July reads:

News makes me sick from Spain. The rebel Fascists seem to be doing
better, & according to the definitely pro-fascist Daily Telegraph –
practically all N. Spain, Morocco, & alot of South is in their hands –
including Barcelona! Toni & Peggy Brosa are staying there too. Let's pray
for better news to-morrow. A big battle is likely to-day or to-night.

In this same diary entry, Britten writes 'After dinner read alot more
Marx. Hard going though edifying.' Grappling with Marx was very
much a sign of the decade. Thus at the end of 1931, Hugh Thomas
reports John Strachey writing to Palme Dutt in these terms:

What I am doing for the moment is to attempt to educate myself by acquiring the grounding of Marxist theory. For example, I am in the middle of the second volume of *Das Kapital*, which, I am ashamed to say, I have never read. A systematic reading of the first volume is certainly a tremendous experience, especially at the moment, when one sees so many of Marx's predictions being uncannily fulfilled [. . .]

(Hugh Thomas, *John Strachey*, (London, Eyre Methuen, 1973), p. 114)

86 To Mrs Britten

Quarryfield, Crantock, Newquay.
[28 July 1936]

My darling,

Thank you for all your letters – that certainly is a record – three in one week! Thank you very much. I am glad you are enjoying your stay with the school[1] – I do envy you as it is a nice place & must be exciting with all the things happening. I think the cup is a splendid idea – Pop would love it I'm sure – & swimming is pleasant too. They hadn't a swimming cup before, had they? I hope parents' day was a roaring success. Tell them I thought about them, with pleasure when the afternoon was fine – a strange occurrence for Crantock as the weather is as treacherous as ever. To-day is foul tho' yesterday was good.

Lennox Berkeley[2] arrived here after all on Saturday – he made alterations in his plans in order to come here. He is a dear & is helping me alot with Our Hunting Fs. The score of that was finished last Friday & I feel very relieved. Now I'm doing a piano reduction for print – to be finished this week if poss. It is very strange to have someone to talk to after all this time! but I'm getting to like it – & getting in practice for when you come down! You'd like Lennox alot – but he has to leave before you arrive. Miss Nettleship says it is O.K. for you to come on Friday – it is not certain where you'll be put yet – but somewhere somehow.

I made great friends with the family here last week – after great feud at the beginning of the week. True, they weren't exactly intellectuals but amusing & very useful with their car and surfboards. We parted yesterday with many protestations of affection. The father was priceless – in the Admiralty – everything was done in nautical terms (often very obstruse) – & he was a true blue of course – we had one or two arguments about the Spanish business,[3] but like practically all his class, he knew nothing about it (or anything that way) & only quoted from the Morning Post – not very difficult to argue with! By-the-way, isn't

it frightful about Barcelona? Toni & Peggy [Brosa] are still there –
he's playing 1st night at the Proms & no Spaniards are allowed
out.[4] Judging by all accounts (& I bought every paper, from Times
to Herald,[5] the last few days) the government is gaining ground
all round. But what about the fascists lining up all the little Popular
Front boys against a wall & putting the machine guns on them?
Imagine English boys of 14 even knowing what Popular Front
means – much less dying for it.[6]

Lennox & I are just going in to Newquay, so I mustn't write
much. The tide is down & so we can walk across the bridge – you
will love this quaint old place. And as for surfing you will go dotty
over it – there is nothing like it in the world. I stay in for hours &
come out solidified with cold.

How's John?[7] I bet he's fine now. I wish I could see him. I have
made great friends with Derek the son of the woman who comes
in to do for us. He is just a month younger than John, but very
lovely.

Love to all of them. I hope the end of term will go smoothly, &
reports will get done well.

By the way how are you getting here. There is a very good train
from Birmingham getting here at 5.20. Could you get on to that
some how? I'll arrange about meeting you.[8]

By-the-way also – you quote a long paragraph about me & films
– but you don't say when or where it was?

Much love – hope you're well & not doing too much,

BENJAMIN

1 Mrs Britten was staying with Robert at his school in North Wales.
2 Lennox Randal Francis Berkeley (1903–1989), English composer, was
   educated at Gresham's (a decade before Britten attended the school)
   and Oxford, where he was a contemporary of Auden's. He studied
   with Nadia Boulanger in Paris, 1927–32. He was knighted in 1974.
   Berkeley and Britten first met in 1936, at the Barcelona ISCM Festival
   (see PFL, plate 83). There are entries in Britten's diaries for 1931 which
   record his hearing performances of Berkeley's works in advance of
   his meeting the composer, e.g. 17 March: 'v. interesting suite [*Petite
   Suite*] of L. Berkeley for Vlc and Oboe (H. Gaskell)'.

   Berkeley had arrived in Cornwall on 25 July at 5.20pm and was
   met by Britten at Newquay:

   Get a bathe in before dinner [. . .] & after dinner a lovely walk on beach
   with Lennox.

   26 July
   I have lunch in with Lennox & after a short read – he, my H.F. [*Our*

Hunting Fathers], & I his Jonah & also Wozzeck (marvellous work) we go
for a glorious walk via Holywell (tea) on to Hoblin Cove – my famous
spot of last Sunday – and even further. He is a dear and we agree on most
points & it is nice to discuss things we don't agree on! Get back for a meal
at 8.30 – talk read & an early bed – exhausted!

27 July
Don't do overmuch in the morning – wander down to the village as usual
with Lennox after breakfast & then back here, where it pours with rain.
I start piano score of H.F. – he writes letters before lunch.

28 July
A mostly filthy morning. It pelts & there is a vile wind so we stay in –
Len. writes letters & I get on with the vocal score – or rather the duets
[piano] portions so as to be able to try them with him. It clears in afternoon
& we have a glorious bathe & then lie together on the beach partly naked
– sun bathing. Heavenly. After tea a long walk down the Gannel to look
for tennis courts – in vain. Work hard after dinner & late bed & even
later to sleep. Lennox has brought with him scores of the new Walton (Bb)
& Vaughan Williams (F min) symphonies & we spend most hysterical
evenings pulling them to pieces – the amateurishness & clumsiness of the
Williams – the 'gitters' ['jitters'] of the fate-ridden Walton – & the over
pretentiousness of both – & <u>abominable</u> scoring. The directions in the score
too are most mirth condusive! It isn't that one is cruel about their works
which are naturally better than a tremendous amount of English music –
but it is only that so much is pretended of them, & they are compared
to the great Beethoven, Mozart, Mahler symphonies.

29 July
After normal down the village jaunt in morning I work & Lennox goes
with Miss Nettleship to see about a piano for us, which we go to in the
aft. but it is a very poor instrument & the effect of Our Hunting Fathers
& Lennox' new organ & piano pieces [Op. 4] on it is beyond description!
[. . .]
   After dinner – much walk & talk with Lennox & then we drive into
Newquay with Miss N. & pick up some friends of hers (mother, aunt,
child) from a concert-hall – & we afterwards till 12.0 odd have tea with
them. Long talks before sleep – it is extraordinary how intimate one
becomes when the lights are out!

30 July
Miss N. takes Lennox in to catch 11.45 up to town. I go with them & we
partake of a very sorrowing farewell. He is an awful dear – very intelligent
& kind – & I am very attached to him, even after this short time. In spite
of his avowed sexual weakness for young men of my age & form – he is
considerate & open, & we have come to an agreement on that subject.
   We have decided to work alot together – especially on the Spanish tunes
[*Mont Juic*]. [. . .] Work again before & after dinner – with a sherry &
coffee from the Banfords (now staying in the bungalow). Early to bed –
but admittedly quite lonely!

   The two composers had become close friends; and the friendship
– which in the event was to be a very long one – was consolidated

by their work together on their joint orchestral suite, *Mont Juic* (see note 2 to Letter 122) and yet further confirmed by Berkeley sharing the occupancy of the Old Mill at Snape with Britten. His furniture was moved in on 13 April 1938, and he rented the Mill after Britten's departure for North America in May 1939. Beth Welford writes in EWB, p. 106:

Lennox Berkeley was also wanting somewhere in the country to work, so Ben asked him if he would like to share the Mill with him. Lennox would pay rent, and the granary was made into a studio for him.

(They had earlier investigated the possibility of a farmhouse in Berkshire, an idea, probably, of Peter Burra's, who wrote to his sister about it.) Berkeley worked for the BBC from 1942 to 1945. Berkeley and Britten remained friends throughout the post-war years, and a number of major Berkeley performances were given at Aldeburgh Festivals, e.g. his operas *A Dinner Engagement* (1954), *Ruth* (1957) and *Castaway* (1967), and the first performance in England of his *Stabat Mater*, Op. 28 (1947), conducted by Britten. His *Four Poems of St Teresa of Avila* (for alto and string orchestra) were performed by Janet Baker and the Aldeburgh Festival Orchestra conducted by the composer at the Aldeburgh Festival of 1960. Berkeley and Britten jointly composed the suite of Catalan dances, *Mont Juic*, which was generated by their trip to Barcelona, in 1936 (see note 2 to Letter 122). While in Cornwall, Berkeley also worked on his oratorio, *Jonah* (see note 1 to Letter 112). Berkeley's eldest son, Michael (b. 1948), one of Britten's godsons, was also to become a composer.

In the same year – 1938 – Britten dedicated his Piano Concerto to Berkeley and Berkeley his *Introduction and Allegro* for two pianos and orchestra to Britten. Berkeley had written in an undated letter to Britten while he was still at work on the concerto:

I hope you will find time to get on with the Piano Concerto. Of course there is no hurry, but I'm so excited about it, and very proud about your dedicating it to me (if you really want to). In a way I feel that I almost deserve it, because you have no greater admirer.

See also Introduction, pp. 39–41, and the following obituary notices: Hugo Cole, 'Music with a French Accent', *Guardian*, 27 December 1989; Peter Dickinson and Roger Nichols, *Independent*, 27 December 1989; *The Times*, 27 December 1989; and Edward Thomas, a supplementary obituary in the *Independent*, 30 December 1989. A tribute to Berkeley by Malcom Williamson appeared in the *Musical Times* April 1990, pp. 197–9.

3 The outbreak of the Civil War. Britten's diary for 1936 is full of references to the 'Spanish business' – the revolution in Spain had broken out in July, and was to lead to the Civil War, the key political event of the thirties. The conflict (which had been preceded by Italy's invasion of Abyssinia towards the end of 1935) played the same role

in Britten's consciousness – and conscience – that it played in the consciousness of his close friends, indeed in the awareness and imagination of a whole generation of artists, musicians and writers. Thus his diary for this fateful year is among the most 'politicized' of the sequence: a commentary on Spain and the Civil War is maintained throughout

On 5 November Britten wrote: 'Madrid bombed by air for umpteenth time. No. of children killed not specified. 70 were killed in one go the other day, What price Facism?' These are words that already embody the preoccupation – the slaughter of children that is part of war – that was to result in Britten's late song-cycle, *Who are these children?*, Op. 84 (1969), in which death from the air is singled out for special attention. This was also the year in which Britten's friendship with Auden powerfully developed. For example, on 7 December, in response to Auden's announcement to the composer (1 December) that he had decided 'to go to Spain after Xmas & fight', Britten wrote: 'He is the most charming, most vital, genuine & important person I know & if the Spanish Rebels kill him it will be a bloody atrocity.' (Auden visited Spain in 1937 and returned unscathed: see note 2 to Letter 92.) There is no doubt that this intensely influential association encouraged Britten to embark on Marx and to make this kind of observation when out for a walk in Cornwall:

[. . .] go for a 3 hours walk in morning over the common to Holywell Bay – a heavenly walk (marred only by the fact that one has to trespass so much – enormous stretches of uncultivatable land marked 'Private' for sale – with no sign of any life on them – oh this capitalist system!).

It was against the background of all this political turbulence that *Our Hunting Fathers* was brought to completion.

The composition of that song-cycle, Auden, Spain and the death of Berg – these were some of the leading themes that made up the texture of Britten's life in 1936.

The *Morning Post* was a daily newspaper of pronounced right-wing opinions, and was later to be merged with the *Daily Telegraph*.

4 Britten's diary for 7 August reads:

Hear from Frank B. that Toni & Peggy are back from Barcelona alright – & have experienced no horrors of any sort. I'm relieved – exceedingly.

Brosa performed the Mendelssohn Violin Concerto with the BBC Symphony Orchestra conducted by Henry Wood at the first night of the Proms, 8 August, at the Queen's Hall, London.

5 The *Daily Herald*, a daily newspaper, published from 1911 to 1964, and associated with the politics and policies of the Labour, Co-operative and Trades Union movements.

6 Rumours of Civil War atrocities were widespread in 1936, and per-

haps this was one of them. Hugh Thomas's *The Spanish Civil War* (Harmondsworth, Penguin Books, 1977), Chapter 16, offers evidence of atrocities committed by both sides which were quite the equal in horror to what Britten describes. The impact such stories were to have on him can be felt in his diary entry for 24 July: 'A long walk after dinner, after which I sketch a bit of a funeral march to those youthful Spanish martyrs.' This funeral march was never completed, but the dead of the Civil War were to be commemorated in *Ballad of Heroes*.

7 Britten's nephew.

8 Mrs Britten reached Newquay on Friday, 31 July.

87 To Alan Bush[1]

Quarryfield, Crantock, Newquay, Cornwall.
[?14 August 1936]

Many thanks for your letter & enclosure. As a matter of fact I have already become a subscriber to Ars Viva[2] so I shall post this copy to another person likely to be interested. I am at the moment frantically busy here – & I want to give your letter consideration; but I will write at the earliest possible moment. I have sent word to O.U.P., & Boosey & Hawkes to send you copies of some of my things – and I will write you something with my comments on your letter.[3] This [is] a heavenly spot, but it <u>will</u> rain so much!

Yours,

BENJAMIN BRITTEN

1 Alan Bush (b. 1900), English composer, studied at the Academy, 1918–22, and privately with John Ireland. He taught at the Academy from 1925. He was (and has remained) a convinced member of the Communist Party and was active in the thirties in left-wing musical circles. It was Bush who conducted the first performance of Britten's *War and Death (Russian Funeral)* for brass band on 8 March 1936 at the Westminster Theatre in a programme given by the London Labour Choral Union. The programme for this event (reproduced in *Alan Bush: An 80th Birthday Symposium*, edited by Ronald Stevenson (Kidderminster, Bravura Publications, 1981), p. 81) describes the work as 'an impression for brass orchestra'. Bush was prominent in organizing, in 1939, a 'Festival of Music for the People', which included the first performance of Britten's *Ballad of Heroes*, Op. 14. In his autobiographical *In My Eighth Decade and Other Essays* (London, Kahn & Averill, 1980), p. 21, Bush writes of his particular association

with Hanns Eisler's *Die Massnahme* ('The Expedient'), with a text by Brecht, the first English performance of which was given in the same programme as Britten's brass band piece: 'I conducted in different districts in London ten performances of *Die Massnahme* in an English translation.' The 1939 Festival was an event that aroused the retrospective wrath of Basil Maine in 1940, who wrote in his *New Paths in Music* (London, Nelson), pp. 92–3:

Whether this was to be regarded as an attempt to drag music into politics or politics into music, the motive in either case was to be reproved. [. . .] The organizer [. . .] was Alan Bush, and [. . .] it is chiefly due to him that this unhappy association of music and politics exists in Great Britain.

A backhander which, we suppose, was a salute of a kind; and even Maine felt bound to add that Bush 'has considerable claim to be considered purely as a composer'. (Even Bridge, in an undated letter, was constrained to write to Britten in connection with his Piano Concerto, '[. . .] I have been wishing for a long time that the art of composition would soon be a part of your subconscious self, instead of an "also ran" with poets in a political net.') During 1940 the BBC's hostility to those on the left of the political spectrum brought about the banning of Bush's music on the air. Following Vaughan Williams's widely publicized support of Bush, the ban was retracted although, as Lewis Foreman has observed, 'exposure of his music on the air suffered, and never really recovered until many years afterwards' (LFBML, pp. 239–40). Britten's relationship with Bush in post-war years was occasional but Peter Pears commissioned a song-cycle from him, *Voices of the Prophets* (1953). No works of his were heard at Aldeburgh until 1977: see *Music of Forty Festivals: A List of works performed at Aldeburgh Festivals from 1948 to 1987*, compiled by Rosamund Strode (Aldeburgh, Aldeburgh Foundation/Britten–Pears Library, 1987).

In November 1936 Bush and Britten, along with Walton and Lambert, were to provide themes for improvisation by the French organist, André Marchal (1894–1980). Britten wrote in his diary on 12 November:

At 7.45 I go up to Bloomsbury & after a meal with Lennox Berkeley we meet Grace & go to a recital of the Organ Music Society – at St. John's [Red Lion Square, London] given by André Marchal, the blind French organist. First part of programme all ord. organ stuff, well played I suppose, but not to my taste. The 2nd half was a Symphony improvised on themes by 4 English Composers (Fugue, Alan Bush – Scherzo, me – Adagio, Walton – Toccata, Lambert). It is amazingly clever & inconceivable since he is blind. My scherzo was a quaint odd little thing, very French & exotic.

An invitation of a similar kind was extended in 1945, when Britten was asked by the BBC to submit themes on which the French organist

Marcel Dupré (1886–1971) would improvise a Prelude and Fugue, on 24 July. The themes were reproduced in *Tempo*, 12, September 1945, p. 233.

2 A journal that never materialized.

3 Britten had received and replied to a previous letter from Bush. He wrote in his diary on 2 August:

> I spend an afternoon writing a letter to Alan Bush who is giving a series of lectures on English Music in Switzerland & wants to include me – so he wants my opinions on music & life in general – very difficult to give at short notice.

The letter has not survived.

88   To Grace Williams
[*Postcard: Newquay, Cornwall*
Boyd, p. 34]

Quarryfield
[Postmarked 28 August 1936][1]

Thank you for the card – it looks <u>quite</u> nice, but nothing compared to <u>this</u> beach <u>and</u> the glorious surfing. I have to start work on Monday & feel sehr traurig -   A commercial film, but it sounds interesting.[2] Sophie Wyss[3] has been staying here a bit, & we have worked at the meisterwerk [*Our Hunting Fathers*]. How are you? When do you return to London?

BENJ

1 In Boyd this postcard is incorrectly attributed to 28 July.

2 *Love from a Stranger* (Capitol – later Trafalgar – Films, 1937), the only feature film for which Britten composed incidental music, directed by Rowland V. Lee and produced by Max Schach. It was based on the stage play by Frank Vosper, derived from Agatha Christie's short story *Philomel Cottage*, and included Ann Harding and Basil Rathbone in the cast. A series of frustrating delays prevented Britten from writing his score until November 1936, when, with Grace Williams's help as amanuensis, it was completed in the space of a few days. The title music to the film, depicting a stormy night in London, is of special interest. It comprises the most extended stretch of music in the score and reveals, in musical character and orchestral technique, a clear anticipation of the 'Storm' interlude in *Peter Grimes*. It was while working on *Love from a Stranger* that Britten first met Boyd Neel, who was acting as the film's music director (see note 3 to Letter 106). See also PR, pp. 148–71 and 482–3.

3 Sophie Wyss (1897–1983), Swiss soprano who settled in England in

1925. She gave the first performances of *Our Hunting Fathers* (see diary for 19 September); *On this Island*, Op. 11 (see notes 2 and 3 to Letter 109; Broadcasting House, London, 19 November 1937, with Britten); and *Les Illuminations*, Op. 18 (see note 2 to Letter 181, first performance of the complete work, London, 30 January 1940, conducted by Boyd Neel). These three works were written with her voice in mind. Wyss (and her husband, Arnold Gyde (1894–1959)) joined Britten in Cornwall on Saturday, 22 August, staying in rooms in the village that Britten and his mother had found for them. She then spent time with Britten rehearsing the new song-cycle. Britten wrote in his diary on 26 August, 'Have a long rehearsal in Village Hall with Sophie at Our H.F. – she is beginning to sing it very well indeed.' See also PFL, plates 88 (where caption ought to read 'Crantock, August 1936') and 89.

Saturday, 19 September 1936
[*London*]

After endless business arrangements I go up to Boosey & Hawkes to sign my contract with Capitol. After that shop at Mappin & Webb[1] (discount thro' B & H) to buy christening present for my god-child! Beth meets me at Waterloo at 1.30 & we go down to Surbiton (sandwiches in train). A very pleasant afternoon with the Gydes – Humphrey is christened & I officiate. At 6.0 we (Beth, Sophie & Arnold [i.e. her husband]) come back to Covent Garden & then begins the most catostrophic evening of my life. Waiting till 8.30 to begin the rehearsal of Our Hunting Fathers[2] – the orchestra (fourth day of 9 hours rehearsal) is at the end of it's tether – no discipline at all – no one there to enforce it. I get thoroughly het up & disparate – can't hear a thing in the wretched Foyer. I get alot of the speeds wrong & very muddled – but I'm glad to say that in spite of the fooling in the orchestra & titters at the work – the 'Rats' especially brought shreaks of laughter – the rehearsal got better & better. But it was impossible & it takes all Arnold's optimism and kindness when he & S. take Beth & me to a nice meal at Strand Pal. to cheer me at all – but I'm feeling pretty suicidal.

1 The silversmiths and jewellers in Regent Street, London.
2 This notoriously turbulent rehearsal was attended by Vaughan Williams, who, according to Sophie Wyss, reproved the orchestra, whereupon 'they pulled themselves together and gave a fair performance'.

Monday, 21 September 1936
[*London/Norwich*]

Up betimes – & to Liverpool St. – meet Sophie W. and we catch
9.48 together to Norwich. Most of the orchestra are on the train
& after Saturday's catastrophe I don't feel too inclined to meet
them. Audrey Sutton (Alston) meets us & we both go out to
Framingham Earl (where we are staying with A) for lunch & she
takes us back to Norwich for a rehearsal ($\frac{1}{2}$hr) in the aft – when I
am relieved to say things improve alot. Back to Framingham for a
high tea (Jack Moeran & Patrick Hadley also there) & then back
to St. Andrews Hall for a grand 'rehearsal' (with packed audience).
I fear I don't take much notice of the audience & rehearse as hard
as the one hour permits. It doesn't go perhaps so well as the aft.
but the orchestra were a bit more tired I suppose. Some people
are very excited over the work.[1]

1 We reproduce Britten's own note on *Our Hunting Fathers*, which
appeared in the Festival programme for the first performance on
Friday, the 25th:

Poems on animals in their relationship to humans – as pests, pets, and as a
means of sport – have been chosen by W.H. Auden as a basis for this work.
To these he has added a prologue and an epilogue.
     The scoring is for soprano solo and a normal concert orchestra (with the
addition of a saxophone).
     Prologue – [*Lento quasi recitativo*]   The words are set in a natural recitative
fashion for the voice – supported by simple chords for the full orchestra. At
'O pride so hostile to our charity' the strings introduce a phrase which
receives considerable prominence in each subsequent movement.
     [A]   Rats Away! – [*Allegro con fuoco*]   Loud fragmentary phrases for full
orchestra, and eventually for the soloist, lead to an emphatic protest from
the wood-wind. The soloist interrupts this with a rapid chant, against a very
light background in the orchestra. When 'St. Kasi' is reached, quick quaver
figures in the flutes and bassoons indicate a more subjective aspect of the
pests. After a slight lull, the chant reappears in a more dignified form. But
this time it is swamped gradually by the orchestra – the fragmentary phrases
(from the beginning of the song) even creeping into the soloist's part. At
the end the wood-wind protest dies away somewhat hopelessly.
     [B]   Messalina – [*Andante Lento*]   Alternating with some emotional string
passages the soloist repeatedly laments 'Ay me, alas, heigh-ho!' Then she
tells the sad story in a simple melodic line, which grows more and more
passionate. A horn *glissando* is the climax, then a long series of heart-broken
lamentations follows – started by the soloist and culminating with the saxophone. A few quiet chords for violas and 'cellos commit the soul to rest.
     [C]   Dance of Death (Hawking for the Partridge) – [*Prestissimo vivace*]   The
soprano runs rapidly through the names of most of the birds concerned in

this hunt, interspersing it often with the cry 'whurret!' The orchestra takes this to a climax. A sudden outburst from the trombones is the first indication that all is not as well as it might be. However with an effort the orchestra recovers, and the soloist launches into a hearty song – 'Sith sickles and the shearing scythes!' At a climax the roll-call is again called, but once more the trombones interrupt. Something depressing appears to have happened, as the succeeding passage is of a wailing nature, with sad 'whurrets' for the clarinet, and dismal 3rds in the bassoons – perhaps a bird has been hurt. But after another bang the movement continues with additional energy, and a big climax follows with a much extended version of 'Sith sickles' on the trumpet and wood-wind. 'Well flown, eager kite!' is sung exultantly by the soloist. At this everyone falls to dancing a merry folk measure, but the trombones interrupt again and with a string *glissando* the movement proceeds with more desperation than before – the soloist is left far behind. The trombones continue with their interruption and eventually overwhelm everyone. The percussion maintains an exhausted roll; vain efforts are made to restart the movement: but the death is sounded by the muted brass. A 'whurret!' from the top of the soloist to the bottom of the double-basses finishes the movement.

Epilogue and Funeral March – [*Andante molto lento*]   A ghost of the hunting song on the xylophone appears at intervals. The soloist sings the words in a simple recitation, with fragmentary support from the orchestra. When the words 'that human company' are reached the fragments gather into a broader theme for violins, which reaches a climax at the word 'anonymous'. The work finishes with a funeral march for the whole orchestra (brass and percussion muted, strings *col legno* and *pizzicato*) with fragments from other movements, and the ghost on the xylophone persisting to the end.

A full-page spread on the Triennial Musical Festival was published in the *Eastern Daily Press* on 22 September and included the following preview of Britten's new work:

The other new work in Friday morning's programme – Benjamin Britten's 'Our Hunting Fathers' – a 'symphonic cycle' for soprano and orchestra, falls naturally to be considered next, perhaps because in almost every respect it is at the opposite pole to 'Five Tudor Portraits'. It is based on a scheme devised by W.H. Auden – one of the most brilliant of the younger school of poets – on the subject of animals and their various human aspects. Mr Auden has taken three old English poems illustrative of the human attitude to animals respectively as pests, as pets and as objects of the chase, and added a prologue and an epilogue of his own commenting on these different attitudes. Of the musical setting I cannot do better than quote Mr Britten's own words. 'The work is difficult,' he says, 'both for orchestra and for the soloist, who has a most exacting part throughout. But Sophie Wyss, who is singing the work, makes light of these difficulties.' Whatever those difficulties may be one thing is certain, that in this work we shall be hearing the music of a young English composer whose strong individuality and marked originality have already brought him exceptional distinction in the musical world. For all that he is still in the very early twenties Britten has twice had the honour of having works chosen for and performed at the International

Contemporary Music Festivals of 1934 and 1936, and both his choral and orchestral music has frequently appeared in the programmes of the B.B.C. Both Dr Vaughan Williams and he will conduct the performances of their own works at the Festival.

Friday, 25 September 1936
[*Norwich*]

Breakfast at 9.0 after which Sophie & I have abt. ½ hrs work on the H.F. & then alot of us go in to the first half of the morning programme in St. Andrews Hall (me already rigged out in full morning dress – most uncomfortable!) I sit with F.B. & E.E.B. – Mum & Beth (1st staying with Mrs. Chamberlain in Surlingham, & 2nd in Lowestoft with Sewells) sitting together somewhere. Jelli D'araigny[1] plays the Brahms (handicapped by Stathams[2] laboured conducting) & V. Williams conducts a very successful show of his 5 Tudor Portraits (1st perf.) – not my music, but obviously the music for the audience.[3] After a hurried lunch at Fram. we go back to the hall – & I conduct 1st perf. of my Hunting Fathers with Sophie Wyss – who is excellent indeed. The orchestra plays better than I had dared to hope – tho' one or two slips. I am <u>very</u> pleased with it & it goes down quite well – most of the audience being very interested if bewildered. A very complimentary & excited gathering in the artist's room afterwards – including F. Bridge &

The cover of the programme of the 34th Norfolk and Norwich Triennial Musical Festival, 1936, and the title page of the vocal score of *Our Hunting Fathers*

Mrs. B., – Vaughan Williams, J. Moeran, Patrick Hadley, Ralph
Hawkes, Basil Wright, J. Cheetal [Cheatle], Rupert Doone, Robert
Medley, Alstons galore, Mum & Beth, Ronald Duncan etc. etc.
Back to Fram. after that – a spirited game of tennis with Christopher
A. before early meal at 6.30 after which we go back to ev. concert of
Delius Mass of Life. Sit with Mum & F.B. – & am very bored. Too
much of same style & mannerisms. Back & a large party – enjoy
myself, but pretty tired.

1 Jelly d'Arányi, the Hungarian-born violinist (1895–1966).

2 Heathcote Statham (1889–1973), organist of Norwich Cathedral, conductor of the Norwich Philharmonic Society and joint conductor with
Beecham of the Triennial Festival. He was educated at Gresham's.

3 But see Michael Kennedy, *Britten* (London, Dent, 1981), p. 22, who
reports that during the Vaughan Williams, 'the bawdy poems of
Skelton caused the elderly Countess of Albermarle to turn purple in
the face and walk out, loudly exclaiming "Disgusting".'

Saturday, 26 September 1936
[*Norwich/Frinton*]

Notices of my work vary from flattering & slightly bewildered (D.
Tel.) – to reprehension & disapproving (Times) – but I am pleased,
because what could be the use of a work of this kind if the narrow-
minded, prejudiced snobbish Colles (forinstance) approved?[1] See
Sophie off in Norwich at 10.23 – & back at Framingham F.B. & EEB
go off at abt. 11.30. Then Christopher & I have a short game of
tennis & after lunch Audrey takes me in to Norwich in her car –
goes on to the Festival (last concert) while I go to see Bill Wakeford
in his 'Gift Shop'.[2] Catch 3.40 to Frinton – meeting Mum & Beth at
Colchester – arr. here at 6.39 (!) & go up to house in the old town-
bus – really a decrepit old horse carriage!

1 A review by Basil Maine of the new work by 'the young Lowestoft
composer' appeared in the *Eastern Daily Press* on 26 September:

The afternoon brought another novelty – Benjamin Britten's 'Our Hunting
Fathers', and again the new music was conducted by the composer and by
the way, conducted very skilfully. This work is a symphonic cycle for soprano
solo and orchestra and appears as Britten's Opus 8. He has taken for text
poems chosen by W.H. Auden to state the theme of 'Man and the Animals'.
The theme is extended by Mr Auden in a prologue and epilogue.
    Both for performers and audience the music is exacting, being uncompro-

mising and of an uncommonly dry quality. But it has the great merit of being positive and individual. It is not in the slightest problematic. On the contrary, the composer makes himself clear in each of the five movements, eloquently so in the episode called 'Messalina', naïvely so in the final Funeral March. The question for the listener to settle is whether the composer, being clear, is communicating to him a vital experience and communicating it with 'the rightness of a god' – for of every creative artist we ask as much.

Of Miss Sophie Wyss, as soloist, it was required that she walk a tight-rope, so to say, and pretend there was no danger. Her fears were not entirely hidden; none the less she made hardly a false step, and for that alone she must be given more than conventional praise.

Richard Capell in the *Daily Telegraph*, 26 September:

'Our Hunting Fathers' is called a symphonic cycle for soprano and orchestra. The text was composed and compiled by W.H. Auden, a poet so little known to Norwich as yet that his name was twice differently mis-spelled in the programme. It is about animals. The central movements, based on texts from archaic sources, consist of an exorcism of rats, a lament for a dead monkey and a falconer's song.

Mr Auden's prologue and epilogue speak in difficult terms of the relations between men and beasts. So difficult, indeed, are these terms that there was some excuse for the member of the audience who took them for clues to a crossword puzzle. Mr Britten's music suggested no sedate English provincial festival, but rather a meeting of the International Society for Contemporary Music.

It is Puck-like music, fantastically nimble and coruscating, having, like Puck, the advantage, if sheer will-of-the-wispness of movement and effect is the kind of activity wanted, of being without flesh or bones. The general impression is a kind of orchestral prank in which the instruments lead a distracted human voice into one embarrassing position after another. The voice in question belonged to clever Sophie Wyss, a Swiss singer, who before she performs the piece again should be coached in some of the niceties of English, for instance, the difference between the pronunciation of 'Ay' and 'Aye'.

The Times, 26 September:

We are not able to say with equal definiteness what Mr Benjamin Britten's suite for soprano voice and orchestra called 'Our Hunting Fathers' has con-tributed. It was kindly received, either because the composer is the youngest of the products of East Anglia represented here, or because he so evidently knows exactly what sort of sound he wants to make at every moment, or because his singer, Miss Sophie Wyss, showed herself almost as clever as he is, or because his audience shares with him some sense of music or of humour, or both, to which we are strangers. Anyhow, we will not be accused of being intolerant (with the accent on the third syllable) like the Lion of his epilogue. Though only now 23 he is no newcomer. His earlier works have made their mark, and perhaps this one will; or, if it is just a stage to be got through, we wish him safely and quickly through it.

The review continued:

This festival is full of local associations. Skelton sets Vaughan Williams writing real folk music, every note of it his own, but music for real people to sing and enjoy, music that is merry and serious at the same time. We wish we knew whether young Britten's music is meant to be either.

This review (in the then *Times* tradition of anonymity) was contributed by H.C. Colles (1879–1943), the chief music critic of *The Times* from 1911 to the time of his death. He was succeeded by Frank Howes.

Among the Sundays, A.H. Fox Strangways in the *Observer* wrote on 27 September:

After Vaughan Williams, struggling in the thicket of his poetic fancies, even in so bluff a work, to come upon Benjamin Britten, lightly unburdening himself of dire nonsense, was a curious experience. Since, however, those parts which W.H. Auden has directly contributed to the text of 'Our Hunting Fathers' remain obscure after a tenth reading, judgement of Mr Britten's composition as a whole would be unfair. But it did seem, all things considered, that what he had done was hardly worth doing, and that, having done it, he would have served his reputation better had he remained like the hunting fathers at the end of Auden's text (or is it the present generation? – or the lion?) anonymous.

The October issue of the *Musical Times* included a review by Edwin Evans:

In the afternoon came another novelty, Benjamin Britten's song cycle with overture, *Our Hunting Fathers,* sung by Sophie Wyss, who sailed imperturbably through the reefs and shoals of its many and formidable difficulties. It is a clever work, clever almost to a fault. Britten evidently likes to 'live dangerously'. He is, however, so sure-footed that he can skirt precipices as he chooses, and it is of his years (23) to prefer them to meadow sweet. In short, this work is teasing, irritating or enjoyable according to the way you take it. I have two faults to find. Lines as recondite as those of W.H. Auden's epilogue do not get over. Song needs more directness; and this section is extended out of proportion to the rest.

Not a single critic betrayed an inkling of awareness of the song-cycle's urgent political, historical dimension: even the startling juxtaposition of 'German, Jew' in the coda of the 'Dance of Death' went unheard and unremarked. This deafening silence remains perhaps the most disconcerting feature of the work's reception.

A broadcast performance of *Our Hunting Fathers* (under Boult) followed in 1937. Thereafter, total neglect engulfed the work until it was revived at Chelsea Town Hall in June 1950, with Pears as soloist, and Norman Del Mar conducting the Chelsea Symphony Orchestra. Thus was a work central to the understanding of Britten's music in the thirties left mute and unperformed for over a decade. See note 1 to Letter 414.

Britten infrequently mentioned the song-cycle, but in a letter from 1957 (17 September), to a correspondent in Buenos Aires (Carlos Pemberton), Britten referred to 'a very early work of mine called

"Our Hunting Fathers" [. . .] rather wild, but I think interesting
[. . .]'.

2 Bill Wakeford was a friend of John Alston's and sold music and
scores at the concert for OUP.

89 To Mrs Britten

Flat 2, West Cottage Road, N.W.6.
Oct. 14th, 1936.

My darling,

No time for more than a tiny mid-week note. It is very very hectic
here now – I'm struggling against time to get the heap of G.P.O.
stuff[1] done by the end of the week, there is a lot of Group Theatre
music[2] still to be written, & there is the shadow of Capitol over
my head, from whom I've still heard not a thing. However things
will be managed I hope.

I hope you are well & have escaped this beastly cold which is
ravaging us all – but of <u>course</u> you have escaped it??[3] Barbara
'phoned to-night & seems much better & voice back all right. I
have had a foul cold that came on very fast (first signs of throat
mid-day, & streaming by the evening – Monday), but it is much
better now. Beth so far has kept clear of it. It's this beastly damp
weather.

We had a very good week-end & seemed to spend the whole
time at the tennis club, which was very good fun. Henry Boys
came on Sunday & I enjoyed having him alot, although Beth got
sick of our talk, I believe!

This week so far has been little else but work. But I go out with
Ralph Hawkes on Friday to the ballet,[4] which ought to be nice.

Mum – please could you send me some of my thick socks . . . I
am running out of them; & also any handkerchiefs that are
knocking about – if there are any.

There is no news. Jack Moeran[5] was in last night, with his new
symphony[6] – long telephone talks with Frank B. – & tremendous
preparations for big recordings (for films) next week. C'est tout.
Hope things are going well with you. What a tragedy about the
mirror, though?

Much love, my sweet. I think alot about you.

Nothing yet decided about the flat – we are trying to get Sprott
to revise his original offer of £4 towards redecoration.[7]

Much love from us both, Beth will write tomorrow.

BENJAMIN

1 Britten was completing several scores for the GPO Film Unit: *Calendar of the Year*, directed by Evelyn Spice (see PR, pp. 134–44 and 471–2); *The Saving of Bill Blewit*, directed by Harry Watt (see PR, pp. 144–7 and 481); and a score known as 'Swiss Telephone' which served four films directed by Cavalcanti: *Men of the Alps, Line to the Tschierva Hut, Message from Geneva* and *Four Barriers*. (See PR, pp. 476–80, and note 3 to Letter 90.)

2 The Group Theatre was founded by Rupert Doone in 1932 and had staged the first production of Auden's *The Dance of Death* in 1934. In 1935 Britten and Auden had met through their work for the GPO Film Unit, and it was undoubtedly through Auden that Britten was first brought into contact with Doone's company, where he rapidly achieved the status of 'house' composer and director of music. His first contribution to the Group Theatre was the incidental music he wrote for a production of *Timon of Athens* (1935). This was followed by scores for plays by Auden and Isherwood, *The Ascent of F6* (1937) and *On the Frontier* (1938), for the translation of Aeschylus's *Agamemnon* (1936) by Louis MacNeice, and MacNeice's own play, *Out of the Picture* (1937). On the same day as this letter was written, Britten entered in his diary:

I have to go up to a Group Theatre rehearsal at Leicester Sq. It is bad, but I cannot arouse any interest at all in this production [*Agamemnon*] – everything is onerous to a degree. Probably because I have so much else to do – more interesting – & it is abominably irritating to be treated like this when one is giving one's services. Because of this I don't exactly hurry to the rehearsals!

Harold Hobson's *Observer* review (8 November) succinctly described Rupert Doone's production and, though not Hobson's customary practice, even mentioned – however briefly and dismissively – Britten's music:

Here was a brave attempt to bridge the backward and abyss of time, and to bring something of the awful splendours of Greek tragedy into the modern limelight. It was impossible to be bored by it, though difficult to be consistently impressed. Mr MacNeice's lively translation often fell musically on the ear, and the speeches of Clytemnestra and Agamemnon were admirably delivered by Miss Veronica Turleigh and Mr Robert Speaight, who have few rivals in the speaking of verse. But for the most part the manner of the production eclipsed its matter.
  The least persuasive of Mr Doone's inventions, I thought, was his disposition of the ancient citizens of Argos, whose dinner jackets, gelatine masks, and formal voices suggested not so much the agents of Greek tragedy as a posse of morticians. The interpolated ballet and modishly archaic costumes were effective. The musical obbligato was Greek to me. And while this story of the deaths of kins eluded both full comprehension and tears, as an example of modern theatrical enterprise and devotion to difficult duty, it

deserved high marks. Those play-goers who lament the sameness and tameness of current theatrical fare might easily go farther and fare worse.

Britten's association with the Group Theatre undeniably had its brilliant and rewarding moments but in general the impatient view he took of the company's organization was to persist. It was through the Group, however, that he first met John Piper (b. 1903) the painter and stage designer, who had joined the Group in 1937. Piper designed and painted the set for the production of Stephen Spender's *Trial of a Judge* (18 March 1938), and it was at Piper's farmhouse (Fawley Bottom, near Henley-on-Thames), during the August Bank Holiday weekend of 1937, that the famous – and turbulent – Group Theatre conference was held, an event (see Sidnell, *Dances of Death: The Group Theatre of London in the Thirties* (London, Faber and Faber, 1984), pp. 178–9) about which Britten wrote in his diary on 31 July (the only entry to include Piper's name):

Business & more work in morning. After an early lunch I meet Christopher Isherwood & catch with him the 3.18 to Henley (& Brian Easdale, whom we meet on the train) – where we are met by various delegates of the Group Theatre Congress which is taking place at Fawley Bottom Farm House (residence of Mr. & Mrs. John Piper – artist). Pretty grim out-look – house filled with people – I have to sleep on floor – no accommodatory luxuries – however Wystan & Stephen Spender arrive, so it may not be so bad. Have first discussion in evening, which is pretty tense as Rupert Doone puts point-blank questions to the Authors (W, Christopher, & Stephen) which have to be answered by an uncompromising 'no'.

The 'Congress' continued on 1 August:

A terrible day of meetings & ultimata. Rupert asks for a guarantee of play-rights from the authors, which of course they are not willing to give – lack of confidence in the present G.T. organisation. Rows – & more rows, – Rupert always taking things personally – but eventually an agreement is arrived at – & a directing committee is formed (by the authors) which to all intents & purposes, will have control of the Theatre. And a good thing too.

We go over to a lovely house nearby for some tennis (lousy) – but this doesn't really relieve the misery.

and ended on the 2nd:

One more meeting in morning – & that, thank God, finishes the business. I smoke two cigarettes (first since adolescent efforts at school) with disastrous consequences in morning. Never again.

Robert Medley, in *Drawn from a Life: A Memoir* (London, Faber and Faber, 1983), p. 140, remembers Britten rising to the occasion by retiring with Auden to vamp hymns on the piano, and then, with special appropriateness, performing 'an ironic Stormy Weather', the poet picking out the tune with one finger, the composer providing a 'brilliant two-handed accompaniment'. Harold Arlen's famous song could well have been adopted as the signature tune for what was clearly a memorably glowering weekend.

The association with Piper in the thirties was to lead to one of the most influential and productive of professional and personal relationships. Piper was to design the majority of Britten's theatrical works from 1946 onwards, and his wife, Myfanwy, was to write the librettos for *The Turn of the Screw, Owen Wingrave* and *Death in Venice*.

Britten attended two performances of *Trial of a Judge*, first on 22 March (with Pears), and again on the 26th, with Berkeley: 'It is 100% better 2nd time. Really grand poetry in it.'

See also Sidnell, op. cit.; Edward Mendelson, *Early Auden* (London, Faber and Faber, 1981); Robert Medley, op. cit.; and DMBA. On Piper, see John Rothenstein, *Modern English Painters*, III, 'Hennell to Hockney' (London, Macdonald, 1984), pp. 69–80. An admirable summary biography was included in the catalogue prepared for Piper's 80th birthday exhibition at the Tate Gallery, London, 1983, pp. 41–7. See also *To John Piper on his Eightieth Birthday*, edited by Geoffrey Elborn (London, The Stourton Press, 1983).

3 Mrs Britten was an enthusiastic Christian Scientist.

4 Diary for Friday, 16 October:

> I change & go out to dinner & to Ballet at Sadler's Wells with Ralph Hawkes. The shows are Rake's Progress – Gavin Gordon – a very effective Hogarth setting with only effective & rather affected music; Beethoven Prometheus music – lovely music is not matched by the choreography, which is not stylised enough; & Tsch. Casse Noisette act 3, dream of music, but very slackly played & consequently not too vivaciously danced. But the Corps de Ballet is on the whole excellent, & [omission] is fine.
>
> The evening itself is my first taste of excessive wealth, & I don't find it over good, tho certainly wizzing thro' London in a 37 h.p. Hispano Suiza has its points! R.H. is supremely natural & charming, but it is a bit ironical to park this kind of car outside the sort of houses that surround Sadlers Wells.

5 E.J. Moeran (1894–1950), English composer of Irish descent. He was a student at the College (1913–14) and later a pupil of John Ireland. He was the son of a Norfolk clergyman and much influenced by his East Anglian origins (he was a collector of folksongs in Norfolk where he lived for some years). The Britten and Moeran families were friendly in the mid-thirties (see PFL, plate 68), which led to Britten's acquaintance with his senior colleague. Moeran and his mother were among the party of Britten's friends who had attended the première of *Our Hunting Fathers*. (See Diary for 25 September 1936, and note 3 to Letter 90).

6 This was Moeran's major orchestral work, his Symphony in G minor (1934–7): see note 2 to Letter 74.

7 The redecoration of the flat into which Britten and his sister, together

with Kathleen Mead (their lodger), were to move a few days later:
559 Finchley Road, NW3.

90 To Mrs Britten

Flat No. 2, [West Cottage Rd.,] West End Green.
[NW6]
Oct. 17th, 1936.

My darling,

Thank you for your nice letter – I am so sorry to hear that the
maid trouble is still with you. It is a pity that the Codling one[1] wasn't
any good, but it might have been awkward if you'd wanted to be
away for long. Perhaps by now you may have heard of someone.
But in the meantime, don't go and ruin your health by working too
hard – much better let the house get dirty & have a good Autumn-
clean when you get someone. Surely Q. can help you abit now as
she is fit to paint.[2]

I have had a bit of trouble since I wrote last; I had a very severe
nose bleed in the middle of Friday night – a real <u>pourer</u> (nothing
like I've ever had before)! It didn't stop oozing all the morning, so
as Barbara & others advised, I saw Beth's doctor and he gave me
good advice. I was worried that it might have continued into next
week which is a really busy one – big recordings[3] & out every
evening. So now I put drops of stuff into the offending organ &
I've taken a complete rest yesterday & today – done nothing, &
enjoyed it alot! It was apparently overdoing it abit last week
combined with excessive vigour in blowing, what done it. But I'm
fine now, so don't worry, will you? Last week was an exceptional
brute, not likely to be repeated.

I had a very wonderful time on Friday night – with Ralph
Hawkes. I had dinner with him in his flat & then went to the
Sadlers Wells ballet with him. It was my first experience of really
great wealth; a lovely Mayfair flat with everything he could want –
and the most superb car imaginable – great long thing that just
oozed thro' London, Front seats at Ballet etc. It is very exhilarating
to do things in such style of course, & he is a really charming
person – but it is wrong that one person should have so much
more than other people. One thing it hasn't spoilt <u>him</u> in the
slightest, & he is delightfully un-snobbish. He is taking me twice
to the Covent Garden Dresden Opera season in the near future.[4]

I am glad that Janie is coming to you. We had Elsie[5] here for the week-end, or rather, just last night. Beth enjoyed the dance last night. Grace came in to see me, & we had a very nice evening.[6] She's a dear.

I've started a new sheet, bother it, as there's no more news & in 5 minutes the Mahler Kindertotenlieder are to begin – what bliss![7]

Do remember what I said about over-work – much better that things shouldn't be done.

Many thanks indeed for the parcel & socks & sweets & things. Very nice & the socks & hankies (esp. the last two days!) are very useful.

Concert's starting – I must go.

Much love & to Q.

be good – (& let who will be clean!!)

BENJAMIN

1 Presumably a maid who was over-protective.

2 Aunt Queenie, Mrs Britten's temperamental and increasingly demanding sister, was presumably visiting Frinton or a visit was planned. She was certainly there in November, as was Aunt Effie, 'two of the down & outs of the family', Britten writes in his diary at Frinton on 14 November, 'it is rather a trial – relations usually are'. It is a theme he picks up the next day:

> Queenie is really a most dreadful trial – she is terribly self righteous, prying, & a general busy-body. She means well, but rubs everyone the wrong way – being a religious maniac, everything controversial (even the subject of U.S.S.R.!!) has to be avoided. One is sorry for her as she must have a lonely life – but by jove she is irritating! Effie is a dear & a brick – works like a nigger, has it is true got funny ways & talks without ceasing (a Hockey failing) – but is a comfort after Q.

3 On 20 October the recording session for three films took place. Britten writes in his diary:

> After much business I go down to Blackheath by 11.30 & correct parts & discuss matters before lunch. In aft. I record incidental music for 3 films (mostly Calendar of Year (Spice), & some for Fishing Village (Watt) & Swiss Telephone (Cavalcanti)). Everything goes swimmingly because of splendid little band of 10 (got together by John Francis [flautist (b. 1908)], inc. Korchinska (harp) & Brosa 4tet – without Toni who's ill) & we finish all this music in 3 hours including a good deal of synchronization.

The next day, 21 October, the composer recorded his music for *Around the Village Green*. He writes:

> I get much cheered up at 6.30 by the recording for the Travel Association (music I wrote mostly back in April) – all arrangements of Folk & traditional tunes (some from Moeran) – lovely stuff, & I must admit my

scoring comes off like hell. Of course we have 16 slap-up players – whole Brosa quartet inc. Everyone's very bucked.

See also PR, pp. 119–47.

4 Britten heard the Dresden State Opera perform Strauss's *Ariadne auf Naxos*, conducted by the composer, in the revised version of 1916, at Covent Garden on 6 November:

As a work it is impeccably written – delicate & refined to a degree & it is a treat to hear such workmanship. But it is 90% of it very thin music, a pale reflection of what [h]as come before. But what vocal writing!

On the 10th, *Rosenkavalier*:

This glorious opera (sickly agreed, but beautifully done, & adorable once in a while) is very well played by the Dresden Co. whose team work is excellent.

The next night, he saw the Dresden *Figaro*: 'This simple beauty (expressing every emotion) is withering to any ambitions one might have – '. A couple of days later he bought a miniature score of *Figaro*, 'which is haunting me beyond words. Wed. night was a land-mark in my history.' See also Letter 415.

5 Elsie and Jane Hockey.

6 Diary for 17 October:

Grace Williams comes for a meal with me, & we spend a pleasant time talking (arguing over Sibelius) & listening to Schönberg Verklärte Nacht – a lovely (tho unequal bit of music!).

7 Britten's expectations were not fulfilled. His diary for Sunday 18 October reads:

[. . .] spend day in doing nothing but read – Compton Mackenzie (Carnival [novel, 1912] – very entertaining), & endless Mahler Berg & Schönberg – & also listen to wireless, deadly programmes except for the Kindertotenlieder in the evening & a very bad show of that, [Alexander] Kipnis [1891–1978, Russian-born bass] being far too clumsy and too close to mike, & Boult as slow, dull & ignorant as is his wont. Even then they stand as supreme – music that I think I love more than any other.

91 To Benjamin Britten
From Mrs Britten

Biltmore, Pole Barn Lane, Frinton on Sea.
Nov 20. 36

My darling Son –

May you have a very happy birthday[1] – I wish I could be with you & give you a big hug – but you will be home again soon. I am sending the birthday cake – the fudge – the socks with my love

& the enclosed. Will you let Beth have some fudge & some buns
– I made them today.

We seem to be getting along pretty well – & don't worry about
us. It will be lovely having Barbara tonight. They – she and Amrid
are to have the spare room. Aunt [Queenie] is in Beth's pro tem.

I wish I had written & wished you good luck today at the French
Embassy – Dear old Benjamin, I wish I could hear you[2] –

Time I stopped for I'm dithering.

Florence is very nice but doesnt like being a General[3] – we shall
see how she goes on –

Very much love & very many happy returns my darling precious
son.

Your loving
MUM

I wish 10/- were £10.

1 Britten was twenty-three.
2 Britten was to have played the piano part in a work of Berkeley's
  but the concert, which Nadia Boulanger was to have conducted, was
  cancelled. A new date was set up but Britten had another commitment, the completion of his score for *Love from a Stranger*.
3 Florence, Mrs Britten's only maid, performing general household
  duties. One remembers that Lady Billows's long-suffering servant in
  Herring was named Florence. (See Introduction, p. 65, note 15.) Likewise the name of the maid in the household of the singer, Joan
  Cross, who created the role of Lady Billows: she too was a Florence.
  Britten's Florence was probably another of his composite portraits.

Thursday, 10 December 1936
[*London*]

[. . .]
The great event of the day of course is the King's Abdication –
announced in the afternoon. Not being allowed to marry the
woman he loved, obviously being incapable (naturally in such a
strained position) of continuing without her, the only course is
abdication. But parliament still have put no charges against her. It
would have been good politically to unite England & U.S.A. –
she would have been an excellent Queen democratically & (being
divorced) typical of the age. But obviously they wanted to get rid
of a King with too much personality & any little excuse surfaced.[1]

Have to work as usual till about 1.0.

1 Britten continued his account of the abdication of Edward VIII next
day:

The event of the evening is the farewell speech of the ex-King Edward
(variously termed, Prince Edward, Mr. Windsor & the Duke of Windsor)
at 10.0 which is really a most moving affair. Very well spoken, very simple
& direct – containing some good home truths only slightly disguised &
ending with a terrifying 'God save the King' that made one shiver in ones
shoes. If he had only been allowed to broadcast a week ago (as he wished
to, but as it now transpires, the Ministers didn't think it 'advisable') there
would have been no abdication.

Thursday, 31 December 1936

[*Frinton*]

In the morning I set some very nice verses of Lamb (Philip's
Breeches) for mixed voices – actually to sketches made in
Cornwall.[1] But I don't think it matters much – but quite nice. Take
Mum out shopping in Lagonda[2] (running well, but a bugger to
start). Sophie Wyss sings some rather dull Balikirev very well 6.40.[3]

Thank God there is no more 1936 to be gone thro'. Of all the
frightful years. Tragedy after tragedy – vile hypocracy of State &
Church – with only the miraculous Madrid stand,[4] & at home F.B.'s

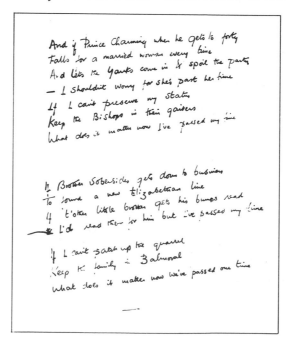

Satirical lines about the Abdication, in Montagu Slater's hand, for the *Pageant of
Empire* (1937)

recovery to brighten it.⁵ Anyhow Lucy Houston's dead, so that's <u>one</u> stumbling block removed.⁶

1 An unpublished setting of the poem by Charles and Mary Lamb. Britten wrote in his diary for 9 July: 'sketch a likely part-song – but can't find any words to fit it yet'. The manuscript is in the Archive.

2 Diary, 27 May:

> Beth and I go down early to Hatch End with John Alston in his car to look at a Lagonda going for £6 at a garage there. Eventually we decide to buy it as it seems in such good condition. Probably foolhardy, but the offer is tempting.

> Alas, the vehicle did not live up to its promise. On 18 March 1937 Britten recorded in his diary:

> [. . .] go to bank & to garage, to arrange about disposal of the Lagonda (We dump heap – we shan't keep it on as it needs too much doing to it to keep it possible to run) [. . .].

> He was always a keen owner of vintage, quality cars, and drove an Alvis until his heart operation in 1973.

3 A group of songs broadcast by the BBC as part of a centenary celebration of Balakirev's birth devised by M.D. Calvocoressi.

4 The siege of Madrid by Franco's army had begun on 6 November 1936, when the government was moved to Valencia. Renewed efforts to subdue the city were made early in 1937 and reported in the press: 'Idealists from all over the world are making their way to fight in the civil war. Most of them are joining the International Brigade, heavily engaged in the defence of Madrid.' In fact Madrid did not surrender until 28 March 1939, the day that brought the Spanish Civil War to an end.

5 On 17 December Britten had written in his diary:

> F.B. has recovered sufficiently to conduct at the B.B.C. tonight. He's looking well, tho' week, but a good deal over. He don't remember anything of his fortnight's wandering of brain – but apparently he was perfectly 'decent' & incredibly lucid in it. – mostly being in Spain – worrying about the revolution & Toni B. – , running thro' music, talking French to Marge, & slanging audiences at Norwich for not taking my 'Hunting Fathers' more seriously!!

6 Unidentified.

Friday, 1 January 1937

[*Frinton*]

A happy new Year! – faint hope of that with the International Situation as black as approaching thunder clouds. Being selfish (a universal failing) I feel it cruel, as I have had a good year & think that next year would be even better – with a very hopeful future, given normal conditions. Ralph Hawkes is a splendid publisher & general patron & I am getting not so bad a number of performances & have lots of ideas for the future. No prospect & little inclination for marriage, tho' unsettled by Beth's proposed change of state.[1] But with plenty of friends old & (mostly) young. However with this religious war upon one – one only prays for courage enough to give one's life to the most useful & necessary cause, & for guidance in that direction. So help me God!

   Letters & rewrite bits of Temporal Suite & 'Phillip's Breeches' in morning and aft. David & Jean Calkin[2] come to tea (aged 15 & 10) & we have a grand time fooling about & playing games. They stay till past 7.0. After supper the Alexanders[3] come in to play Monopoly[4] – which we all do somewhat hilariously till 11.45.

1 Beth and Kit Welford had become engaged on 19 December 1936. The next day Britten wrote in his diary:

   Beth & Kit come back in aft & seem very quiet & moody & it afterwards transpires that they got engaged last night. What momentous days we live in! But I hope she'll be happy, & I think she will, as he's very nice.

2 The grandchildren of one of Mrs Britten's Christian Science friends.

3 The Misses Agnes and Hannah Alexander, Mrs Britten's next-door neighbours.

4 Britten made a characteristic remark about the famous board game in his diary on 28 November 1936:

   [. . .] we have a hilarious evening playing Monopoly a grand new American game (showing up incidently the fatal attractions & hopeless fatuity of Capitalism – but nevertheless very good game).

92 To Grace Williams

[*Incomplete; Boyd, pp. 34–5*]

[Biltmore, Pole Barn Farm, Frinton][1]

[1936/7]

Are you working at all? I'm not – at least not so far – but I may have to go back to town within the next day or two – to see Wystan A., before he goes to Spain[2] – & I shall have to start then again. But I find that films have got horribly on my brain – I wake up with my mind full of ridiculous snippets of the stuff I've done.

   Basil Maine[3] is coming to tea to-day. I'm not pleased as I don't like him or admire him abit; but he lives here & one can't be uncivil – or can one, said he cryptically?

He's a stuck up little blighter too – very ashamed of his father who is a Norfolk draper & a charming little man too – I've met him.

I must stop now & take the dog out. Mum would send her love if she knew I was writing – but she's resting. She <u>does</u> work, you know.

Many thanks again. I hope the family is well.

Love,
BENJAMIN

1 This incomplete, undated letter must have been written between 22 December 1936 and 4 January 1937, when Britten returned to London specifically to see Auden before his departure for Spain.

2 Auden originally intended to leave for Spain on 9 January, but eventually did not depart until the 12th. He left Paris for Spain on the 13th. 'I shall probably be a bloody bad soldier but how can I speak to/for them without becoming one?' he had written in December 1936 to E.R. Dodds. In the event, however, he decided not to become a soldier. He was refused permission in Spain to serve as a stretcher-bearer, and was put to work broadcasting propaganda for a while from Valencia. He then travelled to the Aragon front for some time during February, returning to London on 4 March.

Britten's diary of 8 January records:

Hurriedly do some more parts (Sinfonietta, this time for further reproduction) before meeting Wystan Auden at Tottenham Ct. Road. He goes off to Spain (to drive an ambulance) tomorrow. It is terribly sad & I feel ghastly about it, tho' I feel it is perhaps the logical thing for him to do – being such a direct person. Anyhow it's phenomenally brave. Spend a glorious morning with him (at Lyons Corner House, coffee-drinking). Talk over everything, & he gives me two grand poems – a lullaby, & a big, simple, folky Farewell – that is overwhelmingly tragic & moving. I've Lots to do with them.

On the 10th he writes:

Wystan hasn't yet gone – expects to go to-morrow – because the Medical Unit he was going with was stopped by the Government. Fine non-intervention that, which even stops medical aid as well as arms to the legal Government.

The 'Farewell' – 'It's farewell to the drawing room's civilised cry' – Britten was to use in 1939 as part of the *Ballad of Heroes*. The 'lullaby', 'Lay your sleeping head, my love', he was not to set. Britten was carrying the published miniature score of his *Sinfonietta* with him on the day he met Auden, as well as the published vocal score of *Our Hunting Fathers*. It was on the flyleaf of the former that Auden wrote out the text of the 'Farewell', while he inscribed the latter with

The copy of the miniature score of Britten's *Sinfonietta*, on the blank pages at the end of which W.H. Auden wrote out in pencil his ballad, 'It's farewell to the drawing-room's civilised cry'

the 'lullaby'. See DMBA, pp. 141–4, and p. 165, note 8. It was also in this particular score of the *Sinfonietta* that the composer inscribed (in pencil) an additional horn part, for a performance given by the Edric Cundell Orchestra, conducted by Edric Cundell on 10 March 1936. Britten wrote in his diary:

[. . .] meet Henry Boys for a meal at M.M. [the 'Mainly Musicians' club, Oxford Circus, founded by May Mukle] & then go to Edric Cundell's orchestral concert at Aeolian Hall at 8.30. F.B., Grace Williams & Basil Reeve also come. They are rather a scratch team & some of the wind (horns esp.) are execrable. However they play with Spirit – welcome in these B.B.C. days. They do my Sinfonietta not badly – some of the last movement being good – I can't help liking some of this work. It is absolutely genuine at anyrate.

Cundell (1893–1961), a horn-player himself, was to be the Principal of the Guildhall School of Music and Drama from 1938 to 1959.

3 (Revd) Basil Maine (1894–1972), English writer on music and organist, born in Norwich. His best-known critical study was of Elgar (2 vols., 1933). He was closely associated with the Norfolk and Norwich Triennial Musical Festival. On 19 February 1934 – the same week in which *A Boy was Born* was first broadcast – Maine gave a lecture entitled

'Personalities amongst English Composers', at the Norwich Central Public Library, which included an assessment of Britten. The event was reported in the *Eastern Daily Press*, the next day:

'A pupil of John Ireland', said Mr Maine, 'hails from these parts – from Lowestoft – of whom we shall hear something in the coming years, maybe of his great accomplishment. He is a boy of 19 at the Royal College of Music, and he has had a work chosen for the coming International Festival of Music at Florence in the spring. We have been up to now regarding as the most distinguished of our youngest composers William Walton and Constance [*sic*] Lambert, but there is now another relay on the way, and Benjamin Britten, of Lowestoft, will, I think, be found to be foremost among them. I am not going to prophesy or to be too optimistic, but I think you will find that one of the lights of the future will come from these parts.'

This interesting opinion aroused a good deal of enthusiasm among the audience and was heard with pleasure.

The contents of Maine's lecture provoked a response from Britten's father to the editor of the *Eastern Daily Press*, on 21 February:

With reference to your report of Mr. Basil Maine's lecture on 'Personalities amongst English Composers', there is one very important omission as to Benjamin Britten's musical education. All his early musical grounding, and pianoforte work from the age of seven to fourteen was solely in the capable hands of Miss E.M.K. Astle, ARCM, Southolme, Lowestoft.

So East Anglia has provided the grounding as well as the composer. Frank Bridge took him for composition at the age of 12 and has had him ever since except for a three years' interlude at the Royal College of Music, under John Ireland (composition) and Arthur Benjamin (piano).

Maine's *New Paths in Music* (London, Thomas Nelson, 1940), is interesting for its perception, at that time, of Britten as a 'Left Wing composer' – it is thus that he is identified in the index (p. 148) – and it is in those same terms that he is discussed in the main text. Maine had clearly been rattled by Britten's participation in the 1939 'Festival of Music for the People' and wrote:

Music and the pamphlet make an unhappy association, and although Benjamin Britten's *Ballad of Heroes* proved one of the most impressive contributions to this festival, it would have gone deeper but for the pamphleteering mind of W.H. Auden, from whose poems part of the text of the ballad is drawn. Britten is an extremely spontaneous composer. His mind is fresh and versatile. But when I compare his fine achievement *A Boy was Born* with the music which he has turned out to bolster up the plays and verse of Auden, I fear lest he should dissipate his talent in an unworthy association.

This was a view that was probably also influenced by Maine's experience of *Our Hunting Fathers*, which he had heard at the Norwich Festival in September 1936, and for him, no doubt, was another unsettling product of Britten's collaboration with Auden. A rather similar approach – '*Our Hunting Fathers* [. . .] has its own special significance among Britten's works because it connects him with what was then the forward-looking group of artists in England' – was made by Scott Goddard in his chapter on Britten in *British Music of Our Time*, edited by A.L. Bacharach, (Harmondsworth, Pelican, 1946), p. 211, though in more positive terms. It is of some interest that in his 1963 interview with Murray Schafer, *British Composers in Interview* (London, Faber and Faber, 1963), p. 115, Britten remarked of his association with Auden, 'I think *Our Hunting Fathers* was our most successful collaboration.'

Oddly, there is no diary entry mentioning the Maine visit to which the letter refers. Perhaps it was too discouraging for Britten to write about.

93 To John Pounder

> Biltmore, Pole Barn Lane, Frinton
> as from / 559 Finchley Road, N.W.3
> Jan. 2 1937

My dear John,

I see your letter is dated sometime in October – and I admit that January is a bad date on which to answer it. Still life becomes increasingly difficult every day, as I expect you find too. I want to see you alot some time – there's quite alot to talk about that one can't (or even daren't) write about in letters.

I have finished with films for a month or two & so I am my own master for abit. I return from here to town tomorrow for a week or so, after which I may come back here for a time (nothing settled yet). Perhaps then you could come over for the day – it isn't really far. I'll let you know. You never come to London, do you? at least not until December this year?

I enjoyed your letter alot. It was very nice of you to write. I was certainly very disappointed to have missed you at Norwich. Things were pretty hectic but I kept a look out for you. Lots of people turned up for the show including people like Basil Wright, Rupert Doone, Robert Medley & Frank Bridge (of course) etc. whom you'd have liked to have seen. I'm also very glad you liked Hunting Fathers. I personally think it's opus 1 all right – & alot of people I admire think so to. The BBC. are very slow in deciding to do it. Perhaps the political suggestions worries them. I have seen a tremendous amount of Wystan Auden recently. He stayed with me in town for a week or so & was down here for a time too. He is a grand person, & I am terribly sad about his decision to go to Spain to fight. I agree that is fine & very brave of him – but what the Government wants is not martyrs – she's got enough of them,

but arms & money; & Wystan can do more good back here than
out there. Still one has enough respect for his integrity than to
try & persuade him not to go. But it doesn't make it any the less
annoying. It is also sickening as I have lots of work planned with
him – I'm doing music for his new play F6; discussing an opera &
also talking about a review for a Cambridge theatre with him.[1]

How are you? How's the party? I liked the Xmas card alot, & it
has stood very prominently on the mantlepiece here all the time.[2]
I've got a good family you know – Mum never objects, in fact
silently acquiesces, & my sisters are well trained now! Are you
making any speeches or anything? I met George Atkinson[3] in a Left
bookshop the other day – he seemed nice. David Green[4] I haven't
seen for ages – in fact I've been so busy working at films & things
– literally day & night for two or three months, that I've seen
practically no one. You seem to have had a grand time on the
continent in the summer. I was going to Holland to-morrow, but
the object of my visit (a Mengelberg recording) has been postponed
to March.[5]   I have premonitions about travelling on the Continent
then, though – the tip at Lloyds[6] is, of course, that Germany is
preparing to attack U.S.S.R. in the Spring. One cheerful thought
– how can she attack Russia effectively if she has all those men in
Spain – or vice-versa? I feel most fatalistic now, & never plan
anything beyond this summer. It is hard, isn't it – given ideal social
conditions – life would be so good. In fact even now I am capable
of feeling quite cheerful (with a little drink or — — —[7] to deaden
ones brain). That reminds me, I'm changing my views on Life
(with a capital S[8] abit. There is a plurality – a lack of individuality
about _____ perhaps this had better wait until we meet – one
never knows with letters these days.

Poor Germany this winter.

Be good & let me know how busy you are.

Love

BENJAMIN

1 It was probably as *On the Frontier* (Cambridge, 1938: see note 3 to
Letter 155) that the 'review' took shape. The reference to an opera
proposal is fascinating on many counts. It seems possible that this
is the first documented reference by Britten to an opera project. He
was of course to write an operetta with Auden (*Paul Bunyan*) when
in the USA from 1939 to 1942. But we have not been able to locate
any further references to this 1937 idea, which, if nothing else, is an
early indication of one of the later forms of collaboration the poet

and composer were to undertake and in which both men were to sustain an abiding interest.

2 Presumably a Christmas card with political overtones.

3 A South Lodge contemporary of Britten's and Pounder's, whom Britten probably met at David Archer's Central Books, the bookshop at 2 Parton Place, London, and home of the Parton Press. The same address also housed the premises of Lawrence and Wishart (Montagu Slater's publishers), the Workers' Theatre Movement and the Student Labour Federation, and from April 1936 the office of *Left Review*. See Valentine Cunningham, *British Writers of the Thirties* (Oxford, Oxford University Press, 1988), pp. 108–10, where he writes: 'Parton Street was in its way centrally situated on the small map of London literary and radical–bourgeois political life, so the kinds of youths who frequented it were central to that life.'

4 David Green was also a lodger at 173 Cromwell Road when Britten had a room there during his College days. He was an architectural student from Lowestoft, where his father was an architect. The two young men met and went to some concerts together after the Cromwell Road residence was over. More particularly, Green, who was older than Britten, was able to assist him on some matters relating to his work at the GPO Film Unit, e.g. in his diary for 10 October 1935 he writes: 'David Green [. . .] takes [Auden] & me down to Blackheath – where he gives us some very good technical advice on acoustics for the studio recording.' Green became a well-known architect (the Taylor and Green partnership, in London and Lowestoft). He now practises in Spain. See also Introduction, p. 18.

5 Britten had planned to visit Holland with Henry Boys in order to hear Mengelberg record Mahler's Fifth Symphony with the Amsterdam Concertgebouw Orchestra.

6 The London insurance association.

7 This and the subsequent omission are Britten's own.

8 Sex?

94 To Benjamin Britten
From Mrs Britten

Biltmore, Pole Barn Lane, Frinton on Sea
Jan 14 36 [1937]

My darling, Benjamin –

Welcome home again – I do hope it has been a successful visit – all you expected & more – & that you saw all the lovely places. I <u>long</u> to hear that you are safely at home – & I hope you wont be

17a John Ireland, Britten's composition teacher at the College, where he was a student from 1930–1933

17b Arthur Benjamin, Britten's piano teacher at the College (photo, Royal College of Music)

17c Bridge, Britten and Mrs Bridge, Paris, ?1937

18a R.V. Britten

18b Edith Britten, 26 August 1934: 'Mum in garden' (photo, B.B.)

18c R.V. Britten with Caesar

18d Family line-up: Edith Britten, Benjamin, Robert, R.V. Britten

19a Helen Hurst and Barbara, on the beach, 1934 (photo, B.B.)

19b Robert Britten, H. Marjorie Britten, and their son John, Lowestoft, 1932

19c 'Barbara & Caesar on drawing room balcony' (photo, B.B.)

20a Sophie Wyss, for whom Britten wrote *Our Hunting Fathers*, 1936 (photo, Enid Slater)

20b Ralph Hawkes, Britten's publisher, to whom *Our Hunting Fathers* was dedicated

20c The bungalow at Crantock, in which *Our Hunting Fathers* was composed: 'Bungalow with Mum, Beth, A. Gyde & Miss Nettleship' (photo, B.B.)

21a   Two beach scenes: Britten, Barbara, Caesar and Edith Britten

21b   Britten and Barbara, Crantock, 1936

22a The ISCM Festival, Florence, 1934: Britten, who is carrying the vocal score of *A Boy was Born*, and the composer Arnold Cooke

22b The ISCM Festival, Barcelona, 1936: Toni and Peggy Brosa

22c The Spanish Civil War: the campaign to aid Basque children, Southampton, 1938

23a   A still from the film of Erich Kästner's *Emil und die Detektive* (1931)

23b   A still from *Coal Face* (GPO Film Unit, 1935)

24a   Henry Boys

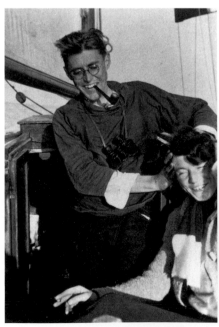

24b   'On <u>Curlew</u> – Oct. 1936. Kit
Welford & Beth' (photo, B.B.)

24c   'Benjamin about to give Beth away at
her wedding, January 1938': B.B.'s caption

25a Boyd Neel (1937), for whose orchestra the *Frank Bridge Variations* were composed

25b Marjorie Fass (1951), the artist and prominent member of the Bridge circle at Eastbourne

25c 'To Benjamin from Hedli, 21–III–38' (source: Hedli Anderson)

26 W.H. Auden in the thirties

27a Britten in a field, c.1937/8

27b Auden, Hedli Anderson and William Coldstream, Colwall, 1937

27c Auden, Britten and Beth on the beach at Shingle Street, Suffolk, 1938: 'To lie flat on the back'

28a The 'AC', with Wulff in the passenger seat (photo, B.B.?)

28b Wulff Scherchen at the Old Mill, 1938 (photo, B.B.?)

28c 'Kit & Piers D. Fooling' (photo, B.B.)

29a   Britten and Berkeley at the piano: a rehearsal in 1938 of the *Binyon Puppets*

29b   Lennox Berkeley and Britten, January 1938 (photo, Howard Coster)

30a Britten, January 1938 (photo, Howard Coster)

30b Trevor Harvey and Michael Mayer in 1939, at 105 Charlotte Street, WC1 (the flat shared by Pears with Harvey and Basil Douglas)

31a Poster

31b *Johnson over Jordan*: the final curtain, with Ralph Richardson

31c Act II, the nightclub scene, for which Britten composed a Blues, 'The Spider and the Fly'

32   Peter Pears, *c*.1939

too weary to take your Rehearsal – Good Luck my darling son –
I'll listen most lovingly[1] –

I hoped to write a card – but didnt think you would get it – so
send this to London –

Flo is with me – came in 5 hours – She is a nice companion and
we are very happy together. Mills[2] has gone to London for a
month to a temporary job.

I am thinking of Beth tonight – Kit is there & I expect she's
happy[3] – come home soon to your

Ever loving

MUM

1 The broadcast on the 16th by the BBC of the *Soirées Musicales* conducted by Joseph Lewis. See also note 2 to Letter 100.

2 Britten wrote in his diary on 28 December 1936: 'Mum's man, who
   is helping us over Xmas as general parlour man, Mills by name is a
   grand success.'

3 On the same day as the broadcast of the *Soirées Musicales* to which
   Mrs Britten was going to listen, Britten wrote in his diary: 'Kit is
   here. Beth goes to bed with temp of 101 at 7.0. [. . .] Phone Mum
   who's coming tomorrow to help nurse.' This may well mean that
   this letter was the last Britten was to receive from his mother.

95 To Grace Williams

[*Picture postcard: Paris
Boyd, p. 36*]

[Postmarked 15 January 1937]

Holland was postponed so I'm here for three or four days.[1] Fidelio[2]
at the Opera last night with Lotte Schöne[3] – it was <u>grand</u>. I have
never been so impressed by any work, I think. When do you
return to work? Hope you're enjoying yourself & working.

BENJAMIN

1 From 12 to 16 January Britten was visiting Paris, with Ronald Duncan
   and Henry Boys. They stayed at the Hotel Indo-Hollandais, in the
   rue d'Haute Ville. He wrote on the 12th:

   We eat in the little restaurant next the hotel (very good and very cheap,
   8 F.). Afterwards decide to go to Opera, but on arrival there discover
   that there is nothing on to-night – so go on to Folies Bergères – but as we
   arrive $\frac{1}{2}$ hr. early, we are taken by one of the commissioners to 'another
   little show' – fools I admit to go, but a mixture of ignorance and curiosity

made us follow. Anyhow we are taken to a large house a few yards away, & there are presented in the most sordid manner possible with about 20 nude females, fat, hairy, unpreposessing; smelling of vile cheap scent, & walking round the room in couples to a gramophone. It is revolting – appalling that such a noble thing as sex should be so degraded. We are given cheap champagne, but decide that we've had enough, & to the disgust of the fat proprietress, take a hasty departure – it cost us 100 F too. After this disgusting little exhibition, we are in no mood for the Folies & as it turns out it is incredibly bad – just chocolate box pornography back stage, alternating with feeble comedy front stage. Besides Josephine Baker is as old as the hills & can neither dance, sing nor act. So we leave here at ½ time & after wandering the streets for abit make our way to Notre Dame, which is indeed a sight for sore eyes. It gives one hope that humans can erect a building such as this.

Duncan's own description of this incident appears in his volume of autobiography, *All Men Are Islands* (London, Hart-Davis, 1964), pp. 133–4.

On the 14th Britten wrote:

Up again pretty late & go (with the others of course) to the Louvre where we stay quite a long time. It is a grand place with the most amazing amount of real achievement on every wall (the Fra Angelicos & Goyas, & Rembrants impress most), but too much to be seen in a year. Then in the aft. we go up to Cimetiére Paris looking for Wilde's grave, which is apparently elsewhere – then to Tour Eiffel, which is shut – an aft. of disappointments. Back here via numerous cafés & of course in a taxi (we are living a life of excessive luxury, never walking or bussing!) & then change, wash & shave & go out for a late meal. Walk, shop & coffee & back here by 11.15.

While wandering the shops, Ronny & I see a Gargantua & Paraquel illustrated ed. by Dubout – limited edition – knowing his name & seeing the quality of the drawings we purchase both vols. not examining them closely till we arrive back, when we do look at them – we are as appalled by the coarseness of it (being still pretty 'green'!), as we are impressed by the skill of it. Certainly we are having some experiences – what is one to make of an animal than can produce the hideous pornography of Tuesday evening, Notre Dame, Fidelio, & give rise to these filthy & brilliant satires?

On 15 January Duncan left for India to meet and talk with Gandhi and Tagore, encounters that influenced him for the rest of his life.

2 Beethoven's opera had long been a favourite work of Britten's; his parents had presented him with a copy of the miniature score on his sixteenth birthday in 1929: the manuscript reads 'To Benjamin/From Mum & "Pop"/November 22–29.' There is added on the verso of this page, 'When the last great Scorer comes to write against your name: He writes – not whether you won or lost – but how you played the game!' He began to make his own English translation of the libretto in a school exercise book. Even in later life his youthful ardour for *Fidelio* was undiminished, and he planned to conduct it

at an Aldeburgh Festival, with Pears as Florestan. He recorded his impressions of this Parisian performance, the first production of the opera he had seen, in his diary of 13 January:

Back to hotel & then off again to Théâtre Champs Elysées for Fidelio [. . .] This is a very deep religious & exhilarating experience. Well as I know the incredible music, I did not realise what a tremendous dramatic thrill it was. Not a weak spot from beginning with the delicious Marcellina (best of all the cast, Lotte Schöne) comedy passing thro' the thunder clouds to the glorious sunshine of the end. The F major 'O Gott, welch ein Augenblick' [Britten here confuses Florestan's aria with Pizzaro's 'Ha! Welch' ein Augenblick'] is the most ecstatic moment of all.

All this too with not too exact performance, but the vitality on the stage made up for some slackness in the orchestral pit. Feeling slightly dazed we wander & then have some coffee before returning.

Between November 1936 and February 1937 the Théâtre des Champs-Elysées gave house room to the Opéra during the latter's period of redecoration. This performance of *Fidelio* was conducted by Philippe Gaubert, with Germaine Lubin, French soprano, as Leonore.

While Britten retained his enthusiasm for *Fidelio*, his general attitude to Beethoven was radically different in the 1940s. For example we find him reported in *Time*, 16 February 1948, p. 68, 'Though a childhood admirer of Beethoven, he now thinks Beethoven's music was too personal. "Let's face it," Britten says. "It was very sloppy music." ' See also his more considered comments on Beethoven made to Murray Schafer in 1963 (*British Composers in Interview* (London, Faber and Faber)).

3 Austrian soprano (originally known as Charlotte Bodestein; 1891–1977). Between 1933 and 1948 she lived and worked in Paris, becoming a French citizen.

96 To Grace Williams
[*Boyd, p. 36*]

559 [Finchley Road, London, NW3]
Tuesday [26 January 1937]

My dear Grace,

The pound for services rendered to Strand Films[1] before Xmas –
Things are pretty bad. Specialist coming again for poor old Beth to-night.[2] Mum is down with a very severe attack of Bronchial Pneumonia.[3] So we've two to worry about. However an efficient aunt's[4] here to do catering. So we sit about & wait.
Hope <u>you're</u> fit.

BENJAMIN

1 The Strand Film production for Southern Railways, *The Way to the Sea* (1937), produced by Jack B. Holmes (1901–1968), directed by Paul Rotha, and with a verse commentary by Auden and music by Britten. The film relates the history of the London–Portsmouth line and illustrates the improved communications between the two cities provided by the electrification of the railway. Britten worked with Auden at the beginning of December, and composed his music on the 11th, with an additional sequence between the 12th and 13th; it was recorded under his supervision on 14th and 16th December. He was paid £52.10s. for his work.

   It was a particularly busy period for him – the important oboe and piano work, *Temporal Variations*, also dates from this time – and Britten sought the assistance of his friend and trusted colleague, Grace Williams, to act as an amanuensis and help him complete the full score on time. Evidence of her hand can be clearly seen on the first page of manuscript, now in the Archive. She was not unused to this kind of work, for she had recently assisted Britten in preparing his scores for *The Agamemnon* (October) and *Love from a Stranger* (November 1936). For further information on *The Way to the Sea*, including a transcription of Auden's verse, see DMBA, pp. 88–93, EMWHA, pp. 430–32 and 671 and PR, pp. 484–7.

2 Britten's younger sister was suffering from influenza, a victim of the epidemic that swept England in early 1937. Before the discovery of modern drugs and antibiotics, this type of infection was serious and possibly fatal. Beth's condition, which lasted from 17 January until late February, was severe enough for a specialist, Sir Maurice Cassidy (1880–1949), to be consulted.

3 Mrs Britten had travelled to London to help nurse her daughter. The sequence of events leading to the tragic death of the mother on 31 January are unfolded, step by step, in Britten's diary. He had returned on 16 January, from his trip to Paris with Henry Boys and Ronald Duncan –

We try & sit up during the sea journey but succumb & descend to the 3rd Class Salon, which has the appearance of a Morgue. There is besides an attendant who is suspiciously attentive, but I wake apparently unharmed(!) [. . .]

– to find

London is dank and dark, & we feel furious at being back with realities again. This feeling is accentuated when I get back here at 8.0 & find Kathleen with the bad Flu plague, & Beth sickening for it. [. . .] Kit is here. Beth goes to bed with temp of 101 at 7.0. [Beth's fiancé, Kit, was then a medical student at St. Thomas's Hospital. It was probably he who arranged the consultation with Cassidy, the specialist.]

17 January
Mrs. Nunn comes in morning to do the invalids – Beth's pretty bad – while

at 11.22 I meet Mum at Liverpool Street. It is a glorious relief to have her
but I must see that she doesn't tire herself by running about too much. Kit
[. . .] is obviously sickening for the plague himself.

On the 18th Britten himself has a bad cold which he fears might
develop into the 'plague'. As a precautionary measure he attends
neither Malcolm Sargent's rehearsal of the *Sinfonietta* at the College
nor, in the afternoon, the memorial service for Harold Samuel, who
had died on 15 January. 'In the evening I have a slight temperature
so have a bath & an early bed. Kathleen's up to-day & dressed. But
Beth's temperature is still high.'

19 January
I get up (not dressed) & come down for dinner. Mum's not feeling too
well (terribly tired) & Beth's no better tho' quite cheerful. To bed about
10.30 & we all spend a very wretched and restless night.

20 January
Beth is much worse – we send for the doctor, who actually doesn't come
till 5.0. Meanwhile Mum is down with the Plague, & so she moves into
my room [. . .] Dr Moberly [a local doctor who practised in nearby Platts
Lane], when he comes at 5.0, says it's pneumonia [. . .] Nurse arrives
after dinner & the Doctor back again. He doesn't seem overworried, but
of course we've got to be terribly careful. Meanwhile he's prescribing the
most drastic treatment – wide open windows – little or no heating.

Britten moves to 'new quarters', with Mrs Hibberd, a friend of
Barbara's, and on returning to the 'plaguey house' next day finds
Beth 'holding her own' but, ominously,

Mum is a good deal worse – accentuated by worrying for Beth, of course
[. . .] This hanging about not being able to do a thing save an occasional
shop is <u>Hell</u>.

22 January
Dr. again says Beth's holding her own, but Mum's no better & a roaring
temperature (104+) [. . .] I'm afraid that I've got this Plague – temp.
102 mid-day: however I don't go to bed as there's nowhere to go! – until
after dinner when I go in the sitting room.

23 January
In bed all day but much better, thank God. [. . .] Beth's holding her own
– of course she's desparately ill – but the illness is taking its normal course.
Mum, we're very worried about. She seems to be developing Bronchitis –
a risky thing when one's her age (60 odd) – her temperature is still way
up in the heights. It is so difficult too when there are <u>two</u> seriously ill
patients in one house.

By the 25th it was confirmed that Mrs Britten was suffering from
bronchial pneumonia & is completely wandering all the time. Beth no
better, but no worse apparently tho' breathing is terribly fast & shallow.
Poor dear it's frightful to see her – indeed both of them.

26 January
A miserable wretched day. Neither patients so well in fact we all are terribly

worried about them. Mum is incoherent all day, but Beth is terribly &
pathetically alert. However the Doctor after his 2nd visit in aft. decides to
call in Sir Maurice Cassidy again & he makes suggestions. Then (in evening)
they give Beth oxygen & this makes a definite improvement & he (Cas.)
also makes reassuring comments. So we feel more cheerful in evening.

But, as the ensuing sequence of diary entries shows, hopes for Mrs
Britten's recovery were to be dashed. See also EWB, Chapter 13, for
Beth's own account of these fateful days.

    The performance of the *Sinfonietta* to which Britten refers took
place on 19 January, a Patron's Fund concert at the College, and is
of some interest as it must be one of the earliest of Sargent's encounters with Britten's music. A later diary entry, 24 February, registers
Britten's disappointment at receiving

a letter from Malcolm Sargent saying he cannot play my Sinfonietta after
all in the Courtauld–Sargent concerts [the prestigious Queen's Hall series,
1928–40] (time limit – he says but I suspect dirty work) – which is a hearty
blow as it would have meant two first rate shows.

See also note 1 to Letter 461.

4 Euphemia ('Effie') Maud Hockey (1876–1944), one of Mrs Britten's
  younger sisters. For a photograph of Aunt Effie (with Britten and
  Robert), see PFL, plate 18.

Wednesday, 27 January 1937

Things do seem abit better with Beth to-day certainly the breathing
is damnably quick & shallow but temperature is down abit. No crisis
yet. Mum not really so good, & tho' lucid at times she is mostly
incoherent.

    Usual kind of day – I finish the scoring of Pacifist March, first bit
of work for weeks – but I cannot really do anything seriously. Kit
is here all day. Read alot – Low Company, by Mark Benny,[1] which
is impressive in its revelation of the sordid life which these people
live, although in no sphere would M.B. be ordinary. It gets out of
its depth abit towards the end, but it is a splendid attempt.

1 Mark Benny, *Low Company: Describing the Evolution of the Burglar*
  (London, Peter Davies, 1936).

Thursday, 28 January 1937

The doctor's evening verdict is that Beth is now out of the wood –
very ill still, but definitely progressing now. Mum is not so well

– but he says there's a fine chance for her. I spend alot of the day with her, but she mustn't talk much, much as she wants to.

I write hundreds of cards in answer to letters that are pouring in by every post. People are very good.

Read lots of poetry (Shelly, Elliot, Auden, & Spender) & also music (principally Mahler). I'm still sleeping down the road with Mrs. Hibberd – Kit in the downstairs room, Aunt Effie in sitting room & Mum in Kathleen's room. Barbara still comes for all the mornings & then from 5.0 for the evenings till Muriel Bond[1] fetches her about 9.0.

1 A friend of Barbara's with a car, who drove her to Finchley Road in the day and ferried her home at night.

Friday, 29 January 1937

Same kind of day – Beth holding her own, & Mum still very bad, but tho' completely delirious, no worse. Kit is here all day & Barbara in the morning.

I go to see Rupert Doone about F6 – the music of which I'm to do – & arrange matters.[1] I get back by 7.30 & find Doctor has been.

1 See note 1 to Letter 100.

Saturday, 30 January 1937

Robert is supposed to be coming up to-day, but as he has 'flu – it is postponed till to-morrow. Barbara is staying in Hampstead this week-end – with Miss MacDonald, her secretary, who has a lovely house in E. Hampstead. I go there for the night too – she is a charming woman. News about the same. Beth still slightly better, temp. coming down. Mum slightly better too – tho completely delirious – still she says 'good-night' to me & apparently recognises me.

Sunday, 31 January 1937

We get a 'phone call at 7.30 in the morning – Mum not so well – Barbara & I half run the distance – taking $\frac{1}{4}$ hr, there being no taxi. Then we find when we arrive that Mum had a heart attack at abt

7.0 & died in about ten minutes without being at all conscious or suffering – thank God. So I lose the grandest mother a person could possibly have – & I only hope she realised that I felt like it. Nothing one can do eases the terrible ache that one feels – O God Almighty –

Poor old Beth mustn't be told, so we have to act, which makes things 1,000,000 times worse. We have to make hundreds of phone calls – luckily Barbara is here to help with & to organise everything – a grand comfort. Get in touch with Nicholson (Lowestoft Solicitor – Mum wants to be buried there with Pop of course), & the authorities here, & of course all relatives. Robert, better but not well yet, is coming up to-morrow. I go back with Barbara with Miss Macdonald, to-night – she is a grand woman very practical.

God – what a day!

Monday, 1 February 1937

The ghastly farcical acting is kept up still – because Beth mustn't know, but she becomes more and more suspicious all day – the deathly silence after Mum's continuous chatter. But by evening the Doctor realises that sooner or later it must dawn on her, & we decide to tell her. The Doctor does it very beautifully & Barbara & nurse stand by. She takes it terribly pluckily – perhaps too pluckily, – tho' it must be a terrible shock. She doesn't shed a tear, until actually I go up myself & considering that we were together so much with Mum (more than the others) she does break down a little. The undertakers come to take the Coffin away to-night – the darling body but that really has no relation to Mum herself. It is the most heartrending thought that I shall never set eyes on her again. Robert arrives at mid-day & comes back to Miss Macdonald with me at night.

Tuesday, 2 February 1937

Another terrible day of hanging about & doing nothing definite. Every day one feels completely exhausted. Beth is not so well – temperature varying abit & Empyena[1] is feared. Cassidy comes again in evening & gives a pretty favourable report. Hopeful anyhow.

Many wreaths arrive – lovely ones – only it is so annoying that

Mum shouldn't see them, as she adored flowers so – of course people say that she can see them, which I only trust & hope she can't; for if she is conscious of earthly happenings, then she realises that the Madrid agony is dragging on & on – besides hundreds of other agonies.

1 Empyeme: a form of pleurisy. The 'operation' referred to in Diary for 3 February, an aspiration to drain fluid from the lung, was performed by Dr Moberly on 5 February under a local anaesthetic. After that, Beth began very slowly to improve, despite 'little periodic collapses'. However, it was not until 21 February that Britten could write, 'Doctor really pleased with Beth today – the lung is at long last resolving & temp. is well down & pulse too. Now for some progress.'

Wednesday, 3 February 1937
[*London/Lowestoft*]

Robert & I come back here before going to Lowestoft with Aunt Effie (& from Ipswich Elsie Hockey) for the Funeral. Barbara we meet at Liverpool Street too. The Nicholsons meet us & feed us before the show. It is a terrible strain – Barbara nearly faints, but we succeed in holding out. It was a fitting service for darling Mum – Mr. Reeve, Mr. Gillespie[1] & Mr. Phillips officiate, & Mr. Coleman plays suitable music (including my little 'Birds' which was written for her.[2] Many people come up to Kirkley Cemetary after.[3] We go back to the Sewells (Laurence) for tea & it is a rest after the strain. Barbara & Robert stay with Nicholsons for the night to do business, while I come back to London with Effie. Have the appalling news when I get back that Beth appears to be forming an Empyena – & operation is considered necessary. Really there is no end to the bloodiness of this hellish world. However Miss MacDonald is comforting when I get back there – but no earthly comfort can possibly fill this ghastly blank.

1 Revd Laurence Gillespie, Curate of St John's, Lowestoft.

2 'The Birds', a song for medium voice and piano, text by Hilaire Belloc, dedicated to his mother and composed in June 1929. It was revised in 1934 and published by Boosey & Hawkes in 1935.

3 In a very late note of Britten's to Pears he writes 'Just had a draughty visit to Lowestoft cemetary – not my favourite form of amusement.' This must, in fact, have been his last visit to his parents' grave.

There is something very touching in the fact that he again mis-spells 'cemetery', just as he had done in 1937.

97 To John Pounder

559 Finchley Road, N.W.3.
Feb 8th 1937

My dear John,

Thank you so much for the nice letter – & you and your parents for the very lovely flowers that you very sweetly sent. Mum was terribly fond of flowers and would have appreciated them very deeply.

It has been a terrible time, old thing, and still is I'm afraid, as Beth is still very ill. But she is progressing well & feeling more cheerful – tho' the Doctor predicts quite another month of bed for her.

It is a terrible feeling, this loneliness, and the very happy & beautiful memories I have of Mum don't make it any easier – tho' perhaps they should, but then I expect there is something wrong about my philosophy of life. Anyhow I'm blessed with a grand family, and things like this bring one very close together.

We have to sell the Frinton house – so that is a tremendous business.[1] I am also beginning the music to Wystan A's new play – to be produced within a week or so. So I'm busy. I hope things are good with you. Very soon I want to come to Lowestoft & see you.

One thing, John, whatever talents I may have in other directions, I'm blessed with a talent of making the grandest friends a person can have _____ and I hope you'll take that as a compliment!

Many thanks & best wishes to you all,
Love,
BENJAMIN

---

1 The house was sold for £1,850. In the final settlement of their mother's estate, each of the four children received the sum of £1,955 17s. 3d.

98   To Montagu Slater[1]

Friston Field, Nr. Eastbourne [Sussex].
[Postmarked 1 March 1937]

I do hope the show (& esp. the P. of E.)[2] has been a grand success
– I've been thinking & hoping alot for it. I'm here till Wednesday
& will 'phone you then. It is damnably hurricany here, but I spend
most of the time in bed, which is grand.

   Is there any chance of me getting seats for the 2nd show next
Sunday?[3]

Hope you & Enid are well.

BENJAMIN B

1   Montagu Slater (1902–1956) and his wife Enid (1903–1988) Slater.
Slater was a poet, playwright, editor and literary critic, prominent in
left-wing circles in the thirties and after. He first met Britten when
both men were working for the GPO Film Unit (Slater, too, was
involved in the making of *Coal Face*) and in subsequent years collaborated with him in a variety of theatrical projects, many of them of a
quasi-political character, e.g. Slater's plays, *Stay Down Miner* and
Easter 1916. In 1938 he wrote a text for the Binyon Puppets (presented
by Helen and Margaret Binyon, twin daughters of the poet Laurence
Binyon) entitled *Spain*, for which Britten wrote the incidental music,
now lost, but the text appears in Slater's *Peter Grimes and Other Poems*
(London, John Lane, The Bodley Head, 1946). (Berkeley also wrote
music for two of these puppet plays.) Harold Hobson's *Observer*
notice of the 'Puppet Show 1938' (26 June) spells out the nature of
the entire production, although it does not identify either composer:

One never-failing charm of the puppet show is its power to create *multum
in parvo*. As one sits in the darkened auditorium waiting for the curtain to
rise, it seems impossible that the tiny proscenium frame – hardly bigger it
looks than the slot in a pillar-box – can contain the phantasmagoria promised
by the programme, or that one will be able to see the performance in detail.
Yet, somehow the miracle always happens. We have seen puppets more
histrionically gifted than this company presented and controlled by the
Misses Helen and Margaret Binyon: but the astonishing illusion which the
Little People convey – the illusion that band-box dimensions have suddenly
expanded to wide open spaces – these immediately communicated. The
scenes – living room, railway station, forest, what not – looked, if anything,
larger than life. Their speech, too – unmistakably *vox humana* – was clear,
since tone and elocution were those of Miss Jean Shepeard and Mr Gonville
Williams, and dialect became them. Their programme, I thought, was a
shade eclectic in inspiration: a medley of morality, farce, ballet, and dream.
Supposing them to be temperamental actors (and everything they do invites
that supposition), it is possible that their occasional languor, refusal to

synchronise voice and gesture, and a tendency to droop may be attributed to their sensitiveness to the weather. For while their unseen human assistants, with speaking and singing voices, violin, clarinet, dulcitone and piano, played their parts impeccably, some of the puppet stars twinkled less than brilliantly.

Slater also wrote a number of open-air pageants for the Co-operative Movement, e.g. *Towards Tomorrow*, first performed at the Wembley Stadium, London, in July 1938. The pageant was a typical and powerful left-wing form of public propaganda prominent during the thirties, often calling for specially composed incidental music, for which the Co-op allotted £1000 per year. Among composers who were commissioned were Alan Bush and Michael Tippett. On Britten's return from the United States in 1942 he invited Slater to undertake the libretto of *Peter Grimes*. One of Slater's last appointments was Head of Scripts in the Film Division of the wartime Ministry of Information, which led to one further collaboration post-*Grimes*: he wrote the script for the original film version of the *Young Person's Guide to the Orchestra* (1946). For further information on Slater, see Donald Mitchell, 'Montagu Slater (1902–1956): who was he?' in PGPB, pp. 22–46, and DMBA, pp. 97–100. Slater's wife, Enid, was a photographer to whom we owe many striking photographs of her husband and Britten, and their circle, in the thirties and forties. See also PR, pp. 194–257.

2 *Pageant of Empire*, Slater's satirical sketch for the Left Theatre revue, was first presented at Collins' Music Hall, London, on 28 February 1937. Britten composed the incidental music – a sequence of eight short instrumental and vocal items in a popular idiom – on 26 February, two days before the performance and itself the day of the première of Auden's and Isherwood's play, *The Ascent of F6*, for which he had also written the music. He did not attend the first performance of the revue as he was staying with the Bridges at Friston Field from 27 February to 3 March. See also DMBA, pp. 97–9, and PR, pp. 238–47 and 518–19.

After his return from the United States in 1942, Britten collaborated with Slater on a further pageant, *An Agreement of the People*, which was performed by the Co-operative Society at the Empress Stadium, Wembley, London. It was subsequently mounted in a revised format by the Bristol Unity Players under the title *Over to You. An Agreement of the People* took the theme of national and international unity against the common enemy, fascism, presented through the eyes of the rooftop fire-watcher; he explains the situation to a character in eighteenth-century costume who is apparently Jonathan Swift's Gulliver. The music for this pageant has not yet come to light. See Colin Chambers, *The Story of the Unity Theatre* (London, Lawrence and Wishart, 1989), p. 246, and Don Watson, *British Socialist Theatre*

1930–1979, Ph.D. dissertation, University of Hull, 1985, pp. 304–6. The inclusion of Gulliver reminds us that it was Swift's satire that had been the subject of a proposed ballet by Slater and Britten in 1936; see Letter 83 and note 2 to Letter 120.

Colin Chambers also notes (p. 184) that in 1939 Britten agreed to take part in the Unity Theatre's 'Development Scheme' at the Kingsway Theatre, London, which sought to stage ballet and opera. Other willing participants included Constant Lambert, Alan Bush, Arthur Benjamin and Paul Robeson. Britten's departure to North America in May 1939, however, put paid to any involvement in this project.

3 Britten did not attend the performance on 7 March, although he did go to part of a rehearsal with David Layton.

Saturday 13 March 1937
[London/Bucklebury]

I catch 10–45 to Reading where Peter Burra[1] meets me – he takes me to his lovely cottage in Bucklebury Common. It is a heavenly day & it is grand to be in the country after all this time in London. We go & look at a charming little cottage nearby – which I'm thinking of taking as it is such a heavenly part of the country. After lunch we go into Thatchington [Thatcham] & Peter initiates me into the wonders of Squash which I find completely captivating & I curse myself for not having played it before. Back here for bath & tea & a long lovely walk over the common after. After dinner play piano duets & talk till a late hour – I have a kindred spirit in thousands of ways (one way in particular) here.

1 Peter Burra (1909–1937), the twin brother of Nella Burra and a close friend of Peter Pears (they were at school together: see PFL, plate 87), who died in an aeroplane accident on 27 April, near Bucklebury Common, Berkshire. During 1936 Pears lived for a time in Burra's cottage. It was Burra's death that brought Britten and Pears into a closer relationship and their joint sorting out of Burra's effects introduced Britten into the Behrends' circle (see note 1 to Diary for 14 March). Britten wrote in his diary on the day of Burra's death:

Go to bed feeling desparate as I've just heard that dear old Peter Burra has been killed in an Air smash near Reading – flying with one of his 'tough' friends. He was a darling of the 1st rank, & in the short year & a bit that I've known him he has been very close & dear to me. A first rate brain, that was at the moment in great difficulties – tho' this is far too terrible a solution for them. Nothing has leaked out yet how it happened. This is a bloody world, & nothing one can do can stop this fatal rot. There is

Franco in Spain blowing thousands of innocent Basque & Castillians to bits [Guernica had been bombed on the 26th]. I'm glad that Peter is out of all that – he felt it so terribly [. . .]

Britten had the news of Burra's death from John Alston, who had read it in the evening paper and told Britten when calling on him later that same evening.

Burra was a gifted and perceptive writer on art, music and literature. While at Oxford he edited a quarterly undergraduate periodical, *Farrago*, for the two years of its existence, 1930–31. A 'Concluding Note' in the last issue read: 'In bringing to a conclusion this *farrago of incongruous kickshaws*, we have no other comment to make than that we have achieved the space of life which was originally proposed.' There was a strong emphasis on music in the periodical, and among the contributors were many whose activities impinged on the lives of Britten and Pears in later years, e.g. Jelly d'Arányi, Cecil Day Lewis, Frank Howes, Herbert Murrill, Desmond Shawe-Taylor, and Randall Swingler. A complete set of this extremely rare journal (published by Simon Nowell Smith), which belonged to Peter Pears, is in the Archive.

Burra's essay, 'The Novels of E.M. Forster' published in *The Nineteenth Century and After*, 116 [1934], pp. 581–94, was much admired by Forster and reprinted in the 1942 Everyman's Library edition of *A Passage to India* (see *Selected Letters of E.M. Forster*, Volume II, 1921–70, edited by Mary Lago and P.N. Furbank (London, Collins, 1985), p. 128).

Britten had first met Burra at the 1936 ISCM Festival at Barcelona, about which Burra wrote as a music critic for *The Times*. On 9 October 1937 he set Burra's 'Not even summer yet' for voice and piano. The poem, first published as 'For a Song', in *Farrago*, No. 4, December 1930, p. 34, was attributed to 'James Salkeld' – Burra's middle names. The first and last stanzas read:

> Not even summer yet
> Can me quite forget
> That still most blessed thing,
> The early spring
>
> But in the lover's ways,
> The summer of his days
> Is come from such a spring
> As poets cannot sing.

Burra's sister, Nella (Nell Moody) recalled the circumstances of the song's composition in a private communication (24 November 1983):

After he was killed a mutual friend Julie Behrend (whose parents owned the cottage at Bucklebury where Pears was living with Peter at the time) suggested that Ben should write the song for me to sing. I sang it first with Gordon Thorne accompanying me at a concert in memory of Peter. I was to do it again at a Wigmore Hall recital with Norman Franklin; in fact the concert was fixed just before Peter died. But I was too emotionally upset and cancelled it.

This unpublished song was revived by Neil Mackie (tenor) and Iain Burnside (piano) at the Wigmore Hall, London, on 22 November 1983.

Berkeley and Britten jointly inscribed their orchestral suite, *Mont Juic* (1937), 'in memory of Peter Burra'. See note 2 to Letter 122.

Sunday, 14 March 1937
[*Bucklebury*]

The glorious weather stops & the awful weather resumes its reign – we have blizzards & then slush. So instead of walking Peter & I go into Newbury & play squash again – this time I progress (I actually beat him about 6–3!) & really enjoy myself alot – so much so that in my over eagerness I sprain my ankle pretty severly & hobble about the rest of the day with a stick – very pathetic, but secretly (I'm ashamed to say) pleased as it draws attention to my prowess at Squash, which Peter is proud of – & which I feel adds to my glamour!!

We have lunch with rich friends of Peters, the Behrends[1] nearby – charming & cultured people who have done a tremendous amount to help artists (besides Peter – Lytton Strachey,[2] & Stanley Spencer among others) in general. We spend afternoon too there – & see Spencers impressive little chapel they erected for him after the war. Back at 'Foxhold' – we play piano & violin (Schumann, Mozart, Franck – swapping parts & making the most extraordinary noise) & then talk till mid-night – Peter is one of the world's dears.

1 John Louis Behrend (1882–1972), and his wife Mary (1883–1977), were friends of both Pears and Burra, and well known as patrons of the arts, in particular of the English artist, Stanley Spencer (1891–1959), who lived and worked in the Berkshire village of Cookham and from whom they commissioned the murals depicting war scenes around Salonika for the Sandham Memorial Chapel which they built at Burghclere, 1926–7. Their niece, Mrs Audrey Harvey, contributed a memoir of her uncle and aunt, to the *Sunday Telegraph Magazine* (date untraced):

They had an immense delight in art, an ability (often livelier than that of the Tate of those days) to recognize early unconventional talent and a passion for helping the young.

For one glorious instance they made possible Britten's first concert – a fact perhaps little known because of their extreme distaste for publicity. [This was probably the first joint recital, which Pears identifies as 'our concert' at the end of his letter quoted below.]

In earlier Hampstead days they were friends of Lytton Strachey, who read them the manuscript of *Eminent Victorians*. It was they who commissioned the huge Henry Lamb [1880–1960, Australian-born painter] portrait [of Strachey]. It hung in the dining room at Burghclere, profoundly disturbing us rather Philistine children. One of their remarkable actions was to build not only the Burghclere chapel but also a small mosque for the workers in a family business in Alexandria.

They were Socialists and Fabians. Mary Behrend, widowed and in her nineties, but eloquent almost to the last, eventually died penniless – one could say from generosity.

They both had wit and an Edwardian sense of fun and many cherish their memory.

After John ('Bow') Behrend's death in 1972, Peter Pears wrote a letter to Mrs Behrend on 10 March which sums up the role played by the Behrends in his life and Britten's:

I would like to be able to put into words just how much Bow and you have meant to me. It was our dear Peter Burra who brought us together. How he loved and admired you, and how quickly I learnt to do the same. The Grey House was the first <u>civilised</u> house I had ever set foot in, and you were the first <u>civilised</u> people I had ever met. So it seemed to me thirty five years ago, and it still does. You and Bow showed me art – at first hand – for the first time. Art as part of one's life – not in a museum. I was <u>very</u> young really and those days were a whole education in itself. One of my prides (and a mighty one) is to have on my bedroom wall the G. [Gilbert] Spencer picture of the boys on the common with the football and the two men – and again the Henry Lamb of the Bivouac in Salonika. They belonged to you and Bow – and now they are are mine. What a joyful pride. Before I saw your pictures, I only knew half of the <u>aura</u> of pictures. And nowadays when people enjoy or come to see our pictures, I would like to feel that <u>I</u> know some of the satisfaction which you & Bow must have felt. Not really pride of possession, certainly not <u>only</u>, but as part of a creative fight for the good and the beautiful and true. And this I learnt from you & Bow.

And then too it was Peter's death at Bucklebury which brought Ben into my life. How can I ever be thankful enough for this happening? Yet, at the cost of Peter? No, it would have <u>had</u> to be. But the picture includes all these shades of tone. All your continued kindness and generosity to us in the war and after – our concert during the War – the String Quartet – and then of course the Opera Group and the Festival. You and Bow have had a great part in our life, a creative one which sets us all an example.

Britten dedicated his Second String Quartet, Op. 36, to Mary Behrend. The Behrends were generous supporters of the Aldeburgh Festival and the English Opera Group and they sponsored the first recital given by Pears and Britten after their return to England from

America in 1942, to which Pears refers in his letter. The recollections of their son, George, who on occasion helped out at Aldeburgh and was Britten's and Pears's driver when on tour in the 1940s and 1950s, were published in PPT, pp. 8–9.

In a letter to Imogen Holst written in 1966, Mrs Behrend recollected that 'Barcelona was where we first saw Ben', clearly a reference to the ISCM Festival held there in that year, and at which the Behrends' protégé, Peter Burra, was of course present as a critic. That may have been good reason for the Behrends' attendance. But it is odd, if Mrs Behrend's memory was correct, that there is no mention of her or her husband in Britten's diary entries about the Festival. Was Mrs Behrend in fact thinking of the first performance of the *Bridge Variations* at Salzburg? See Letter 105. However, there is again no evidence of the Behrends' attendance, something Pears would surely have mentioned in his letter to Britten (No. 107). See also I.M. Rawson, 'Patrons of talent: the Behrends of Burghclere', *Country Life*, 26 October 1978, pp. 1347–8.

2 The English biographer (1880–1932), from whose *Elizabeth and Essex* (1928) Britten was to derive his opera, *Gloriana* (1953).

Monday, 15 March 1937
[*Bucklebury/London*]

Can't move much to-day – so I finish my Reveille[1] for Toni in morning while Peter plays with his new toy, the motor Bike which symbolises his craving for the normal or 'tough' at the moment. Then early lunch – Julie Behrend calls for us both as 12.15 – lunch & then set off for London. Arrive here in time to hear the Scottish Orch. under Guy Warrack do my Rossini Suite – not too well – speeds wrong.[2] They both stay to tea, to which Poppy Vulliamy (a marvellous person, one of the most admirable I know)[3] & Ronald Duncan come. Talk fifteen to the dozen.

Christopher Isherwood comes to dinner – a grand person; unaffected, extremely amusing & devastatingly intelligent. He stays nice & late.

Beth is going on well – but gets very tired.

1 *Reveille*, a virtuoso concert study for violin with piano accompaniment, composed 9–15 March, for Antonio Brosa, and first performed by him and Franz Reizenstein (1911–1968), German-born English composer and pianist, at the Wigmore Hall, London, on 12 April. Brosa was a notoriously late riser, hence the title of the piece, and also Britten's unusual tempo indication, *Andante – rubato e pigro* (*pigro* = 'sluggish, lazy'). *Reveille* was posthumously published by Faber Music in 1983.

2 Guy Warrack, Scottish conductor and composer (1900–1986). He had been appointed conductor of the BBC Scottish Orchestra in 1935.

3 It was Poppy, a friend of Peter Burra's, whom Britten had met the previous December, who was to arrange for a Basque refugee child to be offered a home at the Old Mill in 1938. (See EWB, p. 107, and note 2 to Letter 131.) On 16 October Britten was writing in his diary: 'I am buying clothes (& a football yesterday) for my little Spanish boy – to-day pyjamas & pullover. I am enjoying the responsibility tremendously.'

99 To Clarence Raybould[1]
BBC

at Biltmore, Pole Barn Lane, Frinton-on-Sea.

April 4th 1937.

Dear Mr. Raybould,

Thank you for your letter. I note times of rehearsals, and it is convenient for me to be at the piano rehearsal on 28th at 3.0.[2]

The 'Arthur' music[3] is progressing apiece [sic], but there is an enormous quantity to be done. I hope to deliver it as promised on or about Monday the 12th.[4]

Would you please note that my London address is 559 Finchley Road, N.W.3 – I moved sometime last year, but changes of address are notoriously difficult to sink in!

Yours sincerely,

BENJAMIN BRITTEN

1 Clarence Raybould (1886–1972), English conductor, composer and accompanist. Raybould joined the BBC in 1936, becoming Chief Assistant Conductor of the Symphony Orchestra from 1938 until 1945. At the BBC Raybould conducted the English premières of Hindemith's operas *Cardillac* (18 December 1936) and *Mathis der Maler* (15 March 1939). He wrote music for various independently produced documentary films during the early thirties. Interestingly, Raybould composed a one-act opera, *The Sumida River* (libretto by Marie Stopes), produced in Birmingham in 1916. In 1964 Britten and William Plomer were to draw upon the same source as Raybould – the Japanese Noh play, *Sumidagawa* – for the first Church Parable, *Curlew River*. Plomer brought Raybould's opera to Britten's attention in October 1958, to which Britten responded on 8 October: 'Actually I didn't know that C. Raybould even composed. Don't let it worry us. But what a funny coincidence.'

In 1943 Raybould was to precipitate an incident that suggested that a controversy in 1941 about Britten's pacifism was by no means extinct. On 9 July Erwin Stein, now working at Boosey and Hawkes, sent Raybould a score of the *Matinées Musicales*, in the hopes that Raybould might programme it. His initiative prompted a reply on 12 July that Stein can hardly have expected:

Please do not think me ungracious to your courteous and enterprising firm, for which I have personally the highest esteem; a piano conductor part of the Vaughan Williams, however, is of no use to me, and you may like to use it for somebody else. The other score is of no interest to me because of the composer's personal views and behaviour, I was going to say politically, but expand this to 'nationally'. I have the utmost contempt for the whole gang of young people who are dodging the country's call.

Raybould was to write a personal letter to Britten expressing his 'contrition' for this 'very angry and hot-headed communication'; and indeed his indignation was not to prevent him from conducting the *Sinfonia da Requiem* on 30 September, a performance that led to an exchange of amiable letters between the composer and conductor (Raybould writing to Britten on 1 October, Britten replying on the 13th and Raybould responding on the 15th). But Raybould's broadside of July was to surface again in November, a farcical misunderstanding in which Raybould's intemperate reaction to *Matinées Musicales* was transferred to *The Rescue*:

On November 4th, D.M. [the Director of Music, Arthur Bliss] showed me a memorandum which you received from [Laurence] Gilliam [. . .], in which the latter stated that he had received a telephone message from B.B. to say that I had written a letter to Ralph Hawkes saying that I objected to any dealings with him on the grounds of his being a Conscientious Objector and would only conduct the 'Rescue' music under protest.

This allegation is entirely untrue: I neither wrote to Ralph Hawkes nor did I say to anyone else that I would have no dealings with Britten as a Conscientious Objector, neither did I say that I would conduct 'The Rescue' music only under protest.

[. . .]

Not only have I not refused, either personally to Britten or his publishers, or officially inside the Corporation, to have anything to do with 'The Rescue' music, or to do it only under protest, but on the contrary, it is only a week or two ago that I conducted the broadcast of his 'Sinfonia da Requiem'.

In the event, Raybould was to conduct the first performance of 'The Rescue' on 25 and 26 November, the affair having been 'smoothed over' in the words of R.J.F. Howgill (Assistant Controller (Programmes)), who added however that 'Britten [. . .] apparently does not intend to collaborate in the actual production'. See Letter 437, and note 3 to Letter 375.

2 A piano rehearsal, with Sophie Wyss, for the forthcoming broadcast performance of *Our Hunting Fathers* under Boult on 30 April.

3 Britten refers to the final rehearsal of his incidental music for the

dramatized historical feature, *King Arthur*, by D. Geoffrey Bridson (1910–1980), the English playwright, poet and BBC radio producer. *King Arthur* was produced by Val Gielgud (1900–1981), and first broadcast by the BBC on 23 April; the music was performed by the London Symphony Orchestra, conducted by Raybould. Britten's diary for the day of the broadcast, 23 April, reads:

Early to BBC. at 10.15 for full rehearsal – it goes quite well, apart from a few misunderstandings – tho' the actual play irritates me more than I can say – its stilted dialogue, a pale pastiche of Malory – its dull Tennysonian poetry, & not nearly as good as that either – & its complete divorce from realities or humanities. In the afternoon a further consultation with Raybould (who conducts really very well) [. . .] Then back to BBC for the King Arthur show – at 7.30. It goes very well – but I still feel the same about it. The music certainly comes off like hell & the orchestra & Lennox Berkeley (who comes with me, and with whom I eat at Café Royal after) are enthusiastic about it.

See also PR, pp. 330–60 and 567–74.

4 Britten was first invited to compose the music for *King Arthur* on 12 February 1937, and three days later he held discussions with Val Gielgud and Laurence Gilliam (1904–1964) of the BBC Drama Department. Further discussions took place on 4 March and by the 19th Britten had started work on his composition sketch, finishing it on 2 April, when he began the full score. The score was completed by 15 April and delivered into Raybould's hands the following day, although a final section had to be added on the 19th. Rehearsals took place on 20–23 April. The production was broadcast again on the 24th. See also DMBA, pp. 165–8.

100 To Ralph Hawkes

Biltmore, Pole Barn Lane, Frinton on Sea.
April 13th, 1937.

Dear Ralph,

Will it upset you very much if we post-pone our visit to the Auden play[1] at the Mercury from Thursday to when it is moved to the West End – at the end of the month? I am so sorry, but the wretched BBC. are clamouring for the rest of the King Arthur music & it isn't finished yet – & I must use the evenings for work I'm afraid.

I shall be coming in to see you when I get to town – on Thursday – about one or two minor points – including the Rossini Suite.[2]

I hope things are going well.

Yours,
BENJAMIN BRITTEN

1 Auden's and Isherwood's most successful play, *The Ascent of F6*, which was first performed at the Mercury Theatre, London, on 26 February 1937. The cast included William Devlin as Michael Ransom, Dorothy Holmes-Gore as Mrs Ransom, and Hedli Anderson (see note 2 to Letter 126) as the Singer. Auden had written to Britten from Portugal in the spring of 1936,

> Look here, would you be prepared to do the music for our new play, in which there is a lot. The difficulty is that I dont know how it would be financially. I can only suggest you write it as we wrote our part, and then sell it for what you can. The music is more serious and operatic than in Dogskin. If you would consider the idea, we'll send the text when it's done. Let me know. I've just resigned from the Unit. Hurrah.

In September, when Auden was back in England, the two men met for further discussion of the project. The music, composed in February, included the famous choral number, 'Stop all the clocks' ('Funeral Blues'; see PFL, plate 103) and was conducted from the piano by Brian Easdale (see note 1 to Letter 148), the musical director of the company. A review of the first performance appeared in *The Times*, 27 February, which concluded:

> The real interest of the play lies in its working out, through the medium of a persuasive and unaffected performance by Mr William Devlin, of the dramatists' theory of power. The Abbot gives the key to it. He points to the vanity and peril of achievement, and sets out as alternative the surrender of the will. Does this apply only to individual achievement and individual will, or do the dramatists extend their doctrine to a surrender of the collective will also? If not, the discovery they have made is, as yet, but a halt on the long and familiar journey; but it is an extremely interesting halt, neither combative nor arrogant. The whole play seems to be written less with a desire to wound and condemn than to understand.

Harold Hobson wrote in the *Observer*, 28 February:

> It would be easier to praise this play extravagantly than to do it justice. When a poet gets into the theatre and makes himself heard, his voice is apt to reach the heart and confuse the judgement. Here the poet not only has the first and last words but is never so far from the play's centre as to leave its prosier byways unenlightened. Thus the ascent of F.6 (hitherto inaccessible) becomes an adventure of the soul on which Hamlet might have made pertinent observations, and which Lear might have endorsed. Not that the poet and his prose confederate, while essaying a similar track, rival these prime adventurers. They are less content to leave the way ungarnished. Small, if satirical, comedy, and some of the theatre's flashier, self-conscious experiments bring the groundlings on one side of the footlights into touch with the groundlings on the other. Musical relief, though in itself not uninteresting, tends at times to blur by transmuting the text, and the voice of the doctrinaire to counterpoint the voice of the poet. Yet for all these concessions, diversions, and secular stresses, the play's strength and distinction are clear. The producer, Mr Rupert Doone, has overcome technical difficulties which the text deserved that he should, and his company support

him bravely. The result is an extremely interesting, even exciting, experience. It offers to Mr. William Devlin in particular, histrionic, rhetorical, and nobler opportunities which he takes magnificently.

This first successful run concluded on 17 April, but after a single performance at the Arts Theatre, Cambridge, on 22 April, *F6* returned to London, this time to the Little Theatre in the West End, running from 30 April until 5 June 1937. There is no record in Britten's diary that he and Hawkes ever visited the Little Theatre to see *F6*. For a more detailed account of Britten's involvement in *F6* see DMBA, pp. 97–8 and 118–24, and PR, pp. 509–17. See also EMWHA, pp. 293–355 and 598–652, and John Haffenden (ed.), *W.H. Auden: the Critical Heritage* (London, Routledge & Kegan Paul, 1983), pp. 189–213.

2 Britten's suite of five movements from Rossini, entitled *Soirées Musicales*, Op. 9. Britten had arranged some music by Rossini at the request of Alberto Cavalcanti in July 1935 for the GPO Film Unit's short silhouette film, *The Tocher* (animated by Lotte Reiniger, 1899–1981). (See PR, pp. 446–7, and Eric Walter White, 'Greek Shadow Theatre', in TBB, pp. 185–90.) This first 'Rossini Suite' was scored for flute (doubling piccolo), oboe, clarinet, percussion, piano and a wordless chorus of boys' voices. In December 1935 Britten began to reorchestrate the film suite for small and large orchestra simultaneously, and work continued on and off for the best part of a year, the two-format score being completed on 29 October the following year. From the film version Britten selected three movements for inclusion in the new orchestration: No. 1, *March*; No. 2, *Canzonetta*; No. 4, *Bolero*. The third and fifth movements of *Soirées Musicales* were entirely new. Britten's sources were Rossini's opera, *William Tell* (No. 1), a volume of songs entitled *Soirées Musicales* (Nos. 2–4), and a part-song, 'Charity' (No. 5). The orchestral suite (which format was used is unknown) was first performed in a BBC broadcast concert on 16 January 1937, conducted by Joseph Lewis (1878–1954), senior staff conductor at the BBC from 1930 to 1938. Apart from *Soirées Musicales*, the programme also contained the first broadcast performance of the *Saxo-Rhapsody* by Eric Coates (1886–1957), with Sigurd Rascher (whom Britten had heard in Florence in 1934) as soloist (see also Letter 227). Britten describes the occasion of the concert in his diary for that day:

[. . .] to BBC. Maida Vale Studios where Joseph Lewis rehearses my Rossini Suite – it goes well tho' the conductor is not exactly sensitive. [. . .]
   My broadcast of Soirées Musicales goes well & I love the work.

Soirées Musicales is dedicated 'To M. Alberto Cavalcanti'.
   The first concert performance took place at a Prom on 10 August,

when the BBC Symphony Orchestra was conducted by Henry Wood.
Britten wrote in his diary:

10.0 Rehearsal at Queen's Hall with Sir Henry J.W. & the BBC. of my
Rossini Suite. It goes as well as can be expected in a Prom
rehearsal [. . .] Eat in the evening with Christopher Isherwood – & then
go on to Queen's Hall for second half of Prom concert – when Henry W.
does my Soirées Musicales. It doesn't go so badly – but not a rousing
success with Audience unfortunately. However – there we are. Feel ill &
sick after – so drift about with C. Isherwood – Stephen Spender, whom
we meet – go home for a bit with C.I. & then taxi back here – & straight to
bed & to forgetful sleep!

101   To Mary Behrend

559 Finchley Road, N.W.3.
May 2nd 1937.

Dear Mrs. Behrend,

Thank you very much for your letter. It is a tremendous comfort
to know that when we come down to Reading that things will be so
easy for us. Actually I don't think it will be for a few days.[1] I saw
Peter Piers the other day, & he said that there is no immediate
hurry about the matter. It seems that Mrs. Burra & Nell[2] have gone
down to Cornwall for a short while, and until they return not
very much can be done. But on the other hand we have decided
that there are a few things there that must be done before long,
so when we can make our free days coincide we shall be coming
down. I will 'phone you to see if it is convenient for you – but
please don't bother if it isn't. We could always stay at Foxhold.

Peter Piers says that he has already seen the Chapel notes,[3] &
says he will send them on to you.

It was charming of you to have brought us to town on Thursday.
It was so much more pleasant than trailing up to town in the bus
& train.

Yours sincerely,
BENJAMIN B.

1 The journey was made on 6 May, as Britten recounts in his diary:

After dinner general slack & then Kit drops me at Paddington at 10.45 &
I meet Peter Pears & travel with him in a packed dirty train to Reading
where we arrive about mid-night – & set out for the Behrend's house
(Burclere); on his motor-bike, & the pouring, pouring rain. After
wandering helplessly in the maze of roads over the common – very cold
& damp, to our skins – & me pretty sore behind, being unused to pillion

riding – we knock up people in the only house with a light on we meet at all, & get some rather vague instructions from them. Wander further & quite by accident alight on the house – at about 1.45 or 50. Have hot baths & straight to bed. The Behrends themselves are in town.

Friday 7 May
After a 9 o'clock breakfast Peter & I go over to Peter Burra's house (Foxhold) to spend day sorting out letters, photos & other personalities preparatory to the big clear up to take place soon. Peter Pears is a dear & a very sympathetic person – tho' I'll admit I am not too keen on travelling on his motor bike!

On the same day, Peter Pears wrote to Mrs Behrend:

105 Charlotte St,
W.1.

Dear Mrs. Behrend,
   If you could have seen Benjamin and me arriving last night, you would know how thankful we were to have a warm bath and a comfortable bed. Benjamin says his feet have never been wetter – and if any thing I was the more thoroughly soaked of the two of us. It was chiefly through my stupidity in not remembering which turning off the Common it was!
   We have had a good day's work at Foxhold to-day and really seem to have done everything we can before the final clearing begins. You will be glad to know that the Introductory Essay for the Chapel was there. We worked so well that there seems nothing left to do on Sunday, so that we won't be coming down after all. But thank you alot for asking us.

Yours
PETER PEARS

This, it seems, was the letter that initiated the long friendship with the Behrends of both Pears and Britten, with its many happy and fruitful consequences.

Burra's funeral took place on 29 April 1937. It was attended by Pears and Britten, and Lennox Berkeley, who wrote to Britten on 8 May:

I wonder how you got on with sorting things out at Bucklebury. It must have been a depressing business. That funeral was one of the most heart-rending things I have ever known. A thing like that does make me cling desperately to such religious faith as I have. I'm sure you ought to reconsider all that – it does matter so terribly.

On the 19th, Berkeley must have been among the first of Britten's circle to react to the new friendship: 'I am glad that you survived the motor-bike. I think Peter Pears is charming, though I don't know him at all well.'

The preparations for the Coronation of George VI on 12 May must have provided a strange and disorienting backcloth to the clearing up of Burra's affairs and possessions. On 11 May, Britten writes in his diary:

[. . .] see Ralph Hawkes in the afternoon – but he is too busy on
Coronation matters to be able to concentrate on anything. Incidentally
getting about now is complete hell – walking impossible, with staring
crowds gaping at the literally hideous decorations that are freely strewn all
over the place. Car traffic, because of the apparently now permanent strike,
is colossal – & trains are packed to suffocation.

Peter Pears comes to dinner & we listen to a very dull (inspite of awe
inspiring cast) 'Coronation' Variety Show – & alot of gramophone records.
He is a dear.

And on Coronation day itself:

[. . .] & by jove don't they let us know it! Continuous broadcast of the
ceremony from 1.0–5, & everything one sees & hears is but a repetition
of the same bla, bla, bla – of empire, loyalties one big family (that is 'fine
feeling' if expressed by the upper classes – 'damned cheek' if by the
lower!). We, with Kit who stays here the night, escape into the country
for a picnic lunch, but oddly enough (& valuably too) the weather is rotten,
& it rains solidly from the afternoon onwards after having been
depressingly dull all the morning. Listen to a coronation revue in the
evening. after the coronation address by the King (the poor man masters
his stutter well), & coronation news – in fact spend a coronation evening,
writing coronation letters & retiring to a coronation if lonely bed.

For what the rest of the nation was supposedly thinking (or doing)
on Coronation Day, see *May The Twelfth: Mass-Observation Day –
Surveys 1937* by over two hundred observers, edited by Humphrey
Jennings and Charles Madge, with a new Afterword by David Pocock
(London, Faber and Faber, 1987).

In April 1938, Britten was to be approached by Ralph Hawkes to
contribute to a proposed volume of *Fanfares for Coronation Trumpets*:

You may recall that considerable prominence was given to the Coronation
Trumpet Fanfares, which were played during the Coronation Service in
Westminster Abbey last year.

As a result of this, we have been instructed by the Authorities to manufacture these instruments for sale to all the Regiments. [. . .]

The necessity for providing suitable Fanfares for performance at once
arises and the instrumentation gives good scope for short flourishes or
fanfares of a brilliant character. I would like to know whether you would be
interested in writing one of these.

Other composers who were to be approached included Arthur Benjamin, Ireland, Berkeley, Kodály, Walford Davies and Bliss.

Britten, when returning to Hawkes the corrected proofs of *Mont
Juic*, agreed to discuss the matter of the fanfares, but it seems the
project went no further. He may have been disinclined to accept the
commission, and in any event the worsening international situation
would scarcely have provided a propitious context. In fact, the
volume was never published by Boosey & Hawkes.

2 Helen (Nella) Pomfret Burra, Peter's twin sister (b. 1909), the singer

and actress, who appeared in a number of the important Group Theatre productions for which Britten composed incidental music. She married the actor and director, John Moody (b. 1906), one of the founder members of the Group Theatre, who took the roles of Mr A in *The Ascent of F6* and Oswald Vrodny in *On the Frontier*. Moody was a producer for the Carl Rosa and Sadler's Wells Operas, 1945–9, a Director of the Bristol Old Vic from 1954, and from 1960 a director at the Welsh National Opera where he made many translations of librettos with his wife.

3 The text of an essay by Burra about the chapel the Behrends had built at Burghclere. See also Pears's letter quoted in note 1 above.

102   To Grace Williams

> ~~Flat No. 2, West Cottage Road, West End Green, N.W.6~~
> 559 [Finchley Road, London, NW3]
> [Postmarked 23 May 1937]

Many thanks for sending the scores & Emil[1] back. Things are hectic here. We had a beastly car-smash[2] (with the new car too) & that makes things very difficult. Luckily no one was seriously hurt.

Hope to see you sometime. We don't go out very much at the moment.

BENJAMIN

1 Kästner's novel; see note 7 to Letter 40.

2 Britten and his sister, Beth, were involved in a car accident on 18 May; neither of them was seriously injured. However, that was not the end of the affair. Britten wrote in his diary on 22 May:

The day is completely blighted by the Police notification that they are going to prosecute me for Dangerous driving – blast their eyes. It's infuriating, because I know I was in the right. However with solicitors I may get off – but there is the infernal bother & worry of it all to be faced.

The case was concluded on 14 June:

Mr. Donne, the investigator for Crocker, my acting solicitors, calls for Beth & me at 8.15 & takes us down to Burnham Police-court. There we meet Mr. Edgedale the Council [*sic*] & talk over matters. After a few small cases before the bench – my case comes up: – Two of us – the villain in the grey car (Mr Bartlett) are prosecuted for dangerous driving. I am taken first & all the witnesses give evidence that is 'for' me – & my Council makes great use of that & my case is dismissed without Beth or myself even going into the witness box. The other man is convicted by damning evidence. We both feel very relieved [. . .]

See also EWB, p. 104.

103 To Henry Boys

[*Donald Mitchell*, Gustav Mahler: Songs and Symphonies
of Life and Death *(London, Faber and Faber,*
1985), pp. 339–40]

559, Finchley Road
[Postmarked 29 June 1937]

My dear Henry,

It is now well past midnight & society dictates that I should stop
playing the Abschied.[1] Otherwise I might possibly have gone on
repeating the last record[2] indefinitely – for 'ewig' keit of course.

It is cruel, you know, that music should be so beautiful. It has
the beauty of loneliness & of pain: of strength & freedom. The
beauty of disappointment & never-satisfied love. The cruel beauty
of nature, and everlasting beauty of monotony.

And the essentially 'pretty' colours of the normal orchestral
palette are used to paint this extraordinary picture of loneliness.
And there is nothing morbid about it. The same harmonic
progressions that Wagner used to colour his essentially morbid
love-scenes (his 'Liebes' is naturally followed by 'Tod')[3] are used
here to paint a serenity literally supernatural. I cannot understand
it – it passes over me like a tidal wave – and that matters not a jot
either, because it goes on for ever, even if it is never performed again
– that final chord is printed on the atmosphere.

Perhaps if I could understand some of the Indian philosophies I
might approach it a little. At the moment I can do no more than
bask in its Heavenly light – & it is worth having lived to do that.

– Do come & hear it again soon. I'll be back on Saturday – hear
it then & we'll talk about it all Sunday at the Bridges.[4]

Love,
BENJAMIN

P.S.   Can we catch the <u>10.45</u> on Sunday?

1 The finale of Mahler's song-cycle *Das Lied von der Erde*.

2 The famous Gustav Mahler Society recording issued in June 1937
under the auspices of the Columbia Gramophone Company Ltd., in
a limited edition on seven 78 rpm records, ROX 165–71. The recording
was of a live performance given in Vienna, on 24 May 1936, by
Kerstin Thorborg (1896–1970), Swedish mezzo-soprano; Charles Kull-
man (1903–1983), American tenor; and the Vienna Philharmonic
Orchestra, conducted by Bruno Walter (1876–1962). Britten acquired

his copy of the discs on 22 June when he wrote in his diary, 'Barbara & Henry Boys to lunch – the latter to hear my new (& very good) records of "das Lied [v]on der Erde" – which is too exciting to think of much else to-day.' The recording is now in the Archive. This recording, like that of the Ninth Symphony, was highly influential in moulding opinion in the very early stages of the Mahler revival, as this letter shows. Britten's collection of Mahler scores in the Archive, many of which are inscribed with the date of acquisition, amply demonstrates his enthusiasm for the composer. They include *Das Lied*, the score of which he had acquired in 1936, before the release of the recording in 1937; the Fifth Symphony ('Benjy. Love from me. F.B. Xmas 1936'); the Sixth Symphony (1937); and the Ninth Symphony ('An meinen liebsten Ben. Weinacht 1938. Peter').

Britten had heard the Ninth as early as January 1935, when he wrote in his diary on the 27th about a broadcast:

[. . .] listen to what seems a fine perf. by B.B.C. orch. under Oskar Fried (tho' without the suavity & rhythm of the Wien Phil) of Mahler's wonderful 9th Symphony. I could listen to this for hours. The end is really very moving.

Britten was later to acquire the HMV Gustav Mahler Society issue of the Ninth, a recording made live in Vienna on 16 January 1938, when Bruno Walter conducted the Vienna Philharmonic Orchestra, and for which Henry Boys wrote the analytic notes (see note 2 to Letter 74).

The history of Britten's passion for Mahler is documented in very considerable detail in his diaries. The entries are not only revealing of his relationship to one of the most important of musical influences on him but also give an account of the evolution in England of perceptions of Mahler and his music which were certainly not common at the time. The consequent change in critical attitudes was largely accomplished through the intelligent enthusiasm of a small circle of pre-war admirers, of whom Britten was one of the most articulate.

3 The 'Liebestod' from *Tristan und Isolde*.

4 Britten and Boys were to visit the Bridges from 4 to 6 July. Britten was to write in his diary on 5 July, 'It is grand to see two people click (mentally) like Henry & F.B. They talk for hours, but I go to bed & leave them.'

104 To Nella Burra

Peasenhall Hall, Nr. Saxmundham, Suffolk.[1]
Station: Darsham
as from: 559, Finchley Road, N.W. 3.
July 14th 1937

My dear Nell,

Forgive me for this long delay in answering your letter. I am a frantically bad correspondent but this time I have a good excuse – I have never been so busy in my life. I have been inundated with work, put out with a nasty car accident, & now I'm entirely occupied with house-hunting. So you see – I haven't yet had time to set Peter's song – but as soon as I do it I will at once send you a copy for your approval. I am sure there won't be any bother about copyright. I will get my publishers to make the usual arrangements, & to communicate with Peter's executors – are they your mother & yourself? If you could let me have a line sometime at your convenience to say it would simplify matters.

I hope you are well & working hard. I go to the Behrends for the week-end on Saturday – will you be there? But they will anyhow be able to give me news of you.

I think I have found a good spot to live in – it is an old Mill[2] & house in a quaint old village called Snape near here. It isn't exactly isolated, but it has a grand view and alot of land to ensure its not being built round. But it will be ages before we can move in, as it has to be altered & enlarged, and generally improved.

I do hope your new place is going well. I presume it is the place I shall address this to?

Kindest regards to your mother.
Yours ever,
BENJAMIN BRITTEN

1 Britten was staying with Mr and Mrs Arthur Welford, Beth's future parents-in-law.

2 The Old Mill, at Snape, Suffolk. After the death of his mother, Britten inherited enough money to buy a home of his own (see note 1 to Letter 97). His diary for 29 June reads:

I go down to Peasenhall to stay with the Welfords for four days. Object – to go through the myriads of names sent to me by Agents in my cottage quest. Everyday Mrs. W. & often Mr. W. too take me in one of their cars to visit places – but nothing is any good until we find on Friday [2 July] a

Mill at Snape, which seems to have possibilities – but alot of alterations to be made.

The country is grand – none in England like it – & I feel I'm infinitely wise in choosing this place.

Beth Welford writes in EWB, p. 105:

My future father-in-law, Arthur Welford, was an architect and said he would do the conversion for nothing, which was a great help as Ben had only the £3,000 [c.£2000] left to him by his mother to spend on the building. The plan was to join the mill to the cottage with a single-storey building which would contain bathroom shower, boiler house for the central heating and cupboards for linen, etc. The Mill would become Ben's studio and bedroom. To make it possible to have a bedroom above the studio the roof of the Mill had to be raised several feet. From the Mill there was a fantastic view to the south across to the river and the marshes on one side, with fields to the right, so a long window was placed facing south, inset in the wall to form a balcony one third of the way round the Mill. The granary was already joined to the cottage, so no structural alteration was needed there, except to insert windows and a fireplace. Ben loved to have open fires, so a fireplace for woodburning was built in the studio, but Arthur Welford was in advance of his time in thinking central heating also essential, as the Mill, cottage and granary all had outside walls. Arthur Welford and Ben worked closely together over the planning. It was fun to watch the place taking shape.

The Mill was bought by the composer in July 1937; he occupied it from 1938 until 1947, with a gap between, 1939–42, when he was in the USA. The Old Mill still stands today, overlooking the Snape Maltings Concert Hall, and bears a plaque to commemorate its association with the composer and his most famous opera, unveiled by Peter Pears on the fortieth anniversary of the first performance of *Peter Grimes*, on 7 June 1985.

105 To Mary Behrend

559 Finchley Road, N.W. 3.
July 19th 1937

My dear Mrs. Behrend,

It <u>was</u> a lovely week-end.[1] What with the lovely tennis, bathing, conversation (tho' I fear I overstepped the mark <u>there</u>!),[2] company in general, exquisite hospitality in every direction, & last but not least, the really overwhelming kindness of the hosts – there was everything there civilisation can offer! I do hope you are not too tired after it all, because the amount of work it must have entailed must be considerable.

We had a good run up to town, & Alan was nice & considerate

and spared our rather shattered nerves for motor journeys. We were in before 11.30 though, so it wasn't too slow.

I will let you know when Boyd Neel will be having a full rehearsal of my Salzburg piece[3] – I think it had better be the beginning of August because they will know it better – and I hope that you & Mr. Behrend will come along to hear it. I shall be most anxious to hear your judgement too – because I really set some store by your opinions; you have I feel an instinctive feeling for what's what.

Thank you again so much, & I hope it won't be long before we meet again.

Yours ever,
BENJAMIN BRITTEN

1 The Behrends invited Britten and Beth to spend the weekend of 17–18 July with them. Among the other guests were Peter Pears and Alan George (in the advertising business), who was to drive them back to London.

2 Britten's diary for 18 July reveals the nature of his conversation:

[. . .] interesting talk – which at dinner becomes a regular marathon for me, for I have to stand up to the whole company to defend my (& all our set) 'Left' opinions – the chief protagonist of theirs was a cabinet Minister [Parliamentary Secretary to the Minister of Health], Robert Bernays [1902–1945], who was charming but a supreme parliamentarian & evaser of points! Anyhow, I am not at all vanquished, but maintain my points – & even obtain from him a promise to find anyone I know a job who has left school & cannot find one at all – under the age of 35 too. We'll see!

3 See Letter 106.

106 To Ralph Hawkes

559, Finchley Road, N.W. 3.
July 28th, 1937.

Dear Ralph,

Thank you for your letters. I am glad that the BBC. capitulated to the sum of 50 guineas so easily – re the Michaelmas programme.[1]

About F6 music:[2] I am just going through the whole material – writing it out in proper order & with cues (it got horribly messed about in production) & when that job is finished I will bring it along. The stuff is scored for piano duet (at one piano) & percussion. It looks to me as if the essential parts of it (songs &

such-like) will have to be boiled down to just two hands only –
but not necessarily until they ask for it!

The details of the Salzburg work for Boyd Neel[3] are:
Variations on a theme of Frank Bridge (for string orchestra) –
op. 10.

I will give you the timing of it in a few days. The work is to be
broadcast from Hilversum on Aug. 24th. The rehearsal, I would so
much like you to come to, is at 2.30 on Monday, August 23rd. Is
that convenient?

By-the-way Antonio Brosa is broadcasting a small violin piece
called 'Reveil'[4] on August 15th. What should I do about
assignment for that? I hadn't considered showing it to you yet as
I want to do another one to go with it[5] – an effective couple of
concert solos, I think.

I hope you're feeling better now – & can get away for a decent
holiday. Is Fire-bird[6] in decent repair yet?

I have definitely bought my Mill in Suffolk now – & I want you
to honour the place, as soon as it is ship-shape, with your presence
as one of the first guests!

Yours sincerely,
BENJAMIN B.

1   *The Company of Heaven*, a BBC religious programme compiled by
Richard Ellis Roberts (1879–1953), with incidental music by Britten,
was first broadcast on 29 September 1937 (Michaelmas Day). It was
produced by Robin Whitworth; and featured the actors Felix Aylmer,
Ian Dawson, and Stewart Rome. Britten's music was performed by
Sophie Wyss, Peter Pears, and the BBC Chorus and Orchestra, conducted by Trevor Harvey. Ellis Roberts – one-time Literary Editor of
the *New Statesman* – contributed a short article to the *Radio Times*
for the issue of the week of the broadcast, which explained the
programme's origins:

As with previous programmes in this series – for Christmas, for Holy Week,
and for All Saints – Robin Whitworth will produce the programme, and
Trevor Harvey will conduct the orchestra. With this Michaelmas programme,
however, we have made a change which is, I think, a very great improvement. It is always difficult to give an anthology of prose and verse, however
carefully the pieces are selected, a convincing unity. In my previous programmes the music has been taken from different composers, and Mr.
Harvey has had the ungrateful task of 'joining the flats', which he has
accomplished with astonishing skill.

Some very beautiful music has been composed especially for these earlier
programmes; but at Michaelmas we have what I have always wanted – one

composer has written all the music especially for the programme. He and I have discussed its plan together; and he has, by his music, given to it precisely that unity of thought and feeling which is so desired. The composer is Benjamin Britten, who is known as one of the most brilliant of our young musicians.

Ironically enough, the unity which Roberts sought and Britten achieved initially caused the producer some surprise. Robin Whitworth (in a private communication, 12 September 1989) recalls that

When I first heard the music for The Company of Heaven in its complete form I could not conceal from Britten that I did not regard it as suitable [. . .] There was an awkward situation, – and in face of the adulation of the musicians I felt rather silly! [. . .]

It was intended to be a Feature programme conveying a coherent and continuously developing line of thought, conveyed primarily by words but with music sometimes emphasizing the thought and sometimes playing a main part in its conveyance. The orchestra seems to have appreciated this better than Britten, who, [. . .] instead of troubling to understand the programme [. . .] ploughed his own furrow, and provided [. . .] a straightforward musical entity [. . .]

He may well have been justified in doing so, as the [music] will surely be of greater significance than the long-forgotten Feature! Trevor smoothed out the awkwardness between me and Benjamin, and we remained good friends.

In a BBC internal memorandum dated 13 July a fee of £52.10.0 was proposed for 'The original composition by Benjamin Britten [. . .] of music for chorus and orchestra lasting about twenty minutes'. In the event the score proved to be significantly longer.

Composed during August and September 1937, it contains almost certainly the earliest music written by Britten specifically for Pears, a setting for tenor and strings of Emily Brontë's 'A thousand gleaming fires'. He wrote in his diary on 10 September – Pears had been staying with him for two days – 'Before Peter leaves in the morning he runs thro' my Emily Brontë song (for Michaelmas programme) that he's going to sing – & he makes it sound charming. He is a good singer & a first rate musician.' The only purely orchestral movement from this extensive score – 'Funeral March for a boy' – touches on what was to prove to be a characteristic Brittenesque theme. It also provides the clearest and most fascinating evidence of Mahler's influence, especially of the Fourth Symphony, by which Britten was almost obsessed at this time. But the Mahler influence ranges widely in this work, even as far as the Eighth.

It is clear from a letter Britten wrote to Ralph Hawkes on 6 August that he had not excluded the possibility of eventual publication:

Re the 'Michaelmas' programme for the B.B.C. – I want to be careful not to sign away any publishing rights for the work, because I feel that a short choral work could easily & quite profitably be made out of it for you. When it's done I'll show you & see what you think.

At the outbreak of war in 1939, Trevor Harvey had in his possession the autograph scores of both *The Company of Heaven* and its companion work, the later *World of the Spirit* (1938). As a precaution against air-raid damage, Harvey deposited both scores at his parents' country home, where they lay forgotten until the 1950s, when he rediscovered them, and put together a concert suite from *The Company of Heaven*, which he conducted on 20 May 1956 on the BBC Home Service, with April Cantelo and John Carolan, the BBC Chorus, and St Cecilia Orchestra. See also note 2 to Letter 172, PR, pp. 575–90, and Philip Reed, 'A Cantata for Broadcasting: Britten's *The Company of Heaven*', *Musical Times*, June 1989, pp. 324–31. The work was revived at the 1989 Aldeburgh Festival and recorded on Virgin Classics, VC 7 91107–2. In his diary for 9 September 1931 Britten records his observation of an incident comparable to the imaginary event which gives rise to the 'Funeral March' in his radio score.

2 Hawkes had written to Britten on 26 July:

It is proposed to give performances of The Ascent of F6 at the St. Pancras People's Theatre on October 7th, 8th and 9th, and as I do not know what material was supplied by you for the original production, perhaps you would let me have this information. Apparently, they do not think they could provide more than a Piano. Is there a satisfactory piano part?

On receiving Britten's reply, Hawkes informed Miss Phyllis Kindersley at the theatre that where necessary, Britten would permit the rearrangement of his music. The St Pancras production must have been one of the earliest amateur performances of the play, which was first published in September 1936, with a second (revised) edition appearing in March 1937.

3 In June 1937, Louis Boyd Neel (1905–1981), the English-born conductor, had been invited to bring his string orchestra to the Salzburg Festival later that summer. He was asked to include in the programme the first performance of a new English work, and at once thought of approaching Britten to fulfil the commission. They had already met and worked together in 1936, when Neel invited Britten to compose the incidental music to the feature film, *Love from a Stranger* (Capitol Films, 1937). The chronology of the composition of the *Bridge Variations* can be traced in Britten's 1937 diary:

5 June
Work and odd jobs – including sketching abit of F.B. variations (for Salzburg?)

7 June
Work – at BBC. programme [*Up the Garden Path*: see DMBA pp. 105–6 and 126–7] & at sketches for F.B. Variations in aft.

8 June
[. . .] the sketches for the Variations go pretty badly to-day.

24 June
The Variations are going quite well – a Waltz [*Wiener Walzer*] & Bourée [*Bourrée classique*] were finished to-day.

25 June
In all day working at Variations until afternoon [. . .] Boyd Neel comes to hear what I've done of the Variations – is terribly pleased and decides about them for Salzburg.

5 July
I start to write out the score of the not yet completed Variations in afternoon.

6 July
[. . .] spend rest of day till a pretty late hour copying & writing the score.

8 July
[. . .] work hard at score – deliver most of it to B & H to be copied.

10 July
Stay in all day – working at score, which I deliver (complete, except for last section) before lunch, to B & H. Then sketch the end & fugue in afternoon & evening. Quite pleased.

12 July
I spend the whole of the day writing the score (from a very rough sketch from Saturday) of the fugal end of the Variations. I feel rather proud of my 11 part fugue with canto written straight into score in ink! After a tremendous effort scarcely stopping for meals I get it off to copyist by 6.40 post.

15 July
[. . .] on to rehearsal of the Boyd Neel Orchestra at 2.30. I take them thro' the Variations, which will be successful I think. Much time is spent in correcting parts & things, but the work is grateful to play, & the orch. themselves (a charming crowd) are very enthusiastic.

21 July
Go early to rehearsal of Boyd Neel Orchestra. They spend 1½ hr on my work – Boyd taking them thro' it. It is going much better, but still alot to be done.

28 July
Back here in afternoon – & Peter Pears comes – play songs for him, & also run thro' the Variations for his benefit. [Britten was unable to be in Salzburg for the première. Pears, however, was present and wrote a letter to Britten (see Letter 107) describing the occasion and the performance.]

23 August
My rehearsal (final) with the Boyd Neel Orch. is in the afternoon & it goes excellently. Frank & Ethel Bridge come from the country to hear it – also Miss Fass – & they are very excited – in fact we have celebration – dinner etc.

In his contribution to DMHK, 'The String Orchestra', Neel was to write in 1952:

As I was personally concerned, a word about the birth of this work might perhaps be of interest. In 1937 I was invited to take my orchestra to the Salzburg Festival of the same year and give a concert of English music, one of the conditions being that the programme should include the first performance of a new English work. As it was then May and the concert was to take place on August 27th, the prospect seemed well-nigh hopeless; but suddenly I thought of Britten (till then hardly known outside inner musical circles) because I had noticed his extraordinary speed of composition during some film work in which we had been associated. I immediately asked him whether he would take on the Salzburg commission, and in ten days' time he appeared at my house with the complete work sketched out. In another four weeks it was fully scored for strings as it stands today, but for the addition of one bar. This was one of the most astonishing feats of composition in my experience. I saw at once that we had here, not just another string piece, but a work in which the resources of the string orchestra were exploited with a daring and invention never before known; indeed, it remains one of the landmarks of string orchestral writing in musical history. Here are unprecedented sounds, as astonishing today as they were to that first Festival audience in 1937 when the work caused a major sensation, and was soon to be played all over the world.

The work was dedicated to Bridge – 'A tribute with affection and admiration' – and the theme taken from his *Idyll No. 2* (1906) for string quartet. It was the same theme that Britten had used for his incomplete set of piano variations of 1932. Perhaps the composer had been reminded of his earlier attempt at variations. Britten's dedication of his opus 10 to Bridge was no empty formality. The composition sketch reveals that he thought of this new work as a comprehensive portrait of Bridge, reflecting many facets of his extraordinary personality. On the composition sketch, there are not only the now familiar titles to each movement but also a corresponding list of Bridge's characteristics:

To F.B. – himself		Introduction <u>Lento maestoso</u> and Theme <u>Allegretto poco lento</u>
His integrity	1.	Adagio
His energy	2.	March <u>Presto alla marcia</u>
His charm	3.	Romance <u>Allegretto grazioso</u>
His wit	4.	Aria Italiana <u>Allegro brillante</u>
His tradition	5.	Bourrée Classique <u>Allegro e pesante</u>
His gaiety	6.	Wiener Walzer <u>Lento – Vivace</u>
His enthusiasm	7.	Moto Perpetuo <u>Allegro molto</u>
His sympathy (understanding)	8.	Funeral March <u>Andante ritmico</u>
His reverence	9.	Chant <u>Lento</u>
His skill and	10.	Fugue <u>Allegro molto vivace</u> –
Our affection		Finale <u>Molto animato – Lento e solenne</u>

In Britten's copy of the published score, dated March 1938, he has inscribed a slightly different sequence of Bridge's characteristics: 'His

depth' is substituted for 'His integrity'; 'His humour' for 'His wit';
'His enthusiasm' for 'His gaiety'; and 'His vitality' for 'His
enthusiasm'.

For further details of these dedications and their appearance on
the presentation copy of the score given by Britten to Bridge (in
March 1938), see PHFB, pp. 43–5. Bridge thanked his younger colleague in a letter dated 16 March 1938:

Of course, at first glance I didn't really take it in – or even see clearly – what
was in front of my eyes. But I have now. Your title page really touches me.
I don't know how to express my appreciation in adequate terms. It is one
of the few lovely things that has ever happened to me, & I feel the richer
in spirit for it all, including the charming dedication. Thank you & thank
you, Benjie. What a great pleasure! And "ain't I glad" I love the work itself?
I like to think of you just forging ahead & perhaps the most pleasant reflection is that you should have come into my life just when you did. Of course
I should say our lives because Ethel & I are united in our devotion to you.
God bless you, keep in good health. You'll have lots of prosperity before
posterity has anything to say – thank goodness.

Britten originally intended to include these personal dedications,
presumably in the published score. His diary for 12 September 1937
reads:

Tremendous discussion about my dedication of the Variations to Frank.
Both Mr. & Mrs. B. say I can't put it – but fail to produce any good
reasons – save that of privacy of such things – but Marge [Marjorie Fass]
& I stick out for it.

Bridge's protests were heeded, but Britten had still been able to
pay homage to his teacher through a more direct means: further
quotation of Bridge's music. The Bridge scholar, Paul Hindmarsh,
has observed:

In the Fugue, 'His skill', Britten's singularly appropriate tribute takes the
form of a series of quotations from five of his teacher's most accomplished
scores. These he superimposed in rhythmic augmentation over the scurrying
fugal entries. The fugue subject is derived from the opening of Bridge's
theme, which, in turn, becomes the first quotation. There follows a reference
to the majestic melody that forms the central episode of Enter Spring (H.
174); then the principal themes from Seascape (first movement from The Sea
(H. 100)), the Piano Trio (H. 178), first movement, and Summer (H. 116); and
finally, a reference to the second oboe melody from There is a willow grows
aslant a brook (H. 173). Following Bridge's example in the Lament (H. 117),
There is a willow (H. 173) and Todessehnsucht (H. 181), Britten set the seal on
his tribute by assigning the quotations (i.e. the main melodic material) to
solo strings in unison with the remaining strings sustaining the intricate
fugal accompaniment.

The first performance was a broadcast, given by the Boyd Neel
Orchestra, conducted by Boyd Neel, on 25 August 1937 (not the 24th
as originally intended), from Radio Hilversum, in the Netherlands.

Britten wrote in his diary: 'Listen to Boyd Neel broadcasting the Variations from Hilversum – they go very well.' Three days later the same orchestra and conductor gave the first public performance in the Grosser Saal of the Mozarteum, Salzburg, as part of the 1937 Salzburg Festival. The full programme was:

Henry Purcell:	Chaconne in G minor
Rutland Boughton:	Concerto for Oboe & Strings
	(Solo oboe: Leon Goossens)
Benjamin Britten:	Variations on a Theme of Frank Bridge
Frederick Delius:	Two Aquarelles
Arnold Bax:	Quintet for Oboe & Strings
Edward Elgar:	Introduction and Allegro

4 Britten was to write in his diary: '[. . .] hear a weak & feeble wireless vaguely attempting to pick up Toni's recital. Just hear (Reveil) but only just.'

5 The companion piece was not written.

6 Hawkes's racing yacht, doubtless named after Stravinsky's ballet.

Left: An early draft of the sequence of the *Bridge Variations*, made a few days before work on the composition began; the sequence runs: Intro: Theme; 1. Largo; 2. Recitative; 3. March; 4. Andante; 5. Waltz; 6. Moto Perpetuo; 7. Funeral; 8. Chorale; 9. [Blank]. The notations on the right refer to the purchase of a shirt

Right: The cover of the programme for the Salzburg première of the *Bridge Variations* in 1937

Monday, 23 August 1937
[*London/Crantock*]

Arrive in London early morning. Go to Hairdressers etc. for shaves
– & then I go with Robert to see some school agents. My rehearsal
(final) with the Boyd Neel Orch. is in the afternoon & it goes
excellently. Frank & Ethel Bridge come from the country to hear
it – also Miss Fass – & they are very excited – in fact we have
celebration – dinner etc. & when I go along after to Barbara's flat
to pick up Robert preparatory to our return to Crantock – it is a bit
of a come-down to find them all wild with 'in loco parentis' wrath
at my so-called conceit & bumptiousness – etc. etc. So we have
(R. & I) a first-rate bust up,[1] & part for rest of evening – I to a
restaurant for a meal – & he to wander London. Catch 2.0 train.

1 The relationship between Britten and his elder brother was often
stormy. On 9 August 1936, for example, he wrote in his diary (at
Crantock), '[. . .] I walk into Newquay with Robert – rather a difficult walk as we think differently on practically every subject (politics
especially) & are both very keen on them that arguments are liable
to be extremely fierce!'
    Robert, in a conversation with Donald Mitchell (16 November 1977,
London; Archive), recalled a 'big dispute' with his brother, which
was sparked off by passing the Tate Gallery. Britten claimed to be
able to think of *nothing* worse than the bombing of the Tate. Robert
disagreed. There was, ironically one may think, an explosion.
    Whether it was this particular altercation that was the 'first-rate
bust up' to which Britten refers here, it is impossible to say. It was
certainly the one that lingered on in Robert's memory; while, on
Britten's part, he returned to consideration of the 'bust up' in a later
diary entry, on 17 October, in which he appears in a somewhat
unforgiving mood:
    This row of mine with Robert is subject of a discussion after supper –
    notably with Barbara. I still feel adamant about it – I may have been
    partly to blame, but the fact that it was such a bitter one & such things
    were said by a comparative stranger, shows that there is a complete lack of
    understanding between us. I don't say that we must always be
    melodramatic enemies – but never more than acquaintances.
    The relationship was undoubtedly subject to unusual stresses and
strains, but it was not uniformly tense; and not so, surely much to
Robert's credit, where he might have been expected to be unsympathetic or baffled. There is a particularly interesting diary entry on
4 April, before the big row:

After dinner Robert & I go thro' my records of My 'Boy' – & he is marvellously appreciative. In fact this time I have felt much more warmth towards him, in spite of his obstinate conservatism in so many ways. Actually on our evening walks we have had very intimate discussions & he hasn't been shocked by but even helped with sympathy & advice my 'queerness'.

In his 1977 conversation, Robert remarked that he thought his parents (and he himself) were aware of – and anxious about – his brother's homosexuality at the time (1934: see note 8 to Letter 73), when consideration was being given to Britten's wish to study with Berg in Vienna. It was a reason, he thought, for his father in particular disliking the idea. Was it supposed, perhaps, that *Berg* was homosexual (i.e. 'decadence' = 'homosexuality')? However that may be, it seems unlikely that the chronology of this recollection can be correct in relation to Britten himself, the more so in the light of the diary entry above. As it suggests, and as all the evidence supports, Britten's recognition and acceptance of his sexual constitution belongs to the post-Auden period: close friends unite in remembering that during his adolescence and student years there was no outward sign of a homosexual disposition. This was something Paul Wright, for example, was 'totally unaware of', 'something' – and here he speaks for pre-war society – 'that only happened at school'.

Robert recalled that it was he who had completed his brother's sex education, after an 'ineffectual chat' on the part of his father.

It was Robert's view that the Britten children were over-cossetted. He was unhappy at boarding school because he had been so happy at home, and he thought his sisters suffered from the same sense of deprivation when away at school. But his brother, he thought, was happy at school, though he had no high opinion of Gresham's, where he had been sent because it was thought that music was 'taken seriously there'.

Britten's diaries show that his experience of music at Gresham's was indeed largely painful; and the same sources suggest that while he made a distinct success of his school years, there remained that same acute sense of separation from home that Robert attributed to his sisters and himself. At the beginning of term, for example, Britten confides (on 16 January 1930):

How I loathe this abominable hole [. . .] I simply cannot see how I can bare up through it, & suicide is so cowardly. Running away's as bad; so I suppose I've got to stick it. But 83 days!

And on the 17th:

Usual first day, only much more miserable. Looking at anything beautiful or hearing any good music simply drives me potty, & I can't contain my anguish. Even looking at the stars reminds me of home, & all the darlings

there, & fires (oh, this bitter cold) & comfort, & music & love. Oh! I can't
stand this!

On the 18th:

I'm settling down slowly. To-day's improvement is caused by the receipt
of a letter from my beloved mama contained in a parcel containing clothes
etc. that I had so carelessly left behind.

We have to remind ourselves that Britten was not a new boy, but
had started at Gresham's in September 1928.

Robert himself went to Cambridge, to Emmanuel College, and was
visited there by his brother. He sensed in his brother an abiding
regret that he had not had a university education. A wholly characteristic appearance was made by Robert in TP.

107 To Benjamin Britten
From Peter Pears[1]

Salzburg.
Friday 10.30 p.m.
[27 August] '37

Well, Benjie, I have dashed back to the hotel so that I can write
down at once something about the concert. I think there can be no
doubt about it that the Variations were a great success, as indeed
the orchestra was and Boyd Neel – and I got a very strong
impression that the Variations were the most interesting work in
the programme. One yawned a good deal through the Boughton
(I only got in towards the end of the Purcell) but the B.B. really
kept one's interest the whole time – and more, of course. I was
surprised how superbly the Romance & the Aria came off – the
Romance was really most lovely. Curiously enough the one that
didn't seem to come off altogether was the Moto Perpetuo – it
didn't seem to make its effect, perhaps the performance wasn't so
good.

The Funeral March is very good Benjie. I thought it needed more
strings (get it done by the BBC!) and Boyd Neel didn't quite allow
enough room in it – e.g. the triplets – I think that's one of his
troubles. But I think everyone was very moved by it. The Chant
seemed a bit slight after it (I still rather hanker after the March
repeated). The Fugue got home allright – and I thought the Finale
sounded v. impressive.

The Funeral March was the climax (as it should be, shouldn't it?)
although one didn't feel completely settled till the March (the
Adagio sounded a bit uncertain). The Bourrée and Waltz sounded

just as they should have done. In some of the variations more
Bass tone was needed, but he only had 2 D.B's.

That's all I can think of at the moment – but it really was a grand
show. I'll write some more in the morning, & see if I can get any
press cuttings, & then I'll air mail it to you.

SAT. A.M.

The Boughton, Bax, Delius, and Elgar sounded all really very
much alike in essence – I suppose in being English – but there
wasn't enough variety – The "espressivo" of one was all too like
the "espressivo" of another – There was not enough <u>life</u> – and that,
the Almighty be praised, is what you have, Benjie.

This is the only press as yet[2]. The Viennese papers haven't
noticed it yet, but I will collect what I can for you. I have been
trying to get hold of Boyd Neel but lost him after tracking him
half across Salzburg.

Much love to you –
PETER

1 See note 1 to Letter 113. Peter Pears, on holiday in Europe during
   1937 (with Iris Holland Rogers), attended the Salzburg première and
   wrote this letter to Britten immediately after the performance.

2 'A.', in the *Salzburger Volksblatt*, 28 August, wrote the following notice
   (translated by Paul Wilson):

English Music played by a quite dazzling English string orchestra under the
direction of Boyd Neel, was given on Friday evening in a special concert in
the Mozarteum which, it is said, came about at the suggestion of the Austrian
Ambassador in London. One can only be grateful to him. A dozen and a half
young musicians (two ladies among them) have come together, exceptional
instruments in their hands, in creative chamber music-making of the most
serious artistic intentions and assiduous study, bearing a very personal
stamp. The volume of tone which the conductor elicits from his small ensemble is magnificent, as is the astonishing technique and interpretative
approach which are discernible in every nuance. [. . .] The orchestra began
with a Chaconne of Purcell and then played two Aquarelles by Delius and
a concert piece by Elgar and a quite splendid series of Variations on a Theme
by Frank Bridge of Benjamin Britten (first performance). In the last-named
composition a rather un-English parodistic *élan* was noticeable (e.g. in the
variation 'Wiener Walzer' which is inspired by Ravel), a mood which had
an overwhelming effect. Everything was done with noble articulation and
musical distinction. One is accustomed in mid-Europe to approach English
music with cool reserve – often wrongly in the opinion of the English. On
this occasion, however, a brilliant performance placed the pieces in the
proper light and thus there was much atmosphere and great applause, which
visibly brought pleasure to the sympathetic young artists.

'A.H.A.' wrote in the *Salzburger Chronik*, 28 August (translated by Paul Wilson):

This remarkable ensemble had great success with the rendering of the Variations of a Theme by Frank Bridge by Benjamin Britten. This is a very dexterous piece which knows how to exploit all the effects of the string body to the limit. However, the extent to which English musical sensibility is removed from ours was evidenced by the 'Wiener Walzer' variation. Even when one sets out to write a pastiche it must seem substantially different.

The performance was apparently not reviewed by the Viennese press.

Britten was later to entrust the first performance of *Les Illuminations* (1940) to Boyd Neel and his orchestra, and in 1943 composed the Prelude and Fugue for 18–part string orchestra to commemorate the orchestra's tenth anniversary.

108 To Robin Whitworth
BBC

> 559 Finchley Road,
> N.W. 3.
> Sept. 10th 1937.

Dear Whitworth,

The music for the Michaelmas programme fares apace. I should be delivering the score to the office for copying within quite a few days.

There is one thing worrying me though. As the stuff procedes – the parts for soloists become more & more important – & I am really frightened about entrusting the Soprano part to the tender mercies of the present member of the Singers (B).[1] The tenor – Peter Pears – is first-rate. I've shown him his big number, & he's already reconciled to it. But from what I hear, & from what Trevor himself says, I fear that the Soprano is quite a different matter. Could you please agitate for me to have an outsider? I suggest Sophie Wyss, who broadcasts alot, who I know isnt expensive, & who knows what kind of stuff I write & how to deal with it. I do feel strongly about this.

One especially important movement is the number after the 'War'[2] – 'Heaven is here'[3] – if the soloist isn't first-rate, well – the listener may feel he prefers the other state!

When do you next come to town?

> Best wishes
> Yours sincerely,
> BENJAMIN BRITTEN

1 Section B of the BBC Singers.

2 'War in Heaven', the fifth number from *The Company of Heaven*, is a setting of words from the Book of Revelation, for divided male chorus and orchestra.

3 A setting of an unidentified text for soprano solo, chorus and orchestra.

109 To Kenneth Wright[1]
BBC

559, Finchley Road, London, N.W. 3.
Sept. 14th 1937.

Dear Kenneth,

Thank you for your letter. As I was away for the week-end I have only just found it. Apologies.

I absolutely agree with you about those two little songs Sophie Wyss showed you.[2] They are far too insignificant to stand by themselves. But I have planned & partially written two much longer songs intended to form a group with these two – words also by W.H. Auden.[3] They should be finished quite soon, & as soon as they are done I will show them to you.

By the way, I think the publisher wants to print them pretty soon. Do you want first performance reserved for you?[4]

Glad you liked 'King Arthur' stuff. But I think you'll like this Michaelmas programme I'm doing better.

Yours sincerely,
BENJAMIN B.

1 Kenneth Anthony Wright (1899–1975), Assistant Director of Music at the BBC, 1935–7, who joined the Corporation in the 1920s. With Edward Clark and Julian Herbage, he helped form the BBC Symphony Orchestra in 1930. In the 1930s Wright was responsible for the day-to-day administration of the Music Department's activities. He was acting Director of Music, 1946–8, and later became Head of Music Programmes (Television), retiring in 1959. He was also a composer of light orchestral music and pieces for brass band.

2 'Now the leaves are falling fast', composed on 27 May, and 'Nocturne', composed on 5 May, both copied for Wyss on 3 June. These songs later became the second and fourth songs respectively of the volume of Auden settings, *On this Island*.

3 Wright had already written to Britten on 10 September requesting another, longer song to go with the two that Sophie Wyss had shown

him. Britten had first attempted to compose further Auden settings (excluding the *Cabaret Songs*) on 4 June, as he notes in his diary:

After lunch I start rewriting no. 3 [the third rewrite] of Auden's Fanfare song ['Let the florid music praise!'] – but tho' it is nearer, it isn't there yet.

Later, on 25 September:

Up by mistake rather late, so I don't do all the work I want to. However – I have time to do about 6 versions of the beginning of 'Florid Music' one of W.H.A.'s songs – & all of them N.B.G. – I have never had such a devil as this song.

9 October
[. . .] writing songs – one little one of Peter Burra's ['Not even summer yet'], & a longer one (As it is plenty) of Wystan's.

12 October
I rewrite one Auden song in its entirety (Let the florid music) & write another new one (Seascape).

22 October
I spend all my time in the next few days working at [. . .] (a). copying the Auden songs for Sophie Wyss. (b.) writing new ones (either before breakfast, or just before bed) [. . .]

The new Auden settings were 'To lie flat on the back with the knees flexed' (26 October), 'Night covers up the rigid land' (27 October) and 'The sun shines down on the ships at sea', none of which was published.

For his collection, *On this Island*, Op. 11, he selected five of these eight settings: 'Let the florid music praise!', 'Now the leaves are falling fast', 'Seascape', 'Nocturne', and 'As it is, plenty'. With the exception of 'Nocturne', from the play *The Dog beneath the Skin*, the texts of all the songs (including those unpublished) were taken from Auden's *Look, Stranger!* (London, Faber and Faber, 1936). Britten's copy, in which Auden has inscribed the date of each poem, is in the Archive.

When *On this Island* was first published by Boosey & Hawkes (Winthrop Rogers Edition) in 1938, the collection was described as 'Volume I', implying that there was going to be a further volume. Other projects intervened and the excluded settings remained unpublished, although during his American visit, 1939–42, Britten was to attempt a few more Auden settings, none of which was completed. 'To lie flat on the back' was first performed by Neil Mackie (tenor) and John Blakely (piano) on 23 April 1985, as part of a BBC broadcast recital of unpublished Britten songs; and 'Night covers up the rigid land' was first heard at the Wigmore Hall, London, on 22 November 1985, performed by Patricia Rozario (soprano) and Graham Johnson (piano). See also DMBA, pp. 133–70.

4 Wright replied on 17 September, requesting the first performance.

This took place on 19 November, a BBC broadcast, given by Sophie Wyss with the composer at the piano. Britten wrote in his diary on the day:

Rehearse at BBC in aft. At the Contemporary Concert at 9.0 odd I play the piano part of my 'On this Island' songs (Vol. 1.) – with Sophie Wyss who sings them excellently – tho' her English is obscure at times.

They have a public success, but not a succès d'estime – they are far too obvious & amenable for contemporary music.

Wystan comes & we – with the Gydes, W. Walton, & Lennox Berkeley, have a party after. Wystan comes back to the Gydes after – but as the car misbehaves, we don't get back till past 3.0.

A review of the broadcast appeared in *The Times*, 22 November:

The first of the set, 'Let the florid music praise', is a bold conception with a good sweeping vocal line and a replendent piano accompaniment; the last, called 'Plenty', is at the other pole of expression, jazzy and cynical in the manner of Kurt Weill. In them all the composer has taken the trouble to digest his poem, not merely to set notes to it.

The *Musical Times*, December 1937, p. 1067, published the following notice:

Two new British works were given on November 19th, of which the more interesting was Benjamin Britten's set of five songs to poems by W.H. Auden. [The other work was Alan Rawsthorne's Viola Sonata.] This partnership of two young men had previously produced fruit (if of a rather sour species) in 'Our Hunting Fathers' and the contrast between the two works is illuminating. 'Our Hunting Fathers', written for a popular festival, thoroughly shocked the bourgeois by its elusive and uncompromisingly esoteric atmosphere. The present work shocked equally the up-to-date intelligentsia who frequent the concert hall of Broadcasting House at a late hour on certain Friday evenings, since it was simple, direct, melodious, and not a novelty at all! Once we could get over our pique at being thus cheated, it was possible to sit back and thoroughly enjoy at least three of the five songs. They are scrupulously well-made and immensely grateful for the singer. There is no reason why 'Nocturne' and 'Now the leaves are falling fast' (described by the poet as 'a gloomy little lyric') should not become reasonably popular. The tranquil ending of the latter has real beauty. The final song, a jazz-patter-Holborn-Empire setting of an 'abstract' poem based – how or why? – on a story of Somerset Maugham's* missed fire. Maybe it was of surrealist intention. Sophie Wyss sang the songs admirably, though her

---

* 'His Excellency', which formed part of a collection of Maugham's short stories, *Ashenden* (London, Heinemann, 1928). It is this very story which is listed in that lexicon of Auden's (and his circle's) tastes, *Letters from Iceland* (with MacNeice) (London, Faber and Faber, 1937), p. 220, 'Letter to William Coldstream, Esq.':

> And we read the short stories of Somerset Maugham
>   aloud to each other
> And the best one was called *His Excellency*.

See also Letter 237.

English was not always easy to follow. What the volatile and at times infuriating Mr Britten will turn his lively and fecund pen to next no one (least of all Mr Britten, we imagine) can say.

110   To Leslie Boosey[1]
Boosey & Hawkes

559, Finchley Road, N.W.3.
Sept. 23rd, 1937.

Dear Mr. Boosey,

Thank you for your letter of Sept. 10th. I am glad that you feel printing the score of my 'Variations on a theme of F. Bridge' to be a possibility. But I feel really most strongly, that in a work of this calibre the printing of the <u>parts</u> is the essentiality.[2] This is the kind of work – quite light, & not excessively difficult – that amateur bands in the provinces might like to have a shot at – your Mr. Chapman[3] tells me too that there is a shortage of such material. And players, most of all amateurs, are terribly liable to be put off by M.S. parts – however well copied. After all there are only five parts, & the work is not long. Besides there were inquiries made to Boyd Neel in Salzburg (where he first played it) both from America & Russia.

I may be absolutely wrong, but I feel there is [a] chance of the work being popular (for me!) – judging by the attitudes of the players, the audience at Salzburg, & the press notices. Anyhow if you can be at the Wigmore Hall on Oct. 5th, there is a chance to hear for yourself.[4]

I hope you'll have an opportunity of discussing this with Ralph Hawkes when he returns from his auspicious holiday[5] – next week!

Yours sincerely,
BENJAMIN BRITTEN

1 Leslie Arthur Boosey (1887–1979), English music publisher. He took charge of the Publishing Department of the Boosey company on the death of his father in 1919 and when the latter merged with Hawkes Publishers in 1930 he became Chairman of Boosey & Hawkes Ltd; on retirement in 1963, he became the firm's President. He was elected in 1926 to the Board of Directors of the Performing Right Society Ltd and became its Chairman in 1929. From that date he served the PRS continuously as its Chairman, Vice-President and President. In 1954 he was elected as its President of Honour (for life). He was also a substantial benefactor of the Royal Opera House, Covent Garden.

2 Boosey had suggested to Britten in a letter dated 10 September that the parts might be hired, i.e. not engraved but hand copied.

3 Ernest Chapman (1914–1983), English music publisher, editor and critic. He was a member of the editorial staff at Boosey & Hawkes from 1934 to 1947, where he was also the first editor of *Tempo*, the quarterly house magazine. From 1947, he was an editor for the music publishers, Joseph Williams Ltd. He compiled *John Ireland – a Catalogue of Published Works and Recordings* (London, John Ireland Charitable Trust, 1968). See also LFBML, p. 205.

4 The first performance in England of the *Variations*, given by Boyd Neel and his orchestra. The composer wrote in his diary for 5 October:

Beth comes with me to Wigmore Hall, where Boyd Neel does my Variations – not too good to-night – speeds were pretty cock-eyed. They go down well – much spontaneous applause in the middle.

A note of the concert appeared in *The Times*, 8 October:

The concert given by the Boyd Neel String Orchestra – its first appearance since the recent tour abroad – drew a large audience to Wigmore Hall on Tuesday. It was, as usual, an interesting programme, containing three works which have not previously been heard in London and the playing generally was well disciplined and informed with all the freshness and vigour which one associates with Mr Boyd Neel's conducting. [. . .]

Of the new works, Britten's 'Variations on a Theme by Frank Bridge' was by far the most entertaining. Lars Erik Larsson's 'Little Serenade' was pretty and unpretentious but in no way memorable, and a Suite by [Richard] Stöhr [1874–1967], Prelude, Andante, and Fugue, was mostly rather glib music-making. In contrast Britten's Variations seemed full of invention and wit.

The game is, in effect, the old one of disguising the tune 'in the manner of', and the titles Romance, Aria Italiana, Wiener Waltz, Funeral March, &c., sufficiently indicate the variety that has been extracted from it. It would perhaps have been more creditable to develop the theme seriously, but the results in most cases justify the light-hearted approach. The fancy dress is artfully put on and the charade provides fun both for performers and onlookers.

Bonavia in the *Daily Telegraph*, 6 October, wrote:

No fewer than three novelties were included in the programme played yesterday at the Wigmore Hall by the Boyd Neel String Orchestra. The first, incidentally the best, was Benjamin Britten's Variations on a theme of Frank Bridge. This young composer has qualities which command respect. His idiom is neither old-fashioned nor aggressively modern, with the result that the harmonic texture is always rich yet logical. He takes risks, and very often the result justifies the daring.

His variations disguise rather than develop the theme, but the disguises are varied and there is no mistaking the point of his caricatures. It matters little if the 'Bourrée Classique' does not resemble a bourrée any more than 'Romance' recalls any other romantic piece with which we are acquainted.

What does matter is that high spirits and good technique win the day and that any orchestra possessing the necessary skill must enjoy, as the audience must enjoy, a performance of a score conceived in such a happy mood.

The *Observer*, 10 October (unattributed):

Mr Britten's Variations were worse than we have been told, but better than we had feared. They were clever, and sometimes serious. If we have not the slightest wish to hear them again it is because they still exemplify Mr Britten's particular weakness, that neither his seriousness nor his levity is intense enough.

In the *Sunday Times*, 10 October, 'H.F.' wrote:

[. . .] it was Benjamin Britten who ran away with the honours of the occasion. His Variations on a Theme of Frank Bridge, now given for the first time in England, thrive on their dual personality. Bridge's theme is characteristically tender and smiling, but does happen to possess a pronounced physiognomy. With the rather naughty avidity of the make-up man Mr Britten works upon the face with shrewd strokes of his own, not seldom satirical but always apt. The complaisant countenance is given the complexion and expression by turns of a March, a (sardonic) Romance, an Aria à L'Italienne, a Waltz à la Vienne, a mock-classical Bourrée, a Funeral March. There are nine metamorphoses and a Fugue and Finale, all of a singular freshness, and brilliantly ingenious. Not a 'great' work, but full of life, wit, and health. Technically, the resources of the string orchestral medium are tried rather high: this is no music for the indifferently expert and even in the hand of these clever players some of the effects were only just realised.

The *Musical Times*, November 1937, p. 990:

Their virtuosity suggests them as designed for the Boyd Neel Orchestra and their 'bitty-ness' hints at film music. But there is not a dull bar and the brilliant ingenuity of the scoring provides colours resembling a full orchestra. For the 'Chant' preceding the Fugue and Finale the composer has found strikingly original effects. Were the music as original Mr Britten would have produced a little masterpiece. And he could have done it, for the theme by Frank Bridge is first-rate, and there are passages at the opening and close of the work which well up from the deeper founts of music.

5 Hawkes had recently married and was away on his honeymoon.

111 To Henry Boys

[*Picture postcard: Paris . . . en Flanant:*
La Cité – Nôtre Dame]

PARIS
[Postmarked 4 October 1937]

Just to remind you – & of course you need reminding![1] Back tomorrow – the Exposition is good, but this is better.

See you soon
Love
BENJAMIN

1 Britten visited Paris with the Bridges and Marjorie Fass between 1 and 5 October to see an exhibition of independent modern artists at the Petit Palais, which was part of the 'Exposition internationale des arts et techniques dans la vie moderne'. He writes in his diary on the 2nd: 'The Utrillos, Picassos, Suzanne Valadon (never known by me before) Braques impressed.' Britten begins by mischievously referring to his earlier trip to Paris with Henry Boys and Ronald Duncan: see note 1 to Letter 95.

112 To Mary Behrend

559 Finchley Road, N.W.3.
Oct. 17th 1937.

P.S.   The 'enclosed' will follow
   to-morrow, by book post – easier!

My dear Mrs. Behrend,

All apologies for being so long in sending the enclosed, & also in writing to say 'thank you' for the lovely time you gave me up in Leeds,[1] and also for the cheque – in fact there is so much to say 'thank you' for that I don't know where to begin. Any how please let the impression remain with you that I am really & truly grateful.

Your letter got here yesterday – manythanks for that too. I am afraid that at the moment there aren't any gramophone records of my stuff – one or two possibilities in the near future, but no certainties. I have actually a pretty poor old recording of an old choral work of mine (A boy was born) that is done from time to time, which a friend had done privately for me not long ago. If you'd like to borrow it, do, but I don't think it would be a frightful amount of use.

Also the Auden songs won't be in print until after November 19th when the first performance takes place at the BBC. If you want some M.S. copies to <u>look</u> at, I can get some made, willingly, and send them along. Apart from this the only songs I've got are 12 school ones (Friday Afternoons) published by Boosey. Apart from many <u>part-songs</u> of course, both O.U.P. & B & H. Bits (especially the slow Messalina part) of the Hunting Fathers would go as songs, actually.

How sweet of you about the Mahler; I should love to go with you of course.[2]

Incidentally, if you want to borrow my 'das Lied von der Erde' records while I wander the country, I should love to let you have them. This scribble shocks me more than I can say. All regrets for it, but time is short.

This is the most complicated move I've ever done, & that's saying alot.[3] Trying to decide (a) what one'll never need again – Jumble & waste paper basket   (b) what one won't need for three months – mill, to be stored   (c) what one may need before Xmas – trunks, for Belsize Park   (d) what one must have at once – suit cases, & pockets. Beth & I are in such a state that we almost want to pack each other.

We both send our love to you all.

Yours ever

BENJAMIN B.

1   Britten had travelled to Leeds with the Behrends by car on 5 October, after the UK première of the *Bridge Variations*. They heard a number of concerts at the Leeds Festival. Among the works performed were Rossini's *Petite messe solennelle* ('a grand work', in Britten's opinion), Walton's *In Honour of the City of London* ('desperate – typical W. admittedly – but full of mannerisms & frightful lack of invention') and Berlioz's *L'Enfance du Christ* ('it is a magnificent work – fearfully good – every movement. Must buy & study'). On the final day, the 7th, they heard Berkeley's oratorio, *Jonah* ('which he conducts very, well & has a good show. It has some good things in it & is even more promising for the future').

2   A performance of Mahler's Eighth Symphony which Britten attended with the Behrends on 9 February 1938 at Queen's Hall, conducted 'execrably' by Henry Wood. Britten wrote in his diary, 'but then [as] ever the work made a tremendous impression. I was physically exhausted at the end – & furious with the lack of understanding all around'.

3   Britten was dividing his belongings between London, where he was renting a room from his friends, the Easdales (at 38 Upper Park Road, NW3), 'to use occasionally [. . .] & where we can plonk some of our more frequently used belongings' (Diary, 18 October), and Suffolk, where he took up temporary residence with his sister's future parents-in-law at Peasenhall Hall while awaiting completion of the Old Mill's conversion. He left London on 20 October, writing in his diary,

I am heartily glad to be rid of 559 Finchley Road – it might have been a nice house, but all these memories are too bitter. The loss of Mum & Pop, instead of lessening, seems to be more & more apparent every day. Scarcely bearable.

A further reason for the move was Beth's forthcoming marriage to Kit Welford in January 1938.

113   To Peter Pears[1]

Peasenhall Hall, Nr. Saxmundham, Suffolk.

Oct. 24th 1937

Well Peter,

Have a good time in America. Sing nicely, & come back with lots of money in your pocket.[2] Don't get up too late & miss trains – it makes life difficult, & and, as you know, life's difficult enough anyhow. I envy you alot going all over America – it would be good fun to go – In fact I must go myself before long – One of the thousand & one things I'm going to do before long.[3]

How's Michael?[4] He'll be sad at your leaving. Come back with lots of courage, ready to seize any bull by the horns – & they are fond of it, I'm sure.

Meanwhile I'll go on here. I'll have written about four more vols. of music by the time you come back. More songs, & with luck a piano concerto.[5] I'm feeling on first-rate terms with the Muse at the moment. I shall go up & down to London, & drift around the country: to Christopher next week; Wystan soon after; with Lennox down to Gloucester, & of course to the Bridges. I shall probably run away to the continent for Xmas, because I can't face the prospect of that in England this year.[6]

Yes – you're lucky, my boy. Next year must be the beginning of grand things. Singing & life in general. No more of this messing about with Morning Services[7] (either actually or morally!!) – but la vie-grande in every sense (or perhaps its masculine . . .)

Excuse this – only I'm horribly sleepy after a grand Sunday lunch of Sirloin & home-brew cyder.

All my love & Bon Voyage

BENJIE

1   The first extant letter to Peter Pears (b. Farnham, Surrey, 22 June 1910; d. Aldeburgh, 3 April 1986, at the Red House, the final home he had shared with Britten for almost twenty years), great English tenor and Britten's lifelong companion and musical partner. This is not the place for a full account of Pears's life and career. The best available sources are PPT; the detailed obituary Rosamund Strode contributed to the *R.C.M. Magazine*, 822, Summer Term, 1986, pp. 39–43, and Christopher Headington's *Peter Pears: A Biography* (London, Faber and Faber, forthcoming). What has to be established here is the chronology of the meetings between the two men which finally led to their enduring association. It has been widely supposed

– and was so by Pears himself – that they first met, briefly, at a rehearsal of *A Boy was Born*, which Britten had attended and in which Pears was singing. But this turns out to be unlikely. Scrutiny of Pears's engagement diaries suggests that it was highly improbable that they could have met on the occasion of either of the two BBC performances of the *Boy*, either in 1934 (the first performance), or 1935 (the second broadcast). It remains possible, of course, that the meeting took place at another time at another rehearsal and performance of the *Boy* in which Pears was participating; or perhaps at a rehearsal of some other choral music of Britten's. It is beyond doubt, in any event, that there was an encounter which preceded the serious beginning of the friendship in 1937, following the death of Peter Burra.

Burra was not only an old friend of Pears's; he was also a friend of Britten's: they had been together in Barcelona in 1936 and had met since that date. As we have see, Britten himself had visited Burra in his Berkshire cottage in March 1937, a week after the first mention in Britten's diaries of a meeting with Peter Piers [*sic*]. It is a singular fact that while Pears and Britten had a friend in common in Peter Burra, it was not through him but through his death that Britten's and Pears's new friendship sprang up.

Their professional activities seem to have brought Britten and Pears together initially. Britten's diary of 6 March records his involvement in rehearsals at the BBC of two of his part-songs (he was probably playing the piano), after which he and the conductor of the programme, Trevor Harvey, and Pears (who was then a member of the BBC Singers), returned to 105 Charlotte Street, W1, a flat shared by Harvey, Pears and Basil Douglas (see note 5 to Letter 372). Britten wrote in his diary: 'Lunch with T.H., Peter Piers, & Douglas – at their flat – with interesting tho' snobbish and superficial arguments.' Not, one might think, the most promising start. But undoubtedly it was on this occasion in Charlotte Street that the friendship with Pears began, to which the accident of Burra's death the following month brought crucial impetus.

The friendship developed rapidly – on 8 September Britten writes in his diary, 'He's a dear – & I'm glad I'm going to live with him' – and in March 1938, just one year after their first meeting, Britten and Pears rented their first flat together (see note 1 to Letter 129). Pears had already stayed with Britten for a week (10–16 October 1937) at Finchley Road. There were, too, early musical consequences. In September 1937, Britten had written what was probably his first song for Pears in *The Company of Heaven* and in October there was a run-through by Pears of *On this Island*, after which Britten remarked with typical caution in his diary for 15 October – 'Peter sings them well – if he studies he will be a very good singer.' This comment in retrospect may amuse us, but it makes more sense in the light of one of Trevor Harvey's shrewd observations (Interview with Donald Mitchell, 15 December 1980, London; Archive):

Well, the extraordinary thing was, you see, that in those days I could never conceivably have imagined Peter as an opera singer, or even as a *lieder* singer or anything, because he had a quite small voice. He was frankly pretty lazy and I very seldom ever heard him practising or anything like that at home, and he didn't seem to have any great ambition, and I think – I'm sure – obviously all what happened must have been due to Ben.

This comment reminds us of the youthfulness of these two musicians, both on the brink of careers that were to make them jointly world-famous, and of how much, in the achieving of that fame, they learned from each other. During 1938 and until they left for North America in May 1939 Britten had the use of the London flat, but was also often out of London, at the Old Mill, in close touch with his sister Beth and her family and with Lennox Berkeley, who was spending time at Snape (see Letter 169) and took on the occupancy of the Old Mill after Pears's and Britten's departure.

2 Pears was about to leave on an American tour with the New English Singers. He had returned by 19 January 1938.

3 An early indication of Britten thinking about a visit to the USA well in advance of the European crisis later in the decade and well before the migration of Auden and Isherwood. Another influential factor, we suggest, and one that has been far less remarked upon, was the fact that his revered teacher, Frank Bridge, had visited the States, in 1923 and after, and indeed had enjoyed a success there that was denied him in his own country. On 18 November 1930, Britten had written in his diary, '[Bridge] is still having a marvellous time in America. It is pretty disgraceful that England's premier composer should have to leave his country to get some recognition.' His experience of America must have counted with the youthful Britten, who made a point when in the USA of establishing contact with at least one of his teacher's friends and patrons, Mrs Coolidge (see Letter 206).

4 Michael Patton-Bethune, a friend of Pears.

5 See note 1 to Letter 120.

6 The first Christmas after his mother's death; but in fact, he remained in England.

7 One of the duties of the BBC Singers (of which Pears was a member) was to participate in the daily religious broadcast.

114 To Mary Behrend

C/o. Christopher Isherwood,
19 Pembroke Gardens, W.8.
West. 0509
Oct. 31st 1937

My dear Mrs. Behrend,

Thank you for your card – I'm sorry you've had no luck over the records.[1] Brian Easdale will be in London this week if you could 'phone him – but perhaps I could leave them somewhere for you. I am at the above address until about Wednesday if you could communicate with me.

One other thing: Rupert Doone the director of the Group Theatre 'phoned me yesterday. He & Robert Medley (the painter), with whom he lives, wondered if you have settled anything about Peter's [i.e. Burra's] Cottage. They are looking for [a] small week end cottage – partly for Group Theatre & conference purposes – & they thought of that one. I said I hadn't the foggiest notion of what you had decided, but promised to tell you at once about it.

Probably the best thing would be for you to meet them. They are charming people, & you'd like them awfully.

I am in town altogether for a week. How are you all? I hope that George is better now.

Yours ever,
BENJAMIN B.

1 The recording of *Das Lied von der Erde*.

115 To Edwina Jackson[1]
Boosey & Hawkes
[*Telegram*]

PEASENHALL
[Postmarked 8 November 1937]

MUST DEFINITELY DO HADRIANS WALL[2]   AM IN TOUCH WITH
MANCHESTER RETURNING LONDON TODAY

BRITTEN

1 Ralph Hawkes's secretary.

2 *Hadrian's Wall*, 'From Caesar to the National Trust', broadcast from

the BBC studios, Newcastle upon Tyne, on 25 November 1937. This 'historical survey' was written by Auden and produced by John Pudney, with incidental music by Britten. Auden wrote from the family home in Birmingham on 13 November: 'When are you coming to stay. I want to work on Roman Wall with you.' Britten went up to Birmingham on the evening of the 15th and stayed until the 17th, working with Auden 'at Hadrian's programme' and playing 'lots of Mozart'. The original manuscript score is lost, but from the evidence of the composer's annotated copy of the typescript it would appear that the score comprised some fifteen items, including a choral arrangement of Purcell's 'Fairest Isle' and a vocal setting of Auden's 'Roman Wall Blues' (see *The English Auden*, edited by Edward Mendelson (London, Faber and Faber, 1977), pp. 289–90), the first two verses of which run:

> Over the heather the wet wind blows,
> I've lice in my tunic and a cold in my nose.
>
> The rain comes pattering out of the sky,
> I'm a Wall soldier, I don't know why.

The haunting quality of the blues melody was such that Peter Pears in later life was still able to sing the first few bars. Britten, who conducted his music, wrote in his diary for 25 November:

The show goes fearfully badly. There's a big hitch which makes nonsense of the first part of the programme. But there's good stuff in it I know.

Grace Wyndham Goldie, writing in the *Listener* (8 December 1937, p. 1,254), recognized the quality of the production and also some of its problems:

This was remarkable for four things. One was the terrific vitality of the choruses Mr Auden gave to his Roman Soldiers. These, sung to Mr. Britten's music, were by far the best things in the programme and made it well worth hearing. The second was Mr Auden's ingenious and I thought justifiable use of American slang to differentiate between the speech of the Roman Soldiers and the rest of the cast. The third was the fact that the remainder of the programme was so overcrowded that no clear theme emerged from it. The fourth was that there was an uncomfortable pause during which an actor was told in several very audible whispers to turn to page three.

For a complete text of *Hadrian's Wall*, see EMWHA, pp. 441–55 and 674–6. See also HCWHA, pp. 231–2; John Pudney, *Home and Away – An Autobiographical Gambit* (London, Michael Joseph, 1960), pp. 97–9; 'Britten – A Formative Recollection', in the programme for the New Philharmonia Orchestra's *A Tribute to Benjamin Britten*, 22 February 1977; and PR, pp. 363–78 and 580. Britten's score also caught the ear of Scott Goddard, who wrote about the programme, 'Britten's music for this was unforgettable': see *British Music in Our Time*, edited by A.L. Bacharach (Harmondsworth, Pelican, 1946), pp. 211–12.

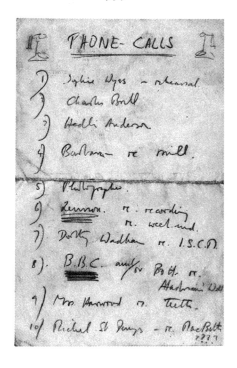

Britten lists the phone calls he was to make: to 1) Sophie Wyss; 2) Charles Brill; 3) Hedli Anderson; 4) Barbara Britten; 5) Photographer; 6) Lenox Berkeley; 7) Dorothy Wadham; 8) BBC and/or Boosey & Hawkes; 9) Mrs Harwood; and 10) Michael St Denys

116   To Ronald Duncan[1]

c/o Boosey & Hawkes, 295 Regent St., W. 1.
[?1937]

Thanks for card – you might be more explicit re. address. I haven't the foggiest idea where you are.

It's all off re my brother – tho' it's very nice of you to think of it. I've had a serious bust up with him & we arn't on communicating terms. I very seldom come to London – & when I do it's mostly a violent rush or silly business things – I've never been busier than I am now – but if you let me know where you are – we might almost meet – or at anyrate telephone each other – I usually stay with Isherwood in London – or in Belsize Park.

As a matter of interest – what has happened to the Townsman.[2] I've heard nothing at all –

Yrs.

BENJAMIN B.

1 Ronald Duncan (1914–1982), the Rhodesian-born poet, playwright and publisher. His friendship with Britten began in the mid-thirties. Duncan was a pacifist and his first collaboration with Britten was in

1937 when he wrote the text for *Pacifist March*, composed for the Peace Pledge Union. A stimulating friendship developed which led in post-war years to his writing the libretto of *The Rape of Lucretia* (1946; see note 3 to Letter 504) and the text for the *Wedding Anthem* (for the marriage in 1949 of the Earl of Harewood to Erwin Stein's daughter, Marion (now Mrs Jeremy Thorpe)). Duncan also helped Britten in some of the difficulties he encountered with Montagu Slater's libretto for the last scene of *Peter Grimes* (see RDBB, pp. 38–9, though Duncan somewhat exaggerates the extent and importance of his contribution). For Duncan's *This Way to the Tomb* (1945; see note 1 to Letter 456), his translation of Cocteau's *The Eagle has Two Heads* (1946), and *Stratton* (1949), Britten wrote the incidental music. He seriously contemplated collaborating with Duncan in operatic adaptations of *Abelard and Heloise* (1944), *The Canterbury Tales* (1944), and *Mansfield Park* (*Letters to William*, 1946), the setting of a post-Hiroshima protest, *Mea Culpa* (1946), and the text for a proposed cantata, *St Peter* (1955). But none of these projects materialized. Extensive documentation of the *Mea Culpa* idea is to be found in the BBC Written Archives Centre. It seems that it was a proposal to which Britten gave serious thought. A typescript of Duncan's text is in the Archive.

The Humanities Research Center, University of Texas at Austin, holds an important manuscript collecton of Duncan material.

The friendship, a very long one, was not without moments of high tension and exasperation on both sides, but the two men remained in touch, if somewhat infrequently, until the end of Britten's life. Duncan's son, Roger, was one of the composer's godsons. For an account (often shrewd, but as often unreliable) of his association and collaborations with Britten, see RDBB. See also his three volumes of autobiography, published in 1964, 1968 and 1977, and *A Tribute to Ronald Duncan by his friends*, edited by Harold Lockyear (Hartland, The Harton Press, 1974). The latter includes contributions from Peter Pears, 'San Fortunato: From a Diary', pp. 96–101, and the Earl of Harewood, 'The Rape of Lucretia: Ronald Duncan as Librettist', pp. 60–9.

2 A quarterly journal that Duncan had started with Ezra Pound's encouragement and for which he had tried to enlist Britten as a contributor. *Townsman*, to the first issue of which Pound contributed, was published between January 1938 and February 1944 (it was later renamed the *Scythe*).

117   **To Harold Walter**
Performing Right Society

c/o Boosey & Hawkes Ltd.,
295, Regent St., W. 1.
Nov. 30th [1937]
Ref. HW/SH

Dear Sir

In answer to your letter of Nov. 24th[1] – I am not aware of any different arrangements made for the performing rights[2] of the G.P.O. Film 'Night Mail'. Being the property of the Stationary Office I gather that the rights cannot be collected. I should be grateful though if you could give Mr. Hudson of the G.P.O. film unit (Gerrard 2666) a ring & get the full details from him.

Yours truly,
BENJAMIN BRITTEN

1   Walter's letter of 24 November reads:

> We have received your letter of 23 November enclosing a notification of your music for the sound films of How Gas is Made and The Men Behind the Meters, and we have noted that you have not granted any performing rights to the producers of these films. Our records are being noted accordingly.
>
> May we remind you that we are awaiting your reply to our letter of 1 November in which we asked you for particulars of your agreement with the G.P.O. concerning the film Night Mail. If you have retained your performing rights, please advise us the duration of the music.

Both *How Gas is Made* and *Men Behind the Meters* were British Commercial Gas Association films made in 1935, the former directed by Edgar Anstey and the latter by Arthur Elton. Britten composed and recorded his incidental music for both these films and a further 'gas' film, entitled *Dinner Hour* (directed by Anstey), during September 1935. See also PR, pp. 453–70.

2   An internal PRS memorandum dated 20 December 1935 had commented on Britten's performing rights as a composer of film music for the GPO. It throws interesting light on the dissemination and distribution of the documentaries:

> The Post Office have three film units which are used in various parts of the country, but quite two-thirds of the performances given by these units are in school class-rooms for the school children as part of the school curriculum. The remainder of the performances are given in (a) Post Office premises, and (b) small halls hired for this occasion.
>
> The performances, apart from those given in school class-rooms number, at a maximum, 500 a year, but they explained that by performance, they mean each actual shewing of a series of films. For instance, in a Post Office

three performances might be given during one day. They could give me no further information as to the actual number of days on which each unit was used during the year for performances, or any other particulars. Then they claimed that so far as GPO films were concerned, the music was specially composed by a staff composer, and was not published music. I explained that if the composer were a member of this Society, then the public performing rights in his music were vested in the Society, but they claim that these composers are in the employ of the Post Office as temporary civil servants, and in accordance with the usual custom, the Crown (HM Stationery Office) claims the copyright in such music. I gathered from them that the composer at present in their employ is Mr Benjamin Britten, and when they engaged him they made it quite clear that the copyright in the music he was to write under the contract of the service was to be vested in HM Stationery Office.

Mr Ford, the author of the memorandum, added the following handwritten note, dated 1 January 1936:

Mr Britten informed me today that he is paid a salary by the GPO. for writing music for their films. He also said they decline to make it a term of the contract that he shall be the owner of the copyright of performing right in the music, but have offered to recompense him for the loss of his PR fees. He asked if we could give him an estimate of the amount, and I told him we could not as these would vary with the number of performances recorded each year.

118   To Ursula Nettleship[1]

At Denshers, Friston, Near Eastbourne.[2]
East Dean 313
Dec. 4th, 1937.

TO BE READ AT LEISURE – SAY, IN BUSES OR TUBES

My dear Ursula,

Forgive the pencil – I am laid up under doctor's orders for abit – 'overwork' she calls it, & I'm rather enjoying the righteous feeling, but not enjoying the lack of sleep.

It was charming of you to write to me about the songs[3] – & I liked what you said about them – except – naturally – the rude remarks about the 'Look stranger'. The trouble is that you are prejudiced against that kind of song – & you have reason to be, because the number of bad editions of it that have been thrust on a suffering public is legion – No, I don't pretend that this is better than all those; it merely shows that for me that kind of song has still vitality, & in this particular case it can be used to conjure up a very real emotion. Only for me – perhaps – but there's no use denying that after every rehearsal I sing it all the way home. Look

at it when you get the printed copy – which should be soon. Ralph
Hawkes is mad-keen to get them out as soon as possible –
probably not before you go on your Winter-sporting – but at any
rate in time for the beginning of next term – sorry, I always think
of the year in terms of school-terms – shows that in spite of
advancing birthdays that one still has contact with one's youth.
Re Mr J.A. Westrup[4] – you can keep him all to yourself. There's no
earthly reason why we should meet. Where's the point of contact?
He obviously loathes all that I admire – no saying he's not as right
(or wrong) as I am – but I <u>cannot</u> be objective about music. Not
like your Bill Franklin[5] – whom I thought nice, & I shall definitely
write some songs for him. I have plenty of new words from
Wystan – I've been staying with him for quite a time, with good
results all round I think. His parents[6] are charming & Mrs. A. &
I are now great friends.

On re-reading your letter I see you offer me a ticket for Dec. 1st
concert.[7] Many apologies for not having answered it – it was very
nice of you, but I couldn't have gone since I've been here for a
week (I'm staying with a great friend of the Bridges – a Miss Fass
whom I think you met at Maida Vale – almost next door to them).
I did listen to the concert tho' – & I shan't tell you what I thought
of the Ireland – it would be libelous – if it's possible to libel that ——
man. I am so disappointed with Willy's new piece – I heard it at
Leeds & on some records he's got of it – but I hope the new fiddle
concerto[8] will be more the goods. But by jove, I thought that
Belshazzar sounded a masterpiece after all that pretentious tub-
thumping, puking sentimentality & really flagrant dishonesty (to
say nothing of the gross incompetance of it). But I won't enlarge
on that. (That's not referring to W.W. – of course!!)[9]

However, thank you for asking me.

My mill, blast it, won't be ready for ages. They've only just
started working on it – owing to difficulties over price. I have
decided to go bust & spend all my overdraft on it – the estimate
was exactly double what I originally said I could afford! March is
as soon as I shall be able to get in I fear. Until then my flying
Dutchman existance will continue. I shall be in London most of
January – unless I go to Spain, with which idea I'm now toying;[10]
it's a good way of stopping work. I also want to go to Prague
before it's blown to bits by those bloody Fascists. I hear that Lord
Halifax[11] has sold it to the Nazis – but I hope & pray I hear wrong.

Do you know the books of Ronald Firbank?[12] Read, if not,
'Eccentricities of Cardinal Pirelli'.

I must stop – or you'll never have time to read this – or at least decipher it. Sorry the writing's so bad – but you know what writing in bed's like – & 'Letters from Iceland'[13] is so darned slippery.

Thank you again for the letter – I'm so glad you got the 'Leaves'[14] – it's easily the best of the lot, & no one seemed to get it.

Yours
BENJAMIN B

P.S.   By-the-way – Lennox Berkeley has just written a fearfully good PSALM for chorus & orchestra.[15] It's the goods all right. You must see it.

1   Ursula Nettleship (1886–1968), trained as a singer in Leipzig and spent much of her long, active life in teaching others to sing. She had a remarkable gift for training choirs, and could inspire large gatherings of quite ordinary people to enjoy themselves by singing together. She and Britten first met at Crantock in 1936 when Britten and Berkeley stayed in her sister's, Ethel Nettleship's, house, and when Britten and Pears returned from the USA in April 1942 (see Letter 373) it was Ursula who provided them with a London home by lending them her studio house at 104a Cheyne Walk (see note 1 to Letter 392). At that time she was the CEMA organizer for the East Anglian region, which led to their giving occasional concerts in the area. *A Ceremony of Carols*, finished on the homeward journey across the Atlantic, is dedicated to her.

When the Aldeburgh Festival began in 1948 it was Nettleship who advised on the formation of a local choir, able to sing *Saint Nicolas*, and she herself acted as choir trainer for the 1949 Festival. She retained her Suffolk friendships and though late in life she broke her hip in an accident (slipping in a punt at a 1957 Aldeburgh Festival event, when listening to Music on the Meare at Thorpeness), her intrepid and courageous nature never admitted defeat. She died just before the opening of the 1968 Festival, and the footbridge over the rivulet at the north side of Snape Maltings is named in her memory.

2   The Sussex home of Marjorie Fass, where Britten stayed for the first days of December, visiting the Bridges and taking a break and a much needed rest. It is clear from Fass's letters from this period that he arrived in pretty poor physical shape:

I shall walk only to lunch at the Brits with Benjy. Who in spite of pills administered by M Fass still has the most revolting breath, though he looks a little less green white. He needs weeks of rest & purging to get him right – & [Dr] Downing saw his discoloured teeth & suggested they were the root of his trouble, but he said, like we all do, he'd a very good dentist & they were being seen to.

Dr Downing was consulted and Fass imposed her own regime of sleep and nourishment – '[I] packed him off to bed with brandy & milk' – reading sessions – 'In the afternoon I read Benjy the Rilke letters from the Nouvelle Revue Française & he adored him' – and restricted listening to the gramophone – Schubert's String Quintet and Beethoven's F major String Quartet (Op. 135 or Op. 59, No. 1?): 'Yesterday I couldn't stop Benjy having a little music on the grammy after dinner – though when Mr B rang up to say goodnight he was furious to hear we were listening to the Beethoven F maj.'

3 *On this Island*.

4 Jack Allan Westrup (1904–1975), English musicologist, teacher, critic, and conductor. After reading classics at Balliol College, Oxford, he worked for a time as a schoolmaster. Between 1933 and 1945 he worked as editor of the *Monthly Musical Record* and was music critic of the *Daily Telegraph* from 1934 to 1939. He was Professor of Music in the University of Birmingham from 1944, and in 1947 he became Heather Professor of Music in the University of Oxford until his retirement in 1971. He was knighted the same year.

Britten always felt resentful, when an aspiring young composer, of what he took to be the unnecessarily discouraging criticism of Westrup. A review that had especially rankled was Westrup's reception of the *Three Divertimenti* for string quartet when they were first performed at the Wigmore Hall on 25 February 1936 (see note 5 to Letter 68).

On Britten's return from the United States in 1942 it must have disconcerted him to find Westrup still in full flow, but this time in the *Listener* ('The Virtuosity of Benjamin Britten', 16 July, p. 93). His subject was the *Sinfonia da Requiem*, the first performance of which in England was to be given on 22 July and broadcast on the BBC Home Service.

The article is singular on more than one count. For example, we encounter an opinion that, to our knowledge, is not met elsewhere in the vast corpus of writing about Britten. 'The fact is', writes Westrup, 'that, in spite of the virtuosity shown in "A Boy was Born", Britten is much more at home with instruments than with voices. He knows exactly what voices can do and how to get the maximum effect out of them. But he is handicapped by a curious insensitiveness to words and by an attempt to exploit vocal colour at the expense of line. This is equally true of his works for solo voice, "Our Hunting Fathers" (1936), the song-cycle "On this Island" (1938), and "Les Illuminations" (1940).'

But it is the first paragraph of Westrup's article that is the most arresting, its first sentence above all. The test must stand as *locus classicus* of a point of view that dominated thinking about music in England between the wars:

'O for a trace of clumsiness somewhere!' wrote a critic of Benjamin Britten's 'Les Illuminations'. The exclamation might seem at first sight peevish. Critics generally have plenty of clumsiness to worry them without wishing there were more. But the point of view is quite intelligible. Britten has published work after work displaying a complete technical assurance; and if nothing but technical assurance were looked for, there would be nothing but praise for his music. What disturbed this critic was the feeling that the technique had become an end in itself and that invention, in the fullest sense, had been left to take care of itself. It is a view that not a few people share about Britten's work, and its prevalence will explain why his music has so often aroused hostility. The hostility arises not from a lack of sympathy or a failure to understand his idiom but from exasperation at what seems a prodigal use of a conspicuous talent.

Westrup's article prompted a letter from M. Bradshaw (London, SW1) that was published in the *Listener* on 13 August (p. 214). The writer protested that 'The technical accomplishment of this gifted musician is something to applaud rather than deplore; it is equalled by the depth and richness of the emotional content of the *Sinfonia da Requiem.*'

It was a view shared, on the whole, by W. McNaught, whose review of the broadcast performance of the work had appeared in the *Listener* on 30 July (pp. 156–7):

The *Sinfonia da Requiem* raises Britten into a new category. For some years past a number of people have been admiring his undergraduate cleverness while wondering when it was going to couple itself with a graduate mind and purpose. This symphony is the answer. Each of its movements is a characteristic and consistent design, and whatever flights of technique or idiom it may indulge in (and some of them are very saucy), they are relevant to the mood and plan of the movement. Britten here draws on the principle, well known to several of the great composers but deliberately set aside by recent fashion, that music is a long-breathed art, most powerful when it maintains a steady backward and forward look.

It looks, then, as if Britten has found himself at last. He joins in the fashion of the age by announcing the fact in terms of the orchestra. He may indulge a pardonable fancy by attaching to his three movements the labels of 'Lacrymosa', 'Dies Irae' and 'Requiem Aeternam'; but in their essence these are essays in orchestral mood and style, and his imagination and ingenuity make of them a satisfying trilogy. The first and third titles may pass as apt descriptive emblems drawn from life; but does the idea of 'Dies Irae' fit its context? The second movement is a Dance of Death peopled by much the same furies and witches as were evoked by Berlioz and Mussorgsky, only more so; and I had thought that the Day of Wrath was to be an orgy, not of evil, but of righteousness. But this is to question only the title, and not the music, which is a remarkable exhibition of orchestral virtuosity, novel, drastic and successful. The third movement I found less easy to size up at a first hearing, except that it is akin to the others in its expressive plane and rounds off a remarkably impressive and individual work.

Thus in three successive issues of the *Listener* almost the whole

spectrum of perceptions of Britten in 1942 was covered. See also note
3 to Letter 389.

5 Henry Cyril Franklin (1908–1973), English bass, known professionally
as David ('Bill') Franklin. He was a notable Commendatore at Glyndebourne in 1936 and a full-blooded Baron Ochs at Covent Garden,
post-war. He retired in 1951.

6 Auden's father, George Augustus Auden (1872–1957), a doctor, and
his mother, Constance Rosalie Auden (née Bicknell; 1875–1941), lived
at 42 Lornswood Road, Harborne, a suburb of Birmingham. Britten
had stayed with the Audens in Birmingham in order to work on
Hadrian's Wall.

7 At the Queen's Hall, London, when the BBC Symphony Orchestra
was conducted by Adrian Boult and William Walton. A vivid description of the group at Friston listening to the broadcast of the concert
was given by Marjorie Fass in a letter to Daphne Oliver:

> You ask abt the concert you missed – Thank goodness you missed it, as you
> were better employed – It was really a disgrace. John Ireland has indeed
> sold his birthright for a Mess of potage. A vulgar, would-be pretentious,
> popular work, which might do for the mob. With no distinction, & only 1
> passage of what even might be called music – indescribably noisy yelling
> clichés, & a tune that was Elgar at his worst & most sentimental mushy –
> Altogether a completely retrograde step – Ireland is off the map if he's going
> to take up that kind of thing. Benjy was surprised at our surprise at the
> vileness of it, because for him Ireland is really bad all through, & he doesn't
> think he's ever written one work worth while, though Mr Brit stuck up for
> the 'Forgotten Rite' – the new Walton was just as bad & screamingly noisy,
> so that the only 'music' & effort of integrity we had in the evening was
> 'Belshazzar's feast', which we've all heard before, & thought wasn't too
> good, but not too bad, by the side of the other works it simply shone as
> something real. But the whole thing was bawling noise, vulgarity & mostly
> cheapness & insincerity from beginning to end. Benjy & Mr Brit were both
> in despair . . . so you did the best thing by hearing a real concert.

The programme comprised the first performance of John Ireland's
choral work *These Things Shall Be* (1936–7), for baritone (or tenor),
chorus and orchestra; Walton's *Belshazzar's Feast*, and Ireland's *A
London Overture* (1936). The final item on the programme was the
first London performance of Walton's *In Honour of the City of London*
(1937), conducted by the composer.

8 Walton's Violin Concerto was completed in New York on 2 June
1939. It was written for, and dedicated to, the eminent violinist Jascha
Heifetz (1901–1987), who gave the first performance in Cleveland
(Ohio) on 7 December 1939, with the Cleveland Orchestra conducted
by Artur Rodzinski. See also note 4 to Letter 176. For Britten's connection with Cleveland and Rodzinski see Letter 343.

9 Britten ignores his own prohibition and after all writes about *These Things Shall Be*, a work Ireland himself came to reject.

10 Britten – a lifelong pacifist – never went to Spain during the Spanish Civil War in any capacity, although he gave concerts in support of Spanish Relief, for example at the Central Hall, Liverpool, on 7 March 1939, 'in aid of Spanish women, children and refugees in Spain and France', about which A.K. Holland, the chief music critic of the *Liverpool Daily Post*, wrote the next morning:

> It was an enjoyable concert, but too long and diverse for it to be possible to say much about the artists concerned. It was a remarkable compilation, which included such well-known singers as John Goss, Sophie Wyss, Norman Walker, Enid Cruickshank, and, in place of Miriam Licette, who was ill, Rena Moisenco, and, in short, it was a brilliant company of artists, who presented a very versatile concert. Lance Dossor, Benjamin Britten, Brosa (violin) were all in grand form. It could not be taken very seriously as a concert, but it could be taken with much seriousness as the combined efforts of a number of very distinguished artists in express their feelings about the Spanish tragedy.

> The programme included Britten's Violin Suite, Op. 6, and a diversity of songs, arias, arrangements (Spanish folksongs among them) *et al*. His thoughts about Spain (see also Letter 155) may well have been influenced at this time by the rapidly deteriorating situation there, and by Auden, who had spent the first months of 1937 in Spain.

11 Edward Frederick Lindley Wood (1881–1959), first Earl of Halifax, English statesman. In November 1937, when Foreign Secretary, he met Hitler, but failed to warn him of the consequences of designs on Austria and Czechoslovakia. In March 1938 Hitler invaded Austria, and, a year later, Czechoslovakia. Halifax served as Foreign Secretary in Chamberlain's government, 1938–40, and briefly in Churchill's all-party administration.

12 Ronald Firbank (1886–1926), English novelist and aesthete, whose final novel was *The Eccentricities of Cardinal Pirelli* (1925).

13 By W.H. Auden and Louis MacNeice, first published in August 1937. Britten was evidently using the book as a support.

As the letters from Fass to Daphne Oliver clearly reveal, Britten was brimming over with enthusiasm for Auden at this time and wanting to share it with his Friston friends. For example:

> After dinner we looked at Wolff [*sic*] songs, & I'd meant him to go to bed early, but it was nearly 11 before I packed him off. He's shewn me a most beautiful love poem of Auden's in 'New Writing' series 3 price 6/- which has prose & poetry in it of all the young writers & if you've not sent Herm [Hermione, Daphne Oliver's sister] a book I think that wld do wonderfully for her. It came out in the spring. No. 1 of last year is pubd at cheap rate now 2/6 I believe – so if 6/- were too much how abt that. Benjy has quite reorganised his mind abt Mozart who is now one of his reigning Gods – &

that particular 5tet that we love one of the most loved of all. He played some Mozart songs too last night, & shewed me his own settings of Auden's words [*On this Island*] that I'd not liked on the wireless.

14 'Now the leaves are falling fast', from *On this Island*. In the meantime, Britten seems to have reversed his opinion of the song.

15 *Domini est terra*, Op. 10.

119   To Sophie Wyss

Denshers, Friston, Nr. Eastbourne.

Dec. 10th, 1937.

Dear Sophie,

Thank you & Arnold[1] so much for putting me up for those three days. I did so enjoy it, & inspite of the concert[2] I really feel alot better & rested for it. I say 'in spite of' because it is always a bit of an effort to play the piano, for I so seldom do it – but I enjoyed it no end; & I think it's an honour to play for you when you sing so beautifully.

I hope the 'teething' is going better, & that you've found a nurse for Humph.[3] He is a grand kid, tho'. I did so like being with him & you all.

I'll see you on Sunday then? Many thanks & love to you all,

Yours,

BENJAMIN

1 Arnold Gyde (1894–1959) was employed by the London publishers, William Heinemann Ltd, between 1918 and 1959. He served on the editorial staff until the outbreak of war and subsequently in the publicity department. He married Sophie Wyss in 1925.

2 See note 4 to Letter 109.

3 Humphrey Gyde (b. 1936), the younger son of Arnold and Sophie, and Britten's godson.

120   To Ralph Hawkes

Peasenhall Hall, Nr. Saxmundham, Suffolk.

Dec. 20th, 1937.

My dear Ralph,

Many thanks for your letter, with kind messages & enquiries. As you see I am now in the depths of the country having a grandly lazy time, doing abit of Christmas shopping, playing abit of ping-pong, but nothing much else. So I ought to be fit soon to get down to the old Concerto for the Prom pretty soon.[1]

I will deal with Lambert and Ballet & talk to him re. story & things.[2] I am glad to hear the Variations made a good impression – but I still combat the idea that they are excessively difficult. After all – is three hours an awful lot for rehearsing a work half-an-hour long?!!

Please, & sorry and all that, I have had the enclosed from the P.R.S.[3] and of course my contract they mention is either in London somewhere, hidden under a pile of clothes, or buried with the furniture in the mill – & I cannot remember what was in it. Do you think you could deal with it for me? I hope you know what usually are the arrangements. Many apologies.

Have good sport in Switzerland. I hope you won't be silly & do anything risky – like Cresta Runs. Hope the snow's good.[4]

By-the-way, I'm going to be very proficient at Squash when I see you next.

Best wishes for Christmas and all that to you & your wife.

Yours,

BENJAMIN B

1 On 14 December Hawkes had written to Kenneth Wright at the BBC, indicating that Britten was keen to compose a piano concerto for the 1938 Promenade Concert Season. Wright was in touch with Britten the same day, inviting him to appear as soloist. Britten agreed (see Letter 126) and began work on the concerto on 7 February 1938 at the Old Mill: 'it dashes along full speed'.

2 Hawkes had written to Britten on 17 December:

The Ballet idea came from a discussion I had yesterday with Constant Lambert, who, I gather, is very considerably impressed with your 'Variations' [the *Bridge Variations*]. He thinks they are fine but he left me no doubt as to his opinion of their difficulty and he considers that with an orchestra containing the finest professionals, at least three hours rehearsal is necessary!! He said that Sadlers Wells could use a new modern Ballet for March but as I knew this would be impossible for you, I suggested that you would be interested to do one for next Winter and told him that you had been 'flirting' with the idea for some time. I suggest, therefore, that you send him an outline of the idea you have, making the suggestion that in a couple of months or so, you will be able to give him a more detailed sketch of the work.

Britten never fulfilled this commission, in spite of toying with the idea of composing not one but three ballets during June–July 1936 (an earlier ballet project discussed with Hawkes in 1935 – 'for which I have a pretty idea' (Diary, 30 September) – came to nothing). Two of these projects were purely speculative: a ballet based on *Our Hunting Fathers* suggested by Rupert Doone and Robert Medley, presumably as a vehicle for Doone; and another mentioned in the diary for 2 July 1936 which was to be a joint venture of Britten's and Montagu Slater's based, as revealed in Letter 83, on *Gulliver's Travels*. One ballet project that was more fully developed was 'Cupid and Psyche', in which the GPO Film Unit producer and director, Basil Wright, was Britten's collaborator. The story of Cupid and Psyche forms part of *The Golden Asse*, the Archive's copy of which is dated 1936.

A letter from Hawkes to Britten dated 21 July 1936 suggests that 'Cupid and Psyche' had been a real possibility:

[. . .] I saw Mr René Blum of the Monte Carlo Ballet, last week and told him about you and Mr. Wright and the ideas which you had, without, of course, giving detailed information. He will be most interested to see your work for I fear that we shall not be able to get in touch with him until early next year [. . .] The idea of the Ballet, therefore, must stand over until that time. I do not think that you could have possibly delivered any sketches in such a short time and it will, therefore, perhaps be advisable to wait until next year.

In April 1938 a further ballet proposal was in the air. Britten writes in his diary for the 6th: '[. . .] dinner with W. Walton & F. Ashton (of Sadlers Wells). There's some talk of me doing a ballet for them.'

In the event none of these ballets materialized, and it was not until 1956 that Britten completed his only full-length, three-act ballet, *The Prince of the Pagodas*.

3 An inquiry about the contract for *Love from a Stranger*.

4 Hawkes was an accomplished skier.

121 To Edwina Jackson
Boosey & Hawkes

Peasenhall Hall, Nr. Saxmundham.
Dec. 27th, 1937.

Dear Miss Jackson,

Many thanks for your letter re Muir Mathieson.[1] As you know I have about ten volumes of film music to my credit (if it be credit!), but which bit is suitable for him I don't know. If he wants large orchestral stuff I've got the 'Love from a Stranger' music. For smaller combinations I have Night Mail (G.P.O.) – & Way to the Sea (Strand) & 6d Abstract (G.P.O.). If he's got a chorus I've got

'Coal Face' (G.P.O.).[2] Could you get in touch with him and ask him? What I suggest, if the hurry is violent, [is] that you wire me here at what time & what number I can telephone him in the evening.

I suppose permission would have to be got from the various film companies? About parts, I suppose that they'd have to be copied – is that on the B.B.C. or us?

I think this is worth bothering about, because it is quite good publicity, & I'm always being told that I should bother about that kind of thing!

Yours sincerely,
BENJAMIN BRITTEN

Best wishes for New Year.

1 Muir Mathieson (1911–1975), Scottish conductor, who studied with Sargent at the College. In 1932 he made his début and two years later became Musical Director of London Films. He was responsible thereafter for the musical direction of over five hundred films, including *Things to Come* (Bliss, 1935) and *Henry V* (Walton, 1944); in 1946 he directed the film of Britten's *Instruments of the Orchestra* (see note 7 to Letter 514).

Mathieson wanted to include some of Britten's film music in his BBC radio series, *British Film Music*, broadcast in March 1938. He met Britten on 10 January 1938, presumably to discuss this proposal. Britten's *Telegram Abstract* was broadcast by the London Film Symphony Orchestra conducted by Mathieson on 26 March. Britten's diary entry reads: 'BBC. rehearsal of my Film music (Telegram stuff for GPO) in morning. Show is in evening. It goes well.'

2 Perhaps the most important experimental film emanating from the Film Unit, the topic of which was the coal industry of Britain. It represents a unique attempt to integrate sight and sound and Britten's score introduced a whole range of ingeniously contrived musical 'effects'. Directed by Alberto Cavalcanti, it was in *Coal Face* that Britten and Auden collaborated for the first time in the setting by Britten, of Auden's lyric, 'O lurcher-loving collier'. See EMWHA, pp. 421 and 665–6, and PR, pp. 70–101 and 439–42.

122 To Ralph Hawkes

Peasenhall Hall, Nr. Saxmundham, Suffolk.
Dec. 30th, 1937.

My dear Ralph,

Thank you so much for the really magnificent present. It was a grand thought, & the scores you chose were very much my cup of tea. I shall have to get you to do a little signing in them when I next come in.

I supppose it was a subtle hint, of course, for me to make my Concerto as good as those masterpieces.[1] Well – sir, I'll do my best, but I can't guarantee it. It's going well though, & at the moment I'm pretty bucked about it.

I hope you had a festive Christmas, with plenty of snow. We had a first-rate one here, with all the appropriate jollifications. I've played a good deal of squash, but I'll need some pretty effective practice before I can challenge you. It's a damnably difficult game – but a darned nice one.

I shall be in town at the end of next week (8th) for the Catalan suite,[2] & will come in to see you.

Many thanks again, & best wishes for 1938.

Yours,

BENJAMIN

1 Hawkes had given Britten a selection of scores of piano concertos as a Christmas present and as a general encouragement to the composer, who was about to start work on his own concerto.

2 *Mont Juic*, Op. 12, a suite of Catalan dances for orchestra, was composed jointly by Britten and Berkeley, and completed on 12 December 1937. In a prefatory note to the published score, Berkeley recalls the work's origins:

The Suite is based on themes that Benjamin Britten and I heard at a performance of folk-dancing in Barcelona where we were both attending the festival of contemporary music in 1936. Mont Juic is the name of the district in which this took place [on 25 April]. We were told later that Mont Juic was also the name of the local prison; however, we decided to keep the title at the risk of its being thought we had lodged there during our stay!

The Suite is in four movements. The first is a stately dance based on two of the themes we heard. The second is a lighter and more graceful tune needing little elaboration. This is followed by a movement entitled Lament (Barcelona, July 1936) – an allusion to the menace of the civil war into which the country was so soon to be plunged. Finally comes, in complete contrast, a gay and carefree piece, somewhat more elaborately scored.

The question who wrote what has often been asked, but we decided, early on, that we would prefer to leave the music to speak for itself, particularly since we discussed the form and orchestration of each piece in considerable detail, so that it would, in any case, have been difficult to disentangle which of us had thought first of any particular feature.

The first performance took place on 8 January 1938, given by the BBC Orchestra conducted by Joseph Lewis as part of a broadcast concert of 'light' music. Berkeley wrote to Britten from Paris on 11 January,

I hope you were pleased with the performance of our joint 'chef d'oeuvre' – I heard it fairly well, but not really well enough to judge the standard of playing, nor quite how successful 'our' orchestration was. [. . .] I must say I thought your two pieces more effective than mine – though I couldn't judge of no. 2 – there were too many passages that didn't come through. [. . .] I thought the last one the most successful – it is exciting and snappy, and the false starts are brilliantly effective.

It was in July 1936, while together in Cornwall (see note 2 to Letter 86), that Britten and Berkeley had decided 'to work alot together – especially on the Spanish tunes'; but it was not until April 1937 that they joined forces at Painswick (Gloucestershire) to achieve their ambition. In Britten's diary entries the chronology of their joint creation and the course of the two composers' friendship are inextricably intertwined:

5 April
Lennox Berkeley meets me & we drive together to Painswick where his friend Miss Bryans is putting me up with him. Spend a pleasant evening playing violin (!) & piano.

6 April
Lennox & I get down to work on the Spanish Suite in the morning. He has sketched two movements which we discuss fully & alter accordingly, & then while I sketch a third (having settled form etc) he makes out a rough score of the first. Everything goes very amicably & tho' of course we don't agree on everything at once I feel the final arrangements are satisfactory. Certainly the music seems nice.

11 April
It is a curse having to go on with this awful bore of Uncle Arthur [*King Arthur*] – especially when we are here especially to work together on the Spanish Suite. However one must live – but we get alot of the Spanish Question settled before lunch.
     [. . .]
     Then before bed – long & deep conversation with Lennox – he is a dear & I am very, very fond of him, nevertheless, it is a comfort that we can arrange sexual matters to at least <u>my</u> satisfaction.

28 April [London]
Tho' feeling desparate [Burra's death in an air accident had occurred the day before] I hurriedly finish off the last Spanish tunes before going to

Lennox Berkeley to work at them all. This we do fairly satisfactorily. Lunch with him. [. . .] See Ralph Hawkes about the Spanish tunes after & he is very pleased indeed.

22 October [Peasenhall]
I spend all my time in the next few days working over at Rhino (the house over the garage) in inimitable quiet (a) copying the Auden songs [*On this Island*] for Sophie Wyss (b) writing new ones (either before breakfast, or just before bed) (c) and starting the score of Lennox' & my Catalan suite which seems to be working very well.

2 November
Lunch with Brosas & Lennox. Play them the Catalan Suite in afternoon. Hair cut.

11 November
To Gloucester – Painswick with Lennox Berkeley. We stay with his great friend Miss Bryans.

12 November
Spend our time playing trios & duets (Vl., Vla, Pft.) & also I do some sketching for Wystan's Hadrian's Wall programme & scoring of the Catalan Suite.

On 28 July Britten had written in his diary:

Dinner with Lennox at his Reform Club – much talk. He is a dear & I'm glad I'm going to live with him.

Berkeley's furniture was moved into store at Snape (while work on the Mill was being completed) on 13 April 1938. On 21 May:

Great International Crisis – war more than ever likely – if only this Government would have a policy. José [Rafaelli] (Lennox's Paris Friend) & L. come down by mid-day train to get his things sorted.

31 May
Work in morning – proofs of Mont Juic.

6 June
Down to Snape mid-day – Lennox is here already. Walk with him in evening. It's glorious here.

Berkeley's name is mentioned for the last time in the diaries on 16 June, which also happened to be the last entry Britten was to make in his 1938 diary:

No more work at [Piano] Concerto – too behindhand with letters. Go to station with Lennox in morning. In aft. I go out to Orford for a picnic tea with D.W. [?Dorothy Wadham] Letters in evening & business.

Thereafter Britten virtually discontinued keeping a diary but for a few scattered entries in 1939, which included a lunch date with Berkeley on 9 March. The history of the friendship was continued in his letters.

As for the division of labour between the two composers of *Mont Juic*, each confirmed on different occasions that the first two movements were Berkeley's, the third and fourth Britten's. The full score and also some of the orchestral parts were in Britten's hand. See also Peter Dickinson, *The Music of Lennox Berkeley* (London, Thames, 1989), pp. 45–6, and an article by Berkeley, 'Views from Mont Juic', *Tempo*, 106, September 1973, pp. 6–7. See also note 1 to Letter 152.

In 1952, Berkeley was to write in DMHK, p. 288:

A similar approach to the problem of composition made such an association possible, and though, after agreeing upon the general shape of the movements, we worked at the different parts more or less independently, I hope I may claim that a reasonably homogeneous Suite emerged. Working with him, as I then did, I was able to observe one aspect in particular of his attitude towards composition. This is his extraordinary flair for what 'comes off' in actual performance, and his readiness to subordinate other considerations to it. I mention this quality here because it has enormous importance in light music. Where the actual material is of slight or limited significance, the manner of its presentation is everything; because Britten realizes this so well, and carries it out so brilliantly, his light music is worthy of serious study.

123 To Ronald Duncan

> Peasenhall Hall, Nr. Saxmundham, Suffolk.
>
> Jan. 3rd, '38.

Dear Ronnie,

You are an irresponsible devil. How you expect to edit a lucid (??) Magazine from the wilds of the Back of Beyond beats me. I get extraordinary communications from time to time from some weird creature announcing the 1st N° of Townsman – then eventually – a letter asking me if I approve – no copy of course, & then a stranger document to a B. Bulter or some such monstrosity, asking for the Tune of the Nocturne[1] – which I suppose is to be thrust on to an unsuspecting public without a word of explanation – actually it is just about as interesting as an Index of First Lines of a volume of Longfellow. Who has done the musical part of No I (if there be such a number)? – Henry [Boys], last time I saw him, was in just as thick a fog as I am.

Cornwall is sufficient for writing biting Xmas cards (many thanks for – by-the-by) – but scarcely for editing magazines.

> All the best,
>
> Love
>
> BENJAMIN

1 'Now through night's caressing grip', from *On this Island*.

124 To John Pudney[1]
BBC

Peasenhall Hall, Saxmundham, Suffolk.

Jan. 14th 1938.

Dear John,

Here's your stuff: sorry it's so late, but I was busy doing 101 other things. I hope it's what you want.[2]

About the 1st section (explanation of 'sections' later) bearing in mind your instructions of a <u>slow</u> piece, preferably dance, & trying to think of an English equivalent of a Sardana, I have evolved a Saraband – fairly stylised & classical, but with brass instruments it shouldn't sound archaic. I hope you'll approve.

Section A –	slow saraband (starting loud & somewhat pompous – with quieter middle section – ending loudly.)
B –	Fanfares with drum rolls.
C –	March – rhythmic & snappy with smoother middle section that loudens somewhat excitingly.
D –	quieter Fanfare than before.
Section E –	Saraband again, but developed & starts very reflectively working up to a big climax to <u>end</u>.

I come to London on Tuesday (mid-day) & will 'phone you for instructions as to recording. Have you been in touch with Ralph Hawkes?

Incidentally, please ask Pratt[3] to have <u>two</u> tenor trombones not <u>one</u> tenor & <u>one</u> bass.

Excuse haste: hope you can decipher the important points of this —

Yours ever

BENJAMIN BRITTEN

1 John Pudney (1909–1977), English poet, novelist and dramatist. He was educated at Gresham's, where he was a contemporary of Auden's. Between 1934 and 1938, he was a BBC staff producer and writer. It was Pudney who, in 1937, had invited Auden to write *Hadrian's Wall*, for which Britten composed the music.

2 In a letter dated 29 December 1937, Pudney had invited Britten to compose incidental music for a series of four programmes produced by Pudney and Leslie Stokes, entitled *Lines on the Map*. On 12 January

Britten wrote in his diary: 'Write some Brass music for BBC. programmes "Lines across Map" – awful muck.' Each programme dealt with a different aspect of national and international communications, and the series was broadcast between January and April. See PR, pp. 581–2.

3 Richard Pratt, Orchestral Manager of the BBC Symphony Orchestra, 1930–46. *Lines on the Map* was scored for two trumpets, two tenor trombones and percussion.

125 To Ralph Hawkes

Peasenhall Hall, Nr. Saxmundham, Suffolk.
Jan. 16th, 1938.

My dear Ralph,

Many thanks for your letter & enclosure. Mr Rosen[1] is dealing with all the "F6" music & would you be so good as to give the letter to him? I have a horrible feeling that the music is already out – & there is only one copy of it. I think it abit unwise to lose these opportunities because – although the direct rake-off isn't stupendous, – the publicity is advantageous. So do you think we might have a photographed copy made? I shall be in town on Wednesday & will ask you what you think then.

I have fixed with my Cabaret singer to come along to you on Wednesday at 5.0 – I think you said that was O.K. for you. Would you mind if Kenneth Wright (of B.B.C. fame) came along too?

I hope you're feeling fitter & that Glasgow was good & riotous,

Yours ever,
BENJAMIN

1 Carl A. Rosen, an employee in the Royalty Department of Boosey & Hawkes. *The Ascent of F6* was to be performed by the Birmingham Repertory Theatre.

126 To Kenneth Wright
BBC

Peasenhall Hall, Nr. Saxmundham, Suffolk.
Jan. 16th 1938.

My dear Kenneth,

I feel very guilty in not having answered a very nice letter of yours of before Christmas. But I've plenty of excuses, because I've been laid up down here, & also in the throes of organising a wedding of a sister.[1] Anyhow of course I should be honoured to

play the old Concerto at the Proms. next season. So far there's not
an awful lot written, but what there is in my head seems to me
pretty satisfactory. I'll let you know from time to time how it goes.

There's one other matter. I did (last year) a lot of Cabaret songs
with W.H. Auden – which have just been sung, with a certain
amount of success in Parties and Caberets and that sort of thing,
by a grand singer called Millicent Hedli Anderson[2] (whom I
believe your audition people have heard & approved). She is going
to sing these just across the road from you – at Boosey and
Hawkes – at 5.0 p.m. on Wednesday next, & I wondered whether
you'd be interested to come and listen, if you aren't at that
moment off your head with meetings & things.[3] Don't bother to
answer this, just come if you feel inclined – but I feel somehow
that you'd be interested.

I do hope that your wife is better – the last news of her I had
was very depressing.

Let's hope that 1938 will bring better news – I personally am
excessively glad to put 1937 behind me.[4]

Yours very sincerely,
BENJAMIN BRITTEN

1 On 22 January 1938 Beth was to marry Christopher ('Kit') Welford
(1911–1973), at Peasenhall Church, Suffolk. The day's events were
recorded by Britten in his diary:

Wedding at Peasenhall Church. 2.15. Recept. at Hall after – about 115
people come. V. good success. I give Beth away – Barb. & Robert act as
Hostesses – 2 small girls (Griffin and Ann White) Bridesmaids – (dressed
ex. like Beth) – 2 Pages – Arnold Gyde & Bobby Sewell (like Kit) very
pretty. Party lasts till 6.30 – with Dancing. [. . .] Sophie [Wyss] sings my
'Birds' in service.

Beth's wedding: her brother makes
an index of his morning dress

2 English singer and actress (1907–1990). She had an operatic training abroad before joining the Group Theatre for Auden's *The Dance of Death* (1934). She later took the role of the Singer in *The Ascent of F6* (1937), when she first met Britten. In 1942 she married the poet, Louis MacNeice (1907–1963), and in 1946 took part in the first broadcast of his radio drama, *The Dark Tower*, for which Britten was to write the incidental music. A major influence on her unique performing style was Yvette Guilbert. Wulff Scherchen, writing in 1988, had a vivid recollection of this remarkable artist:

I often think back to first seeing her on the stage of the old Troc. We'd walked there from the flat, Ben, Peter and I, to collect her after what must have been a Saturday matinée performance. She was the leader of the chorus line and looked absolutely stunning, indeed ravishing. What marked her out from all the others was above all the effect produced by her voice. As good luck would have it, she later at the flat sang for us not only many of Ben's cabaret songs, including 'Tell me the truth about love', but Victorian music-hall ballads she knew well. I recall only one, but with great delight, called 'Up in a balloon, boys, up in a balloon'. I thought she was marvellous, and of course she was.

Wulff Scherchen is remembering the late-night cabaret established at the Trocadero Grillroom, Piccadilly Circus, by Charles B. Cochran (1872–1951) in 1924, a run of shows which continued until the out-break of war (see Cochran, *Cock-a-doodle-do* (London, Dent, 1941), pp. 276–83). Hedli was leading lady in one of the cabarets, *Night Lights*, a suppertime show, for which Doris Zinkeisen was respon-sible for the décor and costumes and Antony Tudor was one of the choreographers. The show – which might well have been the one Wulff attended – included music-hall songs, dance, acrobatics and topical items, e.g. 'The New York World's Fair' (song: 'Everybody's Going to the New York Fair' (words and music by Lorraine)) in which Hedli appeared in the role of the Statue of Liberty. At the same time (but earlier in the evening) she was performing in George Black's revue *Black and Blue* at the Hippodrome (starring Vic Oliver).

On 19 November 1943, in connection with the forthcoming production on radio of Sackville-West's *The Rescue*, in which Hedli Anderson played the role of Athene, the following informative para-graphs, written by C. Gordon Glover, appeared in the *Radio Times*:

I am told that Benjamin Britten has made a first-rate job of the incidental music to the production; Hedli Anderson should find no difficulty in singing her share of it. It was for her that Britten wrote some satirical little 'cabaret songs' some years ago. Hedli Anderson has done most of the things that are expected of singers in these days – opera, broadcasting, cabaret, and revue, in which last she once found herself singing an aria from *Traviata* from the top of a ten-foot pillar.

Hedli was studying in Germany when the Nazi regime asserted itself. This, not surprisingly, she did not fancy, so she returned to England to make, very shortly, her first appearance in opera. *Hansel and Gretel* was the opera, Victoria Hopper and Sydney Carroll her fellow artists. Broadcasting was soon to follow, and listeners may remember her in *The Queen's Lace Handkerchief*, and 'Victorian Music-Hall'.

She broadcast in *Christopher Columbus*, written by her husband Louis Mac-Neice, appears regularly at the famous 'Players' [Theatre], and collects lustre for what she tells me is a pretty lustrous daughter.

The Cabaret Songs to which Glover referred, with words by Auden, were composed during 1937: on 5 May 'Johnny'; and between the 6th and 8th three further songs, including 'Jam Tart' and 'Give up love'. The third song, one is tempted to think, might have been a setting of a 'Blues', dedicated by the poet to the singer, the text of which was first published in *New Verse* in the same month; but despite the inscription, Hedli Anderson replied 'nothing to do with me' on being shown the poem. Around this same time Auden sent Britten 'a ballad' for Hedli, 'My private tune for it is St. James Infirmary.' This was the ballad 'Miss Gee' ('Let me tell you a little story / About Miss Edith Gee', *Another Time* (New York, Random House, 1940)), but there is no evidence that Britten embarked on a setting. Finally in 1937, on 17 June, Britten made an arrangement for solo voice of his 'Funeral Blues' from *The Ascent of F6*. 'Jam Tart' was sung by Hedli at a party that took place on 18 January 1938 at the Hammersmith studio of the painter, Julian Trevelyan, who recalled the occasion in a private communication (24 January 1981):

There was a famous party here, given by the Group Theatre, to say goodbye to Auden and Isherwood when they set out for China (19 January 1938). Ben was asked to accompany Hedli Anderson in some songs he had written to words of Auden, which they both did very professionally. I remember one which started: 'I'm a jam tart' [. . .] The party ended in a bit of a rough-house.

(For a detailed account, including Britten's own diary entry, see DMBA, pp. 127–9. Later, in an undated letter from Shanghai, Auden was to tell Britten, 'I have two albums of Chinese Opera records for you, but I hope they wont influence you <u>too</u> much.')

Britten's setting of 'Jam Tart' has not been recovered. But the text exists, the first verse of which runs:

> I'm a jam tart, I'm a bargain basement
> I'm a work of art, I'm a magic casement
> A coal cellar, an umbrella, a sewing machine
> A radio, a hymnbook, an old french bean
> The Royal Scot, a fairy grot, a storm at sea, a tram
>   I don't know what I am
>   You've cast a spell on me.

It was a song that also caught the ear of the American poet John Berryman who in a letter dated 8 (possibly 10) January 1939 describes attending 'a ball in town', during the Christmas vacation from Cambridge 'where a gorgeous creature sang two of Auden's [sic] new songs', one of which was clearly 'Jam Tart'. The date of the letter would seem to preclude the possibility that Berryman was talking about the same Group Theatre party that Trevelyan remembered. (See *We Dream of Honour: John Berryman's Letters to His Mother*, edited by Richard J. Kelly (New York, Norton, 1988), p. 115.)

The setting of 'Give up love' has, likewise, not been found, but Hedli Anderson remembered Britten setting it and recalled 'vague snatches of tune'. Again, the text exists:

> Cleopatra, Antony
> Were introspective you'll agree
> Got in a morbid state because
> They lounged about too much indoors.
> If they'd gone in for Eton fives
> They wouldn't have gone and lost their lives.
>
> For if you love sport then you won't give a thought
>   To all that goes on in the park.
> Learning to bowl will keep your heart whole,
>   You don't want to go out after dark.
> Love is unenglish and sloppy and soft
>   So be English and stringy and tough.
> If you keep yourself fit you will never want It,
>   So give up love.

At least two further Cabaret Songs are known to have been written. One of them, and one of the best examples of the genre, was 'Tell me the truth about love', composed in January 1938. Exactly a year later, Auden and Isherwood were to leave for North America, and a few months after that, in May, Britten and Pears were to make the same journey. Between January and May 1939, Auden, writing from the George Washington Hotel, New York, sent Britten (still in England), the text of yet another 'Blues', with an (undated) accompanying note:

Dear Bengy,

Here is a blues for Hedli, or whatever you think best. How are you and Wolf. The English papers make me vomit, and the American aren't much better. Busy but poor. Will try to write real letter soon. Copeland [sic] is very nice, I think. Where are the records?

Much love
WYSTAN

Auden must be referring here to the gramophone recordings of the Cabaret Songs made in July 1938 and January 1939, which however were never to be issued. (See note 1 to Letter 165.)

The opening verses read:

Say this city has ten million souls
Some are living in mansions, some are living in holes
Yet there's no place for us, my dear, there's no place for us

Once we had a country and we thought it fair
Look in the map and you'll find it there
We can never go there now, my dear, we can never go there now.

There is no evidence that Britten ever set this 'Blues', though the
fact that he took it with him to America suggests that he may have
intended to do so at some stage. The poem appears in Auden's
Collected Shorter Poems (1966) as the first of Twelve Songs, which also
includes 'Calypso' and two lyrics from *Paul Bunyan*. A setting of the
text, under the title of 'Refugee Blues', was made for Hedli Anderson
by Elisabeth Lutyens in 1942 (along with a setting of Auden's 'As
I walked out one evening'): see also Merion and Susie Harries,
A Pilgrim Soul: The Life and Work of Elisabeth Lutyens (London, Michael
Joseph, 1989), p. 107. After Britten's return from America in 1942 he
had made it clear that he did not want to write any more cabaret
songs and the way was clear for Hedli Anderson to approach other
composers.

However, in a 1946 broadcast (*The Composer and the Listener*, BBC
Radio, published in the *Listener* as 'How to Become a Composer',
7 November 1946), Britten told his audience:

I maintain strongly that it is the duty of every young composer to be able
to write every kind of music – except bad music. That has nothing to do
with high-brow or low-brow, serious or light music. It is a good thing for a
young composer to have to write the lightest kinds of music. I knew [. . .]
a good cabaret singer who asked me to write some songs for her. I obliged
and wrote to the best of my ability some 'Blues' and a Calypso of which I
am not at all ashamed.

The complex history of the Cabaret songs continued when Britten
and Auden both found themselves on the same side of the Atlantic
in 1939, and its documentation necessarily involves details of Britten's
and Pears's travel plans and Auden's personal life. It was in May
that Auden wrote from St Mark's School, Southborough, Massachusetts, to Britten in Canada, 'How fine to hear you are coming to New
York. But we **must** meet soon. I have to come up in June to Toronto
to get on the quota, so we might do it then.' He added: 'I am mad
with happiness, but will tell you all about it when we meet.' This
was a reference to his recent meeting with Chester Kallman, who
was to become his lifelong companion. It seems probable – and one
has to conjecture because Auden's letters to Britten are undated and
Britten's to Auden, with one exception, lost – that this letter of
Auden's generated another:

Dear Bengy

Inspired by writing you a letter, I got out your ms song, which years ago I promised to have a shot at. Here is the shot

WYSTAN

(The contents of what would otherwise appear to be an enigmatic note are elucidated in note 2 to Letter 182.)

It seems clear that Britten must have responded with a letter welcoming the news of Auden's intention to visit Toronto, only to receive a reply in which Auden wrote, 'Don't think I can make Toronto now. No money. When are you coming to the States', and elaborated on the vacation he was planning to take with Chester (his 'honeymoon'). 'Can't we meet before?' he asks, and adds, 'Here is a song for Hedli and you. How lucky her sex is.' The 'song for Hedli' was 'Calypso'.

Britten's reply was Letter 182, dated 5 June, in which he also responded to Auden's 'shot' – the 'Song (after Sappho)' – at providing words for a pre-existing tune.

Britten seems also to have carried to North America with him the text for another song, 'I sit in my flat in my newest frock', which belongs probably to 1937. (A title – 'My love stolen away' – added to the typescript in Auden's hand and a number – 'II' – suggest that at some time he may have thought of the text as an item in a sequence of songs.) It seems unlikely that this was the unidentified song of the three Britten composed in May. If it had been set, why transport the text across the Atlantic? It seems highly probable that this text too was among 'all those cabaret ones' which Britten said he was 'going to get down to' in his letter to Auden of 5 June (Letter 182). Hedli Anderson had no recollection of a setting.

In January 1940 Hedli Anderson proposed to perform 'Tell me the truth about love' in one of a series of films she was making for British Films Ltd entitled *Let's Be Famous*. In the absence of both Britten and Ralph Hawkes in the USA, Edwina Jackson, Hawkes's secretary, gave permission for the cabaret song to be included in the film. The composer wrote to Miss Jackson on 7 February:

I have talked the matter of "Tell me the truth about love" over with Mr. Ralph and Mr. Auden, and there is no objection at all to Miss Hedli Anderson singing this for British Films Ltd. So, I hope she will go ahead and make this film and that we all of us make lots of money out of it and can all retire to the country, which I doubt. Incidentally, the whole business re songs and Miss Anderson is under consideration here at the moment as we feel that these songs should not be restricted to just one artist in the future. However, I shall be writing to her direct about this and will, of course, let you know what we decide.

[. . .] It is lovely having Mr. Ralph over here (he was down at Amityville for the last weekend).

Let's Be Famous, with Hedli Anderson's performance of 'Tell me the truth about love', has not been traced.

Britten's diary for 19 January 1938 reports on the sing-through at Boosey & Hawkes: 'Hedli sings Wystan's and my cabaret songs to Ralph Hawkes with great success.' Only four of the Cabaret Songs have so far come to light: 'Tell me the truth about love', 'Funeral Blues', 'Johnny' and 'Calypso'. They were posthumously published by Faber Music in 1980. There is a final Auden manuscript item in the Archive which must be related to an Anderson–Britten project, a kind of quasi-dramatic *scena* in which the setting of a song in three verses, 'When the postman knocks', each of which ends with a refrain, 'I've fallen out of love with you', would have been interpolated into a witty, sardonic soliloquy, with its own musical potentialities:

> When did it happen? I dunno. It just did.
> The band was playing a fox-trot
> > (do do do dy o do)
> Someone made a joke at the next table
> > (Whoo ha ha Whoo ha ha)
> The Dictators were making speeches
> > (Grrrrrrrr————)
> Mr. Chamberlain was appeasing someone
> > (Cluck cluck cluck
> > cluck cluck)
> Several records were broken on land, water and air
> > (Hip Hip Hip Hurrah.
> > Hip Hip Hip Hurrah)
> The people wrote letters to The Times
> > (I am dear sir,
> > your obedient servant)
> Several thousand people were born
> > (sound of crying)
> Several thousand people got married
> > (Wedding March)
> Several thousand people died
> > (Death March)

The topical references make it clear that this was a period piece, *c.* 1938. There is no evidence that Britten ever attempted a setting of this most diverting text. Was it perhaps intended for late-night cabaret at the Trocadero?

Edward Mendelson in his edition of the *Plays (with Christopher Isherwood) and other dramatic writings by W.H. Auden, 1928–1938* (London, Faber and Faber, 1989), a volume of *The Complete Works of W.H. Auden*, refers (p. 673) to 'one further text, which Britten set in

cabaret-style' and 'seems likely to have been written for a GPO
documentary, although there is no direct evidence linking it to
Auden, or, for that matter, to any documentary film. No one else is
likely to have written it, and the GPO Film Unit is its only likely
origin.'

The text begins:

> When you're feeling like expressing your affection
> For someone night and day
> Take up the 'phone and ask for your connection
> We'll give it right away.

And ends:

> Enter any telephone kiosk O
> Have your say,
> Press button A,
> Here's your number now.

The manuscript of this song, *Vivace*, in F, with the harmony coloured
by an unstable major/minor third, is in the Archive. It is in Britten's
characteristic popular-song vein, less acrid in tone but not so far
removed in style from the cabaret-like setting of the last song of *On
this Island*, 'As it is, plenty'.

Sources: Hedli Anderson, Interview with John Evans, October
1980, Paris; Archive; Elisabeth Lutyens, *A Goldfish Bowl* (autobiography, London, Cassell, 1972), p. 194; Lutyens Work List (London,
Olivan Press, 1975); and Donald Mitchell and Philip Reed, 'Hedli
Anderson', *Independent*, 10 February 1990.

3 Wright sent a member of the BBC music staff to listen but the songs
were never taken up by the BBC and their first broadcast was given
after Britten's death.

4 The year had been overshadowed by the death of his mother in
January.

127 To Mary Behrend

Peasenhall Hall, Nr. Saxmundham, Suffolk.
Jan. 17th 1938.

Dear Mrs. Behrend,

This is only to say that we all hope that your refusal to my sister's
invitation wasn't final, & that after depositing George at school
you will all then come on here to the wedding. It isn't really so far
here, you know, and the affair doesn't start till 2.15. So will you try,
please? It would be grand to have you.

Things are hectic here, as you can guess – & it is terribly difficult to do one's normal work as well, & I have a large amount of that on hand.

I hope you are all well, & had a good Christmas. We had a fine one – I am very particular about my Christmasses, & like them absolutely traditional – trees, stockings, carols & all – although this year we had to forgo snow, unfortunately.

With best wishes to you all for 1938 – from us both; & do try and come on Saturday –

Yours ever
BENJAMIN BRITTEN

128   To Henry Boys

Peasenhall Hall.
[after 26 February and before 2 March 1938]

Henry, my dear,

I am sorry not to have written before, but I have been & still am so lousily busy. It never leaked out about you staying at the flat – & I don't think it ever need![1] I hope you weren't too uncomfy.

I don't know what data you want – anyhow I've written some things on a slip of paper choose what you want. You know more about me, you know, than I know myself.[2]

I feel a bit guilty about Ronnie. Cd. you write him [a] P.C. saying wt. wds. are gd. to set to music? I don't know & don't very much care.

The weather is grand & I'm all hot to start tennis again. Mind you practise hard & we'll march through Lewes.

Much love,
BENJAMIN

I suggest that you write to Ralph Hawkes saying what music you want of mine – & that you've got to do an article on my music for M.M.R. & that it's O.K. by me.

O boy, o boy – the mill is grand.

1 In his diary for 23 February Britten wrote: '[. . .] finally he (H.) comes back to Peter's Flat, because he can't get in anywhere else & sleeps on sofa'. Between living in Charlotte Street and Nevern Square (see note 1 to Letter 129), Pears had the use of Anne Wood's and Iris Holland Rogers's flat in Harley Mews. Britten also occasionally stayed there during the first months of 1938.

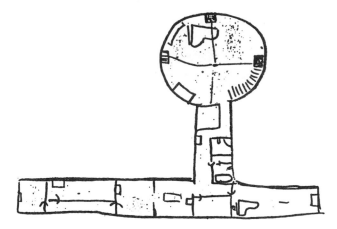

Britten's sketch for the conversion of the Old Mill: he shows the location of his piano and Berkeley's

2 Boys was writing an article on Britten: 'The Younger English Composers V: Benjamin Britten', *Monthly Musical Record*, 68 (October 1938), pp. 234–7. This early essay was the first to point out Britten's particular debt to Mahler, but also acknowledges the influence of Berg, Schoenberg and Stravinsky.

Saturday, 12 March 1938
[*Peasenhall*]

Hitler marches into Austria,[1] rumour has it that Czecho.S. & Russia have mobilised – so what! War within a month at least, I suppose & end to all this pleasure – end of Snape, end of Concerto, friends, work, love – oh, blast, damn . . .

1 On 11 March German troops entered Austria and on the 13th Austria was declared part of the German Reich.

Sunday, 13 March 1938

Beth & Kit go off to London in aft. Glorious day, & bloody news from Vienna – to think of Wien, under Nazi control[1] – no more Mahler, no lightness, no culture, nothing but their filthy, lewd, heartiness, their despicable conceit & unutterable stupidity.

1 Hitler was in Vienna on the 14th.

Monday, 14 March 1938
[*Peasenhall/London*]

Up to London in afternoon – Peter's back from Prague – safely, but with grim news of Germany under Nazi rule.

129 To Kenneth Wright
BBC

43, Nevern Square, London, S.W. 5.[1]
6th April, 1938.

Dear Kenneth,

When I telephoned the BBC at the beginning of the week, I was told you were down with 'flu. I am so sorry, and I hope you will soon be alright and about again.

The second movement of the Concerto is done, and 3rd and 4th movements well away. I am leaving London on Saturday for about ten days. Shall I come and play what's done to you when I come back? So far I'm all elated about it, but I hope it's not a transitory mood, as it so often is!

I enclose list of published stuff as you wished for – hope it's O.K. Get well soon.

Did anything transpire between you and Decca (or Yomans)?[2]

Kindest regards,
Yours sincerely,
BENJAMIN BRITTEN

1 Britten and Pears occupied this flat – their first joint home – from 16 March 1938. For the history of finding the flat, see PPT, pp. 109–12.

2 Walter Yeomans (b. ?, d. 1940), Decca's director of serious music. Britten was seeking to obtain a private off-the-air recording of his *Frank Bridge Variations*, which Yeomans had agreed to organize. Later in 1938, his company recorded the *Variations* (see note 3 to Letter 135). From the 1950s onwards, it was exclusively on the Decca label that Britten's and Pears's performances were issued, to form one of the most important recorded legacies of the twentieth century.

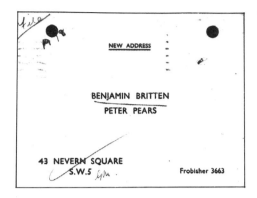

NEW ADDRESS

BENJAMIN BRITTEN
PETER PEARS

43 NEVERN SQUARE
S.W.5

Frobisher 3663

130 To John Pounder[1]

> Old Mill, Snape, <u>Suffolk</u>.
> [Snape 258]
> May 4th 1938

My dear John,

Things are chaotic here. Domestic crisis after crisis. That's why
I've not written before, & now I am afraid it's only a request. I
have had a letter from the owner of my bed (it's not mine
unfortunately!) & it is wanted almost at once. So could you please:
remove all the clothes from it (except matresses, which arn't mine):
tell Mrs Condé that if any one calls for a bed that that is the one
specified. Also – if your wings are sprouting – get Mr. Condé[2] to
bring up Peter's old bed (in one of the basement rooms) & make
up the bed on it for me.

There – there – it isn't as bad as all that.

Briefly; the crisis has been : sacking of a complete family working
here : reorganising of whole house : notice of housekeeper :
pacifying of ditto : Andoni [see note 2 to Letter 131] is going –
which bleeds my heart but it is better on the whole : And the
moods & temperaments connected with all these. It's been h–l. I
come up on Monday – see you then? I hope the test wasn't as
bad as you feared. Many Happy returns of whenever it was.

Any letters or messages? Thank you for forwarding letters.

> Much love,
> BENJAMIN

1 Pounder was in temporary residence at Britten's and Pears's London
   base, 43 Nevern Square, SW5. Pears was at Glyndebourne.
2 Presumably a husband and wife caretaking team at Nevern Square.

131 To John Pudney
BBC
[*Postcard*]

Old Mill, Snape, Suffolk
[Postmarked 5 May 1938]

Dear John,

What rehearsals will you want me for next week?[1] I'm up on Monday or Tuesday. Crisis after crisis here[2] – hope all well with you.

BENJAMIN

1 John Pudney had invited Britten to compose music for a radio feature on Chartism, *The Chartists' March*, by J.H. Miller. Rehearsals took place from 9 to 12 May, with a final rehearsal and transmission on the 13th, when Britten conducted the male chorus for which the music had been conceived. In contrast to many of these radio transmissions, he clearly enjoyed undertaking *The Chartists' March*, writing of the broadcast in his diary: 'It goes well & is exciting to do & listen to.' The manuscript score is lost and no archival recording appears to have survived. See also PR, pp. 582–3.

2 Britten refers to various domestic crises at Snape. These involved his housekeeper, Mrs Hearn, and also the Basque refugee boy, Andoni Barrutia, to whom he had quixotically agreed to offer a home. (In a postcard to Britten from Djibouti, and jointly signed by Isherwood, Auden wrote, 'I hope your mill is becoming a palace fit for your Basque delinquent to live in.') The boy arrived on 22 April and departed on 4 May. The incident is described in EWB, pp. 107–8. Britten seems to have been no more successful in accommodating an East End boy on holiday in Cornwall in August 1937.

132 To Ralph Hawkes

Old Mill, Snape, Suffolk.
May 5th, 1938.

My dear Ralph,

The Radiogram has arrived & to-day the men have been in fitting up aerials & that sort of thing, & it is now working splendidly: any station from Omsk to Tomsk – even the London Regional which is such a problem on the East Coast! I like it very, very much, and it is as nice a house-warming present that one could possibly

wish for – thank you everso much. I do appreciate it enormously.
I hope when you are this way you will come & hear it, and see the
place. It is very pleasant, & once I am through with domestic
worries I shall enjoy it alot. At the moment I am having crisis after
crisis – sacking this person, consoling that, being in fact bread-winner
& house-wife combined – not pleasant, definitely. It's been hard to
work on top of it all – but I have been hard at the big B.B.C. Holy
show[1] & nearly got that off my chest. It may be useful to you. I
have had to put the old Concerto aside for a bit – so your letter
re. Henry Wood was abit of a shock. I wonder if you could use
your proverbial tact & keep him quiet for a week or two to give
me time to finish the sketch, prepare the two-piano version, &
practise the damn thing. Failing this I could play over bits to him
in London next week, but I should much prefer the other. So
please – !

I heard Heward[2] do the Variations last night – not so bad. I heard
a rumour that they are down for the Proms.[3] Which would be
nice. After this I am hot for the ballet I've got a good story & full
of grand ideas – it's going to be a Winner!

I am up next week & shall come & see what you've fixed with
Henry Wood, so don't bother to write.

Thank you again alot for the present – I am really & truly very
grateful & thrilled by it.

Yours ever,
BENJAMIN

P.S.   Could you please tell Chapman that the Fiddle Suite [op. 6]
lasts, as far as I can remember, about 19–20 mins. (or less).

1   *The World of the Spirit*, compiled by Richard Ellis Roberts and produced by Robin Whitworth (who had been responsible for *The Company of Heaven*). It was first broadcast on 5 June 1938 by Sophie Wyss;
Anne Wood (b. 1907), English contralto; Emlyn Bebb, tenor; Victor
Harding, Australian bass-baritone; and the BBC Singers and Orchestra, conducted by Trevor Harvey. Britten's score uses the plainsong
melody 'Veni Creator Spiritus' (a text set by Mahler in his Eighth
Symphony, which Britten had very recently heard). See also GE,
pp. 44–72, and PR, pp. 583–7.

The birth of this Whitsun radio feature was not easy, as Britten's
diary indicates:

2 June
Spend most of day rehearsing at Maida Vale Studios & B. [Broadcasting]

House. It goes fairly well considering lack of time – but a record is made of the last run through which is not good – & consequently the dramatic side complain about the quality of the music.

3 June
The rest of the day is spent in hysterical crises at BBC. The production people <u>won't</u> see that the music sounds bad only because of no rehearsal – finally I threaten to withdraw it – which causes a little sobriety. Very, very disturbing.

5 June
Rehearsal for Whit programme goes well – & they are reconciled – all of them. The evening show goes better – & I'm invited to do the rest of the Series – shows what a little Temperament can do.

Britten was to compose no further radio scores of this religious character. However, a further performance of *The World of the Spirit* was broadcast on 28 May 1939.

2 Leslie Heward (1897–1943), English conductor and composer. He succeeded Boult in 1930 as Principal Conductor of the City of Birmingham Orchestra, a post he held until his death.

3 On 7 September Britten was to conduct the BBC Symphony Orchestra in his *Frank Bridge Variations* at the Queen's Hall, London, his first appearance at the Proms as a conductor. The remainder of the programme was conducted by Henry Wood.
    Britten's principal experience to date as a conductor had been conducting the première of *Our Hunting Fathers* in 1936, when the orchestra had given him a hard time. To prepare for the Proms performance of the *Variations*, he sought lessons from Bridge, when visiting Friston in August. On the 19th, Marjorie Fass wrote about Britten to Daphne Oliver:

He's frantically working today to get some film music written by tomorrow night & then is coming to the Brits for a weekend because he wants Franco to teach him more abt conducting.

A further letter followed on the 22nd:

[. . .] today they worked, Fco [Franco] & Benjy, from the score as the records [conducted by Boyd Neel] are too wrong for Benjy to learn to conduct from. If he goes on for ever he'll <u>never</u> be a conductor – you never saw anything so stiff & held in – Eth or even I cld do better with Mr Brit's marvellous teaching to help us. I was alone here with the 2 this morning – & they didn't mind me being here. It was a privilege.

Fass was wrong in her prediction. But interestingly, though Britten was to become that very rare thing, a conductor of and for musicians, *par excellence*, something of the 'stiffness' to which Fass refers remained as part of his characteristic posture on the podium. (See also note 2 to Letter 11.)

133 To Kenneth Wright
BBC

[*Postcard*]

43. Nevern Square, S.W. [5]
[Postmarked Snape, 28 May 1938]

Dear Kenneth,

The Concerto's going fine – but it's been abit held up by some stuff I've been doing for another section of your Institution for Whitsun – which actually has turned out to be an Oratorio in the grand style. However – the Concerto will be done soon after Whit & I'll be along at once to show it you.

Best wishes,
BENJAMIN BRITTEN

134 To Benjamin Britten
From Peter Pears

I hope to get up on June 20th – can you get me a ticket?[1] Shall I see you?

The Old Cottage
Laughton
Lewes.
[After 30 May and before 5 June 1938]

Benjie my dear –

I was so very sorry not to find you in on Wednesday – I feared that I wouldn't but hoped to. I had the heaviest cold in history and so I fled back here as soon as I could, although I had thought of creeping into a Toscanini rehearsal. How are you, my dear? The flat looked as though you might have been entertaining someone – perhaps Francis?[2] or not yet? Tell me about it.

Things here go on just the same or thereabouts.[3] We started Figaro performances last week and The Don starts on Friday. (I enclose the Pasquale dress rehearsal tickets.) I am enjoying enormously really getting to know my Mozart operas. Figaro really is the most sublime work. The scoring of Susanna's aria "Venite inginocchiatevi" is magical.

I miss you very much, Benjie – and although a nice person called Denis Mulgan[4] has come to live with us, I am bored by everyone in the house and long for congenial company. Basil was down for a weekend which was nice, but it would be lovely to see you.

I'm hoping to go motoring with Mike in July abroad.   Will it come off? I pray it will.

> Write to me again.
>
> Lots of love
>
> PETER

Just as I had finished licking the envelope of this, your letter came. Francis sounds quite fascinating and just the sort of person I should hopelessly lose my heart to.

My racket came very quickly and I am playing a little 3rd rate tennis. But my bloody cold won't go. We have a lot of running about and changing to do in Macbeth and one is always in drafts (or draughts?), so colds stick.

I hope you enjoyed Toscanini.[5] I listened to some, but our set went bad on us. The soloists sounded rather a mixed lot. Roswaenge too Wagnerian? Thorborg a bit flat? Soprano shrill and bass not heavy enough?

Exciting about Osbert.[6] Make him do a Tenor Cantata!!

I'm running mildly after a sweet tough Stage Hand but as usual I can't come to the point!!

I miss you v.v. much. Everyone's opinions here are so very reactionary and capitalist!

Much Love, Benjie darling. Give some to Lennox & Dorothy W. but keep most of it for yourself. Has On this Island Vol 1 appeared yet? Do send me a copy when it does.

I'm doing a little playing for Heddle Nash which is rather funny. I will listen at Whitsun.

1 A Toscanini concert that Britten was to attend with John Pudney.

2 Francis Barton.

3 Pears was singing at Glyndebourne as a member of the chorus. Nancy Evans (also a member of the chorus) remembers him as

tall, fair-haired, reserved and poetic-looking. I was too shy to talk to him much. He was Ebert's obvious choice for the Ghost of Il Re Duncano in Verdi's *Macbeth*, and that scene remains vividly in my mind. Ebert produced us all as individual characters, and in *Don Pasquale* the main chorus scene was encored at each performance.

> (PPT, p. 33)

4 The New Zealand-born pianist and oboist (b. 1915), a member of Glyndebourne's music staff, 1938–9.

5 On 30 May Britten had been at a performance of Verdi's *Requiem*

conducted by Toscanini. Helge Rosvaenge (1897–1972), Danish tenor, was particularly well known for his Italian repertory.

6 Osbert Sitwell, who would provide a text? See Addenda 2, note 8.

135 To Boyd Neel

43, Nevern Square, S.W. 5.
June 21st, 1938.

My dear Boyd,

Just a scribble to say how <u>very</u> pleased I was with the way you did the Variations last night.[1] I am delighted that you eventually did them – it was much wiser – with that shortage of rehearsal, & owing to the fact that your band is so much happier with you than with anyone else.[2] But, besides that, you really understand them so well – and make such a splendid show. The lovely reception that it had was owing to your work & the band's. I do hope you'll do it often again. I'm looking forward a heap to the recording.[3]

I searched every nook & cranny of the BBC. last night for you, both in the interval & after the concert – where did you hop off to?

Many, many thanks, again
Yours ever,
BENJAMIN B

1 The Boyd Neel String Orchestra had performed the *Variations on a Theme of Frank Bridge* in the Concert Hall of Broadcasting House, London, as part of the 16th ISCM Festival, 17–24 June, for which occasion Britten provided the following programme note:

After a short introduction, a solo quartet plays the theme, and the full orchestra repeats it.

Var. I (*Adagio*). Sustained chords in lower strings with interjections from the violins.

Var. II (March). Fast and dotted rhythms.

Var. III (Romance). A tune on the violins with the theme in the bass.

Var. IV (Aria Italiana). First violins 'con bravura' with thrummed accompaniment.

Var. V (Bourrée classique). Heavy and marked. A violin solo in the middle.

Var. VI (Wiener Walz). Many prolonged 'upbeats', and a viola solo in the middle.

Var. VII (Moto perpetuo). Everyone in unison.

Var. VIII (Funeral March). Marked bass with sustained upper parts.

Var. IX (Chant). Violas 'soli' in three parts.

Var. X (Fugue and Finale). Fugue in four sections: (I) fast and light, (II) prominent bass, (III) loud and marked, (IV) muted and pp with Canto Fermo for four soloists. The Finale repeats the tune complete and there is a short Coda.

Alan Frank wrote about the *Bridge Variations* in the *Musical Times*, July 1938, p. 537, in an article reviewing the Festival:

Britten's Variations for string orchestra, brilliantly written though they are, do not wear well, and fail to achieve coherence as a whole. Is it not time that Britten, easily the brightest of the really young English composers, began to settle down again and to start writing music as good as his earliest works were?

Frank continued, 'Lennox Berkeley's new choral work, "Domini est Terra", did not cut much ice [. . .]'.

The same concert included Bartók's Sonata for Two Pianos and Percussion, played by Béla and Ditta Bartók.

In the afternoon of that same day Britten and Bartók had both performed (although not jointly) in a concert of 'Modern Music from catalogues controlled by Boosey & Hawkes Ltd', for ISCM delegates only, at the Music Studio of Boosey & Hawkes in their offices in Regent Street. Britten, with the violinist Frederick Grinke, performed his Suite, Op. 6. The critic of *The Times*, 22 June, wrote:

The difficulty with Mr Britten is to know whether he is being serious or not. Is the march in this suite, for instance, intended to emulate or to parody Anton Webern? Whichever answer is given, this exiguously notated piece proved ineffective in performance. The best movement in the suite is the waltz, about the intention of which there can be no doubt. Elsewhere the music did not produce results commensurate with its cleverness.

The critic of *Musical Opinion*, July 1938, was kinder:

I would like to prophesy that, when he has sowed his (musical) wild oats, he will return like other straying sheep to the fold. Britten is talented, and being a really accomplished pianist, was able, with Frederick Grinke, to interpret his Suite for violin and piano exactly as he felt it. This short panoramic Suite of invention and moods contained a Lullaby of rare imaginative fantasy. Here are the indications of great things by the composer in maturity.

Bartók played a selection of pieces from the *Mikrokosmos*. The concert also included the concert première of Ireland's Piano Trio No. 3 in E. See also Malcolm Gillies, *Bartók in Britain: A Guided Tour* (Oxford, Clarendon Press, 1989), pp. 109–10.

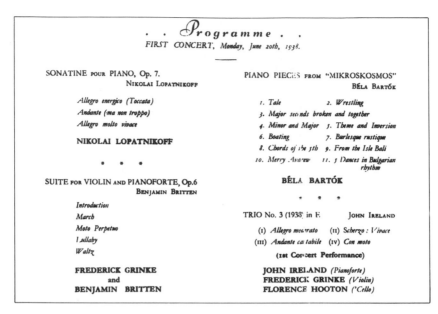

The programme of the first of the Two Concerts of Modern Music, 20 June 1938

2 Presumably Britten had been invited to conduct the performance.

3 Boyd Neel and his orchestra recorded the *Bridge Variations* on 15 July for Decca. The discs were released later in the year on Decca x226–8, with 'descriptive notes' by Henry Boys. Neel re-recorded the piece in 1949 (Decca AK 2307–9) and again in 1952 (Decca LXT 2790).

> **MERCURY.**   **6.30 & 9.**   **THE BINYON**
> **PUPPET SHOW 1938**
> **Words : Montagu Slater.**   **Music : Britten-Berkeley.**

Performances of *The Binyon Puppet Show* took place in June (see note 1 to Letter 98)

136   To Wulff Scherchen[1]

~~The M.M. Club,~~
~~14 Argyll Street,~~
~~Oxford Circus, W.1.~~
43, Nevern Square, S.W. 5.
[25 June 1938]

Dear Wulf,

I do not know whether you will remember me or not – but in 1934 – during the Festival of Modern Music in Florence – we spent a long time together – especially one day in Siena.[2] I have been seeing your father[3] a lot in London this last week, & he suggested that I should write to you.

I have now got a flat in London – but I live mostly in a windmill in Suffolk – not so very far from Cambridge. I should very much like to see you again. I suppose you can't get away from Cambridge during the term?[4] If so I might come & fetch you in a car. Otherwise when do you next come to London? Are you going to Neuchatel[5] for your holidays? If so I might meet you when you travel through London.

Anyhow, do write to me, & I am sure we shall be able to arrange something.

Yours sincerely,
BENJAMIN BRITTEN

1 The son (b. 1920) of Hermann and Gustel Scherchen.
2 At the 1934 ISCM Festival, Britten and Pounder had stayed at the Pension Balestri (though sleeping out at a nearby Pension, as the Balestri was full), where Hermann Scherchen and his family were also in residence. The day after the performance of Britten's *Phantasy Quartet* there was a Festival excursion to Siena. Britten's diary for 6 April reads:

Leave Flor. at 8.45 and go by omnibuses – 5 of them. It pours with rain all day so Siena is rather lost on us. Lunch given by the Mayor etc. – visits to Cathedral. Young Wulff Scherchen (son of Hermann) attaches himself to me, & I spend all the time with him.

Britten met Wulff for a short walk the next morning before leaving Florence for home. He had received a telegram telling him to return, as his father was 'not so well'. In fact, Mr Britten had died on the 6th, the day of the Siena excursion.

The visit to Siena and the rain (see also Letter 139) were remembered by the composer until the end of his life. Over fifty years later, in 1989, Wulff Scherchen also had a vivid memory of the occasion:

A light shower caught us as we walked on towards Siena. Ben happened to be carrying a mac which he insisted we share. He had his right arm in one sleeve I had my left in the other. We found the experience uproarious, as did the rest of our party. Though nothing of any consequence was said or done at the time, it was an occasion of light-hearted and shared contentment which I still recall with fondness & pleasure.

In 1938 he answered Britten's letter the next day:

Wasn't that day in Siena a whole 'family' outing, with the whole orchestra and that wonderful saxophonist Rascher, who is by now professor in Sweden or somewhere? We two went to the piazza something or other and explored the 'guildahalla'. Nein? I was in shorts and sandals (as I am now) and it started to rain. I got thoroughly wet, but it was worth it – 'pleasant reminiscences of a glorious past!' (Excuse my poetic strain.)

On 8 December 1939 Britten wrote to Wulff from New York: 'the Mayers have a photo of that lodge where you & I sheltered from the rain [. . .] It brought back terrific memories!'

3 At the ISCM Festival. On 17 June at the opening orchestral concert Scherchen had conducted the first British performance of Webern's *Das Augenlicht*, Op. 26, for chorus and orchestra, and on 24 June Roberto Gerhard's *Albade, Interludi, i Dansa*. He was favourably impressed by Britten's still relatively new *Bridge Variations*, and decided to include the work in his forthcoming orchestral programmes.

4 Wulff was living in Cambridge with his mother, and studying English, a move influenced by the darkening international situation in Europe. They were helped and advised by E.J. Dent, then Professor of Music at Cambridge, and President of the ISCM, in which capacity he was close to Wulff's father.

5 In Switzerland, where Hermann Scherchen was living and continuing his life as a peripatetic conductor.

137 To Sophie Wyss

Friston Field, Near Eastbourne, Sussex.
June 26th, 1938.

Dear Sophie,

I think you sang simply beautifully on Friday evening[1] – I was everso proud to know you! And you looked grand too – you must <u>always</u> wear white now. Arnold's got grand taste.

I saw the artist Tchelichew[2] on Friday evening & he says that they want us to go to Mrs. Von Hoffmanstall[3] at Hanover Lodge, Regent's Park at 5.0 on Tuesday – instead of to Edward James'.[4] I do hope you can manage it, to come & go through the songs again.[5] I am fearfully keen for Mrs. Von H. to hear the songs – who knows, she is fearfully rich (one of the Astors) & may do something for us – !!! I am getting frightfully political in my old age!

I am back on Tuesday afternoon. Would you care to come to Nevern Square about 4.0–4.30, & we could go on together? Anyhow I will telephone you when I arrive – about 2.30 or 3.0.

Love to you all. I did enjoy last Sunday. When are you coming to Peasenhall for a week-end?

Yours ever,
BENJAMIN

1 Sophie Wyss had taken part in the final concert of the ISCM Festival, broadcast from the Queen's Hall on 24 June. With Parry Jones and William Parsons, the English bass, she had performed excerpts from the oratario *Das Gesicht Jesajas* (1933–5) by the Swiss composer, Willy Burkhard (1900–1955). The BBC Orchestra, with the London Select Choir, was conducted by the Swiss conductor, Paul Sacher.

    The concert also included Copland's *El salón México* (1933–6) and excerpts from Hindemith's opera *Mathis der Maler* (1934–5). It was probably on this occasion that Britten and Copland first met.

2 Pavel Tchelitchew (1898–1957), the Russian-born neo-Romantic painter and stage-designer, and protégé of Edith Sitwell.

3 Alice von Hofmannsthal (née Astor), wife of Raimund von Hofmannsthal, the son of Richard Strauss's librettist. She was a keen patron of the arts, of ballet in particular, and was a close friend and supporter of Frederick Ashton. Britten's diary for 10 May reads:

[. . .] to Sadler's Wells for Gala performance of Ballet – inc. Lennox's new one (Judgement of Paris) – very good. After to party with Freddy Ashton – the dancers – & C. Lambert at Mrs. von Hofmannstall – very good too.

4 A notable patron of the arts who had founded the adventurous, though short-lived, company, 'Ballets 1933'.

5 Probably *On this Island*, which Wyss had first performed in November 1937.

138 To Ralph Hawkes

The Old Mill, Snape, Suffolk.
June 28th, 1938.

My dear Ralph,

    Thanks alot for the letter. The Concerto is now forging ahead. It was held up abit by all the Festivities last week, but I've got down to it again now. The sketch is nearly finished, & the score shouldn't take much more than a week to do. I can promise you a full length show of it by July 14th![1] Could you please tell Mr. Rosen that I'll send him details of length & titles & all that sort of thing at the end of the week?

    I think the Festival went well – certainly the Variations went as well as they could, & if half of the promised performances come off it ought to keep us busy! I met lots of people.

    There's one point – lots of conductors asked me for the score – & I told them where it could be got – but several wouldn't take the hint. I've used up my stock I'm afraid – so what do you think? The two outstanding cases are at the moment: Fritz Busch[2] (the

Opera House, Glyndebourne), & Frederick Ashton[3] (5, Guildford Place, W.C.1.). The first wants to do the work with his Orchestra in Denmark, & probably in South America; & the second shows great signs of wanting it as a ballet (both here and abroad). Anyhow I think they should both have copies – so could you please send them for me, & we can fight about the financial side later!!

M. Cuvelier[4] (who runs the Société Philharmonique de Bruxelles) also writes to know if he may borrow a copy of the score. He wants to do it next season at their concerts. (address: Palais de Beaux Arts de Bruxelles). ????

I'm fearfully anxious for you to cash in on Aaron Copland[5] – the American composer – now without publisher since Cos Cob Press gave up. His El Salon Mexico was the bright thing of the Festival. He's at the moment in Paris, & will be back in the middle of next month. May we arrange a meeting? I feel he's a winner somehow.

You may receive a letter from the Realist Film Unit about me doing a film for them.[6] As the mill is pretty expensive I'd better do it – as long as I needn't start on it before the end of July. Besides it sounds a nice idea, & not too long.

How's Firebird going? Anymore cups? Why didn't you have the gold one on view during the Festival?

Best wishes,
Yours ever,
BENJAMIN B.

1 On which date Britten had evidently promised to play it through to his publisher.

2 Fritz Busch (1890–1951), German conductor and pianist. After a distinguished early career in Germany, he left to begin his long association with the Danish Radio Symphony Orchestra. Busch was chiefly known in England for his pioneering work at Glyndebourne, particularly in the operas of Mozart, from 1934 to 1951.

3 Frederick Ashton (1904–1988), English dancer and choreographer, founder–choreographer of the Royal Ballet, of which he was Principal Choreographer, 1933–70, and Director, 1963–70. He was knighted in 1962. Ashton studied with Massine and Marie Rambert, beginning his work as a choreographer in 1926. In the early 1930s he choreographed for the Camargo Society, creating the one-act ballet *Façade* in 1931. He became chief choreographer of the Vic–Wells ballet in 1935, remaining with the company when it later became the Sadler's Wells and ultimately the Royal Ballet. Ashton was to produce the première of *Albert Herring* at Glyndebourne in June 1947, and choreographed the movement and the ballet sequences for *Death in Venice* in 1973.

4 Marcel Cuvelier (1899–1959), Director of the Société Philharmonique from 1927, and founder of Jeunesse Musicale in Brussels in 1945.

5 Aaron Copland (1900–1990), American composer, pianist, conductor, teacher, and writer on music. Copland and Britten had first met earlier in the month at the ISCM Festival in London, when *El salón México* was performed, an occasion recalled by Berkeley when writing to Britten in the USA on 5 January 1940:

I've got the score of Aaron's 'Salon Mexico'. I think it's marvellously done, and I've learnt a lot from it. It's perhaps in some ways a little too realistic, but it's a grand piece, and so living I shall never forget what a relief it was at that concert, after all that pretentious balderdash that we had to listen to.

For an account of this initial encounter and Copland's later visit to the Old Mill at Snape on 23–4 July, see Aaron Copland, 'A Visit to Snape', in TBB, pp. 71–3. Copland wrote to Britten on 3 August:

You and the Mill and Snape all made a very deep impression – much deeper than a mere week-end would imply. I remember every minute of it with pleasure – and hope you do the same [. . .] If you like to write letters – do write me. It would be nice to keep in touch with your triumphs and 'problems' [. . .] And best of luck on the 18th! [the first performance of Britten's Piano Concerto.]

It was on this occasion that Copland had played through his 'play-opera' in two acts, *The Second Hurricane* (see also note 2 to Letter 174), designed for 'high school' performance, with a libretto by Edward Denby (first staged in New York in April 1937, directed by Orson Welles). The experience left its own deep impression on Britten. There is not only a clear anticipation of *Paul Bunyan*, but also fascinating parallels, e.g. a chorus in the Copland – part of a 'Choral Overture', no less! – the text of which begins 'Once in a while something happens. Something happens, something exceptional.' (Compare the choral Prologue in *Paul Bunyan*, and its refrain: 'But once in a while the odd thing happens, / Once in a while the dream comes true.') In short, *The Second Hurricane* was one of the sources for the composition of *Bunyan*. The two composers' friendship flourished in the USA from 1939 to 1942; Letters 174, 178, 184 and 205 provide ample evidence of the warmth and importance of the relationship, which was also a creative one. Ralph Hawkes wisely accepted Britten's recommendation – 'It was good of you to approach Hawkes for me', Copland wrote on 7 July, 'I appreciate it a lot!' – and from 1938 Boosey & Hawkes were to be Copland's publishers. See also Aaron Copland and Vivian Perlis, *Copland: 1900 through 1942* (London, Faber and Faber, 1984), pp. 247 and 291–4; Philip Reed, 'Copland and Britten: A Composing Friendship', Aldeburgh Programme Book, 1990, pp. 28–9; obituaries by Hugo Cole, *Guardian*; Bayan Northcott, Peter Dickinson and Malcolm Williamson, *Independent*; and *The Times*, 4 December 1990; and John Rockwell, *New York Times*, 3 December 1990.

6 The Realist Film Unit production, *Advance Democracy*, written and directed by Ralph Bond (1906–1989), English film-maker, was made for the four London Co-operative Societies and released in October 1938. Britten's music includes a medley of various left-wing songs. See PR, pp. 489–90. He later composed a motet with the same title to words by Randall Swingler: see note 1 to Letter 159.

In May 1939, Bond once again approached Britten for incidental music for an unnamed film which he was producing for the Realist Film Unit in association with the London Co-operative Societies, unaware that the composer had already departed for North America. Ralph Hawkes, who was dealing with Britten's correspondence in his absence, suggested Lennox Berkeley might be approached.

139 To Wulff Scherchen

The Old Mill, Snape, Suffolk.
June 30th 1938.

My dear Wulf,

I was very pleased to get your letter – & pleased that it was such a nice one. About the start of it, I leave that absolutely to you – although if you dared to call me anything more formal than 'Benjamin' I should be very angry!

It is grand news that you are sometimes free for week-ends. When would you like to come to the Mill? I shall be here both next weekend (9th) & the one after (16th). Are either of these any good for you? If neither of these will do – something might be arranged later on, but I'm not certain of the dates yet. Where are you spending the summer holidays? I shall be here alot in August.

If by any chance you can come next week-end (& I hope you can) – could you get a bus or a train part of the way here – say to Stowmarket or even Bury St. Edmunds? I could meet you there & bring you back here – it would save alot of time. Think about it & let me know.

Yes, I have good recollections of Siena – but chiefly of rain. I don't think that I have ever been so wet. Quite alot of the people there have been in London for the Festival last week – it was nice to meet them again.

No – I'm afraid I cannot claim the music of the 'Taxi Girl'[1] film. I've done alot of film music, though; some quite amusing ones that I think you'd approve of – !![2]

Thank you for the programme of the Festival[3] – it looks as if I shall be too busy to get to it, but will see –

Please give my best wishes to your mother –
& alot for yourself
Yours ever
BENJAMIN B.

The above address will always get me.

1   *The Girl in the Taxi* (British Unity, 1937) – a comic tale charting the downward spiral of the head of a purity League who indulges in a dangerous adulterous flirtation – was directed by André Berthomie.

2   Wulff had written teasingly to Britten on 26 June:

> The day after I received your letter I went to see [. . .] the 'Girl in the taxi' (though how the devil she ever gets there heaven only knows). The musical background, and I suppose, all the off-stage noises, howls, shrieks, had been 'produced' by a certain somebody Britten. I hope it didn't wear all his brains out. The effort must have been terrific. Was it you by any chance?

3   The Cambridge Festival of Old English Music which was held from 30 July to 6 August 1938. Boris Ord (1897–1961) was the Musical Director.

140   To Ralph Hawkes

The Old Mill, Snape, Suffolk.
July 4th, 1938.

My dear Ralph,

Many thanks for your letter, with its numerous points.

The old Concerto is now finished, & I feel quite elated about it – Frank B. approves of what he's seen, & so does Lennox Berkeley – what the 'great unknown public' will think, we shan't know till after the prom. I am now going ahead with the rather boring job of writing out the full score.[1]

Mr. Rosen wanted to know several things about it – could you please give whoever is deputising for him the following data?

1.   Title: Pianoforte Concerto no. 1 in D major.
2.   First performance at Proms.? – quite definitely.
3.   Duration – roughly 30 mins.
4.   Instrumentation:
       2 Flutes (each playing piccolos)
       2 Oboes (2nd playing Cor Anglais)

          2 Clarinets

          2 Bassoons

          4 Horns

          2 Trumpets

          3 Trombones

          Tuba

          Timpani (chromatic)

          2 Percussion players (variety of instruments –
          including Whip)

          Harp

          Strings

          (& Piano Solo of course)

5.   Titles of movements: so far,

     1. Toccata

     2. Waltz

     3. Recitative & Aria[2] leading to:

     4. March

6.   Re publicity, I can't think of anything to say – except it's damn difficult to play!

I'm up on Wednesday to Friday, so I'll telephone you about the other matters.

I'll write to Szigeti,[3] re the Soirées Musicales.

It's fine about Firebird; I'm very glad. Is the 12th the beginning of the Baltic trip? How I envy you! I've just had to put off the Lewes tennis tournament because of the pressure of work – & am feeling very sick about it!

Best wishes & to Mrs. Hawkes,

Yours ever,

BENJAMIN B.

1 The manuscript full score is inscribed: 'Snape – July 26th 1938'.

2 The original third movement. In 1945 Britten substituted a newly composed Impromptu based on a theme taken from the incidental music to *King Arthur* which he had written in 1937. The first performance of the revised version with the new third movement was given at the 1946 Cheltenham Festival on 2 July, by Noel Mewton-Wood (piano), with the BBC Symphony Orchestra conducted by the composer. The abandoned Recitative and Aria movement was revived in a performance of the concerto at the 1989 Aldeburgh Festival. It was recorded for the first time in the same year and released by Collins Classics (1101–2) in 1990. See Eric Roseberry, 'Britten's Piano Concerto: the Original Version', *Tempo*, 172, March 1990, pp. 10–18.

3 Joseph Szigeti (1892–1973), American violinist of Hungarian birth, who wished to collaborate with Britten on a violin arrangement of the *Tarantella* from *Soirées Musicales*. Britten's letter to him has not been located.

141 To Kenneth Wright
BBC

The Old Mill, Snape.
July 17th 1938.

Dear Kenneth,

May I come sometime next Friday to play the work to you?[1] I am in town that day & if it suits you I can come along.

Will it be all right if I leave that little matter of the Radio Times & Alan Frank to you?[2] I've had a card from him, which I won't answer for a day or two.

I hope you are well & not too busy. I am looking forward to a respite from all this writing – but the score ought to be finished in a few days.

Wulff Scherchen, whom I gather you know, is here for a few days & wishes to be remembered to you.

Yours ever,
BENJAMIN BRITTEN

1 Wright replied on 18 July suggesting they meet on the 22nd, when Britten played through his concerto.

2 Britten was unhappy about the choice of Frank as author of an introductory article about the new concerto for the *Radio Times*. In his letter of 18 July Wright proposed that the matter should be discussed on the 22nd. In spite of the composer's objection, it was Frank who contributed an article, 'New Concerto', to the *Radio Times*, 12 August, p. 16:

Britten holds the view – again he is unorthodox – that music should be attractive to listen to: he dislikes this business of dividing music up into light and serious compartments – 'and never the twain shall meet'. (After all, the scherzo of the classical symphony is light music but that is no reason for banning it from a symphony concert.) Britten is no snob in his musical likes and dislikes. Last week, for example, while we were discussing our common enthusiasm for Marx (Bros. not Karl), he suddenly broke off and dived into a full score of *Rigoletto* with the words: 'Do you know that magnificent tune in the first act?'

All this is by way of preparing you for my view that this new Piano Concerto, which Britten is to play at the Proms, derives in spirit from

Tchaikovsky and perhaps Liszt. Not that there is any question of Britten's aping the style or idiom of either. Nothing is more annoying than the habit certain knowing people have of remarking, when they hear a perfectly good, straightforward, warm-hearted tune in a contemporary work: 'What delicious irony!' (Britten himself told me that in the present work he has purposely desisted from labelling the second movement 'Waltz', to prevent its being taken as a parody.) [The programme for the first performance (see PFL, plate 111) and the early published edition of the Concerto did not adhere to the movement titles specified by the composer in Letter 140, with the exception of the Recitative and Aria. Instead, conventional tempo indications were employed: *Allegro molto e con brio* (Toccata), *Allegretto, alla valse* (Waltz) and *Allegro moderato – sempre alla marcia* (March). Britten subsequently preferred to use the original movement titles.]

142 To Wulff Scherchen

~~19, The Mall, Surbiton~~ [1]
As from: The Old Mill, Snape
[July 1938]

[. . .]

The Concerto is not nearly done yet – quite desparate is the situation.[2] However, all my worldly wise friends tell me that most good work has been done under these conditions. I'll take their word for it – but it's damned tiring. The concert of Nazi-banned German music went off very well.[3] I did my part all right – & papers were very nice about it – but it was a nerve strain.

Here I am – wasting my time writing rot to you & the world is champing for my masterpiece – to it, then –

[. . .]

1 The home of Sophie Wyss and her husband, Arnold Gyde.

2 Britten was referring to the preparation of the full score of his Piano Concerto, the completion of the composition of which he had reported to Ralph Hawkes on 4 July. On 10 July he wrote to Hawkes's secretary, Edwina Jackson:

> Here is the 1st movement of the Concerto. I will send the rest as completed. Will you deliver to copyist? Tell them I will send title page at end.

Britten must have shown the concerto to Bridge, who wrote to his younger colleague on 10 July about a particular aspect of the orchestration in the first movement at Fig. 2:

> By the way – just one passing reflection. That rhythmic bass on leaps of a major seventh – if I remember correctly. Even if playable, it is so un-trombonish as not to be worthwhile! I would suggest you reconsider the point. My instinct is against doing this – but forget I've said so.

3 The details of the concert to which Britten refers remain untraced,

but it may have been connected with the 'Exhibition of 20th Century German Art', held at the New Burlington Galleries, London, in July 1938, which showed examples of the art the Nazis wished to suppress. They had denounced much contemporary German art, music and literature as 'degenerate and/or "bolshevist" '.

143 To Wulff Scherchen

The Old Mill, Snape, Suffolk.
August 1st 1938.

[. . .]

It was nice to hear your voice on the telephone last night – it is odd how American[1] you sound 'over the wire' – but nevertheless very pleasant! I hope you had a good journey & are enjoying yourself in Strassbourg – is your mother with you? What are you doing? I suppose that you're working very hard at the old languages. I should think that with your command of German & English & with the present brushing-up of your French you should be ripe for any scholarship.

Excuse the bad writing – but I am writing on my knee being only just allowed up from bed, having been ill for a bit from either (1) over-sunning (2) over eating (3) over-working (4) or over-emotion – anyhow the symptoms were unpleasant enough, & it was made all the more irritating by the fact that W.H. Auden, the poet I told you about, has been staying with me. He is just back from a tour in China[2] & consequently there is quite a bit to talk about – & he has to go to Brussels tonight. And the weather is baking (eminently bathable in). Very annoying.

Well – I can't write anymore now – I am in the middle of writing a description of my old Concerto for the programme on August 18th.[3] Mind you listen in hard – it is a thousand pities that you can't be there – at least I think it is!

I may (only may) go to your father at Neuchatel about September 10th for a few days.[4] But you won't be there I suppose? If I don't go there then I shall expect you at the Mill which is looking forward to seeing you again.

[. . .]

1 The well-known phenomenon of foreign voices, when speaking English on the telephone, appearing to have a distinct 'American' accent.

2 Auden and Isherwood had returned from the trip to China (January–July) which led to publication of their joint account of their

travels, *Journey to a War* (London, Faber and Faber, 1939). Britten was among those at Victoria Station who saw them off on 19 January. They returned to England mid-July, and Auden visited the Old Mill later that month, probably for the weekend of 30 July.

3 The first performance of the Piano Concerto was given in the 1938 Promenade Concerts Season at Queen's Hall, London, on 18 August, when the composer was soloist and the BBC Symphony Orchestra was conducted by Sir Henry Wood. For this occasion Britten wrote what was, for him, an unusually extensive programme note. It is reproduced in full in PFL, plate 111. The concert was broadcast.

4 Britten did not make this trip.

144 To Ralph Hawkes

The Old Mill, Snape, Suffolk.
August 6th, 1938.

My dear Ralph,

This is just to tell you that the first rehearsal went off well yesterday at Q.H.[1] It is still abit rough in spots, but the show with luck will be quite good. It certainly sounds 'popular' enough & people seem to like it all right. The piano part wasn't as impossible to play as I feared, & with a little practice this week ought to be O.K. I delivered the score to Rosen after the rehearsal to be photographed. It has suddenly struck me that a third score might be useful for one or two reasons (I suppose having two copies made is proportionately cheaper than one?) – such as:– if the private companies, you are going to get to record it, want to make a good job of it they ought to have a score to follow so that they make good breaks in it – if, (if), later the work gets performed abit, we might need the third score. But I bow to your judgement in this matter – it's only a suggestion.[2]

The records of the Variations are really fine.

I envy you on the water this week-end – but there doesn't seem to be much breeze for you. It's as hot as blazes here to-day. My bro. in-law was full of admiration of your 194 mile run.[3]

Yours ever
BEN

1 The schedule of rehearsals for the concerto, all held at the Queen's Hall, was as follows: '5th August; 16th (Artists' Room); 17th; and 18th, the final run-through.' Berkeley had written to Britten on 21 July:

I am looking forward to the 18th – I'm sure you're going to have a terrific success; and I hope that you will have a further success afterwards which I know you hope for. If music be indeed the food of love, I think you stand a very good chance.

Auden sent a telegram from Brussels on the occasion of the première on the 18th, 'VIVE LA MUSIQUE A BAS LES FEMMES. WYSTAN.' One cannot be sure that a kind of guide to seduction provided by Auden for Britten's use was related to this particular event, but Berkeley's letter and Auden's telegram make it relevant:

Dear Benjamin,

Nothing to worry about really. As I havent seen him, I can only guess at what happened, but human nature runs along certain lines.

1) You oughtnt to have given him the chance of going to the Corner House.

2) Did you play the piano. Most important.

3) I'm afraid like many people he enjoys a feminine love of power. The correct line is

    a) To appear comparatively indifferent emotionally

    b) To take not the slightest notice of a refusal.

Remember he WANTS to be mastered.

Future Policy

What you did before with such success. A slight coldness. Quite friendly, but cold. And LOTS of music. Suggest a little temporary infidelity.

PERMANANDO VINCIMUS

best love

WYSTAN

(Berg Collection, New York Public Library)

Had Auden written 'permanendo vincimus' we should clearly have translated this as a rallying cry – 'we conquer by persevering'. But the Audenesque substitution of an *a* for an *e*, 'permanando vincimus', leads to the speculation that Auden was sharing a sexual joke with his friend – a *double entendre*, 'we bind by penetrating'.

Later in August Auden returned to the subject of the Piano Concerto and his telegram. He wrote in an undated letter from Brussels:

I hope you got my telegram. I ran all over the place trying to find a radio which would give London Regional without success. I was furious. Do write & tell me about it. I gather from the rather snooty notice in the The Times which is the only one I've seen that it had an enthusiastic reception. And what about its effect on a certain person of importance?

If you are taking a holiday in Sept. why not come here for a few days. I've got something waiting here for you that will make you crazy. 16 tries to pick up a living by singing in the street (tenor Rossignol he calls his voice) Mother dead. Father drinks. Shall I get a photo? Such eyes. O la, la.

Love

WYSTAN

See also note 2 to Letter 164.

2 Kenneth Wright had written to Hawkes on 25 July inviting him to organize a private recording of Britten's performance of the Piano Concerto, to enable foreign conductors to get to know the piece. Hawkes had already arranged for this to be done. The 78 rpm discs made on this occasion are missing.

3 Kit Welford – like Ralph Hawkes – was a keen yachtsman.

145 To Mary Behrend

Old Mill, Snape, Suffolk
Aug. 26th 1938

Dear Mrs. Behrend,

I am so glad you 'got' the Concerto. So many of the beastly critics didn't, & it's so depressing.[1] However the audience seemed to – for a wonder. I can't see anything problematic about the work. I should have thought that it was the kind of music that either one liked or disliked – it is so simple – & cannot make out why it is that they have to hunt for programmes & 'meanings' and all that rot! However, I have three performances already booked, so I mustn't complain. It was disappointing not to see any of you after the show. I caught a glimpse of George – but no more. I suppose you're off on your holiday now. Have a nice time.

I'm looking forward to my September 'off' music. It'll be a change!

Excuse scribble, but I'm just off to London & in great hurry.

With love to you all,
BENJAMIN B

1 What Britten does not mention in his letter – and of far greater interest than most of the reviews that are reproduced below – was the reaction of the Bridge circle, fully reported by Marjorie Fass in a letter to Daphne Oliver that was written the day after the concerto's première:

Thanks, dear Bidy, for the photos returned & for the mushrooms which were eaten by the Brit family for hightea before going to the Prom – & were very good & fresh –

I expect you'll have been as disappointed in Benjy's work as we were & loving him so much made it difficult for us, as we cldn't hurt his feelings before the event, as the knowledge of our opinion would easily have done. In one way, because he has so many young friends who adore & flatter him for his brilliant talent & who only live on the superficial side of life, it won't hurt him at all, but pull him up, if the criticisms in the papers are harsh. The orchestra & Wood liked the work very much – as it's amusing to play

– & every orchestral device is employed with brilliance. – but of <u>music</u> <u>or</u> [illegible: ? originality] there is no trace – And if Benjy develops some day later on, he will see the insignificance of this work as it must be to all real musicians. Poor little boy, he was overworked & tired & played much worse at the show than at the rehearsal. I liked the work too little to want to sit through the 2nd rehearsal – so I went to the German pictures instead, which were as bad or worse – but I felt having a free morning I must go & see them.

Although Fass does not specifically mention Bridge, there can be little doubt that what she wrote represented his views too, though as a later letter (22 August) to Daphne Oliver makes clear, these were views that were not directly conveyed to the composer:

We've had a heavenly Brit Benjy Brosa weekend with the Speyers [Ferdinand and Dorothea, friends of the Bridges from Seaford] to tea yesterday & everything including the sunshine just perfect. Without previous discussion the Brosi & Speyers felt exactly as we did abt Benjy's piano work – & we all utterly agree with the drastic criticisms of The Times & Sunday Times & Observer & Telegraph which is all we've seen – Dear Benjy doesn't know how deeply disappointed we all are, but he will one day. We all adored the Dvorak [Eighth Symphony] after the Benjy work & <u>all</u> said the same thing of it – <u>here</u> is music – & in its degree beautifully made – what a relief – [. . .]

But his friends' negative response must have been evident to him when he played them an off-the-air recording of the concerto's première, an occasion Fass describes in the same letter and which clearly took on the character of a post-mortem, though one may be sure that Bridge did his best to be constructive:

Benjy had brought records of the [Bridge] Variations & of his piano work – Last night we all sat with shut faces while he put on the piano work & Mr Brit followed the score & told him various things about it – & poor Toni & Bill [Mrs Bridge] both got the fidgets & Peggy sat like a statue – & when we had the variations at last we cld smile.

These intimations of disapproval can have made the generally unfavourable press reception no easier to bear.

'F.B.' [Ferruccio Bonavia] in the *Daily Telegraph*, 'Playboy of Music', 19 August, p. 10, had written:

His writing is extremely facile and, if anything, too brilliant. It may be fashionable to use and abuse percussion instruments; but the result lacks finesse and, in conjunction with a solo instrument, balance. There were moments when Mr Britten, who played the solo part, laboured mightily without making an impression against the heavy volume of orchestral sound.

Better things are found here and there. The individual character of the lower strings is exploited very effectively, and the harp is often used in telling and individual fashion. But the concerto, as a whole, does not answer the questions and doubts it prompts.

Its outlook is modern, with many a backward glance; it has the pungent harmony of today and also the broad string phrases of the 'eighties. It is jolly and pleasant enough up to a point – but Mr Britten will do better things and more substantial things when his thoughts turn, as they must, to matter rather than manner.

William McNaught, in the *Musical Times*, September 1938, p. 703, was equally unenthusiastic:

[. . .] Mr Britten as pianist, spent a great deal of his time in rapid splash-work, largely of a harmonic order, and indefinite in outline, that contributed little to the musical interest and was moreover overborne by the orchestra. [. . .] the orchestra was anything but accompaniment. It was the main instrument and source of ideas. This is not a stylish work. Mr Britten's cleverness, of which he has frequently been told, has got the better of him and led him into all sorts of errors, the worst of which are errors of taste. How did he come to write the tune of the last movement? Now and then real music crops up, worthy of the composer of the *Variations on a Theme of Frank Bridge*; but on the whole Mr Britten is exploiting a brilliant faculty that ought to be kept in subservience.

W.H. Haddon Squire, in the *Christian Science Monitor*, [?] August, also drew comparisons between the concerto and the *Bridge Variations*, but in a more positive spirit:

At the recent International Festival for Contemporary Music many were struck by a work called Variations on a Theme of Frank Bridge, for string orchestra. It was one of the successes of the week. The ear was caught by a youthful note of freshness and vitality. A lively sense of humour and a touch of caricature were not the least attractive qualities of a work cast in a form that demands considerable fertility of resource and imagination. The slickness and spontaneity of the writing were in marked contrast to the tortuous cerebration that had gone to the manufacture of certain other festival works, works nearly as festive as a wet Sunday afternoon in Manchester. It was the difference between ersatz and the genuine article, between 'talent-lessness' and actual talent. [. . .]
    This concerto is, in the best sense of the word, youthful; its weaknesses are mostly those of youth. Elderly criticism may be expected to and no doubt will do its duty. But it is also a duty to point out that here is a musician of genuine and unusual talent. In any case, why should not a young composer be allowed to sow his wild notes? One can well believe the statement in the programme – not by the composer – that, 'beginning to compose original music at an age when most young people are struggling with pothooks in their first efforts at handwriting, Britten emerged as an astonishingly mature master of his craft while yet in his teens'. That is the way of real talent. If in this concerto there is an overflow of youthful exuberance, a musical self-confidence on the edge of impudence, there is also an individuality of outlook that flatters neither an admiration nor a fashion. When the serious artist develops to the measure of the craftsman, for which there is plenty of time, one hopes that he will not entirely abandon jest and youthful jollity. There is precious little humour in contemporary music – always excepting the unconscious kind, of course.

The Times, 19 August, carried the following notice:

[. . .] This is the most important work the composer has written, though it still fails to fulfil entirely the promise of his obvious talent. That Britten has a remarkable mastery of technical resources has been evident for some time, and this concerto fully confirms that impression. The writing both for the pianoforte and the orchestra is brilliant and effective. The form, too, in which the work is cast is original without being obscure, even as the harmony is 'contemporary' without being unintelligible at a first hearing. Indeed, the clarity both of form and texture is the best feature of the work.

It is the content that raises doubts concerning the real merit of a work that surely aspires to a higher status than a clever *jeu d'esprit*. There are, indeed, moments of seriousness and genuine romantic feeling at the ends of the first and third movements. The close of the opening Allegro was, indeed, so beautiful that it aroused great hopes of what was to come later. But satire kept breaking in, and, unlike cheerfulness, satire is a dangerous element in music. For one thing it sets the hearer on his guard against taking anything at its face value. For instance, is the end of the third movement, which is rather commonplace in its romanticism, meant seriously, or is the composer's tongue still in his cheek, as it is during the first part of the movement?

The second movement, a valse-scherzo, is elegant, and would make an effective contrast to more serious matter elsewhere, but the Finale seems to have some 'ideological' motive behind it which merely betrays the composer into an angry blatancy. The anger may do credit to his feelings, but its expression does less to his taste. Nevertheless, this is one of the most interesting novelties we have had at the Proms for some time, and its reception by the large audience was genuinely enthusiastic.

Constant Lambert wrote in the *Listener*, 25 August, p. 412:

It was good to hear so enterprising a work as Britten's new piano concerto given the rousing reception it received the other night. The enthusiasm was partly a tribute to the work itself, partly a tribute to the brilliant fashion in which the composer played his own exacting piano part. The concerto has one sterling merit – it is never boring. Wit and invention are to be found in every movement but to one listener at least it came as a slight disappointment after the same composer's brilliant variations for strings. The string variations have wit and invention also, but they have something more besides – a unifying conception of form and style which is what I felt the concerto to be lacking in. The first movement is admirable throughout and the second, a valse, is a fascinating psychological study. It is neither a 'straight' valse nor a 'cod' valse but hovers cynically and convincingly between the two. After the valse the composer seems to lose his grip on the work. There are effective and brilliant things in both the last movements but they sound like essays in texture rather than a direct expression of musical thought. For example the juicy tune in the slow movement sounds to me as if the composer wanted to show us that he could write this sort of thing if he wanted to – I do not feel that it is an essential part of his conception.

I may be wrong in my imputation of motive, and I sincerely hope so. It may only be that Britten, like many composers before him, is finding it difficult to fuse into an artistic whole two apparently opposed sides of his nature. The same criticism that I have made of this work could equally well be levelled at Prokofieff's First Piano Concerto, and we all know how triumphantly he solved the problem in his Third Concerto. It is only because Britten has such undeniable and exceptional talent that one judges him by the highest and most exacting standards. No composer of today has greater fluency or greater natural gifts. For that very reason the temptation to fritter these gifts away must be more than usually great. Britten made both a brilliant and solid beginning at an unusually early age with his choral variations 'A Boy was Born'. Subsequent works showed an increasing brilliancy of technique but hardly an added maturity of thought – that is until we came to the string variations, which are of considerable importance quite apart from their merits as a show piece. It is to be hoped that Britten will develop along the lines suggested by these variations. He need have no fear of being dull or portentous. His natural quick-wittedness will obviously save him from that. His only danger as far as I can see is that of turning out one show piece after another, of being more concerned with texture than with content. Not that anyone but a sentimental amateur despises brilliance of texture but it should be an essential part of the thought – as with Debussy, not a mere surface glitter – as with Respighi.

I should not like it to be thought that what I have said is in any way a denigration of the undoubted effectiveness of Britten's Concerto. Brilliantly written for both soloist and orchestra it is in every way a welcome addition to the very limited repertoire of modern English concertos. It is only because I feel that Britten has it in him to write a really great concerto that I take the trouble to criticise him from what may seem to others an over-exacting point of view.

146 To Wulff Scherchen

Old Mill, Snape, Suffolk.
Aug. 29th, 1938

[. . .]

Thank you alot for your long card – long in content, anyhow. I was pleased to hear that you listened-in to the Concerto, & sorry that it came over badly – as it must have done if the Finale sounded 'pompous' – which I can assure you it is not, whatever else may be! Anyhow I'm glad to know that you recognised the work as mine & that quality about it which reminded you of the Mill. That certainly pleased me!

Critics were varied – but all were heated – in fact there's the devil of a discussion going on now about it, the only person unaffected being the composer! I had a tremendous amount of press, which is the best thing of all. What annoyed one or two critics was that it went down so well with the obviously 'lay' audience!

However ——

You will probably be back about the 1st or 2nd weeks in

September then? You seem to have been working very hard. What exam then? Are you going to Neuchatel?

My plans are this: I'm here, on & off until Sept. 7th when I've got to conduct at the Queen's Hall[1] – I then go to Worcester[2] for 3 or 4 days then back here. I'm ready for you to come here as soon as you wish after that. What about 11th or 12th?

Be a dear & let me have a note saying approximately what your plans are – as I've got to fix things. I <u>may</u> go to Brussels[3] for abit – ditto, Basel & possibly Neuchatel. But alot depends on when (& if!) you wish to come here.[4]

Please excuse the scribble – but I've been writing & still have got to write hundreds of letters about this blinking Concerto – & it's very late now. The Mill is looking very nice – we've got the gate altered & are starting the garden. Some work for you when you come, old thing!

[. . .]

1 See note 3 to Letter 132.
2 Probably to visit his godmother, Julianne Painter.
3 See note 2 to Letter 164.
4 Wulff wrote to Britten on 9 September from Neuchatel:

> [. . .] my father has decided to keep me here till about the 15. or 17., in order to enable [me] to take a few lessons in French here. [. . .] I won't be able to come to the mill, much as I want to. [. . .] I don't suppose you could possibly come down here, to my father [. . .]?

147 To Kenneth Wright
BBC

Old Mill, Snape, Suffolk
Sept. 1st 1938.

Dear Kenneth,

Thank you for your letter. I am sorry not to have been able to answer you by return as you wished, but I was away until late last night – & posts go early in this out of the way spot! However, I dare say this will reach you somehow.

Yes, as far as I know, there has been no Semitic ('Semitic', I believe, being considered the opposite of 'Aryan'!!) blood in our family. But I shouldn't bother about anything in Germany for me or the Concerto – because, even if you succeeded in getting a date for me there, I don't feel I could accept it.[1] Admittedly music has nothing to do with politics – but when politics pokes its slimy finger into music that's a different matter.

Thank you alot for all you are doing – I think you are rendering a great service to music by your grand propaganda methods. I wish I could think that it would make some difference politically – but the world is mad, & nothing less than an earthquake on Berlin (or Berchtesgarten)² will do that.

Best wishes,

Yours ever,

BENJAMIN B.

1 A letter from Kenneth Wright to Arthur Bliss, dated 9 May 1938, suggests that he had Britten in mind as an appropriate British composer for the 1939 Baden-Baden Festival:

> I feel it very important that there should be occasional first performances of British works in such festivals or series alongside Bartók, Honegger, Malipiero and the others. It all helps to line us up – as we can so easily be lined up – with music creation elsewhere. If you can't manage anything for Baden-Baden for 1939 I shall try Vaughan Williams or Britten, but I think you are a much more suitable composer for 'young Germany' in your present form.

2 Berchtesgaden was Hitler's country retreat in Bavaria.

---

246   **THE P.R. GAZETTE**   [JANUARY, 1937.

The Congress of the International Confederation of Authors' and Composers' Societies.

Ine importance attached to the event by the German Government is evident from the fact that Dr. Goebbels, the Minister for Press and Propaganda, acted as Patron of the Congress, presiding over a Committee of Honour consisting of many prominent officials, including Dr. Frank (President of the Akademie für Deutsches Recht), Dr. Gurtner (Minister of Justice), Freiherr von Neurath (Minister for Foreign Affairs), Dr. Walter Funk (Secretary of State), and several others; the musical and literary side being represented on the Committee of Honour by such eminent personalities as Dr. Richard Strauss, Paul Lincke, Dr. Paul Graener and Herr Horst Sander, to name only a few.

Inaugural Meeting.

The formal opening of the Congress took place in the Alte Aula of the University of Berlin on Monday the 28th September, H.E. Dino Alfieri, President of the Confederation, presiding.

An address of welcome was given by the Secretary of State, Dr. Funk, who recalled that the German Government had given proof of the importance which it attached to the defence of Copyright by the promulgation of the Act of 4th July, 1933, and the formation of syndical bodies or Chambers in which were grouped authors, composers and publishers respectively. H.E. Dino Alfieri replied on behalf of the Confederation, in whose name telegrams were despatched to the Chancellor of the Reich and Dr. Goebbels, from whom replies were subsequently received as follows:

" My warmest thanks for the greetings extended to me by Your Excellency and those taking part in the Eleventh International Congress of Authors. Accept in return my best wishes for a fruitful outcome of your work."

(Signed) ADOLF HITLER.

" I thank you sincerely for your telegram, and extend to you my best wishes for a successful Congress in the interests of the art and culture of all nations taking part."

(Signed) REICHMINISTER DR. GOEBBELS.

From the *Performing Right Gazette*, January 1937

148 To Ralph Hawkes

Old Mill, Snape, Suffolk.

Sept. 4th, 1938.

Dear Ralph,

I thought I made it clear to you that I would accept any division of royalties you cared to make with Brian Easdale[1] for his arrangement of the Soirées Musicales. Very sorry if I didn't, & apologies for any delay caused.

I am up in town on Wednesday for the Variations at Q. Hall. Will you be there? I go to Worcester on the Thursday morning.

I see Noreen's[2] been doing some odd things. But you ran second to her didn't you?

Best wishes,

Yours ever,

BENJAMIN B.

Bournemouth's now fixed for Oct. 27th.[3]

1 Brian Easdale (b. 1909), English composer, studied piano, conducting and composition at the College, 1927–33, where he received second prize in the 1930 Cobbett Competition. During the 1930s he composed incidental music for documentary films, among them some originated by the GPO Film Unit, and acted as musical director for various theatres, most notably the Group Theatre, for its productions of *The Ascent of F6* (1937) and *On the Frontier* (1938) by Auden and Isherwood, and MacNeice's *Out of the Picture* (1937), all with music by Britten. In 1948 he composed the music for the Powell–Pressburger film *The Red Shoes* (1948), about the birth of a ballet. The English Opera Group gave the first performance of his opera *The Sleeping Children*, libretto by Tyrone Guthrie, at the 1951 Cheltenham Festival. In 1962 he composed the *Missa Coventrensis* for the newly built Coventry Cathedral. Easdale made a transcription for two pianos of Britten's *Soirées Musicales*, published by Boosey & Hawkes in 1938, and in 1939 a similar transcription of the Piano Concerto.

2 Presumably a racing yacht, like *Firebird*.

3 When the second performance of the Piano Concerto was given by the Bournemouth Municipal Orchestra, conducted by Sir Henry Wood, with Britten as soloist, at the Pavilion, Bournemouth. The concert was broadcast.

149 To Frank Bridge
[*Draft telegram*]

Royal Harwich Yacht Club[1]

[September 1938]

BRIDGE   PARK 5521

BEST LUCK   BON VOYAGE[2]   GOOD HEALTH STOP   BEASTLY JOURNEY
YESTERDAY   FOG.

LOVE

BENJAMIN

1 Britten was presumably sailing with Ralph Hawkes, who was a member of the Royal Harwich Yacht Club. He had sailed with Hawkes on a previous occasion that summer, writing in his diary:

8 June
Up early & leave 7.15 for Harwich by car [. . .] & join Ralph Hawkes on his Firebird (16 metre cutter) for 2 days racing. It is bewildering since I've had nothing ever to do with boats this size – 4 paid hands & 4 more to run her – but it is good fun – Race to Southend. 2nd in.

9 June
Race to day is round Mouse & Naze. Don't do well – but enjoy ourselves. Up to town before dinner with R.H. – he's as grand a publisher as one could have.

2 This telegram, drafted on the blank final page of a letter from Bridge to Britten, is all that survives of what must have been a voluminous correspondence between the pupil and his teacher.

Frank and Ethel Bridge left for New York from Southampton on 9 September, on board SS *Washington*. It was their final trip to the USA, during which Bridge attended the first performance of his String Quartet No. 4 (1937–8), played by the Gordon String Quartet, of which Elizabeth Sprague Coolidge was patron, on 13 September, at the Berkshire Festival of Chamber Music, Pittsfield, Massachusetts. He wrote to Britten after the performance:

Fate in the guise of storm, hurricane & tidal wave, just prevented the New York press getting to the Festival at Pittsfield, but it did <u>not</u> prevent a <u>really</u> first class performance of Qtt No. 4. Such playing as would have delighted you beyond measure.

The performance was repeated at the Founder's Day Concert, Library of Congress, Washington, on 30 October, when Bridge was awarded the Berkshire and Washington Coolidge medals for his services to chamber music, presented to him by Mrs Coolidge, his American friend and benefactor. Britten's First String Quartet was similarly to receive the Coolidge Chamber Music medal, in September 1941. It was through Bridge's mediation that Britten established contact with Mrs Coolidge when he himself was resident in the USA. See Letter 206.

150 To Edwina Jackson
Boosey & Hawkes
[*Typed*]

THE OLD MILL SNAPE
Sept.16th. 1938

Dear Miss Jackson

This is only to tell you that as you can see,Ihave been given an old type-writer as a present! Iam not very hot at it yet, and it takes me years to find thc blinking letters, bul in lime Ihope to becomemore proficient , so that at last you will be able to read the importanter things in my vry frequent letters!

It's rathcr an old maschine, bul it's got lots of excitting gadgits on it:I have got to have it cleaned ,and then everythingwill be grand.

i hope you have had a good hphliday with brigth (I'm sorry about all these little imperfections?, but i'mgetting mz speed up to 90) weather. I'mgoing to stick down here for along time,and widl horses arnr'nt going to make me xxx do any work . . . . $\frac{1}{2}$ . . !
. . !

best wishes
(signed)
Benjimih Brittedn.!

[*Handwritten*: P.T.O.]
P.S.
Please will you give the enclosed to the wrigth person?

151 To Ursula Nettleship

Old Mill, Snape, Suffolk.
Sept. 19th, 1938.

Dear Ursula,

Sorry for the long silence. I've been off my head with work – & also wandering the country in a small Morris 8 – consequently correspondence has been neglected. You must think me rude: but perhaps you'll forgive this like all the other similar faux pas! I don't know what to say about the next two weeks. I should love to see you here, but I think the weather is definitely too cold (& the hill too draughty) for camping. Lennox gets back to-morrow – & so far we've got no spare room at all. There's a nice pub at Saxmundham – I could get you rooms, & fetch you over here. Or, there's a good train in the morning & in the evening – you could manage lunch & tea here. I'm away most of this week, but am back at the end.

Let me have a card – saying what you think –

Yours,

BENJAMIN

R.V.W. was nice about my Juvenilia (Boy was Born) but feels I'm letting down the side by developing – too Continental & all that! The Pig – !!!

152   To Ralph Hawkes

The Old Mill, Snape, Saxmundham, Suffolk.

Sept. 29th, 1938.

My dear Ralph,

There hurriedly concocted is the Note. Alter, add what you please. Sorry I couldn't type it, my machine is being cleaned![1]

To-day we're feeling so much more cheerful that we're going out black-berrying – might even have a next year in which to eat the jam.[2]

See you on Tuesday.

Yours,

BEN

1   The following programme note for *Mont Juic* was enclosed:

Lennox Berkeley & Benjamin Britten were together in Barcelona on the occasion of the I.S.C.M. Festival of 1936. Among the entertainments provided by the Government for the members attending this Festival, was a display of National Dances given in the Mont Juic Park just outside the town. The two composers were immediately struck by the beauty & vitality of the tunes, & noted some of them down on the back of a programme.

These tunes form the basis of the Suite. They have been elaborated and extended, but their shape has been in no way altered. The Suite consists of four dances. In each case the intention has been to reproduce the spirit of the dancing, and in some cases the actual sound of the accompanying band.

The first is a broad & stately dance – somewhat in the style of an eighteenth Century minuet.

The second, in complete contrast, is amusingly reminiscent of the Victorian

Polka.

The third movement is a Lament, with a continuous, heavy, plodding rhythm. In the middle are heard, as from the distance, the strains of a Sardana band.

The last movement is a furious dance in quick Waltz time, gathering momentum as it goes, & ending with Presto Coda.

L.B., B.B.

2 Britten refers to the news that there was to be no war over Czechoslovakia and the Sudetenland. International tension had been at its height throughout September, and by the 25th there was a rush among Londoners for gas masks as the situation escalated. Chamberlain had flown twice to Germany in his attempts to secure peace, while the world prepared for war. At the price of truncating Czechoslovakia and appeasing Hitler, he returned to London on the 30th, waving at Croydon Airport the agreement he had signed at Munich with Hitler, Mussolini and Daladier, and claiming, 'I believe it is peace for our time.' But see also notes 1 and 2 to Letter 169.

153 To Ronald Duncan

The Old Mill, Snape, Saxmundham, Suffolk.

Oct. 3rd, 1938.

Dear Ronnie,

Forgive me for being the cad I am – not writing or anything for ages. Put it down to what you like, only don't forget to include over-work, over-pleasure & the international situation.

Thank you (i) for coming to the Concerto. I was very pleased that you were there, & sorry that I didn't see more of you – but those aren't the most sociable of times.

Thank you (ii) for sending the play[1] – which I am most pleased to see. I have read it thro' quickly – enough to enjoy it & to see that I approve. Later I hope to get down to it properly, & then I'll write you a proper appreciative letter with many suggestions re music.

Thank you (iii) for suggestion re Suite to Olga Rudge.[2] I am doing as you say. Good of E. Pound.[3]

I suppose you are sticking down in Cornwall indefinitely? I should like to see you some time – but I've now finished my holidays & I've got to get down to work again. If it hadn't been for this bloody situation I might have got down to see you – still a week-end might arise later. I shall hear from Henry [Boys] all about its charms, no doubt.

Many plans for future, but nothing very definite. V. much want to go to U.S.A.

Excuse writing & scribble, but I'm just off to London – worst luck.

Yours,

BENJY

1 No play from this period appears in Duncan's *Collected Plays* (1971). See, however, his autobiography, *All Men Are Islands* (London, Hart-Davis, 1964), p. 203. Britten seems not to have followed up this project.

2 The Violin Suite, Op. 6. Olga Rudge (b. 1895), American violinist and musicologist. She first met Ezra Pound in 1920, and thereafter became his lifelong friend. She championed the music of Pound and his protégé, George Antheil (1900–1959). Presumably Pound had suggested to Duncan that the suite should be sent to Rudge.

3 Ezra Pound (1885–1972), American poet and essayist, writer on music and amateur composer. He was knowledgeable about the music of the medieval troubadours and himself composed two operas, *The Testament of François Villon* (1923) and *Cavalcanti* (1932). See *Ezra Pound and Music: The Complete Criticism*, edited with commentary by R. Murray Schafer (London, Faber and Faber, 1978), in which appears an account of a musical event involving Pound, Duncan, Britten and Boys:

> In 1938 Ronald Duncan started a new publication entitled *Townsman*, to which Pound contributed a number of short pieces on music. Following his university studies, Duncan had gone to visit Pound in Rapallo, and Gandhi in India, then returned to England to gain some considerable distinction as a poet and playwright. A close friend of Benjamin Britten, for whom he produced some libretti, Duncan was a sensitive music enthusiast. Pound had given him a note of introduction to Stravinsky, and following his visit to Stravinsky in Paris, Duncan conceived a plan for an anti-war concert with one of the London orchestras, at which Stravinsky would conduct his own works. Stravinsky was ready to donate his services, but the plan fell through when the orchestral managers, and even Stravinsky's British publisher, were indifferent. Pound wrote to Duncan [. . .] assuring him that Rapallo at least stood ready.
>
> Pound also saw Duncan in London in 1938 when he went to sort out the affairs of his mother-in-law, Olivia Shakespear, who had died in October of that year. According to Noel Stock, Pound 'wanted badly to see a Noh play performed in a theatre and to this end Ronald Duncan persuaded Ashley Dukes to lend the Mercury Theatre. Benjamin Britten produced a musician who could play gongs and another of Duncan's friends, Henry Boys, suggested a female dancer by the name of Suria Magito. One afternoon, with Duncan as audience, Pound recited one of his own Noh translations while the girl danced.'

This must have been Britten's first encounter, however marginal, with a Japanese Noh play, though there is no evidence that he attended Pound's recitation.

154 To Wulff Scherchen

The Old Mill, Snape, Saxmundham, Suffolk.

Oct. 3rd 1938

[. . .]

I didn't have time to talk about anything[1] – one thing I particularly wanted to talk to you about. Have you ever thought of writing any serious (not Beachcomber!)[2] poetry? You have a great knowledge of language – you love our really great poets (Shelley & Keats etc.) – & I think you've got great observation. Why not try? There seems to be something at the back of that silly old head of yours – & it might help in getting it out – nicht wahr? You need never show it to anyone – except me – I insist on that! Damn it all – man – I'm writing you a bit of music[3] – do the decent thing & reciprocate with something!

[. . .]

1 Britten had spent the weekend of 1–2 October in Cambridge, staying with Wulff and his mother.

2 The satirical columnist in the *Daily Express*.

3 This might have been the incidental music to Auden's and Isherwood's play, *On the Frontier*. Britten gave Wulff the composition sketch of the Overture and Interlude; Wulff in turn sent Britten some poems. 'Antique', from *Les Illuminations*, was later to be dedicated to 'KHWS' (Wulff Scherchen).

155 To Wulff Scherchen

The Old Mill, Snape, Saxmundham, Suffolk.

Oct. 10th 1938.

[. . .]

First of all, a thousand apologies for the lateness of this. Reason – I was up in London all last week, & really infernally busy – in fact I was out to every meal every day – except breakfast, but including 'elevenses'! I got back here late on Saturday night, & yesterday I spent lazing about – walking – thinking about 'Sturm & Drang'[1] – & in the evening I went over to the Alcocks[2] & we had another lovely session of noise-making. Now I should be

working – writing music for the Cambridge play[3] but the morning
has been upset by a series of events, such as the removal of our
hideous electric-light poles, the arrival of the new trees & hedges,
conking of the wireless, & Lennox has finished his new
masterpiece[4] – so it is hopeless to start writing music; and I'm
writing to you instead. Which anyhow is much pleasanter!

I was very pleased to get the poems. I prefered the 'Death of the
Hero' Spain one. The other has nice ideas in it – but it becomes
a bit 'Slogany' towards the end. Sturm & Drang I was very
impressed (& flattered by!). I follow the working of, what you
please to imagine, your poor bewildered brain! Don't worry, old
thing; we all feel like that sometime – that is, if we have any
imagination at all. Thank God, you have. The storm description is
very impressive – & quite eerie. Reminds me of the Mill. I'm
sorry, in a way, that you allowed the clouds to break in this poem.
I feel it ought to have ended, as it began, in a howl of misery.
'Und' is a nice idea. A ray of hope – what! But that's all dispelled
by the next one. I really feel that abit too deeply to write about
it. When we next meet you must read it, & I'll tell you lots of
things. In the meantime, continue. Write lots more. Read lots
more. I hope you'll like 'Look, Stranger'. In the opinion of many –
myself included – it is the finest book of poetry published these
twenty years.

I must try & get to Rosita's concert on Sunday week.[5] I shall have
to come to Cambridge alot during the next month. I have lots to
arrange about orchestra & what not. By-the-way I have agreed to
conduct the orchestra during the first week![6] I am going to Spain
between Nov. 22nd & Dec. 6th.[7]

[. . .]

P.S.   I may be doing the piano concerto in Paris with your father.[8]
Whatcher . . . – chaps!

1 The title of one of the poems Wulff had sent. In a letter from February
  1939, Britten writes of another batch of Wulff's poems: 'I think the
  last poem is fine – & I want to put music to it only [you] may have
  to (if you will!) alter one or two lines for me.' No trace of any setting
  by Britten of this poem has come to light.

2 Musical friends of the composer who lived at Orford, Suffolk. Britten
  wrote in his diary for 13 June: 'The Alcocks (Mr & Mrs) come over
  to play Chamber music (Pft quartets & String trios) in evening –
  irresistable fun.'

3 *On the Frontier*. On 5 September 1937 Auden had written, 'Christopher and I want to see you as soon as possible to discuss the music

for the New Play which is finished, and is dedicated to you, if we may. There will be a lot of notes to write.' The dedication took the shape of the following verse:

> The drums tap out sensational bulletins;
> Frantic the efforts of the violins
> To drown the song behind the guarded hill:
> The dancers do not listen; but they will.

It was first performed by the Group Theatre at the Arts Theatre, Cambridge, on 14 November 1938. Peter Pears undertook the (spoken) role of the Ostnian Announcer and was also among those listed as singers and dancers, a group that included Nell Burra and Richard Wood, who had previously occupied the flat at 43 Nevern Square into which Britten and Pears had moved. In a letter to Wulff of 17 October Britten refers ironically to his 'new masterpiece' (his score for the play), but adds, 'I think it's got some good things in it.' In 1989 Wulff recollected how impressed he was by the music for the national anthem of Auden's and Isherwood's fictitious countries, Westland and Ostnia:

Wystan suggested an aggressive stance for the marching music of the Dictator's forces and by contrast a thoughtful, almost lyrical quality for the march of the forces of 'Freedom'. Ben turned this into a marvellous exercise in counterpoint, modifying the goose-stepping start by the measured tread of the second group of marchers, which intermingled with and clearly modified the sound of those trampling boots. In my mind's eye I can still hear clearly the two march tunes and their intermingling.

Daryl Runswick has drawn our attention to the opening choral 'Blues', 'The clock on the wall gives an electric tick', the second couplet of which runs:

> The sirens blow at night; the sirens blow at noon;
> Goodbye, sister, goodbye; we shall die soon.

By the end of 1938 the sound of the siren – the air-raid warning system – was already familiar; and with typical ingenuity and precision Britten reproduces the characteristic wail of the siren and sustains it from beginning to end of the 'Blues'. He was to introduce the siren again, but this time at its authentic pitch, in his late (1972) song-cycle *Who are these children?*' in the eleventh song, 'The Children', the text of which describes the bloody aftermath of an air-raid. In the ninth and tenth couplet of the 'Blues' there also appears the 'Johnny' who is the subject of one of the Cabaret Songs:

> You looked so handsome in your overalls of blue;
> It was summer, Johnny and I never knew.
> My mother told me, when I was still as small lad;
> 'Johnny, leave the girls alone'. I wish I had.

See also Letter 393.

Brian Finney, in *Christopher Isherwood, A Critical Biography* (London, Faber and Faber, 1979), pp. 166–7, writes of the play's reception and a bizarre skirmish with the censor which must have confirmed the convictions of the authors and composer that the British government of the day was pitifully weak in its response to fascism:

The play that was performed at Cambridge was virtually identical to the published text apart from various small alterations demanded by the censor to make the parallels between Westland and Nazi Germany less obvious. Scandinavian names were substituted for German ones, and synonyms had to be found for phrases like 'Shock Troops' and 'labour camps'. Such alterations are sad testimony to the dishonesty underlying the official British policy of appeasement in 1938. Not that anyone in the audience was unaware of the parallels being drawn between the Leader and Hitler: the grotesque caricature of the Führer was all too obvious. As T.S. Eliot wrote to Maynard Keynes the day after the opening night, 'I am afraid that Hitler is not the simpleton that the authors made him out to be.'

On the Frontier received a single London performance the following year, on 12 February, when Ivor Brown wrote in the *Observer*, 19 February:

It was odd that the authors of this piece, having doctrine about dictatorship and kindred matters to declare for our good, insisted on putting it in the form most likely to deter the general public. For preaching to the converted their mixture of realism and fantasy, of choral comment and of Left Wing wise-crackery, has been proved, by previous work in other conventicles, a satisfactory method. But surely our dramatists want to reach the people who would be going to the Globe theatre in any case and not merely on Sunday nights and for that purpose a straightforward realistic play, of which 'On the Frontier' has some excellent elements, would be really effective because it would avoid the atmosphere of pretentiousness so tiresome to the average playgoer and so dear to our anti-realists. In this case the singing of choruses (in such a manner as completely to obscure the words) to music which made one fear to be removed to hospital suffering from Percussion, is simply a hindrance. A few of the elect may deem it marvellous, but the average bourgeois playgoer, whose darkness Messrs Auden and Isherwood must wish to enlighten, will only want the players to cut the cackle and come to the Ostnia, Ostnia being a country engaged in war with Westland.

See also PR, pp. 526–31, and John Haffenden (ed.), *W.H. Auden: the Critical Heritage* (London, Routledge & Kegan Paul, 1983), pp. 275–87.

4 Berkeley's *Introduction and Allegro*, Op. 11 (1938), for two pianos and orchestra, first performed at a Promenade Concert on 6 September 1940 and dedicated to Britten. In a letter to Aaron Copland, written from the Old Mill and dated 20 December, Berkeley was to announce:

I'm really going to try to come to America next winter. Ben is probably going in any case to play his Concerto and other things and I have written an Introduction & Allegro for 2 pianos and orchestra which I intend to play

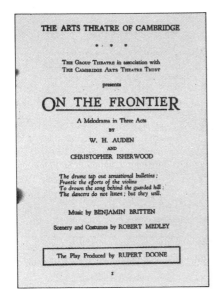
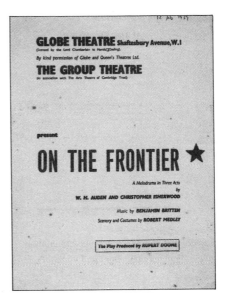

The cover of the programme for the   The first London production, 1939
first production of *On the Frontier*,
Cambridge, 1938

with him. If I could possibly get a performance of that in America, it would be a good excuse for coming. Boosey & Hawkes are going to try to do something about it through their agents, and it occurred to me that if you knew any conductors who would be interested or to whom you could recommend it (all I can tell you is that its a good deal better than anything I have done so far) I can tell them to send a score. I should be most grateful if you could do anything to help.

Benjamin is all right. He is being very successful in all departments of his life and enjoying it all.

Berkeley's hopes did not materialize.

This important letter opened with a paragraph about Copland's 'play-opera', which he had played through to Britten when visiting Snape in July. In the interim the vocal score must have been published:

I have just been reading 'The Second Hurricane' which you sent to Benjamin – I think its terribly good, and that you have succeeded marvelously (sorry, I never can spell that word) in doing a very difficult thing. I thought I would write and say how much I liked it, and at the same time thank you for the letter you sent me after you had been staying here. So glad you enjoyed it – you must come again, and I will try and be here too next time.

5 Rosita Bal, Basque refugee pianist. A 'Recital of Old Spanish, Italian and Modern French Music' was given by Bal and Elisabeth Ravcrat (soprano) at Christ's College, Cambridge, on 23 October. It is not known if Britten was there.

ON THE FRONTIER

Characters in the order of their appearance:

Lessep, *Secretary to Valerian* · · · ·HUGH GRANT
Manners, *Valerian's Butler* · · ·ALAN ROLFE
Valerian, *Head of the Westland Steel Trust*
WYNDHAM GOLDIE
Alving, *A Director of the Steel Trust*
NIGEL FITZGERALD
Corporal Grimm, *of the Guidanto's bodyguard*
IAN DAWSON
The Guidanto, *Dictator of Westland* ERNEST MILTON
Dr. Oliver Thorvald, *Lecturer at Westland University*
TRISTAN RAWSON
Mrs. Thorvald, *his wife* · · ·MARY BARTON
Eric Thorvald, *their son* · · ·ERIC BERRY
Martha Thorvald, *Dr. Thorvald's sister*
EVERLEY GREGG
Colonel Hussek, *late of the Ostnian Army*
CECIL WINTER
Louisa Vrodny, *his daughter* · · ·JULIET MANSEL
Anna Vrodny, *her daughter* · LYDIA LOPOKOVA
Oswald Vrodny, *brother-in-law to Mrs. Vrodny*
JOHN MOODY
Westland Announcer · · · · ·IAN GLENNY
Ostnian Announcer · · · · ·PETER PEARS

2

ON THE FRONTIER.
Time : The Present.

ACT I.
Early Summer.

Prologue: At the gates of the Valerian Works.
Workers: Nella Burra, Jane Connard, Prudence
Wood, Ian Glenny, Cuthbert Matthews,
Harold Child, John Moody, Richard
Wood, Peter Pears.
SCENE 1: Valerian's Study.
Interlude: A Prison in Westland.
Prisoners: Harold Child, Richard Wood, Cuthbert
Matthews, Ian Glenny.
SCENE 2: The Ostnia-Westland Room.

An Interval of fifteen minutes.

ACT II.
A week later.

SCENE 1: The Ostnia-Westland Room.
Interlude: A Dance-hall in Westland.
Dancers: Harold Child and Jane Connard, Nella
Burra and Peter Pears, Richard Wood and
Prudence Wood.
Leftists: Ian Glenny, John Moody.
SCENE 2: Valerian's Study.

An Interval of fifteen minutes.

3

ON THE FRONTIER.

ACT III.
Nine months later.

SCENE 1: The Ostnia-Westland Room.
Interlude: In the Westland Front Line.
Westland Soldiers: John Moody, Peter Pears, Richard
Wood.
Ostnian Soldiers: Ian Glenny, Alan Rolfe, Cuthbert
Matthews, Harold Child.

SCENE 2: Valerian's Study (a fortnight later).

Interlude: The War Correspondents.
Journalists: Richard Wood, John Moody, Jane
Connard, Peter Pears.

SCENE 3: Epilogue.

The Group Theatre's next production will be
Danton's Death, in a new translation by Stephen
Spender and Goronwy Rees.
Production by Rupert Doone and Rollo Gamble.
Scenery and costumes by Robert Medley and John
Piper.
Music by Benjamin Britten and Brian Easdale.
This will be followed by Rupert Doone's
production of *The Hippolytus of Euripides*,
translated by Louis MacNeice.
For particulars of membership apply to the
Secretary, Group Theatre Rooms, 9 Great
Newport Street, London, W.C.2.

4

ON THE FRONTIER.

Scenery built by J. Brunskill.
Costumes for Madame Lopokova, Miss Mansel and Miss
Barton by The Dundas School of Dress Design, 43 South
Molton Street, W.1.
Uniforms by Benjamin.
Uniform for Mr. Milton by Moss Bros.
Uniform for Mr. Dawson by Morris Angel.
Wigs by Spaans.
Electric fittings and effects by Strand Electric and The
Cambridge Electric Supply Co.
Blue Prints by A. West and Partners.
The Ostnian and Westland songs sung by the London
Labour Choral Union and recorded by Decca.
Furniture for Valerian's Study by J. S. Lyon.
Model aeroplanes kindly lent by Imperial Airways.

* * *

Musical Director · · · ·BRIAN EASDALE
Instrumentalists
Piano · · · · · · ·BENJAMIN BRITTEN
Percussion · · · · · ·BRIAN EASDALE
Trumpets · ·SIDNEY ELLISON, BERNARD BROWN

* * *

Stage Manager · · · ·ROGER COLVILLE-WALLIS
Assistant Stage Manager · · · ·ANNE JENKINS
Wardrobe Mistress · · ·CONSTANCE FOLJAMBE

* * *

The Play published by Faber and Faber, price 6/–.

5

On the Frontier, Cambridge, 1938: the cast list

6 Britten refers to performances of *On the Frontier*, which however ran
   for one week only, from 14 to 19 November. While in Cambridge
   Britten stayed with Wulff and his mother.

7 This journey never happened. However, nearly three weeks later,
   on 30 October, Britten was still planning to make the trip to Spain. He
   wrote to Adrian Boult, in connection with the forthcoming broadcast
   performance of his Piano Concerto on 16 December:

   I should certainly very much like to have a run-through with you of my
   piano concerto. I am not sure yet whether I shall be able to do so on
   December the 1st, as your secretary suggested, because I am provisionally
   booked to be in Barcelona at that date. I shall certainly be back on December
   7th [. . .].

8 The performance did not take place.

156 To Wulff Scherchen

[*Typed*]

Group Theatre,
Group Theatre Rooms,
9 Great Newport St.,
London, W.C.2
NOv.10th.1938

[. . .]
   Thank you very much for you nice letter and the poem which I
shall give to Christerpher when I seehim – – – probably to-
morrow.I like it very much – – but I haven't got time to talk about
it now, thinks are hectic here as you can guess.[1] Anyhow   Wystan
and I hope to arrive about tea-time onsaturday.I don't know
whether he'll be able to come to dinner, because he ie staying
with friendsandcan'T make any arrangemenets till he sees them.
I hope he can, and he says he would like to. Anyhow he'll come
to tea I think.
   [. . .]

1 Rehearsals for *On the Frontier* were in progress.

157 To Wulff Scherchen

The Old Mill, Snape, Saxmundham, Suffolk.
Nov. 22nd 1938

[. . .]
   We had a rotten journey back – windscreen wiper failed us –
lights were hopeless – & Lord – how it rained! We were back soon

after five – & found the Slaters here waiting for us. They stayed the night & went off yesterday afternoon – having done alot of work in the garden yesterday morning. They are nice people – husband & wife – he's a play-write – I dont know if you've met them.

I've been working all day to-day – started the new Concerto[1] – it's going fine so far – & it's the best so far I'm sure. I'm feeling cheerful about that – but otherwise <u>very</u> depressed. The strain of becoming a quarter of a century is bearing hard upon me.[2] It's a horrible thing to feel one's youth slipping o – so surely away from one & I had such a damn good youth too. I wish you were here to comfort me!

[. . .]

Written any more poems? Don't forget to let me see them when you do. I've written to Wystan to ask him when he's going to sign your book for you.

[. . .]

1 The Violin Concerto, Op. 15: see note 4 to Letter 175.

2 Britten was writing on his twenty-fifth birthday.

158 To Grace Williams

[*Boyd, p. 37*]

The Old Mill, Snape, Suffolk.
Nov. 28th, 1938.

My dear Grace,

Do forgive this long silence, but I've been away from London alot, & o, so beastly busy. I am coming back to London on Wednesday next, & I should love to see you sometime – & the new piece.

I've been in Cambridge for a bit doing a theatre show (new Auden play) & now I've been here working abit – nothing exciting tho'. How's things with you – what are you writing now? I am moving flats to Hallam St. W.[1] this week, so I'd better 'phone you & fix something.

Hope you're well,
Yours ever,
BENJAMIN

1 Britten and Pears moved into 67 Hallam Street, London W1, in early December.

159 To Ralph Hawkes

The Old Mill, Snape, Saxmundham, Suffolk.
Nov. 29th, 1938.

Dear Ralph,

Sorry not to be up this week, but I am putting off London dates for a few days & staying in the peace & quiet here. Cambridge got me down abit & I have lots of work to get on with. I am in the middle of the Concerto – piano version – started the Violin Concerto & doing the Co-op part song[1] – so there's plenty to do!

I shall be up at the beginning of next week – Tuesday or Wednesday. If you want details of 'On the Frontier' (if you're still interested) – could you phone Rupert Doone – Temple Bar 6382?

I hope you're feeling fit now – & not too many late nights –

Best wishes,
Yours ever,
BENJAMIN

1 *Advance Democracy*, motet for unaccompanied chorus, a setting of words by the left-wing poet, writer and journalist, Randall Swingler (1909–1967), who was the editor of *Left Review*, in its last year, from July 1937 until May 1938. He was a member of the Communist Party from 1934, and active in the Workers' Musical Association: he was himself a skilled flautist. For further details, see *The Times'* obituary, 20 June 1967. *Advance Democracy* was in fact completed on the day this letter was written and published by Boosey & Hawkes in 1939. Britten also composed music for a film of the same title in 1938, but the motet formed no part of the score. He was to set one further text by Swingler: 'You who stand at your doors, wiping hands on aprons', in *Ballad of Heroes*, Op. 14. Swingler was married to the pianist, Geraldine Peppin, and his brother was the Labour MP, Stephen Swingler. See also the obituary of Geraldine's twin sister, Mary – also a pianist – which appeared in the *Independent*, 28 August 1989.

160 To Ralph Hawkes

The Old Mill, Snape, Saxmundham, Suffolk.
Dec. 29th, 1938.

Dear Ralph,

Thank you very, very much for the score.[1] I really am extremely grateful & if you can believe it, there's nothing I'd rather have

had. But it isn't only for Rigoletto that I want to thank you – trying
not to be sloppy – it is for all you've done for me, as Sponsor,
Publisher, Agent, Maecenas – what you will. I don't think any
composer starting out could have met with such luck as I have,
& I only hope that you on your side won't find that you've been
backing a bad loser. And I must say that it is not only in your
business capacity, but in your personal behaviour that I find terrific
encouragement – and that, in these turbulent days, is not as
common as it might be. So thank you, Ralph, thank you!

I enclose cheque from B.B.C. for subtraction of customary 10%.
How are we going to arrange the paying in of these cheques in
the future?

I also enclose letter from Basil Dean;[2] I have answered it myself
saying I can meet him in London after Brussels.

I'll be in town on Monday afternoon, and ready to depart for the
continent when you will. Hope you can come too.

Any news from Alan Bush[3] re Co-operative Society?

Believe it or not, the piano score of Concerto is going ahead.

My regards to the family. Please tell your small step-offspring,
that I will get Emil[4] for her when I get to London. Hope the skiing
goes well.

Many thanks again, & all the best for 1939 – may it be a better
year than 1938 – couldn't very well be worse.

Yours ever,

BENJAMIN

1 Hawkes had given Britten a vocal score of Verdi's *Rigoletto* as a
   Christmas present. The copy, one of 'The Royal Edition of Operas'
   published by Boosey & Co. Ltd and edited by Arthur Sullivan and
   J.P. Pittman, is in the Archive.

2 Basil Dean (1888–1978), English theatre and film producer. It was
   during the 1920s at St Martin's Theatre, London, that Dean became
   prominent, especially with his successful staging of his own dramati-
   zation of *Hassan* (1923) by James Elroy Flecker, with incidental music
   by Delius. During the 1930s Dean was first Chairman and then
   Joint Managing Director of Associated Talking Pictures (later Ealing
   Studios). After his resignation from Ealing Studios in the late 1930s
   he returned to the theatre (always his first love) and was invited
   by the playwright, J.B. Priestley (1894–1984), to produce his plays,
   including *Johnson over Jordan*.

   It was at the suggestion of his son, Winton (the leading Handel
   scholar), that Dean wrote to Britten on 21 December:

You may recall that I met you at Professor Dent's party after the last night of the production of On the Frontier.

I am very anxious to have a talk with you about a new play by Mr J.B. Priestley which I am going to produce early in the New Year. The play is a symbolical work and calls for a certain amount of modern incidental music in the first act. I would like to discuss with you the possibility of your composing this for us, as I think it would be yet another interesting opportunity to introduce your music in the London Theatre. Will you let me know when you can have a talk?

Britten agreed to undertake the commission (see Letter 163) and composed his score during January and February 1939 (see Letter 166) for which he was paid 70 guineas (£73 10s.). Although *Johnson over Jordan* was his major début in the commercial theatre, he had composed a small quantity of organ music as incidental music for Max Catto's mystery play, *They Walk Alone*, first produced by Bertold Viertel at the 'Q' Theatre, London, on 21 November 1938 (see PR, pp. 532–3). A notice of this play appeared in the *Observer*, 27 November 1938:

There is no need to pretend that this is anything else than melodrama, and none to be ashamed of having enjoyed it. A girl, Emmy [Beatrix Lehmann] comes to a Lincolnshire farm as a servant. She is strangely affected by the playing of organ music in the chapel near by, and, from that moment onward, is to be watched suspiciously. The tranquil life of the neighbourhood is desperately disturbed. On several mornings, in the small hours, the organ plays. Soon afterwards young men are found horribly murdered. A dog belonging to one of the victims howls outside the farm; the moor is searched for the murderer; and sometimes we see Emmy, breathless from the dog's pursuit, rush in through the flapping door. She has a power over young men. She has the marks of a dog's bite on her throat. She is small and frail, but has hands and wrists like steel. Two and two are put together, and at last she is trapped. [. . .] Analysis of the play cannot make much of it, but under Miss Lehmann's spell it has astonishing impact.

The music for *Johnson*, however, is substantial and includes a dance-band number entitled 'The Spider and the Fly', orchestrated by Geraldo (Gerald Bright, 1904–1974), and recorded by him and his orchestra for use in the first production of Priestley's 'modern morality' at the New Theatre, London, on 22 February 1939. An article in the *Observer*, 29 January, 'New Priestley Play with Ballet and Music', outlined the play's aims and special qualities in Dean's words:

'The whole gamut of methods of writing is tried at one time or another, realism passing on to symbolism – through hilarious comedy.'

Though Mr Priestley is reputed to have taken two years to write the play, it is admitted to be in every sense 'experimental'.

The devices of ballet and orchestra are to be employed in it. Why music? 'Mr Priestley feels', explains Mr Dean, 'that music is needed fully to illustrate the moods of the play and to accompany its drama.'

Two composers have been engaged on different parts of its score, and there will be an orchestra of twenty. Ballet is to be 'ingeniously welded in with the drama so that it is part of the action'.

[. . .]

The music, like the writing of the play, varies in style. 'The first act demands music of the most modern character. Benjamin Britten is the composer. His piano concerto recently given by the BBC aroused great discussion. It is part of our policy to encourage the younger artists in their various spheres whenever we can.'

'The second act has modern swing music, mainly already established tunes, though at one point Mr Britten will try his hand at modern jazz. For the last act Mr Ernest Irving will select and arrange excerpts from classical music.'

The following notice of the opening night appeared in *The Times*, 23 February:

It is impossible in a few paragraphs driven by time to discuss Mr Priestley's play with the elaboration that criticism of it requires. No one but a fool would venture to say of it briefly either that it is good or that it is bad, for it is a struggling, courageous play, an experiment exciting even in its failures. There is real danger of over-praising its gigantic ambition because ambition of this kind is greatly needed and is a profound relief from the easy trivialities of the theatre, and an equal danger, unless nice distinctions are made, of speaking too harshly of those crudities of treatment which – particularly in the last act – almost bring the piece to ruin. In fact it was not ruined. A magnificently buoyant and imaginative performance by Mr Ralph Richardson sustained it, but it must be admitted that the fall of the last curtain and a kindly reception came like a rescue from the long-impending shipwreck.

[. . .]

The purpose of the cabaret-scene is nothing less than to give an impression of hell. The masks, the dreadful aridity of bought pleasure, and a fiercely symbolic interlude in which Johnson bullies his own daughter in the belief that she is a prostitute do succeed intermittently in producing an effect of terror, but the cabaret is still too much like a cabaret, waves of the common boredom pass over it to the audience, and Mr Priestley says more in one brief and noble soliloquy than in all the contrivances of dance and lighting and violence to which Mr Basil Dean has devoted so much care. And the third act is endangered for a different reason. Here Johnson is re-introduced to the joyful memories of his life – his dead brother; the characters in fiction – Pickwick and Don Quixote – who affected his youth; an old clown, a famous cricketer, an admired schoolmaster; and is permitted to live again early and fragmentary moments of happiness with his wife. That these memories are, in themselves, commonplace is by no means an objection to them, for Johnson was outwardly a commonplace man. The trouble is first that they are a string of incidents that do not contain the continuous impulse of drama; secondly, that their triviality, though justifiable in itself, mixes ill with the splendours of the Prayer Book; the styles of the parish magazine and the Burial Service will not mix, whatever justification there may be, in the play's particular circumstances, for the naiveties of the parish magazine. But one hates to seem to speak even for a moment derisively of such a play as this. It gives Mr Richardson a great opportunity and he carried all its burdens with spring and lightness. It is, moreover, a deeply serious, impassioned, and charitable attack upon a great subject, and that, in the theatre, is more than half the world.

Ivor Brown, in the *Observer*, 26 February, wrote:

Mr Priestley's modern morality might be described as the passage from bowler-hat to heavenly crown. Everyman is here the Cartoonist's Little Man, only since Mr Ralph Richardson plays the part, a size larger. Johnson is an animated cliché, a decent fellow, doing and saying what is expected of decent fellows at the office and in the suburb. Dying suddenly of pneumonia at fifty-one, he is found on his airy way to trans-Jordania, in some Limbo-like area where the lately dead renew, for good or ill, their old acquaintance. It is what the Tibetans call Bardo, a post-mortem dreamland of hallucinations about earthy matters. Johnson is shown undergoing a celestial 'viva' and failing to satisfy examiners who seemed precious hard to please, remembering the ugly lusts which may lurk beneath propriety's black coat, remembering, also, boyhood's delights of sport and reading, and then, rapt from these brief pains and pleasures, he is confronted with eternity, that most terrifying of all human concepts. Death is not to be all reunion with kith and kin, with shadowy cricketers, and Mr Pickwick's ample ghost. Claudio may, after all, be right.

> To be imprisoned in the viewless winds
> And blown with restless violence round about
> The pendant world.

It is a tremendous closing moment when Johnson buttons up his coat, and goes, under summons, into the cold, clean infinite void of everlastingness.

It is a pity, of course, that Johnson lacks a Claudio's tongue. The play cries out for poetry and is given instead the rather familiar mixture of abstractions, masks, and percussive music which Expressionism has been serving up for twenty years or more. If the term be accepted, 'Johnson over Jordan' is at once a powerful example and a damning criticism of the Expressionist outfit. How both at once? Because the play only lives in its living people, its actual facts, its normal speech. The Expressionist Night Club, in which Johnson reveals the thwarted beastliness of normal-seeming man, would be far more impressive if it was full of the dreadful people that one could really meet in that kind of place. By turning all his sub-humans into masked abstractions, Mr Priestley has defeated his own purpose. The masks are cleverly done, but the result does not remind one of a night-club at all, but of a Highbrow Sunday Night at which some earnest drama group is dancing, as it imagines, over the stinking corpse of poor old realism. Well, we need not mourn for realism. For Mr Richardson's performance, which is the beginning and middle and end of this play, is realistic and is vastly moving throughout. No masks for him! I shall not easily forget the driving actuality of his blanched curiosity, his eye frenzied with apprehension, as he turns from the warmth of good earthy memories to the solitudes and immensities of everlastingness. Here was a real man and real acting. The jerky, fidgety Expressionist goings-on of the first two acts, especially of the first, continually interrupted by irrelevant dancers, faded out of mind beneath the strong compulsion of the last.

Johnson was subsequently transferred to the Saville Theatre in a revised version in March 1939. In an interview with Harold Conway which appeared in the *Daily Mail*, 4 March 1939, Priestley described his purpose in writing *Johnson* and the reasons why the production was forced to close at the New Theatre:

My aim in 'Johnson over Jordan' was to make the fullest possible imaginative use of modern stage devices to illustrate a theme which called for spacious treatment.

It has been an experiment which I am well satisfied to have made. I wanted to try certain new ideas – to experiment with one of several possible new forms of dramatic expression. I realised all along that it was a pioneer effort which might not attract a wide public.

In view of the expensive nature of the production and the weekly running costs involved – equal to those of a big musical play – it was essential that the theatre should be practically full at every performance.

This has not been the case. The cheaper parts have been crowded, and usually people have had to be turned away from the pit and gallery. But the stalls have not been so well patronised.

A week later Conway was able to report that the announcement of the play's closure had produced a resurgence of interest at the box office, 'but as another production had in the meantime been booked for the New Theatre, the Priestley play will be transferred to the Saville Theatre' (see 'Priestley Play to Go On', *Daily Mail*, 11 March 1939). See also Vincent Brome, *J.B. Priestley* (London, Hamish Hamilton, 1988), pp. 236–40. It is extraordinary still that not one of the major notices of *Johnson over Jordan* recognized the role that music played in the conception and performance of Priestley's drama or indeed so much as mentioned it.

Ralph Richardson took the main role of Robert Johnson (see Gary O'Connor, *Ralph Richardson: An Actor's Life*, London, Hodder & Stoughton, 1982, pp. 118–21); the designer was Edward Carrick (Edward Gordon Craig), with costumes and masks by Elizabeth Haffenden; choreography by Antony Tudor, and Ernest Irving (1878–1953) was the musical director. Irving was also responsible for the various arrangements of the 'classical' numbers which were used mainly in the last act.

Three BBC radio adaptations were broadcast during Britten's lifetime: in 1940 (Act III only); 1951; and 1955. In 1985 a new radio production was mounted which reinstated all Britten's original music. See Basil Dean, *Mind's Eye: An Autobiography 1927–1972* (London, Hutchinson, 1973), pp. 265–70, where Dean erroneously refers to *Johnson over Jordan* as Britten's 'first contribution to the English theatre', and PR, pp. 258–316 and 534–51.

3 Bush was presumably planning a performance of the motet, *Advance
   Democracy*.

4 Another reference to Kästner's novel.

161 To Enid and Montagu Slater

The Old Mill, Snape, Saxmundham, Suffolk
Dec. 29th, 1938.

My dear Enid & Montagu,

I don't know if you realise the responsibility you've taken upon
yourselves. I am now definitely into my 'American' period, &
nothing can stop me. I hum the tunes & mutter the words all day,
& all my ideas now seem to be that way too – perhaps it's a bad
thing – but I don't care. So for my biographer's benefit: – 'In 1938,
his friends the Slaters gave him the American Songbag,[1] with the
following drastic results . . . . . and subsequent decline . . . .'
etc. But whatever the consequence, I enjoy them no end, & thank
you both <u>very</u> much.

Forgive me writing to you both together – but I've got a few
letters to get done, & I am behind with other things too. Thank
the children for their messages – I meant to get a card to send
them, but before Christmas I was laid up in bed; & then, when
up & about, we were unable to get into the town through snow.
But it did look lovely – & we had alot of snowery – tobogganing
& such like which is my cup of tea. I go to Brussels concertoing
next week – then in London for abit – see you then?

Yours ever,
BENJAMIN

1 *The American Songbag*, edited by Carl Sandburg (New York, Harcourt,
   Brace & Company, 1927). A collection of some 280 songs and ballads
   gathered from all parts of the United States. Britten had clearly told
   his friends about his forthcoming trip with Pears to North America.

162 To Ursula Nettleship

The Old Mill, Snape, Saxmundham, Suffolk.
Dec. 31st, 1938.

Dear Ursula,

Thank you for both your nice letters. It was nice of you to trouble
to write about the Concerto[1] – a few people <u>do</u> write, you know,

after these shows, & it does cheer one. Re the first & more hectic communication – I thought we were both resigned to the weaknesses in my make-up – that I never do ring people up, unless I specifically want something, that I never visit people unless I get phone call, letter or wire commanding me to come at a certain hour, not because I don't want to, but because in London I rush from dawn till mid-night, & when I stop rushing I come here. So please don't be offended – don't think I don't want to see you, because I do enjoy our talking-matches, & enthusings or vices versa (vice versas?) – as you well know.

Anyhow, soon I'll have some new songs[2] to show you. Meanwhile, I dash to Brussels to play Concerto[3] & am in London 6th–10th. See?

Love & best wishes for 1939

BENJAMIN

1 Britten had given a performance of his Piano Concerto (its fourth hearing) as part of a special BBC broadcast concert featuring British composers, with the BBC Symphony Orchestra conducted by Sir Adrian Boult, for which he received a fee of 10 guineas (£10 10s.). The other two works in the programme, both first performances, were Herbert Howells's Concerto for String Orchestra and Edmund Rubbra's Second Symphony.

2 Probably the first of the Rimbaud settings, which were to become *Les Illuminations*. See note 1 to Letter 170. In an interview with John Skiba (*Composer*, Winter, 1976–7, pp. 33–5), Sophie Wyss recollected Britten's first encounter with Rimbaud's poems:

We were travelling back by train after having given a recital together, when he came over to me very excitedly as we were unable to sit together, and said that he had just read the most wonderful poetry by Rimbaud and was so eager to set it to music; and asked me whether I might mind singing it in French, I naturally agreed as it was my first language. He was so full of this poetry he just could not stop talking about it, I suspect he must have seen a copy of Rimbaud's works while he was recently staying with Auden in Birmingham.

Britten had indeed been staying with the Audens in Birmingham in November 1937, and during 1938 gave frequent recitals with Wyss.

3 See note 2 to Letter 164.

163 To Lennox Berkeley

The Old Mill, Snape, Saxmundham, Suffolk.

Jan. 1st, 1939.

My dear Lennox,

A <u>very</u> happy New Year to you! I am sure you're feeling fine
now that you're in Paris & with José & all those friends of yours.[1]
I was going to say that you are now where you really belong, to
cheer you up – but I'm not so sure about that – I think Snape is
really your spiritual home – whatever it is physically!! Anyhow, I
hope you had a good Xmas. Ours was definitely good, in spite
of the very thick snow. It has at last all gone, but the district is
pretty flooded in spots. Peter went last Sunday & Barbara on
Friday. W. [Wulff] is with me for the week-end, & I go up to
London on Monday & to Brussels on Tuesday. I am staying there
with Wystan. I'm back to London on the Thursday or Friday & the
Behrends party is on Monday. I then hope to be back here for the
rest of the month – to do some work – I've done nothing this last
fortnight except write letters – & dozens of them too – I've still
got lots too to do.

Mrs. Hearn is well & abit tired, but she'll recover when left alone
for a week as she will be now. We took her to the Cinema in
Aldeburgh last night & she enjoyed herself I think.

I have been commissioned to do the incidental music to the new
Priestley play for London – I've not read it yet, but it's been sent
me – which may be interesting. Anyhow financially it ought to be
good –

I'm afraid lunch is in – & I must post this.

Much love, my dear; cheer up – I know you'll enjoy Paris alot.

B.

Love to José & best wishes for 1939 – thank him for his Xmas card.

1 Lennox Berkeley had studied in Paris with Nadia Boulanger from
  1927 to 1932. He shared a flat there with José Rafaelli (to whom he
  dedicated his Five Short Pieces, Op. 4, for piano). In 1938, he and
  Berkeley had visited Britten in London and Snape. During the war,
  José was killed while working for the French Resistance.

164   To Wulff Scherchen[1]

[*Picture postcard: Maison du Roi, Bruxelles*]

Brussels.
[5 January 1939]

Having a v.g. time – the rehearsal was a wow this morning.[2]
F. André is very nice & v. good. So I hope you enjoy broadcast.
I saw Weterings[3] this morning & am having tea with him.
[. . .]
   Hoping to see you again before we sail for America.[4]
[. . .]

1 A postcard, signed by Britten, Christopher Isherwood and Jackie
   Hewit (b. 1917, Isherwood's friend), about whom Britten wrote to
   Wulff on 10 January, 'He is a dear, nice creature [. . .] you and he
   [. . .] must meet – you'd like him a lot – he's had one of the hardest
   lives anyone could possibly have had & it's left him extraordinarily
   serene.' See, however, Letter 227.
       For Hewit's own account of his early life and his later friendship
   with Guy Burgess, see Barrie Penrose and Simon Freeman, *Conspiracy
   of Silence: The Secret Life of Anthony Blunt* (London, Grafton Books,
   1986), pp. 200–06. In 1938, 'Hewit went to Brussels to live with
   Christopher Isherwood, but it was a short liaison and he was soon
   back in London with Burgess.' The postcard clearly belongs to the
   months he spent in Brussels. Hewit, in describing (p. 205) the 'gay
   world' in the thirties to Blunt's biographers, said:

   You have to understand that the gay world then had style which it doesn't
   now. There was a sort of gay intellectual freemasonry which you know
   nothing about. It was like the five concentric [*sic*] circles in the Olympic
   emblem. One person in one circle knew one in another and that's how
   people met. And people like me were passed around. I wasn't a trollop.
   Amoral perhaps but not a trollop.

   Hewit's encounter with Britten and Pears and his occupancy of the
   flat at Hallam Street was a precise example of the overlapping circles
   to which Hewit refers. The imbroglio is referred to in Berkeley's
   letters to Britten in the USA. He was to write on 24 September:

   Nicholson rang up the other day to say that there's a spot of bother going
   on at the Hallam Street flat. Apparently Jackie has failed to pay the rent,
   and the landlady can't get hold of him. I said that I had never had anything
   to do with the flat, and that I'd never even met Jackie. No doubt he has
   written to you about it. By the way, what's happening to Peter? Is he coming
   back? You don't mention him in your letter.

   and again on 8 October:

Nicholson says he cant get any answer from you to his letters and in fact hasn't had a single letter from you since you left. It's nothing to do with me, but I think you should be a little less casual – you can't expect the poor man to look after your interests if you won't answer his letters. Then there's a great hullaballoo going on about Jackie – but I think that is Peter's concern. Nicholson is afraid that they might pinch your piano, music etc. but is trying to disentangle you from any responsibility. Your family keep asking me who is Jackie? – what does he do? If they're not careful I shall tell them.

2 Britten was in Brussels for a performance on 5 January of his Piano Concerto, in which he was soloist, with the Belgian Radio Symphony Orchestra conducted by Franz André (1893–1975). He travelled over-night to Brussels on 3 January and wrote to Wulff on the 4th:

> Had a good but bumpy journey – arrived at 10 this morning. Spent day with Wystan & seen Christopher too – hold your thumbs for me tomorrow night [. . .] I'll ring you when I get back. Wystan sends his love.

On the flyleaf of Britten's 1939 pocket diary is inscribed 'Christopher / 29 Rue Stassart', presumably the address at which Isherwood was staying in Brussels.

It was a visit that aroused the anxieties of Berkeley, who wrote to Britten before he left in an undated letter:

> Good luck for Brussels. I hope it goes well. Is Peter going with you? I think you must try and behave nicely there in spite of being in the possession of mysterious addresses. I hate to think of you doing – I mean – oh damn, well you know what I mean. It isn't jealousy this time, but a sort of respect for you and a really very deep kind of affection that makes me want you to be everything that's marvellous and good. It may seem absurd to you but I feel like what your Mother would have felt about that. It would shake the little idealism that I still possess.

Berkeley's words speak eloquently of what undoubtedly seems to have been a period of emotional turbulence and turmoil in Britten's life, along with the release of what had been, until not so long ago, an emphatically constrained sexuality. See Introduction, pp. 16–20.

3 Joseph Weterings (1904–1967), Belgian writer and music critic. Both he and his wife were friends of the Scherchen family. It was Wulff, in a letter dated 2 January, who informed Britten of this connection. Gustel, Wulff's mother, wrote to Weterings to pave the way for Britten's introduction to him.

In August, Weterings sent Britten a scenario for a three-act ballet based on John Bunyan's *The Pilgrim's Progress*. An elaborate work was envisaged, involving dance, solo singers, chorus and orchestra, with Frederick Ashton taking the main role of Christian. Perhaps it was during one of these first meetings with the composer in Brussels that Weterings first suggested the idea. (He had already written a ballet – *Aeneas* for Roussel.) The scenario is in the Archive.

4 This sentence was written in Isherwood's hand and refers to his and
Auden's departure for America later that month.

165 To Wulff Scherchen

The Old Mill, Snape, Saxmundham, Suffolk.

Jan. 22nd 1939

[. . .]

Thank you for your letter & the new pome. Of course I don't like
it as much as <u>mine</u> but there are nice things about it. I like the
1st verse best – the last verse not so much – it's a bit stilted & I
don't like the inversion 'feels loveless life'. I feel that's possible
in German but not in English. However – more later.

[. . .]

Just written a long letter to your Pa. Did you hear Ansermet do
the Variations last night? – it was pretty hot, I must say. The end
was grand.

[. . .]

Hedli & I recorded the songs quite nicely.[1] Glad you like 'm. And
the Spender one.[2]

[. . .]

1 A recording made of two of Britten's Cabaret Songs (with texts by
W.H. Auden) – 'Johnny' and 'Tell me the truth about love' – was
made for Columbia on 18 January. The producer was Walter Legge.
An earlier recording of four Cabaret Songs had taken place on 14
July 1938 for the same company. This included 'Johnny' and 'Funeral
Blues', and the two further songs for which no manuscript sources
have survived: 'Give up love' and 'Jam Tart'. Neither recording was
ever issued and, alas, it appears that the masters were destroyed.

Britten was principal accompanist of Hedli Anderson in his Cabaret
Songs, but in May 1937 his diaries document rehearsals and presum-
ably a performance of the songs in which Henry Boys was the pianist.
Boys was later to run through the Violin Concerto with Brosa in
London when Britten was in the United States.

The Archive is in possession of a recording of the four Cabaret
Songs by Hedli Anderson (source: Corinna MacNeice). We have not
been able to identify the location or date of the recording, or its
motivation, though it is clear that she was not accompanied by the
composer. This is certainly not the Columbia project. Was it perhaps
a demonstration recording of some sort, with Henry Boys at the
piano? Or Arthur Young? See Letter 226.

2 Britten's reference to a setting of a poem by Stephen Spender is of

The programme for Scherchen's 1939 performance of the *Bridge Variations* at Winterthur

special interest since no complete Spender songs seem to have survived, although there is a fragmentary composition of a setting of 'Your body is stars whose millions glitter here' (*Poems*, second edition (London, Faber and Faber, 1934), p. 35). Wulff remembers quite distinctly that the song Britten refers to in this letter was a setting of Spender's poem 'Not to you I sighed. No, not a word' (*Collected Poems* (London, Faber and Faber, 1985), p. 27), and further recalls Pears singing it, in the presence of the poet. He had written to the composer on 19 January after his visit to London: ' "Tell me the truth about love" & the Spender song have completely obsessed me since I returned.' The manuscript was in Pears's possession but seems to be lost. See Addenda, p. 1337.

166 To Wulff Scherchen

[*Two lettercards written on train*]

In the train to Oxford[1]

[17 February 1939]

Volume I

[. . .]

[. . .] You won't be able to read this but this is the only moment I've had for writing this week. I've written something like 90 pages of score in the last three days,[2] as

Volume II

<u>Continued</u> . . .

well as umpteen rehearsals, two concerts,[3] & a certain amount of other fun. So I've been occupied. Hollywood seems a bit nearer – I've got an interview with the Producer on Monday.[4] Hope I get it, that means lot of money & won't we have fun – ! (Writing's better 'cause we've stopped at Reading). I'll send you a wire when I sign the contract.

I had a wire from your father last night; wants me to play with him in Paris on March 14th – think I will.[5] (Here we go again). I've had some wonderful photos taken, by a friend of mine.[6] Make me look wonderfully tough! She took sixty without stopping!!

[. . .]

1 Britten was travelling to Oxford where he was to give a recital with Pears and Pears's cousin, the pianist Barbara (Barbie) Smythe, in the Master's Lodge at Balliol College. See also PPT, p. 47. This occasion is the earliest documented Pears–Britten recital.

2 His incidental music for *Johnson over Jordan*.

3 Britten had appeared as soloist in his Piano Concerto at the People's Palace, London, on 12 February, with the New Metropolitan Symphony Orchestra conducted by Serge Krish, in one of a series of Sunday concerts given by this orchestra which included music by English composers. On the afternoon of the 16th he accompanied Sophie Wyss in a recital for the Anglo-French Society [?].

4 In a letter written earlier in February on the 7th to Wulff, Britten makes a first mention of the Hollywood idea: '(((Shshshsssh . . . . I <u>may</u> have an offer from Holywood for a film, but <u>don't</u> say a word)))'. The possibility of an offer of this kind was undoubtedly one of the reasons for Britten's and Pears's investigative trip to North America. As it turned out, the commission did not materialize. On 9 June Britten wrote to Wulff: 'My Hollywood job is definitely off for the moment. So, I shan't be going there.' See also Letter 202.

5 This probably did not happen in spite of the entry 'Paris' in Britten's diary for 14 March. He was in Snape both on the 13th (see Letter 167) and later that same week, when he was composing 'Marine' and 'Being Beauteous' from Rimbaud's *Les Illuminations*.

6 Enid Slater; see Letter 167.

167 To Enid Slater

The Old Mill, Snape, Saxmundham, Suffolk.

March 13th, 1939

My dear Enid,

I am so sorry not to have written before to thank you for your kindness in putting up with me for those three very enjoyable days. I have had a very hectic time since I got back to London, & I was only down here late on Saturday night. I shall remember those few days a long, long time. Thank you v. much – & Montagu & the children as well.

I was delighted to get your & Bridget's[1] letters this morning. I was going to ask you to send on her great opus – which I was delighted to get. It is grand, I think – & is very promising for the future! Is she less moody now?

Re the German plays – Wulff Scherchen has really pretty good taste, if slightly exaggerated enthusiasms. He could easily (& well) give Rosa[2] detailed Precis (do you spell it like that?) of the plays, & if she wanted them – opinions on them too. His address is: 136 Blinco Grove, Cambridge. It is sweet of you to think of it as he is very broke at the moment, & there is an acute crisis re. education.[3]

I got the first proofs of the Spanish (now 'Peace'!) work the other day[4] – looks nice in print. I suddenly had the jitters to-day over the International Situation – but I hope to regain my equilibrium soon as I've got alot of work to do this week. L.B. bought the new car last week – & I drove her down on Saturday. It is a heavenly thing – 16 h.p. A.C. Coupé & goes like the wind.[5]

I must stop this now & write a note for Bridget.

Much love to you all,

(I'll send cheque when I've worked things out re. photos – could you do say ½ doz. postcard size of each of the three we chose, please?)[6]

BENJAMIN

1 Bridget, the eldest of the Slaters' three daughters. Her sisters were Anna and Carol.

2 Montagu Slater's youngest sister. See also Donald Mitchell, 'Montagu Slater (1902–1956): Who was he?', in PGPB, pp. 23–4.

3 Wulff's father was still transmitting monthly alimony payments to his wife from Switzerland. They did not cease until the outbreak of war, but occasionally the payment was late, thus giving rise to feel-

ings of financial insecurity on the part of Mrs Scherchen. Wulff was nearly nineteen, still at school, and in receipt of pocket money only. It seems probable that Britten was trying to find a way to be of help. As for the crisis in education, Wulff writes, 'The crisis in education was my mother's not mine':

I was blissfully ignorant of it all, until it was brought to my notice. I had just missed qualifying for a Modern Language scholarship to Christ's and was about to prepare for the Oxford and Cambridge Joint Higher Certificate in Modern Languages (German, French, English), in spite of the fact that that would not get me into Christ's, where [J.B.] Trend was Professor [of Spanish], whose secretary my mother was by then. Instead, after getting my Higher Certificate, I was switched back to Engineering and pushed (my mother arranged it all) into Queen Mary College which had just been evacuated from London to, of all places, King's College, where dear old Dent was of course Professor (with Boris Ord as organist). Naturally it didn't work – I'd missed too much Dynamics, Hydraulics, etc., to catch up, and was saved from failing the Inter BSc only by internment and later the Auxiliary Military Pioneer Corps.

4 *Ballad of Heroes*, Op. 14, for tenor solo, chorus and orchestra, composed between 28 February and 4 March (the full score was completed by 29 March), to honour men of the British Battalion of the International Brigade who had fallen in Spain. The work was originally to be called 'Anthem for Englishmen', a title that appears on Britten's composition sketch and used on advance publicity for the concert. The Civil War had officially ended on 1 April. The *Ballad*, for which Britten used texts by Auden and Randall Swingler, was first performed at Queen's Hall, London, on 5 April 1939 as part of a Festival of Music for the People, which had been organized by Alan Bush. It was conducted by Constant Lambert, with Walter Widdop as soloist, the London Co-operative Chorus and the London Symphony Orchestra, and dedicated 'To Montagu & Enid Slater'. The remainder of the programme comprised Beethoven's *Egmont* Overture, the slow movement and finale from Bush's Piano Concerto (with Bush himself as soloist) and John Ireland's *These Things Shall Be*. The Festival (dedicated to Bush) included a Pageant at the Albert Hall as well as concerts at the Queen's and Conway Halls. (See *Tribute to Alan Bush on his Fiftieth Birthday* (London, Workers' Music Association, 1950), pp. 30–31.) The Pageant must have been attended by Edward Dent, who wrote about it to Edward Clark: 'Most of it seemed very amateurish and boring, with the usual graceful young men and lumpy (not very young) women bundling about over the arena in folk dances [. . .]' (see Merion and Susie Harries, *A Pilgrim Soul: The Life and Work of Elisabeth Lutyens* (London, Michael Joseph, 1989), p. 98).

Richard Capell wrote in the *Daily Telegraph*, 6 April, under the heading 'Musicians of the Left: A Spanish Elegy by Benjamin Britten':

The third concert of the 'Festival of Music for the People', conducted by Constant Lambert last night at Queen's Hall, was more coherent than the previous programmes of the series.

Two of the three choral works – Benjamin Britten's 'Ballad of Heroes' (new), and Alan Bush's piano concerto – had this in common, that Randall Swingler had provided the composers with verses. But the best poet of the Spanish war did not fight on the side favoured by Mr Bush and Mr Britten. Their bard has not Roy Campbell's verbal art; and the last dozen lines or so of 'Flowering Rifle' remain for a right-wing musician to discover.

Mr Britten's new Op. 14 is an elegy for members of the International Brigade who fell in Spain. Some of the lines seemed more applicable to another conflict, of which many of us have memories ——

> They have restored your power and pride,
> Your life is yours, for which they died.

It is a pity that other verses (including some contributed to the work by W.H. Auden) should seem too eccentric for a choral composition – thus Mr Auden's incidental jibe at 'works for two pianos'. Then the sense of the exhortation, 'Dry their imperfect dust!', is baffling. A pity; because this 'Ballad' is a good musician's work, serious moving and balanced, if not thematically memorable.

And though Mr Swingler's metaphors can be unhappy (he can talk of 'a bird whose wings beat in a vacuum'), we were made to feel that the hearts, at least, of these young artists of the Left are in the right place. Mr Britten's work is a new augury for his future.

The Times, 6 April:

Britten's resource is astonishing, and every note makes its effect unfailingly. But the work also makes an advance in feeling. The words are occasional, but not tendentious, and do not offer such resistance to musical setting as do some of Mr Swingler's verses in the Finale of Alan Bush's piano concerto, which came after. The ballad has an impulse behind its efficiency which should give it life beyond the occasion which prompted it, just as John Ireland's cantata 'These things shall be', written for the civic purposes of a Coronation ode but included in this programme, proved its worth as an expression of popular aspirations such as this festival was designed to foster.

J.A. Forsythe in the Star, 6 April:

The third and last concert of the 'Festival of Music for the People' at the Queen's Hall, was an interesting affair for two reasons.

There was a new work by Benjamin Britten, and the 'People' showed their lack of enthusiasm in this strange combination of music and political propaganda by leaving a large number of seats unoccupied.

Mr Britten is to be congratulated on composing such attractive music to such grim words as are provided in the 'Ballad of Heroes', written in honour of the British International Brigade.

A.H. Fox Strangways in the Observer, 9 April:

We left this last festival concert at Queen's Hall on Wednesday convinced that it had been worth a whole week of ordinary recitals. The first movement of Benjamin Britten's 'Ballad of Heroes' seemed to mark a crucial point in his development. Until a short while ago many of us felt that he would never be a big composer because he had not quite enough character: he could be neither serious nor stupid with real intensity. The Funeral March in 'Ballad of Heroes', however, has an imaginative rhythm that is irresistible, and also a richness and ardour surpassing both Randall Swingler's poem and anything that Britten has yet given us. A comment at once on the music and on the performance is the wish expressed afterwards by some of those in the choir to 'learn the Ballad thoroughly': the inaccuracies could be forgiven because the work was published too late for serious study. Alan Bush's pianoforte concerto also impressed, though it has not Britten's strength of wing.

Musical Times, May, p. 382:

The Festival of Music for the People comprised three events of which the last [. . .] was the best. This contained the first performance of Benjamin Britten's *Ballad of Heroes*, for the most part an extremely well-written and effective work, of no great profundity, but fittingly direct in its appeal. Its slow sections (the opening Funeral March and the final Recitative and Choral, which make a lovely sound) are preferable to the Scherzo – Dance of Death – wherein the typewriter clatter of W.H. Auden's words makes an intelligible setting out of the question. In this section, too, a certain amount of noisy tub-thumping seemed out of tone with the rest of the work.

Havergal Brian, in *Musical Opinion*, September, p. 1,018:

Though there is much 'pulling faces' at the audience, the diabolical cleverness of the music is indisputable. Only a composer with the outlook of a Berlioz would have thought of doubling the tempo of the Funeral March and turning it into a fast devil's-dance like the Dance of Death. The offering to the chorus is a chorale, in which Britten recognises that to make a chorus supremely effective, the choir must be given the lead. Technically, Britten's music offers no difficulties to good choirs. Of the vision which impelled it: Beethoven, who might have had the same feelings, expressed them far more eloquently in his Third, Fifth and Ninth Symphonies.

5 The Acedes (handmade, to order) was a present – possibly a belated birthday present – from Lennox Berkeley. 'Ben', Wulff writes,

was inordinately fond of it. It was a sort of super or sophisticated toy to him [. . .]. [He] loved driving the AC at speed. It had a highly tuned 12 hp motor and he delighted in putting it through its paces. Could it have been at Easter time that we buzzed down the long straight stretch of the new Brighton Road at over 90 mph, or at a speed that for those times was as scary as it was exhilarating.

See also EWB, p. 104.

6 These are reproduced as plates 79–81 in PFL.

168   To Bridget Slater

[*Written in capitals throughout*]

The Old Mill, Snape, Saxmundham, Suffolk
March 13th, 1939.

DEAR BRIDGET,

THANK YOU FOR YOUR NICE LETTER, AND THE DRAWING OF THE
MILL. THE MILL LOOKS VERY MUCH LIKE THAT – IT IS VERY PRETTY. I
WAS ALSO VERY PLEASED TO GET THE STORY-BOOK YOU MADE FOR ME.
I AM VERY INTERESTED IN THE DOINGS OF THIS DOG CALLED 'REX' –
HAS HE BEEN CHASING ANY RABBITS LATELY? WRITE ANOTHER STORY
ABOUT HIM ONE DAY SOON.

A FRIEND OF MINE CAME TO SEE ME TO-DAY WITH HIS LARGE BLACK
DOG CALLED 'ANGUS', AND AFTER WE HAD BEEN OUT FOR A WALK
(ALL THREE OF US) I TOOK MY FRIEND HOME IN MY CAR. BUT AS IT
WAS A NEW ONE, ANGUS HAD TO RUN BEHIND. BUT ANGUS GOT TIRED
AND SAT DOWN ON THE ROAD, AND SOME SMALL GIRLS BROUGHT HIM
BACK TO THE MILL. SO NOW ANGUS IS SITTING, LOOKING <u>VERY</u> SORRY
FOR HIMSELF OUTSIDE MY WINDOW, WAITING FOR HIS MASTER TO COME
AND FETCH HIM. AND IT IS ALL BECAUSE HE WAS A LAZY DOG AND
WOULDN'T FOLLOW THE CAR.

ALOT OF LOVE TO ANN AND CAROL – I HOPE HER NEW BLACK BABY
STILL LIKES SLEEPING IN THE COT –

AND LOTS TO YOURSELF,
FROM
BENJAMIN

169   To Peter Pears

The Old Mill, Snape, Saxmundham, Suffolk.
[16 March 1939]

My dear Pete,

Isn't everything bloody[1] – just as one was allowing oneself to get
hopeful too – however, I don't think <u>anyone</u> can really trust Hitler
anymore: although N.C.[2] (I wish his initials were W.C.) will have
a good shot at it before he's turned out of power.

However, we're going away. Tho' still no news from Hollywood.
I'll let you know as soon as ever I hear, of course.

Well, the car is a wonder, & I've become suddenly fearfully car-
minded. Spent most of yesterday pulling her (or him!) to pieces

at the garage. I managed her like a school-boy on Saturday – and even you wouldn't have been frightened. I let L.B. drive for a bit and it wasn't <u>too</u> bad. However, re. him we've had a bit of a crisis and I'm only too thankful to be going away. I had the most fearful feeling of revulsion the other day – conscience and all that – just like old days. He's been very upset, poor dear – but that makes it worse! I wish you were here, old dear, because I want terribly to tell to someone. However, I'll see you soon I hope. Ian[3] comes on Saturday and I go to Cambridge on Wednesday – & to town for one night on Thursday (if the Grillers can rehearse with me, i.e.).[4] Will you be round about?

Thanks for the Edinboro' rock, it has been <u>much</u> appreciated. I found it here when I got back – and it <u>is</u> good stuff. And for the letter too. I'm longing to see you again – & scandal away!

Just written a terrific Rimbaud song[5] – with string orchestra – my best bit so far I think. Actually for Sophie at Birmingham – but eventually also for P.P. everywhere!

Just had proofs of [Piano] Concerto.

Any news of Iris – poor dear it'll be hell for her.[6]

Much love,
BENJAMIN

Excuse smudges – just emotion!!

1 The hopes of the Munich Agreement of September 1938 were dashed in 1939 by Hitler's insatiable and unappeasable territorial ambitions. On 15 March his troops occupied Bohemia and Moravia, while on the next day Slovakia was placed under German 'protection'. Later in the month, on the 28th, Madrid surrendered to Franco, thus bringing to an end the Spanish Civil War. On the same day Hitler denounced Germany's non-aggression pact with Poland.

2 Neville Chamberlain (1869–1940), British Prime Minister. He succeeded Stanley Baldwin in 1937 and was replaced by Winston Churchill in May 1940. Chamberlain's government pursued a policy of appeasement of the dictators in the thirties, though one has to remember the warmth of support by the public for the illusory agreement of 1938. Hence the intense disillusionment of 1939.

3 Ian Scott-Kilvert (1917–1989), poet, interpreter and translator, who was educated at Harrow and Caius College, Cambridge, where he was a member of the circle of friends gathered around E.J. Dent and J.B. Trend (1887–1958; Professor of Spanish at Cambridge and writer on Spanish music). Scott-Kilvert joined the British Council in 1946 and was Director of the Council's Literature Department from 1926 to 1977.

4 We have not been able to trace the details of this rehearsal and subsequent concert.

5 'Being Beauteous', which was dedicated to Pears.

6 Iris Holland-Rogers, a friend of Pears and a talented linguist. She made translations of Britten's French Folk-song Arrangements and, for the English Opera Group in 1958, a translation with Pears of Monteverdi's *Il ballo delle ingrate*. She was living in Prague at this time (Pears had visited her there during the summer of 1938) and Britten refers again to the international news and the impact it was likely to have on her.

170 To Wulff Scherchen

> The Old Mill, Snape, Saxmundham, Suffolk.
>
> March 19th, 1939.

[. . .]

Written two good(!) songs this week – French words. Arthur Rimbaud – marvellous poems.[1] I'll show you them later. [. . .]

1 The two songs were 'Being Beauteous', dated 16 March, and 'Marine', dated 18 March. Both songs were ultimately to form part of the orchestral song-cycle *Les Illuminations* (see Letter 181). The songs, in which Sophie Wyss appeared as soloist, were first performed in a midday BBC concert broadcast from Queen's College Chamber Lecture Hall, Birmingham, on 21 April. The programme consisted entirely of music by Britten, the *Bridge Variations* and *Simple Symphony*, played by the Birmingham Philharmonic String Orchestra conducted by Johan C. Hock, and 'Let the florid music praise', 'Nocturne' and 'Seascape' from *On this Island* and 'I must be married on Sunday' from *Friday Afternoons* (in which Britten was accompanist). 'E.B.' [Eric Blom] reviewing the concert for the *Birmingham Post*, 22 April, wrote that the two Rimbaud songs and *On this Island*

showed that Britten is by no means content to exploit a success by repeating himself. There is much that is new in both works, and they astonished one, not only by showing different qualities between them, but by achieving striking originality without showing a trace of deliberate experimenting or shock tactics. They are genuine music throughout, even where they may strike an unadventurous ear as difficult to grasp at a first-hearing.

The Airs are beautiful exercises in the exploitation of vocal technique, very much in the way that Handel's arias were, and except that the idiom is entirely different, there is a kind of Handelian blend of dignity and buoyancy about them. Unfortunately, it was impossible yesterday to make out what the words were about, for Miss Wyss's enunciation was not only too indistinct to convey more than a word here and there; it was so much so that one did not know for some time in what language she was singing. On the other hand, the singer gave splendid value to the grand vocal display, sometimes sustained, sometimes florid, of these songs [. . .].

Britten wrote to Wulff immediately after the event:

You see – the first <u>complete</u> concert of one's music is a pretty good trial – & in fact that it was a great success makes one rather bucked – [. . .]

171 To Mary Behrend

The Old Mill, Snape, Saxmundham, Suffolk.

April 17th [19th] 1939

My dear Mrs. Behrend,

This is only a scribbled note to tell you that Peter P. & I are sailing for Canada on Saturday week. We are both going to work – we may do occasional playing if the occasion arises – but the real reason is to do some really intensive thinking & for me personally to do somework to please <u>myself</u> & not necessarily the BBC or Basil Dean! Peter'll be back at the end of the summer, but I have other ideas & may stay on abit or go to U.S.A.[1] I am so disappointed that I shan't be able to come to Glyndebourne with you, & also that it doesn't look likely that I'll see you before I go. But if you're in London before that I wish you would ring up (Welbeck 9549) – because I may be there. At the moment things are rushed – I go to Birmingham to conduct on Friday mid-day,[2] & back here for the week end. But I should so like to see you.

Yours sincerely,

BENJAMIN BRITTEN

1 In his BBC interview with Lord Harewood (*People Today*, BBC Radio, May/June 1960; Archive), Britten gave his reasons for leaving England, as remembered by him then:

I was very much influenced by Auden, not only in poetry but in life too, and politics, of course, came very strongly into our lives in the late thirties. He went to America, I think it was '38, early '39, and I went soon after. I think it wouldn't be too much oversimplifying the situation to say that many of us young people at that time felt that Europe was more or less finished. There was this great Nazi fascist cloud about to break at any moment and one felt that Europe didn't – nor did it have the will to resist that. I went to America and felt that I would make my future there. It took me a long time to realize that that would not be so, and perhaps it's interesting to say that that realization came partly through illness. I was very ill for a year or so in the early days of the war in America. When the illness cleared, I knew quite definitely that my home did not lie there, that whatever the situation was, that I was a European, and so I came back.

It was, I think, the early days of '42 – yes – it was – I'd tried very hard to get a boat in '41 but, as you might imagine, the boats weren't running very frequently, or easily, in those days, and it took six months to find a passage. I remember the very uncomfortable situation of being packed, having all one's clothes and belongings packed ready to sail at an hour's notice, for more than six months.

Beth Welford recalled that on his departure to North America Britten

fully intended then to take out American citizenship, and of course we couldn't bear the thought of him going away for so long [. . .] nobody knew what was happening in the world [. . .]. Wystan Auden and Christopher Isherwood had gone ahead and they were fully intending to become citizens of the USA, and Ben [. . .] had that intention too [. . .] he had the feeling that Europe was not the place for artists to live in and they felt they'd [. . .] find more of a future [. . .] in the New World [. . .].

(Source: Beth Welford, Interview with Anthony Friese-Greene, 1977, Aldeburgh; Archive)

See also Introduction, pp. 32–9, Lord Harewood's 'The Man' in DMHK, pp. 3–4, and EWB, p. 109.

2 It seems, however, that Britten's role in the concert of 21 April was confined to accompanying.